WEST SIDE MAESTRO

Vol 1

The Creative Spark!

'LENNY' photo by Paul de Heuck

WEST SIDE MAESTRO

A Musical Memoir
of Leonard Bernstein

by

ROBERT MANDELL

Vol 1

The Creative Spark!

PRESSIT PUBLICATIONS

PRESSIT PUBLICATIONS
Leicester, England
www.westsidemaestro.com

For

Ruth

My Dearest Memory of All

WEST SIDE MAESTRO

FOREWORD

After sixteen years of research, interviews, countless listenings to hundreds of CD's and viewings of VCR tapes and DVD's as well as trawling my memory of happenings more than sixty-years past, I have come to the end of a personal journey that I shared with the spirit of a single companion who had been my first mentor, teacher and then professional colleague, Leonard Bernstein.

I first envisaged a single volume of memoirs that would run to about three to four- hundred pages. I viewed that a practical projection since the brief I had set myself was to deal strictly with Bernstein the musician, and only musical matters and happenings related to his career. Reality dawned when I reached and passed the four-hundredth page. I knew then that I had just begun my journey and that to complete a convincing musical portrait of so multi-talented, accomplished and complex a musician would consume an as yet unpredictable amount of time and pages of typed manuscript. There existed no prototype that would enable me to comprehend the vastness of the task at hand. The majority of volumes that fell under the label of Bernstein biography were all of a highly personal nature, barely scratching the surface of his musical accomplishments. How could that be? My researched, documented analysis of the Eliot Norton Lectures that Lenny delivered at Harvard University, one of his most important achievements, filled seventy-two pages of my book.

To truly understand who Leonard Bernstein was, what he stood for and what he represented to audiences amounting to millions of people in every part of the world, you must seek out the musician. The complexity of such an odyssey is compounded by having to tread two paths simultaneously, one which leads to the creative musician, (the composer, writer, original thinker and teacher) and the other to the re-creative musician with whom the majority of people identified, Bernstein the conductor.

WEST SIDE MAESTRO

In the end, years of tenacious dedication to the task produced a first draft of 1100 pages. Editing reduced this number to 900 pages. Decisions had next to be taken as to the final form of the book. The duality of Bernstein's musical gifts tipped the balance towards publication in two volumes. This first volume bears the subtitle, The Creative Spirit. Volume 2, dealing with Bernstein the conductor and his vast output of sound recordings and Video/DVD films, will follow in the autumn of 2012. My writings make constant reference to Video recordings which were a key reference medium for me during my research. Just as the CD replaced the long playing record, the development and subsequent popularity of the DVD has replaced the video cassette. In relation to Bernstein's commercial recordings a large selection of his CD catalogue is still made available by Sony and Deutsche Grammophon. A relatively small collection of his many films released on videocassette can be found in DVD transfers on specialist labels. Fortunately, some of the most important educational films to include the 'Omnibus' series, the Young Peoples Concerts and the Norton Lectures are now available in DVD format. A principal source of up to date information can be obtained on-line from the Leonard Bernstein Society at www.leonardbernstein.com

It is my hope that this book will prove valuable and interesting to both the musician and non-musician, It is generously annotated with footnotes at the bottom of the text page to which they apply to lend further helpful insight to the subject under discussion. A number above a word indicates the footnotes, which also serve as an index. The present technology of E-readers and tablets have different methods for displaying such notes. A popular method is to highlight the number and then click on it to reveal the note. Please consult your users manual for instructions for your particular model.

Robert Mandell,
March 2012
Leicester, England

WEST SIDE MAESTRO

A Musical Memoir of Leonard Bernstein

Vol I: The Creative Spark!

TABLE OF CONTENTS

The Preface is an anecdotal description of the Author's first meetings with Leonard Bernstein and their subsequent professional relationship. It traces the author's three summers at Tanglewood as Bernstein's conducting student and his later appointment as Music Assistant for Bernstein's televised 'Omnibus' lectures and the Young People's Concerts of the NY Philharmonic.

This chapter, again anecdotally and historically, examines those diverse elements that combine to produce the least understood and most controversial of 'star' careers in the music profession. It surveys the early years of the Bernstein career and the musical forces that helped shape it. It probes the historic role of music critics, their influence in launching the Bernstein career, the key role they played in removing Mitropoulos from the position of Music Director of the NY Philharmonic paving the way for Bernstein's accession and finally their turning the full force of their editorials against this same musician who succeeded in reversing the fortunes of the NY Philharmonic and returning it to a position of world class eminence.

WEST SIDE MAESTRO

His sensational NY Philharmonic debut in 1943 made him an overnight celebrity in the insulated world of symphony concerts but his TV debut as highbrow music guru to Middle America for the Ford Foundation television program 'Omnibus' created star status for Bernstein that one formerly associated only with Hollywood celebrities. This chapter details the programs, Bernstein's work habits, and the successes and failures within the five year series. It also details the problems which began to manifest themselves as his fame grew and the concessions afforded him by the Omnibus TV executives resulted in ever more rigorous demands

3. THE NEW YORK PHILHARMONIC YEARS:

This is a capsule, warts-and-all history of Bernstein's relationship with the Philharmonic prior to his appointment as co-conductor in 1957 and afterwards as their Director in 1958. It touches upon the problems experienced by other famous maestros when they faced this temperamental and fierce body of musicians and it details the final years of Mitropoulos's tenure before he was deposed by the man who was reputed to be one of his protégés.

Bernstein's appointment as Music Director of the NY Philharmonic once again attracted sponsorship from Ford for a series of television specials, this time not from their philanthropic foundation but from their commercial Ford Motors sector. With Robert Saudek Associates again as his production team and huge budgets at his disposal, Bernstein delivered fifteen highly varied programs which featured his new partners, the NY Philharmonic, a long list of star performers and backdrops which took him and his orchestra around the world

WEST SIDE MAESTRO

This introduction discusses Bernstein's love of and gifts for teaching. It traces his compulsion to teach from his childhood to his association with Tanglewood, to his innovating use of television as a teaching medium, to his historic six Norton Lectures at Harvard University in which first he predicated inborn human capacities for the acquisition of musical understanding, then examined the present crisis facing contemporary music and its composers and finally predicted the fused amalgam of styles which the contemporary music of the future would reflect.

This section details production meetings, the programs growing pains and the mounting of the televised NY Philharmonic Young People's Concerts. It gives a general overall survey of the fifteen years of programs and of their successes and failures. It provides detailed reviews of 25 Sony Videos chosen from the 53 programs written and presented by Bernstein over its fifteen year history and includes a summation of its importance as an introduction to classical music for both children and adults.

This chapter title describes the series of six Norton lectures which Bernstein gave in 1973 at his alma mater, Harvard University . These were the first Norton lectures ever to be televised. In these complex programs Bernstein attempts to link the aesthetics of music and linguistics in search of innate musical universals of competence within the brain similar to those attributed for language in the theories of Noam Chomsky. Complex linguistic theory and analysis will be avoided although the writings of other noted linguistic scientists with whom the author has been in correspondence will be quoted. This chapter will view Bernstein's key contribution as a catalyst, stimulating further important detailed research into the theories expounded in his lectures. An important segment of these lectures were televised recordings of Bernstein conducting the Boston Symphony in repertoire with which he was closely associated throughout his career. It offers a unique glimpse of the conductor five years after resigning his post with the NY Philharmonic, during which time the bulk of his conducting activities were concentrated with European orchestras, in particular, the Vienna Philharmonic.

WEST SIDE MAESTRO

Throughout his career, with the exception of the Suites from West Side Story, On The Waterfront, On The Town, the three dances from his ballet, Fancy Free and the Overture to 'Candide', Bernstein was the key promoter and conductor of his several large scale symphonic compositions. This chapter will analyse the composer's most recent video/DVD or CD recordings of the three symphonies, the ballets, the stage works including 'Mass' and the opera, 'A Quiet Place', the violin concerto, 'Serenade', 'Songfest', 'Arias and Barcaroles' and the late works for orchestra, comparing them where possible with his earlier recordings with the N.Y. Philharmonic. This chapter will also deal with the controversial television recording of 'The Making of West Side Story' and Bernstein's final attempt to create a definitive recording of his long plagued but brilliant Broadway opera buffa, 'Candide'.

This chapter will sum up Bernstein, the musician, conductor and teacher during the final three years of his life, describing his work and the musical legacy he bequeathed to young musicians in helping to found two new music centres for youth in Europe, The Schleswig-Holstein Festival, [1987 – 1989] in Salzau,, Germany and The Pacific Music Festival, [1990] in Sapporo on the island of Hokkaido, Japan.

A farewell.

In my beginning is my end ...

In my end is my beginning.

TS Eliot *Four Quartets*

This is to introduce Robert Mandell a young man of outstanding gifts

Sincerely,

Leonard Bernstein

LEONARD BERNSTEIN

WEST SIDE MAESTRO

Prelude

"TOOK IT A TEMPO!"

"Is Bob there?"

"This is Bob."

"Is this MY Bob?"

(mustering a tone of gravitas) "This is R-O-B-E-R-T MANDELL. Who's calling, please?"

"It's Lenny!!!!!"

"Lenny WHO???"

"Lenny Bernstein!!!!!"

" **Lenny!!!** How ARE you?"

"I'm doing a new television series called OMNIBUS and I want YOU to be my assistant. ARE YOU AVAILABLE?'

"When do you want me to begin?!!!"

And that's how I left G. Schirmer as manager of the record department of its Brooklyn branch to continue a musical relationship that had begun five years earlier when Lenny attended my debut conducting his groundbreaking musical, "On the Town" at City College, New York where I was an undergraduate majoring in music.

With the exception of Alistair Cooke, host to the famous CBS Omnibus series who addressed him more formally as 'Leonard', to one and all he was 'Lenny'. No acquaintance or musician ever addressed him as Mr. Bernstein or Maestro.

I enjoyed a scholarly and professional association with him spanning ten of the most formative years of his and my own careers, 1949-1959. Our acquaintanceship began in 1949 at my conducting debut, which sufficiently impressed him enough to recommend me to his mentor Serge Koussevitzky, the great Russian conductor and music director of the Boston Symphony, for a conducting scholarship at the Berkshire Music Center in Tanglewood, Massachusetts. Following the sudden death of Koussevitzky in 1951, Lenny agreed to take over the conducting department at Tanglewood. I was handpicked by him to be one of four conductors invited to work with him and to have opportunities to conduct the Music Center's student orchestra. [1]

This was in contrast to the other larger class of non-scholarship and, for the most part, non-performing conductor-auditors who come to Tanglewood each summer from every part of the globe. It was also through Lenny's personal recommendation that I went on to complete my conducting studies at the Juilliard School in New York with Jean Morel.

It is now more than twenty years and three highly researched biographies since Lenny's death. His life ended ignominiously in true tragic hero style. The bright flame that had dazzled the music world for fifty years with its physical presence was robbed of its power and then, in an unguarded moment, snuffed out.

Although over three thousand pages have been written about the man, much of it has focused on his flaws, peccadilloes and troubled lifestyle leaving no secret alone. A notable commercial tribute perhaps, but hardly a proper epitaph for one of the greatest conductor- musicians of any generation.

Of the three tomes, Humphrey Burton's is unquestionably the most authoritative. The Joan Peyser and Merle Secrest volumes portrayed Bernstein as a highly flawed man almost divorced from the musical legacy he represented. Burton, a long time friend and business associate of Bernstein, had the full co-operation of the Bernstein family for his volume. After the raw exposé biography by Joan Peyser, which Lenny was said to have come to fear being published in his lifetime, Burton was probably motivated in part to tell all in detailed fashion to take the wind out of the sails of any author who might be contemplating other volumes based upon Bernstein's profligate lifestyle. Nevertheless, barely a year after the publication of the Burton biography, the Merle Secrest volume appeared in print. If the London Times' choice of Humphrey Burton to review the Secrest biography was ironic, his own biographical opus having just been released in paperback form, Bernstein's 'authorized' biographer[2] did make the important point in

---

[1] For the record, the other three conductors were Lorin Maazel, the Israeli, Elyakum Shapira and the Brazilian, Bernado Federovsky

[2] In the Foreward to his exhaustive Bernstein biography, Burton emphasized that his was *not* an "authorized" volume in the sense that '(he) was not told what to say or prevented from saying what (he) wanted'. The information and sources made available to him, denied to other biographers, point to his book being singled out for its authenticity by the Bernstein family.

WEST SIDE MAESTRO

his review that what mattered most to Bernstein was his music making. What was needed to complete the portrait of this polyglot of music was a study and analysis of his musical talents and output, not a rehash of his indiscretions.

Burton's review prompted me to expand my own extensive research into the body of Bernstein's work as conductor, composer, musician, scholar and communicator as documented in his recordings, music videos and telecasts to a depth not previously attempted. I worked under Lenny's tutelage as both student and professional assistant. My personal knowledge of the man is of his relationship with music. The writing of this musical memoir began sixteen years ago. It is my contribution to the legacy of the musician.

I wrote previously that my musical relationship with Lenny had begun in 1949. If the truth be told, one could say my musical journey with Lenny began after his amazing triumph at the NY Philharmonic concerts substituting for an indisposed Bruno Walter, a concert I attended in 1943 as a young teenager. I would sometimes cut school to sneak into rehearsals of the great conductors I idolized, crouching in the shadows of the vast New York concert halls absorbing lessons in conducting that no class study could duplicate. When I first saw Lenny conduct at Carnegie hall and afterwards regularly with the City Symphony at the New York City Center of Music and Drama, he became the symbol of everything I hoped for in my own future. After meeting him on the best terms possible, having conducted his musical On The Town, it appeared my vision of the future was becoming a reality. I completed three conducting summers studying with him at Tanglewood. Then Lenny and I lost touch for a bit and, with bills to pay and my wife expecting our first child, G.Schirmer became my best friend. With **THE** phone call, however, came a new role and a new title, Special Music Assistant to Leonard Bernstein. My title and name rolled down the television screens of America tuned into CBS for his Omnibus television series for the next four years. With the exception of the summer months, I now found myself in Lenny's company weekly when he was in New York either working at the Robert Saudek offices on technical details for his television programs or meeting with him at the Osborne in his apartment or work studio or attending his rehearsals, usually at Carnegie Hall, which was just across the street from where he lived.

WEST SIDE MAESTRO

With Lenny's appointment as Music Director of the N.Y. Philharmonic in 1957, my work load increased to take on not only the additional duties as his personal assistant and member of the creative team for the televised Young People's Concerts but to perform the same background services for him that he had once performed for Maestro Artur Rodzinski when he was Assistant Conductor at the N.Y. Philharmonic. This job was to examine and appraise the large number of conductor's scores that flooded into the Philharmonic weekly from publishers and composers in the hope of a performance by the orchestra. One day, out of the blue, Lenny bursting with benevolence pronounced that my reward for my years of service would be my appointment as Associate Conductor of the N.Y.Philharmonic following the retirement of Franco Autori, the orchestra's Associate Conductor at the time.

That was it, a young conductor's dream come true. There was no discussion about it before or after. A promise is a promise....

Our working relationship over the OMNIBUS years had been very good and for the most part relaxed. When we worked on a one to one basis, I was permitted to express my opinions freely, which I did even when they differed radically. He valued having someone in his corner with musical credentials he respected who was not a 'yes-man', as was inevitably the case with so many around him on the television side of things. I prided myself, a bit naively, on the privileged place I held being able to challenge my mentor on artistic and musical matters when I believed it was in his best interests.

One seminal occasion stands out when we had a terrible clash. I was reading through the weekly batch of submitted publisher's scores at his Osborne studio. Despite knowing his close relationship with Lucas Foss, I rejected Lucas's choral work, Psalms. Lenny was apoplectic. He would not hear a wrong word against Lucas. I thought the work to be flawed. Imitating Koussevitzky's thick Russian accent, I quipped,

"It jus' 'vouldn't sound, und dat's all!"

Lenny was furious and wasn't listening. He rated Lucas to be one of the great young composers of our time. My frank appraisal was that his opinion was not widely shared by the music world at large.

WEST SIDE MAESTRO

"The work is mediocre and derivative and, at best, not a patch on Lucas' earlier work, "The Prairie."

We ended up agreeing to disagree. I think that was the moment we both marked each other's card. In music history terms, Lucas' "Psalms" did virtually sink without trace. And after the next episode, so did our professional relationship.

By the end of the 1958-59 season, after The Psalm incident, Lenny without warning grandly announced he wanted to have a pool of three student assistants to simultaneously serve the Philharmonic each year for a single season. Lenny graciously extended the first offer of this student apprenticeship to me... but had he really forgotten his promise? This was not the sole Associate Conductor appointment. Compared to the promise of the prestigious ongoing position of Associate Conductor, an offer to be one of three apprentices held little attraction for me My option was to accept his offer to continue as his television assistant as well as serve a one year student apprenticeship with the Philharmonic not knowing where that would lead, or to put his promise behind me and pursue my own conducting career in the concert and recording fields which was starting to take root away from the Bernstein circles. I chose to go my own way and I never looked back.

Despite appearing to be a man of absolute conviction, Lenny was a hopeless procrastinator, prone to moments of benevolence, big gestures and about turns. He could change his mind at any given moment no matter the inconvenience caused to others. He was no fool. He knew an apology from him was as seductive as a promise. His mentor, Koussevitzky, confessed once,

"I'm a very weak man, I promise everybody everything. Thank God, I have the strength not to keep my promises."

How many times had I laughed at this anecdote? When it happened to me, I didn't even crack a smile.

I still had one contract obligation with the Saudek office, Lenny's final OMNIBUS program on opera. At this last telecast, I was sitting, as usual, near the director in the control booth. I had devised a personal system of dealing with musical excerpts on Lenny's programs for those directors who could not easily follow a piano or full conductor's score. The director and I would confer together at a planning session during early run-throughs and he would describe the type of framed visual shots he wished to achieve. I would help him to select the places in the music best suited to his needs and then mark my score two musical measures plus one extra beat before each of the planned shots. If, for example, the music was composed in 3/4 time, that is with three strong pulses in each measure of music, that would amount to 7 beats of preparation, 2 x 3 + 1. The director would alert the appropriate cameraman to the upcoming visual set-up, let us say a four-shot, (a shot containing four people). I would then say to the director but loud enough for the technical director to hear, (for me to address the crew directly would have brought the Union down on our heads), 'On the count of seven' and simultaneously with my pronouncing the number 'seven' the director would shout "Take!" and, with the precision of a Tom & Jerry cartoon, the exact picture and music would harmonize. While working, I noticed out of the corner of my eye Jack Gottlieb- a young composer from my summers at Tanglewood, now serving Lenny in a multiplicity of tasks, from personal valet to music factotum, sitting in a corner of the control room but thought little of it - that is, until the N.Y. Times did a profile on Jack following the first of Lenny's television shows for which he served as my replacement. The television journalist extolled the clever manner in which Jack worked with the director counting out the bars of music prior to each visual shot.

Was I upset? You're damned right, I was! Did I reproach Lenny over this? Not a word. It was better to part on friendly terms. Besides, people may crib your ideas but they can't crib the talent that originated them.

Leaving the "promise" behind me, I flew the Bernstein circles to develop an extensive recording career in England from 1961-1967 in addition to a full schedule of orchestral concerts in the States. In 1968, I made the decision to take up residence with my young family in London. Although it removed me from daily contact with New York circles, I never lost touch with my friends in the Philharmonic during the Bernstein tenure as Music Director These were friendships that dated back to when I was fifteen years old and used to attend rehearsals hidden in an obscure part of Carnegie Hall watching and learning from the greatest conductors in the world.

I was curious now and again how my decision to leave Lenny's 'magic circle' registered with him. As it turned out, we remained friendly over the years as our paths continued to cross at concert halls and rehearsals in the UK and

WEST SIDE MAESTRO

America. From the beginning of our acquaintance Lenny perceptively understood my nature. In an interview he gave during my Tanglewood days, he was quoted as saying that ambition was a key ingredient in a conductor's personality and that one of his students, Robert Mandell, displayed the most burning ambition he had ever witnessed in a young conductor.

Sixty years ago, I was known as an up and coming figure within the field of young American conductors. I was given the rare privilege of working within the Bernstein professional circle for ten years. Having made the decision to break with that relationship, I went on to develop new careers in England both in the recording industry and as a concert conductor. In my post-Bernstein life, I did not trade on our professional connection. My presence in American Bernstein circles is not widely known outside my own musical generation. It did turn up twice in book and film biographies. Both, ironically, involve misattributed Tanglewood memorabilia. The first is a photograph in Merle Secrest's 1994 biography; the second is a film clip of Tanglewood about fifteen minutes into the 1998 superb Public Broadcasting documentary tribute, Leonard Bernstein, Reaching For The Note. Although listed or referred to as representing Tanglewood "in the forties", both are of the same scene simultaneously filmed and photographed at Tanglewood in the post-Koussevitzky summer of 1953, my third year in attendance as a scholarship student conductor.

I attended as many of Lenny's concerts in England between 1968 until his death in 1990 as my own conducting schedule would allow. I became an avid collector of his sound recordings, videocassettes and televised broadcasts. His lectures for his alma mater, Harvard University, "The Unanswered Question", proved especially fascinating in its expanded intellectual challenge to the viewer. The earlier" Omnibus" telecasts were high quality informative entertainments. "The Unanswered Question" was ground breaking television, a seminar of Lenny's, as yet, unproven theories regarding music and the workings of the human brain. In his later years, I noted the development of radical ideas in his music making and I became fascinated in comparing his later Deutsche Gramophone videos and CD's with his earlier CBS/Sony recordings to discern the changes they revealed in his reinterpretation of the classics.

I was also curious to explore how much Lenny was the creation of his own mentor and key formative influence, Serge Koussevitsky. Unlike Lenny,

WEST SIDE MAESTRO

Koussevitzky was not a great musical intellect and was prone to a sometimes incoherent baton technique. Koussevitsky however was natural musician with powerful musical instincts, an unfailing ear for orchestral colour and an extraordinary communicative personality. The man brought to the podium an imperious, unchallengeable will that enabled him to produce performances of breathtaking excitement, beauty and virtuosity.

Koussevitzky in his broken but essentially pithy use of the English language was able to sum up his musical philosophy in very few words:
" A sound is a dolce who have a beautiful round tone."
" Gentlemen, it doesn't sound...it jus' doesn't sound."
" Better und better! There is no 'the end'!"
" Gentlemen, it is very not together."
"Don't hurry! DON'T HURRY! **TOOK IT A TEMPO & KEPT IT!**"

For 24 years Koussevitsky maintained a standard of orchestral performance with his Boston Symphony, (and it was HIS Boston Symphony much as it was with Mengelberg and HIS Amsterdam Concertgebouw Orchestra), which, in its individuality and standard of excellence, has never quite been equaled since his departure. Two world famous conductors taught and influenced the young Bernstein, Serge Koussevitzky and Fritz Reiner. With all of Lenny's vast and superior intellect, it was Koussevitzky, the lesser intellectual of these two conductors, rather than Reiner, the brilliant and meticulously schooled technician, who remained the single greatest musical force throughout Lenny's professional life as a conductor.

On going through the vast output of Bernstein on film one can discern the development and direction his musical thinking and music making took from his youthful beginnings. If his career until 1968 identified Lenny essentially as an American artist, performing principally with American ensembles and totally identified with his early American musical influences, his final years were spent largely abroad conducting symphony and opera orchestras whose musical approach and performing style was the antithesis of the musical impulses and environment that shaped him.

I have been lucky enough to have had stall seats with an icon and one of the great conductors of the 20th century, Leonard Bernstein, attending his rehearsals and concerts as a teenager, as his conducting student, and, finally, as his right hand associate during his breakthrough television career which lead to his appointment as Music Director of one of the world's great orchestras, The New York Philharmonic. I gained unrivalled insights into his studying and writing habits and benefited first hand from his detailed approach to the technique and craft of conducting and to his ideas on teaching.

In the end I trust that my musical account of Lenny's work will allow my readers to reassess Leonard Bernstein's creative contribution to the many areas of music to which he devoted his multi-faceted talents and, as well, to view and listen to his diverse recorded and filmed output with new eyes and ears.

Tanglewood 1951

© Whitestone Photo

(from l to r) **Lorin Maazel, Elyakum Shapirra, 'Lenny', Robert Mandell**

WEST SIDE MAESTRO

PRELUDE 2

"Leonard Bernstein, **who**???!!!" Difficult to conceive, there was a time when a large percentage of Americans posed that question.

My memoir sets out principally to reminisce over a part of Leonard Bernstein's career as a *creative* artist but Lenny's creative talents were always inevitably hinged to his *recreative* talent as a conductor. Yes, there was ***West Side Story*** and...*what* was the name of that stage musical about New York later translated into a Hollywood *cinema-spectacular* with Gene Kelly and Frank Sinatra? The general public, and that's a lot of people, remember Lenny principally from television and as an orchestra conductor. Composing, writing and teaching are private activities, (the latter requiring a job, of course). Conducting requires an orchestra and in the amateur, semi-professional and especially the professional field, there are not many opportunities readily available at any given time.

So to give you a fuller understanding of the forces that shaped Lenny in relation to the career upon which his worldwide fame was achieved, I am going to take you on a short personal and historical journey about Who!What!Where!When!&How! conductors are created. There may be some surprises. All of the conductors we will meet pertinently relate to Lenny because all belong to the breed of *personality* maestros. Of course, all conductors have a personality of some sort but I am referring to **extravert** star qualities. There are other characters to be prepared for as well, the *Demon Kings* of old time vaudeville, the Critics. (Don't get me wrong, some of my best friends are critics.) Finally, awaiting us will be Lenny, whose musical personality has been shaped in one way or other by all of the characters we will meet during our journey.

WEST SIDE MAESTRO

1. CONDUCTORS, CONDUCTING TECHNIQUE, CRITICS & LENNY

There are a plethora of one-liners regarding the profession of Conductor including an oft-quoted spurious comment from the composer Berlioz that 'The hardest thing about *conducting* is finding a job!' Certainly, it is a profession that often mystifies the largest proportion of the concert-going public. In discussion with other conductors, I have found that the question most frequently posed by their admirers is, 'What instrument do you play?' If you correctly answer by stating the obvious, 'I play *the Orchestra*!', you still have to deal with the questioner's flustered but undeterred persistence. 'I *know* that, but what *instrument* do you _PLAY_???!!!' I assume that my colleagues maintain their sense of humour and proportion at this point and rather than simply boorishly turning their back and walking away, they smile outwardly, sigh inwardly, and provide the sought after reply, 'I play the French horn/clarinet/cello/tuba...' or whatever instrument fits the bill. I did receive news of a conductor, whom I knew in his youth to be a 'bit of a nutter'[3], becoming so displeased with a female subscriber's after-concert questions that he gave her reason to ponder his forceful reply from a horizontal position on the floor.

Beyond the claims that mysticism and communion with the spirits of long dead composers are the basis of the conductor's art, lies the simple truth that the indispensable ingredients which form the foundation of a conductor's success with both orchestras and public are to be found in the combination of the non-musical, inborn traits of a communicative personality and a strong will. Musicianship is intellectually acquired over a period of time through personal application. While a necessary part of a professional musician's armoury, its acquisition, even on the highest academic level, is no guarantee that it will be accompanied by a talent to stand before an ensemble of disparately skilled instrumentalists and, with unspoken gestures, weld them into a blended aggregate capable of stirring their

---

[3] 'nutter' - the Oxford Dictionary definition is, 'a crazy person' but in this instance a better definition would be, someone who was 'two sandwiches short of a picnic'.

24

audience to heights of excitement. A happening that illustrates this premise abundantly occurred during my post-graduate studies at the Juilliard School in the conducting class of Jean Morel. One of my classmates, Sam Krachmalnick[4], returned from a concert conducted by Nicolas Slonimsky[5]. We all knew Slonimsky's reputation as an extraordinary musician and as the "piano pounder"[6] who worked with Serge Koussevitzky both in Paris and during the great Russian maestro's early days in Boston helping him to learn his scores. We gathered around Sam to get his impressions and evaluation. "The guy is phenomenal." he said, "He conducted a five pattern with one hand while simultaneously conducting a four pattern with the other." We gasped in amazement. Mine was the next question. "How was the concert?" The reply was short and simple. "It was the worst concert I have ever attended!"

It is understandable if the reader pauses in confusion. How could it be that a musician of Slonimsky's impeccable musical pedigree and culture, (he was reputed among other skills to be the world's leading musical lexicographer), could experience failure despite his prodigious conducting technique and thorough training, while Serge Koussevitzky, a musician with a faulty and sometimes misleading conducting technique and huge gaps in his musical background, could rise to become by virtue of his prodigious drive and almost hypnotic influence over his musicians one of historic figures among conductors, elevating along the way and maintaining for 25 years one of the greatest orchestras in American musical history, the Boston Symphony Orchestra? The answer lies in the character and personality of the two individuals rather than the single factor of technical competence in their chosen field. Indeed, it was said of Koussevitzky that "he was proof that a great conductor need not be a great musician." That remark is quoted from a biography of Koussevitzky by Moses Smith, which the Russian conductor did everything in his power to suppress. That seemingly damning statement was

---

[4] Sam Krachmalnick, (1926-2005) a superbly gifted but neglected American conductor noted for his musical direction of the original Broadway production of Bernstein's 'Candide' still preserved on recording.

[5] Nicolas Slonimsky, (1894-1995) Russian-American musicologist, editor of Baker's Biographical Dictionary of Composers & Musicians.

[6] Slonimsky's description of himself both in his memoirs and Baker's Dictionary.

immediately qualified by his biographer's personal assessment of the conductor. Moses Smith, an exacting and much respected Boston music critic, wrote, "He, (the conductor), must be an artist... And Koussevitzky is certainly one of the very few artists among conductors on the American scene...His very defects have served, by contrast, to highlight his great artistic stature...Applying his *imperious will,* his great musical talents and *his passion for music,* he bent himself (to his task) with a steadfastness and *single-mindedness* that stagger the imagination."[7]

Koussevitzky's was not a lone figure in achieving international acclaim and creating a unique, superb symphonic ensemble in his own musical image in spite of imperfections and gaps in early musical training. Such was also the case with Leopold Stokowski. When Stokowski was studying at London's Royal College of Music, he was not obliged to undertake the full range of musical disciplines in order to achieve his degree as an organist. At every opportunity he seems to have opted for cutting corners to achieve his goals, a personal characteristic which his biographer, Abram Chasins, was able to trace throughout his career. As with Koussevitzky's mode of music making, his interest centred not on an intellectual but an emotional approach to the symphonic literature based upon the creation of a panoply of orchestra colour and sonority. Chasins, in his balanced and best researched biography of this enigmatic figure who, when interviewed, was often 'economic with the truth' in regard to himself, sums up Stokowski's talent in a short paragraph which could equally have been written about Koussevitzky.

"The man was a human dynamo *with unlimited powers to excite other musicians* to achievements far beyond their normal capacities, *to mesmerise* audiences, and to provoke critics and colleagues to unprintable condemnation, even as they extolled his conductorial genius."

In spite of all the controversy surrounding Stokowski, renowned colleagues noted for their impeccable musical backgrounds and culture were his most enthusiastic supporters. George Szell declared him "a born conductor"; the composer, Sergei Rachmaninoff, both a virtuoso pianist and a conductor of

---

[7] Moses Smith, Music Critic/Author. *Koussevitzsky.* Allen Towne & Heath, 1947.

acknowledged brilliance, referred to Stokowski's conducting as "sheer genius" and Felix Weingartner, one of the last centuries' historic classic conducting figures, stated that Stokowski exerted "a magnetic effect on the orchestra and audience."[8]

Both Koussevitzky and Stokowski were aware of their limitations and wisely, like skilled tailors cutting a garment according to the cloth, constructed their careers and musical defences around them. Despite imperfect musical training and having initially bought or impressed their way into their profession, they settled down with an unshakeable purpose to learn their craft. They were not lone figures in the history of conducting whose unusual musical background was often the subject of controversy in their lifetimes. The names of Beecham and Munch, both men of great personal wealth who, without doubt, initially bought their way into the profession, spring to mind. Virgil Thomson, in an article in the Art of Musical Criticism, writes of Koussevitzky, Stokowski, Beecham and Munch as "great artistes all". Of Koussevitzky and Stokowski he wrote, "They contributed more of value to the glory of their art than most of the first-prize-in-harmony boys ever have."

When a conductor achieves sufficient fame to rate a full biography or, at very least, more than a dozen lines in Groves Dictionary of Music & Musicians, invariably, to accompany the bio-profiles, there are interviews or quotes from contemporaries regarding the conductor in rehearsal and performance. These encompass descriptions of gestures and body movements that come under the broad heading of conducting technique which, at some point on his path to fulfilling his career ambitions, a conductor must acquire in order to communicate his musical ideas to the musicians seated before him. The question of what constitutes this technique or even more specifically 'good' conducting technique is a much grainier topic. In truth, anything that works and produces a result that projects an accurate reproduction of the musical, tonal and dynamic ideas of the *'man in the middle'* is a successful form of conducting technique. Music Conservatories from Maine to Moscow list conducting courses, leading to a degree, which offer to teach the craft and

---

[8] Abram Chasins, Composer/Author. *Leopold Stokowski, a profile.* Hawthorn Books Inc. 1979.

prepare the budding conductor for a career.[9] Many of the present generation's established maestros have benefited from this type of educational experience. Nevertheless, the general consensus held within the profession - and most often expressed since conducting was first recognised as a musical craft - is that conductors are born rather than produced via a higher education degree. The unmistakable parallel in the profiles of orchestra conductors since the genesis of modern conducting, dating back to the 17th century composer, Jean Baptiste Lully, the first conductor to 'die for his Art' [10], reveals a kinship of egos with distinctive idiosyncratic characteristics of marked similarity. Indeed, one can draw astonishing parallels between the temperaments and careers of Lully in the 17th century and one of the dominant conducting personalities of the 20th century, Herbert von Karajan. Lully and Karajan, by cajoling, intriguing and ruthlessness in their dealings with both competition and any who opposed them, rose to ultimate positions of dominance, Lully at the Court of the powerful Louis XIV of France, and Karajan throughout all of Western Europe. Both men were driven by a calculating ambition and dealt shrewdly with those in power in order to achieve their ends. Both enjoyed the complete confidence and protection of governing authorities or powerful allies, Lully the Sun King, and Karajan the West German and Austrian Senates plus several international gramophone record cartels that bargained endlessly and fruitlessly for his exclusive services. Both men were perfectionists in all matters relating to performance and used their volcanic energies in creating musical ensembles of such unique discipline that they were the envy of Europe. Lully held monopolistic sway over all the productions of opera throughout France during his lifetime; Karajan, at the zenith of his career, held artistic directorships at Salzburg, La Scala, Milan and the Vienna State Opera and had forged an alliance with the Metropolitan Opera in New York. Simultaneously, he maintained positions as principal conductor of the Berlin Philharmonic, the Vienna Philharmonic

---

[9] Stokowski declared that the mechanical gestures of time beating "could be learned in half-an-hour." The author's Young People's Concert , The Art Of Conducting, does just that in 55 minutes and brings a young member of the audience up on stage to try his hand at it with the orchestra.

[10] Lully used a sharp pointed cane to pound out the rhythm and tempos for his orchestra. While conducting he inadvertently drove the point of the cane through his foot; gangrene set in, and he died of blood poisoning.

WEST SIDE MAESTRO

and the London Philharmonia and later, for a short time, L'Orchestre de Paris. As a final comparison, Lully, in his *Académie Royale de Musique*, later to evolve into the Paris Grand Opera, served not only as conductor for his productions but as director and stage manager as well, as Karajan was to do during his long, autocratic rule of the Salzburg Festival. Both men left behind legacies of intrigue that continued after their death.

Despite the general consensus that successful conductors are more likely to be a product of their genes than colleges of higher learning, the pedagogical teaching of conducting technique has long fascinated educators and filled many volumes of varying size, the early classic texts being penned by three of the most distinguished musicians of the past, the composers Berlioz and Wagner and the conductor Felix Weingartner. Proceeding along the lines of these early volumes, a number of other conducting textbooks have appeared from time to time, some by distinguished musicians, others, by less notable musical authorities. One of the relatively more recent text books on the subject, not by a conductor but by a composer, has been published which in advance publicity avowed to reveal musicological mysteries of the craft unknown since Orpheus strummed the first chord on his lute[11]. It did not

---

[11] The book referred to is Gunther Schuller's *The Compleat Conductor*. It is an exhaustive five hundred fifty page volume whose first hundred pages deals quite interestingly with the esthetics and history of conducting and whose remaining four hundred plus pages deals with the author's painstaking analyses of an endless array of gramophone recordings of eight masterworks by Beethoven, Brahms, Richard Strauss, Ravel, Schumann and Tschaikovsky. The recordings, all by the greatest names in conducting since the turn of the century, are placed under a microscope and mostly found wanting. The author, turned judge and jury, sets his own personal standard of what he would have the reader believe to be objective views on how each of these masterworks *must* be performed. Schuller, for the most part, ignores the personal experience of each listener, condemning, from his lofty heights as a composer, performance after performance for a minutia of detail. Many of the recordings are generally acknowledged to be among the all-time great performances set down throughout the century by its leading conductors. This volume is accompanied by its own recording of two of the masterworks examined *authentically* and competently conducted by the author, correcting all those textual lapses which form the basis of his criticism throughout the text. Both performances prove less revelatory than the premise of the book implies. Mr. Schuller's musical credentials are impeccable but his conclusions shed little light on what makes for great conductors, great conducting or great performances. It is, in the end, little more than another volume of record reviews using a highly selective discography and exhaustive musicological standards of criticism that hold little or no relevance for non-musicians but which might provide an interesting evening of discussion among musicians.

prove to live up to the promise and the best and most comprehensive contemporary textbook, long unchallenged by general consensus, is and will remain Max Rudolph's The Grammar of Conducting, never out of print and now in its seventh edition. It meticulously guides the aspiring young conductor through no less than six variations in beating each of 12 basic rhythmic patterns, *non-espressivo, light-staccato, full-staccato, espressivo-legato, marcato and tenuto*[12]. Then this meticulous musician and educator navigates his novices through the choppier musical rapids of sub-dividing conducting patterns, *ritardandi* and *accelerandi,* (slowing down and speeding up), *fermatas,* (from the Latin *fermare,* to hold; in musical terms, the extending of the length of a specific note indicated by the composer but determined by the musical judgement of the performer), accents and *synchopations,* (the displacement of musical accents from strong to weak beats), the phrasing of music, and on and on even to include the conductor's general appearance, use of the eyes as part of technique and the importance of the independent use of the right and left hands. He does not go as far as Sir Henry J. Wood who, in a highly personal, wonderfully practical and charming, thin volume titled *About Conducting,* includes advice on the proper rehearsal wardrobe to wear including undergarments "always made of wool no matter the temperature, as they absorb moisture and retain warmth, so lessening the chance of chill."

Max Rudolph begins his text with a Preface in which he describes the conductor as "part musician, part actor". He later goes on to remark that "each conductor has his own highly individual manner of directing'" and he expresses the hope that his book will help the student develop an *individual* technique and thus become "equipped to be a musical leader and not merely a time-beater".

Our analysis now moves from the general to the particular and specifically to Leonard Bernstein's technique and style of conducting. Three conductor's have been cited as his principal formative influences, Dmitri Mitropoulos, Serge Koussevitzky and Fritz Reiner. The author enjoyed the privilege of

---

[12] Without expression/ short with lightness/ very short and dry/ expressive and smooth/ marked with accents/ clinging to and savouring each note

observing these three unique and, certainly in regard to Reiner, diametrically different conductors in both concert and rehearsal.

From his early career days with the N.Y. City Symphony onwards, I was also able to observe Bernstein's conducting style and musical development. Our long professional relationship which began for me as his conducting student at Tanglewood, later as his music associate for television and ex-officio assistant at the Philharmonic, then as a first hand observer of his European years from 1968 onwards and, lastly, from the viewpoint of a professional conductor of 65 years experience, has provided me with a specific insight into what made him tick and function as a conductor.

Using Maestro Rudolph's criteria, L[13] precisely fits the bill. He was most certainly "part musician-part actor" and if you could not describe his technique of conducting as "highly individual", how else would one define it? Certainly at no time could one ever accuse him of being "a time-beater". As to his physical movements he remained for the greater part to the very end a composite of Koussevitzky and Reiner.

His theatrical stage persona was given its stamp of approval by his adopted musical godfather, Koussevitzky. The expansive gestures and outward display of emotion and passion which marked all of Koussevitzky's performances equally suited the extrovert Bernstein personality. Another key musical characteristic which marked a Bernstein performance and which he also inherited from the Russian was the endless pursuit of exquisitely coloured orchestral sonorities, transparent textures and wide ranging dynamic contrasts. However, a personality dynamic which the younger conductor never succeeded in emulating throughout his career was the imperial manner and podium dignity of his musical patriarch. It was L's flamboyant physical display, often unflatteringly referred to as "unzipped passion'", that provided many of his detractors with their most potent ammunition. Another characteristic of Koussevitzky's make-up alien to the Bernstein nature was a practised reserve and aloofness that precluded over-

---

[13] From this paragraph onwards, I will substitute an upper case 'L' for the diminutive 'Lenny' to avoid an overuse which could prove to eventually irritate in a volume of this extended length.

familiarity on the part of his orchestra musicians. Such a relationship with his players could never have suited L, he needed too much to be loved by everyone.

From Reiner, he learned traditional baton techniques and the highest standards of music preparation. These would include score reading at sight at the piano; knowing assigned compositions from memory and being able to perform any inner voice part which he might be called upon to sing without notice; to have an awareness of and be able to perform in all national and period styles; and to acquire a broad general knowledge of history and literature, interests which already formed an important part of his intellectual pursuits. L was always to acknowledge the importance of Reiner's formative influence.

All the Bernstein biographies, as well as L's tribute to Mitropoulos, following his Philharmonic predecessor's sudden and dramatic death in Milan while rehearsing Mahler's Symphony No.3, lay stress on the impact of the Greek conductor's arrival in Boston and their first meeting at a Harvard University house party. This meeting and a subsequent luncheon overflowing with sexual overtones were further to intoxicate the young Bernstein. However, there is a large divide between personal intoxication with a charismatic personality and admiration of that individual's fanatic devotion to his profession and professing to find non-existing analogous similarities in the physical mannerisms and musical techniques used by two different and unique conducting talents. As for the much quoted Mitropoulos encouragement of the young Bernstein to make a career for himself in conducting, those ideas were already circling about in his head. He was from the age of fourteen a passionate admirer of Koussevitzky. He had by this time displayed an extraordinary capacity to memorise music of every variety and he was beginning to garner an acquaintance of influential composer friends including Aaron Copland, David Diamond, William Schuman and Marc Blitzstein, all of whom fussed over and encouraged him. As a young teenager he displayed the type of leadership one associates with a conducting personality, organising, training and directing his younger brother and sister along with friends in home grown productions of opera and operetta. At Harvard he constantly manoeuvred to place himself before the public whether as accompanist of the Harvard Glee Club, improvising music to silent films for the Harvard Film Society or writing music criticism for the Harvard Advocate. He composed incidental music for the Harvard Classical Club's production of Aristophanes' *The Birds*. It was with this production that he made his conducting debut. Following one of these performances, it was Aaron Copland who first suggested that he take up the career of a conductor. Not six weeks after the Harvard production of The Birds, Bernstein went one step further than Copland's suggestion by emulating the young Orson Wells in staging, directing and performing as pianist/conductor for Marc Blitzstein's musical satire, *The Cradle Will Rock*. The driving ambition to be in the spotlight was not a character trait that was generated by his meetings with Mitropoulos. It had been part of his makeup from a very young age. The primary factor that drew this wildly ambitious, highly gifted, young musician to the Greek conductor was the constant hope that the series of promises Mitropoulos had made to him would lead to career advancement. In the end, the promises proved to be empty, unfulfilled gestures. As regards conducting technique, the decision to eschew the use of a baton would seem to be the only obvious initial influence. Of Mitropoulos' excessive mannerisms, the 'podium launch' was much later to become manifest in L's conducting vocabulary. In early days it only took the form of a slight rising up on the toes prior to musically climactic moments. It became more intrusive during the latter years of his career. However, at no time did it ever reach the degree of exaggeration as practised either by Mitropoulos or Leon Barzin, George Balanchine's Music Director at the N.Y. City Ballet.[14] Except for L's refusal to use a baton, (much to Reiner's annoyance in early career days), which may or may not have been a conscious imitation of the Greek conductor, Mitropoulos' influence, in retrospect, would seem to relate more to the direction taken in his younger colleague's personal rather than musical life.

---

[14] Leon Barzin, (1900-1999) Belgian-American conductor; flamboyant Music Director of the N.Y. City Ballet (1948-58) Although Barzin's baton technique was superb, his conducting performance before his orchestra was additionally punctuated by stratospheric leaps at regular intervals during the ballet which one more readily associated with a *danseur noble* executing an *entrechat* on stage than to the conductor in the orchestra pit.

WEST SIDE MAESTRO

About Critics, Criticism & L

Thousands of words have been poured onto the pages of biography and the critical columns of newspapers and magazines obsessing upon Bernstein's highly individual style of conducting and the 'larger-than-life' extrovert character of the Bernstein podium personality. It was rare to read a music criticism that did not hash and rehash the gestures, emotional grimaces, pelvic thrusts and aerial dynamic leaps. A disproportionate amount of space continued to the end to be devoted to those physical mannerisms that had long been accepted as an intrinsic part of his psyche and music making. On the whole the American critics during the most crucial period of his career and development, 1943 - 1968, when he rose to become one of the handful of conductors who would dominate the international music world in the second half of the 20th century, tended to be not only denigrating and unkind in contrast to their mostly enthusiastic pro-Bernstein European colleagues but, in blunt terms, unfair, indeed prejudiced, against this upstart who remained the darling of his audience no matter how poisoned the tips of their literary arrows they let fly.

What was his musical crime? Surely not that he restored one of America's great orchestras, brought low by years of lack of discipline under a rudderless leadership, to its former glory; or that, via his television appearances he, if not converting all and sundry, minimally succeeded in bringing classical music into the homes of a massive TV audience addicted mostly to lighter fare; or, that he had written hit Broadway musicals and helped further develop the most original and unique music structure contributed by American composers to their craft, an accomplishment which gave him instant credibility with that vast audience he was attempting to reach.[15] While such may have caused a peripheral irritation to the American critical cognoscenti, I prefer an 'Oliver-Stone' conspiracy theory. I believe, that in the unspoken agenda of a few key American music critics, Bernstein's

---

[15] It is documented that his Broadway connection did jar the sensibilities of Serge Koussevitzky, whose views and influence weighed heavily in the direction his protege's career was to take. Evidence also abounds that Lenny's composing gift for the stage musical also raised the hackles on the self-appointed elite, those 'movers and shakers' whose pervading 'snobbism' has long dominated the classical industry in America.

greatest crime was that he was the first American entry of international potential in a profession previously considered to be the exclusive domain of Europeans. "Ridiculous! Impossible!" would be the shocked and predictable, defensive response from a stung critical fraternity. 'After all, we never wrote in a vituperative manner about Thomas Schippers, Alfred Wallenstein, Thor Johnson, Walter Hendl or Isler Solomon.'[16] The response to such a reply would be that L was a much bigger target. Up until his entrance into the spotlight, the most influential music critics, the Boards of Directors of most major American Orchestras and the concert-going cognoscenti viewed American conductors as strictly second division. By that I do not mean second rate. All the Americans I mentioned were first class musicians and conductors if lacking L's 'candle power'. However, their careers were only permitted to flourish within *quasi* second division orchestras with the occasional major orchestra guest conducting opportunity offered, for the most part, during summer music festivals or as a last minute substitution for an ailing Maestro. Following L's historic national debut with the N.Y. Philharmonic, this predetermined scenario, defining the accepted position to which an American conductor might aspire, changed dramatically.

After his relatively short career as Assistant Conductor with the Philharmonic, the next orchestra with which L was closely identified was the New York City Symphony, which, for all its enthusiasm and *brio*, was very much a second division ensemble struggling with both budgetary problems and maintaining performance standards. During his three years tenure with the City Symphony, it seemed that L could not put a foot wrong as far as the majority of New York music critics were concerned, the most conspicuous

---

[16] Thomas Schippers, protege of composer Gian-Carlo Menotti; international opera conductor; With his Hollywood good looks, carefully sculptured by plastic surgeons, and powerful connections, he was the only American conductor whose musical gifts and career, for a time, threatened to rival Bernstein's. In the end, he opted for a quieter life and settled down as Music Director & Laureate of the Cincinnati Symphony, 1970-77. His life was tragically cut short by lung cancer at the young age of 47. Alfred Wallenstein, American cellist and conductor; Music Director of the Los Angeles Philharmonic and subsequently the Hollywood Bowl concerts, 1943-56.Thor Johnson, Kousevitzky protege; principal conductor of the Cincinatti Symphony,1947-58.Walter Hendl, pupil of Fritz Reiner; Asst. Conductor, N.Y. Philharmonic, 1945-49;Music Direcctor of the Dallas Symphony, 1949-58.Isler Solomon, Principal Conductor later Music Director of the Indianapolis Symphony, 1956-75.

exception being the occasional personal snipe from Virgil Thomson in the N.Y. Herald Tribune. Were his podium manner and technique of conducting at this time other than they had been or were to become as his career developed? Not in the slightest. L was in full flight at every concert. His huge theatrical personality filled the former Masonic temple that had been refurbished and re-launched as *The City Center of Music and Drama*. He and his timpanist, Al Howard, no slouch either in the personality stakes, insured a level of theatrical high jinx which brought the audience almost to a cheering frenzy at the end of each concert. The critics went along with it all and responded enthusiastically. The N.Y. City Symphony was, after all, a relatively new ensemble and not challenging for a place in the first division. The programs, all highly original and varied, were a refreshing change from the standard weekly bill of fare being dished out around the corner at Carnegie Hall. N.Y. critics at this time were still in an empowered position, dispensing their favours and helping build two *second division* careers, that of a young orchestra competing for an audience with the Carnegie Hall monoliths of orchestral culture, the N.Y. Philharmonic, the Philadelphia Orchestra and the Boston Symphony, and that rarest of talented creatures, an *American* conductor of genuine potential. To his audience, however, L, from the first, was a charismatic star in the movie idol sense. He was achieving a power and status which, if he had been blessed with a thicker emotional hide, could have helped to build up a degree of immunity to all the painful criticism which was to plague him throughout his American career.

Roger Vaughan deals with the sensitive topic of music critics in his biography of Herbert von Karajan. Vaughan analyses the broad nature of contemporary music criticism and cites events in Herbert von Karajan's career when unique professional achievements were denigrated and made to seem negative in value by critics chanting a dissenting and repetitive litany decrying a perfection whose shallowness they seemed principally to be the only ones to discern.[17] At events where the general public were moved to

---

[17] Although Karajan's performances were superbly honed and beautifully performed, his critics complained of "a glossy elegance that seemed to militate against spontaneity". Phrases of this nature in an early review soon snowballed into an avalanche of meaningless banalities in an overwhelming number of record critiques of this musical giant's vast gramophone output. Karajan's reply to his critics was, 'Would they prefer if I made the orchestra sound ugly?'

levels of unbridled enthusiasm critics would pick and carp in areas of criticism so rarefied and subjective that they created more confusion for their readers than edification. A similar species of rabid, negative criticism was to plague Leonard Bernstein during his entire tenure with the N.Y. Philharmonic when there was most cause to sing his praises. Although the voice of critical dissent was to echo around him virtually to the very end, it died down to some degree during those years when he worked with the Vienna Philharmonic and other European orchestras, the period when his musical ideas changed radically and most controversially.

It might serve to clarify the roles of the artist and his critics by expanding on Roger Vaughan's cogent thoughts regarding this thorny relationship and relating our conclusions to the change of direction in which, as a result, the Bernstein career was to move and evolve.

From time to time in every century, individuals possessing rare and unique talents appear. As their careers develop their presence becomes a direct challenge to established practices within their sphere of discipline as well as to the capacity of those less talented in a position of authority to recognise, evaluate and document the nature of their gifts. Historically these endowed individuals, not only those possessing musical talents but in all fields of endeavour, have not faired well against critical antipathy which seems to rise up around them like garden weeds intent upon questioning and controlling, if not choking, vast talent and its growth to recognition and full appreciation. The history of music, both in regard to composers and performers, chronicles some of its most renowned personages as prophets without honour in their time, a scenario that the chronology of years has not altered. Conflict between talent and its critics would appear to emanate from a rather primeval source. Let us analyse a prototype scenario. A huge talent explodes on the local scene, a talent whose gifts are both prodigious and unique, but yet without a power base of influence. Who among us is competent to sit in judgement, for example, of a Mozart? The very nature of any talent encompassing such unique individual gifts dwarfs the critic's role as an arbiter of taste. Is it a critic's duty to such an artist and to the public to confine his function merely to constant reaffirmation and encouragement?

WEST SIDE MAESTRO

Human nature being what it is, is it surprising that, faced with the diminution of his formerly powerful role, boredom and resentment are more than likely to set in. Certainly there are more than enough documented instances to support the view that this has a been the timeless response of those in the position to voice their criticism in a large public forum.[18] Add to this malaise possible personal jealousies and insecurities which can and do arise and the historical response of the critic has been to magnify and pick away at whatever flaws can be isolated within the talented individual and dwell upon them obsessively, sometimes in the most deprecating and vitriolic manner. That which the critic may initially perceive as, perhaps, a personality flaw begins to dominate his critical appraisals and, in time, becomes a basis for evaluating the entire nature of the artist's talent and contribution.

American critics tend not to be sycophantic by nature and their treatment of talent has seemed, at times, to go beyond separating 'the wheat from the chaff'. Fortunately, from 1940-68, the years that marked the beginnings, growth and maturing of Leonard Bernstein's musical gifts as a conductor in N.Y. circles, there existed a group of free-lance *second string* music critics and magazine reviewers who generously encouraged and helped young American talent. On the other hand, among the ranks of both first and second string newspaper critics, there were personalities who wielded their power like Lizzie Borden's axe.[19] The worst, drunk with their own self-importance, displayed a vicious disposition combined with, unfortunately, a literate, entertaining writing style; some were composers settling old scores for what they regarded as neglect of their compositions by a particular group of artists; some were commercially minded and used harsh criticism to bring attention to themselves in order to further their newspaper careers; others were unhappy, failed musicians, usually who took their frustration out on the more accomplished who dared to enter the public arena and strive for a career; some possessed a fair amount of knowledge but used as their criteria

---

[18] Slonimsky, Lexicon of Musical Invective. Coleman-Ross Co. Inc., 1965

[19] "Lizzie Borden took an axe/ And gave her mother forty whacks/ And when she saw what she had done/ She gave her father forty-one", a noted children's chant referring to a famous murder which took place in Fall River, Massachusetts in August 1892, later the basis for Agnes deMille's ballet Fall River Legend.

only the false perfection of gramophone recordings and some, providentially, were people of both knowledge and integrity who believed it was their duty to serve the music profession and the public by using their column editorially to try to raise awareness and standards of performance.

In light of this melange of personalities we can justly pose the question as to whether the American critics were expressing strongly held sincere views when, during the Philharmonic years, they tended to denigrate all aspects of Bernstein's musical gifts? Were they merely trying to elevate their own position and assert their power and authority by cutting a unique talent down to size and, if so, whose size? In a slim volume, Conversations About Bernstein,[20] by W.W. Burton, a book that reveals as much about those interviewed as its title subject, some very interesting responses are gleaned from the interviewees, among them Harold Schonberg, retired senior music critic of the New York Times. Burton precedes his first question to Schonberg by describing him as Bernstein's severest detractor. He then asks,' How did you see your role?' Schonberg skirts about answering this simple direct question with the following reply, "Well, first of all, *I never had any argument with Bernstein's talent;* his talent was *formidable - that was never in dispute.* What *I felt* was that *his ego was getting in the way* of his music making. There was a time...when *he could not get a good review in a New York paper*...But *there was never any question about his natural gifts...*"[21]

Throughout his self-serving answer Schonberg absolves himself by privately reaffirming Bernstein's formidable talent that he admits to criticising unrelentingly in negative terms for years on end. He attempts to diminish his responsibility by drawing others into such questionable behaviour by basically saying, 'It was the local sport. Everybody was doing it.' In the footnote to the interviews Schonberg is also quoted as saying, "What difference did an unfavourable review make to him except bruise his ego?"

---

[20] Burton. Conversations About Bernstein. Oxford University Press, 1995.
[21] Authors *italics*.

WEST SIDE MAESTRO

In another of the book's interviews, Joan Peyser, L's *bete noire* because she was the first to pen a 'tell all' biography detailing the most private and personal aspects of his life, comments on Schonberg's disclaimer as follows: "It may not have affected his career but... (there) is the incredible lethal effect of public humiliation in the press... that was not just denting an ego, and Harold Schonberg knows that damn well (!)"

Music critics on both sides of the ocean tended to criticise and, in the case of the American press, ridicule Bernstein's controversial podium manner in a fashion that would lead one to believe that it was unique within the history of conductors and conducting. Yet even the smallest degree of historical research reveals a distinguished list of musicians including Beethoven and Berlioz whose podium deportment caused more than a little critical comment at the time.

Here is Ignaz von Seyfried's[22] description of Beethoven in concert:

"...at a pianissimo he would almost creep under the desk. When the volume of sound grew, he rose up as if out of a stage trap; and with the entrance of the full power of the orchestra he would stand on the tips of his toes almost as big as a giant and, waving his arms, seemed to soar upwards to the skies. Everything about him was active, not a bit of his body idle, and the man was like a *perpetuum mobile.*"

Anton Seidl, a noted 19th century Hungarian conductor favoured by Wagner, spoke of Hector Berlioz's conducting as follows:
"Now he was up in the air, then under the music desk; now he turned uneasily to the bass drum, then he waxed the flautist."

Franz Liszt's mannerisms on the podium almost caused Joseph Joachim, the noted violinist for whom Brahms wrote his D Major concerto, to turn purple with rage:

---

[22] Ignaz Xaver, Ritter von Seyfried, b.1776,d. 1841. Austrian composer and close friend of Mozart.

WEST SIDE MAESTRO

"At the conductor's desk, Liszt makes a parade of moods of despair and the stirrings of contrition and mingles them with the most sickly sentimentality and such a martyr-like air that one can hear the lies in every note and see them in every movement..." (That particular quote reads very much like Harold Schonberg or Virgil Thomson having a go at L a century later.)

Nor were critics any more tolerant of the extrovert conductor in the 20th century. Claude Debussy, writing under his journalistic pseudonym, Monsieur Croche, attended a performance of Wagner's Parsifal conducted by the gifted pianist/conductor Alfred Cortot and penned the following critique:

"Alfred Cortot is the French conductor who has used to the best advantage the pantomime customary to German conductors. Like Nikisch - he has a lock of hair, and that lock is in the highest degree arresting owing to the quivers of passion which agitate it on the slightest provocation. Sometimes it droops sadly and wearily in the tender passages...Then again it rears itself proudly in the martial passages. At such moments, Cortot advances on the orchestra and aims a threatening baton like a *banderillero* when he wants to irritate the bull...Cortot leans affectionately over the first violins, murmuring intimate secrets; he swoops round to the trombones, adjuring them with an eloquent gesture, that might be translated: 'Now my lads! Put some go into it! Try to be super-trombones!' and the obedient trombones conscientiously do their best to swallow the brass tubes."

Finally, let me offer a description of Leonard Bernstein's predecessor at the N.Y. Philharmonic, Dmitri Mitropoulos, which combines my own experience based upon regular attendance at his rehearsals and performances with the Philharmonic over a ten year period and Harold Schonberg's description of the Greek maestro in his book, *The Great Conductors.* "His beat," writes Schonberg, "was jerky, nervous and inexpressive, full of head shakes, shoulder wiggling and body writhings." I would disagree with Schonberg on only one detail and that is that the technique Mitropoulos used was totally expressive but mostly of his own neurotic personality. Everything was tense, highly angular, all shoulders and elbows. His hands, usually clenched fists, would open in legato, expressive passages, stretch towards a particular soloist or section of the orchestra and, palms parallel, his fingers would simulate a motion similar to that of kneading dough. To achieve a diminishing of sound he would crouch down and a crescendo would set his whole body in motion. At its climax he would coil himself like a spring and leave the podium as if shot out of a canon to a height of at least a foot. Virgil Thomson, in a particularly personal review, caricatured another of Mitropoulos gestures, one in which he clenched his fingers and only moved his extended thumbs in parallel motion, as similar to someone riffling a deck of playing cards.

It is inconceivable that New York's chief music critics did not possess sufficient erudition to be aware of all these and many more precedents. Why then, after he was appointed to the music directorship of the N.Y. Philharmonic, did Bernstein's podium manner cause such consternation especially following a heavy ten-year diet of Mitropoulos physical mannerisms and highly personalised gestures? The facts indicate that the first rumblings of dissent regarding the Bernstein podium demeanour date to a much earlier period in his career. A full twelve years prior to L's appointment to the Philharmonic, it was again Virgil Thomson in an influential and highly critical Herald Tribune review of 1946 who not only questioned the sincerity of Bernstein's conducting gestures but the music making behind them. The following is a small excerpt from a lengthy prose piece which began with a reverse compliment stating that Bernstein's "delightful" conducting gifts were being infected with a kind of narcissism as a result of a flirtation the young maestro was carrying on with Hollywood in hopes of becoming a cinema star. It continued:

"With every season his personal performance becomes more ostentatious, his musical one less convincing. There was a time when he used to forget occasionally and let the music speak. Nowadays, he keeps it always like the towering Italian bandmasters of forty years ago, a vehicle for the waving about of hair, for the twisting of shoulders and torso, for the miming of facial expression of uncontrolled emotional states. If all this did not involve musical obfuscation, if it were merely the *prima donna* airs of a great artist, nobody would mind. But his conducting today, for all the skill and talent that lies behind it, reveals little except the constant distortion of musical works, ancient and modern, into cartoons to illustrate the blithe career of a sort of musical Dick Tracy."[23]

Even within this short critique, which ran in total to about 500 words, Virgil Thomson's imperious style, wit and imaginative turn of phrase were challenging and entertaining even though his motives may have been less than pure and open to question. This early review proved to be the turning point in L's relationship with the N.Y. critical fraternity and specifically, at the time of his Philharmonic appointment, with one critic in particular, Harold Schonberg, who was a second string critic on the N.Y. Times when the Thomson's review first appeared in print. The Thomson broadside represented the first major newspaper editorial, (Thomson's reviews were rarely just critiques), to burst the bubble of praise which had hovered halo-like above L since his spectacular N.Y. Philharmonic debut and his joining in partnership with the New York City Symphony. Joan Peyser in her 1987 Bernstein biography reports that L later spoke openly of Thomson's 'vendetta' as being motivated by both personal and professional reasons. I cannot comment on whether L's personal accusation against Thomson contained substance or whether the erudite music critic's professional judgement could be influenced by a rebuff of a personal nature that had little to do with his professional life. I can report Bernstein's antipathy towards Thomson one evening outside the old Metropolitan Opera House at a performance by   Ballet Theatre. Aaron Copland, Morton Gould, Virgil Thomson and L were all scheduled to conduct their own scores to ballets that they had composed on commission from that company. The two men met casually just prior to the performance. The short, rotund Thomson was very effusive and overly familiar, fingering the studs on L's dress shirt and addressing him as "Baby!". L, who was courteous but coldly matter of fact with Thomson, had some uncomplimentary comments to make after the critic departed through the stage door. This occurrence not withstanding, certain more specific evidence lends credence to L's second accusation of professional motivation and malice being behind Thomson's   negative review.

---

[23] NY Herald Tribune, October 16, 1946

WEST SIDE MAESTRO

Examining the program content over L's three seasons with the N.Y. City Orchestra, we note an unusual amount of contemporary music, a large proportion of which were modern compositions by living American composers, (Randall Thompson, Walter Piston, Samuel Barber, Aaron Copland, Mark Blitzstein, Roy Harris, David Diamond and, from Mexico, Carlos Chavez). Nowhere among the list appears the name of Virgil Thomson, a highly respected member of the New York League of Composers. This was not merely an oversight on L's part. He quite openly expressed his dislike of Thomson's music. To exacerbate the rise in the critic's bile that so obvious a slight must have generated, gossip of L's indiscreet, outspoken negative opinions must certainly have reached his ears. To rankle the critic even further was the attention and success Bernstein was garnering as a composer not only within the specialised world of Broadway but with the classical Establishment as well. Thomson had evaluated L's talents as a serious composer in most reserved terms in his Herald Tribune column. This assessment followed the 1944 premiere of L's Symphony No.1, *Jeremiah*. *Jeremiah* had initially lost out in a national competition in which it had been entered. Although the writer Paul Bowles, a second string critic at the Tribune at the time and himself a composer, was later to contribute an effusive review following its public premiere declaring that "it outranks every other symphonic product by any American composer of the younger generation", Thomson was of a different mind. "It is not a masterpiece by any means", he wrote, "but it has solid orchestral qualities and a certain charm that should give it a *temporary* popularity." Despite Thomson's well-publicised reserved judgement, *Jeremiah* went on to win the N.Y. Critics Circle Award for 1943-44. One can only speculate upon the resentment with which Thomson might have viewed this award for a composer and a composition that he, the dean of New York critics, had, for the most part, patronisingly dismissed. It was an open secret in professional music circles that Thomson 'wore two hats' in his Herald Tribune post. Their chief music critic was not above using his exalted position to subtly intimidate or even to stoop to a bit of arm-twisting to *encourage* artists to perform his music. This was borne out to the author 10 years later in relation to the knockout blow a scathing Thomson review had inflicted upon Mitropoulos that began a sequence of events that would eventually remove the Greek maestro from his position as Music Director of the N.Y. Philharmonic.

Mitropoulos spoke of Thomson's review and the pain it had caused him to anyone who would listen. I heard him refer to it on several occasions in company of Philharmonic musicians. He was in no doubt that what had precipitated the attack was his refusal to use his influence on the composer/critic's behalf with the N.Y. Philharmonic Chamber Ensemble. Virgil Thomson, composer, was a man you crossed only at your peril, for behind him lay the authority of the chief music critic of New York's second most powerful quality newspaper.

When one compares a Harold Schonberg review of a Bernstein concert prior to the Thomson review of 1946,
"The atmosphere crackled like the rhythms in a Stravinsky ballet. Bernstein spoke the language of his young orchestra and his young audience.",

or that of Olin Downes, chief critic of the N.Y. Times,
"For vividness, conviction, imagination, we do not expect soon to see this concert surpassed.",

to the change in tone following the Thomson editorial, ie: Olin Downe's review in November 1947,
"...we do not see each gyration of Leonard Bernstein on the platform as essential to the most efficient conducting.",

there seems little doubt that the establishment were taking a more critical assessment of Bernstein's talents based upon the subjective criteria set up by Thomson in his negative editorial in which he accused Bernstein of *"turning ever more firmly away from objective music making and to have embraced a career of sheer vainglory."*

Thomson's accusation is patently absurd on two levels. All music performance is subjective as are all reviews of music performances. 'Objectivity' is an idealised fiction when applied to music makers and music

WEST SIDE MAESTRO

making, a clever turn of phrase long used as a weapon by critics to establish their position as arbiters of taste. Even today's *avant garde* computer composed music, programmed to be performed at unvarying metronome speeds, must initially be set up by a human mind using its own subjective criteria to determine the constituent elements of the program including tempo, phrasing and the gradation of dynamics from very soft, *pianissimo*, to very loud, *fortissimo*. The other, more practical reason, about which Thomson had to be aware and which underlines his personal prejudice and the unfairness of his assessment, was the very limited rehearsal schedule L was allotted with the N.Y. City Orchestra to prepare extraordinarily difficult programs of music virtually unknown to the musicians beforehand. Most of the rehearsal time, simply from a purely practical approach, was spent just getting through the music in the first instance and then rerunning the more difficult passages to provide the players with a degree of performing security to insure the works did not fall apart in performance. L's interpretations were, in fact, quite straightforward without the exaggeration or mannerisms of the meticulously rehearsed, highly personalised readings by conductors such as Koussevitzky. The 'extra something' the City orchestra's presentations did acquire was the product of a combination of a collective Niagara Falls of adrenaline, the constant sheer terror of walking a musical tightrope over an ever-threatening abyss of ensemble pitfalls and L's unbridled energy which he let loose at each performance to inspire and urge on his charges to a successful conclusion. I have attended concerts in later years when the Bernstein podium deportment was, to say the least, 'over the top' and invited criticism. On one of these occasions his exaggerated public demeanour was motivated by fear of a specific orchestra's technical inadequacy. In this situation, L, in his 'angst'-filled desire to cover up collective shortcomings, opted for 'putting on a show'. The concert to which I refer occurred during one of my summers at Tanglewood. L was conducting the newly formed but not yet integrated student orchestra in a performance of the suite from Copland's ballet, *Billy The Kid*. The visual results in concert, especially in *The Gunfight* section, proved highly entertaining but it was quite obvious to all those present sensitive to the orchestra's technical problems as to what was going on and why. Such was never the case at the City Center concerts. Whatever the level of conducting 'razzle-dazzle' to

46

which we were treated, it never deflected from the music but only added to our enjoyment and understanding. Though certainly flamboyant, few, if any of the huge crowd of regulars whose acquaintance one made from concert to concert and season to season, ever voiced the criticism that what was taking place was a phoney display by a young conductor self-aggrandising to the detriment of the music or his musicians. The childlike sense of discovery for audience, orchestra and conductor at those early Bernstein concerts was, in the opinion of many, never duplicated to that same degree ever again in the years to come.

Though the euphoria within the seemingly invulnerable enchanted world of America's wonder boy of music had been temporarily disrupted by the entrance of the black prince of musical journalism, any impression that Bernstein was never to receive another word of critical praise from the American press would be mistaken.

A final altercation at a City Hall meeting during which L stood up and shouted 'Fraud!' at those City Hall politicians who had from the first given only notional support to the City orchestra rather than the much needed proper funding it required, resulted in his severing his ties with the New York City Symphony. He was once again a free-lance conductor. Although his credentials did not produce the immediate offer of one of the excellent second division orchestras within America's 'top-20', it should be noted that there were very few major openings on offer at the time that he would have considered. His celebrity did guarantee continued interest and guest engagements from the various commercial and orchestral managements at home, in Canada and abroad. At the time, there was much speculative talk that he would succeed Koussevitzky in Boston. In retrospect, his ultimate dream of inheriting the Boston Symphony from his mentor was a non-starter from the word go, even with all the influence the Russian maestro brought to bear on his behalf among his powerful Boston acquaintance. The Boards of Directors of American Orchestras were ultra conservative. From the turn of the century, American orchestras had been almost exclusively in the hands of conductors from across the Atlantic. The idea of a appointing a relatively inexperienced young American in preference to a European to the directorship of one of the country's three greatest orchestras was never an odds-on favourite with the cultural bookmakers. Nevertheless, L had already established his credentials abroad in London and Prague and he was about to embark on one of the key ongoing musical relationships of his career and life, that of 'Messiah of music' in the state of Israel. Wherever he went the magic of his enormous musical gifts and charisma continued to cast a charm and good to excellent reviews were the general response. Nor were the storm clouds which gathered in the wake of Thomson's early attack to cast a permanent shadow over his further accomplishments within his New York based career. In the ten-year period prior to his appointment to the Philharmonic his national reputation grew, thanks to the power of films, television and Broadway. At the time of his Philharmonic appointment, Leonard Bernstein was the most famous classical musician America had ever known. His list of successes was varied and impressive. Alongside the commercial successes of his Broadway musicals, *'On The Town'*, *'Wonderful Town'* and *'West Side Story'*, he made a spectacular television debut as America's music guru on the Ford Foundation television series, *Omnibus*. His more traditional music associations as guest conductor with the Symphony of the Air, the N.Y. Philharmonic, the Philadelphia Orchestra and the Boston Symphony were all generally received with enthusiasm by the press. Even the one major failure of the period, the musical *Candide*, brought forth praise for his brilliant and witty score from the majority of critics. He seemed once again in a position where he could not put a foot wrong.

Changes in his relationship with the Press soon after his appointment to the Philharmonic were not precipitated by L but by the retirement of one of his consistent supporters, Howard Taubman, Chief Music Editor of the N.Y. Times. Taubman's replacement, Harold Schonberg, was to become the leader of the pack of critical hounds baying at his heels during the following crucial ten years of his American career. The barrage of negative American music criticism in contrast to his overwhelming reception in Europe in the mid '60's proved to be one of the factors in Leonard Bernstein severing his commitment to the N.Y. Philharmonic in 1968 and, consequently, to his American career. The thorny relationship of artist and his critics led to the change of direction in which the Bernstein career was to move and evolve. As a result, America lost one its important voices and Vienna gained an adopted son with whom they could challenge Herbert von Karajan's European supremacy. Perhaps that was Bernstein's greatest appeal to the Viennese, that he could be their cultural sledgehammer in yet another glorious intrigue in which that city revels. With his cultural transplant, L, in the eyes of many, ceased to grow as a musician and became the pampered darling of Viennese society in which, as a passionately committed Jew, one might have expected him to feel alien and a sense of revulsion. Certainly, he never fulfilled in his own eyes his ambitions as a serious composer. The acclaimed *masterpiece*, which he longed to dredge from the sub-conscious of his considerable intellectual and emotional depths, did result in four important late compositions, an opera, two song cycles and a violin concerto, but, as in the past, acceptance was to be denied him by a section of the critical fraternity whose reviews ranged from begrudging to carping to vicious onslaughts. Acceptance as a serious American composer contributing to the contemporary dialogue equally continued to elude him among his colleagues. It would not be incorrect to observe that his volatile and mercurial personality, consciously agreeing a diary of never-ending over-commitment and his sometime reliance on his facile musical gifts, contributed to the self-deception that such acceptance among the American composer fraternity would prove his destiny. Was the final third of his career, therefore, merely a recycling of the triumphs of the past? Were the changes in his musical ideas and style as a composer along with his music making as one of the world's unique conducting personalities the portrait of an artist undergoing a radical revaluation and questioning of the validity of his past concepts and accomplishments? Were they merely the product of keeping up with changing trends and commercial alliances that required new sounding, competing commercial product to supersede other of the artist's product already flooding the market place? The answer lies in a detailed examination of the substantial quantity of recordings, videos, DVD's and writings documenting the many faceted Bernstein career from the exciting early days of self-discovery to his final recording just a month prior to his death conducting the Boston Symphony, the orchestra which he always believed it was his destiny to lead.[24]

---

[24] Volume 2 of Took It a Tempo deals in detail with an analysis of L's huge catalogue of sound recordings and filmed concerts in his recreative aspect of hid career as a concert artist.

WEST SIDE MAESTRO

2. TELEVISION'S FIRST GURU OF MUSIC

The Omnibus Programs

A Behind The Scenes Look and Analysis

1. Beethoven's Symphony No.5
2. The World of Jazz

I have outlined in my Preface the set of unexpected and, certainly for me, exciting circumstances that led to my becoming Leonard Bernstein's musical assistant. The events which followed his telephone call inviting me to become part of the team for his *Omnibus* television lectures[25] proved to be just as challenging as the main task which I faced of serving as L's musical associate.

The production team that mounted these remarkable, ground breaking first television telecasts were led by one of the broadcasting industry's important program innovators, Robert Saudek. In the early 1950's, Saudek and his associates were as much the new boys on the block within the relatively young television industry as was L. Their famed reputation within the historic annals of the industry is based virtually upon a single series titled *Omnibus* which Saudek conceived and developed for the Ford Foundation TV/Radio Workshop in 1951. *Omnibus* was telecast on the CBS television network for four years but when the Ford Foundation ended its sponsorship, Saudek formed his own production group, Robert Saudek Associates and continued to produce his unique Arts mixture for the next five years, moving first to the ABC and then to the NBC networks. *Omnibus* set a standard for a range of Arts programs which has yet to be equalled much less surpassed. Not the least of their contributions to television and to the international world of music was their launching of a young Leonard Bernstein to present a series of remarkable musical essays which captured the nation's

---

[25] The Bernstein/Omnibus appearances were never referred to at the time as 'lectures' but simply as programs. 1

imagination. It proved to be the jewel in the crown of their brilliant, highly eclectic weekly Arts Program. It transformed the career of this already acknowledged dazzling young musician to that of a television superstar. The Bernstein TV essays drew ever larger audiences and against all trends became a pillar of CBS's proudly heralded Sunday afternoon 'egg head slot'.

His debut television essay examined the first movement of Beethoven's Fifth Symphony. Using Beethoven's own sketchbooks, L reconstructed the formative struggles of genius, clearly exemplified in the sketches by the many varied alternate possibilities which the composer explored alongside other material rejected in violent crossings out. Here was a drama that explored the creative process itself, "a bloody record of an inner battle[26]."

Yet, even the most lucid and beautifully constructed script projected by this most photogenic, velvet voiced young musician with Hollywood good looks would not alone have produced the magnitude of success that this debut program enjoyed. The production values of the program coalesced with the script in a manner to produce a communicative *tour de force* on what at first hand might have been understandably projected to be a remote, esoteric idea appropriate only for educational television rather than for prime time family television viewing. But work it did as L moved about on a studio floor transformed into a gigantic facsimile of the first page of Beethoven's Fifth Symphony populated by instrumentalists who themselves were moved about or dismissed to coincide with the various changes of thought Beethoven underwent as he worked to perfect the famous opening bars of this most powerful of symphonies.

Although L is credited in virtually all existing references as being the sole author of the script of this innovative and ground breaking television program, the name of Arnold Sundagaard, a professional writer, appears on an early pre-edited Bernstein version as being co-writer. Research for another Beethoven program had been submitted to *Omnibus* by the conductor, Wheeler Beckett, closely associated at the time with the presentation of Young People's concerts. In Joan Peyser's biography, L is

---

[26] Unless otherwise noted all quotations in this chapter relating to the Omnibus television scripts are taken from 'The Joy of Music', by Leonard Bernstein, published Simon & Schuster, 1959

quoted as rather ungenerously referring to 'somebody or other doing this segment' prior to his appearance on the scene, a version which the Saudek feature editor, Mary Ahearn, deemed unsatisfactory. However, when I was working on editing the *Omnibus* scripts for what was to become the first best selling collection of Bernstein writings, 'The Joy of Music', I made note of Arnold Sundagaard's name listed on the script alongside L's name as co-author of the Beethoven program. The script, already in a typed working version as distinguished from the typical Bernstein hand written, first thoughts versions, which invariably occupied pages and pages of lined legal sized pads, had obviously been approved and was already being used by the technical crew and director to plan the actual production. As with all of L's shows, there was never such a thing as an absolutely finished script. He would make changes right up to air time, scratching out text and placing his rewrites in the script's wide margins provided specifically for the technical notes of the production and camera crew. So it was with the Beethoven script, which had many crossings out, and new thoughts pencilled in. As L invariably committed these scripts to memory there was never a problem of being confused by a disorganised looking page of script. The only danger lay in a possible memory slip that did actually occur on one of the later programs.

I did not become L's assistant until his third '*Omnibus*' telecast, '*The Art of Conducting*'. The first two programs had proved very successful, the second, '*The World of Jazz*', not quite as spectacularly as the first. With all his book learned knowledge and the influence of several important jazz musician friends, L himself was not steeped in nor, as a performing musician, a convincing exponent of jazz. He could use it skilfully as a compositional tool both in his symphonic writing and his scores to musicals but the results projected only the surface elements of an intellectually contrived jazz rather than its genuine emotional, joyful and natural spontaneous nature. Nevertheless, his Omnibus *World of Jazz*, riding in on the coattails of the extraordinary success enjoyed by the Beethoven program of the previous year, introduced a second season of Bernstein explorations into the many faceted world of music and again captured the imagination of 'middlebrow' America. The *Jazz* script contained all the over generous characteristics that were to mark and, to a degree, mar several of the later televised *Young People's Concerts*. The text is interesting enough but there is an awful lot of it covering, albeit in the typically clear and relatively uncomplicated best Bernstein fireside manner, a whole range of complex technical musical subjects. In this one show his brief encompassed the following: Western scales, 'blue notes', quarter tones, rhythm and syncopation, orchestration, an analysis of the lyrics for blues and popular song, theme and variations, improvisation, counterpoint, tonality plus a potted history of jazz, from whence it came and to where it was going.[27] All this was topped off at the end by a performance of L's unknown, relatively new esoteric work for jazz band and clarinet solo, *Prelude, Fugue and Riffs*, which, despite the presence of its accomplished soloist, Al Galidoro, a well known recording session and Big Band popular musician, must have flown straight over the heads of a large percentage of viewers. Nevertheless, the Bernstein magic, aided by a bevy of skilled jazz performers, first class production, and the Pied Piper quality of the maestro himself, again scored heavily. Even his daring to sing some of the jazz examples in his croaking baritone style only served, after viewers recovered from the shock or stopped laughing, to make him more human and natural to his audience. Most important of all, he confirmed that the mammoth success enjoyed by the Beethoven program the year before was not a fluke, that he possessed genuine television star quality and that he was now on a path of ascendance that would soon establish him as a world figure within the musical Arts.

3. The Art of Conducting

It was with his next televised special, The Art of Conducting, whose production preparation began straightaway after the 'Jazz' show, that I joined L as his assistant. After inviting me to his apartment on 57th Street, conveniently located opposite Carnegie Hall, to generally outline my duties, he sent me off to meet Paul Feigay, an associate producer with the Saudek

---

[27] It was while I was working on editing the jazz script for 'The Joy of Music' that I came to the decision to resign as Lenny's assistant and pursue my own career. Nevertheless, the completed work and comments I delivered on both the Conducting and Jazz chapters were retained by Lenny and his publishers, Simon & Schuster, including the single footnote relating to "blue notes" in the descending jazz scale ('The Joy of Music', pg.99) .

WEST SIDE MAESTRO

Organisation and his long time friend dating back to their professional association with the show, *On The Town*. It was Paul, according to all written accounts, who introduced L to Mary Ahearn, *Omnibus*'s chief feature editor, when problems first arose over a script for a Beethoven project under consideration by the Saudek group. My first meeting with Paul, a tall, overweight, bluff individual who smiled too much and exuded a perspiration quotient that could fill a small swimming pool, was short, shocking and to the point. Three seconds after I introduced myself, he looked up from his desk and barked out percussively, " The job pays $200, take it or leave it!" Despite having had visions of a contract involving thousands, I mumbled, "I'll take it." and beat a hasty retreat back to the Osborne to tell L that everything was settled and to receive his first instructions. To my astonishment, work began as soon as I arrived. There was a script that L reviewed quickly with me, explaining as we read where my background and foreground[28] presence would be required. During this work session, in walked Paul Feigay exuding charm from every pore. "You've met Paul, haven't you?" L asked. My reply was short and to the point, "Yes. *He ran over me earlier today!*" L laughed and Paul, who in private would have easily throttled me for my comment, suddenly became my best buddy.

During production rehearsals my assignments multiplied. What L seemed to appreciate most of all was that I saved him a good deal of personal wear and tear by being able to deal with all the various inquiries which previously had production staff telephoning him at all hours of the day seeking answers to relatively simple technical musical questions. While my contribution was recognised as valuable and time saving, especially as I made myself available at the Saudek offices as well as at the Osborne when L required me, I was treated as somewhat of an outsider by the staff, especially by those who viewed me as an impediment to their basking in the presence and glow of 'the great man'. I possessed little knowledge of the art of career advancement by means of that social technique referred to nowadays as networking. I was young and, in retrospect, extremely naive. I believed a simple, pragmatic approach of working diligently and delivering the goods was all that was

---

[28] My index finger appeared on camera during the show tracing the melody to a Bach Brandenburg Concerto.

required of me. It came as a jolt when, after declining to attend a social post production get-together on the grounds of fatigue and not having been home for three days, I was advised by Richard Thomas, another of the assistant producers, "Don't be foolish, the party can prove as important as the production we just did!" It was left to L, however, to raise my stock and profile with the Saudek executive. Without my knowledge following the dress rehearsal of the 'Conducting' show, he walked into the final production meeting and demanded they pay me more money for the many extra tasks I had been asked to undertake which, by this time, included working with the sound engineer on orchestra balances. [29]

I felt that I now enjoyed L's trust. I had been somewhat self-conscious of the fact that our relationship, till coming to work for him on *Omnibus*, had been only that of teacher/student at Tanglewood, albeit for three summers. He had never been less than friendly and encouraging towards me in the past but I had never pursued him following the Tanglewood summers, as had others, seeking favours. Now as his assistant, I was responsible directly to him on a broader musical basis regarding the quality and professionalism of my work. The question of how much initiative I could or dared to assume in performing my tasks was of deep concern. I was hesitant to do anything that would jeopardise my being asked to serve him or the Saudek people again. One such dilemma tested me during an early camera rehearsal run through of *The Art of Conducting* program. L was analysing various interpretations of Bach's *Brandenburg Concerto No.2*, using recordings to demonstrate how even so straightforward a work could vary from performance to performance. One of the recordings chosen was conducted by the noted Spanish cellist, Pablo Casals, then living as a self-imposed political exile in Prades, France on the border of Spain. Every summer Prades became a musical Mecca to which the world's leading musicians made pilgrimage to work with this most revered musician. Casals recorded interpretation of the Bach concerto proved highly idiosyncratic. The tempo adopted was

---

[29] As a result of Lenny's efforts on my behalf, I began to be given regular assignments by Saudek Associates. These included providing recorded incidental music for many of their drama presentations and working with Agnes de Mille as her Music Director and Orchestrator for the award winning Omnibus television special, *The Art of Ballet*, later exhibited at the Brussels World's Fair.

unusually fast and there had been a questionable substitution of a soprano saxophone for the solo piccolo trumpet called for in Bach's score. While the Casals' recording was played, L proceeded to make exaggerated, cartoon-like conducting gestures which served to further point up the overcharged nature of the performance. I was taken aback as I watched this caricature but too intimidated at first to say anything. The Saudek executive, generally enthusiastic over virtually everything that L did, seemed unconcerned over this breach of professional etiquette. Saudek, himself, who could boast a musical pedigree of parents who were both professional musicians, did not specifically react either. Everyone just chuckled away at L's send-up of this much-loved musician.[30] As the only professional musician on the organisation's staff and, more important, as a conductor, I recognised the potential pitfall and propaganda fallout it might produce. I finally decided to take the risk of broaching the matter.

"Lenny", I asked, "Do you think it wise to mock Casals in that manner?"

"It's only a bit of fun", he replied.

"Casals is God!", I went on, 'When you make fun of him, you are making fun of God."

L's expression changed when he realised the full implications of my remarks. "I'll fix it", he said firmly, and fix it he did. Our working relationship had taken a giant step forward. It confirmed to him where my first loyalties lay and that he could rely upon me in sensitive situations to voice an opinion in which his interests would be my prime consideration. That special frankness marked our relationship up until his full appointment as Principal Conductor of the NY Philharmonic in 1958.

As for 'The Art of Conducting', the telecast again aroused enormous enthusiasm. Every armchair music lover had his fantasy of conducting a symphony orchestra realised. Even better, the entire country had received

---

[30] This pampering and total acceptance of everything Lenny did grew within the Saudek Organisation over the years. It not only ended up costing the network a good deal of money but on one occasion risked Lenny's popularity with his television viewers while simultaneously ruining one of his best television scripts.

free tutelage in baton technique from a young master of the craft. By the conclusion of the program, America's army of 'closet' conductors had been taught the correct conducting patterns for a quick three rhythm conducted one beat to the bar, (Strauss' *'The Blue Danube'* Waltz); a two rhythm, two beats to the bar, (the *Ode to Joy* theme from Beethoven's 9th Symphony); a three rhythm, three beats to the bar, (Schubert's *'Unfinished'* Symphony); a four rhythm, four beats to the bar, (Prokofiev's *'Peter & The Wolf'*); and a five rhythm, five beats to the bar, divided 2 + 3, (Tschaikovsky's *'Pathetique'* Symphony). Having prepared the groundwork, L then outlined the details and subtleties to be added, i.e.: how to beat short, sharp staccato music; lyric, legato music; broad, sustained music; playful or dramatic music. Then he discussed the tempo or rate of speed at which music is played along with subtle tempo modifications such as *rubato*, (from the Italian meaning 'to rob'), shortening one beat and then lengthening another, in a manner, 'robbing Peter to pay Paul'. Most complex of all was an examination and dissection of an orchestral score executed in the best 'I can make the most difficult concept easy to understand' Bernstein style.

The program concluded with a peroration to camera examining the many aesthetic intangibles of the conductor's art whose sum produces the "communicative magic" which inspires both orchestra and listeners to an appreciation and love of music at its deepest level. The viewing audience then was given a behind the scenes glimpse of a conductor at work as L rehearsed the *Finale* to Brahms's First Symphony with The Symphony of the Air, Arturo Toscanini's former NBC Symphony which, having been disbanded, had reorganised, renamed itself and formed a brief alliance with L.

'The Art Of Conducting' proved the equal of and enjoyed a similar impact as his debut program on Beethoven. The *'Jazz'* show had not quite reached those heights and it was important to again prove to the Network that maximum viewer interest could be maintained from show to show. It was easy to recognise the affinities between the *'Beethoven'* and *'Conducting'* scripts and their inherent difference to the *Jazz* script. Both *'Beethoven'* and *'Conducting'* dealt with a single subject. The various other concepts tackled on these programs were merely sub-sections of the main topic which never

deviated from the script's germ concept, in the first instance, Beethoven's own defined musical possibilities for the first movement of his Fifth Symphony and in the latter, all the physical, mental and musical preparation involved in conducting an orchestra. The *Jazz* script was far more complex. Not only was there the huge main topic with which to deal but several important subsections, (Western scales, chromaticism, tonality, rhythm, song form, orchestration, etc.). Each was worthy of exploration on its own merit and, indeed, later on was treated as such for his televised NY Philharmonic Young People's Concerts. Finally, had L chosen to conclude the *Jazz* program with one of his party pieces, such as Gershwin's *'Rhapsody in Blue'*, instead of his own more complex and esoteric composition, *'Prelude, Fugue and Riffs'*, (an understandable self-serving decision made by 'Bernstein, the Composer'), the overall acceptance of the program would have proved more 'commercially' satisfactory. There was simply too much of too many unfamiliar elements to produce the maximum reaction hoped for. Moreover, *'Prelude, Fugue & Riffs'* was to be the harbinger of the future demands L was to make of his employers that would result in a surge in the sale of aspirin compounds for those associated with him.

4. American Musical Comedy

True to their promise to L, my several talents continued to be used by the Saudek organisation for a variety of projects requiring music in one form or other. However, for the next Bernstein *Omnibus* program on *'American Musical Comedy'*, I was passed over. I couldn't understand why at the time but was wise enough not to raise the subject with either L or the Saudek management. I simply took for granted that the bubble had burst and that it was now time to get on with my own conducting career that had begun to flourish in a meaningful manner. In light of such background, my comments on the Musical Comedy show might be viewed as a long harboured case of belated *sour grapes*. The facts are, however, that following the telecast I did express my reservations privately to Dick Thomas, the production associate with whom I worked most closely, that I thought the show was a bit of a 'dud'. After recently again viewing the kinescope, my opinion hasn't changed. The previous summer to this *Musical Comedy* special L was busy preparing for the opening of his much troubled musical, *Candide*. In retrospect, it is a pity that *Omnibus* did not use the opportunity to film this American musical in the process of creation, especially as its composer was, in the musical sphere, their 'star turn'. All the *sturm und drang* surrounding the production of *Candide* would have made for a fascinating documentary. What we had instead was a potted history of the musical in America beginning in 1866 with *The Black Crook*, lingering rather too long and uninterestingly around the turn of the century but to greater effect in the 1920's with the music of Gershwin and then working its way up to Rodgers & Hammerstein's *South Pacific*. The cast of performers, singers, dancers, and musicians was the largest the Saudek production team assembled to date but their use amounted to little more than the production of a second rate review. L's script certainly had its glimmering moments but for the most part it reeled off a lot of names, events and facts and asked questions like, 'Why do we know *Naughty Marietta*, *The Red Mill* and *Eileen* are operettas and not musical comedies?', the answers for which held little interest for the average viewer. All the elements of entertainment were present without the end result being entertaining. It was the kind of happening that would have been fascinating and funny with L seated at the piano in his living room before a small company of friends all laughing, cheering and singing along while he, with the aide of his brilliant *show-biz* pals and long time collaborators Betty Comden and Adolph Green, performed all the parts. Those were not, unfortunately, the ingredients he presented for his national audience.

5. Handel's 'Messiah'

Following his Musical Comedy lecture the telephone did ring again and I was asked to rejoin L's team at a considerable rise in fee. It seemed that the musically inexperienced office staff assigned to the *Musical Comedy* program to duplicate my wide range of tasks for the *The Art Of Conducting* were less than co-ordinated and there was an overspend several times the amount they had hoped to save from my relatively small fee. I was happy to be back and appreciated the positive comments of the television technical staff, all of whom expressed pleasure that I had returned to do what they viewed as a necessary specialist job. If I had possessed a crystal ball when the Saudek office again contracted me, I don't think I would have been quite so enthusiastic.

L had been asked by Robert Saudek to conduct a performance of the so-called '*Christmas*' *Messiah* consisting of Part 1 of Handel's famous oratorio concluding with the birth of Christ, followed by the *Hallelujah Chorus* as a finale to this favourite annual musical presentation celebrating the greatest historic event of the Christian calendar. This particular *Omnibus* special has been virtually ignored in all of the major Bernstein biographies because it was produced to be a purely musical, unscripted performance. It represented, however, another ground breaking credit to be added to the Bernstein brochure. Historic music practices up to that time had been the property of small, specialist music societies and musicologist conductors. Now on national television a young, major American conductor dared to take a fresh look and approach to a sacrosanct classic of the choral repertoire. L, working from the Ebenizah Prout version, spent a good deal of time creating his own edition. The Prout publication held the advantage of being a scholarly amalgam of the original Handel, of which at least five different versions exist, a later Mozart orchestration and the editor's own realisation of the figured bass organ and harpsichord continuo parts. Most would view the Prout edition as the height of Victoriana, but L never intended to use it in its original form. He employed a very small orchestra for the vocal arias. This increased in size for the choral ensembles for which L used Mozart's edited orchestration. The choir, about thirty-six in number, was about the same size as the one Handel used for the oratorio's Dublin premiere in 1742. This single feature alone was an important departure from contemporary convention which, since the second quarter of the 19th century, had employed massed choirs numbering from a hundred to several hundred voices to perform the *Messiah*. L recorded the *Messiah* for CBS Masterworks[31] the following year and for this complete recorded version he worked out his ideas in even greater detail. His most interesting and revolutionary decision, which he had been considering at the time of his

[31] This recording has been digitally remastered and is now available in Sony's Bernstein Century edition.

WEST SIDE MAESTRO

Omnibus telecast, was to return to the baroque practice of employing a solo male alto voice rather than opting for the long accepted Victorian custom of a female alto voice. The choice of the earlier tradition, which dated back centuries when the *castrato* singer was in vogue, proved much too daring an experiment for his television *Messiah* and L, wisely, opted to use a female alto voice instead. However, for his performances at the Philharmonic and the subsequent recording that followed, L did indeed substitute a specialist in baroque vocal music, the noted male alto, Russell Oberlin. This recording, heard with modern ears in light of the enormous advancements made in baroque scholarship over the past fifty years, sounds somewhat old-fashioned with its over-rich romantic string playing and *plummy* sounding choir. Nevertheless, there is much musically to be admired and the drama of the Christmas story is wonderfully caught by L. The importance of the *Omnibus* telecast of the *Messiah* and the subsequent public performances and recording that followed is that it underlines L's curiosity regarding early performance practice twenty-five years before Phillips Records turned its attention to specialist, early instrumental ensembles, creating from them a multi-million dollar earner for its record label.

An Introduction To Modern Music

The next scripted program embarked upon was originally titled, *Crazy Modern Music*. L's text, at that stage, existed partially in hand written, partially in typed form. From what was outlined to me at a somewhat tense first Saudek script conference, it was again set to break new ground. I better understood the reason for the tension observed at the Saudek meeting and the depth of meaning of the understated phrase "breaking new ground" when I met with L to receive his instructions. The concept he outlined to me was more akin to an impending seismic disaster of 9.7 on the Richter scale. The entire program, he informed me, was to be structured around a single work, Stravinsky's *'Symphony of Psalms'* for chorus and a most unusual orchestral ensemble. L cautioned me of the Saudek staff's opposition to the concept but, after he had spoken with Mark Blitzstein[32], Mark had convinced him to hold his ground. I certainly was in no position to add my two-pence

---

[32] Mark Blitzstein, American Composer, 1905-1964, one of an inner circle of Bernstein friends and, along with Aaron Copland, one of the formative musical influences in Bernstein's life.

worth into this highly volatile situation. My instructions were to contact Hugh Ross, the noted choral conductor of the *Schola Cantorum*, whom I knew from my years at Tanglewood, and to start putting together a choir. In addition, I discovered that I was now also responsible for booking the orchestra, something I had never attempted on a professional level though I had some experience at this kind of organisation on a non-professional level as a student at City College and post-graduate at the Juilliard School of Music.

Contracting an orchestra is a well paid but the least enviable job within the music profession, ideally suited only to a masochist with the emotional epidermis of an elephant and the thirst for power of Genghis Khan. Unless you are one of the handful of much feared contracting giants whose fingers are tightly wrapped around the throats of those musicians who expect to earn an important percentage of their annual income in return for their unswerving loyalty, you are well on your way to your first ulcer. The *occasional* Contractor, which I most certainly was, discovers that the more prestigious the musician you book the greater the possibility that he will telephone you the morning of the first rehearsal with some feeble or obscure excuse to inform you that he will be unable to do your *gig*.[33] The variety of excuses can be simple or elaborate, in most cases having to do with health or a death in the family to include the dog. The actuality is that he or she has been offered another equally or better paying job by one of the full time contractors whom a musician refuses at his/her peril. Nevertheless, undeterred and without any additional financial incentive offered by my employers for this new and exasperating task, I started dialling around. With my private directory on my lap listing the cream of my Juilliard and Tanglewood instrumentalist chums, I began putting together an orchestra of young superstars. My contracting task was somewhat unusual as the Stravinsky's *Psalmes* employs a most unique orchestration,

5 flutes, 5 oboes, 4 bassoons 4 horns, 5 trumpets, 3 Trombones & Tuba, Timpani, One Percussionist, Harp, **2 pianos (!)**, cellos and basses

---

[33] A 'gig' is musician's parlance for a paid engagement ranging from a wedding to a concert with the London Symphony Orchestra.

WEST SIDE MAESTRO

<u>No</u> clarinets and <u>no</u> violins or violas!.

Whenever stuck for a specialist instrumentalist, I telephoned a close musician friend, Raymond Sabinsky, a member of the N.Y. Philharmonic, and he would either suggest a few names or place a few calls on his own to help me out. It was fortunate that I knew many young, lesser known but outstanding musicians as the week of our *Omnibus* telecast there were no less than three other televised musical spectaculars, the premiere of Rodgers & Hammerstein's 'Cinderella', the Ed Sullivan Variety Show and a ballet spectacular. All four telecasts were employing huge orchestras and I had cornered the market on some of the best young woodwind and brass players in town.

My job as librarian appeared simple. L, at this point, had only mentioned the single Stravinsky work. Renting the music and collating it for the orchestra would be quite straightforward. I could now concentrate on my other key tasks. The contracting of the orchestra appeared well in hand so, relatively trouble free, I was able to sit with Hugh Ross while he auditioned singers for the choir. Hugh projected as a modest and very proper *olde worlde* Englishman from the days of the Raj. It was therefore left to me to pose the necessary *show-biz* questions relating to the televised aspects of the show, which would have caused him embarrassment. They were principally addressed to the potential Tenors and Basses. By modern employment standards, my impertinent probing would have seen me up before a panel of magistrates for discriminatory employment practices. "Do you own a toupee? Will you shave your beard? (only *weirdoes* or eccentrics wore beards in 1955), Do you have lifts to give you a bit more height? etc., etc." These auditions and questions went on for three days. Work for freelance choir singers in the 1950's was thin on the ground. A large majority of the auditioning singers were students who had to hold down one sort of job or other, mostly non-musical, to pay their bills. We were asking them to take off time from work to make several non-paying appearances at our auditions. Yet such was the pressure on these young people to find work in their proper profession that there was never a word of complaint.

WEST SIDE MAESTRO

It was midday on the Thursday, just nine days prior to our first orchestral rehearsal and eleven days before the telecast itself, when, without warning, the proverbial roof fell in. Richard Thomas entered the audition room and said he had to speak urgently to Hugh and myself. Requesting our present batch of auditioning singers to leave the room, we turned to the rather tense associate producer and asked to be let in on the problem. Richard informed us that L had just telephoned. He now viewed his original idea to be a non-starter. He wanted to change the entire program using a traditional symphony orchestra playing a wider range of known contemporary repertoire. **No choir!**

I broke the deafening silence with two words, "I quit!" "You can't quit", pleaded Richard. "You're the only one who can talk to him." Hugh was completely flustered but, brave man that he was, he called all the auditioning finalists back into the room to announce the news. He made the usual vague promise that the Saudek Organisation would use them all at the first opportunity and that he had some work coming up and that they would all be given first preference. Again there was total silence and, as a measure of the times, not a single word of protest from any of these gifted and now much abused young singers was spoken. They just put on their coats and quietly departed.

I headed straight over to the Osborne to see L. He was sitting with his head in his hands, obviously stressed and somewhat panicked. "These are the pieces I have decided to use", he said, proceeding to dictate what seemed an endless list of repertoire and specifying the excerpts from each work that would be used for examples. There was no mention made of the enormous contrast in instrumentation required for this newly chosen repertoire or of the many extra instrumentalists hired specifically for the Stravinsky choral symphony or the immediate need to acquire at least 26 violins, eight violas and a clarinet section in the nine days before our first rehearsal. He was unaware of the other competing television spectaculars and, other than allowing myself the indulgence of a well-deserved moan, I knew it would be pointless to bring the matter up. I headed back to the Saudek offices and brought everyone into the picture listing my requirements to get everything in place for the first orchestra rehearsal barely nine days away. It was

WEST SIDE MAESTRO

already past 4pm in the afternoon and the Thursday working day was coming to an end. I sat alone in the conference room with my pad and pencil and set out a work schedule for myself. One of my attributes has been a brain that has served me as a musical garbage dispose-al, carrying about in it all manner of music information, especially in regard to publishers and their publications. My priority at that moment was to get on the phone and start ordering the raft of new music required. Before 5.30pm, the close of the day's business, I had rented or purchase all the music required and had arranged to have it delivered by express post or messenger. I then began telephoning all the *fiddle* players I knew as well as asking my NY Philharmonic pal, Ray Sabinsky, himself a violist, to help put together a viola section for me. The next day I put in calls to all the major contractors in charge of the competing TV specials, men whose names struck terror into the hearts of musicians at their very mention, and began to bargain as if I were in an Arab bazaar. I traded off my now unneeded extra flutes, oboes, bassoons, trumpets and pianists for violinists and clarinets. My contracting colleagues needed what I had to offer as much as I needed their help, so everything was carried off in a highly co-operative spirit without my feeling any sense of being the underdog in the situation. I was helped to no small degree by the fact that I was carrying out my task for Leonard Bernstein, whom the contractors, with their sharp sense of smell for money, viewed as a potential future client. Each of them ended our conversations with, 'Give my regards to Lenny!' The weekend arrived at last and after a hectic two days everything seemed, more or less, again under control.

On Monday, before going to the office, I went to the Osborne to give a progress report and, no doubt, show L what a clever boy I had been. He looked pretty terrible the last time we spoke and quite despondent. I felt a bit of good news wouldn't go amiss. He was still in bad shape when I arrived. Obviously, he had been writing the new script the entire weekend and he looked pretty well done in. For the first of two times during our ten year working relationship I heard him speak the phrase, "I've never been in so much trouble." I uttered a few words of encouragement and assured him that everything was under control from my end and would be ready for him on Friday. "This is not what I wanted the program to be about", he said. To which I replied, "Lenny, the program is about *you. You* are what the people tune in for." I'm not sure he wanted to agree with or even hear this correct commercial evaluation of the situation but, for the moment, it did seem to help put things into perspective. His original idea would no doubt have produced a brilliant personal *tour de force* but with a minority audience. For the network, the sponsors and the Saudek association it would have produced *clicks-ville*, the onomatopoeic description current within the TV industry of all of America tuning off at one go. At this time in his career, L's instinct warned him to step back from the precipice and, on this occasion, he wisely did. As he gained in position and power, however, he became more reckless and suffered the concomitant predictable results.

The responsibility for this present sequence of events was not entirely L's fault. This incident didn't just occur; it was an accident waiting to happen. The one characteristic shared by the senior figures in L's personal and business life is that they all indulged him. What no one seemed to realise, something patently obvious when L's career is viewed in retrospect, is that he did his best work when his energies and talents were channelled by other strong personalities whom he respected. That is why *On The Town, Wonderful Town, West Side Story* and the ballet, *Fancy Free* are the massively successful amalgam they are. George Abbott and Jerome Robbins unquestioned control of all aspects of their shows may have angered, maddened and depressed their associates from time to time, but it produced absolutely the best from all of them. L, out on his own, as a loose canon, invariably caused problems for himself.

Having left him beavering away in slightly better humour than when I found him, I headed for the Saudek offices. Music had begun to arrive and kept arriving all day. There was now a huge amount of librarian work to be dealt with involving organising and marking the parts according to L's instructions. I began straightaway. By evening, all the parts had arrived and I decided to begin collating them into separate folders for the orchestra. Having completed the string books, I was horrified with the result. The large number of selections when collated into one folder would never sit on a music stand. I considered opting for two folders for each musician but all that juggling about during the show or even the sight of the second batch of

WEST SIDE MAESTRO

folders laying casually on the floor next to each stand waiting to be used would never be found acceptable and, in the end, all the fingers would be pointed in my direction as the responsible party. There was nothing to do but copy out by hand the shorter extracts onto single sheets of music paper, thus eliminating the need for the original twenty page part, the greatest portion of which was not being used. I headed home in a taxi with a mountain of music. I kept a large stock of music manuscript paper at home and I could work through the night in relative quiet. By the next morning, I was exhausted and had barely scratched the surface of the work to be completed. For those works from which an extended excerpt was to be played, making an extracted copy simply wasn't practical. There was not enough time. Those parts had to be carefully prepared with paper clips so that the musician could open to the required page. A *Cue* number and where to start and where to finish. then had to be carefully marked in pencil.

I didn't leave the house and I didn't sleep for the next seventy-two hours. Early Friday morning, sporting a three day growth of beard, I headed back into Manhattan to one of the established music copying services. I had telephoned them the previous day to say that I would be arriving at 8am for a rush job for the Bernstein television special. The magic of L's name sparked immediate agreement and I was assured that someone would be there waiting for me. In preparing the extracts, I had made only a single copy of each string part. Sufficient copies had to be made for the entire string section. Nowadays, photocopying these parts would take a matter of minutes - not so back in the 1950's. Everything took time. While the music was being reproduced, I sat at a typewriter working on an orchestra routine and cue sheet, which, itself, had then to be copied. Everything completed by 10am, I made my way to the rehearsal studio. It was about 10:15 am and the rehearsal was not scheduled to begin till 11.30am. Happily, no one as yet was about. The orchestra stands and chairs had all been set up according to a diagram that I had left at the Saudek offices on Monday.

Using the floor as a huge table, I began collating all the music in sequence according to my orchestra cue sheet. The single page extracts had reduced the volume of each folder considerably. Each now sat comfortably on its proper music stand. At about 11am the musicians slowly began to drift in. I looked a bit of a mess but I put on a big smile, greeted all of them, assigned them to their appropriate places and then awaited the arrival of L. Members of the Saudek staff along with Robert Saudek himself were the next to arrive. At 11.27am, L whirled through the door wearing the famous cape bequeathed to him by Serge Koussevitzky. There was a great stir in the room. I approached him. As he looked over this sea of unknown musicians' faces he whispered, "Who *are* all these people?" "Give a downbeat and find out", I replied, handing him a cue sheet.

L opened the collar of his cape and dramatically tossed it across the room. He energetically hopped up on the podium, gave a downbeat and, with every part and extracted cue clearly marked and in its proper sequence, he powered through the entire program in an hour. I had in the meanwhile dragged myself over to a quiet corner to collapse and try to take some satisfaction from the accomplishment of the most exhausting week of my life. As L gave a last flourishing cut off to the orchestra, everyone leaped to their feet cheering and applauding. An enthused Saudek Associates rushed over to him praising his genius. As I lay quietly in my corner I heard L reply, **'You see how easy it is when you know what you're doing!'**

The script to the *'Introduction To Modern Music'* proved to be among the most valuable of L's writings. It was later to form part of two future scripts for the Young People's Concerts and to be the cornerstone of his Norton Lectures, *'The Unanswered Question'*, at Harvard University. The *'Modern Music'* script again called for cleverly conceived graphics to help simplify difficult musical concepts. In this instance a baseball diamond was used to explain the thorny subject of tonality. "Home base" of the baseball diamond represented the *tonic* or principal note. Other notes were related to and dependent upon the *tonic* home base, but were free to use the other three bases of our baseball diamond, running around them in sequence or even skipping among them arbitrarily. Eventually, however, they always returned to their *tonic* home plate. For his musical example showing how the *relative* notes returned home to the *tonic*, L used as his musical example the popular American patriotic tune *'America'*, (which also happens to serve as the national anthem of the United Kingdom, *'God Save The Queen'*).

WEST SIDE MAESTRO

As one can see by the above example, the tonic (**T**), in this instance the marked G natural, is stated twice at the start of this tune. It is surrounded by four of its 'relatives', other notes, which move around and about it, never failing to keep in touch. Eventually, their wanderings lead them back to precisely where they began, to their 'G natural', **T**onic home base.

This simple explanation was followed by a somewhat more complex concept, the law of physics known as the Harmonic series, more commonly referred to as *overtones*. *Overtones* are a sequential pattern of musical tones produced when an object capable of vibration is set into motion by being struck. For example, when a wood hammer attached to a piano keyboard strikes a metal string which sounds the note, low C, the ear hears not only the basic tone struck but a whole series of tones produced by the vibrating string which rise sequentially in an order dictated by the natural physical laws of sound[34].

L next demonstrated and identified the order in which overtones are produced, the first being an octave above the basic tone, the second a fifth higher than that, the next a fourth above that followed by a third above that and so on until the sequence of notes become so close together and faint that the human ear can no longer distinguish or detect them. Conjuring up a variety of different melodies from imaginary primitive man onwards, L showed the changes which occurred in musical patterns as future generations became subconsciously aware of more and more pitches in the overtone series. Great emphasis is placed upon the interval of the major third, the fourth overtone. When it became part of music's vocabulary, musicians had at their disposal the three notes which make up the common chord. As L so aptly put it, Man was now in possession of the "bread and

---

[34] L was much later to refer to the overtone series in his Harvard Norton Lectures as a "musical universal" analogous to *language* universals which are shared by the world's cultures and which, according to the theories expounded by the linguistic scientist, Noam Chomsky, form part of the evidence that language capacity is an innate brain activity.

butter of Western musical culture". The inclusion into Western musical culture of more and more notes from the overtone series is dealt with at some length. Special emphasis is placed upon the evolution of the pentatonic or five note scale upon which folk music of several different countries is demonstrated to be based. Having finally introduced all twelve tones which form the Western chromatic scale, L concluded his exposition by returning to the importance of the 'tonic', pointing out that in examining the music of the past three hundred years one could now understand that somewhere among all twelve tones there had to be a tonal center, "a home plate, a point of reference, a point of repose, a focus, a locus, what you wish, but in any case a place to get back to, no matter how skittishly you may have been running around all those other bases."

Although the complexities of this script were vast and varied, everything moved along at a quick pace. When L introduced the concept of *modulation*[35], not the simplest of topics to explain to a non-musically trained audience, his chosen musical example could not help but hold every American's attention. It was the national anthem, *The Star Spangled Banner*. Later, when avant-garde elements were introduced, they proved fascinating and were handled with brevity and clarity. For the topic of *dissonance*, the word most closely associated with contemporary music, well-known excerpts from Beethoven, Brahms, Chopin and Tschaikovsky were used as examples. "Music we love most", L explained, " couldn't exist without dissonance. The dissonant note is one that doesn't belong in a chord and for that reason it will always be the most expressive note in the chord precisely *because* it doesn't belong" Wonderfully clear! Wonderfully simple!

Moving past Richard Wagner whose "music was so dissonant, so expressive, so chromatic, so wandering in its modulations from key to key that the poor listener had almost lost his tonal bearings", we arrive at music at a crossroads. We encounter Arnold Schönberg whose music led to the renting of tonality - music composed with no sense of key at all, "no home plate, no bases to run, just music using the twelve tones." L had arrived at a pivotal point in his script. No longer was he merely our guide. Behind his words was

---

[35] modulation - to pass from one key to another using proscribed rules of harmony and tones common to both keys .

the protagonist for tonality in music. This undeviating stand to which he cleaved his entire working life was later to form the basis of his Harvard Charles Eliot Norton Lectures.[36] Three questions are posed, carefully slanted to influence the listener towards L's own bias as a committed tonal composer:

1. Is Schönberg's non-tonal music denying a basic law of nature when it denies tonality?
2. Is the human ear equipped to take it all in?
3. If the human ear can take it in, will the heart be moved??

The third question was, of course, the most loaded one of the three, totally appealing to the viewer-listener's emotional subjectivity and worded in a way to encourage a prejudiced response.

As a contrast to the ultra modern ideas and sounds of Schönberg, L introduced the composers who set out to save tonality. From the solo flute introduction to Debussy's orchestral *'Prelude to the Afternoon of a Faun'* we move to the cool, dispassionate, *objective* music of Satie and then on to the music of Maurice Ravel. Originally, it was to the music of Stravinsky that the script logically should have proceeded. It was Stravinsky who lead the crusade to revitalise tonal music. It was Stravinsky to whom the younger firebrands of music looked for inspiration. But in this particular script, it was the moment when the entertainment factor took precedence over historic reality. It had been a particularly complex subject that L had undertaken and he had handled it skilfully to this point. But the show now needed something special to hold the interest of that part of the viewing audience who were not classical music enthusiasts. L provided it in spades. In previous shows, he had displayed his gifts as a pianist in short excerpts to demonstrate various points of his text. Now he appeared as a full- fledged soloist as well as conductor in the final movement of Ravels brilliant and jazzy *Piano Concerto in G Major*. If the concerto itself did not move the premise of the

---

[36] The ideas already presented in this groundbreaking program and much of what will follow will again be encountered in highly expanded form twenty years later when L stands to address the students and faculty of Harvard University and subsequently his television audience in six lectures, 'The Unanswered Question', which were to be the pinnacle of his career as an innovative thinker, educator and communicator.

script one jot forward it certainly served to showcase the full brilliance and breadth of L's talents. If anything, it underlined my comment to him the previous Monday, "The program is about you, Lenny. *You* are the reason people tune in."

Having included the Ravel as a highly entertaining five-minute break from his thorny subject, L did not permit himself other indulgences in dealing with the remainder of his script. Most of the musical examples which followed were certainly less austere than his original plan of using only the Stravinsky *Symphony de Psalms*, but, in general, the script remained uncompromising. Moving on past Satie's cool objectivity, the addition of satire by means of "funny wrong notes" is touched upon with a bit of help from Shostakovich. Then, having demonstrated how composers cleared away the cobwebs of romanticism, the ushering in of neo-classicism with Stravinsky as its leading spokesman occupies most of the rest of the program. L describes how composers began to seek inspiration by looking backward to the musical forms and composers of the 18th century and beyond to reaffirm the supremacy of tonality in the 20th century. The use of old fashioned scales or the early Greek modes and the elimination of that excessive chromaticism which had given rise to the twelve-tone nightmare was a first cleansing step. A resurgent interest in melody followed. Extracts from works by Roy Harris and Serge Prokofiev serve as demonstration models. Everything was being done to make tonality sound fresh and new and yet still modern. Turning again to 'The Star Spangled Banner' and 'America' (God Save the Queen), L performs them simultaneously on the piano pointing up the dissonant clashes that occur between the two melodies. "One could", he explains, "iron out all these clashes by altering one melody or the other", (he demonstrates), "or, to be *modern*, just leave them as they are". L has lead us into the world of modern counterpoint and music of the noted composer and teacher, Paul Hindemith. The opening of Hindemith's *Concert Music For Strings and Brass* is dissected swiftly and used to demonstrate how each of its two individual musical lines sound wonderfully melodic and unchallenging when performed in isolation. When played together, however, they create an exciting and tense modern sound of great freshness. L identifies this new, dissonant sound as *bi-tonality*, two tonalities functioning at the same time. Using Strauss's *'Blue Danube'* Waltz we are treated to a piano demonstration of bi-tonality reminiscent of one of Victor Borge's[37] funniest routines as L performs the right hand melody in C major while his left hand accompanies in a totally different key, E flat major. L returns to a discussion of Stravinsky and his use of bi-tonality in his early masterworks, the ballets *Petrouchka* and *The Rite of Spring*. The *cross rhythms* of jazz are now introduced in Gershwin's popular tune *'Fidgety Feet'*.[38] Jazz *cross rhythms*, so evident in the music of Gershwin, became a popular tool for contemporary composers such as Aaron Copland. (L performs an extended excerpt from one of Copland's most light-hearted and popular jazz influenced compositions, *El Salon Mexico*).

The new sounds, colours and instrumental combinations used by 20th century composers moves this long, complex but riveting program to its conclusion. The final text serves as both an affirmation of the personal creed of Bernstein, the composer, and a challenge to his colleagues, "If the *tonal* composer has *something fresh to say* then perhaps he will not have to resort to Schönberg's twelve tone system for guaranteed originality."

We are reminded that daily around us we are absorbing different kinds of new contemporary art. It might be in a chewing gum ad that employs a Miro or Mondrian-like design, or in background music used for television drama which might be by Bartok, or in film scores which use *avant-garde* compositional techniques to heighten the drama of the projected image. The script ends with an apotheosis. It is a summation of the underlying theme that has threaded its way through the entire program:

"It's only a step from films to the concert hall, from Wrigley's gum to the Modern Art Museum, from the drugstore novel to James Joyce's *Ulysses*.

Be glad for modern art ...(be glad for) modern music. It is your music."

---

[37] Victor Borge – concert trained Danish pianist famed for his one-man show, *ComedyIn Music.*
[38] In Gershwin's 'Fidgety Feet' the melody creates the feeling of three beats, (accents), in each bar while the chord accompaniment against the melody maintains a regular pattern of two beats to the bar

WEST SIDE MAESTRO

7. The Music Of Johann Sebastian Bach

The *Omnibus* special devoted to *'The Music of Johann Sebastian Bach'* followed hard on the heels of *'An Introduction To Modern Music'*. L's appearances on television were by now an established and a much awaited part of television's culture. In resolving to devote an entire program to the first of the 'Three B's' of music, he again chose to walk a tight rope high above his public without the aid of a safety net. The other 'two B's' had written music that the general public knew even if not everyone could attach the composer to the composition. Everyone in America knew Beethoven's Fifth Symphony, if only for its famous opening motive identified during World War 2 with the Morse code, 'three dots and a dash', representing the letter 'V', extended in meaning by propagandists to represent the nationally popular 'V for Victory' slogan. When L made his television debut program devoted to the famous first movement of Beethoven's *'Victory'* symphony, the sounds of its stirring opening measures resounded in the memories of anyone in America whose lives had been touched by that terrible world conflict. It had been heard daily for years on end on national radio introducing news or current affairs programs. It was incorporated into every cinema background score for war or spy films and its use was a *sine qua non* for the filmed newsreels reporting the war. As for Brahms, virtually everyone was familiar with and had hummed or perhaps even sung to a child his famous 'Lullaby'. Several of his Hungarian Dances were bizarrely used to choreograph the antics of our favourite cartoon characters. Johann Sebastian Bach had become known to the general American public in the 1940's mostly through one composition, the organ *Toccata and Fugue in D minor* which had been transcribed for orchestra by the charismatic maestro-turned-film-star, Leopold Stokowski and included in Walt Disney's 1940 animated foray into classical music, *Fantasia*, (not one of the Disney studio's most popular successes at the time). To most Americans, Bach was one of three composers spoken about in boring school music appreciation classes as part of a triumvirate of great composers identified by the convenient cliché, *The Three B's* of music.. How does one sell this to 'middle America'?

L attacked the problem head on in his introduction.

WEST SIDE MAESTRO

'BACH! A colossal syllable, one which makes composers tremble, brings performers to their knees, beatifies the Bach-lover, and apparently *bores the daylights out of everyone else*.'

How could every viewer not be taken with such total ingenuous honesty and not give their television guru of music a chance, at least ten minutes, before '*clicks-ville*'. Five minutes was all L ever needed to fill anyone listening to him with his own excitement for whatever he was enthusing about. The public listened and watched in its millions and another historic telecast was chalked up.

From the start L addressed himself to his musically inexperienced listeners, encouraging those new to Bach's music to open themselves to its "power, majesty, charm, delicacy, warmth and joy". To underline the point musically, he then 'joyfully' launched himself into the brilliant fanfare-like opening of Bach's choral masterpiece, *Magnificat*, whose text is a song in praise of the Blessed Virgin.

As with the *Contemporary Music* special, I had again been assigned the task to assemble the musical forces for the program, in this instance a small freelance chorus and orchestra. Freelance musicians who depend on the excellence of their last performance to secure their next engagement can be depended upon to always give that little bit extra. Under L's enthusiastic direction, the performers did most 'joyfully' project the opening chorus of the *Magnificat*. At its conclusion, L expressed a regret that most of his audience probably had never heard this work before. As a word of reassurance, he admits that even to those familiar with Bach it is difficult music to come to know.

The script continues autobiographically. L goes on to describe his own difficult experience as a youngster in coming to understand and love the music of Bach. He confesses that it had meant very little to him before the age of seventeen. He then began studying the composer's monumental setting of the *Saint Matthew Passion*. Previously, he had found most of Bach, including works assigned to him for his piano lessons, "pretty monotonous stuff". Only the virtuoso challenge of the *Chromatic Fantasy* and the deeply moving melody of the slow movement of the *Italian Concerto* spoke to him with their immediacy. The rest seemed to be "nothing but endless pages of notes, chugging along like a train." Even over-interpreting the music assigned to him never raised his interest because his artificial manner of performance only seemed to point up the 'basic dullness' of the music. L, needless to say, demonstrates his point with great theatricality at the piano.

The special quality of all of L's programs was his ability to *teach by stealth*. An example of this is his analogy to Bach's music with a subtle beauty which lies hidden beneath the surface at first contact but which, in time, is revealed to embody qualities that produce a lasting experience.

L examines the reasons Bach's music seems less immediate, less dramatic than that of, for example, Brahms or Tschaikovsky. What follows is a three minute seminar for the non-musician on *contrast* and its use by composers to create *a duality* of character between the themes or the emotions contained within a single work or movement. Examples from Beethoven and Rachmaninoff illustrate such duality. Bach's music, we are told, represented the last stand *against* this dualistic concept. A single Bach movement is concerned only with a single idea. Once the theme is stated, "the main event is over". Bach may elaborate, reiterate and discuss this principle idea but it is done without change of mood, slowing of tempo or yielding to any emotion which would alter our perception of the theme in its original presentation. The only contrasts to be found are restricted to dynamics, (loud or soft), changes of key or the varying of instrumental groupings. OK, says L in essence, it's tough going, but "let's pull in our belts, take a deep breath and get to know Bach on his own terms." A lesson learned from my many years of studying and working with L was that if you powerfully communicate with your audience with total confidence, asking them to come along with you that 'extra mile', they will respond positively in most instances. The viewing ratings achieved by this esoteric program certainly seem to support this approach.

L's script moves on to *counterpoint*. He re-introduces the example of counterpoint from his *Modern Music* program, *'The Star Spangled Banner'* played simultaneously with 'America'. Nothing to be afraid of here, we are told, counterpoint is nothing more than a set of rules for making two or more melodies go well together. In this instance, it means altering a few notes of 'America' to make the combination of tunes work together but no great harm is done and the results prove pleasing. But why does one need to complicate things with *counterpoint*? The music we hear most of the time consists only of melody supported underneath by chords. L explains that in earlier times people listened to music differently. "The ear was conditioned to hear *lines*, simultaneous melodic lines, rather than chords. Counterpoint came before harmony." He makes the observation that Bach was the representative great model for the creation of long, continuously running melody and for that reason jazz players, whose performance art is primarily involved with *horizontal* melodic improvisation, love his music.

Touching upon the affinity between Jazz and the music of Bach not only humanises the giant of the Baroque era but it provides the novice listener a sense of contemporary relevance to his music.

An extended part of the program is now devoted to understanding Bach's use of linear, (horizontal), melody in his music. We are shown how the fusion of four melodies, Soprano, Alto, Tenor and Bass, in a Bach choral creates an interaction that is simultaneously melodic, (horizontal), and harmonic, (chordal or vertical). The played and sung examples now come thick and fast and include Bach's settings of popular Lutheran hymns and one of the baroque master's most beautiful and known compositions, the chorale prelude, *'Jesu, Joy of Man's Desiring'*. Having by the end of this section presented in some detail what L describes as "the four corner's of Bach's musical world, the chorale, the chorale-prelude, the canon[39] and the fugue[40]", L undertakes an examination of Bach's *St. Matthew Passion*.

If his audience thought they were by now familiar with the full extent of the Bernstein talents, they were now to discover yet another of his gifts, one that

---

[39] Canon - a melody in one voice imitated note for note by one or more other voices starting after the first voice. Two famous examples are *Frere Jaques* and *Three Blind Mice*.
[40] *Fugue* - A musical form derived from the simple melodic imitation of a *canon* but developed with great complexity, tangential wanderings and intervening musical episodes.

was to serve him well with his Young People's Concert audiences, that of a supreme story teller. While analysing and performing large chunks of the Bach 'Passion', L relates the story of Christ's journey beginning on the evening of the Last Supper to His betrayal, His trial and His enforced march to the Cross. It makes for riveting drama.

Speaking over the final chorus to the passion - a farewell to Christ in His tomb - L delivers his peroration.

"Oh, if it were only possible to show you *all* the wonders of this work...only one in the vast catalogue of Bach's output ...(the camera reveals the complete edition of the Bach *Gesellschaft*, some forty-odd huge volumes containing all the Baroque master's composed works - later presented to L by Robert Saudek as an extra *perk* for this remarkable show, making it one of the most expensive props ever viewed for a mere ten seconds on television) "... For Bach, all music was religion; writing it an act of faith; and performing it an act of worship. Every note was dedicated to God...This is the spine of Bach's work: simple faith...He played the organ, directed the choir, taught school, instructed his army of children, attended board meetings, kept his eye out for better paying jobs. Bach was a man, after all, not a god; but he was a man *of* God, and his godliness informs his music first to last."

The closing choral music underscoring L's final speech, in actuality more than double the length of the abridged text version quoted, swells to an emotional conclusion as the program credits roll up the television screen

Who could not help but be moved? No one, I would project, except myself who at the time was busy conducting the orchestra and chorus off camera during this lengthy final speech. I was sheet white and my heart was racing. What all of America didn't know was that L had 'dried', as we say in 'show-biz', that is, he had a total lapse of memory. Instead of his original text, which had been carefully timed to Bach's music during rehearsals, he began to ad-lib for more than forty-five seconds. That may not seem a long time but when you have rehearsed and timed music and text to fit exactly, forty-five extra seconds seems like several lifetimes to the man conducting the underscore. Fortunately, having memorised L's speech, I instantly realised what had happened. Raising my left hand with the unquestioning authority of 'Robo-cop', I lurched forward on the podium in a manner to draw everyone's attention. Two and a half measures from the end of the piece, with the orchestra members' eyes collectively glued upon me, I indicated firmly that everyone hold a specific chord. This posed little problem for the orchestra as only the strings were playing at this juncture. Fortunately, none of the woodwinds were forced to contend with having to sustain a long held chord. Such was not the case with the Choir who sing straight through to the end. They paused with me exactly as I had hoped at the appointed place along with the strings. I signalled them with a previously untried semaphore and, to my relief, they seemed to get my unspoken message to stagger their breathing so that their sound continued in a sustained, wordless B flat major chord for what seemed an eternity. My eyes were now glued on L as the single chord sounded under his extended text. Finally, it was obvious that he had come to a full stop and I gave both orchestra and chorus the signal to move on to the final cadence. It was the most triumphant execution of these concluding two and a half measures of music in the entire history of performances of the *Matthew Passion*.

The show was over. L sat huddled on the floor in the last position from which he delivered his final speech. I approached him not knowing his mood in light of what had taken place. Finally, I plucked up enough courage to speak. "Are you OK?", I asked. He grabbed me by the shoulders and hugged me. "I've never had anyone in my life help me the way you have," he said. For a young conductor like myself trying to prove his worth every minute of every day, this was a memorable moment for me. L, however, was later quoted by his biographer Humphrey Burton[41] as drawing a blank in an entirely different show. In the revisionist version, the memory lapse occurred in the middle of 'The Art of Conducting' program. He describes himself as standing in the middle of the studio not having a clue for a full forty seconds as to the next line of his script. Only by walking over to the piano to sneak a peak at a cue sheet "pasted somewhere where the camera couldn't see it" was he able to rescue the situation. It is difficult to conceive

---

[41] Leonard Bernstein: Video Man by Humphrey Burton, an essay for a collection of writings about Leonard Bernstein titled Bernstein Remembered. N.Y.: Carroll & Graf

that a mind as sharp on detail as L's would forget the exact time and circumstances of so traumatic a moment, now documented in the DVD of the Bach program. Whatever his reasons, L, at that juncture of his life, did not want to appear to have been in need of anyone to rescue him from a problem resulting from a chink in his professional armour. Altering the course of events allowed him to produce a scenario where alone he was able to extricate himself unaided from a difficult and what he must have come to perceive as a professionally embarrassing happening.

8. What Makes Opera *'Grand'*?

In the autumn of 1957, a year later, L delivered his final *Omnibus* essay, *What Makes Opera 'Grand?* In the first eight months of that year, *West Side Story* had occupied a good part of L's time and attention. In the summer of '57 he had signed his contract with the N.Y. Philharmonic to become joint Principal Conductor with Dmitri Mitropoulos for the 1957-58 season and then, in the 1958-59 season, to become sole Music Director. In December, he and Felicia headed for Israel where L conducted the inaugural concert for the newly built Fredrik R Mann Concert Hall in Tel-Aviv. A travelogue of this journey was later presented as a half-hour feature on *Omnibus*.[42] In January 1958, while still Music Director-elect of the Philharmonic, he initiated the first season of a series of critically acclaimed televised *Young People's Concerts* which, over a fifteen year period, was to grow to fifty three in number, be dubbed into twelve languages, shown in forty countries and glean virtually every award television could bestow upon an Arts program. For eleven years, from 1957 onwards, the emphasis of the Bernstein musical career dramatically shifted from that of nomadic free-lance performer to that of 'establishment' figure within the stabile, regal environs of Carnegie Hall and then Lincoln Center's Philharmonic Hall[43] as director of one of the country's oldest established front rank orchestras.

---

[42] *Bernstein: A Musical Travelogue* is reported on more fully in the video/film section on Documentaries.

[43] Renamed the Avery Fisher Hall in 1973 following a $10.5 million donation to the NY Philharmonic by the philanthropist.

WEST SIDE MAESTRO

One might have projected from such a scenario of impending activity that the pledge to write and perform a major television special on opera not specifically related to his vast new commitments to the Philharmonic would have, understandably, been given short shrift. Not only was this not the case but *'What Makes Opera Grand'* proved to be the climax of his innovative series for Robert Saudek.

Of the seven Omnibus specials, an analysis of the *Opera* program appears on the surface quite the most straightforward of them all. The bulk of the program followed a single format based upon the script's principal proposition that there is no stronger way in theatre to project the weight of drama, the story line or an emotional situation than to *sing* it. In order to palpably demonstrate this, L chose the entire Third Act of Giacomo Puccini's *'La Boheme'*, that most immediate of operas, as his laboratory guinea pig to prove his thesis. The format proved to be as brilliant as it was simple and was to serve him on two further occasions for his later series of specials for the Ford Motor Company.

To begin, L demonstrated how human emotions when sung are magnified to a larger-than-life dimension. To illustrate the emotion of love he chose a large excerpt from the Second Act Love Duet from Wagner's *'Tristan and Isolde'*, accompanied by the Metropolitan Opera Orchestra.. This was followed by shorter excerpts from a variety of operas, all accompanied by L at the piano, to illustrate jealousy, hope, despair and the exaltation of evil.

Now began the development section of the program which consisted of an analysis of the third act of Puccini's *La Boheme*. The formula was as follows: A segment of a scene would be examined in a straightforward theatrical analysis, i.e.: the place, the time of day, the weather, the characters involved, what they were thinking, feeling, etc.; the text was then performed in an English translation by professional actors; Puccini's version of the same scene followed, sung in the original Italian; finally, L, accompanying himself at the piano, examined, analysed and passionately sang in his unique gravel baritone fragments from the same scene analysing for his viewers the various techniques Puccini used to intensify pictorial and dramatic aspects through his musical setting.

WEST SIDE MAESTRO

A Trio late in the Act, involving Mimi, hidden behind a tree listening and commenting upon her lover, Rudolfo speaking with his best friend Marcello discussing her illness and the impending end of their love affair, was one of L's most graphic examples. A spoken English version using three actors delivering their lines simultaneously predictably projects only unintelligible confusion. The sung Puccini version, however, reveals the miracle of music. As succinctly stated by L, "notes are born to sound together as words are not. Reality has been expanded by music into a richness of lyricism whereby we can actually perceive three emotions at the same time." After analysing Puccini's contrasting emotional setting of not only each character's vocal line but the accompanying orchestral part, L performed the Trio in its entirety clarifying, underlining and reinforcing the various dramatic features he previously indicated.

Next to be spotlighted were two musical techniques, the use of assigning characters a musical label, a *leitmotif*, and the expansion of time through music at a key moment of drama.

As the scene continues, the Trio is interrupted by the appearance of Musetta, Marcello's coquettish and inconstant girlfriend whom Puccini first introduced in Act 2. While Rudolfo gently comforts Mimi, the orchestral accompaniment plays the melody to Mimi's principal aria in Act 1. Mimi, almost fainting, is reflected in a theme created specifically to depict her illness. Musetta sweeps onto the scene and we hear the theme that recounts her boisterous laughter, first heard in Act 2. L explains that these are *leitmotifs*, (motives assigned to each character), which reached a pinnacle of perfection in the operas of Richard Wagner and their depths in their indiscriminate use by Hollywood composers in the 'click track'[44] cinema scores of our favourite films.

The expansion of time through music is graphically illustrated by having the actors perform Mimi and Rudolfo's short scene of farewell. A spoken version

---

[44] 'click track' - a metronome beat added to film to insure absolute accuracy of tempo during the dubbing of the music track so that there is an exact synchronizing of the film's visual events with composed matching musical effects. The music tracks that match cartoon animation movement and ever -scripted violence which one character inflicts upon another represents the ultimate use of 'click' track.

of the scene requires a mere 36 seconds. L points out that such a scene cannot in those 36 seconds plumb the full depth of the emotions of the characters. Puccini, however, stops time by giving Mimi an aria of farewell lasting three and a half minutes. The words she sings are the same as those spoken by the actor but now the emotional power of the scene has grown and been expanded through the dimension of music. What seemed only small details in the spoken version have now been underlined to permit the character to project their full emotional meaning. This is one of the most powerful moments of L's highly original script. If only for one brief moment, it must have turned scores of Americans who had never previously heard a note of opera into opera lovers.

L has reached the final scene of Act Three, a quartet contrasting the two pairs of lovers. Mimi and Rudolfo have decided to stay together till spring but Marcello and Musetta, in a comical dispute, quarrel, shout names at each other and separate in anger. All of Puccini's dramatic techniques are shown to be present in abundance. Time is expanded; *leitmotifs* abound, there is the simultaneous contrast of lyricism with comedy, all bringing together a panoply of polarised passions, moods and events.

This musical *tour de force* does not signal the end of this brilliant script. Indeed, L moves his thesis one step further. So far he has examined how the *spoken word* can be elevated to greater heights and depths through music. Now he examines the opera form elevated to the point where words are almost rendered unimportant, "where the music is so communicative that the merest general knowledge of the dramatic action is enough to provide the key to a rich enjoyment of the work." We have already been shown how opera can alter time and space. Now we are offered the possibility of it transmuting meaning itself; communicating on a plane which transcends even the written text. At that level the ultimate success of opera for the listener becomes the extent to which he or she is willing to enter its sphere, accept its conventions and join with those to whom breathing its rarefied air has become one of life's enriching, ennobling experiences.

To conclude this epic final *Omnibus* program L conducted an abridged, sweeping version of the final scene of Wagner's *Tristan and Isolde*, a scene of voluptuous lyricism. Tristan, mortally wounded awaits the arrival of his beloved, Isolde. He struggles in his delirium to rise from his stretcher. Isolde enters and rushes to his side. He dies in her arms. Isolde's final Love-Death, *Liebestod*, in which she sings of their being united again in death, concludes as, transported by the ecstasy and rapture of the moment, she herself expires falling across the body of her dead lover.

In bringing his remarkable *Omnibus* lectures to an end, *What Makes Opera Grand?* proved a fitting climax. to the panoply of musical essays L had contributed for five seasons to this unique and peerless ground breaking Arts television series. *Omnibus* led its field in television broadcasting for nine years leaving all competition light years behind. Now, virtually fifty years since its final telecast, this series has yet to be equalled. In the present climate of the dumbing-down of all aspects of television, including its commercial-breaks that seem the last vestige of originality, it is doubtful that anyone will any longer even pretend to make the effort. If one considers *Omnibus*'s vast range of varied and imaginative projects within which the Bernstein programs were jewels in a crown encrusted with all manner of jewellery, the mention of but a few of the presenters and artists along with a sampling of projects undertaken will provide a tiny indication of the scope of Robert Saudek's vision: the choreographers, Agnes de Mille, Gene Kelly and José Limon; the actors, Orson Welles, Peter Ustinov, Hume Cronin, Jessica Tandy and Danny Kaye; the plays, *King Lear, Oedipus Rex, Dear Brutus, Androcles and the Lion,* the underwater naturalist, Jacques Cousteau, the noted lawyer, Joseph Welsh, examining the American Constitution, musicians, Leopold Stokowski, Pablo Casals, Yehudi Menhuin and even Dr.Seuss - and I haven't even begun to scratch the surface. There were classic plays and brand new commissions, dramatised adaptations of books, history, in depth current events coverage and interviews with those making the news. What made the total accomplishment even more remarkable was that, unlike virtually all of television production today, it was live. Each week an hour and a half program was mounted, edited and presented live at prime time on a national television network.

For L's final show, the Saudek organisation denied him nothing. The historic Metropolitan Opera House on 39th Street and Broadway was taken over for the production. The Metropolitan Opera Orchestra and Chorus along with the services of a distinguished group of opera soloists and actors were secured. Additional cameras and crew, a most expensive production item, were squeezed out of a tight-fisted Network. Nothing was spared. As recounted in my Preface, because of the complexity of the music in relation to planning the visual presentation of the program, I spent hours with Charlie Dubin, the director, not only plotting the shots but working out the new method, previously described, which would enable him to capture all the subtleties of the drama and music with razor sharp precision. So much could have gone wrong on a program of this scope and intricacy, but I cannot recall a single major musical or technical mishap. Everyone involved knew as the last credit of the crawl rolled up the screen that something extraordinary and very special had taken place. Robert Saudek himself wrote me a letter afterwards thanking me not only for my contribution to the many *Omnibus* shows over the years but to this show in particular. Though a welcomed souvenir, it paled in comparison with the memory of having had the privilege of assisting L in one of his and television's greatest achievements.

3. <u>THE N.Y. PHILHARMONIC YEARS</u>

Part 1: OVERTURE

Prior to his appointment as co-conductor of the N.Y. Philharmonic in 1957 and then Principal Conductor in 1958, Merle Secrest in her biography documents a six year hiatus during which Bernstein 'had not been asked to appear as guest-conductor'. This in no manner reflects the reality of the situation. This hiatus was Bernstein's choice. He had had a serious falling out with the orchestra and had no desire to appear with them. As I was only one of two observers at the rehearsal during which the problem occurred[45], it was never a matter of public record. Quite obviously Bernstein's biographers did not find it documented in diaries and the only two outside sources to whom L spoke of it at the time, other than perhaps members of his family, would seem not to have volunteered to make mention of it.[46] Relating the matter in detail will not only shed light on the importance the appointment to the Philharmonic held for L but on the enormous authority he was able to assume with the orchestra from the very first day of his return.

L was appearing as a guest in the 1950-51 season. On his first program, he was scheduled to perform and the following week record Stravinsky's *Le Sacre du Printemps* (The Rite of Spring). It was now two years since the 25 year reign of Serge Koussevitzky as the unquestioned music director of the Boston Symphony had come to an end. Koussevitzky was perceived to be L's protective father figure within the professional community much as Toscanini was seen to serve in a similar role for Guido Cantelli.[47] After Koussevitzsky's retirement the more aggressive members of the East Coast orchestral fraternity with whom L's guest conducting centred viewed him as vulnerable to the settling of old grievances. While his talent was not to be

---

[45] The other observer was the Associate Conductor of the Philharmonic, Franco Autori.

[46] David Oppenheim, CBS Records Executive and close personal friend and Helen Coates, Bernstein's Private Secretary.

[47] Guido Cantelli (1920-56), brilliant young Italian conductor tragically killed in an airplane crash at Orly Airport, Paris as he was flying to America to conduct a series of concerts with the N.Y. Philharmonic

denied by one and all, he was still resented by a small group who viewed him as a 'smart ass kid' who had the nerve to treat them like students at his rehearsals. In every orchestra there exists such an aggressive minority, a kind of musical *Mafia*. They dominate and influence the atmosphere during rehearsals and are invariably the strong-arm men in the Musicians' Union Committee appointed to every orchestra. They feed on the power they attain and can be very brutal in the manner in which they use it. They are set apart from the majority of orchestra players who, opting for a peaceful life, come to rehearsal to play their assigned part under the direction of, hopefully, a reasonably competent, relatively pleasant conductor, keep their heads down, stay out of trouble and, at the end of the day, go home to their wife and 2 .5 children.

Like the masks of comedy and tragedy these 'musical mafiosi' display two faces. To the initiate conductor or *routinier* they can be cruel and challenging, ridiculing with exaggeration every musical request. In contrast, when a figure of unchallengeable authority and indomitable will appears who is favoured by the Board of Directors, the orchestra's subscribers and an international record conglomerate with lucrative contracts on offer, these same 'bully boys' become all smiles, displaying a consummate skill in both the 'posterior pucker' and a diplomacy to rival the most skilful politician.[48]

---

[48] To name but a few of the most famous maestri the mention of whose name alone could strike terror in the hearts of musicians, one would without contradiction include Serge Koussevitzky, Fritz Reiner, Artur Rodzinski, Leopold Stokowski and George Szell. As an example of the black humour which reveals the power and fear these men could generate among their players, I was standing on the stage of Carnegie Hall at the conclusion of a Philharmonic rehearsal speaking with my friend, the violist Raymond Sabinsky, when Fritz Reiner approached us. Raymond and Reiner were old acquaintances. At the age of 16, Raymond played viola and solo saxophone with the Pittsburg Symphony under Reiner's direction. Even more recently he was a frequent guest in Chicago at the home of one of the Chicago Symphoniy's wealthiest patrons where he and Reiner had often met socially after concerts. In a grand and effusively broad Hungarian manner Reiner questioned, " Well, Sabinsky, when are you coming to play for _me_ in Chicago?" "I didn't know you had an opening, Maestro." Raymond replied. "I don't," continued Reiner "but at the end of the season I am expecting a few *resignations!*" As he spoke the word 'resignations', his eyes narrowed in a manner which absolutely turned your blood cold. Indeed, an often told annecdote about Reiner is that he fired two of the pallbearers at his funeral.

WEST SIDE MAESTRO

In the acrimonious Philharmonic incident of the 1950-51 season, L was the innocent victim. Not only was there nothing in his behaviour to precipitate what took place, on the contrary, he was at the time being his most musically brilliant, funny, friendly self. He began the rehearsal with the *Danse Sacrale*, the complex finale to Stravinsky's *Le Sacre du Printemps* in which the composer varies the signature and rhythmic patterns from measure to measure with terrifying frequency. Conducting from memory, L whizzed through a detailed rehearsal of this portion of the music in less than 25 minutes.[49] Having broken the back of the most difficult section of the work and with the orchestra razor sharp in their response to his requests, L turned to the beginning of the ballet to begin a comprehensive run-through. As a matter of professional courtesy, he asked the Principal Bassoon whether the player would prefer, after a discreet indication to begin, to perform the opening notoriously difficult unaccompanied solo on his own or have it conducted throughout. The player requested that L conduct it. The lone bassoon solo that opens *Le Sacre*, marked *rubato*[50], begins with a crochet (quarter note) followed by 4 semi-quavers (16th notes):
Example:

Stravinsky, *The Rite of Spring*

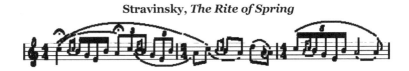

The player, interpreting the composer's *rubato* indication in relation to the semi-quavers, held the first of the four notes rather long and then rushed the other three. L stopped and requested that only the notes which the composer specifically indicated should be extended in length. In addition, L pointed

---

[49] In light of the N.Y. Philharmonic's standard weekly subscription concert schedule of four preparatory rehearsals, each 2 1/2 hours in duration, this was a very economic use of rehearsal time. One which virtually guaranteed that all the preliminary detailed work for 'Le Sacre' could be completed by the end of that first morning.

[50] rubato from the Italian verb, *Rubare*, to rob; a free, expressive manner of performing a passage or phrase of music during which a performer may stretch out certain notes and then rush others to compensate. It's a musical version of 'Robbing Peter to pay Paul!'

out that Stravinsky, by clever rhythmic variation, had actually composed the *rubato* into the musical notation, eliminating the need for further elaboration. Would the player please play the four semi-quavers evenly, no single note being held or emphasised more than any of the other three; in simple terms, to play the phrase exactly as written on the page. They began again. The second time through the bassoonist distorted the playing of the four semi-quavers even more. L stopped again and, addressing the player in a friendly manner by his first name, not only again patiently explained what he wanted but sang the passage as he hoped it would be performed. They began a third time. This time the player caricatured the passage in a manner that caused laughter in the orchestra. L stopped yet again and in an amused fashion said, 'Well, maybe I'm crazy?' The bassoonist snapped back, "**YOU CERTAINLY ARE!**" and then all hell broke loose. The first Oboe, the most respected, articulate and invariably outspoken member of the orchestra asked, 'Why are you always trying to give us lessons?' The first viola, another orchestra chieftain and not the most pleasant man on the best of days, could also always be relied upon to stir things up. "We know the piece. Just let us play through it," he chimed in. "We'll give you what you want." The dam had burst. Shouts could be heard from every quarter of the orchestra. The rehearsal was in chaos. L closed his score and walked off the stage. I found him sitting in his dressing room visibly shaken. He had telephoned David Oppenheim at CBS to cancel the recording sessions of *Le Sacre*. He was trying to fathom the unfathomable, what had made the orchestra behave in that manner risking the cancellation of the upcoming recording and the additional income which all of them welcomed and needed? That is the question invariably asked when orchestras pursue a path of action against their personal interest. It has been posed but never answered since the organisation of the first ensemble.[51]

To try to understand how such a sequence of events could have taken place, a short review of labour/ management relations within the N.Y.

---

[51] The author was for 15 years an elected lay representative to the British Musicians' Union serving at local, regional and national levels. Bernstein's experience of the N.Y. Philharmonic musicians acting contrary to their own interests is not a rare occurrence. The targets of the wrath of musicians are, unfortunately, not for the most part those who cause individual musicians, ensembles and even the profession itself the most harm.

WEST SIDE MAESTRO

Philharmonic's organisation will prove revealing. The orchestra seems always to have enjoyed an historic reputation of striking fear into the hearts of all but those ruthless conductors whose body epidermis was composed of pure elephant hide. Its ranks over the years have been populated by some of the greatest virtuosi among orchestral musicians. Great virtuosi have monumental temperaments and egos and can often be unruly and uncontrollable. On the management side, the Board of Directors for 30 years, (following the merger in 1928 of the best players from the National Symphony, the Philharmonic Society and the New York Symphony to create The N.Y. Philharmonic-Symphony Society), maintained a firm grip over the orchestra by using its sweeping powers to dismiss players and, sometimes, even conductors summarily. Within the playing ranks of the orchestra spies were encouraged who regularly reported goings on at rehearsals to the Management whose Chief Executive since 1922, Arthur Judson, was one of the most feared personalities in the concert world. Judson was a man who exercised a power and influence nationally in American music circles unparalleled either before or since. Even today, when the undisputed rule of a 'dictator of the baton' such as a Toscanini is an anachronism, there still exists, between the Principal Conductor and Management on the one side and the rank and file musicians on the other, an inherent cloud of suspicion along with a 'them and us' atmosphere which engenders fear, resentment and insecurity within the orchestral ranks. One must add to this constant siege mentality an artistic history which has fluctuated from great critical acclaim under historical musical figures, Mahler, Mengelberg, Toscanini, Stokowski, Rodzinski, Walter, Cantelli and Bernstein to an excoriating barrage of criticism performing under lesser talents or conductors whose career advancement has been orchestrated by an international gramophone record company. Two exceptional musical figures who possessed the gift of greatness but who nevertheless came in for the harshest of criticism during their Philharmonic tenures were Sir John Barbirolli and Dmitri Mitropoulos. They failed in New York for diametrically opposing reasons. Barbirolli, still relatively young and inexperienced, inherited the unenviable task of having to follow Toscanini's brilliant ten year reign at the Philharmonic. Barbirolli's natural gifts and secure musical credentials found its admirers both inside and outside the orchestra but the timing of his appointment was not in his favour and only after his return to his native England did his career flower and world-wide recognition follow. Mitropoulos, on the other hand, was temperamentally and, in some degree, musically unsuited to this most demanding and difficult position. Despite enormous charisma and inspirational qualities, he lacked the ability to maintain either musical or personal discipline in the orchestra during his tenure.

Prior to his appointment as Principal Conductor of the N.Y. Philharmonic in 1950, Dmitri Mitropoulos had been a guest conductor with the orchestra from 1947-49 and then shared the position of Principal Conductor with Leopold Stokowski during the 1949-50 season. By nature, he was a very gentle man. He adopted an almost passive role in dealing with the ongoing key task facing any leader, that of retaining the respect of those who work for him while maintaining the required discipline and standards to accomplish the task at hand. This relaxation of personal discipline within the Philharmonic was certainly at the root of the orchestra's unprovoked outburst during L's rehearsal.

Mitropoulos was an enormous contrast to the autocratic Artur Rodzinski, his predecessor, whose tenure began with the dismissal of 14 musicians including the concert master[52]. It ended with his resignation mid-season three and a half years later amid a raging controversy with the Management.

As a guest conductor, Mitropoulos had initially galvanised the orchestra to great musical heights. His feats of memory seemed astonishing. He would not only rehearse his programs without a score but call out all the rehearsal reference numbers at any point at which he stopped to make comment. At first the Philharmonic musicians were agog. As his presence became an every day affair, noticeable chinks in his musical armour began to appear. His rehearsal technique involved, for the most part, running through the

---

[52] Concertmaster – derived from the German *Konzertmeister*, it is the American designaton for the Principal first stand violinist who holds the overall responsibility for leading the entire string section, to include the complex task of working out bowing not only for the violins parts but, when applicable, for the violas, cellos and basses as well.

score several times from start to finish without stopping to correct obvious mistakes in pitch[53] or ragged ensemble. While acceptable, even desirable

from the musicians' point of view if he is struggling with unfamiliar, contemporary music, such an approach over an extended period wreaks havoc with orchestral ensemble in the performance of standard repertoire. In light of the new and exciting repertoire he was presenting, his musicianship and the variable quality of orchestral performance went unquestioned by both his musicians and the critical establishment. However, when he began to conduct the classic repertoire, his musical taste came under closer scrutiny. Every composition seemed to be approached in the same highly emotional fashion no matter its style or content. In rehearsals charged with an electric atmosphere similar to that of a performance, the batonless conductor would run through his unique repertoire of gestures, arms flailing, body writhing, sudden crouching to achieve a pianissimo or great leaps into the air at the fortissimo climaxes. When taken in small doses as a guest conductor of unusual repertoire the effect Mitropoulos achieved could be very stimulating. As a regular, every day happening, it was exhausting and wore thin quickly. The power brokers in the orchestra began to test their arm, openly questioning his musical taste in the classics that older members had performed under Toscanini and which Bruno Walter, the renowned German conductor, now often came to conduct and record. Instead of asserting his authority, Mitropoulos would crumble when challenged and would end up apologising to the player who had confronted him. At rehearsals widely attended by professionals and members of the public, not only the orchestra but the Management began to challenge him in a conspicuous manner. A regular occurrence of this related to overtime. In the past, were a Toscanini or a Stokowski to demand overtime to prepare a difficult work, no one would have dared to question or deny them. Mitropoulos, however, desperately in need of an extra half hour at the end of a rehearsal of monumental works unfamiliar to the orchestra, such as Alban Berg's opera, *Wozzek* or Milhaud's opera-oratorio *Christophe Colomb*, would be summarily stopped by the orchestra manager clapping his hands

---

[53] Wrong notes in the orchestra parts were invariably corrected during rehearsals by Franco Auturi,.the Assistant Conductor.

and dismissing the players without reference to the conductor. It was the same at his CBS recording sessions. Equally compliant, he would cram in as much music as possible in single run-throughs during the scheduled three-hour period allotted.

He resorted to retakes only if the orchestra broke down.[54] What saved his position again and again was his astonishing ability to pull a rabbit out of a hat at the concerts after even the most traumatic of rehearsals. The combination of his unusual programming and the sheer visceral excitement that he could conjure up in performance worked for him when the opposing forces in the orchestra were not free to interfere without exposing themselves to criticism.

These were the circumstances that initiated Bernstein's self-imposed exile from the N.Y. Philharmonic. It was to last until the announcement of his appointment as Mitropoulos's co-director in 1957 and his successor in 1958.[55]

In the intervening years the orchestra was to descend into some of the worst artistic times in its history. Mitropoulos control in rehearsal continually lessened and he was treated like a pawn by the collective forces that surrounded him. His occasional brilliance distracted the public momentarily from the general low standard of playing which marked many of his concerts and bought him a bit of breathing space with New York's powerful circle of music critics. The professional concern for the Philharmonic, however, no

---

[54] The acid test when listening to even Mitropoulos's most noted NY Philharmonic recordings is to play them at low level. In the recording studio such a general critical test also incorporates the use of small, so-called *granny* speakers, that is, speakers of a size associated with modest home radios. Such a test reveals ensemble imperfections with the cruelest clarity.

[55] The exceptions to this 'exile' were a series of recordings made in the summer of 1952 with 'The Stadium Symphony', actually the N.Y. Philharmonic during its summer season at Lewisohn Stadium. The sessions, all of which I attended, took place at midnight at Carnegie Hall following a public concert which featured the work to be recorded. The recordings, released by American Decca, were produced by Jerry Toobin, the Manager of The Symphony of the Air. Toobin was to establish an important professional relationship with Bernstein in the following years. L also agreed to deputize for Guido Cantelli, who had been tragically killed in 1956 in an airplane crash outside of Paris.

longer centred on its position in the 'top five'[56] but whether, in light of its persistent poor public showings, it deserved to be considered in a league with the other four.

It was Virgil Thompson, the most eminent and powerful of the music critics, who performed the *coup de grace*, albeit with mixed motivation for doing so. In a brilliant, utterly vicious and what could be characterised as the bitchiest review ever penned, Thompson, writing in the N.Y. Herald Tribune, took Mitropoulos apart gesture by gesture. Oscar Wilde at his most capricious could not have penned such literary acid to greater effect. In fact, it was neither the previous night's performance nor even the justice and need of bringing to public consciousness the deplorable state to which a great orchestra had been reduced that motivated this outpouring of bitchery. Mitropoulos, in his typical altruistic fashion, had informed Thompson that it would be improper for him to use his influence to persuade the N.Y. Philharmonic Chamber Ensemble to perform one of the critic/composer's compositions at their noteworthy series at New York's 92nd Street 'Y'. Thompson's response was to teach Mitropoulos a lesson he would never forget. The effect of the review was immediate and devastating. Mitropoulos suffered a nervous collapse and was taken into hospital. When he was well enough to return to the Philharmonic, he seemed a shadow of his former self. Music scores to the works he was to perform were now in obvious evidence on a music stand placed before the conductor's podium. If one had the opportunity to speak to him at the rehearsal interval or afterwards, he would invariably turn the conversation to Thompson's review working himself up into a highly emotional state. Thompson's review was to be followed by Howard Taubman's historical N.Y. Sunday Times full-page editorial of April 1956, "The Philharmonic - What's Wrong with It and Why". The article sent shock waves through the N.Y. 'establishment'. The then president of the N.Y. Philharmonic was quoted as saying that it tore them to bits.

The time was ripe for a revitalisation that would reverse the orchestra's fortunes and ever diminishing audiences. A restoration of its musical

---

[56] Boston, Philadelphia, New York, Chicago and Cleveland

WEST SIDE MAESTRO

disciplines under new leadership that would emulate its performance standards during the golden era of Toscanini was to be the first priority. With musical credentials that cut across all age and social barriers, with youth, movie star good looks, charisma and, to top it all, a new kind of celebrity as America's most famous classical musician television personality, Bernstein became the front runner and obvious choice.

Let us briefly flash back to the 1950-51 season and the incident that strained L's relationship with the Philharmonic. Like the proverbial elephant, conductors have long memories of past injuries. When, in 1956, L agreed to substitute for the late Guido Cantelli, the personnel within the orchestra was virtually unchanged from that of the '50-'51 season. There was more than a bit of anxiety in the air with L's arrival. Orchestra musicians the world over all have a tale to tell regarding a conductor's capacity for extracting revenge. Certainly, no one was going to attempt to challenge L at any level at this time. On the contrary, there was a collective desire within the Philharmonic to play its very best for him, not only to restore its tarnished reputation but to help it and their soon to be Music Director put the past behind them.

This was the setting for L's return. However, what set the seal on his unquestioned authority was the manner in which he dealt with the principal bassoon whose outburst had started the chain reaction of chaos and insults that L was forced to endure six years prior.

The Principal Oboe and Principal Viola, men of no small intellect and craftiness, had already begun their own campaigns to ingratiate themselves with L. The Principal Bassoon, however, was not the cleverest of politicians. He was of the old school, a first class player with a certain amount of hard edge acquired during his many years as a member of the power brokers within the ranks of the orchestra. He assumed, incorrectly as it turned out, that if he maintained a high standard of performance and kept his head down, L would come to forgive and forget. Unfortunately, that turned out to be an extremely naive view.

WEST SIDE MAESTRO

L's revenge was brilliantly conceived and quite subtle. Week after week he programmed repertoire containing all the notoriously difficult and exposed bassoon solos. It soon became obvious to all what was taking place. L never showed his displeasure or stopped smiling. He just kept pouring on the pressure, going to great pains at rehearsal to get the bassoon solos to be performed exactly as he wished even if it meant keeping the whole orchestra waiting while he repeated the solos again and again. Within two months the bassoonist's nerve began to crack and, much to his later regret, at a rehearsal in which L was being very exacting, he gave vent to the stress he was experiencing with yet another outspoken outburst. "We're doing the best we can", he declared loudly, trying to turn the attention from himself to the orchestra in general, probably hoping that his colleagues would support him. Everyone knew in that instant that it was all over. Later that season the player requested that he be moved in the section from first to third bassoon and soon afterwards he took retirement from the Philharmonic moving to a position for a relatively short time in the Metropolitan Opera Orchestra.

One can only begin to imagine the degree of control L now held over the Philharmonic. No one in the orchestra, in management or in the recording company executive were to, certainly in the early years of his tenure, either challenge him or deny him what he asked. In this atmosphere of strength, L produced year after year adventurous concert programs, young people's concerts, recordings and network television specials which were not only evidence of his continued growth as a musician and communicator but of his capacity to rebuild and maintain, as had his mentor, Serge Koussevitzky, one of the world's great orchestras.

WEST SIDE MAESTRO

THE NY PHILHARMONIC YEARS
Part 2: AFTER *OMNIBUS* :
Ford/LINCOLN presents
Leonard Bernstein & The NY Philharmonic
Beethoven's Ninth Symphony

On November 30,1958, the first of four televised specials launched Leonard Bernstein as the newly appointed music director of the NY Philharmonic. Sponsored by Lincoln, a division of Ford Motors, it was independently produced by Robert Saudek Associates. Although not associated with the broad Arts mix that was the Saudek flagship, *Omnibus*, it could be said to be a direct outgrowth from L's earlier groundbreaking programs for this same organisation and was aimed, in musical terms, at creating *super-Omnibus* programs. One of the features L had instituted upon becoming Music Director of the NY Philharmonic was a subscription series which he called *Previews*. These concerts served several purposes. It allowed the orchestra, as its title suggests, an opportunity to preview that week's new concert program before an audience *without* critics being present[57]. The generally

---

[57] This was a fully rehearsed performance and not merely a dress rehearsal. The NY Philharmonic always suffered a slight disadvantage at its home base, Carnegie Hall. The Hall represented the summit venue for all touring orchestras. Two of America's greatest orchestras, the Philadelphia Orchestra and the Boston Symphony, gave annual subscription concert series at the Hall. These visiting orchestras shared a distinct advantage over their New York colleagues. They arrived with sure-fire programs, meticulously rehearsed and performed a multiple of times for their own home-base subscribers and on tour before bringing the concert to the *Big Apple*. The Philharmonic, in contrast, was presenting a new program four times weekly, sometimes with a change of program for their popular Saturday night subscription series, for forty consecutive weeks each concert season. This was accomplished on four rehearsals per program with a single extra rehearsal for the occasional new Saturday night program. In addition, recording commitments had to be squeezed in on days off or during their weekly rehearsal schedule. The mettle of this much-overworked orchestra was tested at the first concert of each week's change of program. Prior to L's instituting *Preview* concerts, the critics would attend and write midnight deadline reviews of the program, the featured solo artist, the conductor and the orchestra's standard of performance throughout the

98

conservative Philharmonic audiences benefited from L's unique expertise at explaining and simplifying the more complex music programmed. Finally, along with his now televised Young People's Concerts, it served to amplify his image as America's most unique music guru to audiences of all ages.

L telephoned Saudek's chief feature editor, Mary Ahearn, and invited her to dinner to discuss his new project for television. That evening he spoke to her regarding the televising of his Philharmonic *Previews*. Ms. Ahearn, not only a brilliant editor but also a most practical lady, envisaged, from a media point of view, the limitations that mounting such an extensive compendium of music in a live concert setting would engender. A studio environment would allow for a less technically problematic and more visually interesting program. From their agreement in principle to his new approach, it was only a short evolution to a program concept based upon individual ideas rather than the overgenerous brief that the Bernstein *Previews* would encompass. That is a Readers' Digest version of the genesis of this next development in L's strengthening his grip on both the Philharmonic management and orchestra. Not only would these programs focus a new national and international attention on the orchestra but it would also prove a major money-spinner for everyone involved. Not least of all they would reinforce L's teaching-via-television persona, which was to be centred for the next twelve years around his position as the NY Philharmonic's Music Director and, after his resignation, as Conductor Emeritus. The *Young People's Concerts* and the *Ford/Lincoln Presents* specials would climax in 1973 with his now recognised revolutionary televised Norton Lectures at Harvard University, which took as its theme 'human innate perception of music'.

The debut program of the Lincoln series was the first of several television specials spanning the next thirty years devoted to an examination of Beethoven's final symphonic statement, the Ninth (*Choral*) Symphony. This was certainly an impressive subject with which to launch his new series. It echoed back to L's notable debut on *Omnibus* with his groundbreaking examination of Beethoven's Fifth Symphony which explored several

---

evening. The Philharmonic invariably suffered in reviews and editorials by comparison with the meticulously prepared visiting orchestral ensembles.

alternative possible constructions for the first movement of the Fifth Symphony based upon preliminary sketches taken directly from the composer's own notebooks. On the surface all boded well for new standards to again be set in television presentation for the Musical Arts. In retrospect, however, several of the programs reveal weaknesses in scholarship less meticulous in comparison to the high standards applied to his *Omnibus* programs. The very first program was a case in point. Contradictions, sketchy factual presentation, even a revisionist approach to historical fact are to be noted throughout L's script.

The program's introduction promised much, especially for those who remembered the powerful opening of L's debut *Omnibus* show on Beethoven. Would L again go to the sketchbooks seeking out other possible documented options which Beethoven was considering for the finale of his Ninth Symphony? Such an approach must have appeared self-recommending and it is inconceivable that such a suggestion did not surface at one point. In light of the brilliance and impact of his earlier program, it would have made for riveting television, especially as documents, manuscripts along with the sketchbooks reveal that immediately preceding the composition of the Ninth, the years 1816-17, the composer was not considering the inclusion of a choral finale to his Ninth Symphony. Certainly, a setting of Schiller's *Ode to Joy* had been very much on Beethoven's mind since 1798. As late as 1811, melodic sketches of a rather banal setting of a short phrase from the *Ode* were discovered within the pages of his hand-written manuscripts of his seventh and eighth symphonies. Next to the sketch appeared the following notations: "Finale, *Freude schöner Götter Funken Tochter Elisium*. The symphony in four movements; but the second movement in 2/4 time like the first. The fourth movement may be in 6/8 time - major - and well fugued.".

These early choral references, however, were not to be part of the structure of the Ninth Symphony. Beethoven's initial design for this symphony included a purely instrumental finale. Notebook sketches for the finale confirm this. Indeed, the composer later used these sketches for the finale of his String Quartet opus 132, in A minor. Yet, much of the legend surrounding the Ninth would have us believe that the creation of a 'choral' symphony was part of Beethoven's grand plan from the first. This also proved to be L's implied approach although, historically, it is without foundation. This choral movement, long considered one of the crowning achievements of Beethoven's output as a symphonic composer, gave him such cause for regret not long after its creation that he voiced the opinion that his choice of a choral finale was "a mistake" on his part. It is inconceivable that L was unaware of these facts. However, as a performance of the choral finale to the Ninth was to be the cornerstone of the first *Lincoln Presents* program, we can only conclude that L made the decision to ignore the historical background by not volunteering information which would have vitiated the approach for which he had opted, i.e., that 'the choral finale was a joyous vision of brotherhood which kindles emotions of love and unites its listeners through a common emotional experience' - certainly true in retrospect if not reflecting the composer's view towards this same movement at the time of its creation.

L's broader, less historically driven premise dominates the entire script. His opening foray from which he proceeds is fuelled by the overall question regarding the Ninth Symphony, "What makes this mighty work so mighty?" Unlike a Mozart or a Schubert, both of whom produced virtual final versions of their compositions from the moment they set pen to manuscript paper, the act of composing for Beethoven, was an endless struggle with musical ideas and forms. Never before his Ninth Symphony, L tells us, had this composer probed so deeply into the structural possibilities of his musical material. At the height of his powers, the progression of notes one to another unleashes a power analogous to a "musical chain reaction.". This is Bernstein in full flow at his most communicative.

The implication of the brief set by the overall posed question and the terms "musical ideas and forms, structural possibilities, the progression of notes one to the other" points the way towards a more technical approach rather than an historical view of this monumental, hybrid work.

WEST SIDE MAESTRO

And this is confirmed as L moves quickly to what he does best, working with the music itself, colourfully explaining its mechanisms and functions and opening new possibilities for informed and pleasurable listening for his viewers. He begins with the principal theme of the first movement which he breaks down into nine component parts. Then, taking a single component, he goes on to trace its transformations in the many variants created from within Beethoven's ever probing musical vision and imagination. He does the same with the second movement *Scherzo* theme, (which he characterises as the laughter of demons). We are shown, at this point, one of Beethoven's sketchbooks dated eight years prior to the composer beginning work on the symphony. In it the composer first notated the *Scherzo* theme. Again, we are treated to a simple but wonderfully clear explanation of the musical evolution of this single idea. L proceeds to the contrasting *Trio* section of the *Scherzo*. He, quite reasonably, describes it as a kind of Austrian village band effect. Then, quite unreasonably, from the existing historical evidence, he subjectively depicts it as another kind of demonic, grizzly humour. This Trio, however, was meant by Beethoven to serve as a rather happy contrast to the unrelenting, high spirited grotesquerie of what had gone before. The sketchbooks reveal a direct relationship between the *Scherzo Trio* of Ninth Symphony and the *Scherzo Trio* of the composer's Haydn influenced Second Symphony. In wanting to thrice underline an idea he was putting forward, L was here applying a revisionist approach to historical fact. Neither historical evidence nor the evidence of our ears seems to support such an interpretation. Even L's own descriptive analogy, a *Scherzo* of "demonic laughter", is far removed from Beethoven's own mood at the time. In the autograph sketch of this movement the composer wrote in the margin his favourite German proverb, *Morgenstund hat Gold im Mund,* (lit: "The morning hour has gold in its mouth", which we better identify as *The early bird catches the worm*). Such an expression of mood seems light years away from 'demonic laughter' and 'existential' despair', which are L's overall views of this movement. Scholarship was here giving way to the overall emotional thesis for which L had opted. It should be added that glitches of questionable scholarship did not stand in the way of his enormous success in television which lay in the conviction of his presentation which swept all before it. How many of his viewers knew or cared about matters of scholarship when the results were so entertaining and, in a majority of musical ways, so correct and interestingly informative.

L's description of the third movement as "a wondrous kingdom of peace" is all of that and more, an outpouring of melody with variations that bring calm following the turbulence of the first movement and the driving brilliance of the *Scherzo*. That peace is shattered, in any case, by a savage outburst that introduces the final movement. This finale becomes the focus of the remainder of the program.

Ignoring Beethoven's letters and sketchbooks, L script concentrates on the parochial view of the choral finale as a revolutionary, symphonic hymn to brotherhood. To accomplish this he piles hyperbole upon hyperbole. "Beethoven calls upon every force available...the *biggest* orchestra he can conceive of, a *vast* chorus, *four* soloists, *operatic* and *concerto* elements, and *the utmost freedom of form*..."[58] Again, the script's claims are at odds with the reality. Except for a minor use of percussion in the *Turkish style*[59] in the final movement, the size of orchestra used for the Ninth Symphony is no larger than that for the composer's Fifth symphony. Regarding the handling of the orchestration for the large instrumental and vocal forces at Beethoven's command, far from revolutionary it was accomplished in the highly traditional classical manner of Handel and Haydn, carefully using only sufficient numbers of instruments to accompany the diverse vocal combinations and always taking care never to overwhelm the vocal elements or to pit the entire orchestra against them.

Regarding the revolutionary hybrid nature of the movement, ten years before he began contemplating material for a Ninth Symphony, Beethoven had already begun experimenting with hybrid symphonic forms. In an earlier work, the Choral Fantasy op.8o, he radically combined the elements of a piano concerto, a *sinfonia concertante* and a massive choral hymn in

---

[58] Author's italics

[59] In the *Turkish style* refers to the use of bass drum, cymbals and triangle. Mozart's opera *The Abduction from the Seraglio* and Beethoven's own *Turkish March* from his incidental music to *The Ruins of Athens* provide two well-known examples.

praise of Music and Art. This earlier work is often viewed as a precursor to the composer's later setting of Schiller's *Ode to Joy*.

Certainly, the challenge of creating an overall unity for his Ninth symphony caused Beethoven to devote special consideration to the form which a newly imposed choral finale would assume in relation to his previous three contrasting movements. (One must not forget that when work on this symphony began in 1817, the composer's intent was to create a traditional four movement instrumental symphony). In light of the tragedy, unremitting joy and transcendence of the first three movements, what the composer came to seek was a triumphal resolution, a finale which would rise above all that had come before. This is precisely what he accomplished by eventually heightening communication in this final movement not only through Schiller's words but also through the use of a musical/literary allusion which established a connection with all that had come before.

Within an extended ninety-one bar 'fantasy' introduction, the themes of the first three movements are re-introduced and one by one rejected. Beethoven remarkably effected this in his final version in purely instrumental terms. In Beethoven's original plan, however, following the violent instrumental introduction to the movement, a solo voice rebuked the outbreak of violence and then proceeded to reject the offering of each of the previous movements, rejoicing finally only in the appearance of the new *Ode to Joy* theme. This was sketched by the composer in oratorio recitative[60] style using a text that he himself had composed. In the end he rejected this solution in favour of solo cellos and basses performing an instrumental recitative simulating speech which, through skilful dramatic and dynamic characterisation, projects the same implication of rejection and final acceptance as his original sung text. This was Beethoven's truly novel contribution to the form of this movement. None of this fascinating aspect of Beethoven's creative thinking in shaping this movement is referred to in L's script.

---

[60] Recitative, declamation in singing, notated musically but without definite meter except where imposed by an orchestral accompaniment.

WEST SIDE MAESTRO

Also not mentioned is that less than half of the Schiller *Ode* is set to music and that the verses chosen by Beethoven do not follow the sequence of the original poem. L does, however, make an interesting and important observation before devoting the final segment of the program to a performance of the choral finale to Beethoven's symphony, "A painting or a statue can be seen in a second. Further attention only adds to the first impression through the study of detail. You can't do that with music. You can't judge the whole until you reach the end of the final movement."

Urging his listeners to concentrate for the next twenty plus minutes without permitting distraction of any kind, L presents for them what I view as the best overall performance of the final movement of Beethoven's Ninth among the five recordings of this symphony which L directed in full or in part for disc, television or film over the next thirty years. The NY Philharmonic is in top form with four first class soloists, Leontine Price, Maureen Forrester, Léopold Simoneau and Norman Scott, and a well-trained Schola Cantorum choir prepared expertly by their director, Hugh Ross. This inspired performance transcends all the peripheral visual and sound problems, which include rather prosaic camera visuals of the vast array of music forces and dynamic conductor and a choral balance leaning prominently towards the lower bass voices. Musically, L's reading is a very well proportioned although his inclination is to adopt rather overheated quick tempos. The *alla marcia*[61], the seventh of this movement's variation form, and double fugue that follows are examples of this. Although pressed that bit too hard, the Philharmonic, an orchestra almost too virtuoso for their own good, make light-weight of the challenge. The only musical blemish, one could even characterise it as shocking, is the immense retard suddenly imposed upon the final two measures of the symphony. L's tendency of underlining to an audience that a work was ending was usually accomplished by a physical gesture, either an arm flourish or an exaggerated body movement.[62] No last second excess, thankfully, could spoil what was an auspicious launch to an

---

[61] The seventh variation, *alla marcia* - The chorale finale to Beethoven's *Ninth* is constructed as a set of Theme and Variations. *Alla marcia* means in the style of a march.

[62] As seen in his many videos, these large physical movements tended to have the opposite effect sought for. Instead of achieving an immediate reaction, the audience, who, for the most part, knew when the work ended, tended to be startled which adversely caused a delayed response.

important new Arts series which was without duplication in its time and for many years afterwards.

Jazz In Serious Music
(Telecast: 25/01/59)

The combination of the word *Jazz* in the title and the presence of Leonard Bernstein to impart new insights and thoughts into a subject with which most listeners must have felt at home certainly must have initially insured a large and interested listener's rating for this unusual but, from a commercial point of view, risky experiment. Of course, the risk did not involve the presence of *Jazz* as much as the presenter's choice of compositions to demonstrate its use in *Serious Music*. The bulk of the program was designed to be dominated by the performance of two sixteen-minute compositions, the first of which was a shocker to say the least and the second of which was a sure-fire winner. I have not been able to trace the original newspaper advertisements for this TV special but, sight-unseen, I would place a sizeable bet that it listed in large print under the title of the show, 'Leonard Bernstein conducts and performs Gershwin's *Rhapsody in Blue*'.

This fascinating but risky script was designed by L in what must have been one of the most confident moments in his career. New Testament miracles extend to walking on water. L boldly attempted something riskier with this program by walking on quicksand.

Down-home words like *jazzy, honky-tonk, ricky-ticky, shimmy, square, snoozing,* along with familiar images and analogies are scattered throughout the script to help prepare and soften the impact of what is to come. The folksy opening line of his script points the way, "If this were a program called *Name That Noise*, or something, and you had to identify the following musical excerpt, you might have a bit of trouble." The allusion to that most popular of big money game shows, *Name That Tune*, predictably evoked recognition and, no doubt, smiles from his coast to coast viewers. As it turned out, there was nothing to fear, for the *Name That Noise* musical excerpt turned out to be a bouncy bit from Aaron Copland's *Third Symphony*, which L described as *very* symphonic and *very* jazzy. If such was to be the degree of musical noise to which the audience would be exposed, who had anything to fear?

Even the typical, colourful, Bernstein comparison between jazz and symphonic music - " it's all right to talk during jazz, or laugh, or dance, or leave the room for a minute, but with symphonic music - not a word, don't move, head in hands, eyes closed in wondrous dreaming - or maybe in just plain *snoozing*." - served to further put his viewers at their ease.

Next, as was the formula for his programs, came the short but always entertaining history lesson complete with examples performed with oodles of personality by L at the piano. During this segment L traced the exhausted state of serious music at the beginning of the twentieth century, the explosive proportions to which the orchestra, and the length of the works being composed had grown and the grandiosity of emotional levels composers felt free to express. "It had to stop somewhere or bust." The only solution was to start afresh with fresh material and every new musical device upon which one could get one's hands - new scales, new ways of looking at tonality, atonality, seeking out the music of other cultures, the Far East, the Near East, Africa. Any kind of music that was "not the Mozart-to-Mendelssohn-to-Mahler triple play that the Germans had going for more than a hundred years."

This short historic interlude brings L to the first extended musical highlight of the program, an example of Ragtime, "bred in New Orleans and out of African drumming and French military Marches and Polish polkas." Ragtime's appeal, according to L, was not from some special musical gimmick. "The thing that made it irresistible was that it had *life*...it swung...spicy, light, effervescent; it was *Sal Hepatica*."[63] A music cue if ever there was one for L to analyse and then perform Scott Joplin's *Maple Leaf*

---

[63] *Sal Hepatica*, an effervescent stomach remedy very popular in America and a noted sponsor in the heydays of situation and comedy radio broadcasting.

Rag. Of course, his performance demonstrated that Ragtime *did* have a *gimmick*, a rock steady marching bass against its bouncy, highly syncopated melody.

In the post-World War I years, the rage for ragtime crossed over into classical music. (Stravinsky's 1918 miniature, *Ragtime for 11 Instruments* serves as L's example). In the 1920's Ragtime gave way to Jazz.[64] This new Black music had an especially exciting welcome in Paris. France could justly claim to be the first country to recognise jazz as a genuine art form. Its leading composers along with the leader of the Parisian intellectuals, Jean Cocteau, demanded the Arts Establishment recognise Jazz as an art form on a par with the cinema and modern painting. Satie, Ravel, Auric, Poulenc, Martinù, Milhaud and others, began incorporating elements of jazz in their music. Milhaud is the name with which we must concern ourselves as it is with the introduction of his sixteen minute ballet, *The Creation of the World,* that L entered an area of musical quicksand alluded to earlier. Milhaud's short ballet score was, in fact, a totally justifiable musical choice to fully demonstrate the incorporation of jazz into a full-fledged classical art work. However, its *avant-garde* aspects risked compromising L's relationship with his established viewing audience. Milhaud's polytonal, polyrhythmic, highly contrapuntal and highly dissonant *Creation of the World,* even by sophisticated listening standards, is a 'strong cup of tea' whose musical caffeine levels rise at times to atomic proportions. Jazz elements not withstanding, it is hardly the ideal first choice with which to introduce an uninitiated audience to either contemporary music or jazz. Doing so is spoiling for trouble especially where prime time commercial television interests are involved. Certainly, there existed several other French examples of the same period all incorporating elements of jazz which would have been more immediately accessible to a neophyte audience, ie: Milhaud's jazz ballet on South American themes, *The Bull on the Roof,* Stravinsky's pre-1920 *Octet* or his ballet, *The Story of a Soldier,* the finale to

---

[64] Leonard Feather, (1914-1994), in his *Encyclopedia of Jazz*, (Bonanza Books, NY, 1960), describes succinctly the synthesis out of which Jazz evolved. Jazz is a synthesis of six main sources, rhythms from West Africa, harmonic structure from classical European sources, melody and harmony from American folk music, religious music, work songs along with minstrel show music, all overlapping

WEST SIDE MAESTRO

Ravel's *Piano Concerto in G Major*[65] or Jaques Ibert's delicious *Divertissement*. All would have worked as a comfortable jazz contrast to Gershwin's Rhapsody in Blue. Whatever his reasons, the Milhaud was a choice which risked compromising his relationship with his established viewing public who tuned in specifically to be entertained by his multi-faceted talents as teacher and performer in accessible concert repertoire that never challenged to any degree one's lack of musical background. Milhaud's *Creation* ballet in the concert repertoire at the time L performed it for television was and, in fact, remains today that of an antique curiosity of the '20's. It never achieved the popularity of other of the composer's earlier and more accessible 1920 jazz oriented compositions The paradox to all this is that had L been giving a seminar on the same subject to a musically sophisticated audience the choice of the Milhaud would have been, among many possibilities, the most apt. Milhaud's *Creation* is a rare early example of a serious European composer influenced by the international rise in the popularity of jazz and his own personal enthusiasm for this new craze to create an entire composition out of its idiosyncratic elements[66]. Nevertheless, it was less than good judgement to program it for the television family audience L had been carefully developing and nurturing over the years. It was an ill chosen, headstrong decision just as Stravinsky's *Symphony of Psalms*, his original planned major work for his *Omnibus* special on modern music, had been equally ill conceived. In the latter instance he came to that realisation, albeit at the eleventh hour, re-conceived the entire musical portion of the program and ended up producing one of his best television shows that, while remaining challenging, both communicated with and entertained his listeners. All the headaches and problems his warrantable, if panicked, last minute change of mind caused were vindicated by the end result. This re-evaluation did not occur in relation to his choice of the Milhaud. It could have been motivated by his pedagogical passion "to grab you by the lapels...to convince an audience of the beauty of what he was doing, of the clarity of *why* he loved (a work) - a

---

[65] L had performed the first movement of the Concerto on his 1957 *Omnibus* program, *An Introduction to Modern Music.*

[66] L hears no hint of jazz at the opening of Milhaud's score while the author identifies the featured opening saxophone melody as pure blues.

WEST SIDE MAESTRO

love he wanted to share"[67]; or it could have been yet another example of the precipitate headstrong behaviour which caused him on occasion to make decisions and act in a manner which were contrary to his own interests. I had been witness to willful behaviour of this nature during our ten year professional association His elevation to the Philharmonic, bestowed upon him unchallenged power and authority that he had never previously enjoyed. The fact that the Lincoln/Ford programs were his concept, instigated through his efforts and based upon his central presence in the project, enabled him to make and enforce any and all musical decisions without question. It is not surprising, considering the strength of his position at this time, that all music decisions upon which he had set his heart brooked no dissenters.

To his credit, L did everything he could to help the novice listener grasp the Milhaud work using instrumental excerpts to amplify his explanations. He analysed each of the several sections of the ballet. He compared the work's opening and the fugue that follows to Bach. He used jazz-speak to describe certain instrumental happenings such as a trumpet *lick*, a *break* and a *fill*. He used the adjectives "savage, percussive, mean" to describe Milhaud's jazz fugue but avoided words like harsh and dissonant which complete the description. He underlined the scholarly nature of the work's construction. Few listeners, however, would have been able to remember these various described subtleties when he finally performed the ballet score in its entirety. He again took the opportunity to make use of his much exploited but invariably successful *gimmick* of setting words to a well known, easily identified tune or phrase contained in a classical work. In this instance, it was a familiar, easily spotted four note motto which all of America could immediately recognize as *Good Evening Friends*.

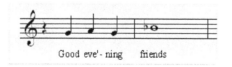

---
[67] Quote from Schuyler Chapin, (1923-2009) Columbia Artists Mgt. & CBS Records executive), *Leonard Bernstein, Reaching for the Note,* American Masters, PBS film

WEST SIDE MAESTRO

This musical motto is demonstrated, complete with blues inflection, to introduce one of Milhaud's key themes. To Americans, this *Good Evenin' Friends* tune was identified as the familiar cliché-ending to a wide variety of popular big band instrumentals of the 1940's and '50's. It could also be heard weekly on national radio, used by comedians, such as Jack Benny and Fred Allen, to break the tension in comedy situations involving a clumsy happening or embarrassing moment. Even with all this precedence, it might have seemed merely an out of context detail to L's audiences except that, happily, he points out later in the program that Gershwin uses precisely the same cliché phrase throughout the *Rhapsody in Blue.*

L and an ensemble of Philharmonic virtuosos deliver a superbly accomplished performance of Milhaud's *Creation,* which is sadly hindered by inferior engineering sound balances. L first conducted this work during his student days at Tanglewood. He remained devoted to it, leaving us no less than three superb recordings and a telecast version during his career Unfortunately, his devotion to the work and his superb interpretation did little to make any of its sixteen minute, action-packed, *avant garde* qualities any easier listening for the musically inexperienced viewers of his *Jazz in Serious Music* show. In a sense, this work would have been preferable to the opening Copland work for the imperative, *Name that noise!*

The program proceeds to a short comparison between Milhaud and Gershwin, composers at either end of the musical spectrum. *Rhapsody in Blue* was written, after all, only one year after the Milhaud ballet. While each composer's approach was different, "both were...making a conscious effort to fuse jazz with long-haired music." Milhaud was superimposing jazz elements onto his personal, carefully schooled and manicured composing style while Gershwin was struggling to contain his highly developed jazz understanding and *Tin-Pan-Alley* melodic style within a classical symphonic structure in which he was, at that moment in time, relatively unschooled. Of the two new European schools of musical thought which were now waging war under their generals, Stravinsky and Schönberg, Milhaud, the neo-classicist, was one of the anti-romantic representatives of the Stravinsky brigade. In contrast, Gershwin, an established star among popular American composers, was dealing with lush sounds and harmonies accompanying expansive romantic melodies. By Milhaud's standards Gershwin's approach represented an old-fashioned, reactionary view in a dramatically evolving world musical scene. As we know, Gershwin's ideas were to develop in an exciting fashion and with astonishingly rapidity in the ten years of life remaining to him.

L, at the piano, does a quick survey of the *Rhapsody* and of the various techniques which Gershwin employed. We encounter our *Good Evenin' Friends* motive again and again, each time placed in a different key rising ever higher in pitch. This is a typical and simple musical device called *sequences*, (for the record, Tchaikovsky was the supreme master). L next plays the ragtime theme from the *Rhapsody*, the second half of which is none other than our *Good Evenin' Friends* tune yet again. This too is given a sequential treatment but in the more virtuoso style of Liszt, complete with a splashy cadenza. Having succinctly described the entire work's structure as "one section after another loosely strung together by cadenzas", L makes a most arresting observation, "The *Rhapsody* is so sectional and choppy that you can cut it, interchange the sections, leave out half of it, play it backwards...but whatever you do it is still the *Rhapsody in Blue*." If the *Rhapsody* is as rambling as L's description, how does one account for its immense success and durability? For L, its greatness lies in its tunes and sheer invention and, search as one may for loftier reasons, one could not put it better or more succinctly.

Following a flashy performance of the *Rhapsody* during which the Bernstein personality explodes out of the small television screen, L begins a summation of his program. He speaks of the many American composers who have turned to jazz, absorbed it and transformed it into a language that has become indefinably American. He also speaks of a new generation of composers equally at home with jazz as with classical forms. They do not have to 'borrow' Jazz as Milhaud did or symphonic forms as did Gershwin. "Perhaps", poses L, " the future of American music is in their hands." This concept of eclecticism was to dominate L's thinking in the coming years and reach the apogee of creative expression in his *Mass* of 1970 and his thinking and concerns in the Harvard Norton Lectures of 1973.

The Infinite Variety of Music
(22/02/59)

This television lecture demanded of L his most persuasive and charismatic powers to keep his audience from switching channels within the first five minutes. Certainly, it began in the most glamorous fashion with the sophisticated, sensuous and seductive sounds of the music of Maurice Ravel, the Dawn sequence, a passage lasting a mere seventy-five seconds, from the hour long ballet, *Daphnis and Chloe*. It turns out to contain, L informs us, no less than 16,206 notes composed entirely from permutations of the twelve chromatic tones that are the melodic and harmonic basis of traditional Western music. That, in essence, is what this entire program will set about demonstrating, the seemingly infinite mathematical permutable possibilities of the chromatic scale which exist for the composer using the wide variety of musical techniques at his disposal, (harmony, rhythm counterpoint, higher or lower registers, repetition, etc.). The number of permutations possible, we are informed, transcends the concept of mere billions and involves a mathematical identification so large that a new word had to be created to encompass its concept, *googol*.

Happily, if his viewing audience had remained patient and loyal following this cerebral introduction, they found they were now in for a treat in the form of musical game playing in the best Bernstein tradition. Once having made his point, which really was a complex but relatively short explanation of how it was mathematically possible for the many great composers over the centuries utilising the same twelve note scale to produced so many different sounding and totally individual compositions, L then set to work not only showing us how it was done but, in the examples chosen, how it could be accomplished using only four notes. Of course it's all a bit of a conjurer's trick, but the most wonderful and enlightening bit of musical magic you will ever come across. The four notes chosen outline a little ditty which in that part of the English speaking world enjoying an occasional tipple, is affectionately sung to the words, "How dry I am".

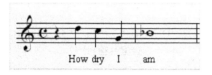

These four tones which, crucially, harmonically imply the basic tonic and dominant chords, "the cornerstone of tonal Western music"[68], provide a starting point for a wide variety of familiar melodies, classical, folk and 'pop'. L demonstrates several of these, beginning with the French folk song, *There was a shepherd,* and continuing with such familiar classical favourites as Smetana's *The Moldau* and the Hornpipe from Handel's *Watermusic.*

We learn how the shape of a tune can dictate our response. Certain notes emphasised or extended in one version may be given weak and less important roles in another. What is most important, of course, is what follows our four 'how-dry-I-am' notes. It is what follows that completes and delineates the character of the tune.

To make his point, L must shift the goal posts, not just once but several times. He not only alters the order in which the notes of our 'dry-I-am' motto are played but adds auxiliary notes which he characterises as "*simple dissonances, permutations.*"! And so they are, but not merely of a tune titled, *How dry I am.* More importantly, this four note sequence outlines the 3rd, 4th, 5th and 9th overtones of the harmonic series, the strongest relationship in tonal music, that of *the tonic* and its *dominant.* As the *tonic* represents the *home base* starting point to which melodically we will inevitably return, it should come as no surprise that the notes which make up the *tonic chord* form an especially appealing way to begin any theme. These four notes make up four sevenths of any major, minor or modal scale and are the most important four notes in any of the scales mentioned.

---

[68] This quote again formed a pillar within L's much later Norton Lectures.

WEST SIDE MAESTRO

L demonstrates how composers over the centuries used these four tones to create many of their famous themes and mottoes . Permutations which shift the order in which our four tones appear turn up in Brahms, the operas of Wagner and Richard Strauss, the symphonies of Prokofiev, even that song favourite of barbershop quartets, *Sweet Adeline,* as well as the imposing chimes of London's *Big Ben.*

THE CHIMES OF BIG BEN

It should be emphasised that composers may have used the same four notes in a variety of sequential patterns but one should not consider the resulting tunes as 'the same'. They are not even a variation on the same tune be it *How dry I am* or *Sweet Adeline.* Such a thought never came into the minds of the various composers. They are, however, examples of the mind-boggling, mathematical variety that can be achieved about which L spoke at the very beginning of his lecture.

Once the composer was free to expand his vision to include all twelve tones of the chromatic scale, of which the tonal relationship inherent in our four note *How dry I am motto* would continue to represent the most important third, he was able to "surf the network" of possibilities which then multiplied to the *googol* degree. In the historical development of Western Music, L declares the possibilities to have been increased virtually to infinity, not only by the variations which can be achieved using a chromatic application to music in the major keys but to include *all the minor keys as well*[69]. Then, permutating our four tone motto into a *minor* key by chromatically changing a single note, L demonstrates a variety of examples by Beethoven, Ambrose

---

[69] L wisely does not 'over-egg' an already exotic musical pudding by including all those yet unmentioned modal scales and patterns and *non-tonal* twelve tone permutations so beloved by composers of the twentieth century or the exotic scales from which tribal, folk and Art music the world over have long been constructed.

WEST SIDE MAESTRO

Thomas and, most importantly, Dmitri Shostakovich. It is with the final movement of Shostakovich's Fifth Symphony, which begins and concludes with a theme built upon our four note motto quoted in both minor and major modes, that L also brings this fascinating television essay to a conclusion.

In his typical unabashed outpouring of enthusiasm, L declares that Shostakovich has built the whole of the final movement of his Fifth Symphony on the *How Dry I Am* fragment. While one could hardly demur from agreeing that the opening of the movement is a powerful presentation of our fragment in its minor mode form and the closing section a juxtaposition of the theme first expanded in the minor then transformed into a flags flying, drums pounding, brass braying pompous finale of endless repetitions in the major, what happens in-between is what most analysts agree to be an extensive development of new material. Of course, having taken this position, I now expect a spectral visit from L dragging Shostakovich behind him by the sleeve to prove to me that every note of the entire movement is nothing more than a permutation of the first four notes. It is certainly true that the composer puts our motto theme through its paces. He shrinks it, stretches it, reverses it, breaks it, up into little pieces and hides it within masses of other notes and, in general, explores all its musical possibilities via his fertile and creative mind. L worked so very diligently to explain and expand upon what I view as his most difficult television thesis for the uninitiated layman, that one really ought not begrudge him this bit of analytic hyperbole.

It all comes right in the peroration. L projects that he may have finally worn our patience thin with his *How dry I am* fragment so insistently presented in his final performed excerpt. He points out, however, that in the footsteps of Handel, Beethoven, Brahms, Wagner and Strauss, a Shostakovich in 1937 could still take inspiration from a sequence of four notes that has found inspired reincarnation in endless forms over the centuries. He refers to it as the "miracle of the inexhaustible fertility of the human mind, the infinitude of man's creative spirit." He speaks of Shostakovich's "tremendous creative spirit" overcoming the "banality of the theme" to create "a new artistic utterance."

Of course, this astonishing act of musical legerdemain is only a tiny particle of what this program has illustrated. It was logical for L to choose works by Handel, Mozart, Beethoven Brahms and Wagner, geniuses one and all, whose names carry a certain familiarity to the virtual novice viewer. Their particular gifts have been shown to elevate our simple musical atoms to exceptional heights. Not to be forgotten, however, are the long list of accomplishments of those composers who are less than household names. Their inspiration, also, at times, rose to levels of greatness, and they too undoubtedly discovered and developed permutations of our now familiar four-note *motif*. Its seeming endless mutability has, because of its underlying harmonic relationship, intrinsically linked to the way that ultimate computer, our brain, organises and interprets music. It has permitted this fragment to enjoy a chameleon existence over centuries. It goes without saying, four notes in themselves do not begin to tell the story. This was an area of the initial premise of this highly original program which, intentionally, did not attempt to plumb the depths. That would have been impossible to achieve in the time allowed. In the end, it is the manner in which all these composers proceeded beyond these four notes that reveals the way they have expressed their endless musical vision of Western music using only the twelve notes as their basic vocabulary; twelve notes that, until recently, have been the sole productive seeds of a thousand years of musical history[70]. That is the real "infinite variety of music" about which L has been speaking.

The Humors of Music
(Telecast: 22/03/59)

---

[70] Through the adaptation of Eastern scales as well as the facilities available to composers working exclusively with computer generated compositions, the interpolation of quarter tones is now a practical reality although Western ears are not yet trained to readily respond to music thus designed.

WEST SIDE MAESTRO

My first reaction to this telecast was that it was an expanded follow-up to the Young People's Concert on *Humor in Music* for which I served as musical assistant. This program begins with the Finale to Mozart's *Musical Joke* which ends with three hopelessly dissonant chords representing "village musicians", who are supposedly performing this deliberately cliché work, collapsing not only in sheer exhaustion but sheer incompetence. "Are you calmly secure in your *bunny slippers?*", asks L. He then proceeds to explain the shock and illogic of these final three chords which is the final topping bit of humour of this amusing work.

L examines three categories of musical humour:

1. musical humor which is funny to some but not to others
2. musical humor not intended to be funny at all
3. music that comes across as being funny because it is attached to *funny* words

As an example of the third type of humor he accompanies himself in a performance of the Executioner's aria from Gilbert and Sullivan's *The Mikado*. L analyses the G&S excerpt and shows that without Gilbert's words there is nothing whatsoever funny about the music. The music is funny for *non-musical* reasons. Once you take away the story elements, the elements of humour disappear with them.

L next demonstrates music which deliberately starts out to be funny. His examples are Ibert's *Divertissement*, (a truly funny work), the *taxi horn* effect from Gershwin's *American in Paris*, (slightly amusing), and Paul White's *Mosquito Dance*, (A typical, light hearted, Boston Pops encore). These three works represent music that is funny for musical reasons such as funny *wrong* notes placed next to *right* notes. L then takes an ungenerous jab at the twelve tone music of Schönberg which he comments has so many dissonances, that is, *wrong* notes, that to the untrained ear all the notes sound *wrong*. Milhaud's ballet score, *The Bull on the Roof*, on the other hand, is a clear example of running into the surprising *wrong* note that can produce a smile. This latter example demonstrates the essence of all humour which is the *set-up,* (a jolly Latin American dance), followed by the *knock-down,* (all those surprise wrong notes).

Now we move on to *funny* colours (sounds), both instrumental and vocal. The bassoon demonstrates its genuine comic flair via its famous solo from Dukas' *The Sorcerer's Apprentice.* Other examples of *funny colours* are the "mocking low trumpets" in Prokofiev's Fifth Symphony, the violin *glissandos,* (sliding from one note to the next), in the Scherzo from Shostakovich's Fifth Symphony and the squeaky, jazzy E flat clarinet solo from Copland's *Music For The Theatre.*

Next on our humour agenda are "overstatement" and "understatement". Beethoven's *Fifth Symphony* and Stravinsky's *Octet* serve as L's contrasting examples of *over* and *understatement.* Certainly when directly compared to each other they make the point admirably but whether they would be recognised as such when performed individually would be another matter. In the demonstration of *satire* and *parody,* however, L is on solid ground. His good friends Betty Comden and Adolph Green provide a song of unbridled enthusiasm, *Carried Away,* from their first Broadway collaboration with L, *On The Town.* The musical setting here is a satirical parody on the Italian opera duet. The next parody example provides L with a solo turn performing Shostakovich's Second Piano Concerto. This work parodies the famous Hanon *dull-as-ditch-water* piano scale exercises we were all made to practise for hours on end as children.

Now L places "humour in music" into a larger frame. "Where does great music come into the picture?", he asks. "Can a serious composer afford to be humorous?" L allows himself the widest latitude in answering these questions. "Every symphony must have its comic relief," he continues, "not to be *funny,* but to provide those moments of relaxation essential to every large musical construction." The *scherzo* from the classical symphony represents such comic relief, albeit in its highest sense. The *Scherzo* movement from Beethoven's Third (*Eroica*) Symphony serves as his example. L underlines that this music is "not funny but *fun...* Five minutes of fun...yet serious enough to belong in so monumental a symphony. Humour at its highest estate." What really struck me as funny was that L conducted his example of this humorous movement looking like grim death.

The program concluded with the same work chosen to end his Young People's Concert, *Till Eulenspiegel's Merry Pranks* by Richard Strauss. This work follows musically "note for prank" the humorous adventures of a practical joker named *Till* who is eventually caught, tried by the Courts and hung. L lists for his viewers all the characteristics that bring humour to this graphic musical tale, overstatement, understatement, jokes, squeaky clarinets, rude bassoon noises, abrupt louds and softs, wrong notes - all the elements discussed throughout this program. Ten minutes of brilliant analysis follows touching upon all the score's subtleties. L declares the work to be "a magical piece of construction and invention, humorous just in the magical way the notes are put together." He clues us in to all the things to listen for in "Till's game of notes", from titters to a triumphant shout. His final summation of this very entertaining program is that "Humour is the fountainhead of Art and a mainspring of civilised society."

Till now, I haven't devoted much space to L's podium manner in my summaries and analyses of the *Ford/Lincoln Specials*. I would not have in this instance either if everything had proceeded throughout in the ordered, sane way in which it had begun. L's conducting throughout was controlled and straightforward though, as to be expected, with bags of personality. He certainly embarked upon shaping a first class performance of Richard Strauss' masterwork in a classically controlled fashion with the NY Philharmonic displaying its best form. Suddenly, however, without warning, at the climax of the work, the point where *Till* is captured and hanged, L began to leap wildly about the podium. The tempo was thrust into high gear and this up-till-now gorgeous performance was suddenly transformed into a cluttered mess. There seemed no stopping him as he pushed the orchestra to the limits and beyond. Fortunately, Strauss, the composer, cools things down compositionally before *Till* is heard launching the final energetic, ghostly prank which closes the work. This enabled the performance to end in good order. After viewing this videotape, I was left to wonder whatever possessed L to take such risks live on air which, on this as well as other occasions I had witnessed, ended up ruining what promised to be a truly marvellous performance. The answer I arrived at was that the risks were all an intrinsic part of who and what Lenny was. Without them he would probably have become bored and stale. By constantly taking chances without a safety net beneath him, there was always the possibility that he could arrive at and conquer a peak of a musical Everest that he had never previously scaled.

Leonard Bernstein and the NY Philharmonic in Moscow
(Telecast: 25/10/59)

The scene is the Great Hall of the Tchaikovsky Conservatory in Moscow. The audience is composed of students, faculty and the general public. L enters greets his audience in Russian addressing them as "friends" and then conducts the national anthems of Russia and the United States. Several Moscow musicians now join the orchestra to supply the additional instrumentation required for Shostakovich's massive Seventh Symphony which is the featured work on this program. The only other substantial work to be examined will be Aaron Copland's Suite from the Ballet, *Billy the Kid*.

The underlying theme of L's script is "hands across the sea". In the course of this program one point will be stressed again and again, 'Look at how much we Americans and you Russians have in common.'

L's first step on this self-appointed mission of world diplomacy is the question, "What is it that makes two peoples so alike despite obvious differences?" The answer for him is found in the music of the different countries. Americans and Russians love each others' music. He speaks of Gershwin's *Porgy and Bess*, which enjoyed an enormous success during a State Department sponsored tour of Russia. As he plays a strain of *Summertime* there is a murmur of recognition from the audience. He returns the compliment with positive noises about the music of Tchaikovsky, Rimsky-Korsakov and Rachmaninoff. He performs several American popular songs whose melodies were borrowed, (stolen would be more accurate) from these composers. He then correlates Shostakovich's

WEST SIDE MAESTRO

Leningrad Symphony to Copland's *Billy The Kid* as examples of music which make a serious statement to a wide audience in a musically nationalistic language. The physical grandeur which both works project is a reflection of the large physical presence which both countries represent. He performs the ending of both works to demonstrate this sense of grandeur. Neither ending evokes applause. Russian audiences show themselves different enough from their American counterparts not to respond to demonstration examples which would certainly have brought a response in an American concert hall.

Much of what L was saying was going straight over the heads of a large percentage of his audience who either spoke no English or possessed a minimum comprehension of the language. Though a Russian interpreter provided an instant translation to L's text, the text itself was too complex to follow with any degree of accuracy except by someone with some fluency in English.

L compares the ethnic make up of the two countries. With borders touching upon Europe, Asia, the Balkans, Antarctica and the Near East, Russia contains within her own vast country more than one hundred different nationalities. America also has earned a reputation as a great melting pot of peoples. Copland's score to *Billy the Kid* exemplifies these diverse ethnic influences. Its synchopations and cross rhythms reflect African influences that evolved into Jazz.

L lists humour and frankness as both American and Russian qualities. There is also the love of percussion and strong sounds and a reverence for folk song and folk legend. L's unashamed, ecumenical outpouring reiterates other points of commonality, the affection for the primitive past, an emotional expansiveness, the sense of fun, frankness, vigour and the tremendous variety which are the characteristics of both countries. Ignoring the possible breach of political protocol, he states, "We are similar people, natural friends who must not let prejudices keep us apart."

One cannot comment at this distance in time upon the reaction of officialdom on both sides of the arctic circle to this naive if heartfelt attempt to solve the problems of East/West politics with a fifteen minute appeal delivered at a concert in Moscow. But we can comment on how L's sponsor, the Ford Motor Company reacted, for at this moment in the telecast there was an interruption in the continuity. During this interlude, we were not delivered 'a short word from our sponsor' but something much more subtle at the time if obvious in long term perspective. The figure of the noted lawyer, Joseph Welsh[71], filled the television screen. He appeared standing in Independence Hall, Philadelphia, the home of the Liberty Bell. For the next few minutes, he delivered a short commentary on America's Bill of Rights, the Declaration of Independence and the Constitution. Thus the Ford Motor Company made clear that their sponsorship of this black and white telecast contained not even the slightest hint of "pink".

The telecast then returned to Tchaikovsky Hall in Moscow, with L still holding forth. He moved on to the most substantial musical extract of the program, the first movement of Shostakovich's Seventh Symphony. He introduces the composer who is in attendance. The audience response is enormous. Shostakovich, acknowledges the applause from his seat in the hall, but so sustained is the applause that he finally comes to the stage to accept the adulation of his countrymen. Later, the composer had some harsh words to say about certain of L's public comments during the New York orchestra's visit to Russia. On this day, however, he could only be thrilled with its performance of his most maligned and misunderstood symphony. The orchestra's playing was inspiring. The wonderful blending of the woodwinds, the powerful but never forced string tone, the whole internal balance, - it was all faultless. As for L's reading, he had over many years come to understand, appreciate and present this symphony in a manner that made a nonsense out of the constant carping and brickbats hurled at it by the musical press. On this day, not only did he offer the Muscovites a supreme reading but an opportunity to witness his charismatic talents in full flight, displaying his entire range of dramatic gestures and emotions. In

---

[71] Joseph Welsh was famous throughout America as the man credited with sounding the death knell for Senator Joseph McCarthy and his feared House on Un-American Activities Committee which thrived during the Eisenhower administration wreaking havoc throughout the Performing Arts of America with its blacklist which destroyed the careers and lives of performers, writers and technicians along with hundreds of other innocent Americans.

every sense of the word, he delivered an heroic performance. Throughout, close-ups of the audience, both children and adults, allow us to witness the full effect of the music upon them. At its conclusion, there is a stunned silence – then, a seemingly endless cheering and deafening applause began thundering through the hall threatening to bring down the ceiling. The concert had taken on the aspect of an extraordinary event. L, in voice-over commentary, launches yet another anti-war plea. Then we are backstage. L and Felicia are greeting Boris Pasternack who had made a rare public appearance to attend this concert. The telecast ends.

One cannot treat this program as one normally would a musical event. The events of this day had transformed it into a unique *happening*.

Ford presents
The Ageless Mozart
The NY Philharmonic in Venice
(Telecast: November 22, 1959)

This program, the second in the newly renamed *Ford presents* series, was televised during the 1959 NY Philharmonic tour of Europe and Russia with L as their recently appointed Music Director.

The overture to Mozart's comic opera, *The Marriage of Figaro* opens the program. This very well known classical *lollipop*[72] makes extremely demanding requirements of the orchestra both in terms of technique and dynamic control. The ability to perform its virtuoso *pianissimo* opening to perfection requires the entire string section to play with minimum pressure of the bow while, simultaneously, bringing to every note produced a maximum clarity and importance within the ultra-quiet dynamic demanded. The NY Philharmonic reveals itself in superb form in the company of their new chief maestro. L dedicates their performance of the Mozart overture to all their American friends as " a most affectionate postcard...from this

---

[72] *Lollypop* was the designation given by Sir Thomas Beecham to a much loved classic of relatively short duration which he could serve up as an encore.

glorious city of Venice."[73]. Then, as with the majority of his television 'specials', the formal script begins with a question, "Why are we *Americans* playing *Austrian* music in an *Italian* theatre?" The connection is the interior design of the Venetian theatre in which they are performing, *La Fenice*, (The Phoenix). L describes this historic theatre as "the embodiment of what we think of as eighteenth century beauty", aristocratic elegance, intimacy yet with grandeur, lightness and airiness, delicate gaiety, refined ornamentation and, lastly, precise, tasteful elegance. He correlates all these qualities to Mozart. He goes as far to suggest that the visual experience of *La Fenice* initially produces in one's thoughts and inner ear the music of Mozart with its similar "elegance, wit, daintiness, intimacy, and the rest."

Why Mozart? Other contemporaries of Mozart are named but, as L explains, none of them rise to a genius that is universal, capable of capturing not only "the spirit of his age but also the spirit of man, man of all epochs, man in all the subtleties of his desire, struggle and ambivalence."

The remainder of the program is a paean to Mozart, reaffirming the universal elements of the man through examples of his music, the solo compositions for piano, the late symphonies, the opera, *Don Giovanni*, and, lastly, in longest excerpt, the second and third movements of the Piano Concerto No.17 in G Major for which L serves as both soloist and conductor.

L expands on the universality of each musical example as it is presented. Mozart's *Fantasy in C* could easily be Beethoven; the G Major Piano Concerto is "replete with Tschaikovskian sighs and longings"; the C Major Piano Concerto is "one of the special treasures of all musical history: timeless, ageless." though "it rests on a rigid, formal, eighteenth century pedestal." Even eighteenth century ornamentation, that "elegant icing" which adorns melodies of the period, develops deeper musical values becoming "emotional music in Mozart's hands...more meaningful and moving..." The Minuet from the late G minor symphony reveals" a rhythmic variety and surprises...typical of a twentieth century composer", while the finale of his last symphony "looks back to Bach." His opera, *Don Giovanni*,

---

[73] Except if otherwise specified, all further quotes in this essay are taken from L's script.

has Verdian overtones as well as the depth and power of Wagner. Music from the final scene from *Giovanni* has even been described by music analysts as "the first twelve tone music ever written." For L "Mozart is *all* music; there is nothing you can ask of music that he cannot supply."

The program concludes with the second and third movements of the G Major Piano Concerto. L gilds the lily just a bit in ascribing to its Andante "the tranquillity of a Schubert Lied, the filigree of a Chopin, *the brooding of a Mahler!*"[74] However, it is not hyperbole when he depicts the *Finale* as the essence of rococo, "bathed in the glitter that could only have come from the eighteenth century...And yet, over (which) hovers the greater spirit that is Mozart...a spirit that knows no ages, that belongs to all ages."

No part of this script could be considered 'ground-breaking' or revealing of aspects of Mozart's music new to anyone with an appreciation of classical music. One must consider, however, that a large majority of the viewers of L's television specials were not classical music devotees as such. Many must have been the youngsters and their parents first attracted to classical music through his televised Young People's Concerts. Others may have first become interested in serious music via the earlier *Omnibus* programs. Still others may have been drawn to these specials by the charisma and extraordinary multi-musical gifts of its presenter. Even for those who could recite, whistle or hum a litany of Mozart's tragic history and miraculous musical output, it was never less than an enjoyable experience to spend an hour in the company of so vital a musician. An interesting footnote to this program is in regard to the venue in which it was filmed, *La Fenice*. This magnificent theatre, named after the mythical Phoenix, was again destroyed by fire for the third time in its history in 1996, and remained for many years a burned out ruin, a derelict monument - yet another victim of political in-fighting and corruption in a country that seems ever in political paralysis. However, characteristic of its namesake, the Phoenix, this historic opera house rose yet again from its ashes in 2003 to take its place as an international temple of the Arts.

---

[74] Author's italics

WEST SIDE MAESTRO

Christmas Startime
(Telecast, 22/12/59)

This is about as upmarket a Christmas Special as one could conceive. International in flavour, its cast of talent was drawn from England and America. The concert program was devised to appeal mostly to "longhairs" and families with serious cultural leanings.

The noted lawyer, Joseph Welsh, served as linking narrator throughout the program. Welsh had established close ties with the Saudek Organisation as a presenter of historical programs for *Omnibus*, such as its award winning series on the American Constitution. His introduction transports us to London and St. Paul's Cathedral. A fanfare by the trumpets of the Royal Horse Guards Regiment introduces a processional of the choir of St. Paul's. To the sounds of the carol, *O Come, All Ye Faithful*, we are treated to magnificent views of the interior of the Cathedral and of the choir as they move to their places at either side of the altar. Following the carol, the venue shifts to Stationers' Hall in London. L is seated at a harpsichord surrounded by young members of the St. Paul's choir. He chats amiably with them, discussing their family backgrounds and getting them to improvise each of the verses to *The Twelve Days of Christmas*. It's all very informal, carried out in the spirit of fun. When it works its lovely and when it doesn't it is equally charming and natural. These are youngsters having a friendly time with the world's musical *Super Dad*.

Back in New York, we are introduced to Marian Anderson, one of the most famous contralto singing voices of the twentieth century. With her accompanist, Franz Rupp, she sings the carol, *Behold that star*. Miss Anderson was well on in years when she appeared on this program but her voice still responded well in carefully chosen repertoire. Her second selection, the spiritual, *He's Got de Whole World in His Hands*, delivered in the rich, velvet tones of her lowest vocal register, was no less than sensational.

The Schola Cantorum of New York with soloists Lee Venora, soprano, Betty Allen, mezzo-soprano, Russell Oberlin, counter tenor, and Charles Bressler, tenor, join the NY Philharmonic under L's direction for a performance of J.S. Bach's *Magnificat*, a Latin setting of the hymn of the Virgin Mary, "My soul doth magnify the Lord". The set designed for the *Magnificat* consisted of a huge triptych frame placed upon an altar. The choir, in renaissance costume, was positioned in the two outer wings of the triptych. The central wing was used for various frozen tableaux mounted in the style of famous renaissance paintings based upon the life of the Virgin. Each tableaux reflected the sung text of the *Magnificat*. L introduced and translated the text of each section.

The musical performance of this lengthy cantata incorporated a dichotomy of styles and traditions. On the one hand there was an attempt at period authenticity, the counter-tenor, Russell Oberlin, whose voice recreated the ancient tradition of the castrato male alto. He was joined by the tenor, Charles Bressler, an expert in baroque performance. The women soloists, though wonderfully accomplished, were more traditionally selected. The orchestra was equipped with replica examples of baroque instruments, ie: piccolo trumpets, an Oboe d'amore, (wonderfully played by the NY Philharmonic's *cor anglais* soloist, Engelbert Brenner), and a Viola da gamba, (bass viol) and baroque pipe organ to accompany the recitatives. The remaining, overly large group of players all performed on modern instruments. L made several other halfway-house musical decisions along the way. The choir, Hugh Ross's *Schola Cantorum*, were encouraged to sing in a lush, romantic, Victorian manner. Old fashioned huge retards, (exaggerated slowing down), were applied at the end of each section. The joyful opening and closing movements of the *Magnificat*, both assigned the precise same music by Bach, were taken at tempos at marked variance to each other.

A Bible reading by Joseph Welsh followed the Bach, then a return to London for more superb views of the interior of St. Paul's. The choir carols *Good*

WEST SIDE MAESTRO

King Wenceslaus, *Greensleeves*, (What Child is This), and *Ding-dong, Merrily On High*. In quick succession there is a return to New York for a very unsteady rendition of *Silent Night* by Marion Anderson now accompanied by the Schola Cantorum with the NY Philharmonic under L's direction and a final return to London for more carols by the St. Paul's Choir. The choir processes out singing *Hark! The Herald Angels Sing* as our closing visual again captures the Brass of the Royal Horse Guards Regiment.

Other than to discuss present changed musical attitudes towards Bach performance, it is really pointless to subject this Christmas entertainment to criticism. The tele-visual option to semi-stage Bach's *Magnificat* ended up being *kitsch*[75]. Tableaux depicting scenes from the life of the Virgin based upon renaissance paintings was a fine idea on the drawing board but proved otherwise in practice. The studio settings were all very plush and over-Romanticised, a kind of Tiffany version of Christmas. In retrospect, the best and most enjoyable musical selections were the two simply presented Marion Anderson choices at the opening and the carol singing of the Choir of St. Paul's Cathedral.. This program was an attempt to create a televised Christmas celebration with a difference. With its huge budget and high profile conductor, it ended up a rather overblown, pompous affair, somewhat snobbish in appeal.

The Creative Performer
(Telecast: 31/01/60)

The Creative Performer provided an examination of the inter-action between the hieroglyphics of music notation, lacking or accompanied by a limited or large number of instructions from the composer, and the human factor, the performer, whose task it is, thorough training, knowledge of period style, musical instincts and an individual talent and personality, to find a way of bringing life and communicative meaning to the printed record.

---

[75] kitsch - vulgarised or pretentious art usually aimed towards popular appeal.

WEST SIDE MAESTRO

In a somewhat overstated summation rather late in this generally entertaining and interesting show, L brashly asserts that the manner in which we translate and perform the music of dead composers is all based upon "guess work." In light of the enormous degree of musicological, historical research already going on within the time frame of this telecast, such a declaration was more than overzealous, it was self-defeating. Had L substituted the idea of *'informed* intuitive preference', spoken about throughout the program, for the phrase 'guess work', his summation would have been less contentious and not opened to predictable criticism from within music circles. The artist as an innovative, informed personality is what this program is about. Someone capable of taking the printed sheet of music and personally infusing it with individual ideas of shape, colour, dynamics and choice of tempo that will project an "inevitable rightness" to the listener, perhaps even the sense of that which the composer himself might have had in mind.

Beginning with Beethoven's Third Symphony played as if by two conductors of different temperament and backgrounds, L presents us with a fierce, hard driven performance of the opening moments of the first movement followed a slower, gentler, less aggressive playing of the same section. Which interpretation is the 'correct' one? What are conductors A & Z looking for? What was Beethoven seeking? The composer has provided both a descriptive word hint, *Allegro con brio,* (Fast and lively), and a metronome mark instructing a speed of one bar of music per second or sixty bars of music per minute. In addition Beethoven has added many irregularly placed accents and contrasts in dynamics. Since there are 691 bars of music in this movement, or 691 seconds in terms of time span, the section of the symphony should take *eleven and a half minutes* to perform. Yet, L notes that he could not find a recorded performance of this movement under *thirteen* minutes. "How could this be?", he asks. "Did Beethoven give wrong information?" "Did the performers ignore his wishes?" His answers to these questions are what the rest of the program is about, the *human factor.* Personally demonstrating or with the aid of three star names from the classical firmament, the pianist, Glenn Gould, the soprano, Eileen Farrell, and the composer, Igor Stravinsky,[76] and a varied repertoire of Bach, Ponchielli and Stravinsky, L reveals how the various elements of music, tempo, dynamics, style, and phrasing are inter-related and capable of affecting the tempo as well as the very character of the music itself. He then examines the unknown factor, the artist's instincts demonstrating through his guests that no matter to what degree any a composer goes to instruct the performer, each artist still must seek out a performance which incorporates themselves into the equation, what L refers to as "the artist's demon". Certainly, his three invited guests demonstrate this *demon* factor admirably.

Glenn Gould's chosen work, the D Minor keyboard concerto by J.S. Bach, provided the soloist with the least amount of performing information. Bach was one of many baroque composers whose music was written exclusively for their own use. As these composers were in charge of the preparation of each performance, there was little need for writing instructions in their music. Communication took place directly with musicians who were in regular employ and with whom the composers had already established preferred performing practices.

L prefaces Gould's performance by demonstrating how the work might sound blandly played with neither expression nor nuance. He then performs it a second time with all manner of exaggerated shading. To truly know a work, L points out, one must become acquainted with the whole before coming to any conclusions. Gould then performs the first movement of the concerto in his own individual fashion playing each note in a short detached fashion, *staccato*, with great clarity achieved between right and left hands and beautifully shaped phrases.

The work chosen for Eileen Farrell is the *Suicido* aria from Ponchielli's opera, *La Gioconda*. This represents music for which the composer has provided an overabundance of information. What can an artist add to this? A great deal as it happens. In Farrell's case she pours on the drama, adds a tear in her voice and sings with wrenching passion, all a reflection of her

---

[76] Both Glenn Gould and Igor Stravinsky were making their American television debuts on this program.

knowledge of the character she is portraying and the complex plot situation described in the aria. The last of the three guests, the composer, Igor Stravinsky, can show us precisely how he wants his music performed. He conducts three movements, the *Infernal Dance, Berceuse* and *Finale*, from his 1947 suite to his ballet, *The Firebird.* The NY Philharmonic provides sterling service for all three soloists as well as their music director. In the case of Stravinsky, who was new to television and seemed somewhat nervous, they gave that bit extra when his beat proved not always to correspond with the music he was conducting.

This program was produced with theatrical flair and allowed the uninformed viewer an entertaining behind the scenes glimpse of the artist as interpreter.

Rhythm
(Telecast: 13/03/60)

This script is one the most imaginative and complex that L ever attempted to construct for his adult television audience. His core theme deals with the larger aspects of rhythm, how a fundamental pulse of undifferentiated beats can be structured into regular groups to create a metrical pattern; how a metrical pattern can be grouped to form a phrase; how a phrase can be enlarged to form a period, that is, a larger section; and finally, how these larger sections can be combined to form larger groups which can themselves be combined to form an entire movement. This basic but huge concept of musical structure will be explained through a "principle of *doubleness,* **the concept of <u>two</u>**". L's core statement upon which the rest of his script will be structured is, "All the music we know, *in one way or another*, is built on a duple concept.

This program begins with the visual of a human heart beating. Its pulsing beat, alternating systolic and diastolic contractions, is translated into the rhythm of the opening movement of Beethoven's Seventh Symphony. The image dissolves to L conducting the NY Philharmonic performing a fragment of this first movement containing this pulsing heart rhythm. The underlying dupleness that is the symmetry of the human body is given as a principal example of the *two-ness* in the world around us, two eyes, ears, arms, hands, legs, feet, the way we breathe, in/out - in/out, the way we walk, left/right - left/right, day/night, hot/cold, etc.

With the purpose of demonstrating that what happens above a basic meter is that which creates musical interest, ever more complicated rhythmic patterns are superimposed over a steady metric pattern.. During a musical detour we examine the two contrasting elements that delineate the structural essence of Ravel's *Bolero,* the ever repeating two bar *bolero* pattern played on the snare drum and the various solos and combinations of instruments which play a rhythmically free flowing melody against this rhythm. From this relatively straightforward tangent, we leap to another tangent far more complex. L needlessly and confusingly, in my opinion, introduces into the scheme the aesthetic of Poetry. Using the poetry of Shakespeare he seeks a parallel in the use of language comparable to the structural contrasts of Ravel's Bolero. His purpose is to demonstrate that Shakespeare builds variety directly into the structured meter of his poetry. That is, one does not read a Shakespearean line structured in iambic pentameter in a stilted *ta-dum/ ta-dum/ ta-dum* fashion but with free expression, savouring the meaning, drama and expressivity of the words. Explaining how this is done, however, ("...by the inversion of the first iambic foot into a trochaic foot") risked losing his audience. What L had to say with this digression, although interesting, is light years away from where he is heading. While adding variety to his script it also adds an element of confusion to that which is already a very difficult concept to get across. Happily, the spotlight quickly returns to matters musical. To help hold his audience's attention and underscore his various points we have short musical examples taken from well known classics performed by the NY Philharmonic and, as always, L at the piano.

Where is L heading? The notion expounded in the remainder of his script appears relatively straightforward and simple but defines, in fact, one of the most important and complex pillars upon which the architecture of Western music is constructed, *symmetry*. L demonstrated this as follows: Taking a Beethoven melody in duple rhythm, he shows how its first bar, containing *two* beats, is melodically incomplete,   requiring a complementary second bar. But this *two* bar segment is also incomplete, not yet a phrase much less a sentence, so we add *two* more measures to complete the phrase - a phrase consisting of *two* 2-*bar* fragments. We now have a 4-bar phrase but it too is incomplete. To make it complete we must balance it with a complementary 4-bar phrase to give it a sense of symmetry. We now have arrived at an 8-bar musical statement which consists of *two* 4-bar phrases or, viewed in a somewhat more complex manner by L, 2x2, (two 2-bar fragments creating a 4-bar phrase) x 2, (our 4-bar phrase and its 4-bar symmetrical balance), to create an 8-bar musical statement. But, as L points out, Beethoven has not completed his thought and so to this 8-bar statement he adds a balancing, complementary 8-bar statement. Now we have the full 16-bar theme made up of *two* 8-bar statements, or examined in more detailed complexity, 2x2x2x2!

Up to this point barely a quarter of the program has been consumed and the lesson in musical mathematics has just begun. Now L takes on the more difficult explanation, triple meter, (three-beats-to-the-bar), with which we are most familiar in its waltz form. There can be no biological, (physical), analogy to be made in this instance. "Three is an *invented* number", intellectual in concept, even mystical in origin, (the *Holy Trinity*, the triangular shape of the pyramids or the two superimposed inverted triangles which comprise the *Star of David*).

L views this as the critical point to understanding Rhythm in all its complexities. From this point onwards all rhythmic considerations to be examined will "result in one way or another from the interaction of physical-2 and intellectual-3: either 2 + 3, or 2 x 3, or 2 *against* 3 or whatever." Just as mathematics can be reduced to basic elements of two and three, (4 = 2+2; 5 = 2+3; 6 = 2x3; 7 = 2+2+3 etc.), so it is with music. L takes the theme from Johann Strauss' *Emperor Waltz* and, just as he did with the Beethoven melody,   builds up his complete sixteen bar theme by adding a complementary second bar to his first, adding two more bars to complete his phrase, four more to complete his musical statement and eight more to balance and complete his theme. The only structural difference with the Beethoven theme is that instead of the meter for each bar being 1/2, 1/2, 1/2, it is 1-2-3, 1-2-3, 1-2-3. Nevertheless, as L points out, despite all its *three-ness*, the Strauss waltz remains architecturally a slave to *two-ness*. L's explanation is as simple as it is obvious. "The waltz is a dance, and a dance is performed *with two legs*." Despite its triple meter the architectural structure of a waltz turns out to be as duple as a march. L repeats this feat of metrical legerdemain with Wagner's *Ride of the Valkyries* whose meter is 9-beats-to-the-bar. This turns out to be just another 3-to-the-bar structure, each beat consisting of three pulsations, (3x3=9). L repeats the same symmetrical balancing act with Wagner as with Beethoven and Strauss. What all these pieces have demonstrated is an unfailing symmetry which L relates to an aesthetic demand created from a biological need derived from "the physical biformity of the human being", or more simply, that famous left/right concept which he set out in detail at the start of the program. So universally felt has been this concept that it has defined the structure of Western music up to the 20th century. A short analysis follows of the final movement of César Franck's *Symphony in d minor*, characterised by L as "a super *duple* symphony" and "a hymn to symmetry". Having performed only snippets from a variety of masterworks thus far, the substantial finale to the Franck Symphony comes as a welcome relief to all the mathematical formulas and repetitive examples of symmetry. It is a particularly good choice, although not mentioned by L, as its symmetrical structure deals with music composed in both duple and triple rhythm. It's an even better choice because it is an exciting, dynamic work from beginning to end, with great tunes, tremendous energy and big climaxes guaranteed to excite and hold any viewer/listener, even one hearing it for the first time. An all-stops-out performance of the Franck brings us to the end of the first half of the program.

Sitting in my small viewer's booth at the unique Museum of Radio & Television in New York City waiting for the second half of this teletape to begin, I was left to wonder whether this idea might have been better served if presented as two separate programs. Although one tries not to fault such a vital concept devoted to bringing a deeper understanding of great music to many who never conceived the endless pleasures that could be derived from the *long-haired* side of the *Top-Ten* list, I could not avoid the sense that this difficult concept with all its accompanying analyses and analogies was too much to be taken in at one go, even when reduced to the simple, clear terms which was L's gift of proven expertise. My musing was interrupted by the explosive sounds of the NY Philharmonic performing a most rhythmically complex extract from Stravinsky's shocker ballet of 1918, *The Rite of Spring*. The second half of the program had begun and not only had the goal posts been moved but one found oneself in a totally different stadium. L was now speaking of "forces that all but annihilated the comfortable symmetries of yesteryear." Working backwards he traces through composers of the past similar examples of unequal meter and rhythmic patterns in music of Brahms and Tchaikovsky. As it turns out even with the odd appearance of a meter with five beats in every bar, as was the example chosen from Tchaikovsky, the overall structure of the music in each case was still bound to *duple* conventions. L proceeds to early examples of asymmetry in the music of Stravinsky less radical than the example that opened the second half of the program. He chooses the coda to the ballet, *The Firebird*, which is composed in a 7-beats-to-the-bar meter, which Stravinsky permutes into alternating divisions of 3+2+2 and 2+2+3. In this instance, as it turns out, with all its complex internal asymmetry, the structure of the passage as a whole still conforms to the same classical balance we found in Beethoven, Brahms, Franck and Tchaikovsky. With the next musical example L moves beyond this conformity to a point where meter in modern music changes from bar to bar, from six to five to seven, etc., shattering the convention of duple symmetry.

The remainder of the program is devoted to a single work by Aaron Copland, his eleven minute musical souvenir of Mexican life based upon recollections gathered during a trip to that country in 1932, *El Salon Mexico*. L performs an especially disjunct rhythmic passage from *El Salon* at the piano in which bars of six, five, seven, three, two and eight follow and alternate in quick succession. This is the rhythm of the twentieth-century, filled with surprises and unpredictable - no balanced duple-ness here.

WEST SIDE MAESTRO

At this point, L brought to mind my philosophy professor at university. No sooner had he by logic and example proved a specific point to which we, his students, felt no recourse but to concede, then he began to unwind his whole theory and prove the very opposite. This is precisely what L does through a statement and a challenge: the statement, "I think we have come to depend in the past far too much on symmetry, even sometimes mistaking symmetrical balance for beauty" and the challenge, "Why should we remain forever slaves of our two-leggedness?" L's argument is that 'beauty' is more related to *balance* than *symmetry,* and that *"balance* is not necessarily symmetrical." He points out that Copland's music is the product of someone "nurtured on jazz as well as Stravinsky and Brahms." Through excerpts from *El Salon* he demonstrates that Copland's music, far from being an example of some wild-eyed revolutionary seeking to destroy all that came before, is an amalgam of the past with the addition of the new ideas which have stirred the imaginations of twentieth-century composers. Copland's *El Salon* is shown to contain both simple and complex elements, *duple-ness* and "waltzy" *triple-ness,* and various balanced combinations of these two elements used both simultaneously and in alternating fashion. The 'newness' comes when he begins to use 2's and 3's in unpredictable, highly irregular patterns. That, for L, is what makes it music "uniquely of our time." A quick two sentence summing up and L and the orchestra are into a complete performance of the sparkling Copland work that ends this unusual and demanding program.

Rhythm is one of six scripts reprinted in a volume of L's collected writings titled, *The Infinite Variety of Music.* For its publication, six years after this telecast, he wrote the following postscript. It reveals his mood at the time and even a bit of personal despair. He writes of how rhythmic innovation has gone far beyond the complexities of Copland and Stravinsky, how the avant-garde have multiplied the complexities of rhythm to the point of producing "rhythmlessness". He speaks of a "static" quality which he views in certain of the contemporary music of that time which he relates to the use of rhythm in such a construct, i.e. so many different rhythmic patterns sounding at the same time, that it tended to cancel out its function. In his closing statement, he picks up the standard which he was to carry into his personal battle as a tonal composer in the years to come, "...we must take our leave of rhythm as we have known it on this program, much as contemporary music has taken leave of tonality."

Leonard Bernstein and the NY Philharmonic
in Berlin
(Telecast: 20/11/60)

This performance was staged expressly for an audience of upper school and university students in West Berlin. The kernel work around which the entire program was constructed was Beethoven's Concerto No.1 in C Major for Piano and Orchestra. To put his young audience at its ease L begins light-heartedly by caricaturing the opening phrase of the concerto as performed by a Frenchman, a Russian, and finally a jazzy American. There is much laughter and applause[77]. Having now warmed up his audience, L proceeds into the substance of his lecture, the universality of Beethoven's music as well as the music of other German composers, (Bach, Brahms, Schumann, Wagner). What is it, he asks, that makes German music basic and universal? He offers two musical suggestions, a folksong-like Minuet from Haydn's *Surprise* Symphony and the "student-drinking-song-like" Trio from Beethoven's Seventh Symphony. These everyday folk and school reminiscences form peripheral supplements to the core element of the universality of classic German music. This core element, he suggests, is the *Goethe* mind which in turn has produced the German mind that probes and examines each idea no matter how small, dissecting, testing and proving, ever striving towards a universal truth. In music, this intellectual process can be found in any *development section* of the large-scale compositions of the great German composers. To clarify, L chooses a non-musical analogy to demonstrate this process, the city of Berlin. His chosen point of enquiry is, "Why is it so noisy?" He then proceeds to analyse the reasons for the noise, then the reasons for the reasons, and then the reasons-for the reasons-for the reasons. This style of enquiry is a simplistic parallel to the manner in

---

[77] L was emulating his close friend, the composer Lucas Foss, whose party piece specialty was to perform the *Ode to Joy* theme from Beethoven's 9th Symphony in the style of a half dozen noted and stylistically varied composers.

which a composer might approach the development section of a composition.

L then proceeds to analyse the Beethoven piano concerto to be performed. He speaks of a series of transformations that will take place and the specific order in which this will be carried out. He goes through all the transformations of the first theme showing how one change of idea leads to another, which itself is further transformed.

Now, having completed as much analysis as time allows, he devotes his remaining moments before beginning a performance of the complete concerto for a "heart to heart, mind to mind" appeal reminiscent of the talk he delivered in Moscow the previous year. He speaks of that very day in Berlin on which they are gathered together to listen to Beethoven's universal music. It is the Jewish High Holiday of *Rosh Hashonah*. He delivers a Benediction in Hebrew to his young audience. It is the one spoken at the close of a synagogue service, "May the Lord lift up his face to you and give you peace."

The performance of the concerto proves notable. The long orchestral exposition reveals the NY Philharmonic displaying their highest standards of performance. It is not a matter of accomplishment in the face of technical difficulties; the concerto poses few if any for the orchestra. The orchestra's performance transcends standards of immaculate playing and perfect ensemble, both qualities immediately apparent from the starting note. It represents the sheer joy of music making, the combination of the colouring and shaping of phrases, of wonderfully judged dynamics, of blending and balancing within the ensemble. What we are witnessing is the product of a collective imagination operating at its highest aesthetic capacity. The challenge to L to match such musical eloquence is great and, indeed, he proves somewhat tentative on his first entrance. However, within a page of music he has grabbed the nettle and is matching the orchestra phrase for phrase. His is a clean, well articulated performance of this early Beethoven work which still reveals the influence of Haydn. L does imbue the long first movement cadenza with an heroic cast, more associated with later

Beethoven. He displays a wide palette of pianistic colours that combine strength and power with contrasting sections of lightness and mystery.

The Second movement follows virtually without pause. This highly contrasting, lyrical movement is presented simply without indulgence of any kind. The third movement enjoys a performance of great *bravura*[78]. Although this concerto was the one L had most often performed in concert, he had obviously taken additional care not only to prepare himself technically for this occasion but also to re-examine its musical content. [79] At the conclusion of the concerto, there is an enthusiastic reception. L thanks his young audience in a short farewell speech making special comment upon their concentration and attention throughout.

This is among the noteworthy Ford Specials, less for its word content than for the exceptional performance of the Beethoven Concerto and the opportunity to observe L communicating with a level of young, developing minds many stages beyond the youngsters for whom he had served as musical godfather in his Young People's Concerts.

Romanticism In Music
(Telecast: 22/01/61)

This no holds barred, no expenses spared telecast offered a stellar list of performers from all areas of the Arts. From opera there were the sopranos Birgit Nilsson, Leontyne Price and Frances Bible, from the ballet, Edward Villella and members of the NY City Ballet, there were actors to read the poetry of Edgar Allen Poe and John Milton plus a choir and the NY Philharmonic to round out this extraordinary gathering of talent representing the world of the Performing Arts. To fuse this diverse group of

---

[78] bravura (Ital.) here it means brilliant in the face of great technical demands.

[79] I have written additionally of this performance in Volume 2 in the sub-chapter, The Unitel Video Collection, The Music of Beethoven: The Concertos

performers together there was Leonard Bernstein presenting one of his best scripts.

The program opens with L, seated at the piano, performing music we closely associate with the *Romantic period*, a Chopin *Nocturne*. His brief is to explore and pinpoint the essence of *Romantic* music. First, he lists qualities generally associated with romantic music - warmth, melody, amorous yearnings, moodiness, atmosphere, passion, even "swaying palm trees in moonlight." L's exploration, however, is not of some single subjective quality that might suggest romantic overtones but of *Romanticism* with a capital *R*, the nineteenth century historical movement that took the Arts by storm.

The eighteenth century revolutionary fight for freedom from tyranny in France and America culminated in greater freedom of expression for the individual in the nineteenth century. L lists the great leaders for such freedom in the Arts, Goethe, Schiller, Beethoven, Byron, Keats, Shelly, Pushkin, Victor Hugo, among others. Each of these revolutionary personalities fought not only for individual freedom but freedom from the restrictions of formalisation and stylisation in their creative output. L introduces examples of dance, poetry and music that illustrate and contrast the several revolutionary changes that took place.

The proclaimed right to self-expression placed the creative personality for the first time in a position of dominance. However, this proved to be a pebble that also stirred the waters of artistic egotism. Soon the *recreative* performing artist was also asserting the right of self-expression based upon virtuoso levels of accomplishment. Thus was created within the Arts a constellation of performers, the star actress, the matinee idol, the prima ballerina, the personality conductor, the instrumental virtuoso and the opera diva. L quotes

Pushkin's brief but powerful call to arms for the new humanistic cult of the individual, "*You* are the Czar!" This emotive as well as highly entertaining exposition featuring an array of talent from the theatre, concert, ballet and opera now concentrates specifically on the musical Arts in the *Romantic* era.

WEST SIDE MAESTRO

L's examines the techniques that helped effect this new wave of freedom of expression for composers. He classifies them as the four *musical* freedoms,

"freedom of tonality, freedom of rhythm, freedom of form and freedom of sonority." [80]

L reviews and demonstrates each of these new nineteenth century developments in music. Beginning with Beethoven and carrying through to the turn of the century and beyond, he outlines how music became more and more *chromatic* in the pursuit of greater intensity and expressivity. He illustrates through the music of Berlioz, the epitome of nineteenth century *Romanticism,* chromaticism's elusive and mysterious appeal to romantic composers and the new ambiguity it brought to chordal relationships in harmony.

Not only harmony, however, but also rhythm was to find greater freedom in the hands of a Beethoven, Berlioz, Schumann, Chopin and others in this *romantic* era. Tempo within a movement was allowed to change at will, rhythmic flow was interrupted, different rhythmic patterns were juxtaposed against each other.

Rhythm provided only the second of the new freedoms. *Form* was also reshaped in this search for the new. Berlioz's *Romeo and Juliet* symphony proved so non-conformist in its overall shape that the composer felt the need to qualify its description by calling it a *dramatic* symphony, stressing its extra-musical content and effect over strict classical form.

Music was now extending its brief to encompass other aspects of the arts to include literature and drama. Out of this was to grow a new musical genre of composition whose emphasis on content rather than form, on stories, scenarios and characters, would find an encapsulated meaning in its broad

---

[80] This television script is of particular importance among L's writings. It later served as the foundation for many of the ideas that were expanded for his Norton Lectures delivered at Harvard University in 1973.

WEST SIDE MAESTRO

description as *program music*. L analyses Liszt's use of the *leitmotif*, (leading motive), which had been brought to public attention earlier in the century by Hector Berlioz[81]. Liszt's three movement *Faust* symphony provides L's laboratory. He researches its principal themes which represent the characters of *Faust*, *Gretchen* and *Mephistopheles* and reveals how they are musically transformed and made to interact in a fashion to parallel their dramatic progress in Goethe's epic drama which inspired the composer.

This recycling of themes through the various movements of a symphony was defined as *cyclical form* - "a form in which the material keeps returning in cycles". This technique grew in popularity in the second half of the 19th century, especially with composers of opera. L shows how cyclic, motivic techniques employed by Bizet and Verdi were used to identify characters and events throughout their operas. It was left to one composer, however, to develop and perfect the use of the *leitmotif*, Richard Wagner. Wagner, in whom the German Romantic movement was raised to its most complete expression, *die heilige deutsche Kunst,* (the holy German art), composed operas which were massive vocal symphonies that were organically developed on a vast number of motives which represented characters, symbols, circumstances, emotions and even geographical localities. These symphonically conceived operas were designated by their composer as *Music Dramas*. This multi-talented composer who was also a poet, a stage designer and director and a conductor, represented for L the ultimate romantic ego.

---

[81] In Berlioz's unusual five movement symphony, a reoccurring *leading motive*, (idee fixe), appears which represents a musical image of an artist's beloved as he delusionally visualises her while under the influence of drugs. Her theme reappears and is developed in each of the first four movements of the symphony. In the fifth movement, *The Dream of a Witches Sabbath*, the theme of the beloved returns in a highly grotesque guise which again is reworked in a manner to mirror the composer's specific program story outline. The use of such a germinal phrase cyclically to interlock the various movements of a sonata or symphony into a unified whole did not begin with Berlioz, although Berlioz, Liszt and Wagner are the three composers who have come to represent the supreme development of this technique. Examples can be cited in the sonatas, suites and canzonas of the 7th century. Other models are to be found in the sacred works of Bach and Mozart, in the instrumental works of Handel and Haydn, and in the chamber music of Schubert and Beethoven. The most famous early 19th century instrumental example of thematic transformation to establish cohesion in a multi-movement form is Beethoven's Fifth Symphony. Brahms' Third Symphony, Mendelssohn's *Italian* Symphony, Schumann's Fourth Symphony and Franck's D Minor Symphony are all well-known examples which employ this *cyclic* technique.

WEST SIDE MAESTRO

"Where is all this leading?", he asks. His answer is the musical form, the *symphonic poem*. Historically, L should have referred back to Liszt at this point, who is credited with having fully developed this form. Liszt's *Les Preludes* is, in fact, a masterpiece of the cyclical *symphonic poem* form in miniature. Instead, L's script moves us forward towards the *symphonic poem* in its extended form as exemplified by the mature orchestral works of Richard Strauss. Unfortunately, it was not one of these extended, mature Strauss works which L chose for his example but one of the composer's very early tone poem dating from 1889, *Don Juan*, written when he was barely twenty-five years old. The radical post-Wagner changes in Strauss' music, i.e. richer and more dissonant harmony and the expanded use of huge orchestras populated by an array of unusual instruments, (oboe d'amore, Heckelphone, saxophones, all manner of clarinets, thunder and wind machines, Wagner tubas, etc.)[82] in compositions of extended length, did not occur until after the turn of the century. *Don Juan* is a work no more complex in form or longer in duration than Liszt's *Les Preludes*. Though it could not by any stretch of imagination be placed in either a trend setting or radical category, it was a work inspired by and which reflected and expanded upon what had come before, specifically Liszt symphonic poems and Wagner's *Ring* operas[83] and *Tristan and Isolde*[84]. It served several practical purposes for this telecast. From a timing point of view, it was of a practical length and it displayed an undeniable brilliance of orchestration, (L's *fourth freedom*, "the freedom of sonority, of musical colour"). Its central thematic and harmonic core were certainly undeniably *romantic* from start to finish Though a bit of a cheat, L's use of it ended up making his point convincingly.

Don Juan also provided L with a needed simile, that of a musical image depicting the final death shudder of the sword-pierced Lothario which he

---

[82] Strauss' *Alpine* Symphony calls for 150 instrumentalists.
[83] *The Ring of the Nibelungs*, four operas based upon the Nibelungen Norse sagas by Richard Wagner. The four operas, connected dramatically and thematically by the composer, require a performing time which exceeds fifteen hours.
[84] Another post-Wagnerian development glossed over in L's script was the expansion of *symphonic form* encountered in the massive symphonies of Bruckner and Mahler.

compared to the shuddering death throes of the *Romantic* movement soon to be replaced by a twentieth century in which all things new, efficient and scientific would sweep away the old.

There was enough material in this telecast for two programs, the first on *Romanticism* in the nineteenth century and the second on the turn of the century musical revolution that ushered in radical modern trends in music and the collapse of tonality. But to encompass that huge brief would have opened a veritable *Pandora's box.* As matters worked out, future Ford programs did carry the story of contemporary developments in music forward but for now L wisely turned from elaborating further on the complexities of the twentieth century and returned to tidy up any loose ends of his script on *Romanticism* in the nineteenth century.

"Why do we (continue to) yearn for Schubert, Schumann and Wagner...Brahms...Tschaikowsky?", is the question with which L introduced his brief summing up. His answer, expressed in picturesque, poetic imagery tied the neatest of bows on this wonderfully entertaining program. "The *Romantics* give us back our moon...which science has taken away from us and made into just another airport...We are all still 'romantics' at heart...but the way we live is no longer romantic; and so, when we are sorely pressed, we look backward, and we play Schumann."

The program then concludes with the slow movement of Robert Schumann's Second Symphony.

Whatever musicological faults one may find in the script, this telecast represents top drawer Bernstein. With a huge cast of star performers for which few Arts programs could budget, along with its unique presenter, it placed on display a coherent panoply of the Fine Arts structured within an historical context. L's script was lucid, crisp and direct, his choice of music highly communicative without resorting to obvious 'safe' choices. The topic chosen was extremely broad in scope and the period covered one of the most distinguished in the history of the music. It was a lot to condense within the time allotted and challenging for a musically untrained television audience.

However, full marks should go to L and the Saudek Associates for mounting this entertaining and informative production. I would find it hard to believe that those viewers with even a very limited interest in classical music did not stay with the program till its introspective, richly romantic, musical conclusion.

Drama Into Opera: Oedipus Rex
(Telecast: 02/26/61)

This is the first of two Ford Specials that made use of a format L had developed for his *Omnibus* telecast, *What Makes Opera Grand*. In this instance L contrasted Sophocles's tragedy *Oedipus Rex* with Igor Stravinsky's opera/oratorio based upon the same myth. Actor's performed scenes from the Sophocles tragedy and solo singers, male choir and the NY Philharmonic performed duplicate scenes from Stravinsky's opera. L, as in his Omnibus special, then analysed each in turn comparing the individual approach of playwright and composer.

The program opens with a classically robed male choir standing before a simple setting of Corinthian columns. They sing the dramatic first four phrases which open Stravinsky's *Oedipus Rex*. This ensemble will serve both as a narrative Greek Chorus and the people of Thebes. L explains that the Stravinsky work is not actually an opera but an oratorio sung in Latin that can be staged with costumes and scenery.

He then turns to the original Sophocles text. The Greek playwright assigns the role of the narrator, who will carry the drama forward, to a single, dominant acting presence. The Stravinsky setting, in contrast, uses a large, anonymous ensemble that sings its text in Latin, an archaic language. This depersonalises the narrative role for modern audiences twice over [85].

---

[85] The Stravinsky *Oedipus* calls for spoken narration. Unlike the sung Latin text of the oratorio, Stravinsky's narrator speaks in the language of the country of performance, (France, England, Japan, Germany, etc.) The libretto, created by Jean Cocteau, was conceived entirely in French. Only later, Stravinsky decided to have the sung text translated into Latin, leaving only the spoken narration in a form which could be directly understood by the audience..

WEST SIDE MAESTRO

We see the actor Keith Michel in crown, doublet and cape, seated upon a throne mounted on a huge half Greek column. He speaks with great emotion to the people of Thebes of his restlessness. He tells them that he has sent his brother-in-law, Creon, to Delphi to consult the Oracle. He worries that Creon has been gone too long. In contrast we now view the duplicate scene in Stravinsky's oratorio. David Lloyd, who sings the role of *Oedipus* is dressed in a simple, colourless, draped toga. He resembles a granite statue. While Sophocles' speech of pride was filled with emotion, Stravinsky's setting for his sung *Oedipus* is restrained, idealised and monumental. Everything is simplified, crystallized, magnified. Its unfamiliar Latin text again makes what is taking place impersonal, once removed from its audience.

We return to the Sophocles drama. Oedipus seeks out the blind prophet, Tiresias. There is an angry dialogue as Tiresias, unresponsive to Oedipus's insistence for answers, is accused by the king of conspiracy. Tiresias angrily turns upon his accuser   and warns Oedipus that revealing the truth will seal his destiny. In the Stravinsky setting this scene consists only of two monolithic arias. L's analysis of Stravinsky's opera/oratorio reveals the twin foundations of the composer's setting, a condensation of the spoken text and a clear exposition of the neo-classic style, which the composer developed following his early flamboyant Russian style that climaxed with his ballet, *Le Sacre de Printemps*.

Sophocles' scene between Queen Jocasta and Oedipus is crucial to L's comparative analysis. It is the point towards which not only the drama is heading but the place of maximum contrast between the original Greek playwright's retelling of the legend and Stravinsky's contemporary setting. Jocasta pleads with Oedipus, "Let us have no more of this dread questioning." Keith Michel's Oedipus, possessed by his destiny, goes to meet it exultantly shouting, "I *will* know my birth." This is followed by the famous scream when Oedipus learns of his unholy matriarchal marriage and in penitence blinds himself. L speaks of this moment of catharsis, so well understood by the ancient Greeks, as the moment of cleansing. Through pity and terror, filled with emotion and trembling, the observer as well is cleansed. He compares this with Stravinsky's frame for the same dramatic events. None of the tension of Sophocles' high drama is experienced in the Stravinsky. All is neo-classic self-restraint, "like a religious rite." There is no scream, no overt emotion of any kind. In theatrical terms, this is *playing the reverse*, as powerful in its depiction of tragedy through restraint as is the original in its overt display of emotions. In the Stravinsky, it is the observer who is made to suffer for the unseen *Oedipus* as the gruesome events are dispassionately recounted by the massed chorus. It is the observer who must supply the compensating emotion for that which is not openly expressed on the proscenium.

This script provided a compelling presentation from start to finish. L's explanations were wonderfully clear and in depth in regard to both versions of the drama. The casting throughout could not be praised too highly. Keith Michel's *Oedipus* was heart rending as his self-discovery moved him ever closer to self-destruction. Irene Worth's Jocasta and Paul Stevens' Tiresias both made powerful contributions.

Musically, I found this version of the Stravinsky's oratorio far more powerful and theatrically effective than the version later created for L's *Norton Lectures*. Of course, the later version was complete while the *Ford* version was cut, the spoken narration having been eliminated in its entirety. The professional choir for the *Ford Special* was superb. Their phrasing, accents and linear singing brought great depth of meaning to the drama. The NY Philharmonic contribution was cleanly delivered with Stravinskian bite and sharply chiselled rhythms. The solo singers, David Lloyd as *Oedipus*, Inge Borkh as *Jocasta*, Paul Stevens as *Tiresias* and Bramwell Fletcher as *Creon* delivered Stravinsky's monumental music in an equally monumental fashion. Not all the camera work comes off, especially those moments during L's analyses when the director opted for complex visual solutions to problems better dealt with simply. Despite this quibble, the Saudek production team comes in for the highest praise. This was great television and contemporary generations should be given a second opportunity to view the best of the programs in this series.

WEST SIDE MAESTRO

Leonard Bernstein and the NY Philharmonic in Japan
(Telecast: 02/06/62)

This highly original program televised in *black and white* begins with the National Anthem of Japan. L announces his desire to share with his tele-audience a broad two-sided view of the two weeks he spent in Japan with his orchestra. We will accompany him as he seeks out Japanese music and compares it with Western music. The program begins in the Hall of Music of the Imperial Palace in Tokyo. Imperial Court musicians performing on instruments that date back to the *Tang* dynasty demonstrate the ancient Court music, *Gagaku*. Next we view *Bugaka,* which is a danced version of *Gagaku*. This dance pantomime dates back to the Eighth Century. L's narrative carries on throughout the segment, which distracts somewhat from the visual experience of this remarkable historical pageant. The Court Orchestra then perform traditional music for formal occasions called *Etenraku*. Again in voice-over, L explains its differences to Western ears. He describes the various ancient instruments being used. The music being performed has been relegated to little more than underscore. Obviously someone did not believe Western viewers would find the extraordinary sounds being produced to be of ample interest to hold one's attention.

L, seen sitting cross-legged within the orchestra, asks individual players to demonstrate the qualities of their unusual instruments. This proves the most fascinating part of the demonstration as we are given the opportunity to listen without distraction to the unique diversity of sounds being produced. We hear them in ensemble for a thirty second extract. L's narration again takes up. He speaks of this music as a relic from the past.

The scene changes to the Festival Concert Hall in Tokyo. L introduces Seiji Ozawa, then a twenty-six year old assistant with the NY Philharmonic. He conducts the *Bachanale* of Mayuzumi, a contemporary Japanese composer. The work, the least interesting music on the program, bore no relationship with the ancient traditions of Japanese music. It revealed a parade of influences from Stravinsky, the French composers of the 1920's[86] to contemporary American jazz of the 1950's. Combining Latin Americana with the brutal elements of Stravinsky's *Le Sacre de Printemps*, some French *Impressionism* with a bit of Bartokian *Night Music* thrown in, it was noisy enough to guarantee a response from the audience.

The scene moves to the city of Nagoya. The Philharmonic is again in concert. L introduces and conducts for Jennie Tourel the first of three songs, *Asie* (Asia), from Ravel's orchestral song cycle, *Shehérazade*. The French text is sub-titled for the television special. The camera visuals of MS.Tourel, L and the orchestra are extremely simple and are intercut with reaction shots of the audience.

The scene shifts to a beach at Catagai. Japanese women are seen hauling in huge fishing nets. They sing a three-note work song with racy lyrics, which, nowadays, would require a "Parental Guidance warning for under 16 year olds". Children are seen on the beach with traditional dancers and then viewed in a class taking lessons on the *Koto*. Their Master, who teaches them this ancient instrument, speaks English. He demonstrates for the cameras a melody used to teach the children.

Our next port of call is Osaka to visit the puppet theatre. This is the most fascinating and exciting part of the program. We watch the puppet masters, hooded and swathed in black, manipulate their exquisitely created half human-size puppets. Their hands inserted in the costumes bring the puppet characters to life by means of subtle and delicate hand gestures. A single voice sitting with the orchestra takes the parts of all the various characters. In contrast, we then view the westernisation of Japan via its many nightclubs.

In the two final sequences, we first join L, seated at the piano, coaching a group of young Japanese singers in his one act opera, *Trouble in Tahiti* and then in the concert hall conducting the final movement of Beethoven's

---

[86] Debussy, Ravel and *Les Six*, (Durey, Honegger, Milhaud, Tailleferre, Auric and Poulenc).

Seventh Symphony. The symphony is taken at a very quick tempo and several interpretive modifications are to be noted throughout the performance. At the Coda, he accelerates the tempo even further but the orchestra never falters. The work ends in a burst of brilliance and the audience, predictably, goes wild.

In a final postlude, L reviews his long tour with the orchestra, South America, Russia, East Berlin, Istanbul and, finally, Japan. Japan, he says, was the most gratifying because "the gap to bridge was the greatest." He believes genuine communication took place. The program ends with flashback clips of the Katagi fisher women, Shin-ichi Yaize, the *Koto* teacher, the Puppet Theatre of Osaka and the music of Mayuzumi conducted by Seiji Ozawa.

The Drama of Carmen
(Telecast: 3/11/62)

The Drama of Carmen was the last in the series of Ford Specials. As with the *Oedipus Rex* telecast, L again structured his script on his Omnibus *What Makes Opera Grand* formula. It will not, therefore be necessary to deal with the production aspects in great detail, as the reader is already well familiar with the techniques involved. L's hypothesis was that, by going back to the Prosper Merimée novel upon which the opera is based as well as the original *Opera Comique* version, which had spoken dialogue between each aria, one could flesh out the real nature of Bizet's characters and the true drama of Carmen.

L compares *Carmen*, with its "humour, wit, mockery, irony and plain fun" as a tragedy deserving to be placed in company with Shakespeare's *Macbeth* and Wagner's final Ring drama *The Twilight of the Gods*. From its opening bars the opera deals with the fatal aspect of immanent death. A principal character in *Carmen* is *Escamillo*, the toreador. L speaks of the bullfight as "a courtship with death". In essence, Carmen herself carries on a courtship with death from her first entrance onto the scene.

WEST SIDE MAESTRO

For L, *Carmen* is a kind of nightclub entertainer over which destiny hangs. There is a tragic humour that surrounds her character. With brevity, neatness, surprises, and comic elements, Bizet constructs the paradoxical tragedy of Carmen through his music. L's investigation concerns itself with this paradox.

He examines the original *opera comique* version of Carmen which employs spoken dialogue. Nowadays, Carmen is mostly performed as a grand opera using sung accompanied recitatives composed by Ernest Guiraud[87] in place of the spoken dialogue. This through composed version was created following Bizet's tragic death at the young age of thirty-eight just three weeks after the failed Paris premiere of the opera. L states his preference for the original version with spoken dialogue because it presents the plot and the characters with the passion and violence of the Merimée novel.

As with his *Omnibus* opera program and the previous year's Ford special on *Oedipus Rex*, the telecast studio was transformed into a theatre laboratory which would allow for a comparison of the two versions of Carmen side by side, a spoken drama with an acting Carmen, Jose and other characters, and a sung Carmen with opera singers.

L introduces the scene between Jose with his superior officer, Lieutenant Zuniga. First we hear it sung using the Guiraud's composed recitatives. The same scene is then performed in the *comique* version by actors. The spoken scene proves more human, projecting the characters with greater warmth and detail. We learn that Jose had to flee Navarra because he accidentally killed a man in anger. Despite this act of violence in his past, his character still projects as being naive. L now has the opera Jose perform his famous *Flower Aria*, inspired by a flower which Carmen flirtatiously tossed at him shortly after their first encounter. Contrasting the naiveté displayed by the actor Jose, we find that the singing Jose projects as both pompous and stuffy. Additional insight into the Jose character comes with the Carmen's second entrance. Carmen enters under arrest for having attacked with a

---

[87] Ernest Guiraud, French composer, (1837-1892), professor of composition at the Paris Conservatory and teacher of Claude Debussy.

knife one of the other cigarette girls at the factory. The acting Jose is now seen to display humour and possess insight. We witness him loosely tie her wrists. As the scene continues, the acting Jose and Carmen find each other when she tells him that she too is from Navarra. This is dramatically conceivable in the *comique* version since, despite a letter from his sick mother asking him to marry his childhood sweetheart, Michaela, Jose never declares his love for Michaela. That story line was added after Bizet's death in the text of a new Guiraud recitative for Jose. Throughout the entire opera the acted version reveals much more detail and truth about the characters and why they act and interact the way the do. The actress Carmen's greeting of Jose in Act Two is lively, effusive and bitingly witty but in the opera version it is very formal. In the *comique* version there is a knife fight between Jose and Escamillo, the toreador, during which Escamillo spares Jose's life. This is cut entirely in the opera.

This is a well-researched and produced Bernstein program. It is worth noting that L's final program for the *Omnibus* series was *What Makes Opera Grand* and now, three years later, he chose to use the exact formula for his final *Ford presents* program. Though the various elements of this production were well presented and it enjoyed a strong script, the repeat of this format only one season following its similar use for the *Oedipus Rex* special may have vitiated its dramatic impact. The ideas put forward in this program came, in fact, to fruition for L just over ten years later when he conducted *Carmen* at the Metropolitan Opera incorporating many of the scenes from the opera comique original with the later Guiraud version. This Metropolitan Opera performance was the first link in the chain of his new recording alliance with Deutsche Grammophon which would be contractually formalised three years later. The DG recording of *Carmen* went on to become one of the best selling opera albums in its catalogue.

The Lincoln/Ford series ended in 1962 but it, along with L's distinguished *Omnibus* programs, was to form the backdrop of L's extensive televised or filmed teaching activities that climaxed with his 1973 *Norton Lectures* at Harvard and continued into his final year of life.

WEST SIDE MAESTRO

WEST SIDE MAESTRO

THE NY PHILHARMONIC YEARS

Part 3: TELEVISION'S PIED PIPER

The Need To Teach

Teaching became an important part of L's life at the age of twelve. He needed to earn money to help pay for his own piano lessons. As a result he began to teach piano to other neighbourhood children charging one dollar per lesson. One of his pupils was Sid Ramin, who was much later to play an important part with Irwin Kostal and L, himself, creating the orchestrations for *West Side Story* as well as assisting on *Mass, 1600 Pennsylvania Avenue* and *A Quiet Place*.

L not only taught the neighbours' children, he also insisted on tutoring his sister, Shirley, in piano even after she had given up taking formal lessons. With Shirley and neighbourhood friends, he began to produce, direct and choreograph, (which is another form of teaching albeit on a grander scale), home grown, personal adaptations of Bizet's *Carmen* and Gilbert and Sullivan's *The Mikado* and *HMS Pinafore*. The *Sharon Players*[88] created sufficient neighbourhood interest for him to charge his growing audiences a small admission and to eventually move his productions from his own living room to the Sharon Town Hall. When a local jazz *combo* was formed L was at its center. The pattern for leadership and the need to interact and communicate his ideas, the mark of a teacher, was there from the beginning. In whatever form or forum it manifested itself in the future, from the breakfast table sitting across from his own children teaching them in the manner his father had imparted knowledge to him; or at Tanglewood where he, having learned his craft and found a teacher/mentor in Koussevitzky, became the teacher/mentor for new generations of young musicians not only in the Berkshires but at new music festivals for youth which he was to help

---

[88] The young group took their name from their home town, Sharon, Massachusetts.

found throughout his life; or on coast-to-coast television communicating to all of America; or standing before every orchestra he ever conducted, teaching was his compulsion. I can speak about this with authority from my own experience as a student in his private conducting classes of only four students during the three summers I attended at Tanglewood.

Flamboyant public persona played little part in L's classes for the *active* conducting students at Tanglewood. He was as demanding with his privately conducted class of students as Fritz Reiner had been with him during his student days at the Curtis Institute[89]. With the exception of Lorin Maazel, who attended Tanglewood during my first summer and, though in age our contemporary, was already a highly sophisticated musician and a conductor of reputation, we were all students still attending various conservatories or universities. We were at Tanglewood to learn and, hopefully, gain some public credibility as young conductors of potential. To this end, L gave to us from his knowledge and experience enthusiastically and unstintingly. He loved both the idea and the role of being a teacher. Always seated at the piano in Koussevitzky's brightly lit studio within the grounds of Tanglewood, he would be our orchestra, playing with gusto and brilliance the scores we were assigned to conduct while correcting our baton gestures and posing musical questions to challenge the thoroughness of our preparation and knowledge not only of the work at hand but a large range of works in both the symphonic and operatic repertoire which posed similar musical and technical conducting problems. His own voracious appetite for music of all styles made him respond even more enthusiastically if he perceived that your knowledge of the repertoire was not limited to the 'all-time top 50 favourites'. The lessons became much more than merely learning how to conduct a single, assigned work. They represented a panoramic approach to music aesthetics and the study of orchestral scores from the widest musical and historic perspectives For that small handful of 'active conductors' who had been given the privilege of working with the student orchestra from week to week, it was a continual test of one's mettle and posed the broadest of musical challenges.

---

[89] Fritz Reiner, A Biography by Philip Hart; Northwestern University Press

WEST SIDE MAESTRO

L attended all of our rehearsals, observing us from within the ranks of the student orchestra surrounded by a large group of auditing, non-performing conductors who were attending Tanglewood simply to observe and be a part of the festival's halcyon atmosphere. Although L never interrupted us during our rehearsals to correct or make suggestions[90], he would carry on a non-stop dialogue with the auditors commenting on musical elements we might have missed, a gesture that might have precipitated an imperfect ensemble or the obvious influence on our baton technique by established maestros such as Toscanini, Koussevitzky, Walter, Ormandy, Reiner, etc. For some of my colleagues it proved to be unnerving but, and, perhaps, that was the point behind it all, it was to see whether you would keep your nerve under pressure or become rattled.

The auditing conductors for their part maintained most cordial relations with those of us in L's private conducting class. The greatest part of their schedule was occupied with singing in the Tanglewood choir, attending the student orchestra and Boston Symphony rehearsals and concerts and working in a weekly class under the observant eyes of L, Lucas Foss and, the pianist/conductor, Seymour Lipkin. These weekly sessions involved a discussion and no-holds barred criticism of the previous week's concert of the 'active' conductors and dealt with specific conducting problems contained within works to be conducted in the following week's student orchestra concert. Most important of all, these classes allowed volunteers to reveal their conducting prowess by demonstrating their skill in dealing with problems in complex repertoire such as Stravinsky's *Rite Of Spring* and *A Soldier's Tale*, Walton's overture, *Portsmouth Point*, Copland's *Billy The Kid*, etc. Occasionally an obviously gifted auditor conductor was given an opportunity by L to work with the student orchestra and conduct at a Friday night concert. To indicate the esteem in which the auditing class at Tanglewood was held within the fraternity of ambitious young conductors,

---

[90] His later method of working with student conductors, as demonstrated in the video documentaries recorded at the University of California, Salzau, Germany and Sapporo, Japan, would change radically. In these documentaries L is seen at the students shoulder, next to or even on the podium. He interrupts freely and even personally demonstrates various points.

WEST SIDE MAESTRO

no lesser personages than Christoph von Dohnanyi and Herbert Blomstedt were among the auditors during the three summers I attended.

Although memory can be a deceitful mistress, the practical importance of my three years at Tanglewood with L along with my further studies at the Juilliard School with Jean Morel, an extraordinary conductor and teacher to whom L had recommended me, proved of inestimable practical value throughout my career. In short, L was, outside the spotlight blazing on his own career and the future hyperbole to be generated by his television lectures, a natural and inspired teacher. Both he and Jean Morel followed a similar pedagogical approach. Principal for both men was the demand for the most complete intellectual and aural knowledge of the notes of the score plus the historic context which dictated its style of performance. Next was the application of a baton technique which would not only engender rhythmic precision but be grounded in shaping long phrases of music which encompassed all the subtleties of colour, dynamics, accents and note articulation. Most important of all, neither L nor Mr. Morel ever attempted to develop their students in their own image. Each student was allowed to be different and to develop a technique that reflected his own personality. Considering L's total commitment to his Tanglewood conducting students, I found it extraordinary to later read a number of quotes and to hear public interviews given by several of the more volatile conductors who later made up the small annual army of N.Y. Philharmonic *student* assistants, (three per year during L's tenure), to the contrary. All complained that L rarely allotted them any of his personal time during the year they served at the Philharmonic. Moreover, that virtually none of the conducting tuition of the kind I described, which marked the Bernstein Tanglewood years during which he passionately undertook to carry on the Tanglewood vision of his great mentor, Koussevitzsky, was ever offered to them.

I sat in on L's discussions with several of the composers attending Tanglewood to study with Aaron Copland, Ingolf Dahl or Luigi Dallapiccola. As wonderful a teacher as he had proved to be for conductors, he seemed hopeless with composers. He would become so competitively involved with every note in the first measures of their scores that a half hour later a single page had yet to be turned. I remember specifically such a happening regarding a violin concerto written by Leonard Rosenman, a gifted American composer who went on to provide scores for a number of noted Hollywood films starring James Dean and the revolutionary twelve tone score for the Lauren Bacall film, *The Cobweb*, as well as a much loved television theme to the series *Marcus Welby, M.D.* The two "Lenny's" were arguing back and forth for an hour, the senior wanting to change everything and the junior defending every note of his score. They remained reasonably friendly over that summer although Rosenman spent a good deal of his time freely expressing his less than flattering opinions of his senior's music, which the still youthful Bernstein accepted with equanimity but which the Bernstein elevated to the music directorship of the NY Philharmonic would have quickly silenced with, "Who asked you?!!!"

L's teaching career was to blossom in a new way during his association with the weekly television Arts show, *Omnibus*. He would emulate the Talmudic atmosphere of his own upbringing during which the taking of meals represented yet another opportunity for the Bernstein children to absorb wisdom from their knowledgeable father on a myriad of subjects. Through his own unique communicative personality, L would now expand the family circle in his home to a television family of unseen millions on whom he would bestow enlightenment on matters musical, much in the same enthusiastic way he had been taught by the two father figures in his life, Sam Bernstein and his musical father, Serge Koussevitzky. The *Omnibus* shows, which he devised, were not merely glorified, glamorised versions of the music appreciation classes we all suffered through in junior and senior high school. They were the prototype model for the communicating of technical aspects of music in non-technical terms by opening doors to new kinds of notions and, even more important, curiosity. No quarter was given to the inexperience of the viewer. If you were willing to stick around long enough to go through that first door there lay ahead of you *a yellow brick road* which would lead you on a journey as exciting as one that would take you to the *Land of Oz*. While no one denied L's pedagogical gifts, many were left wide-eyed as to how he actuated this continued national mass interest if not always total conversion to the more complex disciplines of the musical arts. I

WEST SIDE MAESTRO

will try to explain via my own experience a very basic way to establish contact with one's audience, even a remote television audience, and, if you can capture its interest, how you can convince them to stay committed to and even participate in what is taking place.

I tailored my own Family concerts very much along the lines of L's television specials, starting with a unifying concept based upon which all the music was chosen, then writing a linking script and finally, acting as my own presenter. Employing all these elements allowed me to establish a one to one relationship with my audience. Even my stage appearance was more *show-biz* than concert conductor, to be precise a huge variety of superbly tailored jackets each of a different colour crafted from embroidered metallic brocade. My unusual style of concert wear combined with my between selection musical explanations and historical or personal anecdotes inspired one critic to describe my concert persona as a combination between André Previn and Liberace. I was thus able to remove that invisible barrier between conductor and audience symbolised by the back of a conductor's tail coat, which is the standard audience view of a maestro during formal concerts.

During a stint as guest conductor with the City of Birmingham Symphony Orchestra, I determined to have the audience join with our soprano soloist in the final well-known vocal selection. Before introducing the finale I made up a fanciful tale that our two-hundred voice choir intended to accompany our soloist was stranded in their coaches on the motorway. To make up for such a grievous loss, I had decided to substitute a *two thousand* voice choir, that is, everyone sitting in the hall. However, it would not be enough for them merely to join in the chorus, which I was confident they knew, but that I wanted everyone to cross their arms, join hands and sway in time to the music as they sang. (Please understand that I was addressing a most conservative British audience). When the appointed time came the hall was filled with sound and a thousand couples gripped the hands of total strangers and did, indeed, sing and sway in time to the music. The only thing the scene lacked was a spinning mirror ball on the ceiling.

WEST SIDE MAESTRO

When I left the stage the orchestra manager was waiting for me *gob-smacked*[91]. "How did you get them to do that?", he asked in astonishment. To which I replied with typical American *chutzpah*, "Never for a second did I believe they wouldn't do it." In a very true sense, when L addressed any audience, and he addressed the toughest audiences of all when he walked onstage to present his Young People's Concerts, could he have accomplished what he did without absolute faith in the project and his ability to bring his audience with him.

That short, hopefully instructive and highly simplistic insight into conductor's megalomania, brings us to the two peaks of L's career as a teacher, the televised *Young People's Concerts of the NY Philharmonic* and the *Charles Eliot Norton Lectures* at Harvard University. The YPC's occupied L's attention for fifteen seasons. The concerts were sold out from the first and there was a waiting list for tickets that would have filled the hall twice over. The telecasts were watched in millions of American homes and, if one judges by the audience in Carnegie or Philharmonic Hall, by as many adults as children. The 1967 Christmas Day concert stunned the executives at the television networks by topping the Neilson ratings with an audience of twenty seven million. If L had become a music guru to the adults who sat glued to the *tube* during his *Omnibus* programs, he became the *Pied Piper of Hamlyn* to the young people who flocked to attend his concerts and even to the youngsters who were frog-marched to either the concert hall or the television set by their parents and told to pay attention because 'it was good for them!!!' The telecasts, dubbed into twelve languages and shown around the world, deservedly gathered virtually every educational television award going. L had smashed the *Mary Poplins* children's concert formula to smithereens. There were "spoons full of sugar" from time to time but not before he had stretched the capacity of those young minds to come to appreciate a genre of music and to arrive at a musical understanding of concepts never previously considered possible for a musical event for children.

---

[91] A good, old bit of British slang, *gob* referring to one's mouth and *gob-smacked* being an exaggerated case of one's jaw dropping to the floor in astonishment.

WEST SIDE MAESTRO

With the Norton Lectures, L raised the musical stakes even higher. This was not the typical Bernstein bill of fare of an hour long musical essay based upon a single subject or piece of music of general interest explained or analysed in simple, straightforward terms, picturesque analogies, graphic visuals and mostly short, musical examples which transformed the opaque into a transparency. Each of the six lectures was the equivalent of a narrated university thesis which was of two to three hours in length, used musical examples which ranged from entire classical symphonies or movements from symphonies, to Stravinsky's oratorio, *Oedipus Rex*, along with examples of both tonal and non-tonal music covering two centuries of music. The six lectures traced the development of music from the utterings of a hominid baby to Mozart to Wagner to the revolutionary split between Stravinsky and Schönberg. The different disciplines of physics, linguistics and poetics were used to correlate a possible innate human capacity for music recognition and learning which related to and paralleled the brain's innate functions for language cognition.

Although the audience that attended his Harvard lectures, held in a cinema theatre prior to the later videotaping of each lecture in the intimate surroundings of a television studio, could be described as mixed, a large number of seats were occupied by faculty from the surrounding universities, university students and noted musicians, composers, music theoreticians and critics - not exactly the typical cross section of America attracted to his popular television essays.

The lectures created controversy no less volatile than many of the political causes L embraced in his lifetime. In attempting to create a correlation between the innate acquisition of language and the brain's cognitive ability to understand, organise and interpret music, L specifically confined this innate cognitive ability solely to *tonal* music. His thesis went one further controversial step forward by suggesting that the brain's tonally selective cognitive music function relegated non-tonal music to a higher intellectual learning process on the outer edge of cognition, the equivalent to mastering higher mathematics or chess. The complexity of such a thesis predictably garnered a much narrower audience profile when the Norton Lectures were aired on television. In retrospect they can now be viewed as a key contribution to the enormous strides made in the years since to an understanding of the workings of the human brain. They also proved to be a red flag waved before an angry bull, the bull being the school and adherents of non-tonal music, specifically those followers of the composer, Arnold Schönberg, who occupied seats of power within the musical arts establishment at the time,

I have devoted extended chapters on each of L's pinnacle television achievements, the *Young People's Concerts* and the *Norton Lectures*. In both, the body of work now can be seen to transcend not only the controversy that was stirred up but the lavish praise as well. They are bequests of inestimable value from a unique teacher from whom the entire world continues to benefit through his recordings, videotapes and DVD's.

WEST SIDE MAESTRO

<u>THE NY PHILHARMONIC YEARS</u>

Part 4: The T.V. Young People's Concerts
Analysed & Reviewed

L was not the first conductor of note to undertake Young People's concerts. Walter Damrosch was a household name for 12 years conducting weekly broadcasts on the NBC network especially aimed at schools. Leopold Stokowski turned his hand at children's concerts for the N.Y. Philharmonic and was adored, cod-Polish accent and all. Prior to L, Wilfred Pellitier, a noted conductor and broadcaster for the Metropolitan Opera, had been in charge. In England, Sir Malcolm Sargeant was rightly considered the musical hero of the country's young people. To his last brief appearance at the BBC Proms, the young cheered him to the rafters.

Extraordinarily, the thought of taking on these concerts at first struck panic in L. His tenure with the Philharmonic as Rodzinski's assistant was too short for the management to even begin to consider him for such a role, although with many American orchestras it is invariably the assistant conductor who undertakes responsibility for the children's concerts. He was, therefore, more than a little interested in discussing my own experiences with this special genre of concert. He and I would kick around possible concert formats at his work studio in the Osborne apartments where I was spending my afternoons reading through and making notes on scores submitted to the Philharmonic for L's hopeful approval. Having regularly conducted the children's concerts for two of the four orchestras I was associated with at the time, I was already reasonably experienced in this field. The ideas we discussed were tossed into a pool of production ideas which helped shape to a degree parts of the six concerts for which I served as his assistant. My discussions with L all involved a linking script as I, myself, had been influenced to adopt his *Omnibus* format for my own children's concerts. My suggestions, however, were biased much more heavily towards a large number of complete musical examples to illustrate a lean text, a proportion of two-thirds music to one-third script. L, however, felt more comfortable with his detailed *Omnibus* format, a tested and proven success, that had established him on television not as just a personality but, in his eyes, as a teacher to all of America. Soon the large number of musical examples I suggested was whittled down and more and more text was added.   It reached the point where I believed the approach was becoming counter-productive. We were working at the time on the program titled, "What Is Orchestration". The script opened well with a spare three-minute introduction. L then was to conduct the final movement, the *Gypsy Scene and Fandango*, from Rimsky-Korsakov's *Caprice Espagnole*, a brilliant and exciting work from the pen of one of the classic masters of orchestration. So far, sensational! Then, for the next 40 minutes, neither a complete piece of music nor even extended excerpt was to be performed. What was structured into the script were 45 musical fragments, many of which were as short as two seconds, the large majority rarely over 30 seconds in length and none of which were longer than a minute. These fragments were to be used to illuminate and punctuate a long, lucid text that seemed to me to be directed towards a more mature mind capable of a far longer attention span than the large majority of young children are capable of sustaining. A short two and a half minute audience participation link followed, an aspect of programming for young people which I consistently supported both in private conversation with L and at our open production meetings, and then the program was to end with Ravel's *Bolero*. I commented that the program was supposed to be a concert and that all we, in fact, were offering the children were two imposing musical bookends between which were stacked little more than pamphlets. Although my criticism was public and struck at the program's intrinsic value for children in its present format, resistance to my comments came not from L but from others in the production team who, in my young, aggressively concerned mood, seemed to spend most of their time just nodding 'yes' to whatever L said or did and then, afterwards, moaned and groaned in private. L, however, was quite taken with my simile, which appealed to his literary turn of mind. His reaction was, "What a very clear, poetic concept." In the end the program remained unchanged. In viewing it again after the passage of almost 30 years, I found it exhausting and to judge by the director's cut away close-ups to audience, so did many of the youngsters in attendance.

WEST SIDE MAESTRO

I continued to serve L till the Spring of 1959 as his link-man with the director for television, Charlie Dubin[92], with whom I had worked on *Omnibus*. During the actual telecasts, my assignment was to sit with orchestra score in hand working with Harold Bridges, the sound engineer. I attended and participated in all script discussions. L would deliver his scripts written in longhand on octavo sized yellow legal pads, of which he seemed to have an endless supply. Any resemblance, however, to Merle Secrest's description of his work habits on these programs bears little affinity to reality. Scripts were certainly not delivered weeks in advance. Due to his endless procrastination in getting down to work, our production meetings would invariably take place in the wee hours at his Osborne work studio only days prior to the actual telecasts. L was often faced with only a minimum amount of time to learn scripts which had been brought to a final draft barely one or two evenings prior to the telecast. This is underlined in the early concerts when he is clearly seen to be self-consciously script bound. (Tele-prompters were not yet available to help feed him the lines of his long, complex scripts.) L's first six concerts, for which I served as his assistant, are all included among the first series of 15 videos released by the Sony Corporation for their European edition and are included in the more extended American edition. In them, you can witness the growth of script from show to show. Music, except for the opening and closing selections, was relegated to short illustrative excerpts, many of which were performed by Bernstein himself at the large grand piano at which he was seated when not conducting the orchestra. Audience participation, one of the keys to maintaining the attention of the younger audience members, was used well but sparingly and not always as imaginatively as one would expect from a mind as creative as L's.

In assessing the strengths and weaknesses of these programs, one is faced by a tidal wave of statistics and industry propaganda. The annual four-concert series occupied L's attention for fifteen seasons. He conducted fifty-three televised concerts in all. The concerts, which debuted at Carnegie Hall and later moved with the Philharmonic to their new home at Lincoln Center,

---

[92] Charles Dubin (1919-2011) noted television director serving L's Omnibus programs and Young People's Concerts.

were sold out from the first and, astonishing and bizarre as it may sound, there was a waiting list of two thousand children some of whom had been registered by their parents at birth. The average viewing audience for each telecast numbered ten million and the YPC, 'A Toast To Vienna' aired Christmas Day 1967, claimed a staggering audience of twenty seven million. The telecasts were dubbed into twelve languages and distributed in forty countries. They garnered virtually every major award in the field of educational television. They seemed to hold a special place in the Bernstein list of priorities. L was quoted as saying, 'the Young People's Concerts are among the favourite, most highly prized activities of my life.' Part of this enthusiasm for this genre of concert, without doubt, stemmed from L's self-absorption, one might venture the word obsession, with his image as a teacher. However, it was not only children and the 'unwashed public' at large over which he wished to spread his intellectual net but, with less success one must observe, every orchestra he conducted as well. One of the most notable examples of his failure to communicate some of his more controversial concepts to either audience or orchestra occurred when he came to London in 1982 to conduct the BBC Symphony in a performance of Elgar's *Enigma Variations*. Following a perplexing performance of interminable length, L broke through the *chutzpah* barrier by declaring that British conductors, among whom he included the illustrious name of Sir Adrian Boult, "didn't understand what Elgar was about." Humphrey Burton in his biography tried to rationalise this incident as merely a cultural gap between a great intellect who saw Elgar's position in terms of the totality of European Romanticism and those who did not have the capacity to grasp the truth of this concept. Using a warmly worded if, in my opinion, misguided appraisal of L's performance by Yehudi Menhuin, (an unkind word seems rarely to have crossed Menhuin's lips about any of his colleagues), regarding a studio recording of the *Variations* made following the live concert by the same forces, Burton puts a gloss on the entire incident which leaves the reader with a sense that if Menhuin, who knew and worked with Elgar, approved of L's performance, perhaps those who have been critical of it should have a re-think. I found this equivocation most unusual for Burton who, in general, takes a very even-handed, warts-and-all approach to his subject in his biography. The deference by colleagues and commercial management to L's every word and idea had been part of an *Emperor's New Clothes* atmosphere which generally surrounded him since the mid-1950's. It served, in the end, to allow flaws to scar his concerts and television presentations.

In analysing and reviewing the twenty-five Young People's Concerts on video[93], I have used a more exacting criterion in examining each in relation to format, content and scholarship than has been previously applied. In doing so it has not been my intention to discredit these much heralded and deservedly award winning programs but to provide the reader with greater insight into their internal workings gained as a member of the program's original creative team, as L's chosen personal musical assistant and as a highly experienced conductor in my own right totally conversant with a genre of Young People's Concerts built upon the same model. I have divided the various programs into specific groups in order to compare like with like as well as to comment on the changes and developments from year to year over the course of the fourteen years represented on the programs commercially available on videotape.

---

[93] Now available in DVD format.

WEST SIDE MAESTRO

YOUNG PEOPLE'S CONCERTS VIDEOS (DVD'S)

Sony Corp - 15 VHS S15HV 48444 (15 concerts) for the UK and Europe
       10 VHS (24 Concerts) SHV7428 - SHV57437 for North America

Programme title	Timing	Date of Transmission
1. WHAT DOES MUSIC MEAN?	59min,52sec	Jan 18,1958
2. WHAT MAKES MUSIC AMERICAN ?	59min,20sec	Feb 1,1958
3. WHAT IS ORCHESTRATION ?	58min,57sec	Mar 8, 1958
4. WHAT MAKES MUSIC SYMPHONIC?	60min,02sec	Dec13, 1958
5. WHAT IS CLASSICAL MUSIC	59min,40sec	Jan 1,1959
6. HUMOR IN MUSIC	59min,59sec	Feb 2,1959

On all of the above programmes, I served as L's musical assistant. It was, therefore, with special interest that I viewed the videos after a passage of 28 years. My memory of most of the text proved remarkably accurate. A published edited and illustrated series of the scripts to the Young People's Concerts helped fill in the gaps. They also provided a handy reference and, in some instances due to editing, greater script clarity than certain of the televised programmes which steamrollered their way to their conclusion with L issuing a torrent of new and difficult words and concepts as he went.

These programmes evoked unanimous praise. They established the series as unique presentations within their genre and a giant step forward for television as a medium for mass education. They also confirmed Leonard Bernstein as a media super-star.

Critics, queuing up to write the next rave review, created a euphoric atmosphere of success which served, in my view, to work against the important honing, reshaping and improving of the format in the early days. After all, in America they invented the phrase, 'If it ain't broke, why fix it?' The problem lay in that praise was coming from adults not children or to be more specific, those under-ten-year-olds who formed a large segment of L's initial audience. Getting down to basics, what do adults really understand about what stimulates and - L to the contrary - *entertains* the young people who attend or are dragged to children's concerts. *Children* know about children's concerts! **'I loved it!/I hated it!'; 'It was terrific!/It was boring!';'Take me to another one!/I never want to go again!'** Black and white, that is the way children view experiences of this nature. What a parent hopes for in taking his child to designed events of this kind is that the sounds and melodies will link up to the young minds and fantastic imaginations; that they will want to repeat the experience not only in the macrocosm of the concert hall but the microcosm of the home, listening to the radio, recordings or watching music videos and even, hopefully, continuing to practice their piano, guitar or recorder with new enthusiasm and without the need for that special brand of nagging which we parents refer to as *encouragement.*

For a conductor to make instant communication with a young audience, the youngsters must instinctively view him as one of them, a grown up child who understands and is at home in their world of imagination. On that single level, Leonard Bernstein was the perfect candidate to launch these new N.Y. Philharmonic Young People's Concerts. On presentation alone L scored a dead centre bulls-eye in his first concert, WHAT DOES MUSIC MEAN? Strikingly, his text begins upon a premise that is opposite to the title of the programme, dealing not with what music means but with what it *doesn't* mean. "Music is only notes, never about anything," (A statement borrowed from Igor Stravinsky) he states at the opening. The idea he is selling to his young audience is that while music is about nothing, it is still fun to listen to.

The script is presented at a breathtaking pace and sprinkled with short, colourful musical excerpts which, more often than not, contradict the premise, but no matter. No one can match L's enthusiasm when he is in full flight. The audience knows it is in for a great time from the moment the program begins with the familiar strains of the Finale to Rossini's overture to *William Tell*. The Philharmonic is in great form, blazing away whenever they are given their head to perform, which, unfortunately, is not that often.

Later in the program, using the passage from Richard Strauss's *Don Quixote* where the *Man from La Mancha* charges a herd of sheep believing them to be an enemy army, L invents a wild fantasy about Superman rescuing his 'pal' from jail. He tells how Superman has "a secret whistle" which tells his "pal" he is coming. Meanwhile, his pal spends the whole night in jail practising the kazoo while all the other prisoners are sleeping and snoring. Superman charges into the prison yard on his motorcycle, "bops the guard over the head", grabs his friend and, while the prisoners continue to snore, carries his friend away to freedom. Strauss's vivid music first played in illustrative excerpts by the orchestra and then as a complete fragment, lends itself perfectly to this far out, concocted adventure tale. The children adore it. They love the words *pal* and *kazoo* and *bop*. These are words that belong to them and their world.

L then relates the actual story behind the music, playing all the excerpts once more, this time at the piano, and then conducting the entire fragment with the orchestra. He repeats this same analytical process again, this time using Beethoven's '*Pastoral*' Symphony as the musical example which connects material imagery to the music. This is, unfortunately, overkill as he has already substantially made the point with the Strauss excerpt.

The children couldn't care less, if any of them even noticed, that L has contradicted his initial thesis. The Strauss music may not be about superman or a hundred other made-up stories but its picturesque musical language is certainly about something other than the mere abstract movement of one note to another. What difference does it make? The kids are having too good a time laughing, singing away in audience participation segments and shouting answers to questions posed to them from the stage by the *Pied Piper* himself. They probably also haven't noticed that thirty minutes have passed and the orchestra has yet to play the first complete pieces of music on the program, two short movements from the Mussorgsky-

WEST SIDE MAESTRO

Ravel, *Pictures at an Exhibition.* L uses 'child speak' to introduce these two excerpts imitating the chant one child might use when calling another and the taunting, teasing whine, 'nya, nya -nya, nya'. (When I was a child we sang, " Shame! Shame! - Everybody knows your name", to this same tune.) This is followed by a highly cut version of the finale to *'Pictures'*, *The Great Gate at Kiev.* There was so much that was right and worked wonderfully well in this program that it was a pity that L was unable to step back and allow the music to exert its own form of unique magic without words. Given the choice at this time, he invariably chose to extend his script and cut the music. In retrospect, this, in my opinion, is the *Achilles' heel* of many of these programs.

L now moves towards his conclusion. Using fragments from the 4th and 5th Symphonies of Tschaikovsky, he speaks of the emotions of pain, happiness, joy and triumph that they evoke. That to L is the nub of what music is. "It's *the way it makes you feel when you hear it...without knowing anything about sharps and flats.*" Well, (pick!pick!pick!) if it's about a wide range of feelings, it is about something much larger, more complex and more abstract than "a lot of beautiful notes and sounds put together so well that we get pleasure out of hearing them." L may have shot himself in the foot again but, no matter, the kids are having a whale of a time.

The program concludes with a performance of Ravel's *La Valse* advertised as 'complete' but in fact with a huge cut reducing it to two thirds its length. The orchestra performs it magnificently and is razor sharp in its response to its new music director.

One extremely distracting sound problem haunted this first program. There was a non-stop litany of L grunting and groaning which spilled through his personal microphone when he was either playing the piano or conducting. It would have done little good to comment to him about it. He would just have said, 'I can't help it. I've always done it. I don't even know that I am doing it. You'll have to put up with it and do the best you can...' or words to that effect. There were areas of conflicting opinion where one could not shift him.

WEST SIDE MAESTRO

Anything that he interpreted as criticism of any aspect of his conducting or performance would be a signal for him to dig his heels in. I could have told the sound man to shut off his microphone when he was playing the piano or conducting but one never knew when he might ad-lib. If text were lost due to an action I had taken without consulting the director or producer, all hell would have broken loose afterwards In the hierarchy of the production staff, I was assigned an enormous amount of work responsibility but remained low man on the totem pole. The best solution was for L to watch a *kinescope*[94] of the show afterwards and come to his own realisation of the problem and its necessary solution. This he quite obviously did. From the moment he began to conduct at the start of our second program, WHAT MAKES MUSIC AMERICAN ?, it was noticeable to all that extraneous sounds from the podium were virtually non-existent.

I will deal with the next two programs in the series together as they both underline the same problem, too much script and too little music. WHAT MAKES MUSIC AMERICAN ? gets off to a fine start with a large seven and a half minute helping, about half, of Gershwin's *An American In Paris*. L's success in his debut concert in controlling the audience participation segments, something that initially he anticipated with terror, emboldened him to include three more such segments in the American Music concert. These provide some of the best moments in the program, totally involving and holding the attention of the young audience. The premise of the program is as follows:

The most talented turn of the century American composers were little more than carbon copies of the great European composers such as Brahms, Schumann and Wagner. Not until the emergence of Jazz following the First World War did something that could be identified as a truly American folk idiom take hold in the music of American composers such as George Gershwin and Aaron Copland.

---

[94] *kinoscope* - term used to describe copies of early television programs

WEST SIDE MAESTRO

History lesson over, L introduces and explains *syncopated* rhythm and, in another short audience participation segment, gets his young audience to handclap a syncopated Charleston dance rhythm with a bit of help from the percussion section of the orchestra. As a further demonstration of syncopation, L has a solo organist perform the esoteric *Prelude* by Roger Sessions. This was an extremely doubtful choice of music for relatively inexperienced young listeners even if the audience did consist of, as the pianist Glenn Gould irreverently projected, 'little kids specially imported for the occasion from the Westchester[95] Home for Insufferable Prodigies.' Not content with having shell-shocked his young audience with the Sessions organ *Prelude*, L moves off on another intellectual tangent. Gone is the childlike persona of the debut concert; gone is their *pal* who spoke their language, communicated with them and made going to a concert fun. In his place, is an intellectual 'toff' endlessly talking and throwing all manner of high-flown concepts at them. He compares the poetry of Shelly with the poetry of the American, Kenneth Fearing. This, he says, is to demonstrate "English spoken with an American accent and American rhythms". His young audience are expected to understand this very adult concept as an analogy of how "American composers superimposed their culture and rhythms subconsciously on learned European traditions."

We are now 44 minutes into the concert and the total musical content has been 14 minutes of musical fragments, eight minutes of which were performed at the very start of the program. Cut away shots to the audience show children out of their seats chatting to each other. The parents, who make up one out of every three in attendance, are engrossed, but L seems to have lost contact with the younger members of the audience. More short musical fragments drowned in text follow. Only the introduction of Aaron Copland to conduct the final movement of his own *Third Symphony* comes to the rescue. The movement, which begins with the *Fanfare For The Common Man*, all brass and percussion, restores the audience's attention. It is the only complete work on the entire program and the only substantial amount of music performed since the eight-minute segment from American

---

[95] Westchester - A posh middle to upper class New York suburb.

174

WEST SIDE MAESTRO

In Paris that opened the program. Were Bernstein a lesser personality, were the audience made up from a greater social mixture of New York society, were there not such a plethora of parental control in the audience, one could project that both conductor and orchestra would have been pelted with hard candy by children gone native from sheer boredom. Happily, the Copland work and the composer's sunshine personality and vigour as a conductor rouse the audience to great enthusiasm and the concert ends in fine style.

WHAT MAKES MUSIC AMERICAN? and the concert that followed, WHAT IS ORCHESTRATION? are two sides of the same coin. The '*Orchestration*' script is again overly long, even more verbose than the previous concert, and the music played desperately meagre. I have already described the structure of this concert at the beginning of this chapter. Launched with the final two movements of Rimsky-Korsakov's *Spanish Caprice*, a healthy seven minutes of exciting music, it then consists of an illustrated script for the next forty minutes. The text, while highly informative, is simply too ambitious. The audience have come to hear a concert not receive a diploma in orchestration at the conclusion of a seminar. L has lost sight of the purpose of most successful Young People's Concerts, *to educate by stealth*. Pruning this script to half its length and illustrating key orchestration techniques, (i.e.: the contrast of bowed and plucked strings, open and muted brass, tuned and un-tuned percussion, etc.) with complete short works of music would have produced not only a more satisfactory but more exciting and stimulating result. The concert in its present form, however, is not without its pluses. There are two and a half minutes of audience participation where the children, by vocal means, attempt to simulate the sounds of an orchestra. This evokes both interest and pleasure in his audience. L's *tour de force*, however, is the final segment which is so good that it could be extracted from the program and developed on its own as a short music documentary. It consists of a performance with analysis of Ravel's *Bolero*. Using a voice-over technique during the playing of the first four minutes of *Bolero*, Ravel's musical essay on orchestration, L explains, as they occur, the various elements that make up the composer's musical and orchestral design. By the time the first theme has completed its first full cycle via the flute, clarinet, bassoon and E flat clarinet, the explanation seems almost another instrument in counterpoint, so cleverly and precisely is it handled. In the clearest, simplest terms L reveals how Ravel will develop these elements purely by means of orchestration to a huge climax. His narration closes with the following encouraging words, "...Before (this piece) is over, you'll have heard all kinds of delicious sounds, colours and combinations...It makes an exciting trip through the world of Orchestration. Bon Voyage!"[96]   Now turning to his orchestra, he conducts the remaining nine minutes of the work. The kids go wild at the conclusion.

When he was in top form, such as in this Ravel segment, there was no one to touch Lenny.

The next Young People's Concert took place in the winter of 1958. Mitropoulos had resigned and L was now the official Music Director of the N.Y. Philharmonic. Between his much publicised television appearances and his photograph appearing on the cover of every major national magazine, he had become the most famous musician in America. One cannot have this much attention lavished on oneself and remain unaffected. L was enjoying a position of real power for the first time and, when 'push came to shove', he began to use it. The improvement in the Philharmonic's performance as an ensemble was already garnering compliments from the press but it was accomplished at a cost to the orchestra that was already becoming apparent to the discerning members of the music profession who watched the televised Young People's Concerts. All was not sweetness and light. As the camera techniques used for the televised concerts were quite simple and as L's presence and lengthy scripts dominated the proceedings, the camera concentrated for the most part on him. Indeed, during the rehearsals for the first telecast, the director became so obsessed with L's image that it evoked another of my outspoken comments. I suggested that a fortune could be saved if we used a cardboard cut-out of the orchestra and played recordings which L could conduct at the appropriate times. I was young, L's soon to be, so I thought, assistant conductor designate at the Philharmonic and I viewed

---

[96] Leonard Bernstein's Young People's Concerts; Cassell - London, 1970

my loyalties not to CBS Television but directly to him. My caustic comment was a rather risky attempt to protect him. "Would you show Rubinstein without his piano", I asked, "or Heifitz without his violin? Similarly, you shouldn't show a conductor without his instrument which is the orchestra." The penny must have dropped, as the use of incessant close-up shots diminished and a wider-angle shot was adopted which more often showed L in relation to the orchestra. Wide angle shot or not, L remained the centre of interest. During the early telecasts, one could not help but notice the black looks he was casting about the orchestra as they performed. There was an almost aggressive, challenging manner in his style. His tempos were at times unbelievably demanding, pressing the orchestra to the point where another lesser ensemble would have broken down. It was all part of a well-planned process, despite a good deal of smiling, of showing them who was boss.

Everyone was looking forward to this second season of telecasts, not least of all the orchestra who were earning welcomed additional fees from the new commercial work L's presence was attracting. I continued my two-tier job as L's musical assistant for both *Omnibus* and the *Young People's Concerts*. I had earned L's trust for the way I carried out my duties on his behalf and he knew that he could depend upon my loyalty. It was on this basis that I continued to make both private and public comments to him when I felt some action or direction he was adopting would prove counter-productive. It was with this sense of freedom that I had criticised the Orchestration script of the previous season as shortchanging the audience on music content. Whether such criticism ever influenced L when he was planning YPC's one can't really say. He was his own man and only when his back was up against the wall, as happened on two occasions involving the *Omnibus* series, did I ever feel that he specifically reached out for help and support. Both occasions were preceded by him uttering precisely the same statement, "I've never been in so much trouble in my life." This was certainly not the case when his Autumn 1958 season began with the Philharmonic. He couldn't have been flying higher. Nevertheless, in his first show, WHAT MAKES MUSIC SYMPHONIC?, there was a complete turnabout in the script's format. Music was used for the first time in a 2 to 1 ratio to script. What resulted was not only one of the best concerts in the entire series but one of the best children's concerts ever. It proved a brilliant mixture of music and script performed at fever pace throughout, without a boring moment or a bored child to be found from start to finish.

The script deals with the most complex of musical forms, *development*. "*Development* in music", states L, "is any change, growth or blossoming out. *Development* is the main thing in music, as it is in life." Having connected the development of musical ideas with the life-force within Nature and Mankind, L ties these two concepts even more firmly together with several simple, practical analogies. *We* might change by *developing* muscles or good teeth or *developing* a good mind. Music, like people, has a life of its own, with a beginning, a middle and an end. Within that musical life all the themes and melodies and musical ideas, however small they are, grow and develop into full grown works *just as babies develop into full grown adults.* Hey! Presto! Magic!

Moving straight on, L introduces Mozart's '*Jupiter*' Symphony, No.41 in C Major. This symphony contains one of the greatest examples of development in the whole history of music. L picks out on the piano the four note motto which opens the final movement and asks his young audience "to try to follow the fascinating life that blossoms out of those four notes as the piece develops". A stylish and brilliant performance follows. The audience explodes into extended applause at its conclusion.

L then asks, "How did these four notes grow into a mighty work? How did that development actually work?" Taking the simple folk theme which follows the dramatic introduction to the fourth movement of Tchaikovsky's Fourth Symphony, L demonstrates all the changes it undergoes, played softly, then loudly, in different keys, by different instruments, twice as slow and then twice as fast. "It's always the same tune", he says, "but it is always changing and it always sounds different."

That demonstration takes a little over a minute but it has opened a door in the minds of his young listeners. L conducts the complete Tchaikovsky fragment with much applause at the end. He goes on to explain development via *repetition* employing a small group of instrumentalists from within the orchestra performing *Dixieland* jazz. Next comes development by *variation* and the example chosen is the last movement of Beethoven's '*Eroica*' symphony, which gets the full Bernstein treatment. Music and explanation intermingle. All the musical excerpts are substantial. Development by *sequence* is next on the list with more Tchaikovsky, some Gershwin and a repeat of the development section of Mozart's 'Jupiter' Symphony. Development using *imitation* and *counterpoint* brings in the always-valuable fun segment, audience participation. *Frere Jacques* lustily sung as a four part round puts the young audience in an especially good mood. The educational *tour de force* of this segment of the program is development that builds up *by breaking down*. Using another theme from the *Finale* to Tchaikovsky 4th Symphony, L demonstrates how Tchaikovsky takes his theme and builds tension by breaking it in half and using the new broken fragment in rising sequences. Then by breaking the fragment itself in half again, the composer is able to increase the tension. Not stopping there, yet again the fragment splits like an amoeba building the continuing climax on only two notes of the original melody. Finally the tiny fragment disintegrates altogether into a flurry of whirling scales. Our original theme has become dust. L's descriptive summation of this last segment is 'making music by destroying it!' A truly stunning image!

In the concluding segment of the programme the Finale to Brahms Symphony No.2 in D Major is placed under the microscope. L analyses the development of all the main themes, which begins with their first statement. The clarity and simplicity of language used to carry off this difficult task are superb. This Brahms portion lifts this wonderfully illuminating program to even greater heights. The performance of the entire movement by the NY Philharmonic brings the concert to a fitting conclusion. This program stands as a monument to a unique educator of young people.

———————————————

WEST SIDE MAESTRO

In reviewing WHAT IS CLASSICAL MUSIC?, despite former claims for my long-term memory, I will confess to have recalled almost none of the program. If my name hadn't flashed up on the screen at the end, I wouldn't have remembered working on the show. After watching the video three times, I fully understand the reason why. It is the most frustrating and infuriating example of a great talent drowning in self-indulgence. The script is endless, the presence of substantial music in a 60 minute program almost non-existent, occupying less than 25% of the running time of the program.

The concert opens with a one-minute fragment from the Hamilton Harty arrangement of Handel's *Water Music*. L then sets out his opening thesis using the same formula employed for the WHAT DOES MUSIC MEAN? YPC. For the next twenty minutes the discussion centers upon what the term 'classical music' *doesn't* mean. Having determined what classical music *isn't*, L takes us on a journey to determine what classical music *is*. The preliminary conclusion is that it is a musical work in which the composer provides as much exactitude as possible, i.e.: the exact notes, the exact dynamics, the exact instruments or voices required to perform the piece and, in general, as many guiding directions as the composer can conceive to help the performer give an exact performance. L, having brought in the performer, moves onto a short tangent to show how different artistes can differ in their interpretation of the same notes in a given work. By demonstration the audience is shown that even when the artist adds his own inflections, a work's classic nature is not changed if none of the notes, rhythms, etc. have been altered. Putting on his 'seated-at-the-piano-Mr.Show-Biz' hat, L compares the exactitude required of a classical artist with the freedom enjoyed by a 'popular' performer. What follows are wonderfully funny imitations contrasting the different styles of Louis Armstrong and Fred Waring[97] singing, 'I Can't Give You Anything But Love, Baby'. The introduction of popular music into his YPC's always proved a high point for the audience. In this instance, it produced much laughter and applause, especially from the adults in the audience. The point of the demonstration was that classical music is what 'pop' music is not, *exact* music.' Another tangent is slipped in for later use, a reference to *Romantic* music in the form of a four bar fragment from

---

[97] Fred Waring, famous American choral conductor of popular music

WEST SIDE MAESTRO

Rimsky-Korsakov's *'Scheherazade'*. 'Is this classical music?', L asks. 'Yes!', shout back the audience. 'Wrong!', says L 'Classical music refers to a very definite period in the history of music...from about 1700 to 1800!' 'Wrong, again!', one must comment. The topic under discussion is, 'what is meant by the generic term *classical music*?' Had the subject of the program been 'Music of the Classical Era', L's tangent into the 18th century would not have been a tangent at all but the very substance of the script. We might have had to sacrifice the Louis Armstrong imitation but *you win a few and you lose a few*! Twenty-five minutes into the concert and L has again shifted the goal posts. Depending on the degree of importance placed on the question of scholarship and script consistency determines how one views this major shift in concept.

As for the musical substance, with the exception of the overture to Mozart's *'Marriage of Figaro'*, we have had only bits and pieces from Bach and Mozart and a strong visual analogy that building a fugue requires the same exactitude as building a Ferris wheel with an erector set.

Haydn and musical humour are next to be discussed with L rather than Haydn getting most of the laughs. As we move towards Beethoven the association with Romanticism again rears its head and off the path we stumble once more, encountering Chopin and Schumann before finding our way back. Fortunately, this somewhat confusing and unfocussed script has run out of words. L uses the remaining time to perform Beethoven's overture, *'Egmont'* to closes the concert.

The single positive plus of this YPC is the NY Philharmonic. Their performance of the few works they are required to play is stunning. They are again in marvellous form, razor sharp in their attacks, transparent and light in their playing of the Mozart and Haydn excerpts and substantial in sound when matching the drama of Beethoven's *Egmont*.

All credit is certainly due L in so quickly restoring the orchestra to its rightful place among the leading American orchestras.

WEST SIDE MAESTRO

For educational purposes, dividing this text into short segments will most efficaciously serve those teachers interested in making use of this particular concert in the classroom. For the individual viewer, this program may prove of minimal interest.

HUMOUR IN MUSIC was the last program on which I served as L's Music Assistant. Regretfully, no production credits appear at the end of this video. It is among the outstanding Young People's Concerts within the entire series.

There must have been a good deal of flak following WHAT IS CLASSICAL MUSIC? as the program on 'Humour' is its antithesis. Most important among the several changes to the format is a leaner script illustrated by a large amount of substantial music, not merely short fragments. This program contains complete works by Piston, Haydn, Prokofiev, Shostakovich, Copland, White and Brahms as well as chunky excerpts from Rameau, Mozart, Mahler, Wagner, Richard Strauss, Dukas, Kodaly, Gershwin and Gilbert & Sullivan. The length of the list of composers alone is an indication of how this program was much more akin to a concert than any of the previous concerts to date.

L's public image through the Young People's Concerts had reached an immediacy and unequalled popularity throughout North America. He was like no other conductor before him, much more than just a maestro with matinee idol good looks and a brilliant mind. This musician told funny jokes, used funny accents, imitated Elvis Presley, John Lennon and Louis Armstrong and, in the present program, added Greta Garbo and Katherine Hepburn to his list. No classical music snob, he played boogie-woogie, rock & roll and jazz and took the parts of both the male and female characters in opera and Gilbert & Sullivan excerpts which he sprinkled into the scripts of various programs. In short, he was an *entertainer*! L would have gone ballistic if any of his production team had even mooted such blasphemy. *His* young people's concerts were going to be "important" and not trivialised with gimmicks like others. As he told Roger Englander, his producer, in no uncertain terms, 'A concert is *not* a show.' But, of course, it *was* a show; a very superior low budget Arts show, (except for the cost of the host-conductor), which could get away with minimum production values because the 'star turn' was a superstar. It was the *Lenny* Bernstein Hour and *no bad thing that was, either.*

The audience enjoyed a rare old time during HUMOUR IN MUSIC. There was much laughter and an enormous amount of extemporaneous banter and musical interplay between L and his audience. He was so relaxed and lay-back, he was practically prostrate. Except, however, when he was conducting. What the audience couldn't see were his eyes flashing about the orchestra with irritation if even the slightest thing displeased him. He speaks to his audience of how, when he first heard Prokofiev's 'Classical' Symphony on the radio, he rolled about the floor roaring so with laughter that tears came to his eyes. Yet, when he conducts two movements of the symphony, barely the flicker of a smile passes his lips. There can be little doubt that L was making his presence as 'the boss' felt, though he did it in a subtle enough manner so that only another conductor or experienced player would catch the signals.

The HUMOUR script, while not as 'wordy' as the previous five, still suffers from a *word* problem. Here it involves specific words and their complex inferences and subtleties. They come rolling at the audience like a mini-linguistic avalanche, *wit, satire, parody, caricature, burlesque* and, most stressed of all, *incongruous.* While L has been rightly praised for his clarity and simplicity in explaining difficult concepts, a weakness in several scripts is that, having enlightened his young listeners momentarily, he was off onto some other difficult idea before the previous one has had time to sink in. Another chink in his pedagogical armour were the often absurd assumptions he made on behalf of his young audience in order to make a point in his script or play a particular obscure, (to his audience, at any rate), piece of music. 'You probably all know *Bach's Italian Concerto,* he interjected in the concert on MELODY; or, in this HUMOUR program, he brings in Richard Strauss's opera, *Der Rosenkavalier,* "in which the composer is describing passionate love in a comic way using a *parody* of the most passionate love music in history which is, *naturally*, from Wagner's opera *Tristan and Isolde*. I'm *sure*," he continues confidently, "you *must* have heard the music of *Tristan*." In script after script, he indulges in similar unrealistic assumptions or manipulates his text to justify playing a composition or dealing with a subject which may be inappropriate but which he fully intends to include no matter the opposition, of which, in my day, there was very little.

In the programme on *Humour*, L was equally *sure* that his young audience, after the passage of more than a month since the previous concert, had remembered all he had said about Haydn and the use of wit in relation to his music He recapitulates by rattling off in ten seconds a dozen of his mostly forgotten comments which now fly straight over the heads of his audience. I quote the final words of his script on *humour*, "All humour doesn't have to be a joke or make you laugh. It can be strong and important and make you have deep emotions. It's still humour because it makes you feel good inside." While the young audience were still trying to digest this bit of philosophy, he conducted the third movement of Brahms 4th Symphony, the last piece you would have expected in a program on humour.

Discussing this script in detail would serve little purpose. Having posed the question, 'What makes music funny?, and answered it with, "the unexpected and the shocking - the same thing that makes a joke funny.", L takes us on a semantic journey explaining and then demonstrating with musical examples wit, satire, parody caricature, burlesque and that which is plain clowning around in music. It is a video that would require a youngster several viewings to gain a proper understanding of all the subtle inflections of the text which is directed more to a mature teenage mind. Nevertheless, it can be enjoyed straightaway for the music performed superbly by the N.Y. Philharmonic under Bernstein's always-vital direction.

WEST SIDE MAESTRO

WHAT IS A CONCERTO? (28/3/59)

Seated on the stage is a small ensemble of just over 20 musicians as L enters and begins his program. Unusually his eyes are glued to his script reading the text rather than, as was his usual custom, speaking mostly from memory in an extemporaneous fashion and keeping his script tucked away inside the piano for a rarely required memory prompt. What follows are four minutes of soul searching regarding the efficacy of his YPC's before he finally turns to his chosen topic of the day. Then, via an extended tour around the word *sonata*[98], L provides a six minute explanation of the words "concerto' and 'concerto grosso' based upon musical scholarship that was, at very least, sketchy and incomplete. L delivers the contemporary definition of 'concerto' as derived from the Italian word *concertare* meaning 'concert' or 'agreement', such as *to act in concert*. He ignores an earlier and more relevant 17th century meaning for *concertare,* which is *"to dispute"* or *"compete",* a more apt description of the contrasting and challenging roles between soloist and accompanying ensemble in a concerto. Further, in explaining 'concerto grosso' first in literal terms as 'a big concerto', then as a work usually in three movements written for a big orchestra with a little orchestra attached "just like the earth which travels through space with its little moon travelling next to it.", he creates a faulty analogy which is opposite to the musical reality. It is the *concertino*, the small orchestra of soloists within a Concerto Grosso ensemble, which is the dominant musical entity rather than the larger mass of instruments whose music, taken from that written for the solo group, was simpler and whose function was secondary. If an analogy is to be made between the Earth and the Moon, it is the Concertino that represents the Earth and the larger mass of accompanying instruments that must be viewed as the satellite.

Ignoring the 16th century origins of the instrumental concerto in the *Sacrae Symphoniae* of Giovanni Gabrieli and with only the briefest mention that the words symphony and concerto were interchangeable for almost a century, L introduces the first of five substantial musical works to demonstrate the *concerto* in its various metamorphosed states over two and

---

[98] 'What Is Sonata Form?' is to be the subject ten years later of an outstanding YPC.

WEST SIDE MAESTRO

a half centuries, Vivaldi's *Concerto for Diverse Instruments and Mandolins*. First, however, we get a capsule biography of Vivaldi as composer-in-residence and Director of Music at a school for girls in Venice for whom he wrote a seemingly endless list of concertos to suit their astonishingly varied instrumental and musical talents. Then, complete with pictorial illustrations, we are given a short history of all the original *concertino* instruments for which this concerto was originally scored, none of which, with the exception of the two mandolins, is being used for that day's performance. The audience, who have sat long and quietly through a lengthy, complex and not always clear introduction, become restless as L moves to the Harpsichord to conduct one movement from the Vivaldi Concerto. At the conclusion, there is deservedly warm and enthusiastic applause for this utterly beguiling work.

More string players enter and seat themselves. L uses their arrival to make the point that with the passage of time the orchestra grew in size and instrumental variety. All perfectly true in relation to the Classical Period and the music of Haydn and Mozart but for the next programmed work, the third movement from J. S. Bach's *Brandenburg Concerto No.5*, totally unnecessary since its *ripieno*, (the name of the larger accompanying ensemble in a Concerto Grosso), was historically no bigger than the one used by Bach's contemporary Vivaldi. The Bach receives quite a neat performance. One cannot help but feel, however, that its presence after the Vivaldi is a bit of Baroque overkill. The movement, featuring a solo Flute, Violin and Harpsichord, is not the most ideal listening experience for a young audience. Built upon a fugue, it is a complex discourse of musical ideas and instrumental textures complete with a lengthy cadenza for Harpsichord.[99] It neither moves us musically or historically forward from the Vivaldi concerto. Its presence does serve a twofold purpose, it uses up a good chunk of time and it gives L a solo work to perform.

More players enter. L moves on to the Classical era and introduces the slow movement of Mozart's *Sinfonia Concertante* for solo violin and viola. In his

---

[99] J.S. Bach's 5th Brandenburg Concerto had long been one of the handful of works that L performed in public. He had many years before recorded the complete concerto with members of the Boston Symphony performing the harpsichord part, as was his custom, on the piano.

introductory remarks to this program, L deplored the general use of complicated technical terms to explain music. He has, he tells us, avoided using them "whenever he could do without them." Despite this early disclaimer, a list of formal musical terms along with the archaic names of long discarded baroque instruments have thus far featured heavily in this script. With the introduction of the Mozart, he adds two more technical terms, *cadence and cadenza*. Earlier, we had been told that designations of works as 'concertos' or 'symphonies' or 'sonatas' had been very loosely and interchangeably used. The chameleon-type forms a sonata could assume included: a trio, a quartet, a quintet, an octet and even *a symphony*. To move us logically to his YPC topic, L added, " A symphony that features a soloist or a little group of soloists separate from the big orchestra is called a concerto." Actually, L's definition more accurately describes a *sinfonia concertante* than a concerto, which, like the term *concertante*, defined not only the solo aspects but the formal musical structure of the work as well.

The Mozart Sinfonia Concertante, here performed in a slightly truncated version, again features the Concertmaster of the N.Y. Philharmonic, John Corigliano, who has appeared as soloist in each of the works presented thus far. He is joined by the orchestra's principal violist, William Lincer. This beautiful music receives a straightforward reading well shaped and controlled by Mr. Corigliano with his violist partner. It is well received by the audience.

Enter more players, yet another cosmetic increase in the number of performers to again emphasise the continued growth in size and diversity of orchestral instrumentation over the centuries. However, the orchestra for the next work, the final movement of Mendelssohn's *Violin Concerto in E minor*, is, in truth, no more varied instrumentally than a late Mozart piano concerto or the earliest of the Beethoven concertos. L's script has also placed emphasis on the ever-diminishing number of soloists employed for concerto-like compositions, i.e.: the opening Vivaldi work employed twelve soloists, the Bach only three and the Mozart only two. What is glossed over is that Bach continued to write concertos for widely varied instrumental groups of different sizes, Mozart wrote an alternate *Sinfonia Concertante for*

WEST SIDE MAESTRO

Oboe, Clarinet, Bassoon and Horn while Beethoven wrote a Triple Concerto for Violin, Cello and Piano. It is perfectly true to state, as L did, that the solo concerto dominated the form but that had been true since the time of Bach and Vivaldi. The emphasis on the solo star virtuoso performer in the public spotlight, however, is the next topic L is to explore. This again was far from a unique development of the 19th century. Seventeenth and eighteenth century composers enjoyed public solo careers. Vivaldi and Mozart are two noted examples from these periods. They toured Europe featured as soloists in compositions they had written specifically to demonstrate their virtuosity. "The solo concerto had come to stay", states L. (When had it ever left?) However, the technical accomplishments of the soloist in the virtuoso concerto, as especially demonstrated in the extended 'flashy' solo cadenza, became the central purpose behind a particular genre of composition rather than the mark of creative inspiration. Nevertheless, a great composer, such as Mozart or Beethoven, despite the fashions of the time, was always capable of writing a concerto that displayed the full range of a soloist's talent and still be recognised as music of the highest quality. Such a concerto was Mendelssohn's *Violin Concerto in E minor,* a work that combines all the virtuoso 'flash' one would wish for and yet remains serious, great music. L speaks of the orchestra's role in the Mendelssohn concerto as being more interesting in content and no longer merely a secondary musical element kept well in the background.

One cannot but totally agree with this statement but again point out that some of the most sublime moments of interplay between soloist and orchestra were to be found repeatedly in the slow movements of Mozart's piano concertos written more than fifty years before the Mendelssohn. John Corigliano is again the soloist. His marvellous performance in the Third Movement of the concerto receives the most sustained applause of the concert.

One would be remiss not to comment that in this YPC John Corigliano has represented a musical presence equal to that of L. His contribution underlines the highest quality of instrumental accomplishment and musicianship required of a Concertmaster of a world ranking professional ensemble. The glimpse of him exercising his authority via bow movement, eye contact and body language to bring about a faultless ensemble between himself and his musical partner in the Mozart *Sinfonia Concertante* is an absolute revelation into the role of a Leader of the strings of a symphony orchestra. L pays tribute twice to his outstanding Leader, first by commenting how hard John has been working during the concert and second with the satirical aside 'Here is the climax of our Corigliano Festival' just prior to beginning the Mendelssohn Violin Concerto.

We have arrived at the final pages of the script. Every chair on the stage is now occupied by an instrumentalist. Musically we have moved a century forward. L speaks of the renewed interest by contemporary composers in the old forms such as the *Concerto Grosso*. While solo concertos continue to be written, they have now become so big and complex that many composers have turned to the simpler forms of classical days. These composers have been labelled 'neo-classic' composers. With them developed a 'new' form called a *Concerto For Orchestra*. L adds the truism that the concerto for modern orchestra, which is huge, is very different from the concertos of Bach and Handel which were small. However, if L is assessing the contemporary 'concerto for orchestra' to be the evolutionary child of the earlier smaller concerto grosso, it is a contradiction of his statement that the 'concerto for orchestra' was a new form. Indeed, looking back to the opening work on this program, one could make the case that the Vivaldi Concerto for Diverse Instruments seems a direct ancestor of the modern Concerto For Orchestra. Examples quoted of contemporary 'concertos for orchestra' include works by Walter Piston, Paul Hindemith, Ernest Bloch and Igor Stavinsky. Both Piston and Hindemith did compose virtuoso works for orchestra under that title but neither Stravinsky nor Bloch did. The latter two composers did, however, write works for string orchestra in the concerto grosso form. Happily, L side-steps all this somewhat garbled background information with a short description of the two movements from Bela Bartok's Concerto For Orchestra with which the program will conclude. He speaks of the Bartok work as "the most showy, effective and beautiful of all" in that form. It is a work which "lights up" every section of the orchestra giving each a "chance to shine."

What follows is a typically virtuoso performance from the Philharmonic. No tempo, no matter the speed, finds them wanting. They take it all in their stride and stride away they do in great style. It is a display of collective virtuosity that one can compare to the technique of the greatest of solo artists. As for L's podium manner, he has been a restrained figure throughout this program. The Bartok, in which you might have expected him to go to town, is, for him, sedately presented. The rhythmic and tempo variants are all clearly and simply set out and the understanding and communication between conductor and orchestra are total. This is an ideal presentation of this particular work by a conductor who knows how truly to introduce audiences to the enjoyment of contemporary music. It receives an enthusiastic reception by his young audience whose taste in music has broadened and grown up considerably since first attending these programs.

One is of two minds regarding this YPC. On the one hand, it contains more music than most other programs whose scripts call for short extracts from a variety of sources in distinction to those YPC programs in which the script is built around a single extended composition[100]. On the other hand, the pedagogical content of this script is not up to standard. L's eyes appeared glued to his text during the telecast[101]. Having worked closely with him and being totally familiar with his television work patterns, my educated guess is that the program was thrown together very quickly or radically changed at the last minute. Everything about the script points in that direction as well. The opening of the program consists of ten minutes of chat that wanders all over the place from a defensive statement of inner soul searching to a digression into "what is a sonata?[102]". This leads to several incomplete and

---

[100] 'What Is Impressionism?', 1/12/61; 'Happy Birthday, Igor Stravinsky', 26/03/62; 'Berlioz Takes A Trip', 25/05/65; 'A Birthday Tribute To Shostakovich', 05/01/66; 'Two Ballet Birds', 14/09/69; 'Fidelio, A Celebration Of Life, 29/03/70
[101] In the early days of the YPC, L was required to commit most of his script to memory as teleprompters were not yet widely in use.
[102] Virtually all of this same material is again used, far more cogently, in LB's 1964 YPC, 'What Is Sonata Form?'

challengeable historical and musicological explanations concerning the words Concerto and Concerto Grosso. Regarding this lapse in the quality of scholarship, it is not that the facts lack total substance but that, in several instances, incomplete historical background is presented in order to make the point at hand.

One can, of course, find mitigating reasons for the lapse in standard of this YPC if you search for them. Since January of 1958, L had set himself a gruelling schedule. His life now was dominated by a whirlwind of official and social Philharmonic activities on a demanding level equal to that of the previous year when West Side Story had dominated his career calendar. His debut season as co-Director of the Philharmonic with the soon to be departing Dmitri Mitropoulos included the creation of YPC while he was still committed to the very difficult and time consuming Omnibus television lectures. In April 1958 while immersed in his Philharmonic duties, he agreed to conduct the premiere performance at the NY City Opera of his one-act opera, *Trouble In Tahiti*. At the end of April, he embarked on a gruelling seven week tour of Latin America. Although the tour was to be shared with Mitropoulos, L dominated the tour dates and Mitropoulos, who nevertheless scored a great success, served mostly as a fill-in conductor for those concerts L chose not to conduct. The 1958-59 season, his first totally in command, involved a general survey of American music from its very beginnings. This required learning or restudying a vast amount of repertoire, which he not only conducted but also analysed for the audiences who attended his new Thursday evening Preview Series. In addition, there lay ahead of him television commitments for what was to be his last season of Omnibus lectures and his ongoing Philharmonic series of Young People's Concerts. As this was also the last season I worked with L, leaving just prior to this final YPC of the 1958-59 season, I can testify not only to his overcommited schedule but to his exhausting weekly Philharmonic routine. In working to rebuild his much maligned, demoralised orchestra, his rehearsals became endurance contests during which he picked apart, measure by measure, every work rehearsed, even the most well known standard repertoire. As each final rehearsal prior to a concert approached, one wondered whether there was going to be sufficient time to put all pieces back together again.

WEST SIDE MAESTRO

Needless to say, he succeeded and critical acclaim for himself and his newly rejuvenated orchestra followed. Of course, something had to give with all this mounting pressure. The preparations for the Omnibus show were becoming more and more fraught. We began to work later and later into the night, not finishing sometimes till two or three a.m. A similar pattern was emerging for the YPC at the end of an exhausting and demanding season. Judging by the 'thrown together quality' of this YPC, everything must have come to a head just after I left.

One must understand that, despite the critical success of the YPC, L was still not totally comfortable with the programs or his audience. In private, he would express his dissatisfaction and in viewing the overall series there can be little doubt that he continued to experiment with its form and content. A criticism levelled at him over the years was that he was facile and that his work sometimes lacked depth. Be that as it may, he was still the best 'swashbuckler' around. To judge by the repertoire selected for this particular YPC, which included Bach's 5th Brandenburg Concerto, a standard Bernstein 'war-horse', along with other works recently performed and recorded by the orchestra over the previous season, he may have decided, having run out of time, to 'swash a buckle'. It's good to hear the orchestra playing so consistently well, especially in the Bartok, in this still relatively early stage of their relationship, and it is also good to witness the non-flamboyant, precise way L produces from them such superb results. The quality of the camera work remains unchanged - unimaginative and sometimes confused. However, the music is attractive and there is lots of it. You won't learn much useful information regarding 'what is a concerto?' than you probably already knew but you are sure to have a new and enjoyable listening experience with Vivaldi's *Concerto For Diverse Instruments and Mandolins* and the two movements from Bartok's *Concerto For Orchestra*.

WEST SIDE MAESTRO

FOLK MUSIC IN THE CONCERT HALL
(09/04/61)

The first phrase of the Trio from the Minuet to Mozart's *Symphony No. 39* opens this entertaining and music filled YPC. What never ceases to amaze is L's supply of varied images. He describes Mozart's simple tune as something you might sing around the campfire. It's attraction is not that it is a folk tune but that "it is *like* a folk tune."

Folk music expresses the nature of a people, the rhythms, accents and speed of the way they talk.[103] To illustrate this, L sings for us a Hungarian folk song with its strong accents, like the spoken language, on the first syllable of each word. Then he sings a French folk song which, like the spoken language, is smooth. This same smoothness of melody , (legato), also finds its way into the symphonic compositions of the great French composers. As an example he conducts an ultra legato fragment from Ravel's ballet *Daphnis and Chloe*. Instances of musical stress to mirror spoken language continues with examples in German, Spanish, English and American-English, The latter is drawled out first in a ballad sung cowboy western style and then in New-York-ese via a fragment of the *Fugue for Tinhorns* from the musical *Guys & Dolls*. The audience greets it all with peals of laughter. Whenever his uninhibited frog croak breaks into a Beatles or any other pop tune with which he is making some musical point or other, his young audience comes to adore him even more.

Returning to Mozart, L conducts a complete performance of the Minuet & Trio from the 39th Symphony with which he opened the program. Again the emphasis is that its melodies are not derived from folk tunes though they sound as if they were. To prove the point, he sets the words to the well-known folk song, Strawberry Fair, to the Mozart melody. Up till now, we have not heard much from the orchestra. From this point on, they begin to participate virtually non-stop till the end of the program.

---

[103] The theory that music expresses the nature of different peoples and incorporates the rhythms, accents and speed of the way they talk was to form one of the basis of the Bernstein's Norton lectures, 'The Unanswered Question' at Harvard University ten years later.

WEST SIDE MAESTRO

From the Austria of Mozart, we take a leap of almost two centuries to the music of Mexico in the 20th century, the *Senoia India* of Carlos Chavez. L explains and demonstrates at the piano the pentatonic (five note) scale, which is a feature of the folk music of Mexico. He then demonstrates the pentatonic structure of Chavez 's themes. As with the melodies in the Mozart symphony all the Chavez themes are original though they sound like authentic folk melodies. What *is* folk in origin, we learn, are the complex rhythms that Chavez employs. A complete performance of *Sinfonia India* follows. Although it is a four-movement symphony, all the movements are composed to merge with one another, giving the effect of an extended eleven minute overture. It is a marvellously colourful work utilising a huge and unusual percussion section playing all manner of exotic Mexican folk instruments. *Sinfonia India* had long been a Bernstein speciality dating back to the days of the N.Y.City Orchestra. The performance by the Philharmonic is so exciting that it is worth securing a copy of the tape for this alone. Happily, more wonderful music is to come.

L welcomes and turns the stage over to Marni Nixon, a marvellous singer who, during a long career in Hollywood gained fame as the singing voice for Deborah Kerr and Audrey Hepburn in the films of 'The King & I' and 'My Fair Lady'. Ms. Nixon charmingly explains and sings three folk songs from the Auvergne area in France. While the songs are authentically folk, the orchestral settings by Joseph Canteloube are highly sophisticated. The performances by singer, conductor and orchestra are glorious and the audience is both enchanted and enthusiastic in their reception

In the final part of the program, L turns to music of the United States. Rather than concentrating upon native folk music in its original settings, he chooses a symphony by the early avant-garde American composer, Charles Ives, who often used folk songs and folk dances in his complex compositions. The last movement of Ives' Second Symphony concludes this concert This movement incorporates several well known folk melodies such as *Turkey In The Straw*, *Long, Long Ago*, Stephen Foster's *Camptown Races*, *Columbia the Gem of the Ocean* and even the military bugle call with which the army wakes its troops - *Reveille*. Ives, in his highly personal and revolutionary style, pits these themes simultaneously against each other in different keys, creating clashing dissonance. As L enthusiastically characterises it, "it all adds up to a rousing jamboree, a Fourth of July celebration."

I absolutely adored this program. It is a real concert, very daring with extended, uncut exciting and unusual music. It is informative and clear without any of the explanations straining the audience's patience or endurance. It has introduced fresh contemporary sounds along with complex harmonies, rhythms and tonal relationships - and the young audience remained enthralled from start to finish.

As for L and the Philharmonic, one cannot praise their performance too highly. Hearing contemporary music performed with such precision, verve and understanding offered a top-flight experience for those who were fortunate enough to be in the Hall or watching their TV screens at the time.

WHAT IS IMPRESSIONISM
(01/12/61)

A short comparison between 'a suggestion' and 'a direct order' ushers in a program whose degree of success, I venture to guess, took both L and his production team completely by surprise.[104] This 'comparison' moves L to a discussion of "what *is* Impressionism?". Two views of the Rouen Cathedral are displayed, one a sharp edged photograph and the other one of the twenty diffused views Monet painted of the cathedral facade in the changing light of day. The effect of this visual image serves to underline the direction the

---

[104] This format was to become the prototype of several future programs, all of which enjoyed different degrees of success but one of which, A BIRTHDAY TRIBUTE TO SHOSTAKOVICH, was to stretch the boundaries and revolutionise concepts regarding Young People's Concerts as never before

script is to take and the inherent truth in the cliché, "a picture is worth a thousand words".

From Debussy's *La Mer*, [three symphonic sketches of the sea], the orchestra performs excerpts from the first movement, *From Dawn To Noon On The Sea*. L translates these musical excerpts into descriptive poetic images for his audience. The first excerpt describes the stillness of the ocean before dawn, the next, the first rays of the dawn light, others, the cries of the seabirds, the stirrings of the waters as the breezes rise, the sun rising over the horizon and, finally, the blaze of the sun at high noon.

All this is accomplished in two and a half minutes. It is precise, clear and fascinating, awakening the imagination of the young audience to this work which is filled with evocative and exciting exotic sounds. L then conducts the orchestra in the complete first movement. During the performance the camera cuts away to the audience showing the faces of involved and concentrated young people in absolute rapt attention. As the orchestra sounds the final chord, the audience bursts into applause spontaneously before the chord has concluded. Less than one third into the concert one can sense the level of excitement and interest that has been generated.

L speaks of impressionistic music as tone painting, i.e.: "painting for the ear instead of the eye." At the piano, he demonstrates the "hazy, dreamy sound of impressionism" with the Debussy prelude, *Sails*. He explains Debussy's use of the *whole tone scale* and its differences from the *chromatic* and *major* and *minor* scales. In a brilliant pianistic display using as his example the attractive Debussy tango, *The Port of Wine*, he elucidates in a clear, simple fashion the even more complex subject of *bi-tonality*. He tosses in for good measure a fragment of the *Gollywog's Cake-walk*, which brings a hum of recognition and giggles from the audience. The last multiplex scripted demonstration dealing with a variety of highly sophisticated technical subject matter has taken ten minutes but his young audience remains a picture of concentration.

WEST SIDE MAESTRO

L returns to the podium. He uses orchestral fragments from the second movement of *La Mer*, *The Play of the Waves*, to explain not only its imagery but to remind his audience of the various impressionistic chords he was demonstrating at the piano. A complete performance of the movement follows.

The format of a Bernstein YPC concert imposes certain stumbling blocks for the participants. The stop and start nature of music-making leads to unsettling the orchestra. L, himself, rushes the opening of the second movement before settling down. The Philharmonic musicians, sitting without playing under hot television lights during the long piano demonstrations, begin to manifest problems with orchestra tuning. However, the professionalism of everyone involved, the obvious careful musical preparation which had been given to this program and, I'm convinced, the growing realisation by all that they were participating in one of those magical musical happenings that has become an all too infrequent event in concert halls, quickly brings everything quickly back under control. At the end of the second movement there is another enthusiastic response of approval from the young audience.

With barely a thirty second link, merely to announce the title of the third movement, *Dialogue of the Wind and the Waves*, L conducts the work to its conclusion. The obvious outpouring of pleasure underlined by the sustained applause at the end must have been a source of great satisfaction mixed with astonishment for all involved.

Reviewing all the YPC videos from their inception in calendar order, one cannot fail to notice that the age profile of the audience has moved into the young 'teens'. Very young children, the 'under-elevens', no longer constitute the majority of the audience. Nevertheless, the programming of a complete contemporary work, even one whose modernism was of a conservative nature, was a very daring gesture on L's part. The sophisticated manner in which the youngsters received it certainly seemed to have caught him by surprise and pleased him. This is underscored by his momentarily leaving his script to comment on how quiet and attentive everyone remained for such a long, difficult, new work.

L turns to the music of Maurice Ravel, another composer who was a world leader in the '*Impressionism*' movement. He underlines that all the elements to be found within the music of Debussy, whole-tone scales, modes, bi-tonality, will be encountered in the music of Ravel. With that short introduction, the program concludes with the finale, the *General Dance*, from Ravel's ballet, *Daphnis and Chloe*. This excerpt, which usually takes just over four and a half minutes to perform, is played at a furious pace, cutting a full minute off the conventional timing. The orchestra copes amazingly well. Though the speed at which it is taken certainly generates an artificial excitement, the fragment of music, by its nature a "bleeding chunk" from a much longer work, becomes distorted. There is a burst of applause at the end but it is less enthusiastic than the reception given to the thoughtful, well-proportioned reading of *La Mer*. My own reaction was that it made little musical sense. It made me wonder whether the excessively fast tempo taken for *Daphnis*, especially following L's ad-lib comments on the attentiveness during the performance of *La Mer*, wasn't originally opted for in anticipation; that, perhaps, his young audience would be somewhat restless after the long Debussy work. If so, in retrospect, it proved a miscalculation.

What elements produce 'magic' in a concert? For without doubt, nine tenths of this concert was sheer magic. First of all, having Leonard Bernstein and the N.Y. Philharmonic in brilliant form as your star turn is a good beginning. The music, though probably new to the greatest part of the audience, contained a panoply of unusual and fascinating sounds which were received with concentrated interest and judged by the audience to be both beautiful and exciting. L's text, though breaking new ground, was very controlled in its length so that the proportion of music to talk was 3 to 1. This, as well as the modest length of each of the movements of the Debussy, presented no challenge to the attention span of the youngsters, the single greatest problem in the presentation of any Young People's Concert. Add to this the indefinable, that certain 'something' which only those present during a 'live' concert event can experience to the full, and you have, at least, a partial explanation of what made this YPC one of the finest of the series.

WHAT IS MELODY?
(21/12/62)

"The meat and potatoes of music is *melody*", L explains, "a series of notes that move along in time one after the other". He sits at the piano and plays one note. He adds another, and then another, eventually forming the introductory sequence to Mendelssohn's *Wedding March* from the incidental music to *A Midsummer Night's Dream.* The N.Y. Philharmonic promptly strikes up completing the phrase begun on the piano. This old-fashioned 'cue-the-music!' introduction delights his audience. Would that the rest of the program had followed the example of this concise and sparkling introduction. Instead we are given a program bulging with interesting ideas but bogged down in a quicksand of words and musical and aesthetic concepts which are too much for even the most inquisitive young mind to take in at one go. It is certainly reminiscent of earlier Bernstein *Omnibus* scripts directed more towards adult audiences.

L continues, "Isn't any string of notes 'a melody'? They can be many different things", he explains, "a tune, a theme, a short motive, a long melodic line, a bass line or even a somewhat concealed inner voice within a musical work. Most people think of a melody as a tune that is complete in itself; that you can remember and can go out whistling. As with songs, melodies should consist of a beginning, a middle and an end.
(The ideas contained within the above paragraph are the embryo of this program).

Now L moves into gear. In *symphonic music,* we are not concerned with 'tunes' but *themes.* 'Tunes' are complete in themselves but *themes* leave something to be said and cry out for further development and *Development* is the main thing in symphonic music. *Themes* are the seeds from which *develop* symphonic trees.

L conducts examples of symphonic themes. The first is the opening passage from Beethoven's 5th Symphony, which we later learn is so brief a musical statement that it is not really a theme but a *motive*, next is the theme from the 2nd movement of Beethoven's Seventh Symphony, which he points out is "mostly harping on one note", and last of all comes the big D Major theme from the 1st movement of Tschaikowsky's *Pathetique* Symphony, which is "practically a whole tune in itself". Next we learn the 1-2-3 *construction of themes*, '1' being a short musical idea, '2' the repeat of the same idea with a small variation and '3', the launching of the idea' into a flight of inspiration'. In a short flight of inspiration of his own, L compares '1,2,3' theme construction to the countdown in a race: **1.** 'On your mark; **2.** Get set; **3.** *Go*!'; or to target practice: **1.**'Ready; **2.**Aim; **3.***Fire!*'; or the direction in a movie studio: **1.** 'Lights; **2.** Camera; **3.** *Action*!'

It is simple but brilliant teaching! However, to be noted is that 15 minutes have gone by and we have yet to hear a complete piece of music.

Fragments from the opening of Wagner's *Prelude to Tristan and Isolde* follow, illustrating the construction of a Wagnerian melody from different short overlapping *motives* which, when connected, create a single extended theme. Moving to another fragment at the end of the *Prelude*, L shows how the three motivic elements from the opening of the *Prelude* are juxtaposed *contrapuntally* to create an exciting climax. He asks whether this is "too much melody for a human ear to catch all at once?" but adds with confidence that he would "bet" that *his*[105] young audience can hear it all - "every note."

In current American parlance this is what is known as 'laying a heavy number' on the youngsters in attendance. L's daughter, Jamie, then ten years old, was said to be his inspiration for this YPC. Her endless curiosity was reported by her distinguished father as being a constant stimulus to him. In his desire to satisfy his daughter's curiosity, of which L seems to have

---

[105] Author's italics

lost track, is that the young people who were attending his Philharmonic concerts, average ages ranging from 7 -15 years, did not enjoy the distinct advantage of having Leonard Bernstein sitting across from their bowl of cornflakes at the breakfast table.

Following a breathless performance of the Tristan excerpts which must have set some sort of world speed record, L reassures his audience that they need not be "scared of that frightening word, *counterpoint*" since *Counterpoint* is not the absence but the abundance of melody. "It doesn't erase melody, it multiplies it."

(If only in practice the solution for one's auditory nerve and brain was as simple as this true but somewhat misleading over-simplification leads one to believe).

We have thus far dealt with the multiple concepts of what is a melody, the difference between a melody and a symphonic theme, how a symphonic theme is constructed, what is a motive and how it is possible to join two or more motives together to create a theme plus analysing a three voice contrapuntal passage one voice at a time and then listening to the entire passage attempting to tune one's ear into hearing all three elements sounding simultaneously **and we have not reached the half way stage of the program or been treated to a complete work.**

Now we come to the first composition on the program to be performed in its entirety, the 1st movement of Mozart's Symphony No.40 in G Minor. It might have been good judgement in light of the many complex ideas already put forward to have listened to this work through before dealing with further analysis but that is not the format developed for these programs. Fortunately, much of the new inquiry recapitulates concepts and musical techniques encountered earlier in the program, i.e.: the 1, 2, 3 structure of a theme, the use of tiny motives and counterpoint. This is helpful, less taxing on the audience, and very sound pedagogy. One new topic, however, is encountered, *what is un-melody?*. This deals not with the absence of melody, as one might think, but the need to learn to listen for themes obscured by counterpoint, buried within complex textures in the middle of an ensemble, assigned to instruments at the extreme top or bottom of an orchestra or constructed of such tiny motives that they don't register as tunes. All aspects of this latest analysis are clearly illustrated using appropriate fragments from the Mozart symphony played by the orchestra.[106]

A rather routine performance of the Mozart follows. Sitting around on a concert hall platform for a half hour under hot television lighting having barely played for five minutes creates all kinds of technical, physiological and psychological problems for an orchestra. The musicians are obviously trying their best but their concentration seems far from at its peak. L's podium deportment is controlled; his baton technique is clean and precise. This is simple, classical conducting without flamboyance or exaggeration of any kind.

Now begins the most complex and challenging part of the program. L's moves into an extended discussion of 'what is *un-melody*.' He begins with the notion that for most people what makes a melody is what their ears are used to hearing and what they have come to expect - "in other words, their *taste*." Repetition plays a great part in our learning and identifying a melody. "What happens", he asks, "when we hear melodies that don't repeat at all?" He chooses as an example of a melody without repetition, the 2nd movement of Bach's Italian Concerto for harpsichord, a work he studied at the age of 14. At the time, he tells us, he couldn't understand the work. "It just seemed to wander around, with no place to go. *Do you know it*???"', he asks.

Earlier on he asked the same question regarding an excerpt from the Cesar Franck Symphony in D Minor. Before playing the excerpts from *Tristan* he stated with conviction, 'You've all heard the *Prelude* to this great opera, I'm sure.' This pattern of presumption or implied presumption by L in relation to a great number of compositions which young people within the age group

---

[106] If I appear to be dwelling upon the erudition of this program for a young audience, one need only point out that parts of this analysis of the Mozart symphony were again used by L for his Harvard University lectures, The Unanswered Question, more than ten years later

attending these concerts would hardly be likely to know runs throughout the entire series of Young People's Concerts.[107] Certainly, in this instance, it was highly unlikely that even those members of the audience who had been taking piano lessons would have come across Bach's Italian Concerto.

L plays an extended excerpt from the Bach work and asks, "Do you find it wandering and aimless? *I find it one of the glories of all music –* now *– today,-* but I didn't think so when I was fourteen[108]. I was still young enough to think that every melody had to be a *repeating tune*, because that's what my brief musical experience had taught me to expect." To follow the Bach, L and the orchestra perform a four-minute excerpt from the slow movement of Hindemith's Concert Music for Strings & Brass as a second example of a long, non-repeating melodic line.

In earlier camera 'cut away' reaction shots of the audience, the under 12 year olds were already seen to be restless. I would venture that following the Hindemith some of the parents, who made up more than a third of the audience, were themselves beginning to question the complexities of this esoteric program.

Following the Hindemith, L's comments are reminiscent of those which followed the Bach, "Whether you like it or not, *that* is a great melodic line, and there are four minutes of these beautiful curves, arches, peaks and valleys."

From my own experience self-justifying comments of this nature which crept into the script usually were generated by critical remarks or questioning which L may have encountered during production preparation. By lending his seal of approval via hyperbole, "one of the glories of all music", or force of

---

[107] To use a mixed metaphor, this is *verbal body language*. Whenever L knows that he is walking a knife's edge in using examples which may be obscure to his audience, he invariably uses the technique of implied presumption. It's a form of flattery to maintain interest even though it is hardly likely that you have acquaintance with what he has implied or unequivocally presumed you to know.

[108] The age of the average teenager in his audience.

authority, "like it or not, <u>that</u> is a great melody", he attempts to deflect possible critical flack which may follow.

Nevertheless, the point he was trying to put over was perfectly valid. What is judged as ugly and un-melodic in one generation may be viewed as charming, everyday stuff to the people of another generation. If L's audience found the Hindemith work un-melodic, awkward and graceless, those were the same words written about the music of Brahms fifty years before.

The final movement of Brahms 4th Symphony closes the program. Again analysis precedes performance. It is short and precise but complex. L describes a set of thirty variations and coda. Each variation is eight bars in length and is constructed upon a six note scale plus a two bar cadence which introduces the movement. He comments that basing an entire movement on a six note scale and a cadence does not sound melodically promising but Brahms' genius in employing all the techniques they have been examining, (counterpoint, motives, repetition, the 1,2,3 theme structure, the theme in the bass or placed within other textures), produces a magnificent outpouring of melody. In this concise conclusion L has used word and idea repetition skilfully to help tie his program together. It is one of the great strengths of this most complex script.

Unfortunately, L adds the following last minute coda of his own which must have created some confusion and threatened to put the whole premise of his script into question:

' If you're still wondering *What is Melody?*, just listen to this (Brahms) movement and you'll realise that *melody is exactly what a great composer wants it to be.*'

This enigmatic truism could mislead us to conclude that *'melody'* is any subjective sequence of notes declared to be a melody by its composer. This is obviously not what L meant to imply. Rather, that *great* composers have the genius to transform the simplest of materials into a thing of beauty.

WEST SIDE MAESTRO

The performance of the final movement to Brahms 4th Symphony is everything it should be. There is no concession made to the age of the audience or the possibility that the majority of them are hearing this complex work of the mature Brahms for the first time. No attempt is made to drive the tempo to create an artificial excitement. The YPC audience is presented with a stylish, well-proportioned classic reading. The orchestra responds superbly and sensitively to L's clear direction. Special mention must be made of the outstanding solo of John Wummer, the orchestra's long serving Principal Flautist, in the movement's 13th Variation as well as the beautiful balanced chording of the horns and trombones throughout. L's tempi are judiciously chosen with each phrase imaginatively shaped. Hints of rubato inflect the long, melodic lines as one variation flows seamlessly into another. The conducting style is extrovert and emotional but never exaggerated or over the top.[109] One notes also that the overall sound balances have improved considerably and credit for this must go to John McClure, L's record producer, who had joined the production team to supervise the sound.

Because of the many caveats I have expressed in this critique regarding the length and sophistication of the script, the commercial video proves critical. It can be repeatedly watched, allowing the young viewer time to absorb and understand its variety of complexities over a series of viewings. For the interested youngster, it will test both his patience and sustained interest. The video helps solve many of the problems begot by its chef in 'over-egging' his musical pudding for the young appetites of his original concert hall audience. Just as L reminds us of "how important repetition is in making a melody easy to latch on to" so repeated viewings of this program can and will bring its many valuable concepts to be understood, absorbed and enjoyed. This in turn will lead to greater and more knowledgeable listening pleasure of a wider range of music for its young viewers.

---

[109] Dmitri Mitropoulos had died suddenly and dramatically two years prior to this concert. Comment at the time was that L was beginning to incorporate the excesses of Mitropoulos's podium manner into his own technique, particularly jumping into the air at moments of musical climax. It is to be noted that virtually none of the Mitropoulos mannerisms were to be observed in Bernstein's conducting for his YPC's over the many years that he presented the series.

WEST SIDE MAESTRO

WHAT IS SONATA FORM?
(6/11/64)

L begins by stating that he has avoided the subject of *Sonata Form* not because of its difficulty but because of the mystique of complexity it has gained through those music appreciation classes which treat it like a course in map reading complete with strange place names like *exposition* and *recapitulation.*

If, by this introduction, the viewer believes that he is going to learn about Sonata form using the Bernstein method and thus avoid terms like *exposition, development* and *recapitulation* a certain amount of disenchantment will set in by the end of this program. However, it should be added straightaway that if he is hoping to gain this knowledge by the least painful, simple yet crystal clear explanations and examples, this video is just the ticket.

The first music we encounter is Mozart's *Symphony No.41*, the *'Jupiter'* Symphony. L tells us just prior to performance that he is going to repeat this same piece at the end of the program at which time he hopes that his audience will be hearing it with new ears.

Before conducting, L sets about unlocking the first of many doors to the complex *sonata form* structure we are to examine in this YPC. He projects that we are probably wondering why, if our purpose is to learn more about *sonatas*, he is playing a *symphony*? With L about, enlightenment cannot be far behind. "A *symphony* **is** a *sonata*." A *sonata*, we are told, is any piece of music, usually of several movements, following a certain form. When that form is used in a composition for any solo instrument, i.e.: flute, violin, etc., with piano accompaniment, it is called a *Sonata*. The same form used in a piece for three instruments is called a *Trio*, for four instruments a *Quartet*, for five instruments a *Quintet*, etc. When the composer makes use of the form in a work for full orchestra, it is called a *Symphony*. "A *Symphony* is a *Sonata* for orchestra. **Simple!!!**"

WEST SIDE MAESTRO

Explained that way, it really is simple.

The program then makes a healthy start with a good chunk of a Mozart masterwork.

It is not only the choice of music that sets the standard but the orchestra playing as well. Although 'original instrument' execution has come in recent years to dictate the style of performance in repertoire from Bach to Beethoven, L's 'big orchestra' Mozart would hold up under comparison and find a welcome in any of the world's concert halls. It is clean, precise and transparent, overflowing with phrases beautifully shaped and performed with a singing tone. The intonation of the orchestra is superb, their ensemble well nigh perfect and their dynamics carefully graded. The Bernstein gestures are controlled with only tiny extravagances being glimpsed within a baton technique that is economic in gesture but never lacking in clarity and communication befitting the composer he is serving and period style in which this music was composed.

Following the performance of the Mozart, L moves to the subject of, 'Form', which is an understanding of the shape of a musical composition. He warns us that this is the subject most people find hardest to understand. One remembers a tune, or rhythm or other musical details of a piece but grasping its 'Form' involves taking in or *hearing* its structure all at one go. Unlike looking at a painting or a church building, which exist in space and whose overall form your eyes can survey virtually instantly, *music only exists in time* so it is impossible to hear an entire work all at once. This takes time. To work out the musical *Form* you have to remember all the notes you've heard while listening all the time to new notes, so that at the end of the piece you can add up what you know and then determine its overall shape. While that sounds impossible, it's not *if* you know something about its structure in advance, i.e.: if you know the piece is in *Sonata Form*, you can virtually predict the musical shapes you are going to encounter. That is the task in hand, to find out what a *sonata* is.

WEST SIDE MAESTRO

L's exposition, a word soon to take on great significance, is not the easiest of concepts for a young mind to grasp in so short a time. However, while remaining relatively simple and graphic in his explanations, L painstakingly unwinds this many knotted problem of '*sonatas* and *Sonata Form*'.

Sonata, he informs us, is from the Latin *sonare*, 'to sound'. It meant any music that was sounded by instruments. In the past two hundred fifty years, however, it has acquired the additional special meaning of describing the *Form* of a piece of music, - in particular, the first movement of a work. This first movement *Form*, which became known as *Sonata Form*, laid the foundation of the structure of the *symphony* for composers from the mid-seventeenth century to the present day.

L now sets out to explain the popularity and growth of Sonata Form and, particularly, what makes it both satisfying and complete to the listener. The answer, he says, lies in its *Balance and Contrast*, specifically its *three part* balance and its exciting, contrasting elements. L gives us several graphic examples of three part design which are all around us; a bridge with its two rising towers at either end connecting the long span between them, a tree with its central trunk and branches to either side or a human face with nose and mouth in the center and eyes and ears mirrored on either side. The obvious conclusion, a form so basic and natural in life must be equally natural in music.

L moves on to the simplest of examples of *Three Part Song Form*, *'Twinkle, Twinkle, Little Star'*. He reduces it to an A/B/A formula of Balance and Contrast:
(A) Twinkle, Twinkle, Little Star - How I Wonder What You Are?
(B) Up Above The World, So High - Like A Diamond In The Sky
(A) Twinkle, Twinkle, Little Star - How I Wonder What You Are?

Most popular tunes stick strictly to this A/B/A pattern with the slight embellishment of repeating the 'A' Section straightaway before the contrasting 'B' Section, altering the pattern to A/**A**/B/A. The music remains the same only the first part, 'A', is played twice in succession. The example L chooses to demonstrate this expanded song form, again section by section, is the Beatles tune, *And I Lover Her,* which he sings with great sentimental charm at the piano sounding a bit like an out of tune Liberace.

L's great love of singing and total lack of inhibition to give forth in public despite a truly terrible singing voice for which every song seemed just that bit too high or too low was something we had laughed over together in earlier days. I shared an equal enthusiasm for vocal music but was similarly plagued by a singing voice that let me down. I remember saying to him after the YPC, WHAT IS CLASSICAL MUSIC, "Don't ever die! If you die, **I'll** own the ugliest voice in the world." Nevertheless, his singing of 'pop' tunes used as examples to explain difficult musical concepts throughout the entire YPC series humanised and endeared him to his audience. They laughed, applauded and idolised him.

Following the Beatles tune demonstrating the 'extra deluxe feature' of the repeated first 'A' section, L proceeds to operatic examples to demonstrate the further growth of *three part song form.* The young black soprano, Veronica Tyler, sings Micaela's Aria from Bizet's *'Carmen'.* As L points out before beginning, this more sophisticated example doesn't "break up quite so neatly" into an ABA Form but he is confident that his audience will follow it as easily as they did the Beatles tune.

The six minute aria that follows, sung in the original French, might have raised a few eyebrows at the time regarding its appropriateness as the clearest of examples but Miss Tyler's beautiful voice and youthful, exotic appearance combined with Bizet's lovely melodies brings it off. Whether the youngsters actually followed the French composer's rather more obscure and extended use of A/A/B/A form or not is a separate question.

If what has gone before has seemed relatively "child's play", (unintended pun), what comes next is the real "grownup stuff". Explaining that three part *Sonata Form* is just an expansion of three part *Song Form,* L embarks on a miniature seminar analysing the form. We encounter those "nasty road map names", *Exposition, Development and Recapitulation* that L declared to be the source of much complication and confusion in his earlier implied criticism of the teaching of music appreciation. As simply stated by L, *Exposition* is the 'A' of our A/B/A Form. In it the composer states or 'exposes' the themes of the movement. This is followed by the *Development* or 'B' section in which some or all of the Themes are 'developed' in different ways. Finally, we have the *Recapitulation* which is the 'A' section repeated all over again. "But," L emphasises, "whatever words we use, the idea of those three parts remains clear". It creates that feeling of *balance* we get from the two similar sections, 'A' & 'A', situated on either side of the central 'B' section.

L reminds us that earlier he emphasised that there were *two* secrets to the Sonata. He had just explained the first, *balance,* but there was also *contrast,* which is just as important as *balance*. *Contrast* is what gives the sonata both drama and excitement. Somewhat apologetically, he tells us that he'll "have to get technical for a minute or two", (actually for the next 12 minutes), but he has something very important to show us, indeed, "the root of the whole *Sonata* business."

Now begins a discussion and analysis of *Keys* and what constitutes *Tonality*.

(This portion of the script now being delivered to a young teen-age audience was appropriated from L's Omnibus script An Introduction to Modern Music written for an adult audience).

Most music, we are told, is in one *Key* or other. The Beatles tune played earlier was in *F Major*, but it could have been in *G Major* or in any one of the twelve different keys represented by the white and black notes on the piano keyboard. A *Key* is a center or home base for a musical composition. It is the place from which it starts out and to which it returns. Home base itself is called the *Tonic,* (L demonstrates), the *Tonic note* is the first note of its scale, (another 'demo') and the *Tonic chord* is built on and begins with that note, (another 'demo'). Though all the other notes in that scale also have names, the only other one we need be concerned with in today's lesson is the 5th note of this scale, (or any scale), which is called *the Dominant*. In C

Major, the key in which L is demonstrating, this fifth note is 'G' and on this 'G' we can, as we did on the Tonic note, build another chord, which we call *the Dominant chord*. L discusses the close relationship between these two chords. He demonstrates that if he plays a *Tonic chord* followed by a *Dominant chord*, one is left with an unresolved, unfinished feeling and a desire to return to the *Tonic*. Whereas, if he plays a *Dominant Chord* followed by a *Tonic Chord*, one instantly has a feeling of satisfaction, of completeness. In a clear analogy, he describes the Tonic to be like a magnet. One can leave it, go to other chords, other tonal centers, (L improvises as he speaks), but, in the end, the magnetic pull of the Tonic draws you back. And with an explicit final word regarding Sonata Form, L sums up by telling us that "out of this magnetic pull-away from and back to the Tonic, Classical Sonata Form is built."

Using as his example the entire first movement of Mozart's *Sonata for Piano in C Major*, L sets to work to demonstrate how all that we have learned so far about *Sonata Form* actually works. Analysing and performing at a breathless pace, he lucidly takes us through the short *Exposition* with its *First Theme*, clearly *in C Major*, (the *Tonic* Key), and from which, in a feat of musical sleight of hand, Mozart instantly lures us away to his *Dominant* Key of *G Major* for his new or *2nd Theme*. The Exposition ends with a little *Fanfare* still in *the Dominant Key* of *G Major*. In a classical sonata, the composer here usually indicates a sign for the performer to repeat the Exposition from the beginning. This is the equivalent of the immediately repeated 'A' theme in the A/'**A**'/B/A song form we encountered earlier in the Beatles' tune.

L returns to his 'magnet' analogy comparing the Exposition to the first Act of a three Act drama in which we run away from our *Tonic* home center, freeing ourselves from its strong magnetic pull. In Act 2, the *Development*, the drama heightens as we wander further and further from our *Tonic* home travelling to ever distant *Keys*. In the 3rd Act, the *Recapitulation*, the drama is resolved as we give up all our wanderings and return unequivocally to our home *Tonic*.

WEST SIDE MAESTRO

L does not spend a great deal of time trying to unravel the *Development's* complexities except to tell us that, ignoring both his opening themes, Mozart chooses only the little Fanfare which closes the Exposition and "puts it through its paces". L, in top pianistic form, then likewise puts the Development passage 'through its paces'. At this point Mozart's genius proves unpredictable. Earlier L explained that in the *Recapitulation* all the themes return in the *Tonic Key*. Mozart, in this instance, breaks the rules and begins his recapitulation in a foreign key before finally succumbing to the irresistible magnetic pull of his home *Tonic* to bring the movement to a satisfying conclusion. L shrugs this off as merely a surprise played on us by a genius who doesn't always play the game according to the rules but who often affords us more pleasure by breaking them.

L now embarks on his own *recapitulation* of *Balance and Contrast*. The *Balance,* he reminds his concert hall classroom, was provided by the three part Form - (A)Exposition, (B)Development & (A)Recapitulation - and the *Contrast* was provided by the shift of Keys - from Tonic to Dominant.

Highly simplistic, of course, but no more complex than it need be in explaining very difficult concepts for the first time to young minds. It should also be mentioned that the journey has been musically stimulating and highly entertaining along the way. The audience has been attentive throughout.

If only L had left it at that. Perhaps out of concern of criticism over the very simplicity that made his explanation so effective, he muddies the water by adding a whole series of caveats that would have been best left for another program or not mentioned at all.

In a thankfully short detour, L chooses now to volunteer the additional information that the contrasting Key is not always in the Dominant, that rules get broken left and right and that additional extra sections can be added at the beginning and end of a movement called Introduction and Coda. Fortunately, having already clearly made his main points, he quickly dismisses this series of additions and exceptions as something to be discussed at a later time. He goes on to say that his audience now has enough information to recognise and follow any classical Sonata Form movement. To prove it, he conducts for them the last movement of Prokofiev's *Classical Symphony* which, though a modern work, adheres strictly to 18th century classical *Sonata Form*. The performance is usefully screen captioned to enable the listener to follow its strict A/A/B/A Form. The captions indicate the shift in the Exposition (A), from Tonic to Dominant Keys, the repeat of the Exposition (A), the Development (B) section and, finally, the return in the Recapitulation (A) of all the themes in the Tonic Key.

The Prokofiev is 'meat and potatoes' for the Philharmonic. It was a great favourite of Mitropoulos, who even programmed it for the orchestra's down market two-week, four- shows-a-day stint at the Roxy Theatre, a famous New York cinema that featured an hour long stage show between showings of the feature film. This miniature symphony, in spite of its short twelve minute length, is one of the most fiendish technically difficult pieces in the repertoire and, no matter how many times one performs it, it never gets easier! Even at L's 'hyper-drive' tempo, the orchestra tosses off the final movement as if it is the simplest of works. The playing of the difficult woodwind figures is virtuoso to a point that defies description. L's conducting is again straightforward and simple, all smiles but very watchful, using for the most part tiny gestures and, sometimes, barely conducting at all, again in the style of his first conducting teacher, Fritz Reiner. Only the great final flourish on the last beat of the movement, simultaneously whirling about to accept the applause is the kind of *echt*[110] Bernstein which would have brought a narrow-eyed glance of disapproval from the martinet teacher of his youth.

The program now moves swiftly to a conclusion which, in terms of production values, is unique to this series of concerts. L prepares his YPC audience for the final work to be performed, a repeat of the work that opened the concert, the first movement of Mozart's '*Jupiter*' Symphony. Having expressed his confidence that they are now ready to enjoy listening

---

[110] *echt* - German adverb: really, truly - (not always used in a complimentary fashion).

to music even more by being able to follow the *Form* of a piece as well as the tunes and rhythms, he has nevertheless decided to give them a bit of extra help with this Mozart Symphony because it is a much more expanded and complex work than they have examined thus far. He has, therefore, enlisted the help of nine music students divided at the back of the orchestra into three groups, (similar to Three Part Form), who will hold up signs one at a time as the various elements of *Form* the audience has learned about earlier occur in the music. Finally, he tells them, they are on their own and that he hopes that, as he had expressed at the beginning of the program, they will now hear this piece "with new ears".

The program ends with another beautiful performance by a totally rejuvenated N.Y. Philharmonic.

Among the available YPC Videos, there are a handful of 'What is ...?' programs encompassing topics of such complexity that one ponders the rationality of those involved, above all L, in choosing to tackle them. In virtually every instance, each of these programs has proved to be among the most remarkable and educationally well-*conceived* presentations of the entire series. The only reservation that can be noted is covered in the 'dust jacket' of the book of the series, 'Leonard Bernstein's Young People's Concerts'. It reads, 'This book is written for young people ages 12 to 18." When the concerts were first debuted the age profile of the audience in the early years was certainly much wider. Many children looked to be no more than seven or eight year olds. As parents from year to year held onto their subscriptions with the tenacity of a Silas Marner, many of the youngsters grew up with the series from children to young adults. At the time this program was performed camera glimpses of the audience revealed that in addition to an abnormally large percentage of parents, the dominant age profile consisted of young teenagers. While there were aspects of this program that very young children might enjoy, unless those youngsters were serious music school students or were fortunate enough to have a private instrumental teacher disposed to imparting more than just a degree of technical proficiency on an instrument, these programs probably flew straight over their heads and tested their notoriously all too short attention span. For those who attended who were able to get the message, this program offered a marvellous learning experience presented in a simple and clear but also entertaining manner.

MUSICAL ATOMS - The Study of Intervals
(29/11/65)

This is the only YPC to open with an encore. Avery Fisher Hall, the home of the Philharmonic at Lincoln Centre, had turned out to be an acoustic nightmare. It had been the architect's bright idea to use, as the predominant structural material for the performing stage area, concrete blocks. The sound produced was hard and the balance, chameleon-like, changed as quickly as you changed your seat to another part of the stalls or tiers. There was a wonderful story of spurious origin circulating regarding an acoustical testing of the hall that is, nevertheless, worth retelling to indicate the problems encountered early on. Leopold Stokowski, considered a musical authority on hall acoustics, was said to have been called in with an orchestra of 100 players put at his disposal. Rather than requesting glamorously scored works by Wagner, Rimsky-Korsakov, Respighi and Ravel, Stokowski requested a single composition, Beethoven's 'Eroica' Symphony, a work written for a classical size orchestra with no trombones or percussion other than a single timpani player. This unusual request caused some confusion and concern among the architects and engineers. Nevertheless, the librarian was instructed to put only the Beethoven on the music stands. Stokowski entered, mounted the podium and immediately called out, "The first two chords only." He gave a downbeat and the orchestra responded with an incisive performance of the two E flat chords which announce the first movement. There was silence. "Again!", instructed the white haired Maestro. Once more the two chords resounded throughout the hall. Another extended pause followed. "Yet, again", was the demand from the podium and once again this huge assembled ensemble played only two solitary chords. Stokowski stood pensively without moving while the army of sound specialists shifted nervously in their seats waiting for him to begin his next test. Stokowski suddenly wheeled around and scowled, "You called me in too late!" Throwing his cashmere topcoat over his shoulders, he stalked out of the hall.

Despite the glamorous opening of the Philharmonic Hall in the presence of the President's lady, and the famous televised coast to coast perspiration laden kiss which L bestowed on the Camelot princess, the topic spoken about in musical circles the following day was the disappointment with the hall's acoustic. The worst aspect of it was the complaint by the Philharmonic musicians that they could not hear each other when they were performing, an absolute vital ingredient in a hall's acoustic properties for achieving good ensemble. The upshot was that after the furore had died down and a respectable amount of time had passed, Philharmonic Hall was closed down and the stage was entirely rebuilt, this time using a wood structure to produce a more congenial reflecting surface for music performance.

L celebrated his new concert stage with his YPC audience on the occasion of his MUSICAL ATOMS concert, conducting the Philharmonic in a showy performance of the Prelude to Act 3 of Wagner's opera *Lohengrin*. The audience for these concerts had never been much interested in the hall's acoustic. They came to see their hero. As long as they could hear and observe him in seats of relative comfort, that was good enough for them. The gesture of playing a work at a Bernstein YPC simply to show off the hall's new acoustic was most probably either a bit of publicity requested by the Philharmonic management or, more likely, it was intended to fill in time for a script which, in its completed form, ran a few minutes short of the total time slotted for the television broadcast. Whatever the truth of the matter, it proved a good excuse to test the Hall's new properties in front of a large audience on national television and, simultaneously, a positive way to fill out the shortfall of time without padding the script unnecessarily. It proved an excellent decision.

Acoustic demonstration over, the proper concert began in earnest. One cannot imagine a more difficult musical concept to teach to children in one hour than the one L had chosen that day, *intervals in music*. What could be more boring or dry! Right??? **Wrong!!!**

One feared the worst as L began by making an analogy of a single note to a proton or an electron and to two notes consecutively as an atom. You almost expected to hear a tiny voice from the back of the hall shout, 'Help!' However, within the space of the next 60 seconds, L, magician that he is, begins pulling musical rabbit after musical rabbit out of a metaphorical hat. Before five minutes have gone by, he has explained and demonstrated the concept of intervals in a lucid, simple and graphic fashion that any young mind would understand.

Teaching this complicated musical concept is child's play in his hands. In a happy audience participation segment, L has his audience singing all the intervals within a major scale from the interval of a 2nd to the interval of a 7th. Expanding upon his subject, he then demonstrates simultaneous intervals, (two notes played at the same time), as the beginning of harmony. Extending the concept further to three notes sounding simultaneously, he forms a chord.

L next plays a melody of four descending intervals, each a *major 2nd* apart. He plays this melody three times, each time with a different set of vertical intervals, (chords), underneath. Having asked his young listeners if this sounded familiar and receiving no response, he then repeats the descending intervals and chord accompaniment while singing the title song from the Beatles' film *Help!*. The young audience squeals with delight and explodes into applause.

L enlarges upon the subject of intervals to include *inversion*, yet another complex subject. He creates an arithmetic game complete with magic formula that automatically reveals what an interval changes to when you *invert* it, (make the lower note the top note). This truly is having fun with music and L accomplishes it in barely thirteen minutes. Included within this brief action packed musical roller-coaster ride are graphic visuals, such as the stretching of a tape measure one foot at a time while pitches an octave apart rise from one instrumental section to another in the orchestra, beginning with the lowest instruments playing their lowest notes and moving upwards to the highest instruments playing their highest notes. "Measuring the distance from one note to another", (in this case an octave), L explains," is how we use the word interval in music."

L devotes the next third of the program to an analysis of the first movement of Brahms' *4th Symphony*. Seated at the piano, he demonstrates Brahms genius by showing us how the composer constructs his melodies for the entire first movement on the interval of a *3rd* and its inversion, a *6th*. From a teaching point of view, this three-minute segment is top draw Bernstein. It is crisp, clear, fast moving and totally comprehensible to a young mind.

L moves on to discuss the chromatic scale. This is the complexity of complexities. Again using his trusty tape measure, he now reassigns to each foot of distance not merely the **eight** *tones* that make up the *octave* of a major or minor scale but all **twelve** *chromatic* **half** *tones* which are also contained within that same octave.[111] This examination of the chromatic scale relates to the final work to be performed on the program, the 4th movement of Vaughan Williams' *Symphony No.4 in F Minor* in which the composer thematically juxtaposes intervals of both major and minor *2nds*. L prepares his audience to recognise how these two intervals, although sharing the same name of a *2nd*, contrast in sound. The script, colourful and filled with imagery, never falters.

Not content with merely using illustrations from the scheduled 4th movement, L, at a breathtaking pace, analyses the entire symphony melodically. The language remains simple and clear as he contrasts the grim sounding melodies of the first three movements, built upon *minor 2nds*, to the triumphant resolution of the symphony's tensions in the final movement with melodies built upon *major 2nds*.

---

[111] For the non-musician, if someone will point out the note C or A on a piano and, starting on either note, you play a rising scale containing eight adjacent white keys only, you will produce first a C Major scale octave and then an A minor scale octave. If you start on any note on the piano and play the next twelve notes to include both black and white keys, you will produce a chromatic scale.

WEST SIDE MAESTRO

Unfortunately, the return at the very end of the symphony of the dramatic, tense music which opens the first movement doesn't quite fit into the Bernstein script. His explanation of this, which he admits is merely an assumption, is pithy and facile but without factual relevance; for it to be otherwise, would send him off on a long, wordy tangent not wanted at this juncture. What is wanted is for the youngsters to hear the music and try to remember and identify some of the new ideas they have learned from their remarkable teacher. This they are able to do via a performance of immense clarity and exact execution. The orchestra, themselves, enlightened by the 'boss's' explanations, seem to make extra efforts to clarify those thematic elements in their parts, which were spoken about in L's analysis. L, himself, is totally absorbed in his task. His conducting is full of passion but not exaggerated, over the top or playing to the cameras. It is exemplary in every way. The music, often considered a thorny listening experience for adults much less children, comes across with enormous energy and colour. The entire hall erupts at the end. This is another remarkable video from the Bernstein team, worthy of being nominated among the top half-dozen of the series.

A TRIBUTE TO SIBELIUS
(19/02/65)

The year 1965 had been declared Sibelius year by President Lyndon Johnson to celebrate the 100th anniversary of the composer's birth. The YPC, A TRIBUTE TO SIBELIUS, was one of several sequels of that year of celebration.

L's text begins with the historic background in which Sibelius' most popular work, *Finlandia*, was composed. He describes Finland's political domination by czarist Russia and cultural domination by Sweden. He tells of the rise of Finnish Nationalism at the turn of the century, of the re-emergence of the

WEST SIDE MAESTRO

Finnish language which had been submerged in preference to Swedish, the choice of educated and upper-class Finns, and of the final recognition of the dramatic folk sagas, epics and poetry of Finland as great and important literature. The audience is attentive as they hear of the patriotic fervour that followed the first performance of *Finlandia* and of how Russia, Finland's conqueror, so feared the music's power to stir the Finnish people that it was banned from performance for many years. L concludes by dedicating the Philharmonic's performance of *Finlandia* to the freedom loving Finns.

What follows after all this hyperbole is an under-rehearsed, sloppy performance conducted in a halfhearted fashion by L. It is a routine rendering for what, for the most part, turns out to be a routine YPC.

A regular feature of these YPC's over the years was the showcasing of "Young Performers". A finalist but not a winner at the 1965 auditions was a 20-year-old Romanian born Israeli, Sergiu Luca. On the basis of his impressive audition, L invited the young violinist to perform on the Sibelius tribute program. He was assigned the first movement of Sibelius's *D Minor Violin Concerto*. Luca in appearance is very far from the image of a young protégé, looking five to ten years older than his announced age. His stage demeanour is straightforward, totally lacking in histrionics. His performance of the seventeen minute first movement of the concerto displays passion and technical competence but little more. The concerto is a work of haunting beauty but it does not provide the kind of visceral excitement that one readily associates with the Tchaikovsky or Mendelssohn concertos or the flamboyant, virtuoso display of a work like Sarasate's *Carmen Fantasy*. It is an appropriate choice for a Sibelius celebration program but it is the wrong work for a YPC audience. During the performance, the camera inadvertently catches one child dozing off. At its conclusion, even with Bernstein rushing his young soloist to provide a bit of needed extra fire, the young audience applaud the soloist respectfully but, except for some adult friends or relatives in the audience shouting, 'Bravo!', something which rarely if ever occurs at a children's concert, there is no rush of excitement.

WEST SIDE MAESTRO

Up to this point, except for the short program note about Finlandia, this has been a straight concert. In the final twenty-one minutes, L returns to form with a clear and interesting analysis followed by an exciting uncut performance of the last movement of Sibelius's Symphony No.2. What is telling is that L manages to do in eight minutes what it has taken him as long as forty minutes to do on earlier shows, to analyse, complete with orchestral musical examples, the melodic and development techniques used by a composer to construct an entire symphony. The text, which pithily deals with Sibelius's use of a three note motive, its inversions, augmentations, diminutions and rhythmic variations and extensions, is clear and fast moving. It provides a fascinating contrast to his much-extended format of earlier programs acclaimed by adult critics on behalf of children as the most outstanding concerts of their kind ever produced. It gives one pause for thought.

The other question raised by this program is the choice of soloist for young people's concerts. Is it not more exciting and inspiring for young people to listen to and watch an accomplished young musician closer to their own age? Not all of the youngsters may rush home from the concert and begin to practice eight hours a day, but, for those who are pursuing the serious study of an instrument, it certainly provides a clear example of what persistence and practice can produce.

Finally, a word must be said regarding the production values and especially the sound balances on this show. The Sibelius program was recorded in 1965. Television had, by that time, made great technical strides. Nevertheless, over the years Roger Englander, YPC's producer/director, seems to have made no attempt to improve the visual images seen by the home audience. Unimaginative does not adequately describe them. It must be noted that by this time L himself was very much in control of everything he did. He was obsessed with the idea of the concerts never coming over as 'a show'. Although, he always made claims to the contrary, as I reminded him at a crucial point in the changing of the format to the *Omnibus* show on modern music, changing the program did not change the show's focus since, in truth and fact, *he* was the show's focus. Perhaps he was, by this time, satisfied that the show, very much his own creation, was successfully capturing his persona and ideas and those elements in themselves satisfied the production needs for television.

Lastly, the sound for this show is a bit of a mess, muddy throughout with microphone balances distorted by a constant shifting from a very distant to a very close perspective.

Except for the Sibelius symphony sequence, this is one of the few shows in the series that is dull and, to a degree, pedestrian.

WHAT IS A MODE
(23/11/66)

The televised program begins on a glamorous note. It is the introduction of colour to these otherwise staid presentations. L enters, welcomes his audience to this their 10th Season of YPC's and their first season with the addition of colour to their TV transmissions. This is why, he comments, he is wearing such a 'modishly' coloured tie. That phrase links him to his topic, *What Is A Mode?*. He goes on to explain that musical modes have nothing to do with neckties, dresses or even fashions of a musical kind. Modes are simply scales. The inspiration to present this unusual subject came from L's then fourteen-year-old daughter Jamie who was struggling to find the correct guitar chords to a Beatles' tune. He explained to her that the tune she was working on was modal in construction and that she needed to understand the modal scale on which it was based in order to find the correct chords. Enthused with her new knowledge, she encouraged her Dad to explain and demonstrate Modes to his YPC audience as he had to her. So, as she was the instigator of today's program, "they could blame it all on Jamie", he adds rather ungenerously.

WEST SIDE MAESTRO

L goes to the piano and demonstrates how scales are simply a way of dividing up the distance of any note and the same note repeated an octave higher. The difference between major and minor scales, which have dominated most Western music over the past 200 years, is the public perception that *Major* sounds happy and *minor* sounds sad. The real difference between these two modes, however, is the special and specific order of *the intervals*[112]that constitute each of their octave scales, that is, *the sequence* of *whole* and *half tones* within an octave which make up and are unique to the structure of a *Major* or a *minor* scale. One can, therefore, construct a major or minor scale by beginning on any note and then following the proper arrangement of intervals unique to each mode.[113] The entire explanation, complete with copious examples takes five minutes and is done in the simplest fashion making it both interesting and immediately accessible to the young mind.

L introduces one of Debussy's Three Orchestral Nocturnes, *Festivals*. He explains that the work is based upon modes that are neither major nor minor. Without explanation, he states that Debussy used all kinds of other modes that his audience will not know about. For the moment, however, all that is important is that they listen to the work and enjoy the beautiful sounds, which may seem "a bit strange and ear tickling." He announces that at the end of the program he will repeat the work after discussing all the modes other than Major or minor. He hopes that they will be able to listen this second time with greater understanding as to what is going on.[114] He now gives a non-musical description of the music; 'nightime, celebration, fireworks, dancing, an approaching procession, a grand climax during which the music of both the procession and dancers fuse, the dispersing crowd as the hour grows late and, at the end, the final echo of the night's festivities which hang in the air and end in a whisper.'

---

[112] Intervals represent the distance between two tones as defined by the number of half and/or whole tones between one note and the next. L devoted an entire program to this subject the previous season titled, 'Musical Atoms'.

[113] See footnote 111 regarding the construction of a C Major and A minor scale

[114] L successfully used the technique of concluding a YPC with a repeat of the opening work from an earlier program, 'What Is Sonata Form?', (November 6,1994).

WEST SIDE MAESTRO

What follows is a beautifully controlled, superbly executed performance of Debussy's six and a half minute masterpiece. The projection of the music's orchestral colours is vivid and the textures transparent. L's conducting technique is virtually pure 'Fritz Reiner' in style, full of personality yet simple and clear. It is conducting of a kind that would have confounded his critics, emulating the classic styles of the master maestros of the century to whom he had often been negatively compared. As for the Philharmonic, while the success of the marriage between Bernstein and themselves had been evident from the beginning, their playing now reached a level of unanimity of blended ensemble combined with a vast palette of sound colour and hue that was reminiscent of the Boston Symphony under Koussevitzky.

The nature of the whispered conclusion which brings Debussy's *Festivals* to an end often causes audiences to react in a muted fashion. So it proves again to be the case at this YPC. L tries to buoy things up with one of his over the top comments. It is the same knee-jerk reaction we have witnessed in other programs of this series when the audience response was less than enthusiastic. "How's that for an exciting piece", he gushes, " I find it positively *goosefleshy*!"

L goes straight to the piano and demonstrates what he has designated as the 'dance music' in *Festivals*. He plays the scale pattern on which it is constructed describing it as the *Dorian* rather than the invariably *Major* or *minor* mode. Rather than getting bogged down in complex technical explanations, L talks about the history of the *Dorian* and other Modes in Ancient Greece. In doing so, he makes this seemingly dry topic both interesting and immediately accessible. He relates how the Greek Modes were taken up in the music of Ancient Rome and later by the Catholic Church during the Middle Ages, where they were used as the basis of church *Plainsong*. The members of the Philharmonic quite wonderfully demonstrate by singing an example of *Plainsong* in the *Dorian Mode*. It is a marvellously humanising gesture that evokes an immediate reaction from the audience who applaud the orchestra spontaneously and enthusiastically. "I'll bet you didn't know they could sing, too", slips in L, getting an additional quick laugh.

WEST SIDE MAESTRO

Returning to his teacher persona, he again sits at the piano and in a few carefully chosen words explains that if you start on the note 'D' on the keyboard and play only the next eight ascending white notes, it will produce a *Dorian* scale. In fact, by starting on any given white note on the piano keyboard and playing an ascending octave only on white notes, you can construct all of the Greek modes.

L swings into a four bar intro and then croaks out a nine bar vocal of *Along Comes Mary*. As ever, the audience adore it and him and explode at the conclusion in the biggest response to anything as yet performed on the program. This song, he explains, which they know so well, like Debussy's *Festivals*, is in the *Dorian Mode*. This is not only communicative teaching at a high-octane level, it is the prototype of the rare teacher who inspires.

The revival of ancient Modes, L continues, was the result of both classical and 'pop' composers seeking a fresh sound from the major and minor modes which had virtually dominated all of Western music since the time of Bach. The unfamiliar Modes created a flavour and atmosphere of the ancient, the primitive and the oriental. He moves from the piano to the podium and conducts the opening phrase of Sibelius' *6th Symphony*, also in the *Dorian Mode*. He asks his young audience to listen for a kind of ancient, brooding quality which, in this instance, expressed for Sibelius the music of Finland.

Back to the piano for another technical analysis, examining the differences in structure between the Dorian and the standard minor Mode. In each case this involves the *7th* and *8th* steps of the octave. With the *minor scale* there is only *a half tone* between the *7th* and *8th* notes. This 'leads' to a convincing resolution, whereas in the *Dorian* scale there is a *whole tone between these two key notes* creating the feeling of an unconvincing resolution. Beginning then on the note E, L outlines the next ascending white note octave. This, he tells us is the *Phrygian Mode* which projects the quality and atmosphere of Gypsy music. He demonstrates this by playing the opening passage of Liszt's *Hungarian Rhapsody No.2* and then has the orchestra demonstrate

WEST SIDE MAESTRO

Phrygian Mode passages from Rimsky-Korsakov's *Scheherezade* and a Brahms Symphony.

Next is the *Lydian Mode*, the scale from F to F on the white notes of the piano. This Mode, we are informed is related to the *Major* scale with the exception of one alteration. The audience is asked to clap when they hear the place where the two modes differ, which occurs in this instance between the 3rd and 4th tones of each scale. The youngsters identify the difference with enthusiastic accuracy. Short orchestral illustrations follow, Prokofiev's *Lieutenant Kije* and Sibelius' Fourth Symphony. Both demonstrate the *Lydian Mode* and the contrasting inflections it can give to melodies constructed upon its scale with its raised 4th step. In the case of the Prokofiev the effect is comic, sounding like a deliberate wrong note, but with the Sibelius the effect is a brooding and distant quality. This "distant quality" is the reflection of those more remote parts of the world in which the Modes evolved, the Middle East, Greece, Bulgaria, Russia and especially, in the case of the *Lydian Mode*, Poland, in whose folk music it is a dominant feature. L plays a short excerpt from a Chopin mazurka, one of the many piano compositions based upon Polish national dance rhythms in which Poland's greatest composer used the *Lydian Mode*.

We are now at the half-way stage of the concert and, although well paced and filled with fascinating information, one is again longing to hear an entire piece of music. L must have sensed this as well in constructing his script as, with only the shortest of introductions, he is back on the podium to conduct the entire *Polonaise* from the 2nd Act of Mussorgsky's opera, *Boris Godunov* which, of course, is in the *Lydian Mode*.

The *Mixolydian Mode*, from G to G on the white notes of the keyboard, is the scale popularly used in the fields of jazz, Afro-Cuban music and rock-and-roll. For his *Myxolydian* demonstration piece L chooses *'You Really Got Me'* by the Kinks, which he renders in his inimitable vocal style to the loudest applause so far. This is followed by about five trees worth of *Norwegian Wood* by the Beatles as another example followed by a further thirty seconds of Debussy's *The Sunken Cathedral* to show that the *Myxolydian Mode* is not the private dominion of Pop Music. L then conducts *Danzon*, dance music he composed in an Afro-Cuban style using the *Myxolydian Mode*, which is part of his score to the ballet, *Fancy Free*.

Even the conducting of his own very flamboyant music does not tempt L into excess. He conducts the *Danzon* in a clean, clear and straightforward manner. The orchestra's performance is excellent but it is obvious that, especially in this work, their eyes are glued to his every gesture to pick up the slightest nuance.

L disposes of the final three modes, the *Aeolian*, the *Locrian* and the *Ionian* Modes, rather quickly. The *Aeolian*, which starts on A, is almost like the minor mode and is often referred to as the 'natural minor'. Like the *Dorian* and *Frigian* Modes, its special feature is the lowered *leading tone*, the *7th* tone leading to the octave. As for the *Locrian*, L points out that virtually no music has been written in this Mode. Its unsatisfying and inconclusive aspect stems from its unstable, unsettled *Tonic* chord formed from the first, third and fifth tones of its scale.[115] There is no need to spend further time upon it. Of all the Modes, L informs us, it is our last mode, the *Ionian* Mode, which has survived the evolution of history better than all of the others and "has emerged in glory as king of all Western Music for 200 years." Starting on C and playing up the octave we discover, lo and behold, that the *Ionian* is none other than the *Major* Mode. As an example of the *Ionian/Major* Mode with a vengeance L conducts the final minute of the Coda from Beethoven's *5th Symphony.* .

L now returns to Debussy's *Festivals*. Using a variety of orchestral excerpts, he demonstrates the several Modes which, sometimes in quick succession, are used by Debussy in this colourful work. Then, before embarking on the second scheduled hearing of this work, L expresses his hope that, now that

---

[115] The tonic chord of the Lochrian mode is unique in that it is composed of two intervals each a minor third apart. In contemporary harmony this forms a diminished chord which is, indeed, very unstable in nature. Its instability makes it particularly valuable when modulating from one key to another as each of its notes can function as a 'leading tone'.

they know a bit more about Modes, they will enjoy listening to the work twice as much as when they heard it earlier in the program.

L conducts what comes over as a rather overheated second reading of *Festivals*. Though the running time of this second performance is only ten seconds faster than the first, the effect is one of breathlessness with the Woodwind Section being pressed to the limits of their technique in their many exposed passages. The Philharmonic musicians make light work of the challenge. Their response to their conductor is of breathtaking virtuosity. One can only think back to the period just prior to L's appointment and all the criticism that was heaped upon the orchestra. At the time this program was filmed who could doubt that the N.Y. Philharmonic had again joined the ranks of the world's greatest orchestras and that, in terms of its technique and brilliance, it was in a class by itself.

This program could have been as dry as dust. The subject, presented in a straightforward fashion, would have either put the audience to sleep or sent them rushing out the doors. The fact that they didn't do either is a personal tribute to the clarity and simplicity of L's presentation. More than any of the other YPC commercially available, this program is a true personal *tour de force* for L. It is far from above criticism, especially regarding the woeful shortage of music of any substantive quantity performed. Nevertheless, the choice of short excerpts to demonstrate the different Modes, many of them from hit tunes performed by the top rock groups of the day, absolutely captivated the audience and kept them with him throughout. The script itself could not have been more lucid and its delivery more entertaining as L again displayed his unique talents as a natural educator and communicator. For young people who maintain a continued and serious interest in music, this program represents a key primary learning experience although only a secondary listening experience. It deserves multiple viewings by those even remotely interested in its subject matter and will prove a great aid in paving the way for anyone seeking a deeper understanding of how to listen to music.

Regarding the Production for this series, the sound engineering has improved considerably and the 10th season begins with the orchestral sound projected with the quality of a commercial recording. One should not dwell or continually comment on the visual production as it is much the same from season to season, straight on camera shots of individual instrumentalists or sections as they perform solos or carry the principal theme, a long shot in the full orchestral *tutti's*[116] and an understandable majority of close-ups of L at the piano or conducting. The close-ups of audience reaction are not always the most flattering especially among the very young members whose span of attention tends to be shorter than the young 'teens' in attendance. No interesting angles of the orchestra in performance are attempted and one is not aware of an evolving point of view focused upon the projection of the video pictures as an enhancing educational tool of the production.

BERLIOZ TAKES A 'TRIP'
(25/05/69)

BERLIOZ TAKES A 'TRIP' is the second program in the series of YPC Composer profiles. The 'street' title with its reference to hallucinations brought on by the consumption of hard drugs must have created quite a stir at the time, not the least of which concerns whether the overdosing on drugs is a suitable subject for a young people's concert. Is it being prudish or out of touch in presenting a program along the lines of the Bernstein script to cosmetically alter the accompanying Berlioz text so that the opiates which cause the protagonist, a young artist, to fall into a trance are referred to as a potion or a sleeping draught? It doesn't change the story or its nightmarish development in the slightest. It only robs you of a title with an effective *sound bite*. I could not help but wonder whether some member of the production team did not put this point of view forward. If such were not the case, and the addition of this script to the latest revised edition of the book of the Young People's Concerts seems to confirm this, what streak of stubbornness and self-justification possessed L to persist? Parents must have been sensitive to this issue as a camera scanning the audience at the opening of the concert reveals an inordinate number of empty seats. This for

---

[116] *Tutti-* Italian plural of *tutto* meaning 'all'. In this instance, *tutti* refers to the whole orchestra.

WEST SIDE MAESTRO

a series that was over-subscribed with a waiting list of 2000 hopefuls makes one wonder.

L enters and without spoken introduction begins to conduct the first minute of the fifth movement of Berlioz's *Symphonie fantastique*, 'The Dream of a Witches Sabbath'. He turns to his audience. "These sounds", he declares, "come from the first *psychedelic* symphony in history. The first musical description ever made of a *trip*." I pressed the reverse on my remote control and played this passage a second time to make sure I had heard it correctly. L then goes on to read Berlioz's own program note. "A young musician of morbid sensibility... has poisoned himself with opium in a fit of depression..." "Of course," continues L, in the first of two self-conscious apologies, "Berlioz did not take opium. His *talent* was his opium." From that moment on, having gone past what he must have finally acknowledged was a highly risky introduction, a typical skilled Bernstein analysis of the entire symphony begins. He explores the 'fixed idea', (*idée fixe*), a reoccurring theme which represents the 'beloved' of the young artist who is the cause of his depression and drug taking. Then, skipping the long, slow, atmospheric introduction of the symphony and beginning at the Allegro, L performs short and then extended excerpts from the first movement titled *Reveries and Passions*, which depicts the Artist's various emotional states as he dreams while under the influence of an opiate. All the excerpts are presented in overdone, highly exaggerated style to illustrate L's text. The script is graphic, the examples are well chosen and yet the initial reaction to the analysis of the first movement is one of curious dissatisfaction. I believe this results from the episodic nature of the first movement structure. Its inevitable logic only unfolds when one is allowed to follow the procession of ever rising and subsiding musical tensions that, at the conclusion, fall back to a kind of religious calm as we become aware of a progression of 'amen' chords which close the movement.

In a succinct one minute and fifteen seconds, L colourfully outlines the program for the second movement, *A Ball*. The luminosity and precision of his text is so impressive that it again gives rise to the peripheral question of why he had not, in general, chosen to use his gifts for clarity of language and vivid image to such positive, economic effect. It would have allowed for the programming of a far more substantial amount of music on a large majority of the YPC programs. The second movement is performed in its entirety.

Using substantial excerpts L lucidly reviews the program of the third movement, *A Scene in the Country*. He presents a highly abridged, Readers' Digest account of this movement. In its original form the work runs just under seventeen minutes. Here it is cut to barely eight minutes. As a marriage of text and music to create a satisfying total entity, however, this segment could not be more successful. Communication from the podium is at its highest level.

The fourth movement, *March to the Scaffold*, is introduced in a blaze of purple prose and sparkling imagery lasting barely a minute and is then performed in its entirety.

In a three minute narration well sprinkled with musical examples, the final movement, *Dream of a Witches Sabbath*, is introduced. Before he goes on to perform it, however, L adds an epilogue which, no matter how good a face you try to put on it, is little more than a self-conscious anti-drug abuse speech positioned at this point to justify the YPC undertaking the whole questionable project. I quote the entire Epilogue:

"Our hero is left in the clutches of his opium nightmare. It is brilliance without glory. That's the problem. I can't honestly tell you that we have gone through the fires of hell with our hero and come out nobler and wiser. But that's the way with 'trips' and Berlioz tells it like it is. Now there was an honest man. You take a 'trip'. You wind up screaming at your own funeral."

L certainly meant well in embarking on this project. It represents another example of his passionate commitment to a variety of causes both worthy, which this was, and, at times, unworthy upon which he pontificated from time to time. When they backfired, as they sometimes did, he sought to self-justify or simply blame others. The use of a NY Philharmonic's televised YPC on this occasion even for this worthy cause was, in my view, ill-conceived and represented monumental bad judgement.

Having pointed out the negative aspects of what I view as a wrong-headed project, I do not hesitate in stating that this is a fascinating program for a mature audience. It just isn't and, in my opinion, shouldn't be a young people's concert. The script, in form, is a carbon copy of the successful Omnibus programs L devised in the 1950's. It wouldn't come as a surprise to discover that this program was originally envisaged for *Omnibus* and had lain gathering dust in a trunk for years until, in an ill conceived decision, L decided to exhume it for a Young People's Concert. The final judgement is that while this script represents top drawer Bernstein it is more suitable for an older target audience than the one at which it was aimed[117].

A concluding word regarding L's podium demeanour for this show, recorded one year after he had resigned his position as Music Director of the Philharmonic. His gestures are less controlled, more flamboyant than in other shows in this filmed series. He is often airborne during climactic moments in the music and his two handed conducting gesture, (both hands clasping the baton, simultaneously beating time), about which much discussion has been generated among conductors, is very much in evidence.[118] The orchestra's performance is both flawless and thrilling.

---

[117] *Berlioz Takes A Trip* has now been released specifically for an adult audience on a *Bernstein Century* CD combined with a performance of the *Fantastic Symphony*.

[118] L has often been accused of being eclectic as a composer. However, his eclecticism was not limited to the field of composition. He was equally eclectic as a conductor. If he observed a gesture by one of his colleagues that he viewed as effective and, even more important, theatrical, he would adapt it for himself. Such was the case in point with the 'two-handed' gesture. In *Conversations about Bernstein*, David Diamond quotes L as saying the gesture came about through a physical necessity. 'My shoulders are in such vices... if I don't pull my arms forward, I'll never get through the rest of the work.' In truth, L pinched the gesture from Lorin Maazel. Lorin, when a student conductor at Tanglewood, was assigned Stravinsky's *Symphony of Psalms*. In the final *Laudate*, a batonless Maazel, hands pressed together in prayer resembling the famous Durer drawing, conducted the entire last section of the work using this devotional gesture. It was wonderfully over the top and suited the Bernstein *personna* to perfection. L started using the gesture almost straightaway. However, it was only when he began to use a baton that the gesture became sufficiently disguised to become solely associated with him.

WEST SIDE MAESTRO

YOUNG PEOPLE'S CONCERTS - ADDENDA

The following nine Young People's Concerts are available in an American format which consists of three concerts per videotape, unlike the European edition containing one concert per video:

1. Who is Gustav Mahler?	Telecast on	07/02/60
2. Happy Birthday, Igor Stravinsky!	"	26/03/60
3. The Latin American Spirit	"	08/03/63
4. Jazz In The Concert Hall	"	11/03/64
5. The Sound of an Orchestra	"	12/14/65
6. A Birthday Tribute To Shostakovich	"	05/01/66
7. A Toast To Vienna In 3/4 Time	"	25/12/67
8. How Musical Are You?	"	26/05/68
9. Two Ballet Birds	"	14/09/69
10. Fidelio: A Celebration Of Life	"	29/03/70

These concerts fall loosely into the following categories:

a) Brilliantly scripted and presented:
   A Birthday Tribute To Shostakovich
   Fidelio: A Celebration Of Life
b) Entertaining in varying degrees, but of a modest educational value:
   Happy Birthday, Igor Stravinsky
   Two Ballet Birds
   The Latin American Spirit
   A Toast To Vienna In 3/4 Time
c) I am going ahead with these three scripts, whether you agree to them or not! :
   Who Is Gustav Mahler?
   Jazz In The Concert Hall
   The Sound Of An Orchestra
d) Short, without much substance, but the audience loved it! :
   How Musical Are You?

WEST SIDE MAESTRO

I will begin with Category B, as I do not believe any of the programs in this group require detailed close scrutiny. Two of the four programs lean towards the 'old fashioned' children's concert, that is, a large music content accompanied by a story telling element. They are *'Happy Birthday, Igor Stravinsky'* and *'Two Ballet Birds'*. Both programs are dominated by a single masterwork composed by Igor Stravinsky, the 'Happy Birthday' program by the ballet score to *'Petruchka'* and the 'Ballet Birds' program by a concert suite drawn from *'The Firebird'*. While these programs include some pedagogical element, the bulk of the script to each concert is taken up with the story that inspired the music.

The 'Birthday' program opens with Stravinsky's own orchestration of *'Happy Birthday To You'*, which he wrote for Pierre Monteux, his lifelong colleague and champion, in celebration of Monteux's 85th birthday. Short, contrasting examples of Stravinsky's early, middle and late styles, from *Le Sacre du Printemps*, the *Dumbarton Oaks Concerto* and *Agon*, illustrate the 'ever changing, ever new, ever young *King Igor*'. L quite rightly parallels Stravinsky's musical experimentation and evolution with that of Pablo Picasso. All that takes place in the first ten minutes of the program. The rest of the program is devoted to an annotated performance of the complete ballet score to *Petruchka*. Prior to performing each of the three musical Tableaux that make up the ballet, L relates the story using short musical excerpts to underline specific dramatic imagery. It is all done in a wonderfully simple, straightforward manner. Talk is kept to a minimum and the graphic musical illustrations illuminate this highly accessible contemporary masterpiece for its young audience. The performance by L and the Philharmonic is both clean and brilliant. Tempos tend to be, in general, quick but not overtly so and the complex Stravinsky rhythms are tossed off as casually by the performers as if they were playing a work by Mozart.

WEST SIDE MAESTRO

'Two Ballet Birds' is modelled very much on the Stravinsky *'Birthday'* concert. Its script, short, clear, interesting and entertaining, avoids getting bogged down in technical terms. The bulk of the program is taken up by a performance of the complete concert suite from Stravinsky's ballet *'The Firebird'*. As in the previous Stravinsky Birthday program, L displays his gifts as a storyteller *par excellence*.

Ballet Birds opens with the Prelude to Act 2 of Swan Lake. 'Who says ballet music isn't any good without the ballet?' is the initial question posed. L announces that his program will contain music from only two ballets, both by great Russian composers, Tschaikovsky, representing the 19th century, and Stravinsky, representing the 20th. The ballets are *Swan Lake* and *The Firebird*. This leads him into a digression regarding "man's age old dream to fly" and why ballets with stories about birds are both popular and a natural symbol of the art of dance since so much of dance is a defiance of gravity. Happily, he doesn't dwell for more than a moment on this nebulous thesis. He returns to deal with a comparison of the two ballets he has chosen and their dance structure. L points to their story similarities. Both have romantic themes with mystical overtones of magic, their hero princes both discover their enchanted heroines while out on a hunting expedition and, finally, the villains of each tale are defeated in the end by all-conquering love. These are stories bathed in the fairy tale atmosphere of myth and legend.

Now comes the main thrust of the script, the two different genre of ballet that exist, one that tells a specific story and one that is abstract, "dance for its own sake, for the delight of movement, pattern and form and for the interpretation of music through the motion of the human body." We learn that *'Firebird'* is an example of a ballet in which every note is intrinsically linked to the story but that *Swan Lake* is a combination of both story ballet and abstract ballet. Although much of the action within *Swan Lake* progresses the plot forward, it is also filled with a number of set pieces, dances that have almost nothing to do with the story. These momentary diversions or entertainments create within *Swan Lake*'s narrative plot an abstract element. These dances are expendable and have a history of often being shifted about interchangeably by different choreographers. At the same time, these plotless virtuoso numbers give *Swan Lake* its place within the classic tradition of ballet, which is dance for its own sake. As an example of a "plotless" set piece, L chooses the *Black Swan Pas de Deux* from Act 3. He explains the musical and dance forms of a classical *Pas de Deux*, i.e. an *Adagio* danced by the two leading characters but featuring the woman, a *virtuoso variation* for the Principal Man, a lyric *variation* for the Principal Female and an applause getting brilliant *Coda* danced by both Principals. L relates that the music for the *Black Swan* originally appeared in Act I of the ballet but was later moved to Act 3. This, L says, underlines its rather loose connection to the main story line and justifies the changing of our perspective towards it as superfluous to the plot.

While it is true that this *Pas de Deux* is the conclusion of a long string of abstract folk dances staged in the ballet purely as an entertainment by the Prince's mother for her son's birthday celebrations, giving weight to L's argument that its function is purely abstract, in fact it is the only segment of this extended *divertissement* that actually furthers the plot. It serves as a dance of deception and seduction of the Prince by Odile, (the daughter of the evil magician of the story), who appears in the guise of the Prince's enchanted love, the Swan Princess, Odette. Throughout the *Pas de Deux* Odile receives instructions from her evil father on how to keep the Prince from turning his gaze towards the window where the image of the real Odette is frantically trying to attract his attention. Indeed so successful is Odile in tricking the Prince that at the end of their dance duet he asks for her hand in marriage and in doing so sets in motion circumstances that will bring about the death of Odette and the suicide of the Prince in the final act.

Although the choice of the *Black Swan* duet as it is used in the ballet was far from ideal in making L's point in regard to abstract, plotless Classical dance sequences contained within a romantic story ballet, L would have been absolutely correct in his analogy if he had chosen either classical *Pas de Deux* from Tchaikovsky's *Nutcracker* or *Sleeping Beauty* ballets or mentioned that the *Back Swan* is often extracted from the ballet and performed as an abstract virtuoso dance duet. An extrovert performance of this Tchaikovsky excerpt is delivered by the Philharmonic. It comes replete with a superb violin solo in the 2nd Variation for the ballerina performed by David Nadian who had succeeded John Corigliano as concertmaster of the orchestra. L's interpretation underlines his special feeling for music for the stage.

L moves on to Stravinsky's *Firebird*. While it is true, as he points out, that he has spent the first twenty or so minutes of the program on the music from *Swan Lake* without telling the story, it is equally true that it would not have served his purpose to have done so, (especially in light of his equivocal choice of the *Black Swan* as his example). The contrasting point that he now wishes to emphasise is, unlike the score to *Swan Lake* which was constantly changed and revamped at the will of choreographers, how intrinsically bound together with the Stravinsky ballet music are both story and dance. Not a single note in this score is superfluously wasted. The music and story are of one piece. L then recounts in detail the fairy tale of the Firebird, part woman, part bird, with whose help and magic Prince Ivan destroys the evil magician, Kastchei, releasing the Princess, the Tsarevna, from her enchanted captivity and returning her to the Prince's Court where they are married in a dazzling ceremony depicting the pageantry of old Russia. However, as L reminds us, the real feeling of the legend of the Firebird, the sense of very ancient times, of a primitive fantasy world of wonder, is above all most vividly projected by the magical tapestry woven by the Stravinsky score. Although he has already recounted the entire tale of the Firebird, L again pauses between movements of the concert suite to describe the progression of the story as it relates to each individual section.

The performance of the *Firebird Suite* is a display of subtle and brilliant musical colours and rhythmic panache by the Philharmonic and their conductor. It is the mark of their great musical partnership. As throughout the performance of *Petrouchka* in the 'Birthday' program the audience sits in rapt attention to a single extended masterwork responding warmly at the conclusion of each movement and then virtually exploding with enthusiasm at the end. To have created this rapport between his young listeners and the unusual contemporary music with which, from time to time, he challenged them was one of the lasting accomplishments of this series.

WEST SIDE MAESTRO

The Latin Americn Spirit

In the early part of 1963 an LP of Latin American music numbered among the huge schedule of recordings to which L annually committed himself and the Philharmonic. All the works scheduled for this recording had long been a part of the Bernstein repertoire. This same LP repertoire forms the musical skeleton of the YPC, "*The Latin American Spirit*". As a program, it is highly entertaining, jam packed with music which is colourfully scored for an orchestra loaded with percussion players creating all kinds of magical sounds with claves, bongo drums, gourds, rasping sticks and a myriad of other exotic instruments. The script for the most part is superficial, dominated by the typical standard children's concert 'instrument demonstrations' and potted biographies with a bit of Latin American history thrown in. It couldn't have taken L more than a day to plan and write. Its value lies principally in the variety, quantity and quality of music performed. Three of the compositions are by Brazilians, Oscar Fernandez, Camargo Guarnieri and Heitor Villa-Lobos, one is by the Mexican, Silvestre Revueltas, and the final two are by Americans, Aaron Copland and L himself.

The Fernandez and Guarnieri works are strictly in the 'pops' category, light listening but highly enjoyable. The Villa-Lobos *Bachaianas Brasileiras No.5* is a masterwork. Scored only for eight cellos and soprano, it is an unusual and enchanting work. This "Brazilian piece in the manner of Bach" is in two movements. The opening movement features the soprano voice blended with a solo cello first singing and then humming a long, wordless melody to the pizzicato accompaniment of the other seven cellos sounding very much like an amplified guitar. This movement has always enjoyed popular appeal and even the 'pop' singer, Johnny Mathis, attempted a recording of its haunting wordless melody early in his career. In the second movement of the Villa Lobos the spirit of Bach has moved to the background and Brazil to the foreground. Very rhythmic in nature and projecting the feeling of a native folk dance, its musical language is contemporary. It is a tribute to these concerts that the young audience, seen in many close-ups, sit engrossed, receiving this, for them, new and somewhat esoteric work in rapt silence, reacting only at the end with enthusiastic applause to show their approval.

The music of Revueltas provides the only other challenging listening experience for the youngsters in this program. Revueltas, born in Mexico at the turn of the century, became an assistant in the late 1920's to Carlos Chavez, the noted composer and conductor. Chavez, who was the dominant force in music in Mexico for more than forty years, was the first to encourage Revueltas to compose. He also dominated and controlled his colleague's life and career development. Revueltas, a broken man and an alcoholic, died tragically at the young age of 40, cutting short the brilliant career of one of the most gifted and original talents Mexico has ever produced. *Sensemaya* was the last of Revueltas's orchestral works. Originally cast as a work for voice and orchestra inspired by a poem by the Cuban poet, Nicolas Guillen, it was later rescored for large orchestra with a huge percussion section performing on all manner of unusual instruments. It is constructed upon an *ostinato motif*[119] which builds in various orchestral guises to a huge climax. Although a highly sophisticated, complex work, it is both violent and dissonant in nature in its depiction of a primitive tribal ritual involving the killing of a poisonous tropical snake. In its dissonance and disjunct rhythms, it recalls Stravinsky's early masterpiece, *The Rite of Spring*. This work, long a favourite with L, is given a marvellous performance and again the audience give it their full attention. A difficult work on first listening, it is only reservedly received by the youngsters.

The repertoire for the LP upon which this YPC program was based featured the *Sinfonia India* of Carlos Chavez. This work, however, was performed three years previously in the YPC, *Folk Music In The Concert Hall*. Therefore, for the final two works on the concert, L substituted two American compositions which have more to do with the 'spirit' in the title of this concert than 'Latin America', Aaron Copland's *'Danzon Cubano'*, also contained on L's LP, and the dance music from his own 'West Side Story'.

---

[119] Ostinato - from the Italian meaning 'persistant' or 'obstinate'. A musical figure, traditionally in the bass part, which is repeated many times unchanged and over which melodic variations occur.

WEST SIDE MAESTRO

A colourful description complete with small gestures and body movements of a Cuban *Danzon* as it is performed on its native soil is demonstrated by L. Needless to say, the kids adore the demonstration. What follows is a riotous performance of this gay, extrovert, sometimes jazzy dance piece inspired by Copland's visit to Cuba in the early 1940's. Copland, both L's close friend and mentor, is the American composer who has been most celebrated and performed at these concerts.

For the final work, L conducts a short suite from his Broadway musical, West Side Story. The Suite contains the Mambo and Cha-Cha-Cha from the Scene at the Gym, the 'Cool' ballet music from Act 2 and 'The Rumble' which closes Act 1. While the Mambo and Cha-Cha have obvious musical connections with the program's Latin American theme, 'Cool' and 'The Rumble' have virtually none. It is a lone example of careless, one would be tempted to say self-indulgent programming. The most astonishing result is that its audience reception, considering West Side Story's immense popularity and the fact that it is a work composed by their favourite conductor and 'pal', proves somewhat indifferent.

Up to now I have not commented to any degree upon the music making in this program other than to praise the execution by the orchestra. Regarding L himself one might expect that a program of such an extrovert nature would tempt him to throw caution to the wind, pull out all the stops and, as the critic, Virgil Thomson, once penned, "shimmy and shake" his way through this colourful repertoire inspired mostly by exotic dance rhythms. Just the opposite proves true. Even in his own 'West Side' music, his podium manner is very controlled. Looking back over all 25 programs filmed, one cannot help but observe that throughout L maintained a relaxed, fatherly-type teaching manner towards his audience that never failed to communicate even in those shows that misfired. Only rarely did he throw dust in the eyes of his young devotees by putting on a display of exhibitionist conducting in order to, in my opinion, try to cover up his lack of security regarding the program's musical content, which I believe was the case with the YPC *Jazz in the Concert Hall*. There was so much about L that resembled a grown up child that perhaps before a young audience, once he overcame his initial fears, he never felt the need to have to prove himself. He was one of them. He could truly act as a surrogate big brother and teacher becoming a conduit for the music without attempting to impose his physical presence in any manner that could be viewed as self-serving. While one could disagree with the choice of music on occasion, one could but rarely criticise the care that he took to insure its ideal communicative presentation. Musically speaking, L and the Philharmonic were consistently in top form.

There is one niggling quibble that asserts itself as one views the audience in each of these videos. It is a surprising one considering the degree of social conscience with which L identified himself and publicly vaunted. As the camera surveys his audience of children, teenagers and adults one cannot escape the reaction that these concerts are presented not just for middle income families but a social fabric favouring upper middle class families. It is true that television made these programs more widely accessible but in the late 1950's and early '60's not every family could afford a television set. Moreover, a television screen could never serve as a substitute for the excitement of a live event.

A TOAST TO VIENNA IN
<u>3/4 TIME</u>

A Toast to Vienna in 3/4 Time is a kind of hybrid concert entertainment staged, it would appear, to pay off a number of personal debts. L's musical affair with the Vienna Philharmonic was now in full bloom. That year both the Vienna and N.Y. Philharmonics were celebrating their 125th anniversary. The Viennese orchestra had come to N.Y. to open the season as a tribute to their American colleagues and to present them with their coveted Golden Ring of Honour as well as raise money for the N.Y. Philharmonic Pension

WEST SIDE MAESTRO

Fund.[120] In return, the N.Y. musicians were "honouring"[121] their Viennese colleagues with this Young People's Concert celebrating their music.

By 1967, the audience for these concerts, as revealed on camera, is mostly dominated by teenagers who have literally grown up with this unique series.

To begin, L embarks on a potted history of the rich musical heritage of Vienna based upon music all in 3/4 time composed both before and after Johann Strauss. To launch the program with the proper spirit and dedication to the man who immortalised and internationalised the rhythm of 3/4, L conducts the Philharmonic in a marvellously idiomatic rendition of the waltz, *Vienna Blood* by Johann Strauss II. The only serious quibble, and this holds true for most of the *before-Johann-Strauss* composers performed at this concert, is that the music is heavily cut.

As for the text, which is plentiful, we progress quickly from the designation of Johann Strauss as the composer of the 'pop music of his time', to a purple phrased description of the waltz which includes the much used adjectives 'hypnotic, bittersweet, elastic, lilting, hesitant, swooning and irresistible.' We then get a quick survey of the "holy forefather Patron Saints of Vienna", Mozart, Haydn, Beethoven and Schubert followed by a second period of Viennese glory in which the great musical personalities were Brahms, Bruckner, Mahler and Richard Strauss who were then followed by the three great radical forces in contemporary music, Schönberg, Berg and Webern.

---

[120] Although L described these two supreme ensembles as 'fraternal twins, brother orchestras', one can only begin to speculate about the behind the scenes wheeling, dealing and arm twisting that must have taken place to bring this sequence of events about. A large percentage of the N.Y. orchestra were of Jewish heritage, men who had served in the Armed Forces in World War II. The pro-Nazi leanings of Austria during the war especially centred in Vienna. This, combined with the long history of Austrian anti-semitism, caused much resentment within the ranks of the American orchestra not only towards the Viennese players but towards L himself, a Jew and the broker of the deal. There was the additional resentment that L was soon to leave them not to devote himself to developing his other musical gifts as was the claim but to switch conducting allegiances to Vienna taking with him the huge recording and television contracts that had made even a rank and file member of the Philharmonic the envy of the profession.

[121] "Honouring" the Vienna Philharmonic seems a less than appropriate phrase. It did not reflect the strong feelings of resentment within the New York orchestra.

WEST SIDE MAESTRO

Having set the perimeters of the program, L returns to discuss the origins of the waltz in both the peasant country dance called the Ländler[122] and the aristocratic court dance, the Minuet. The musical examples chosen are Mozart's *'Sleigh Ride'* from the *Three German Dances* and a heavily truncated Minuet from the same composer's *'Jupiter'* Symphony. Along the way we get a quick survey of three part, ABA, form as it relates to a Classical Minuet, i.e. Minuet / Trio / Minuet. We move on to Beethoven and his speeded up transformation of the Minuet, the Scherzo, from the Italian word for 'joke'. In a sense, the word 'joke' is appropriate. What follows is a two and a half minute version of the eight minute scherzo from Beethoven's Seventh Symphony. In fairness, one must point out that the cut-away shots of the teen-aged audience reveal faces in rapt attention. The performance of this excerpt is clean but a heavy tendency to underline musical points has crept into L's performances.

For an authentic Viennese touch, L invited two of his 'Viennese pals' along, the noted then-married husband and wife team of Walter Berry and Christa Ludwig. Earlier L assured us that "we would recall some of the moments of (Viennese) glory not in a school-teacherish way, as this, after all, was a birthday party, but in the spirit of Johann Strauss." Do we now hear our singing couple render some of the glorious songs from Viennese operetta in which they were so famed and expert and which the young audience would have adored? Not a note. Instead, using the Gustav Mahler connection as both a noted Viennese composer and as a one time conductor of both the New York Philharmonic and Vienna Philharmonic, we hear three songs from Mahler's orchestral song cycle, The Youth's Magic Horn', the last of which, written for solo voice, is divided up between the singers to create the semblance of a duet. It is well enough performed but received indifferently by a somewhat bored audience. There is much hugging and kissing of hands at the conclusion and a typical L comment when things haven't gone strictly to plan, **"Pretty great stuff!"**

L's next scripted comment is very telling and underlines not only his own reservations about this program but the flak he must have been getting from

---

[122] Ländler from the German adjective 'ländlich' meaning 'rural; rustic; from the countryside.'

all sides. "Offhand', he says, 'it would seem the worst kind of programming to have all the pieces on a program in 3/4 time and yet one never tires of it." Considering that around the orchestra some of the pundits were referring to this program as "the almost Great Waltz'[123]", a certain weight was added to the sage observation that what sometimes appears a good idea on paper often proves to be the reverse in practice.

The script continues with the anomaly between the continued fascination with triple rhythms and the natural impulses, structures and general duality of the human body, i.e.: two eyes, ears, hands, legs etc. Next follows a paean of praise for the "special touch" the Viennese possess for "drei - viertel takt", (three quarter time), and the unique lilting swing they, (alone), impart to it. Comments made to me by Philharmonic players afterwards indicated that remarks such as these which set the performance of another orchestra above theirs, whether they occurred privately in rehearsal or publicly, in this case to a viewing audience of 25,000,00, were highly resented and viewed as ungrateful after the many years they had consistently given of their best to L in concerts on home ground, on the strenuous tours to South America, Europe and Russia, and at hundreds of recording sessions. The results of whatever resentment they may have been feeling at the time of this telecast manifested itself in the closing item of the program, the waltzes from Richard Strauss' opera, 'Der Rosencavalier', (The Cavalier of the Rose), which L proposed as "a farewell, bittersweet toast to our brothers, the Vienna Philharmonic." The orchestra really pulled out all the stops to *out-Viennese* the Viennese. It is quite the most riotous, virtuoso display that anyone could desire for this extrovert work, complete with that special 'drei-viertel takt' (three-four time) lift that only the Vienna Philharmonic were supposedly capable of achieving.

I have placed this program in the 'entertaining to a varied degree' category and it certainly does possess entertainment value. The script, however, is very superficial and, as I indicated in my opening paragraph, purveys an air

---

[123] The Great Waltz: The 1934 American version of Waltzes From Vienna, a spectacular1931 Viennese operetta loosely based upon the lives of Johann Strauss, father and son, later to become a famous musical film starring the noted soprano, Miliza Korjus and still enjoying revivals.

of a 'paying off of debts', in this case a propaganda exercise by L to further cement relations between himself and his soon to be virtually full time 'Brüder', the Vienna Philharmonic. A final word regarding L's podium demeanour in this concert. From the description quoted in Humphrey Burton's biography, "he looked as if he might dance off the podium at any moment", one expected to view uncontrolled flamboyance. Actually, for such extrovert music as the Johann and Richard Strauss waltzes, L's podium manner is quite controlled and, at times, very economic of gesture. All praise, as always, to the Philharmonic musicians throughout this concert.

What can one say about the YPC titled, *'How Musical Are You?* The concert was only forty five minutes in length, short changing its ticket paying audience, the script must have taken all of an hour to conceive and the concert itself contradicted L's unequivocal dictum to his Producer, Roger Englander, that 'a concert is *not* a show!' Had the title of this program been 'Fun With Music, an afternoon's musical romp with Lenny Bernstein', it would have more aptly described what took place at Lincoln Center. The program was a kind of kitsch résumé purporting to test the knowledge acquired by the YPC audience after eleven years of loyal patronage. The music performed, all eighteen minutes of it, was very well known and had been played at one or more of the concerts. A large number of the questions posed were deliberately simplistically designed to evoke laughter and fun. Virtually all could have been answered correctly at the first concert in 1957 by most of its young, highly sophisticated, upper middle class audience who had patronized this series since its debut. Having stated all this, I can assure you that there was a 'feel good factor' enjoyed by every child that left the hall, with perhaps only a 'niggle' from the older, more sophisticated teenagers, that any political party in the world would give its eye teeth to engender among its constituents. L pulled out all the stops as a presenter, I would even venture the word 'entertainer', and there was more laughter and fun in Avery Fisher Hall that day than I dare say has been heard there since.

WEST SIDE MAESTRO

Of course, being a top drawer L-'swash buckle', although quickly thrown together and rather empty in terms of content, the concert had one sure-fire thing going for it, the personality, huge charm and popularity of its presenter. Editorial contradictions were ignored and tended to pop up from time to time. An example of this occurs at the beginning of L's quiz. Having reassured his audience that his music test will have very little to do with book knowledge, that is, " with straight information on composers, titles, themes, dates, that sort of thing", L then asks the following five questions concerning the first musical work to be performed:
1. What is the composer's name?
2. What is his nationality?
3. What is the approximate date he lived?
4. What is the style of the music, (Baroque, Classical, Dixieland, etc.)?
5. What is the form of the music, (Sonata form, Song Form, Variations, etc.)?

Not only does he ask these typical school test music appreciation questions at the beginning of the program in relation to the opening work, the overture to Mozart's 'Marriage of Figaro', but again later in the program in regard to the first movement of Prokofiev's 'Classical Symphony'. Having long learned the lessons about audience participation and the chaos that may ensue if the questions are too difficult or require more than a single word answer, L supplies the answers to all his questions himself. This also has the advantage of allowing him to pile on the jokes, behave in an over-the-top, extrovert fashion guaranteed to maintain a relaxed atmosphere and divert the audience's attention from the shallow content of a rather thin script.

As a taste of L's stand up comedy, he includes an alto saxophone solo in another batch of simplistic questions regarding the Mozart overture that evokes a tremendous laugh. Then, having asked the audience to whistle the opening to the overture, he tells them that if you *can* whistle it "you are either a genius or some sort of vaudeville act", (much laughter). He then makes an obviously absurd effort to whistle the overture himself and the audience explode with glee. More super-simplistic questions follow under the heading, "What's wrong with this picture?" In one of several mimes L conducts in an exaggerated pianissimo fashion while the orchestra plays *forte.* "I was the culprit", he says, "Anybody who didn't get that **deduct 169 points!**" (Huge laughter!).

The final 'wrong picture' again utilises the Mozart overture. It involves all the percussionists on stage hitting every instrument on which they can get their hands. The event proved to be a kind of sub-text salute to Victor Borge. One may look down one's nose at it but no one was seen rushing for the doors to demand their money back.

One is again reminded of L's protests during the Omnibus telecasts regarding last minute decisions to change the script or choice of music. "It's not what I wanted this program to be about", was his private complaint. My riposte "Lenny, the programs are about you. That's what the public tunes in for." would certainly, be applicable in regard to this musical Quiz show, (please note that I did not use the word 'concert'). Every aspect of L's talent was showcased, Conductor, Pianist, Teacher, Raconteur and Humorist and even sometime singer of 'pop' songs. I don't think the video can even begin to recreate the incredible atmosphere in the Hall that day. Without that 'magic', the value of this video is negligible to the young viewer. There is, however, the superb playing of the N.Y. Philharmonic in Mozart, Prokofiev and Rimsky-Korsakov. It should be added that all the works performed by the orchestra are available in performances found on other Young People's Concerts in the series.

Who Is Gustav Mahler?
(07/02/60)

In his biography of L, Humphrey Burton recounts a happening related to him by Carlos Mosely, the then assistant manager of the N.Y. Philharmonic. The orchestra, on tour, was in the city of Denver, Colorado. He and L were walking in one of the public parks when "a little boy of four of five marched up to L and hit him. The little boy said, 'You didn't say good night to

WEST SIDE MAESTRO

me!...You were talking about Mahler!" It seems that the YPC on Gustav Mahler had run overtime and L didn't say his usual farewells at the end. It's a wonderful story but surely something must have got lost in the retelling.

My own slight acquaintance with Carlos Moseley during the two years I assisted L at the Philharmonic revealed to me a man of great charm and impeccable manners not given to telling *porkies*[124]. I could understand a child of four or five beating up on L for having put him through an entire program of Mahler's music but, as is implied, that a five year old sat riveted to his television so entranced by the esoteric German Lieder programmed by his television musical guru that he cried himself to sleep that night because there hadn't been time at the end of the program for an *'Abschied'* - well, that does tend to stretch the imagination just a bit. One feels embarrassed to point out that L never said 'goodbye' at the end of his YPC's, he simply summed up his program's theme, announced and performed the final work, took his bows wordlessly with the Philharmonic and left the stage.

If I've given the impression that I was somewhat underwhelmed with the YPC, *'Who is Gustav Mahler?'*, I more than hinted at that in my earlier summing up when I placed this program in the 'like it or not, *that's* the program!' category. I'd often seen L dig his heels in when opposed. Only last minute panic would alter his previously 'unalterable' decisions. Obviously, he maintained his convictions right to broadcast time in this instance.[125] This program must have been the hardest going for his young listeners in all the fourteen years of presenting YPC's. The script is very long, filled with psychological musings profiling Mahler's internal manic/depressive, schizophrenic struggles as a learned and sophisticated, world famous conductor who, as a known and equally committed composer, searched to recapture the purity and innocence of childhood in his music. Of course, *who* better could understand Mahler's struggle *than L*? "I ought to know", he says, "because *I have the same problem myself*. It's like being two different

---

[124] *porkies* - short for 'pork pies' which is cockney slang for 'lies'.
[125] L recounts to his audience just before the concluding work, the 'Abschied', (The Farewell), the final song from Das Lied von der Erde, (The Song of the Earth), that his colleagues tried to convince him that this was an ill chosen choice for a young audience and that it would be met in stony silence.

men locked up in the same body and they are both one fellow called Mahler *or Bernstein!*" Whether this pronouncement was, at this point in L's life and career, a conscious or subconscious projection, it is certainly true that he held a strong personal identification with Mahler which soon developed into an obsession. He again and again drew parallels between their two backgrounds and careers. Within the first two pages of this YPC script, he mentions the conductor/composer parallel, Mahler's association as principal conductor of the N.Y. Philharmonic fifty years previously and twinning their names when describing Mahler's internal struggles as a composer.

A short excerpt from the first movement of Mahler's Fourth Symphony opens this program. L uses the contrasting gaiety of this movement to underline the personal unhappiness that Mahler suffered both externally and internally throughout his life even as he composed such happy music. As an example of Mahler's "crying voice amidst all that happiness and gaiety", L conducts an intensely dramatic and sad moment from the same symphony's *Adagio* movement. All this, we are told, is the result of the duality which manifested itself in every area of Mahler's life and career. Happily, the young audience is spared the variety of Mahler's duality which L made much of when publicly drawing attention to the close affinities between Mahler and himself[126]. L now begins to construct a dialectical hypothesis on the key to Mahlerian duality. Other composers, Mozart, Beethoven, Bach wrote happy and sad music - how does this differ from Mahler? L's answer, "...no composer goes quite so far in each direction - *so* happy and *so* sad! When Mahler is sad, nothing can console him. *It is like a weeping child* (my italics)". This is the linchpin statement not only to L's explanation of

---

[126] L and Mahler, both of Jewish heritage, began their musical careers as pianists who turned first to composition and then to conducting Both scored important breakthroughs in their conducting careers as young men. Both were men who loved and were deeply involved early in their careers in theatre, Mahler in opera and L in Broadway musical theatre. Mahler had converted to Catholicism to ensure his appointment at the Vienna State Opera, L, of a strong *Hassidic* background, married a Catholic to lend an air of respectability to his private life and thus make him eligible for consideration for important conducting positions such as the Boston Symphony or the N.Y. Philharmonic. Both men faced a reluctant musical establishment in their efforts to establish themselves as serious and original composers.

WEST SIDE MAESTRO

Mahler's nature but why he believes that young people, above all, should respond to his music. (The entire language of the script has, so far, been very 'folksy' with a large sprinkling of jargon like, "original stuff", "jolly stuff", "terrific", "being a double man", "feel like whistling", "be on top of the world", "heart-broken-sounding", *Christmassy* sleigh bells", etc.). Now comes a flood of statements in which the words and images all express the sense of childhood, i.e., "child", "childlike", "children", "young people", "sounds of nature", "birdcalls", "forest murmurs", "purity", "innocence". This is the focus and thrust of an entire page of text. It is the beginning of a subtle propaganda campaign to convince his audience why it was right to have *his* young people come to this Mahler birthday celebration. "I believe", says L, "young people understand Mahler's feelings even better than older people. Once you understand that *secret*", (kids love *secrets*), "of his music, *the voice of the child*, you can really come to love his music. Mahler was struggling all his life to recapture *those pure, unmixed, overflowing emotions of childhood.*" The script goes on like that for over two minutes with some allusion to childhood in virtually every sentence.

To close this first segment of the program, the final movement of Mahler's Fourth Symphony is performed. The movement takes the form of a song about a child's dream of Heaven. The singer, a soprano voice, "must be bright, clear and young, *like a child's voice.*" L charmingly translates the poem which is to be sung in German. The performance, for a conductor so identified with and seeking to be so specialist in the music of Mahler, is rather colourless, lacking the kind of magic and imagination to which L has constantly been making reference. The rushed tempo would seem to point to insecurity in regard to his audience's attention span. Despite the translation of the poem, listening to Lieder in a foreign tongue for a young, inexperienced audience must have created cause for concern. This musical example, in light of the previous explanation and build up, proves of little relevance to the audience except as a work written by Gustav Mahler. It is immediately noticeable that L's style of conducting is bigger, flashier and much more extrovert than at previous YPC's.

WEST SIDE MAESTRO

The second segment of the program begins with a three sentence recapitulation about Mahler's internal struggles between Mahler the conductor and Mahler the composer, between the young, happy nature lover and the tragic, tormented grown-up and between the smart grown-up and the innocent child. We then embark upon further of Mahler's inner conflicts. The script adapts a more adult tone as L speaks of Mahler's social background. Born in Eastern Europe, Mahler was to integrate his Gypsy, Slavic and Jewish heritage with the more sophisticated cultures in the capital cities of the West in which his career as conductor and composer was to develop and mature. L also speaks of Mahler's fascination with Chinese poetry and the presence of a Chinese-like tune in the Fourth Symphony. How, after writing eight huge Austrian symphonies, which followed the traditions of his great predecessors, Mozart, Schubert, Beethoven and Brahms, Mahler turned to poems dealing with Chinese concepts and wrote an hour long song symphony based upon them, which featured two solo voices. L declares this Symphony, *The Song of the Earth*, to be Mahler's greatest and "best known"(!) work. Any argument regarding the greatness of Mahler's epic song symphony has long since ended but as for its being the composer's best known work, that bit of hyperbole relates to L's script in which *The Song of the Earth* virtually dominates the rest of the program. No reference of any kind is made to Mahler's First Symphony which is, indeed, the composer's most popular and best known work.

What follows are three of Mahler's songs with orchestra, two are movements from *The Song of the Earth* and the third is *St. Anthony's Sermon to the Fishes* from the song cycle, *The Youth's Magic Horn*. There is also a short duet for Soprano and Alto, an extract from the final movement of Mahler's Second Symphony. All are sung in German. Also included from Mahler's Second Symphony is a short excerpt from the third movement which is an orchestral version of the previously performed *St. Anthony* song. It provides the second of only two purely orchestral works performed on this entire program.

It is by now clear that I hold strong reservations regarding this, in my opinion, misguided and misguiding program. Let me *cut to the chase*. The workings of L's mind in programming this concept for his YPC and then, even after second thoughts which raised misgivings, stubbornly going ahead with a script that he publicly admitted was opposed by the editorial team that worked with him, are hard to fathom. I had experienced a similar situation first hand during our working relationship. Changes in L's perception of the power he could wield became progressively more obvious with the announcement of his appointment to the Philharmonic. I wrote earlier of the free exchange of ideas which he permitted in our working relationship. As was the case with most of those who worked with L, I held a genuine concern for his welfare and the need at times to try as unobtrusively as possible to protect him from himself. In my situation, this might involve the thrust of those scripts for which I served as his Special Musical Assistant. My comments were always made privately and invariably involved something L had written which might be misinterpreted, reflecting badly upon him. Just before we parted professional company such a situation arose. L's appointment to the Philharmonic had quite naturally caused a flurry of publicity. One could walk down any street and see his picture splashed over the cover of one or several important national magazines on the newsstand. His stock in the music world had risen to astronomic heights. We were working together at the time on a television script when I brought what I felt might be a sensitive issue to his attention. For the first time he snapped back, "Who asked you?!!!!!" I replied quietly, "No one", and made no further comment on the subject, which, wisely, was eventually cut from the script. This Mahler program retains all the same earmarks of L in his most entrenched, headstrong, mode. In light of his confessed opposition of his staff, he recognised, that he was treading on thin ice. In the end, when it was too late to go back, he employed several tactics to try to lessen the impact of the idea backfiring disastrously. His conducting style became notably flamboyant and *showbiz*, something, which, till then, had been virtually absent from the Reiner-like baton clarity, he had employed for his YPC's. He also added a concluding peroration combining flattery with emotional blackmail to win the audience to his cause. As mentioned in an earlier footnote, L had chosen to close this program with a twenty minute long excerpt from the final movement of *The Song of the Earth*, which is a thirty minute song of farewell sung by a *mezzo-soprano*. This decision, L confessed, had produced the most vocal negative reaction from his colleagues. He then applied the emotional screws to his young audience.

"People were amazed", he said, "when I told them I was going to play this for you today. They said, 'What?!! Are you crazy?!! You are going to play that *long, slow piece'*, (preparing his audience), 'for young people? You're crazy! *They'll get restless and noisy'*, (alerting the considerable number of parents in the audience to keep their kids under control). Now came the challenge to his young listeners. "They won't understand it. It's too highbrow and it doesn't even end with a bang-up finish. (Another warning). It just dies away quietly. *Nobody will clap*!!!"

(Here beginneth the emotional blackmail). "**Well - I know *my* young people!** I'm not afraid to play this music for you. I know *you'll* **understand it** and **even *love* it** because *you already know more about Mahler than most people do*", (after half an hour, that's pretty good going), "and you'll understand all those *double-Ness's*, all those fights in him." L continues in this vein recapitulating the various conflict-creating duality's within Mahler's personality and along the way finding a few new clashing duality's to toss in. Then, after translating the text of the final song, he speaks of the very end of the Mahler song symphony and of its sad musical farewell in which the soloist repeats the German word *"ewig"*, (forever), again and again. L concludes, "It's almost like magic, this marvellous ending. You really have the feeling it goes on and on even after it stops. And if this magic stillness at the end makes *you feel like **not** clapping*, then don't. **I'll understand!!!'**

Of course, L had nothing to fear. The large percentage of parents in the hall and the general upper class profile of the audience virtually guaranteed that. His worst concerns were more logically audience boredom and low TV ratings. The former would be noiseless and the latter was a minimal risk as once his TV audience had tuned in, the chances were more than likely that the parents of viewers would not switch channels for the fifty-five minute length of the show especially since they were probably as interested if not more so than their children. There also existed a possibility he hadn't touched upon, that the audience in the hall would applaud enthusiastically at the end of the *Abschied*. And so it proved. Before the final chord of the Mahler had faded away, before most adult audiences would know if or when to applaud, from the very back of the hall a few individuals began to applaud vigorously. This quickly spread to the rest of the hall and before you knew it the concert ended much like all the others, with smiles, much handshaking and bows for conductor, soloist and orchestra.

As the production credits rolled past a voice-over is heard informing us that Leonard Bernstein's Young People's Concerts has received the Thomas Alva Edison Award for the Best Children's Program on television.

Jazz In The Concert Hall
(11/03/64)

Jazz In The Concert Hall opens with five seconds of avant-garde jazz played by a trumpet, two saxophones, a string bass and kit drums.[127] Over the audience's predictable reaction to these strange, less than comprehensible musical sounds, L begins. 'Now that's about the last sound in the world you would expect to hear in Philharmonic Hall.' So begins a well intentioned, interesting idea for a YPC which, unfortunately, fails in most part due to the choice of music and in part due to L's desire to stretch the borders of his YPC's just that bit too far, too soon. The judgement to go ahead with this program in the form we now view on video, as in the case of the Mahler YPC, again posits questions regarding L's use of his authority to force past his band of knowledgeable editorial assistants, his director/producer of the YPC's and the Philharmonic Management ultra radical decisions regarding program content for the YPC which carried with it a high degree of risk for the series' reputation. In the end, there was no alternative other than the gamble of losing L altogether to the YPC project. One had to take the good with the chancy. In retrospect, the benefits ended up far outweighing the

---

[127] kit drums - known in the U.S.A. as 'traps', this is the collection of percussion instruments played by a single player principally in dance orchestras or jazz 'combos'. It consists of a bass drum, played by means of a foot pedal, a snare drum, tom-tom, an assortment of cymbals of different sizes plus smaller specialized instruments such as cow-bell, wood block, temple blocks and triangle.

disadvantages and the occasional failures, of which this program is a notable example.

Jazz In The Concert Hall mostly concerns itself with *Third Stream* jazz that, as L succinctly states, "mixes the rivers of jazz with other rivers that flow down from...the mountain peaks of twelve tone or atonal music." The sound and feeling of jazz, his young audience is told, has become progressively more a part of serious American music for, (at the time of this telecast), the past forty years. This is followed by the puzzling statement that despite efforts to combine jazz and symphonic music "*the two music's have somehow remained separate*, like two streams that flow side by side without touching or mixing *except every once in a while...*" The phrase "except every once in a while" is the escape clause. It permits L to defend so broad a premise that is contradictory to the history of Jazz in relation to its assimilation and wide use in serious music composition from World War I onwards. One can only project that had not L decided to build his script upon such a specific premise which stretched historic reality, he could not have justified the choice of music by Gunther Schuller and Larry Austin, both distinguished musicians and leaders within the fringe *avant garde*, *third stream* movement, but, in terms of public perception, little known. In terms of jazz based serious music of immediate accessibility, certainly not high on the long list of distinguished world composers whose jazz based compositions would have been far more meaningful to a naive, inexperienced young audience.

The presence of Gunther Schuller both as composer and a guest conductor on this program speaks volumes. It becomes obvious during the course of this program that his influence was the major force behind this concert right down to the choice of Larry Austin's "Improvisations For Orchestra" as the major work to close the telecast.

I knew Gunther in the early '50's as the Principal Horn of the Metropolitan Opera Orchestra and as a producer for Everest Records for which the N.Y. Philharmonic recorded from time to time under their summer *nom de plume*, the *Stadium Symphony*. His father, with whom I was also acquainted, was a long serving principal member of the string section of the

WEST SIDE MAESTRO

NY Philharmonic, holding a position on the first desk in the Second Violins for many years. Gunther's work as a composer was first championed by Mitropoulos in 1956. He was asked to lecture at Brandeis University in 1957 and organise and oversee concerts of *third stream* compositions, a term he first coined at Brandeis. L had held a visiting Professorship at Brandeis from1951- 55 and maintained continued close associations with the University even after his resignation. He certainly must have been interested in Gunther's Jazz oriented Festival as he had himself instituted jazz symposiums at Brandeis as early as 1952. By 1959, Gunther had given up playing Horn to begin successful careers as both a full time composer and conductor. He formed important relationships within the field of Jazz, the most important of whom was John Lewis, a noted player associated with jazz greats such as Dizzie Gillespie, Charlie Parker, Miles Davis and Ella Fitzgerald. It was Lewis, himself a composer, who was to form the Modern Jazz Quartet in 1952 which was to be in the forefront of the presentation of contemporary jazz for more than twenty years. Lewis and Schuller established the School of Jazz in Lenox, Massachusetts, the small town adjacent to Tanglewood and the center of all summer social activities outside the music centre. By 1962, Schuller was a member of the composition faculty at Tanglewood and in close association with L. By 1964, when the YPC 'Jazz In The Concert Hall' took place, he had become a force within American music if never a household name. He was one of the authorities on Contemporary Jazz. He had been appointed Head of Contemporary Music Activities at Tanglewood for the 1965 season, within two years he would be appointed President of the New England Conservatory of Music and within five years the Co-Director of the Berkshire Music Centre at Tanglewood.

After his short opening statements on *'third stream'* 'Jazz in the Concert Hall', L floridly introduces Gunther Schuller to his audience. He describes him as a 'total musician' who writes, lectures on and conducts all kinds of music and who is the center of a group of young composers who look to him as their leader and champion. The first work performed is Schuller's *Journey Into Jazz* which, switching roles, the composer conducted and L narrated. *Journey Into Jazz* is a kind of *Peter and the Wolf* in *third stream* jazz terms. Like Prokofiev's *'Peter'*, it calls for a narrator with orchestra. In this instance, however, the orchestra includes the presence of a modern jazz *combo* that is called upon to improvise during the course of the performance. It begins in a rather conservative contemporary style but as the piece progresses the textures and musical language become more complex and aggressive. The best one can say about the narration, written by the noted writer on jazz, Nat Hentoff, is that it is simple. It lacks the charm, clarity and humour of Peter *and the Wolf* and, due to the more abstract, complex textures of the composer's musical language, it does not wed well with the music. A technical problem regarding balance between text and music that seems not to have been anticipated nor compensated for by the composer becomes quickly apparent. In order to match the text to the appropriate music, L, even with amplification, is forced to shout a good deal of the time.

The story is basically this; Peter Parker learns to play jazz on the trumpet by listening to and then copying recordings. Three times he tries to join a jazz *combo* in his neighbourhood. Each time he is sent away for a different reason, first because he can't improvise, second because he doesn't integrate his playing with the other players and third because he only plays intellectually rather than with feeling and emotion. Peter returns home and his anger at being refused a third time produces the emotional musical stream of consciousness about which the *combo* spoke. The *combo* recognises upon his next attempt that he is now a fully formed jazz musician. This takes the construct of a long 12 tone improvisation superimposed over a kind of Charles Ives string cluster accompaniment. Peter once again heads home, this time a happy and complete jazz musician who welcomes one and all to enter his room, something he had previously forbidden, to enjoy the new, marvellous music which has made his musical soul soar.

In Joan Peyser's biography of L, she recounts that Schuller told her that L insisted on a number of changes in the work and that Gunther, under time pressures and L's overwhelming personality, acceded. One wonders what L could have wanted to and, in the end, did change and whether it made a jot of difference to this charmless, un-amusing work, (at least as it seemed as a work for the concert hall). I again came across *Journey Into Jazz* as an animated cartoon produced for German television and, with the soundtrack perfectly balancing narration to music, one could at least understand what the composer was attempting. Even the ending, which just fizzles out, was made to work within its cartooned version. In the end, however, the animation remained far more interesting than the work itself.

L moves to a more substantial, less *'gimmicky'* jazz influenced work which was ground breaking and revolutionary at the time of its composition in the mid 1920's, Aaron Copland's Piano Concerto. After recounting its controversial premiere in Boston with Koussevitzky conducting and the then 26-year-old composer as soloist, he introduces the now 64-year-old composer who, for the third time, makes a special guest appearance at these Philharmonic YPC's, this time as piano soloist in his own Concerto.

The presence of the composer along with L at his most charismatic and flamboyant produces a level of intense listening from the audience. This is a marvellous work with which to introduce young audiences not only to jazz but also to accessible American contemporary music that was *avant garde* in its time and has still not lost its bite. Alongside its dissonant modernisms are wonderful, lyrical blues themes. The work is rhythmically and explosively alive with climaxes of genuine grandeur. Deservedly, it receives an excited, sustained reception from the young audience.

Larry Austin's *Improvisations for Orchestra and Jazz Trio* concludes this YPC. Austin, then in his mid- 30's and an assistant Professor of Music at the University of California was among a group of fringe, intransigent, modern composers who utilised a form of graphic musical notation and verbal directions in their compositions. His presence on this program and particularly his *Improvisations* provides the final bit of evidence that Schuller most probably extended a strong editorial influence on this mostly *third stream* YPC. Both *Journey Into Jazz* and Austin's *Improvisations* received their premieres two years previously at a *Festival of Jazz* in Washington, D.C. organised and conducted by Schuller. Schuller enjoyed a professional association with Larry Austin dating back to 1960 when he travelled to visit the academic in California to survey his music. The result of that visit was a commission to Austin to write a full-scale work for a large

WEST SIDE MAESTRO

jazz ensemble that Schuller later conducted. In 1962, Schuller began his association with the Berkshire Music Centre at Tanglewood. In light of this background, is it too far a leap of the imagination to conclude that during the next two years he introduced the idea of including a YPC *Jazz In The Concert Hall* to L during their Tanglewood summers together and that he influenced the choice of program to include two *third stream* works that he had just premiered amidst a flurry of national publicity? Had L been left to his own devices, it is my view that he would have dealt with the Jazz theme otherwise and created an effective learning experience for his devoted YPC audience.

L's introduction to the Austin work is filled with patronising, apologetic comments that reveal his concern such as:
"...He,(Austin), is an **assistant Professor of Music**, *so this is no tossed off stuff!*"
"...it is...a serious piece, *in spite of its jazz combo and hair raising ending.*"
"...you may not even realise that there is even jazz in it...!"
The last statement alone makes one wonder why L would include such a work in a concert *introducing* a Young People's audience to symphonic jazz.

What follows is a work which in the first ten seconds reminds you of the sounds Schönberg was creating as far back as his *Five Orchestra Pieces*, opus 16. Thereafter, the composer's musical voice becomes his own. It is one which only aficionados of the fringe *avant-garde* would profess to *enjoy*. One is reluctant to trivialise the work of a highly schooled musician such as Larry Austin. That is not my intention. The question does arise as to whether all the pointillist *squeaks, squawks, bangs, belches* and other bodily function sounds which inhabit *Improvisations,* no matter how skilfully one can analyse the correctness of each note at jazz seminars, justifies its presence in a Young People's Concert purporting not only to teach certain basics about an important international cultural and musical movement but to engender an excitement and curiosity about the subject which will lead its young listeners to further explore the subject on their own. In fairness, a second question arises as to whether the young are more broadminded where music of this nature and difficulty is concerned. On this occasion, the aesthetic appeal of the work seems to have centred on the unremitting violent noise of its outer movements, the mixture of Bartok-like *night music* and Chinese exoticism in the slow, middle movement and the excessive head shaking, wild arm waving and jumping about of their usually well controlled, albeit dynamic conductor.

With a powerful advocate like Schuller to guarantee further performances, the Austin work may appear from time to time in concert programs under his direction, especially on the 'university circuit'. One doubts that it will ever make a further appearance on a YPC. Among the many Bernstein YPC's, this program, except for the presence of Copland's *Piano Concerto*, could most generously be described as unfortunate.

The Sound of an Orchestra
(14/12/65)

The educational aspect of this program purported to be, 'what *should* constitute the sound of any orchestra?'[128] The program gets off to a rocky start with L's basic premise that to identify an orchestra by its particular sound is misconceived by those who consider it a plus factor. 'If an orchestra has its own sound, how can it have the composer's sound? The sound of a great orchestra is one that can change at will from one style to another.' The key word in the last sentence is, of course, *style*. All music making begins with understanding and recreating the correct style of performance for any given work. The identifiable sound qualities of the performing group of instrumentalists, assuming that it is of an acceptable quality, whether string quartet, chamber ensemble or orchestra is peripheral to the question. There is no such thing as a neutral sound from which all ensembles begin to construct their performances. Yet, this is what L seems to point to as the ideal. The sound qualities of an orchestra, the specific brief of this concert, will always reflect the training and temperament of its players, the quality of

---

[128] Author's summary and italics

the instruments they play upon, and the discipline and traditions which the collective acquires under the direction of its conductors. For example, Stokowski and Ormandy after him developed the strings of the Philadelphia Orchestra to display a particularly rich sound. Similar characteristics of beautiful string tone could equally be attributed to the strings of the Vienna Philharmonic. Yet, in comparing the tonal qualities of these two orchestras, they could not be more different. That such is the case should not be a surprise to anyone. L was simply in his *devil's advocate* mood and making a bit of mischief. His stated point was that there should not be an individual orchestra sound only a Haydn sound, or a Mozart sound, or a Beethoven/Berlioz/ Brahms/ Debussy/ Ravel/ Stravinsky sound. He is absolutely correct except that the word 'sound' is being incorrectly used here when *style* is what is meant. There is nothing incompatible in adapting the cultivated, individual sound of any orchestra to a work by Haydn, Mozart or any of the other composers mentioned. If the conductor is thoroughly aware of the traditions that stylistically shape the performance of each named composer's music and carefully prepares the music accordingly, it will sound as it should. The overall tonal characteristics of the particular performing orchestra will only serve to add an extra dimension of individuality to the performance. In the end, it is down to the conductor. If he is a fine musician, well schooled in all periods of the symphonic tradition, there should never be a problem. The sound the orchestra produces only comes under question when the authority in charge applies the wrong style to the music at hand.

This YPC opened with the slow movement of Haydn's Symphony No.88. L had instructed the full orchestra at rehearsal to perform in an un-stylistic fashion with an overly rich string tone, exaggerated accents and huge dynamic contrasts. This being the NY Philharmonic and the children not informed beforehand what to listen for, the end product was most probably thought to be marvellous by everyone. L takes an inordinate amount of time explaining the list of incorrect instructions that he gave to the orchestra. Then he conducts a series of demonstrations pointing up each of his requested exaggerations, which starts with his choice of a string section far too large. Then L performs the original Haydn excerpt again, this time with all the stylistic corrections. The reaction of the audience proves not of a kind to indicate that the repeated performance sounded much different to them. It also struck me as a bit of overkill to make a point that, from the first, had been initially flawed. In fact, L admits that he has been exaggerating and that you don't usually hear orchestras perform Haydn as he had instructed his orchestra **but** "that *sometimes* you do", at which point I wrote in my notes, "Never!"

L goes on to explain and demonstrate other aspects of style, such as "the roughness, crudeness, rage, humour and wild celebration" in the symphonies of Beethoven; the rich, warm sounds produced for Brahms; and the difference between the sound of French music and German music. Along the way L provides short analyses of the atmospheric transition to the final movement of Debussy's *Iberia* and compares its sound to the transition in the final movement of Brahms First Symphony, from an equally atmospheric slow opening to the main *Allegro*. It struck me that for the first time L had written a YPC script that was unclear and at times too abstruse for the young mind.

The next excerpt performed uses only seven players. It is the March from Stravinsky's 1918 ballet, *The Story of a Soldier*. It is another demonstration of style, in this instance the dry, clean, sharp, unromantic style of Stravinsky. It is followed by an excerpt from Gershwin's *An American in Paris*, with L again making points regarding style. Using the *Charleston* theme that is initiated by a solo trumpet, he has his player perform it as if written by Brahms. Bill Vacchiano, the Philharmonic's long serving first trumpet had played this solo in its original jazz form a hundred times and his Brahms interpretation, not unsurprisingly, does not stray very far from Gershwin. L's final demonstration is built around country fiddling. His example is the *Hoedown* from Aaron Copland's ballet, *Rodeo*. L has the Philharmonic strings perform the excerpt in the style of Bach, Haydn, Beethoven, Brahms, Debussy, Stravinsky and Gershwin - underlining his point that the job of an orchestra is to deliver the *sound*(???) reflecting the composer. For the last time, what he means is *style*. The program ends with a complete performance of the *Hoe-down* from *Rodeo* delivered in true Copland style but with a Bernstein/NY Philharmonic sound - and a very appropriate sound it is, too.

For a program about 'sound', the actual technical engineered sound was sub-standard, sometimes downright poor. The camera work had some bright moments but the director kept losing his way, calling the visuals late, resulting in instrumentalists being photographed after their solos were finished. The orchestra was not at its best on the day, either. L took a hopelessly fast tempo in the closing section of Debussy's *Iberia* creating a scramble for notes and the playing of the Stravinsky *March* was scrappy with dirty looks being showered on the orchestra by their conductor. This was not a particularly good day out for any of those involved.

A Birthday Tribute To Shostakovich
(05/01/66)

Five years separate the final two of the nine YPC films, *A Birthday Tribute To Shostakovich* and *Fidelio: A Celebration Of Life*. If nothing else, they confirm that bursts of inspiration and daring which stamp the entire YPC series as the most original ever undertaken by any orchestra were sustained to the end of the series. In my analysis of the program, *How Musical Are You?*, I refer back to my comments to L that his enthusiastic reception by his TV viewers was a personal tribute to him above his script. That is even more the case where the YPC's were concerned. No other musical personality of this century could have duplicated this extraordinary effort. This was certainly not for lack of intellect or ability to communicate in a public forum by other conducting personalities. André Previn, Michael Tilson Thomas and Leonard Slatkin have all since proved themselves highly adept as music presenters who became familiar television figures on the world's most powerful communication medium. L more than anyone else simply had it all. To his Young People's audience he was musician, conductor, pianist, teacher, raconteur, writer, big brother and friend. How many conductors would have felt so at one with such a young audience as to potentially reveal themselves to the world on international TV as a croaking, uninhibited, failed singer of popular songs. This Achilles heel only served to endear him to the young. His multiple personal and musical gifts were projected by a communicative personality which could laser its way through 6 inch thick armour plate. It displayed the audacity of a high wire act a hundred feet above the ground without a net. He dared to fail and at times he did, all credit to him, pretty spectacularly, never in a pussyfoot manner. When he succeeded, as was certainly the case in both the *Shostakovich* and *Fidelio* programs, the success was not only equally spectacular but served to set new standards in terms of what could be attempted and accomplished with young audiences.

The *Shostakovich* script is quite straightforward. There can be no denying that the writing is sophisticated in dealing with an equally sophisticated but accessible masterwork of contemporary music.[129] As such, parts of the text must have been a bit above the heads of the younger members of the audience. However, the majority of the audience, loyal patrons over the years, were by now in their young to middle teens. For them, this subject was another logical step along the path they had been treading for ten years following the Pied Piper wherever he lead them.

The script begins with a short profile of the composer which L dubs "a sort of after-dinner speech" to honour the genius of Shostakovitch. In this personal birthday toast, L recounts the Philharmonic's recent tour to Russia and the meeting he had with the great Russian musician. He contrasts Shostakovitch the reserved and shy individual with the assured international composer whose compositions reveal a confidence, ease and boldness. This points up how artists can reveal a different personality in their everyday lives from the art they create. L dwells on this contrast between Art and its creators underlining that Shostakovitch, though shy and withdrawn, had a lot to say "musically" and that very often what he had to say was noble, original and deeply moving. As a link to the introduction of Shostakovitch's *9th*

---

[129] L was to again use a shortened version of this script for his Unitel VHS of 1987 which featured two Shostakovich symphonies, Nos. 6 & 9.

WEST SIDE MAESTRO

Symphony, L points out that its creator was famous for his sense of humour and that his music includes some of the "most downright funny to be heard." Therefore, to celebrate the composer's 60th birthday in an atmosphere of fun, they are going to perform one of his gayest and most amusing works. L then begins an analysis of the Shostakovitch *Ninth Symphony* presented on two levels. The first is historical, involving the mystique surrounding the writing of any *ninth* symphony by composers who have reached this creative stage and output and who view Beethoven's monumental statement to be the benchmark to which all "*Ninth*" symphonies' must aspire. The second is a layman's analysis of the Shostakovitch symphony in terms of form and content, illustrating all key musical points with short excerpts played by the orchestra.[130]

L reviews Shostakovitch's career at the time of the writing of the Ninth. Having previously produced two large-scale symphonies, the *Seventh*, the *Leningrad Symphony*, and the *Eighth*, the composer chose to move in a totally opposite direction to the monumental Beethoven Ninth approach adopted by other noted composers. [131] His '*Ninth*', in contrast, is a miniature, lightweight affair which maintains its intent as a serious work of Art while still leaning heavily on punning references, surprises, and a general joke filled atmosphere virtually throughout. The composer does seem to tip his hat to Beethoven at a moment of feigned drama in the fourth movement when he uses a bassoon solo to paraphrase the dramatic bass recitative heard at the opening of the 'choral' movement of the Beethoven's masterwork[132]. The bassoon soloist, however, transforms this interlude of seeming drama into a little circus tune which, without pause, introduces the final movement of this deliciously satiric work.

---

[130] L uses this same script formula in his 1987 video presentation of this Symphony conducting the Vienna Philharmonic. Extraordinarily, in this video specifically made for commercial release, he does not play through the work from start to finish but, as with his YPC, explains and then performs each movement individually after each analysis.

[131] Schubert, Bruckner and Mahler all produced famous examples.

[132] Shostakovitch also quotes Mahler's 9th Symphony which underlines LB's premise regarding the composer's homage to the mystic proportions attributed by his colleagues to "9th Symphony's".

While not to be compared as a listening experience on level of difficulty with Larry Austin's avant-garde *Improvisations For Orchestra* featured on the *"Jazz"* YPC two years previously, Shostakovitch's Ninth is, nevertheless, a work of the twentieth century which, although tonal and melodic, uses a contemporary musical idiom not immediately accessible to the novice. L attacks the challenge head on. With clarity of language and stimulating word imagery, carefully chosen musical examples, enthusiasm and humour, he lucidly and entertainingly scores all his various musical points as he opens up a new world of listening for his young audience.

The Philharmonic's performance along with L's interpretation and conducting of the Shostakovitch symphony are everything one could wish for. The audience's response leaves little doubt that they have had a whale of a time.

FIDELIO: A Celebration of Life
(29/03/70)

Fidelio: A Celebration of Life opens with a brief excerpt from its overture. L introduces the opera as "one of the greatest works containing some of the most glorious music ever conceived by a mortal". He then proceeds to list all the weaknesses of this celebration of love, life and liberty. It was viewed by critics as flawed, a failure and a bore. Though often performed in Europe, *Fidelio* has never achieved popularity on the opera circuit that even begins to measure up to a *Carmen* or *Aida*. The composer, himself, was so dissatisfied with his efforts that he wrote no less than three different versions with four different overtures. Still, after all this effort, the opera remained a flawed masterpiece.

Despite his recognition of the works inherent weaknesses, which relate in most part to the libretto rather than to Beethoven's music, L sums up his own feelings towards Beethoven's only opera and also establishes why, against all odds, this program will prove in the end successful with his audience. "When it's good", says L, "it's very, *very* good. And when it isn't, - it's *still pretty wonderful!*" Thus nailing his colours to the mast, L sets out with total conviction to convince us of the greatness of this blemished masterwork. From the beginning of his first narration, which is to last fifteen minutes, there is the heat of passion and conviction. He picturesquely relates the main plot of *Fidelio*. We have already experienced L's gifts as a storyteller in other YPC's but nothing to date matches the prowess of his performance on this day. As he reveals to us the key weakness of its naive sub-plot, he evokes a huge laugh when he takes the part of the character of the young ingénue, Marzelina, and utters only a non-descript "Oh!" when she discovers that Fidelio, the disguised wife of our imprisoned hero with whom she has fallen in love, is, in reality, not a man, as she thought, but a woman.

Having contrasted the drama of the main plot with the insubstantial sub-plot, L demonstrates with short excerpts how Beethoven's musical treatment of the two story lines contrasts and differentiates the one from the other. The sublime nature of the *Fidelio* story, with its celebration of human rights and freedom of speech, its hymn to the beauty and sanctity of marriage and its affirmation of faith in God, is mirrored in a sublime score the equal of Beethoven's most inspired creations. The lightweight aspects of the sub-plot, dealing with the lives of the opera's secondary characters, receive a comic opera treatment one might expect from Haydn. We are treated to L singing and acting a fragment of two of the opera's lightweight solos arias in his best German. The audience, if not yet entirely won over, is well on the way.

Our attention at this concert, L tells us, will be directed towards the inspired music Beethoven composed to project the drama of *Fidelio*'s main plot. The four musical examples chosen to demonstrate Beethoven's genius are contained within the sequence, which opens Act Two. They consist of the prison aria of our hero, Floristan, in which he reaffirms his faith in honour, duty and a merciful God; a Duet, beginning with spoken dialogue underscored by music, sung by Fidelio and Rocco, the prison jailer, as they dig a grave for Floristan who is about to be murdered by the villain, Pizzaro;

WEST SIDE MAESTRO

a Trio, in which Fidelio, finding her husband, Floristan still alive, convinces Rocco to allow him a sip of wine while she, in a sacramental gesture, offers the starving Floristan a bit of bread for which he expresses his gratitude; finally, a Quartet in which the four main characters, Floristan, Fidelio, Pizzaro and Rocco, confront each other. Fidelio reveals her identity as Floristan's wife, Leonora. The King's Minister of Justice arrives in time to save Floristan from Pizzaro's knife. Lastly, a great hymn of salvation is sung by our hero and heroine as our villain curses his fate and Rocco, the jailer, sings of his relief that everything has ended well.

That is the substance of the entire program. What one cannot begin to describe is L's performance as narrator, atmospherically setting each scene and then, with breathless excitement, performing the parts of all the characters as he translates the texts before the singers and orchestra take over. As Beethoven's surrogate storyteller, he is irresistible. His total commitment to *Fidelio* and his eagerness to communicate and create for others a musical experience which will engender an enthusiasm for it mirroring his own combines with his flamboyant conducting style, (which includes mouthing every word along with the singers), to produce a musical event of inspired intensity. The NY Philharmonic seems a bit tentative in its attack at the start. This could be accounted for by the obvious changes which had appeared in L's baton technique or, more personally, by his change in allegiance to another orchestra. Since resigning as Music Director of the New York orchestra, L had been devoting a large proportion of his conducting schedule to the Vienna Philharmonic. In relation to his somewhat altered conducting style, the Vienna orchestra's legendary late reaction to the downbeat of its many conductors is best described in the spurious tale of the conductor who brought his baton down for the opening chord of an overture, went out for a cup of coffee, and returned in time to hear the chord first sound. L, having adjusted his baton technique to suit the late response of the Viennese orchestra, was now slightly anticipating each beat with the New York orchestra which, for ten years, were accustomed to playing exactly *with* his beat not *after* it. Even so, following an unsteady start, the orchestra quickly settles down to provide superb accompaniments in what was, for them, totally new Beethoven repertoire. Orchestras are very resourceful creatures and the adjustment to their former conductor's new 'Viennese' style is quickly compensated for by the employment of body and head signals among the various sections, especially obvious among the woodwinds, to insure a secure ensemble.

In his final words before the program's musical finale, L describes the Quartet as a transcendent creation, abstract, pure and sublime, depicting the triumph of good over evil in the highest poetic sense. One cannot project how much if any of that statement was understood by his young audience. What becomes obvious, however, following the final chord of the Quartet ending the concert is that something extraordinary has taken place. There is an explosion of applause and sustained cheering unlike anything at the conclusion of other Young People's concerts.

This program seemed on the surface to be a sceptic's delight, dealing as it did with opera, the least popular form in music for listeners coming to it for the first time, both the young and the more mature. Compounding the problem was L's choice of work. *Fidelio* would not appear to be the first choice to convert young music lovers to opera. Further, his decision to have it sung in German, a language virtually no one in the audience understood, could predictably be anticipated as a recipe for failure. Indeed, prior to the concert, had you done a feasibility study of a thousand knowledgeable instrumentalists, conductors and orchestra administrators regarding the projected potential for success of a YPC based upon Beethoven's only opera which would consist of fifty per cent spoken text and the other fifty per cent a sequence of four musical numbers from the Second Act, a solo, a duet, a trio and a quartet, all sung in German, except for some radical revolutionary among your survey team, the overwhelming if not unanimous response would most probably have been a prediction of disaster of cataclysmic proportions. By all previous experience in the field of children's concerts, such a program would have been judged to have nil chance of success. Moreover, it might further be projected that the participants would be lucky to escape from the stage in one piece, having been pelted by a non-stop machine gun spray of hard candy from an angry young horde emulating the uncontrolled mob spirit of those who stormed the gates of the Bastille. Such a concept simply wouldn't - *couldn't* work. That the opposite proved true, and quite spectacularly so, elevates this concert to a triumph of the most extraordinary proportions. On this basis alone, among all the YPC's, *'Fidelio: A Celebration of Life'* must be counted among the most remarkable if not *the* most remarkable of the entire series! L's passionate love of this work, his fervent desire to communicate and transmit this love to others combined with his ability to inspire his forces to perform it at a white heat level, produced an absolutely unique musical experience for his audience at Lincoln Center. One would be hard pressed to find another musician of stature skilled in the ability to communicate in a public forum, and I am thinking specifically of André Previn, Michael Tilson Thomas and Leonard Slatkin, all highly adept and proven music 'presenters', who could have succeeded so completely with this material and this audience. *'Fidelio'* must be counted as a truly astonishing Bernstein document

Although criticism has been expressed in several of my analyses regarding the lack of substantial musical content in a number of these YPC's, how many of the hundreds of Young People's Concerts produced annually world-wide can boast that they have successfully introduced their young audiences to complete performances of Debussy's *'La Mer'*, Stravinsky's ballet suites to both *'Firebird'* and *'Petruchka'*, Aaron Copland's *Piano Concerto*, the music of Charles Ives and Vaughan Williams, a complete Shostakovitch symphony and extended excerpts from Beethoven's opera, *'Fidelio'*.[133] These programs represent the listening summits of the Bernstein YPC's. They tower above the stereotyped children's concert bill of fare which, though successful on a basic level in introducing an interested minority of young people to *serious* music by means of classical *lollipops*, have rarely stretched either the possibilities for diversity of enjoyable and exciting listening or the imaginations of their young audiences. On this level alone, the Philharmonic concerts, warts and all, are in a class of their own.

---

[133] This list does not begin to touch upon the variety of shorter works and movements from symphonies programmed by L which included composers, such as Mahler, Hindemith, Villa Lobos, Holst and Richard Strauss, rarely encountered in the vast majority of programs designed by orchestras for its young audiences.

WEST SIDE MAESTRO

POSTLUDE

The entire fifteen year YPC series consisted of fifty-three programs. Nine of these programs were straightforward showcases for talented "young performers." In essence, therefore, the twenty-six videotapes commercially available represent more than half the scripted programs devoted to examining specific musical subjects or the lives and works of famous composers. Of the eighteen remaining unreleased videos, three celebrate Aaron Copland, the composer most represented throughout the entire YPC series. One Copland YPC consists of a complete performance by students from New York's High School of the Performing Arts of his opera, *The Second Hurricane*, another is a birthday tribute and the third is a musical biography celebration, *A Tribute to Teachers*. [134]. We can move quickly past five other programs whose content one can quickly surmise from their titles, *Unusual Instruments of Past, Present and Future* (1960), *Overtures & Preludes* (1961), *The Second of a Hall* (1962), *Alumni Reunion* (1967), and *The Anatomy of an Orchestra* (1970). That leaves us with ten important concerts whose captions make one hope that sooner rather than later they will be added to the twenty-six YPC's now available. Their designations wet one's appetite, *The Road to Paris* (1962), *The Genius of Paul Hindemith* (1964), *Farewell to Nationalism* (1964), *Charles Ives, American Pioneer* (1967), *Forever Beethoven* (1968), *Fantastic Variations: Don Quixote* (1968), *Bach Transmogrified* (1969), *Thus Spoke Richard Strauss* (1971), *Liszt and the Devil* (1972) and *Holst: The Planets* (1972).

While these programs taken as a whole represent a unique body of work, many of the scripts of the later years were not as searching or consistently of the inspired level of the earlier "What?" programs, (*What Does Music Mean?*, *What Is Impressionism?*, *What is a Mode?* etc.). The program's format had as much to do with this as anything else. There are just so many broad musical topics, sonata form, orchestration, melody, modes,

---

[134] This was a subject to which L was to return in Humphrey Burton's 1987 biographical video *Teachers and Teaching.* In this later video of reminiscence, L acknowledges his debt to the three most influential conductors in his life, Koussevitzky, Fritz Reiner, and Dmitri Mitropoulos, to his piano teachers, Isabel Vengerova and Helen Coates, to his professors of music at Harvard, Edward Burlingame Hill and Walter Piston, and to, once again, Aaron Copland.

impressionism, jazz, etc., upon which to script a YPC. Once they have been exhausted the next fertile area becomes either the music of a single composer, *"A Birthday Tribute to..., The Genius/Celebration of..."* or a single unusual work placed under a microscope, *"Fantastic Variations* (Don Quixote), *Berlioz Takes a Trip, Liszt and the Devil,* etc.". When time becomes pressing there are fillers to get you out of difficulties, *Young Performers Nos.1 - X,* Quiz Concerts, etc. Coming up with fresh, interesting ideas which would capture the imagination of young minds was the ever-challenging problem and it was a problem of L's own making. He had, after all, set his own standard at the highest level. Once other time consuming demands and commitments began to capture his interest, creating a drain on his inspiration, energies and enthusiasm, it was the international aspect of a televised YPC which had to provide the catalyst for him to continue to come up with at least one top-notch, blockbuster program per season. It was this inexorable pressure to maintain the reputation not only of the series but the world's perception of him as the foremost innovator in music presentation for young people that challenged him to his final concert in the series. Following his resignation from the NY Phiharmonic, he reduced his concert commitment to the televised YPC's to three appearances per year for the next two years, a single YPC in 1971 and two in his final year of participation, 1972.

Having worked with L from the beginning on this project and having from the first based my own children's concerts upon his *Omnibus* format even before coming to work on the NY Philharmonic series, I can personally testify to how time consuming, creatively draining and frustrating the procedure of putting such a concert together can be. It is so much simpler to program a handful of sure-fire classical *Pops* and perform them with little or no comment. Young People's Concerts are rarely more than sixty minutes in length, (if they are, they *shouldn't* be), and the *back-to-back* music approach was the way most concerts were done '**BL**' - *before Lenny!* Nowadays, most organisations feel required to provide more than a string of great and exciting 'tunes' for the children of their subscribers. Movie and television personalities are invited along, sometimes dressed in elaborate costumes, (the actor who played Darth Vador in the *Star Wars Trilogy* has even done his share of concerts), to do their star turn when the conductor prefers to limit his role to conducting the music. Only a knowledgeable, really gifted conductor/communicator, (i.e. Tilson Thomas, Slatkin), chooses to emulate L's educational approach. The shadow he has cast is simply too large.

How best can this series serve music educators and the general public? While these are outstanding examples of superb musical events for young people from the ages of 12 to 18 years of age, they resist, in many instances, being categorised under the general heading of 'concerts'. Many of them are, in fact and form, musical seminars for young minds of reasonable sophistication. Though L resisted, indeed loathed, the phrase 'music appreciation', that is precisely how many educators would view them. In the early programs, the overwhelming emphasis was placed upon a script illuminated by illustrative but mostly short musical fragments. In the course of some of the hour long programs on quite technical subjects, complete musical works or movements from symphonies occupied as little as 15 minutes of the total running time. The Oxford Companion describes "a concert" as "*the performance of music* by a reasonably large number of instrumentalists (or singers) before an audience." The early Bernstein programs may have been about music but the emphasis was overwhelmingly on discussing and analysing it rather than performing it. This changed in later years when several programs featured entire works, some of quite an esoteric nature for young ears. The variety and scope of the repertoire covered over the entire series, as continually underlined, was both astonishingly wide and challenging.

Of interest to parents is whether these programs will convert or at very least influence the musical interests and tastes of their children? I cannot envisage a young person switching from a steady diet of *rock*, *pop* and *heavy metal* to listening with his friends cross-legged in a circle to the 'three B's', waiting impatiently to discuss afterwards the musical forms, modes and subtle orchestration employed. Much depends on the young person's overall interests and the musical environment within the home. If, however, one evaluates these videotapes on a broader basis, as an inspiration for children with a musical background then they could prove an excellent stimulus in opening up new areas of music exploration for them. For instance, if your youngster is a budding instrumentalist with a burgeoning love for classical music and a desire to learn more about those 'nuts and bolts' that make pushing down a key on his clarinet even more exciting, I would recommend WHAT MAKES MUSIC SYMPHONIC, MUSICAL ATOMS: The Study of Intervals, and, though its musical content is a bit sparse, WHAT IS A MODE? The first two recommendations are not just superb music events for young people, they have to rate as among the best planned and executed music programs for the young ever conceived. I don't think these tapes will make much of a dent on a child under 12 unless listening to classical music is part of the home environment, or the child has already shown interest in other like educational videos and CD ROM programs or his Christian and middle names are Wolfgang Amadeus. There are, however, other programs in the series, of a less technical nature and with a substantial music content, that more closely resemble straight concerts. These can be enjoyed by children as young as ten. If I were planning to take a child to his or her first orchestra concert, a careful choice from the wide selection of programs available in this series, perhaps one in which L tells the story behind the music performed, could prove an exciting visual introduction to what he or she could expect to hear and experience at the concert hall.

On the broader educational level, these programs are a *must* for any junior or senior high school or recorded music public lending library. For the imaginative music educator these programs open a myriad of possibilities to expand and develop a broader range of listening and thinking for young children with a genuine musical curiosity. They certainly provide a more productive, interesting and challenging way to spend time in a general music studies class than for the teachers to sling a record on the turntable to keep students reasonably occupied and quiet while both watcher and watched catch up on unfinished or unprepared homework for their next class.

Adult education is on the rise, especially among the senior retired. This large group within society who hunger for a bit of extra knowledge and are easily identified by the oft used phrase, 'I don't know anything about music/art/opera/theatre, (circle the appropriate word), **but I know what I**

like!' would derive an immense pleasure and mental stimulation from the YPC teaching videos, (the WHAT IS.../WHAT MAKES... series) especially under the guidance of a knowledgeable teacher. They represent a doorway to knowledge that, from my own observation, boosts the confidence, receptivity and understanding of the adult listener new to classical music.

Lastly, these videotapes are a *sine qua non* for any orchestra conductor whose brief includes the devising and performing of Young People's Concerts. Though not all the programs can be viewed an unqualified success, each one is, nevertheless, an outstanding example of thematic programming. The discerning conductor can readily see what works and what doesn't. Using the Bernstein approach as a starting point, conductors can adapt it to their own style of presentation and to suit the age, educational level and musical experience of their own young audiences.

Those unfamiliar with these filmed concerts may be taken aback at first viewing. These YPC videos should be acquired for their content not their 'look'. The quality of the early black and white images tends to be very grainy and crude by modern standards. The first method of recording television programs when the industry was in its relative infancy was primitive. The now famous Toscanini videos were created by merely pointing a film camera at a television screen The early Bernstein efforts were recorded electronically but do not yet benefit from the vast improvements that were made in television recording and sound as the series progressed. The largest drawback remains, even in those recordings made in colour much later in the series, in the lack of visual variety and imagination in the use of the medium to translate the live experience in the hall into a larger than life experience for those watching a truncated, selective visual conversion onto the comparatively small television screen. Roger Englander, the producer and later also the director of the YPC's, described them as visually probably the most straightforward shows on television. For the consumer, translate 'straightforward' as a polite term for visually repetitive. It was only after I came to live in England that I witnessed on BBC TV a truly original and exciting approach for translating musical events of this nature onto the television screen.

WEST SIDE MAESTRO

Finally, these videotapes provide fascinating insights into Bernstein the conductor at the beginning, during and after his directorship at the Philharmonic ended. We observe the radical change in his conducting technique before and after he began using a baton. There is an unmistakable new economy and clarity. We witness the high candlepower and authority of his charismatic persona. We witness the razor sharp response of his musicians to his most subtle and not so subtle hand and body movements and sudden tempo modifications. This is caught in the majority of these YPC videos. After he began using a baton, we observe that it is not the Koussevitzky or Mitropoulos influence which projects, but that of his teacher during his time at the Curtis Institute in Philadelphia, Fritz Reiner, one of the great technicians in the economy of use of the baton. Lastly, we see L's return to a more flamboyant style of conducting at the YPC's following his resignation from the NY Philharmonic and the shift in his conducting activities to European orchestras, especially the Vienna Philharmonic. As for the music making, other than the paucity of music programmed in the first four years of YPC concerts, many of the early performances are very hard driven. This changes from about 1961 onwards, by which time it seemed to me that L appeared much more at ease with his young audience. The performances after 1961 are more reliable and reflect the kind of imaginative music making one had come to expect of him at his weekly adult subscription concerts with the N.Y. Philharmonic. For a panoramic view of his fifteen years as conductor of the Young People's Concerts which combines superior teaching, a wide variety of music and a portrait of the great musical partnership that was Leonard Bernstein and the NY Philharmonic here is my recommended sampling, WHAT MAKES MUSIC SYMPHONIC?, WHAT IS IMPRESSIONISM?, MUSICAL ATOMS, FOLK MUSIC IN THE CONCERT HALL, HAPPY BIRTHDAY IGOR STRAVINSKY, TWO BALLET BIRDS, and especially, A BIRTHDAY TRIBUTE TO SHOSTAKOVICH and FIDELIO: A CELEBRATION OF LIFE.

4. THE CHARLES ELIOT NORTON LECTURES AT HARVARD

THE UNANSWERED QUESTION

Prelude

Leonard Bernstein's most significant contribution to television as an innovative educator were the remarkable Charles Eliot Norton Lectures at his former *Alma Mater*, Harvard University. The time during which he delivered these talks represented a watershed in his artistic life. His many pronged career as pianist/conductor/composer/teacher and, most important of all, musical revolutionary was to alter in the years following. The main thrust of his career was to change radically. His many faceted musical talents that earlier constantly rivalled for his time and commitment were now placed to one side to be called upon only on special occasions. The creative artist would now principally devote himself to the re-creative role of conductor, re-recording his key repertoire during live performances for his new commercial European alliances using the most modern sound recording techniques developed for the now dominant commercial medium of compact disc. For posterity he would emulate Herbert von Karajan and leave his image for future generations to view by simultaneously committing to film his live concert recordings for concurrent release on video cassette.[135] Leonard Bernstein continued to be a star international figure and principal player within the musical Arts till his sudden, untimely end, but it was as a performer rather than as a symphonic composer of the first rank, his burning ambition, and the revolutionary leader, innovator and catalyst in those several fields in which he had broken new ground and set the standards for others who came after.

Up until this chapter, I have been justified in presenting my musical portrait of Leonard Bernstein as a personal *memoir*. The closest I can claim to even a remote professional relationship to L's lectures at Harvard would be my particular familiarity with large chunks of his text which also formed the

---

[135] A number of video recordings, including the Young People's Concerts, and the Norton Lectures have been made available in DVD format.

basis of several Omnibus and Young People's Concerts scripts for which I had served as his assistant. Also, as a student, I had attended several panel discussions at which L had expressed views regarding *tonality* which paralleled the underlying theme of the Harvard lectures. Nevertheless, this chapter will still qualify as a memoir but one in which the memory and experience of others will, I trust, serve to shed light in corners previously obscured by partisan prejudices which took various forms. The Norton Lectures were among the most discussed and argued over undertakings of the Bernstein career. In retrospect they can now be viewed as a key contribution to the enormous strides made in the years since to an understanding of the workings of the human brain and particularly to what now seems incontrovertible, that man does indeed possess among others mental capacities a specific innate cognitive ability for music best understood as an analogue parallel to Noam Chomsky's revolutionary theories regarding the human innate capacity for language.

The invitation to L announcing his appointment to the Charles Eliot Norton Chair of Poetry represented the ultimate Establishment accolade. This bi-annual event held at Harvard University could with understandable pride boast its historical roster of the most important contemporary writers and musicians active within the Arts of America. To this distinguished roster was to be added the name of Leonard Bernstein.

Previous Norton Lectures were technically simple, straightforward affairs. The guest lecturer stood at the podium and expounded upon his chosen subject of expertise. Afterwards, Harvard University Press produced an unadorned book reproducing the texts of the lectures. Needless to say, such was not to be the pattern regarding the Bernstein lectures. With his invitation, the 'media-machine' went straight into action. Not only were the lectures to be televised nationally but also a no expenses approach was to be adopted. In contrast to what might have been expected, L. moving between a lecture podium and the piano to demonstrate his various musical references, the full Boston Symphony and the Harvard Glee Club were drafted in to perform substantial works from the concert repertoire chosen to illuminate the text. These included complete symphonies by Mozart and Beethoven and

WEST SIDE MAESTRO

Stravinsky's hour long oratorio, *Oedipus Rex* along with generous servings of Wagner, Berlioz, Mahler, Debussy, Ravel and Charles Ives. These performances were all committed to film in advance for a multiplicity of practical and technical reasons relating to a smooth, uninterrupted flow from text to music example. The Mahler excerpt, the final movement from his *Ninth Symphony*, was extracted from an existing video film of a live concert in Vienna with L conducting his new orchestral alliance, The Vienna Philharmonic. The book of the lectures, when it finally appeared three years later, was a lavish affair which additionally encompassed action photographs taken during the video tapings, reproductions of most of the musical examples referred to in the text in piano reduction format and three seven inch LP's of music which the amateur pianist reader might view too complex for his or her limited musical technique. These recorded examples were carefully banded to facilitate their co-ordination with those places in the text to which they were applicable.

The Lectures themselves were held initially in a large cinema in Harvard Square and then repeated the following day at WGBH-TV where they were videotaped before a smaller, more select and sedate audience. Ray Jackendorf, the noted Professor of Linguistics at Brandeis University, reported that the Harvard Square performances of each lecture, attended by university faculty and students, noted musicians, music critics and the general public, were over-subscribed and that the audience responded attentively as well as vigorously and that L appeared to "love it all".

L titled his series, *The Unanswered Question*, after a short work by Charles Ives for chamber orchestra composed in 1908 in which the American composer anticipated many of the radical innovations of the musical revolution about to sweep Europe under the opposing leaderships of Arnold Schönberg and Igor Stravinsky. Despite an elaborate metaphysical subtext which Ives ascribed to this relatively short work, L. was convinced that this early *avant-garde* pioneer was posing the question, "Whither music?" Ives own clarification of the purpose behind the conception and composition of *The Unanswered Question* was, in fact, less soul searching than L.'s projection. "The work," he stated," was intended merely as a musical experiment in the logical combination of consonance and dissonance." The revelation that the fundamental question, "Whither music?", emanated from L's own inner musical concerns and conflicts rather than Ives' neither vitiated nor rendered less important the legitimacy of the enquiry. As L. was to correctly assess, this question, which began surfacing within the consciousness of the musical world after the premiere of Wagner's *Tristan and Isolde*, was to continue to dominate musical thought throughout the century to follow.

Though L presented the thrust of his overall subject matter of the six lectures to be "Whither music?", the foundation of his text was based upon a lifelong defence of tonality in music and his advocacy of it in face of the growing threat to its disintegration posed by the rise to prominence of the non-tonal *Method* used by a new army of composers who looked to Arnold Schönberg, its creator, as the true leader and innovator within 20th century music, as well as those other *avant-garde* composers who worked within non-tonal musical idioms, such as the computer dominated school of electronic composition and the musically indeterminate school of aleatory composition.[136]

In a complex series of six lectures L. diagnosed the malaise of the twentieth century's musical crisis as the struggle between tonality, which he believed to be the innate and universal root basis of all music, and *atonality* or non-tonality, which treated all twelve tones of the chromatic scale equally and independently, deliberately avoiding any reference to a governing tonal center. This struggle augured the disintegration of tonality and the fragmentation of stylistic coherence. To support his theory regarding the innate nature of tonality and the need for a tonal universe, L sought to establish that there existed a phonology of music complete with musical syntax that connected all musical language via common and discernible roots. This exploration for possible musical universals was inspired by and

---

[136] Aleatory, (from the Latin *aleae* meaning risk, hazard, uncertain). In this *avant-garde* school of composition certain creative decisions are left to the performer in regard to the ordering of and improvisation on composed fragments. In some instances conventional music notation is superseded by graphs or long lists of written instructions relating to the chance aspects which would govern performers in creating the sound combinations to be played or improvised.

attempted to parallel the work of the noted linguist Noam Chomsky[137] in his revolutionary pursuit of innate language universals. For this series, Leonard Bernstein's television persona moved into a new gear which took America's music guru down a road leading away from the mass audience which he so assiduously courted from the moment he had taken on the mantel of a super-star Mr. Chips[138] of classical music for public communications' powerful TV medium. His long-running, freewheeling balancing act between the world's of Broadway and Beethoven had tended to stamp him with a facile, somewhat lightweight, popular, (in the Kellogg's Corn Flakes sense), image. This caused him no end of personal *angst*. He wanted to be perceived and accepted as an intellectual heavyweight, not so much with the unwashed public at large but with the 'movers and shakers' in the worlds of the Musical Arts and Literature. He certainly must have viewed his appointment to the Harvard University's prestigious Charles Elliot Norton Chair of Poetry a heaven sent opportunity to accomplish this. The 'Chair', already established for more than four decades, had been occupied by predecessor's that read like an Arts *'Who's Who'*. They included composers, Igor Stravinsky, Aaron Copland, Paul Hindemith and Roger Sessions and poets T.S. Eliot, Robert Frost and e.e. cummings.

None of L's previous professional activity caused as much polarisation of attitudes among his friends, acquaintances or intellectuals within the musical or literary Arts. Even in one of the more recent volumes, Westbrook Burton's *Conversations About Bernstein*, the issue of the Lectures twenty

---

[137] Noam Chomsky, Professor of Linguistics, Massachusetts Institute of Technology. Chomsky represents one of the great innovative minds in the field of Linguistics. His early publication, Syntactic Structures, in which he developed his theories of generative grammar, is considered a turning point in 20th century linguistics. Chomsky's theories on human cognition sought solutions to the way our mental processes enable us to use language. Going beyond the study of individual languages he went in search of linguistic universals encompassing all languages from which he could derive a grammar which set out rules from which all the grammatical sentences of a language can be constructed. Chomsky's approach encompassed the notion that language universals are biologically derived and innate to the human mind. As such they have been an important contribution to the Chomskian argument that the explorations of innate universals are a step forward in the understanding of human intellectual capacity..

[138] Goodbye Mr. Chips, 1939 MGM film about the ultimate benign teacher's lifelong devotion to his students.

three years after the event resurfaces in a conversation with Jonathan Miller, the English theatre and opera director and BBC's resident medical intellectual[139]. Miller had directed a successful production of *Candide* for Scottish Opera in 1988 at which L attended both rehearsals and performances. The director, whose mostly negative comments are repetitively peppered with the word "vulgar", paints his not-too-disguised view of L's intellectual capacities as being shallow and uses the Norton Lectures as a key example. I quote Miller, (the italics are mine):

"He rather mystified and repelled everyone. They were filled with awe and horror at the same time...Of course, he was very intelligent and he had that sort of omnivorousness which enabled him to pick up all sorts of references and cross-references, and which would have helped him, for example, to give those lectures at Harvard. But *I find the Norton Lectures rather shallow. Those references to [Noam] Chomsky I think were all nonsense.* In my opinion *he really didn't understand what Chomsky was on about at all.* He just got a sort of showbiz version of it, and people were rather staggered to hear the composer of *West Side Story* mention Chomsky."

This entire sad interview reflects throughout the badly dented ego of a re-creative talent of dominant personality accustomed to being the center of attention whose nose had been put badly out of joint by the sudden arrival of a vastly more creative and talented individual possessing a far more commanding personality. Miller's interview is worth quoting, however, because it represents a proportion of the uninformed view regarding the Lectures that over the years has found its way into print and cast a shadow over what L was attempting to accomplish at the time and what, in fact, his efforts did eventually produce. Of course, Miller's vacuous opinions at this later date count for little and cannot be compared in scale with that of the music critic, Michael Steinberg, whose editorial assessment of the Lecture

---

[139] Jonathan Miller, who holds qualifications as a doctor of medicine, came to fame as an undergraduate at Cambridge along with Dudley Moore, Peter Cook and the playwright, Alan Bennett when they devised and launched at the 1960 Edinburgh Festival the brilliant satirical review, *Beyond The Fringe*. Miller directed a successful production of Bernstein's *Candide* for Scottish Opera in 1988 which accounted for his inclusion in Burton's thin but entertaining volume.

series in the Boston Herald back in the autumn of 1973, later reprinted in the New York Times, deeply wounded L and caused him to comment to his business director Harry Kraut that Steinberg's spur was personally motivated and that he had been sitting in wait to make just such an attack. Paranoid as that may appear at first glance, enough information exists to confirm L's view. Certainly, Steinberg received little joy from either Noam Chomsky himself or Morris Hallé [140]. In speaking to Steinberg, Chomsky had merely described his relation to music as that of a passive listener and he would not be drawn to comment upon or criticise L's efforts to seek an innate capacity for the human acquisition and understanding of music parallel to his own theories regarding language acquisition. Morris Hallé on the other hand had met and spoken to L prior to the lectures. Prof. Halle quickly recognised that though L's formal concept of linguistics was sound it had nothing new to say regarding linguistic science itself and L, not being a full time academic, had neither time nor patience to work out some of his more interesting ideas to their possible conclusion. However, he was equally quick to recognise that L's chief arguments were both sound and courageous. They raised questions related to the concept that the mind is not infinitely plastic; that one writes music for human capacities and that not every formal experiment is a justified experiment. This same view was echoed by Ray Jackendoff, one of Chomsky's most brilliant and knowledgeable advocates in the field of Linguistics whose credentials in analysing and assessing the important contribution of L's Norton Lectures included a sound theoretical knowledge of music along with instrumental performing talents at a virtually professional level.

That the Lectures proved so controversial and resulted in L becoming 'target of the week' is not surprising when one considers the chosen scope of the undertaking. His purpose, as stated previously, was to attempt to apply the linguistic methodology of Noam Chomsky's theory of *transformational grammar* to music, specifically in search for musical universals analogous to the linguistic universals of commonality within the world's languages. He

---

[140] Prof. Morris Hallé - noted linguistic authority in the field of Phonology and the person responsible for bringing Noam Chomsky to the Massachusetts Institute of Technology where they formed a formidable partnership.

hoped to extend Chomsky's argument regarding innate human cognitive abilities to include music. One would imagine that as outlined L had bitten off as much as common sense would prescribe for the perimeters of his six lectures but I have only begun to describe their breadth of content. L logically states early-on in his first lecture that to arrive at any answers to the question "Whither music?" one must first ask "Whence music? What music? Whose music?" This is about as broad a base one could take for one's platform. Add to this that L had begun by stating that his approach to his subject would make use of interdisciplinary methods of investigation to shed further light and understanding which would involve "quixotic forays into such fields as poetry, linguistics, aesthetics and...a bit of elementary physics" and it is astonishing that the 'rocket ever left the launching pad'.

As can be imagined from L's stated purposes, the preparation for these lectures exceeded every demand that had ever previously been placed upon his time and intellectual gifts. The invitation from Harvard to serve as Charles Eliot Norton Professor of Poetry was formally extended in 1972. It was to cover the 1972-73 academic year. The invitation embodied much more than the six Norton Lectures that we now singularly associate with the prestigious honour offered to him. The appointment also involved living at the college for two semesters as well as taking seminars and holding student consultations. This was to be the climax of his pedagogical career after twenty years as teacher to the parents and children of televisionland's *kultur-korner*. Although he was paid handsomely for his television lectures and the Young People's Concerts, L's passion for teaching was so consuming that he always gave you the feeling that, despite all the *sturm und drang*[141] and crises that seemed an intrinsic part of the production of all his television lectures, he would have gladly volunteered his services *gratis* just for the opportunity of communicating his ideas to a large public and especially to young people.[142] This passion for teaching was an echo of the Talmudic[143]

---

[141] *sturm und drang* - storm and stress

[142] L subsidised a portion of the television production and recording costs of his Norton Lectures.

[143] The Talmud - a monumental compendium of sixty-three books containing the debates, dialogues, conclusions and commentaries of scholars who for over a thousand years interpreted the first five books of the Bible, (The Five Books of Moses), applying its teachings to problems of law, ethics, ceremony and tradition.

atmosphere that had permeated his childhood within his family home and with which he identified his father and the family's distinguished religious ancestry.

Previously, format and time restrictions had always structured his televised teaching efforts. Commercial network considerations proved the key controls which held his boundless, over-the-top enthusiasm for his various subjects within reasonable confines and prevented his volatile mind not only from running on uncontrollably but moving off into unproductive and sometimes contradictory paths. No such strictures were to be applied to his Harvard lectures. It was a once in a lifetime opportunity to present his musical views unfettered and uncensored and he was going to make the most of it.

Although Humphrey Burton reports that L's "next two years were to be dominated by preparations for the Harvard lectures", one would have to interpret "dominated" in a relative sense. The list of activities undertaken peripheral to the lectures seems so long one wonders where he found time to ever complete his commitment to Harvard. L was collaborating with Jerome Robbins on the ballet, *The Dybbok*. He had begun discussions with Alan J. Lerner on their future collaboration, *1600 Pennsylvania Avenue*. He flew to London in the Spring of '72 where he succeeded the late Igor Stravinsky as president of the English Bach Festival and conducted the London Symphony in a telecast Stravinsky memorial concert for London Weekend Television. L. also served as narrator for a documentary film celebrating Stravinsky's key role in the music of the 20th century which preceded the concert. Then he was off to Vienna to conduct Mahler's *Third*, *Fourth* and *Fifth Symphonies* with a reluctant Vienna Philharmonic. From there he flew to Israel to conduct and record Mahler's *Das Lied von der Erde* as well as to accompany mezzo-soprano, Christa Ludwig, in a filmed Brahms song recital. In June he was in Washington DC to attend the second season reopening of his *Mass*. By the summer of 1972, Burton reports, not surprisingly, that the Norton lectures still remained unwritten. L was now forced to revise his schedule. He cancelled appearances in London and Vienna but continued to work with renewed vigour on the ballet for Jerome Robbins and to move forward his plans to collaborate on a musical with Alan J. Lerner. He also agreed to open the Metropolitan Opera's fall season conducting six performances of a new production of Bizet's *Carmen* which was then to be recorded. [144]

Despite finding himself in the position of having written no substantial amount of organised text for his spring lectures, L took up residence at Eliot House in the autumn of 1972. He soon made the acquaintance of Irving Singer, Professor of Moral Philosophy at Harvard and Tutor at Eliot House at that time. Professor Singer proved to be one of L's great allies and advisors during his stay at Harvard.[145]

Production decisions were moving forward even if scripts were not. Orchestral excerpts were to be filmed in advance and projected onto a screen during the lectures. L's new business manager, Harry Kraut, recruited from the Boston Symphony, would handle the commercial aspects related to television, recording and book rights. Robert Saudek, executive producer of L's *Omnibus* lectures was brought in to administer a similar role and Mary Ahearn, Saudek's chief editor, and Thomas Cothran were to serve as L's script and research assistants. Boston's educational station, WGBH, had agreed to make their facilities available for the recording of the lectures under studio conditions.

L. was feted during his autumn stay at Harvard. Although fulfilling some of his educational commitments to the students, his concentration seemed devoted to luxuriating in being the man of the hour. The scripts to the lectures remained unwritten when he left to resume his professional career. The inevitable consequence was that by the Spring of 1973 it became obvious that he would not be ready to deliver the lectures as planned. Such a happening would have been unthinkable in relation to his earlier television commitments to *Omnibus* or the NY Philharmonic. Deadlines were there to

---

[144] Following the Carmen recording L parted company with CBS Records to join Deutsche Grammophon. He did make a final recording for CBS of Stravinsky's *Oedipus Rex* with the Boston Symphony which did serve to help prepare this work for the later television recording used in his final Norton Lecture.

[145] In the Author's Note to the book edition of the Lectures special thanks is expressed to Prof Singer by L.

be met even if it meant, as it often did, burning the midnight oil for days on end. Now L's celebrity had made him a law unto himself and the degree of indulgence which he expected and which was conceded to him became characteristic within his professional life. It reflected badly on his integrity and professionalism but that never seemed to enter into the equation or deter him. Harvard proved no different than other authoritarian figures encountered in his career. His schedule was rejuggled without a word of protest so that he could fulfil his pedagogical duties in the late spring and then deliver his lectures the following autumn.

In the spring he was back at Harvard with his team of editors and an army of typists setting about in earnest to complete his lectures. Humphrey Burton writes of L's countless drafts that kept the staff busy typing and re-typing and indicates that by the end of May "only the finishing touches to the lectures themselves were still awaited." This report is directly at odds with descriptions of the state of affairs by Irving Singer and Mary Ahearn. According to both Prof. Singer and Ms. Ahearn, the scripts did not reach their final form till just prior to each lecture, which to me rings true and is a replay of the scenario of virtually every telecast for which I served as L's music assistant. L's mind was too volatile to let anything sit undisturbed for more than a day. There were always improvements to be made, new ideas to be integrated, flashes of inspiration which involved discarding whole blocks of text and rewrites. Life was never Arcadian during the formative period which shaped a Bernstein project.

A vast amount of research and editorial responsibility was delegated to Tom Cothran and Mary Ahearn. As a result, in the case of Cothran, it has been alluded in print and was certainly grist for the gossip mill at that time that his participation in assisting L amounted to a degree of co-authorship of the Lectures. Mary Ahearn personally made it unequivocally clear to me that such a suggestion was "preposterous". She described L as agonising over the deductions he was making, that he was ever aware of the important questions that his presented conclusions might raise for further study. The famous trademark of all his lectures, a small mountain of yellow legal pads all containing his original hand written drafts, are testimony to this and are now available for research purposes in the Library of Congress.

In the midst of all the activity L was equally busy doing a good deal of supplementary homework deepening his understanding of Chomskian linguistics. L's admiration of Noam Chomsky verged almost upon hero worship. It was not only the intellectual brilliance of the social scientist that evoked such strong emotion but Chomsky's undeterred commitment to political action. The combination of intellectual heavyweight and social activist mirrored a role that L would have chosen for himself had not career compromises dictated safer paths along the way. L was a late convert to Chomskian linguistics and psycholinguistics[146]. He first read Chomsky's *Language and Mind* in 1969 which contains the large proportion of ideas to which he would make reference in his Norton lectures. L was deeply concerned with the correctness, authority and manner with which he presented Chomsky's theories of *transformational grammar* and innate linguistic competence. If he intended to construct persuasive relevant analogies from them, which could equally be seen to point towards the existence of a similar innate *musical* competence, his knowledge and presentation of Chomsky's theories had to be convincing and not carry the stigma of superficiality or the accusation of dilettante. To this end, he devoted himself to acquiring a considerable knowledge on the subject for someone who had never been trained over a long period of time in linguistics. It was Prof. Donald C. Freeman, formerly of Harvard and now on the faculty of the University of Southern California, who, at the time, helped L. clarify the linguistic aspects of the Norton texts. During my research, Prof. Freeman wrote to me in enthusiastic terms of the remarkable amount of effort L put in to realise a firm grasp of linguistic theory.

For those in his audience relatively unfamiliar with the work of Noam Chomsky upon whose theories he would construct his own musical thesis, L. expounded upon and provided in his first three Lectures a potted version of

---

[146] Psycholinguistics is the branch of linguistic studies which deals with the relationship between language and the mind, focusing principally on how language is acquired, stored and, at times, lost.

the three disciplines of Linguistics, phonology, syntax and semantics[147]. The emphasis of the final three Lectures was predominantly on music, specifically tracing the crisis which developed out of the nineteenth century's unceasing search for "bigger and better harmonic ambiguities" which climaxed in Wagner's *Tristan und Isolde* and brought about a crisis which was to split musical thought into two opposing camps for the whole of the 20th century.

In writing about the Lectures, I found myself faced with a conflict of historical writing styles. As the videotapes, from which I principally worked, represent a moment frozen in time, I have chosen to describe the Lectures and L's performance as recorded live on video in the present tense. The historical background to the Lectures themselves plus the additional material that I have added to amplify the musical personalities or eras spoken about will be treated in the historic past.

---

[147] Phonology is the study of sounds and combination of sounds in a given language Syntax is the arrangement of words into larger units, i.e.: phrases, clauses, sentences Semantics is the study of meaning in language

WEST SIDE MAESTRO

Fugue

I will begin with an overview of the content of the Lectures themselves and their place, relevance and importance in the multiplicity of activities within the Bernstein career. In their totality, they represent simultaneous in-depth portraits of the musician, conductor, instrumentalist, composer and voraciously curious intellectual. L's natural gifts as a teacher had already been confirmed and documented in his *Omnibus* lectures and *Young People's Concerts* telecasts.

One has to agree with the caveat expressed in Burton's Bernstein biography regarding the Lectures when presented in live forum. Humphrey Burton, in commenting on the length and complexity of each lecture was not being over-critical when he assessed the text with its many interdisciplinary cross-references to not only have been beyond the capacity of the average listener but "tough going even for Harvard students" who were in attendance. Nevertheless, having accepted Burton's assessment as accurate, we now have the advantage of gaining a greater understanding of the multiplicity of ideas poured out during the course of the Lectures via a marvellously annotated book of the texts, (sadly with the recorded musical examples no longer on offer as a supplementary feature), and six videos, (now available on DVD), of the original lectures themselves, which, for the truly interested, provides an indispensable companion to the printed text, recreates the level of excitement and adrenaline experienced by those in the TV studio audience and includes all the musical examples performed by L at the piano or conducting the Boston Symphony. These accurate journals permit one to ponder and absorb L's various fascinating ideas and projections at a pace which is far more rewarding than was allowed to those who had to grasp at the initial go "a rich melange of brilliant and wild theoretical speculations, illuminating descriptions of a variety of musical phenomena and just plain personality - a multi-media, multi-disciplinary happening."[148]

---

[148] From a review article by Ray Jackendoff of the book, 'The Unanswered Question' by Leonard Bernstein; Language: Volume 53, No.4 (1977)

WEST SIDE MAESTRO

In the first three Lectures, L explored the way classical music from the 18th and 19th centuries could be analysed and understood using ideas and techniques analogous to those envisaged by Noam Chomsky's when he conceived his linguistic theory of *transformational grammar*.[149] L's search was aimed at determining a genetically innate capacity for music parallel to Chomsky's revolutionary projection of an innate human capacity for language. Does the human brain possess, as Chomsky projects for language, a built in set of rules, which, in the case of music, would be a pre-existing *musical* grammar, which enables us from the earliest age to respond in an organised fashion to music? If it does, as seems incontrovertible in the case with language, there must be present *musical universals* that can be traced within all the world's cultures. L's passionate cause, and passion is the operative word, was his unshakeable belief in the innateness of *tonality* in music. It is the underlying theme of the entire lecture series. For him, summing up his beliefs in his final peroration, "Music, no matter the style, emanates from a genetically formed innate response in the human subconscious wherein are rooted the universals of *tonality* and language." If L's beliefs could be proved it would therefore follow that *tonality* in music was not only an immutable fact but a universal one as well.

The opening three Lectures formed a neat package, each Lecture examining aspects of music using techniques employed in the three disciplines of Linguistics, *Phonology*, *Syntax* and *Semantics*. The first Lecture explored music and language via their sound, their *Phonology*. It was the obvious place to begin a search for *substantive musical universals* comparable to *phonological universals*, (musical sound patterns comparable to the language sound patterns shared by the world's languages). The presence of such *substantive universals* would immediately point to the existence of an

---

[149] *Transformational grammar*: a model of grammar which attempts to replicate and explain the linguistic abilities of native speakers on two levels, a deep structure level and a surface structure level and which then sets out to clarify how these two levels relate to each other. The transformations themselves represent mental operations of addition, deletion, transposition and substitution within sentences or parts of sentences which convert them from their deep structure form to their surface structure form. A prototype example of transformation is seen in the relationship between active and passive sentences, i.e.: The cat ate the mouse (Active form); The mouse was eaten by the cat (Passive form).

innate musical competence parallel to the linguistic competence predicated by Chomsky.

L's began by posing two questions for himself, "Where do ...notes come from?" and "Why do our ears select certain notes and not others?". For L, a ready-made answer was to be found in what he viewed as a preordained *musical universal* within Nature, the acoustical phenomenon called the *harmonic* or *overtone series* from which the entire grammar of tonal relationships and harmony in Western music were eventually developed. It was a subject upon which he had already expanded fully in an *Omnibus* television lecture.[150] Indeed, when I spoke to Mary Ahearne in New York she told me that L was at first reluctant to rehash a thesis that he had previously dealt with in some detail on television. Nevertheless he felt his argument gained in power by being able to immediately show the existence of a *musical universal* that possessed psychological as well as physical relevance. Thus it became one of the foundation pillars of his first Norton Lecture and a first step in his journey to prove the innate nature of *tonality* and the need for a *tonal* universe.

The first Lecture encompassed, among a variety of explorations, an introduction to *monogenesis*, the theory that all languages spring from a single source. Imagining himself a hominid[151] baby, L presents us with a theoretical speculation of the genesis of the sound *Ma* stretching from the hungry infant producing the sound *Mmm-* to attract attention to that instant when baby opens its mouth to suckle producing the sound *MMM-AAA*, which evolved to be among the first proto-words, that for "mother". L further suggests and demonstrates how a wide variety of human emotions might have found expression through pitch variation, upward or downward, to these proto-syllables. It's worth purchasing the video for this segment alone. Its pure show-business and in turns wonderful, interesting, stimulating and informative as L proceeds to explain other words developed

---

[150] L demonstrated the overtone series without Chomskian associations in his *Omnibus* lecture of 1957, An Introduction to Modern Music.
[151] hominid - in this instance a member of the family of fossil man

from proto-syllables like *mal* and *grrr* which we now associate with either *smallness* or *something bad* and *largeness*.[152] .

A discussion of overtones and the development of ever more complex harmony and harmonic relationships follows. L presents an extended analysis of overtones from a single *fundamental* note to the *tonal* relationship between the *fundamental*, (which was given the name *tonic*), and its first *different* overtone a fifth higher (designated the *dominant*). With the discovery and absorption of more overtones into usage, more complex relationships arose. The major triad, formed from the first four overtones, was destined to become the cornerstone of Western music. Thus the beginnings of tonal music were fashioned from the basic notes of the harmonic series. "Elsewhere", as L's argument continued, "the genetically endowed capacity for musical competence allowed the world's peoples to interpret and utilise this same preordained universal overtone series in various ways to suit their own cultures." [153]

L demonstrated how, in Western music, the techniques developed from these relationships whose seeds originated in the overtone series eventually allowed composers to move freely from key to key and then back again to their original *home tonic*, providing their music with greater chromatic variety while still maintaining it within a system of strict tonal controls. The concept of *ambiguity* in music was next introduced as a further device to create greater expressivity through the employment of juxtaposed opposites,

---

[152] *mal, màlenki* and a large variety of other words beginning with the prefix *mal* in all the Slavic languages connote *small* or *few* while *mal,malo* in the Romance languages alludes to something *bad*. *gr* prefixes a wide variety of words in many languages to connote largeness: *grand* in English or French, *grande* in Spanish, *gross* in German, *groot* in Dutch, etc. all connote largeness

[153] L was not the first Norton lecturer to dwell on the subject of the harmonic series. In his 1949-50 lectures, the distinguished composer and teacher Paul Hindemith discussed the harmonic series in extended mathematical detail. Hindemith's lectures, in which his long held unremitting negative views upon Schoenberg's dodecaphonic system are stated in detail, must have had a profound influence on L. L had first come into extended close contact with the composer at Tanglewood during the summers of 1940 & 1941 and had been a great advocate of Hindemith's music which he performed and recorded throughout his career.

such as *chromaticism* and *diatonicism*.[154] To demonstrate these techniques in practice Mozart's *Symphony No.40 G minor* served as L's example. The plethora of technical references sprinkled throughout his text gave notice that a full understanding would require a greater knowledge of music than was ever previously demanded of his listeners.

The previous fifty lines of summary of the first Lecture don't even begin to scratch the surface of L's brief in its detail and complexity. But it was simplicity itself in comparison to the lecture that was to follow.

The second Lecture set up working analogies with language via the discipline of *Syntax*, sounds into words and words into sentences. At this point, there must have been more than a little surprise and frustration in his audiences to encounter the focus of L's text leaning principally towards linguistics. Their expectations must surely have been for a greater concentration on musical matters.

L believed it would be simpler and clearer to discuss his theories by creating analogies between musical functions and comparable language functions which people encounter and use daily. A good deal of the highly speculative theoretical material from the first three scripts was, in essence, L thinking out loud. The second Lecture is filled with absorbing propositions and dead-end speculations. The additional effort required to come to understand even those hypotheses which led L down several cul-de-sacs in his search for parallels between language structure and music structure still proves interesting. It serves to create a more complete picture of the enquiring mind of one of the leading musicians of the 20th century. However, it would also be less than honest not to comment that this Lecture must have been extremely thorny for those in attendance lacking previous technical knowledge in music or linguistics. L's effort to compensate was to provide a twenty-five minute primer on Chomskian linguistics. Brief musical examples

---

[154] *diatonicism* - refers to music which exclusively uses notes belonging to the octave scale of one key or mode. *chromaticism* - the division of the octave scale into twelve equal parts each a semitone apart. It has been a feature of music dating back to Ancient Greece whereby diatonic music was embelished by non-diatonic sub-divisions.

were sprinkled throughout to illuminate the text including attempts to construct musical analogies comparable to various linguistic sentence transformations. (Ponder, if you will L demonstrating the musical equivalent of a positive statement, then a negative statement, then a question followed by an equivocation, etc.). The density of concepts and the enormous variety of material involved have, in retrospect, made the publication of the book and the videos mandatory for proper comprehension.

Just prior to the interval of the Lecture, a key detour moves us into an examination of poetry as an aesthetic parallel with music. Both these art forms primarily deal with sound and manipulating elements over a structured time span and both are a result of the expression of human creativity on what L terms "a transcendental plane where musical and verbal thought become comparable." The relation of poetry to music is to surface throughout the Lectures and is an essential element of the final Lecture.

The second half of this Lecture is again devoted to Mozart's *G minor Symphony* but in this instance involves only a review of the first movement. Viewing the entire movement of the Mozart masterwork as the equivalent to the *surface structure* of a poem, L sets his task to try to discover or invent a *deep structure* from which the final symphony *surface structure* might have been derived[155].

What follows is a highly detailed and complex but clearly expounded analysis of the relevant component parts which make up the *deep structure* which, transformed, result in Mozart's final *surface structure* of the first thirty measures of his symphony. It is soon demonstrably clear that the components are so numerous in number that it is impractical for L to continue as he has begun. He therefore limits himself to extrapolating the deep structure from one point of view only, *symmetry*, which he declares and defends with multiple examples to also be a *universal* concept. A list of

---

[155] Deep and Surface structure - In Chomsky's *generative grammar*, sentences are analysed at these two levels of organisation. The 'deep' structure is the abstract representation which displays all the factors that govern how its meaning should be interpreted. The surface structure is a more concrete representation of a prose phrase, what we would expect to hear if the phrase were spoken.

the symmetrical dualism that is so much a part of ourselves and our every day lives prefaces an examination of the structural symmetry of the opening and other selected passages from the Mozart symphony[156]. Earlier in the Lecture L expressed the hope that his hypothesising and speculation would strike a nugget or two. The structural analysis of the Mozart symphony upon which he embarks in this second lecture is one of those nuggets he had hoped to strike and I will return to this when discussing the long term impact and importance of the Lectures.

One does not know where to begin to discuss the many complexities of this structural analysis on its several musical and aesthetic levels. Its most striking and important overall aspect is that it draws attention to what a listener intuitively hears and mentally organises when he listens to a piece of music. A problem of L's own making is that in his enthusiasm he persists in pursuing musical analogies with linguistics even in areas where his musical theory is sound enough to stand on its own and does not require analogy. Ray Jackendoff pointed to "L's great insight into the essential issues" in his review of the book of the Lectures. When he gets bogged down trying to make all the specifics of linguistics, not his given field, fit his musical examples one does at times get the uncomfortable feeling of square pegs being forced into round holes.

The theme of the third lecture is Musical Semantics, (*semantics*, the study of meaning, being the third discipline of linguistics). In both the highly complex second Lecture and this more accessible third Lecture, L has used the technique of playing 'devil's advocate' to himself. His timing seems best summed up by the line most quoted from 'B' western movies, *'We'll head 'em off at the pass!'* What I mean will become clear after three examples.

In the second Lecture, after a short introduction in which L introduces Chomsky's theory of innate language faculty, L poses the question, "What has syntactic investigation to do with music?" He has with this question anticipated the unspoken question of all those who came to hear Leonard

---

[156] L deals much in the same terms in great detail regarding the subject of *symmetry* in relation to music composition in his YPC *Rhythm*.

WEST SIDE MAESTRO

Bernstein speak on music not on linguistics. Having asked the question, however, we allow him time to deliver his answer.

His answer as it turns out is long and complex involving a huge chunk of *transformational grammar* accompanied by attempts to find even more musical analogies that are comparable to word relationships in language. When several of the analogies are seen to fail, the time has again come to play 'devil's advocate',

"...transformation, deletion, embedding, prenominalization: what, **I** ask again, (he, of course, means *you* ask), has this to do with music?"

The question again allows him a breather and another concession on our parts to be led further into the argument. And, indeed, L does leads us into a truly fascinating comparison between poetry and music followed by a complex analysis of the aesthetics of music structure. Then again at the crucial moment our 'devil's advocate' again steps from the wings.

"So what?", he asks again on the listeners' behalf. "Why burden us with all this pedantic hair splitting? Isn't this all stuff for the musicologists?"

Encore! We have been 'headed off at the pass'. I'm sure you get my point by now. This well-worn psychological technique has once again proved really useful in 'keeping the natives from getting restless'. The incendiary heat and passion that accompanied each of L's answers swept his audience along even when the speed at which concept after new concept was thrown at them sometimes lead to a degree of confusion.

I mention this because the entire introduction of the third Lecture involves L reporting that he had been challenged by some anonymous young female in regard to his various theories of existing analogies between *transformational grammar* and musical *transformations*. This reported question and answer session allows him to quote a classic Chomskian example of *ambiguity* and to use an excerpt from Stravinsky's ballet, *Petrouchka* as a further musical analogy to his Chomskian model. With barely time to catch one's breath, we are introduced to the subject of *metaphor* as a key to understanding, specifically *metaphor in poetry* analogous to *metaphor in music*. This demonstration proved to be one of L's most effective forays into a language/music comparison. It must have proved equally convincing even to those in the audience who came to scoff. I will discuss the overall importance of Poetry within the six Lectures in detail as part of my analysis of the final Lecture.

The second half of the Lecture is devoted to Beethoven's *Symphony No.6*, the *Pastoral*. An analysis identifying linguistic parallels of Beethoven's compositional techniques is truly stunning. It represents L in his best and most communicative teaching form and certainly served to recapture the imagination and interest of some who may have been ready to fall by the wayside. It was followed by a filmed performance of the complete symphony.

The final three lectures, which lean more heavily on musical analysis than linguistics, move us into the Twentieth-Century. L traces the crisis in tonal ambiguity brought on by the ever increasing employment of chromaticism during the course of the 19th- century by composers such as Berlioz, Chopin, Schumann and Liszt and culminating in the operas of Richard Wagner. L poses the question, "How far can music romp through new chromatic fields without finding itself in uncharted terrain?" By the end of the century the burgeoning of ever greater tonal ambiguities had, in fact, given rise to *the* crisis question in the musical arts, "Was containment to be found nowhere?" Those committed to tonality struggled to accomplish this but ultimately the crisis did arrive and at the time of L's Lectures, after more than half a century, remained unresolved. To begin to trace how this occurred L uses the final third of his fourth Lecture to analyse and perform Debussy's *Prelude to the Afternoon of a Faun*, one of the last-ditch stands of tonal containment which, at the same time, was a work that epitomised the search for 'bigger and better' tonal ambiguities. He draws specific parallels between the poetry of Stéphane Mallarmé, whose poem inspired Debussy's *Faun*, and the musical construction of the orchestral Prelude itself. He points to various phonological and structural parallels which, although of different genres, the two art works share. Mallarmé's language is as chromatic, perfumed and phonologically vivid as Debussy's sensuous melodies. Debussy's seeming musical vagueness is ever protected by classically established and stabile compositional techniques and so, equally, is Mallarmé's often elusive text. Both the poem and the music succeed in maintaining a clarity of structural articulation in spite of all the vagueness deliberately inherent to both works.

It was L's fifth Lecture which opened a floodgate of hostility from musicians who had inherited Arnold Schönberg's mantel. Certain of L's loaded statements, which in essence were a repetition of sentiments expressed in his Omnibus lecture on Modern Music almost twenty years earlier, tended to overshadow the larger and more important part of his text which traced, explained and analysed in relatively simple and straightforward terms the development of Schönberg's ideas from his earliest *atonal* compositions to the reformulation of his procedure of composition in the 1920's which was re-christened the *twelve tone* or *dodecaphonic 'method'*.[157]

In the Omnibus telecast L posed three questions:
1. Is this kind of music, (*dodecaphonic*), denying a basic law of nature when it denies tonality?
2. Is the human ear equipped to take it all in?
3. If the human ear can take it in will the heart be moved?

The first two questions echo a challenge laid down by Paul Hindemith in his Norton Lectures of 1949-50. Hindemith's position was that for composers to try to avoid tonality was as fruitless a pursuit as trying to avoid the effects of gravity. However, Hindemith accepted that composers working in the *twelve tone* method did succeed to the degree that they were able to arrange their melodies and chordal harmonies so that the *tonal centers* to which they refer *changed too rapidly* to be interpreted by the human ear, leaving the listener floating in a kind of musical 'no-man's land'. Hindemith believed, however, that tonality was inescapable, that the intervals, which form the building

---

[157] Schonberg's twelve tone system simplisticly explained consists of presenting all twelve tones of the chromatic scale in a pre-established order, (*tone row* is the designated technical term applied), with no tone repeated until all other eleven have been sounded. The *row* can be used both linearly, as melody, and vertically as harmony but the principle that no note is to be repeated until all other eleven are used remains inviolate.

blocks of melody and harmony, are automatically perceived instinctively in tonal groupings. This instinctive automatic tonal grouping referred to by Hindemith is demonstrated by L in his analysis of Schönberg's strict twelve-tone *Waltz for piano, opus 23*. L reveals harmonic implications throughout the entire work, specifically an augmented triad that is outlined in melodic and harmonic form in each permutation of Schönberg's original *twelve-tone row*. To L this represents 'the fascinating ambiguity between the planned anti-tonal function of the *twelve-tone row* and the inevitable tonal implications that *innately* reside in it, _do what you will_!' This is what L views as the result of an ambiguous tug-of-war between being rooted and *partly* rooted (in *tonality*). Tonal grouping was not the only point of similarity in the views of these two distinguished musicians. Both also took as a central theme in their Norton Lectures that the natural harmonic series (*overtones*) was the key factor that enabled us to understand the organisation of tonal music. Indeed, to L, the overtone series was an example of a *substantive universal* such as those sought by transformational grammarians like Chomsky.

It would be instructive at this point to seek out Schönbergs views on the natural harmonic series and tonality. Schönberg believed "that all musical phenomena can be referred to the overtone series, so that all things appear to be the application of the more simple and more complex relationships of that series."[158] This is not very far away from L's or Hindemith's view. Where the master certainly parted company with L and Hindemith was in his view of tonality. "Tonality is not something which the Composer unconsciously, (subconsciously), achieves, which exists *without his contribution*[159] and grows of itself, which would be present even if the Composer willed the opposite. In a word, tonality is neither a *natural* nor *automatic consequence of tone combination* and therefore cannot claim to be the automatic result of the nature of sound and so an indispensable attribute of every piece of music."

---

[158] All the quotes attributed to Arnold Schoenberg are taken from his article 'Problems of Harmony' (1934), reprinted in Arnold Schoenberg: Style & Idea, Selected Writings edited & revised by Leonard Stein, Faber & Faber, 1984

[159] Author's italics

WEST SIDE MAESTRO

This last statement is diametrically opposed to the theorem L had set out to prove, that tonality was a *substantive universal* and an inherent part of human genetic innateness. As can be noted from the Schönberg quote, tonality for the brilliant revolutionary was merely the end product of a definite 'art-means', (i.e.: a constructed theory of chordal harmony). Moreover, as he went on to write, firm application of these 'art-means' had to be applied at every point in a composition "to give the key, (tonality), unequivocal expression."

Schönberg refuted the label *atonal* in regard to his own music. "*Atonal* can only signify something that does not correspond to the nature of tone. A piece of music will *always be tonal* in so far as a relation exists from tone to tone, whereby tones, placed next to or above one another, result in a perceptible succession. The tonality might then be neither felt nor possible of proof, these relations might be obscure and difficult to comprehend, yes, even incomprehensible. But to call any relation of tones *atonal* is as little justified as to designate a relation of colours *aspectoral* or *acomplementary*. Such an antithesis does not exit."

Indeed, it was Schönberg's view that if audiences and musicians did not permit themselves to be influenced by slogans or striking terms in regard to a "technical peculiarity" associated with a style of composition, (ie: impressionistic, expressionistic, *atonal),* but rather listened with open ears and inquiring mind in search of originality and whether the composer has something new and worthwhile to say, within a few decades they "would recognise the *tonality* of this music called *atonal.*" It would only then be a matter of the gradual recognition between the "tonality of yesterday and the tonality of today." The article from which I have quoted ends on a most positive statement of faith in his ideas and their future.

"That which is tonal", wrote Schönberg, "is perhaps nothing else than what is understood *today*, and *atonal* is what will be understood in the future."

WEST SIDE MAESTRO

There is yet the third question L posed in his *Omnibus* Modern Music telecast to be dealt with in its revised Norton Lecture version. "If the human ear can take it in, will the heart be moved?" was to take on the more confrontational form of "Is this perhaps why Schönberg has still, to this day, not found his mass public - a large, concert-going public who *loves* his music?" L goes on to suggest that the compositions of Alban Berg, Schönberg's most famous pupil who, with Anton von Webern and their teacher were the leaders of the Second Vienna School of composition, are listened to with innate emotional response while those of his teacher are perceived as too self negating to be grasped by the listener whose ears are tuned to innate predispositions. L's answer to this contradiction is that Berg, within the ultimate musical ambiguity that is *twelve-tone* music, had found a personal form of expression that had reintroduced tonal implications within *dodecaphonic* techniques.

Stating that one can not come to "love" serial music seemed obdurate at a time when it was not only in its ascendance with tonal music in retreat but was represented on the world's scene by protagonists who were the 'movers and shakers' within the musical Arts, Pierre Boulez, Luciano Berio, Karlheinz Stockhausen, Milton Babbitt, Hans Werner Henze and, most extraordinary of all, Igor Stravinsky, the Pope of tonal modernism who, following the death of Schönberg, began to compose exclusively using the twelve-tone method. L compared Stravinsky's musical change of allegiance to "the defection of a general to the enemy camp, taking all his faithful regiments with him."

L's challenge to the validity of *dodecaphonic* music was guaranteed to produce a vigorous counter response from Schönberg's followers. They responded, as did their leader back in 1934, that time and exposure would bring audiences not only to understand their music but to "grow to *love* it." This, interestingly enough, conforms to the behaviourist theory espoused by such great thinkers as Leonard Bloomfield whose theories profoundly influenced Noam Chomsky's teacher, Zellig Harris. Bloomfield's linguistic theory of *behaviourism* as applied to 'meaning' is something that can be deduced solely from a study of the situation in which speech is used - a *spoken stimulus* which results in *a response to that stimulus*. As can be seen, a clear analogy exists between this linguistic theory and the aspirations of the Schönbergians. However, in regard to the behaviourist argument, Ray Jackendoff points out that "Kohler in 1927 and Chomsky in 1976 published the following: "There are two different modes of learning: trial-and-error learning, which obeys the behaviourist learning curve, and rapid learning on limited exposure, guided by innate ability." Jackendorf continues, "It is fairly clear that the assimilation of principles of simple tonal music, like the learning of language, lies in the latter domain, since nearly everyone learns to sing such music with some degree of skill. It is an empirical question, however, whether an arbitrary new way of organising music can be so assimilated - or whether, like chess or quantum mechanics, its mastery is somewhere at the extreme limits of human ability, or even beyond them."[160]

Was not L stating the very same idea when he opined that the rules of Schönberg's method "not being based upon innate awareness, on the intuition of tonal relationships" were like the rules of an artificial language which must be learned; that in spite of all conditionings and reinforcements the human ear still found the ambiguity posed by *twelve-tone* music too huge to be grasped. This is the concept of "the mind not being infinitely plastic" which Morris Hallé viewed as one of L's important contributions to the argument.

Lest it be thought that this lecture was in the main a vinegary polemic against Schönberg and the school of thought he founded, which indeed was the music critic Michael Steinberg's charge, just the opposite was true. L spoke of Schönberg's commitment and genius in a manner that was "more than respectful." It was tinged with the kind of reverence one reserves for a "father figure" which the Viennese master most certainly represented to generations of composers. Gunther Schuller, a noted contemporary composer, educator and founder of the school of *third stream* jazz[161] was quoted as author of the above phrases in a NY Sunday Times letter to the

---

[160] Ray Jackendoff, Review Article, Language: Volume 53, Number 4 (1977)
[161] 'Third stream' - the combination of classical forms with the improvisatory elements of jazz which maintains the disparate elements and character of each style within the synthesis.

WEST SIDE MAESTRO

editor from Professor Irving Singer written in response to Michael Steinberg's negative critique of the Lectures. Schuller, who composed, although not exclusively, in the *twelve-tone* style commented on L's treatment of Schönberg as follows,

"I thought that Bernstein handled the difficult subject of Schönberg's role in 20th-century music very beautifully. It was more than respectful: it was a moving account of Schönberg's links to the past and a sympathetic view of the innate complexity of Schönberg's thought, which is after all the real problem, not, as is often presumed, the surface problem of Schönberg's use of *atonality* or the *twelve-tone* system."

One might imagine that this immensely complex lecture had run its course by now. It had begun with a performance of Feria (Holiday) from Ravel's *Rhapsodie Espagnol*. The setting chosen was the year 1908 and the Ravel work, bursting with confidence, seems to project an unconcern and unawareness of a crisis brewing in music that will split musical thought for the rest of the century. In this same year of 1908 Mahler will produce his *Ninth Symphony*, Sibelius his brooding and a-typical *Fourth Symphony*, Scriabin his daring and wildly chromatic *Prometheus* and, most important of all, Schönberg his prophetic *Second String Quartet* which will mark his departure from tonal methods of composition. The title of the lecture series, *The Unanswered Question*, re-emerges but this time in its original form, a short work for chamber orchestra featuring a solo trumpet, wind quartet and strings. It too has been composed in the year 1908 but by an unsung American composer, an original named Charles Ives, 3000 miles away from the centre of the musical conflict lurking upon the European horizon, in the state of Connecticut. Ives, who interestingly enough also looked to the music of Mahler for inspiration, had begun to compose in a style that will mark him as a pioneer of the *avant-garde* in America.

The next hour is spent in a discussion and analysis of Schönberg, the composer, teacher, thinker and one of the two key revolutionary figures of the 20th-century. L performs all the musical excerpts at the piano, which includes singing and *sprectstimme*[162], where required, in his inimitable *rough-and-ready* style so familiar from his Young People's Concerts days. This segment includes a discussion of Alban Berg, a cursory discussion of his method of composing after Schönberg and a quick analysis of a portion of the final movement of his *Violin Concerto*, the pertinent section of which is then played via a gramophone recording. One certainly had enough 'food for thought' by this time.

Nevertheless, after a wonderfully pithy summing up of more than an hour of his text in the following manner,

"Is it enough to have examined its (the Ultimate Ambiguity) origins, to have identified the great tonal split, to have traced one side of the split into the development of a Method that changed the history of music, to have attempted a dispassionate assessment of Arnold Schönberg - only to have Alban Berg walk off with all the honours?"

L springs his surprise and we realise that this Lecture is far from over.

"No," he continues, "there *is* further light to be shed, and that light is to be found in the mind and the prophetic soul of Gustav Mahler."

Following the interval the Lecture takes a very dark turn and the discussion of Mahler becomes a discourse on death, Mahler's obsession with death and its depiction in his music, Mahler's knowledge of his own impending death, the death of *tonality*, the preoccupation with death by the century's great minds in the fields of Arts and Sciences and the impending actuality of genocidal war with all its consequences, the extinction of the human race and the death of the planet. L sums it all up in one emotive, perfumed phrase, "Ours is the century of death, and Mahler is its musical prophet." L depicts Mahler as a latter day Jeremiah who saw all that was to overtake the century back in 1908. A powerful, moving statement and certainly true in part if not in its totality. Certainly much of Mahler's music has been tinged

---

[162]*Sprectstimme* - (*spechgesang*), speech-song, when used in reference to Schoenberg's compositions. It involves speaking in specific rhythms on approximate specific pitches.

with aspects of death. The *First* and *Fifth symphonies* contain funeral marches, the *Second Symphony* deals with resurrection, the *Fourth* with a child's vision of heaven, in the *Sixth* the hero is struck down by three hammer-blows of fate and both the *Ninth Symphony* and *Das Lied von der Erde* are symphonies of farewell. During one of the happiest periods of his marriage, with his children playing outside his studio door, he wrote his *Songs on the Death of Children, (Kindertotenlieder)*. In the last years of his life Mahler had been diagnosed with a serious heart ailment and a lifetime of outdoor physical activity in which he revelled had been totally forbidden him. This preyed on his mind and without doubt affected the nature of his musical output. It is one thing, however, for a brilliantly talented man of a morbid disposition to be preoccupied with death, especially his own, and another to elevate him to the status of a prophet and depict his life's musical output as internationally shunned for fifty years because it projected to the world an apocalyptic vision. The facts simply don't bear out this thesis. And it is a shame it was presented in this manner because the message would have remained just as powerful and convincing if L had puts his case for a death-wish obsessed 20th-century as an accurate, historic retrospective view of the century rather than Mahler's.

Let us examine the reality of the situation in terms of known evidence. Mahler's last two completed symphonies, the *Ninth* and *Das Lied von der Erde* are both a valediction to life but by someone who, at the time of their writing, had come to terms with his impending death and who still savoured what time remained. This is underlined in a letter to Bruno Walter[163] written in 1909 from New York during his NY Philharmonic season:

"I have been going through so many experiences for the last year and a half that I can hardly discuss them... I see everything in such a new light and am in continuous fluctuation; I shouldn't be surprised to discover that I had acquired a new body (as Faust does in the final scene). *I am thirstier than ever for life and I find the 'habit of life' sweeter than ever.*" (my italics)

---

[163] Bruno Walter (1876-1962) - Internationally noted German conductor. Mahler's protégé and closest associate and collaborator in Vienna. After Mahler's death, he gave the first performances of *Das Lied von der Erde* in 1911 and the *Ninth Symphony* in 1912.

WEST SIDE MAESTRO

This was written only two years before his death and at a point where *Das Lied* was in the final stages of completion and he had begun work on the *Ninth Symphony*. If anything his song cycle symphony reflects his calm resignation. In the final *Farewell* movement of the song symphony are verses which are Mahler's own words substituted for the original poem. It is the composer himself who speaks to us of his passion for life and calm acceptance of his death to come:

O beauty!
O intoxicated world of eternal love - life!

I shall no longer seek the far horizon,
My heart is still and waits for its deliverance

The same atmosphere of the song symphony pervades the *Ninth Symphony*. Indeed, Michael Kennedy in his excellent short biography of the composer, his life and music, perceptively suggests that the *Ninth Symphony* is an extension of *Das Lied*, almost a symphonic commentary upon it. Although one meets the spectre of death in several guises during the course of this massive eighty minute dark work, especially in the allusion to the very act of dying with which the symphony concludes and which L so brilliantly and movingly describes in his introductory remarks to a performance of its final movement, one cannot proclaim an encounter with death in every bar of music as has been asserted in much musical criticism over the years.[164] There are to be found Mahlerian musical quotes alluding to the approach of death throughout the work[165] but these quotes serve as a unifying element as much as they reinforce the work's extra-musical meaning of farewell.

---

[164] This critical over-preoccupation with a continuous message of death may have taken as its source a letter written by Anton von Webern to his fiancée after studying the score to the first movement in the summer of 1910. In it Webern describes the movement as permeated by premonitions of death which continually crop up and in which all other elements of earthly visions culminate till, finally, in the midst of a 'colossal passage...of almost painful joy in life, Death itself is announced.'

[165] Mahler incorporates in his first movement an allusion to the 'Leb wohl' (farewell) motif from Beethoven's *Les Adieux* sonata, Op.81a and in the closing bars of the symphony a reminiscence from his own *Kindertotenlieder* (Songs on the Death of Children). Farewells in the form of quotes or allusions to his earlier symphonies and *Das Lied von der Erde* are scattered throughout.

WEST SIDE MAESTRO

Mahler foreseeing the death of tonality is again a questionable projection. That Mahler was both a beginning and an end, as L historically describes him, is certainly an accurate description of the composer's historical position. In Egon Gartenburg's excellent one volume study of Mahler, the author perceptively states a like view when he sets up a comparison between Mahler and Beethoven.

"Beethoven straddles the 18th and 19th centuries, leading the way from the classicism of Haydn and Mozart to classic romanticism, leaving the form and sound of his illustrious contemporaries to amplify and augment in both departments and usher in a new era in music. Mahler straddles the 19th and 20th centuries and again augments and enlarges on anything the music of the romantic century had achieved before him...Through his contributions...he led music into the 20th century...(However) Mahler was the end of that line of development...No further enlargement ...was possible after his symphonic giantism."[166]

That Mahler was a vehement supporter of Schönberg who was to usher in the revolutionary challenge to tonality is historical fact. He was among the first to recognise publicly the obvious musical and intellectual brilliance of the young composer. Alma Mahler describes her husband's efforts to protect Schönberg from "the brutality of the mob." Nevertheless, Mahler confessed to his wife after a performance of Schönberg's (still *tonal*) Chamber Symphony, "I don't understand his music but he's young and perhaps he's right. I am old and I daresay my ear is not sensitive enough."[167] These words do not project a futility in his own art, only a recognition in a new and different art of another composer whom he respected but did not comprehend.

By the year 1909 when Schönberg had forsaken tonality altogether with his *Three Pieces for Piano, op.11*, Mahler had already left Vienna to embark

---

[166] Egon Gartenburg: Mahler, The Man & His Music, pub. Cassell & Co.Ltd, London, copyright Schirmer Books, 1978
[167] Alma Mahler: Gustav Mahler, Memories & Letters, pub John Murray, London 1946

upon new careers in America, first with the Metropolitan Opera in 1908 and one year later as the chief conductor of the NY Philharmonic. Although he returned to Europe at the end of each season to rest and devote himself to composition at Toblach in the Dolomite mountains and at Goding as the guest of friends[168], he did not return to Vienna until the final weeks of his life[169], all during which he was hospitalised. He never stopped being of assistance to or concerned for Schönberg, including lending him a considerable sum of money at an hour of desperate need for his young colleague, but there does not appear to be documentation regarding whether he ever heard any further examples of this *music of the future*. Mahler continued to compose in a tonal, indeed, at times, diatonic and triadic style for both his Ninth and unfinished Tenth Symphonies parallel to Schönberg writing in a far more advanced manner. Certainly, Schönberg was initially influenced by elements in Mahler's symphonic writing, (especially the *Fifth*, *Sixth* and *Seventh Symphonies*), specifically the austere contrapuntal textures, the huge interval skips in the melodic lines and tonal ambiguities pushed to their limits.

As for anticipating "the impending actuality of genocidal war with all its consequences", along with "the extinction of the human race and the death of the planet", this may have been planted in L's mind by evaluations of the mood of the times by writers such as Gartenberg:

"When Schönberg, Berg and Webern eventually ushered in a new age in music...it was on the ruins of that nineteenth-century romanticism which had prevailed long after outliving its *raison d'être*...A chasm inevitably began to open between the Vienna of Johann Strauss and that of

---

[168] *Das Lied von der Erde* was composed at Toplach during the summer of 1908, the *Ninth Symphony* begun at Toblach and Goding in the summer of 1909 and the uncompleted *Tenth Symphony* begun at Toblach the summer of 1910.

[169] There were, of course, short forays into the city, the most important of which followed the overwhelming reception he received in Munich conducting the premiere of his *Eighth Symphony* in 1910. At this time he went to visit Prince Montenuovo, the Emperor's Lord Chamberlain of the Household who was Mahler's protector and friend when he was artistic director at the Imperial Opera. Weingartner, Mahler's successor at the Opera, had proved a failure and was soon to resign. Prince Montenuovo again offered Mahler his old post. It is speculated that, had he lived, Mahler would certainly have accepted.

WEST SIDE MAESTRO

Schönberg...Only the men of music, Schönberg and Webern, intuitively felt the coming of the Great War and in their music mirrored their fears."[170]

As for Mahler, the historical record of this great but contentious musician is of an artist moving from one volatile professional confrontational problem to the next in his dual career as opera artistic director/conductor and symphony conductor while, in the final years of his life, having to come to terms as well with a life threatening illness. His personal concerns centred on establishing a financially secure future while trying to maintain some semblance of a marriage-in-crisis with a brilliant but volatile, free spirited wife who was pursued, before, during and even after death had ended their union, by a parade of Europe's most brilliant minds in the fields of art, architecture, literature and music. There would have been little time at best to even superficially contemplate world politics on the scale suggested by L. Once Mahler had forsaken Vienna, he had also removed himself from the atmosphere of the Viennese coffee house where he was accustomed to argue these radical matters dialectically late into the night with the young firebrands who looked to him for leadership. In addition to his huge career commitments, he devoted every spare moment he could steal for himself to composing and, until his illness forced him into a sedentary existence, communing vigorously with nature. The scenario, then, of Mahler pushing a mountain of professional and personal problems to oneside while he contemplated an Armageddon of proportions which threatened planetary extinction is but an extravagant projection of Kafkaesque high drama to add to the reality of the powerful real life drama contained within the auto-biographical symphonic movement of the *Ninth Symphony* L was to about to present to his audience.

Yet one final detour mixing historical fact and fiction moves L away from his own powerful message which culminates in a most moving analysis of the *Ninth Symphony* followed by a filmed performance of its final movement with L conducting the Vienna Philharmonic. This involves L's theory that "Mahler, the prophet of death" was "telling something too dreadful to hear"

---

[170] reference: footnote12

and that this was "the real reason for the *fifty years of neglect* Mahler's music suffered after his death."

Putting to one side that mounting a Mahler symphony is no small task making huge financial demands in terms of rehearsal time and the expanded personnel required as well as calling for a public of some sophistication, what other composer of this century could boast the list of distinguished champions to equal Mahler's: Bruno Walter, Otto Klemperer, Willem Mengelberg, Felix Weingartner, Leopold Stokowski, Sir Henry J. Wood, Clemens Krauss, Jasha Horenstein, Dmitri Mitropouls, and extending to a young Eugene Ormandy, John Barbirolli and Leonard Bernstein. And this takes us only to the end of World War 2!

We know that Bruno Walter continually championed Mahler's music during his entire career, giving the premieres of both *Das Lied von der Erde* and the *Ninth Symphony* after Mahler's death. Mengelberg, already an established champion of Mahler's music during the composer's lifetime, maintained all the Mahler symphonies in his repertoire till his Nazi sympathies cost him his long serving position as chief conductor of the Amsterdam Concertgebouw Orchestra. A special mention must be given to Stokowski's historic performances introducing both Philadelphia and New York audiences to the Eighth Symphony in 1916 in perhaps the greatest and most important success of his career which put both the conductor and the Philadelphia Orchestra on America's musical map. In the 1920's, Klemperor scheduled a work by Mahler in each of his seasons. In 1930 Clemens Krauss conducted a retrospective of all the Mahler symphonies with the Vienna Philharmonic. Mahler's music continued to be performed throughout Europe in the 1930's until Nazi dictum decreed it banned because of Mahler's Jewish heritage. Nevertheless, Henry Wood in England who since 1903 had been introducing Mahler's music to British audiences continued to perform Mahler's most demanding symphonies, especially the *Eighth*, till 1940 when the war years restricted the size of revivals such as the *Second* and *Eighth* symphonies. We move on through the '40's to 1947 when a young Leonard Bernstein with an equally young N.Y. City Symphony bowls New Yorkers over with his performance of Mahler's monumental *Resurrection* Symphony to open his season. I don't wish to beat this 'neglect' issue into the ground, which really stems from a statement Mahler made that "it would be fifty years before the public would grasp his ideas and the importance of his position in music history", but if we take one further moment to examine early Mahler recordings one has to be astonished at the number of 78rpm recordings of Mahler's music which were undertaken by the leading commercial record companies at a time when, unlike today's monthly releases of a hundred CD's or more, only thirty albums of classical music were released per year. What do we find? In addition to a 1920's recording of the *Adagietto* movement from the *Fifth Symphony* by Mengleberg and his Dutch orchestra, there are recordings made in the 1930's and '40's of the first five symphonies, the *Ninth Symphony* and *Das Lied von der Erde*. Once we enter the era of the long-playing record the list of Mahler recordings and repertoire grow. With the emergence of the CD, especially after L's ground-breaking recordings of the complete *Nine Symphonies* and *Das Lied von der Erde*, a virtual Mahler industry has emerged and has carried on to the present day.

One must ask the question, "In face of the reality, why did L take this tack?" L makes so many valid points that it is a pity he vitiated his argument by exposing himself to criticism for speculation and inaccuracies that could be easily checked and criticised using even the limited amount of research material available at the time. Mahler, the composer, was everything he described him to be, a beginning and an end, and his music provided the gateway through which would burst a radical musical revolution into the new century. Our century is everything he described, death-ridden-*plus* with the future of our planet hanging on mankind's seeming inescapable ability to repeat their worst mistakes while seeking escape in the various -*isms* which have proved to be little more than placebos. Much of the great literature of this century has centered on death and despair and much of Mahler's life was touched by death in the most heart-rending way. As L states, "the facts are potent enough."

Why, then, invent new ones? I believe it had much to do with L's personal obsession with Mahler, some connection of re-birth in which he believed that he had been chosen to fulfil some Mahlerian destiny. His reinforcement of his arguments are accomplished by making himself part of the Mahler equation. The meeting and subsequent acquaintance with Alban Berg's widow in Vienna and his meeting with Alma Mahler which took place during a rehearsal of Mahler's *Fourth Symphony* with the NY Philharmonic at which I was present, all of this culminates in the statement, "I began to feel myself *in direct contact* with Mahler's message."

Though I have spent a fair amount of time and words pointing out the inaccuracies it was for the purpose of putting them to rest. They are unfortunate but they are not the nub of this outstanding if complex lecture. To end it as a tribute to the human spirit which represents the Ultimate Ambiguity, is to reveal the complexity of the Mahler personality. Without consciously making the link between his own creativity and that of Schönberg, Mahler handed on to his young colleague the torch that lit his way into the future. Schönberg proved himself one of the great examples of the human spirit in the twentieth-century, the "prototype of the Ambiguous Man" who engineers his own destruction while simultaneously flying on into the future.[171]

At this point L briefly but vividly gives his personal programmatic description of the first three movements, (not performed), and then a more extended and moving account of the final movement with its incontrovertible description in music of the very act of dying. The lecture ends with a final paraphrased quote from Keats *Ode to a Nightingale*,

> We are now in love with easeful death...
> now more than ever seems it rich to die,
> to cease upon midnight with no pain...

to which L adds, "And in ceasing, we lose it all. But in letting go, we have gained everything."

---

[171] This last paragraph on the human spirit paraphrases L's brilliant summation of the essence of Schoenberg's personality and the drive that enabled him to survive and conquer in a life filled with incredible hardship and frustration.

WEST SIDE MAESTRO

(A performance of the final movement of Mahler's *Ninth Symphony* follows)

The final lecture begins with a manufacturer's warning, "This lecture is going to be a long one; if you think the others were long, you've got another *think* coming...!" Certainly L is true to his word, the lecture proving to be a mini-marathon lasting virtually three hours. It is a highly complex affair which deals on several levels with a variety of key issues both new and previously encountered . As with any concluding chapter of a series that has spread its net so broadly and involved many personalities and ideas, a key final goal is to bring the various loose threads together and to tie the entire package into a tidy bow.

To accomplish this L must deal with the other half of "the great divide". The fifth Lecture had explored the *Gotterdämerung*[172] of Romanticism and the emergence of the Second Viennese School of *atonal* composition under the leadership of its architect, Arnold Schönberg. Now was the turn of the other great revolutionary, Igor Stravinsky, who for more than forty years had lead a great rescue operation to save tonality from those who had turned their backs on it, rejecting its further validity. With his extraordinary mind, talent and consummate musical skills, equal within the Arts only to another of the century's greatest revolutionaries, Pablo Picasso, Stravinsky devoted his gifts to finding ever-new ways of keeping tonality fresh, alive and relevant.

It appears that L's original design for this Lecture was to be purely musical. He would discuss in detail Stravinsky and his tonal "fresheners", (relating to the composer's source material, his unique handling of harmony and melody and, most important of all, rhythm), followed by an analysis and performance of the composer's opera/oratorio, *Oedepus Rex*. The Lecture would conclude with a summing up of L's thesis on human musical innate capacity and his view as to what he believed to be the inevitable course of the music of the future in relation to his initial *Unanswered Question*, "Whither music?". This alone would have been both a demanding and commanding

---

[172] *Gotterdämerung* - The twilight of the gods, the title of the fourth of the cycle of Wagner operas based upon the legend of *The Ring of the Nibelungs.*

agenda to have occupied L's creative mind for the entire final script. However, this final lecture is so much more than this that the mind *boggles*[173].

L takes up the story with Stravinsky an already respected and admired part of the Paris art scene. The composer had virtually become an expatriate following the 1910 Paris premiere of his ballet score, *The Firebird*, by Diaghilev's Ballet Russes, for whom he was also to compose two other supreme masterpieces of his so-called *Russian* period, *Petrouchka* and *Le Sacre du Printemps,* (The Rite of Spring). Although he continued to visit his home city of St. Petersburg, he chose to live in both France and Switzerland between 1910-20 and thereafter in France until 1939, becoming a French subject in 1934. While he was to become the most influential composer on the French scene, one cannot underestimate the degree to which he himself was influenced by the sophisticated milieu in which he lived, travelled and socialised. The composer's historical heritage, innovative musical techniques, development and influence form the largest part of the first half of L's text.

Le Sacre was the culminating work of Stravinsky's *Russian* period. Its massiveness and invention pushing at the very frontiers of musical and rhythmic dissonance, as in the case of Mahler, proved to be a dead end. Stravinsky had to look elsewhere for a personal solution that did not march him into the ultra radical Schönberg camp of non-tonal music which he vigorously and vocally opposed. There was a need to re-impose order and to seek out a fresh approach after the excesses of the recent past. What L labels as "the great save" which could impose the order Stravinsky was seeking for tonal music was to be found in *Neo-classicism*. This L defines in its broadest sense as the application of the contemporary, (to include the *vernacular*), to whatever forms and styles any given society *regards* as *classical*. L goes on to show that as Stravinsky began so he was to continue, ever stretching musical frontiers. Reaching far beyond the vernacular of his Russian youth, a variety of examples demonstrate the vernaculars both old and new that Stravinsky now embraced to include jazz, salon music, popular and

---

[173] boggle - be startled or baffled, Oxford Dictionary, Clarendon Press, Oxford

sophisticated dance music from all countries and even ragtime. They were all grist for his *freshener* mill, L explains, put to the service of codifying his new version of *neo-classic* musical art. In addition to his harmonic and rhythmic innovations, trivialities of the vernacular validated through his immense intellect and musical wit were elevated to the legitimate materials and building blocks of Stravinskian *neo-classicism*. His techniques, which also served an army of others, were to be in a constant state of revision and updating in his search for the 'new' to meet and fulfil his own creative needs.

With the exception of a fascinating detour paralleling neo-classicism in poetry at the turn of the century, the rest of the first half of the Lecture is devoted to analysing and demonstrating the music and revolutionary concepts of Stravinsky and his followers and the consolidation of the *neo-classic* movement in music.

Poetry continues to dominate at the opening of the second half of the Lecture. The shift in emphasis to language relates to the musical example chosen by L to display the breadth of Stravinsky's influential contribution to musical thought in the twentieth-century, the opera/oratorio, *Oedipus Rex* . It is the first of the larger works analysed by L that involves the setting of a text to music. L had devoted parts of his second and third Lectures in seeking correlations between language and music. He had obviously given a great deal of thought to the aesthetic problems involved. He put forward the concept that there was no correlation between the surface level of ordinary language prose and music. Only on a higher, super-surface level of poetry was a correlation able to be found. Now he suggested a further metaphorical leap upwards to a *supra* level where the very essence of music and poetry reside and intersect. It is at that level of Creativity, L proposes, that the union of words and music comes to exist. L emphasises that such a concept infers a union of well-matched components.

The congruity of words and music that L projected as coming to exist on a metaphorical *supra* level is challenged by a work such as Oedipus Rex. Oedipus Rex is considered by many to be a keystone work in the composer's output, marking a shift in emphasis from Stravinsky's early *neo-classic* period. It represents a juncture when a fusion of new ideas were to be observed more stylistically personal in nature than those which marked the composer's earlier works. It moved Stravinskian *neo-classicism* to a new plane. It also marked the first of a trio of large scale works for chorus and orchestra to be composed on monumental themes over the next six years.[174]

L performs and analyses a number of excerpts from *Oedipus*. In each excerpt he points out the obvious incongruity between the text and its musical setting. He speaks of having had new thoughts about and problems with this work when re-examining the score after being away from it for more than a year. He tells of one incongruity among the huge number to be found virtually on every page which he could not identify. He describes how it began niggling away at him. It was somehow connected to the opening four note motif and the theme of "pity and power", the textual substance of the opening chorus to *Oedipus*. This motif plus other musical signposts eventually pointed L in the direction of Romantic opera and specifically Verdi's *Aida* from which the motif proved to be a direct quote. Robert Craft who was Stravinsky's protégé and devoted amanuensis later acknowledged L's insight into the Stravinsky-Verdi connection[175] Underlining Craft's statement is that Stravinsky, having borrowed from *Aida* the musical motive for "pity and power" for his own setting of text based upon that same theme, then adapted it both orchestrally and vocally in the opening Act I chorus to *Oedipus Rex* much in the style of Verdi's dramatic Act I opening storm chorus from *Otello*.

Stravinsky's use of a Verdi motif and orchestration were only clues to the larger question L was seeking to answer. Could Verdi and Stravinsky, in contrasting text settings at opposite ends of the spectrum, effectively depict the same theme of "pity and power"? Verdi's opera had used all the well-matched musical, language and visual components one would expect to express human emotions. This was a clear example of L's projected *supra*

---

[174] *Oedipus Rex,* (1927); *Symphony of Psalmes,* (1930); *Perséphone,* (1933)

[175] Five years after the Lectures, Robert Craft confirmed L's perceptive connection between Stravinsky and Verdi. Craft, in his 1978 book written in collaboration with Vera Stravinsky, writes, 'Mr. Bernstein was right...Stravinsky knew and loved Verdi's operas...'

level of Creativity where *well-matched* components intersect. Stravinsky's opera, conversely, used austere, *ill matched* word, music and visual components. *Oedipus Rex* was light years away from the Verdi approach to opera yet one cannot deny that its comic-tragic *ill matched* elements astonishingly combine as effectively as those by Verdi to make *Oedipus* a powerful and moving experience. This challenged an extremely important question of aesthetics.

Unfortunately, Michael Steinberg, critic for the Boston Globe, did not quite see it this way. In a generally negative review of the entire lecture series, he pounced on the *Aida* connection as an example of 'tune detection' much in the style of a noted music writer, lecturer and radio personality of the '30's and '40's, Sigmund Spaeth, who was known as the "Tune Detective". Of course, the discovery of Stravinsky's use of Verdi's *pity-and-power motif* was not a matter of "tune detection" for L. Stravinsky had been borrowing from other composers for years. Steinberg had totally missed the quite important point L was making about *ill-matched* components.

Indeed, Steinberg, a respected critic, having initially written a positive review following the first Lecture, seemed to go out of his way afterwards to misinterpret, misquote and deprecate much of what took place in reviewing the entire lecture series. He summed up L's achievement as "little more than good theatre and generous entertainment" but dismissed the cultural and intellectual worth of the Lectures out of hand. Moreover, having failed in his efforts to elicit negative comments on L's presentation from either Noam Chomsky or Morris Hallé, M.I.T.'s[176] *big guns* in linguistics, Steinberg then selectively quoted in his review from a telephone interview with Ray Jackendoff, a Professor of Linguistics at Brandeis University, to create a supporting negative establishment view of the Lectures. Prof. Jackendoff found it necessary to refute Steinberg's misuse of his statements in a letter to the Boston Globe, the paper in which the criticism originally appeared. When Steinberg's article was reprinted in the NY Times, the editors redressed its negative bias by publishing a 1500 word letter of rebuttal three weeks later from Prof. Irving Singer which point by point not only corrected

---

[176] M.I.T. - The Massachusetts Institute of Technology

the wide variety of Steinberg's misstatements but also contained parts of Ray Jackendorf's letter of clarification to the editors of the Boston Globe. Steinberg chose not to respond to Professor Singer's stinging reply.

L's lecture series concluded with a valediction. There were "summaries...conclusions... the present musical moment to be generalised upon (and) the future to be guessed at."

L's summary begins with Schönberg's death in 1951. With Schönberg gone, the way was clear shortly afterwards for Stravinsky to desert tonal composition for another new challenge, Schönberg's *dodecaphonic* method. Many who looked to Stravinsky for guidance followed, adopting the Schönbergian *method* as well. While Stravinsky survived the conversion, many of his followers did not. For some the *method* refreshed and enriched their musical vocabulary. For others the *method* produced sterility; "still others stopped composing altogether." The preceding quote must have produced a great sadness within L for surely it referred to Aaron Copland. In L's book, *Findings*[177], written ten years later, his "Intimate Sketch of Copland at 70" tells of Copland's flirtation with twelve-tone composition. At the premiere of Copland's *Inscape*, an uncompromising twelve tone work, the composer lamented that not one young composer had attended or seemed interested in a brand new work that "he had laboured over." L asked his former mentor, this gentle man who had been one of his loyal, key allies and formative influences, "Of all people, why you...? Why are you bothering with tone rows...?" Copland's answer had to be one of the saddest of replies, "Because I need more chords. I've run out of chords." After four more compositions, Copland ceased to compose altogether.

L reports to his audience that by the mid-1960's his outlook for music was quite bleak. He outlined his pessimism in a book, *The Infinite Variety of Music*. By the time of the Harvard Lectures, however, his outlook had quite changed. Commercial music, the only thing he could find to admire during his depression in the '60's, now seemed to him passé, even grotesque; *jazz* was enjoying a renaissance; *avant-garde* techniques had taken on a new life;

---

[177] *Findings* by Leonard Bernstein, pub. Simon & Schuster, N.Y.1982

lastly, and most important, *tonal* music was no longer dormant. With the death of Stravinsky in 1971 a crisis within the musical arts broke out. Left to their own devices the young composers returned to their roots, what L terms as "their innate and long-denied sense of tonality." What before had been the Great Divide, a split into two camps now became a fusion of the two, one style feeding the other. For L this represented a return to the *supra*-level of abstract semantics where mismatched components could unite in a new eclecticism. However, L adds the caveat that "such a union can only take place...if it is embedded in a tonal universe." L followed this statement, certainly confrontational to some in his audience, with an ecumenical appeal that he surely hoped would produce a positive response. L described composers to be in a refreshed, relaxed state. He felt the time had come for a new synthesis, a new eclecticism. He spoke of bitterness coming to an end and a time of reconciliation, all of which he said he discerned in the music of recent years. With *tonality* again in the air, there was the positive atmosphere of rejoicing and a sense of brotherhood among composers who were now freely crossing the line to include either *serial* or *tonal* techniques in composition styles that previously strictly adhered to one style or the other. L believed this had all been made possible by the re-acceptance of *tonality*, the fertile ground from which diversity springs. No matter the style or intellectualised approach, all music qualified as poetry if it was *rooted in the earth* (of *tonality, of* course).

The final Lecture ended with a credo stated in rather flowery, poetic terms which I have reduced to six key points, re-interpreted in places in language which I believe expresses their intention in less obscure terms:

1. From the Poetry of the Earth, (innate *human* capacity), emerges a musical poetry, (an innate *musical* capacity),which by the nature of its sources, is tonal.

2. These sources, (Nature, itself), cause the existence of a phonology based upon and evolved from the universal known as the harmonic series, (overtones).

3. There exists a universal musical syntax, (set of rules), which can be codified, (classified), and structured in terms of symmetry, (balance), and repetition.

4. The devising of certain musical styles whose surface structure (i.e. twelve-tone or aleatory) is remote from their basic origins, (tonality), which can be strikingly expressive (communicative) 'as long as they *retain their roots in earth'* (a poetic way of referring to 'tonality').

5. Our deepest emotional responses to unique 'expressive musical styles', (non-tonal styles), are influenced by our innate tonal musical capacity but this does not preclude deriving (full) pleasure from them through conditioning or learning.

6. All languages influence one another and combine into new idioms, (crossover styles); that these idioms will ultimately merge into a new speech, (L suggests a *neo*-neo-classicism), sufficiently universal to be accessible to all and that the expressive distinctions (styles of composition) among these idioms depend ultimately on the dignity and passion of the creative voice, (in a word, 'talent!').

WEST SIDE MAESTRO

Riffs

Except for Peter Gradenwitz's biography of L, virtually all other biographies have devoted little space to examining these important Lectures that represent the culmination of L's revolutionary ideas for using the world's most dominant mass media, television, to provide music education for a wide general public at a level and popularity unequalled previously or afterwards. This is not to underestimate the outstanding work of three other American conductors who have also enjoyed a high degree of success explaining and presenting serious music for television, Andre Previn, Leonard Slatkin and Michael Tilson Thomas. However, as in many of the projects with which he was associated in the last half century of his life, L was the leader who set the standard. The Norton Lectures sum up all his musical and teaching gifts and reveal one other for which, up to that time, he had been given little credit, that of an original thinker. There were the standard cache of PR words used by both his publicists and detractors. *Genius*, in terms of his imaginative and creative capacity, would not overstate the case but it was not the kind of genius one associates with a Mozart, a Beethoven or, much as he would have dearly loved to be true, a Mahler. *Charisma* was perhaps the most overused term, '*clever*' was the perfect begrudging adjective to deny his mental gifts and capacities, and '*big talent*' was the opt-out phrase with which to deny him maturity and greatness.

L was the most controversial of figures and his lifestyle and unbuttoned public behaviour served to fuel the fires of those who refused him recognition for his enormous accomplishments. These Lectures were a case in point. With few, happily important exceptions, there were many colleagues and critics who denigrated the enormous effort that went into preparing and presenting them. It is no secret that the linguistic community were not enamoured of his efforts to wed music with their science. To describe the general atmosphere among them as initially hostile would not be overstating the case. Indeed, the word 'dilettante' in relation to L was widely tossed about over cocktails. Noam Chomsky, whose theories on language were the source of L's own theory on innate musical capacities, did not attend any of the lectures which certainly set tongues wagging. Chomsky, contrary to what many projected, was frank and accurate in his own assessment of his relationship to the project. Where music was concerned he considered himself a passive listener at best. His presence at the Lectures would have placed him in the invidious position of being besieged by questioners at every turn mostly hoping for a juicy negative quote. He never satisfied these opinion seekers because, to quote his letter to me:

"When Lenny Bernstein was here, we met a few times and talked about various things. For what it is worth, I thought his basic instinct was plausible and probably correct, but I didn't feel competent to comment on the execution."[178]

What Prof. Chomsky did say privately at the time of the lectures but which, for obvious reasons, was never stated publicly was that he viewed those baying for L's blood most rabidly to be motivated by jealousy. There is no doubt that Chomsky was aware of what was taking place at the lectures from Irving Singer, a colleague at Harvard and a friend of both L and the distinguished linguist. In addition, Prof. Morris Hallé, Chomsky's closest associate at MIT, attended the Lectures, as did Chomsky's distinguished pupil and colleague Ray Jackendoff, whose name and quotes have appeared throughout the previous chapter and about whom more is to be written. Jackendoff's particular expertise in the field of music must have added great weight to his reportage.

I want now to discuss the Lectures in aspects not already dealt with in detail in my overall view of the series, the musical analyses, the pre-recorded musical performances with the Boston Symphony and the long-term impact from L's innovative theory relating to human innate capacity for music parallel to human innateness for language.

Lastly, I would wish to examine contemporary attitudes towards tonal and serial music, the two sides of "the great divide", and the progress, if any, that has been made in the thirty-nine years since L presented his Norton

---

[178] Letter from Noam Chomsky to author, May 31, 1996

WEST SIDE MAESTRO

Lectures towards a reconciliation of the two principle schools of musical thought of this century.

First, let us take an overall look at the various musical analyses that peppered each Lecture whether in an incidental way or as a major feature. Those who remember the Omnibus lectures or the Young People's Concerts will already be familiar with the format and L's manner of approach. The major difference between the Norton Lectures and what had preceded them is that the language involved is much more dense and technical. For example, to fully comprehend L's harmonic analysis of Mozart's *G minor Symphony* one does need a degree of technical musical understanding to follow the argument closely. As in the past, L's unbridled enthusiasm helped carry the day but there surely existed a percentage of his Harvard and television audience who felt slightly disenfranchised during the various analyses and pleased at the final arrival of the filmed performances of the complete musical works discussed with L conducting Boston's world famous home town orchestra.

As the first three Lectures set goals seeking to explain music and musical innateness via analogy with linguistic disciplines and procedures, L chose short and vivid musical examples analogous to linguistic techniques such as *inversion, fragmentation, repetition, embedding, conjoining* and *deletion*. Even more ambitiously, he attempted to depict a variety of spoken sentences, such as declarative, interrogative, positive, negative and equivocating, in musical terms. He suggested that chords could inflect a meaning just as adjectives do in language. Choosing three adjectives, *cruel*, *kind* and *tricky*, and the noun, *fate*, he substituted the music of Wagner's *Fate* motive from his Ring operas for his noun and then harmonised it in three different ways with chords which seemed analogous to each of the adjectives proposed. This short intermezzo proved higher in entertainment value than in scientific import. However, an interesting and provocative examination of the relationship between poetry and music as aesthetic parallels in the second, third and sixth Lectures proved highly challenging in terms of the questions it raised for further exploration by professional linguists. The obvious connecting link was that both poetry and music are aural arts and both manipulate their component elements over a structured time span.

Mozart's *G minor Symphony* was used in both the first and second Lectures to demonstrate how various techniques employed by the Viennese master could similarly be described using linguistic terminology and methodology. The first Lecture took an overall general view of the entire symphony using old fashion harmonic analysis. Having taken his audience on a brief historical musical journey from the acquisition of more and more overtones from the harmonic series to an ever enriched musical language complete with an established hierarchy of relationships and rules, L showed how Mozart was able to exploit these relationships to freewheel from his home base to distant harmonic areas and then back home again. All this freewheeling was done at a price and that price was the creation of *ambiguity*. Yet *ambiguity* brought with it greater expressiveness. As long as the *ambiguity* could be strictly controlled through the rules, composers had a powerful musical device at their disposal.

The return of this same *G minor symphony* in the second Lecture was closely tied to linguistic methodology. I have detailed these in my overview of the Lectures themselves. In summary, the initial analysis of the symphony was approached in terms of Mozart's handling of harmony and harmonic relationships. This second analysis deals with a multiform structural analysis of the first movement with an emphasis on *symmetry*.

The density of detail and complexity of the brief undertaken in these opening three scripts leaning so heavily towards disciplines other than music, principally linguistics, with which the majority of his audience were certainly unfamiliar, must have proved a source of disappointment. Expectations must have been for a greater concentration on musical matters. One would be hard put to deny the frustration experienced when the language of the text became particularly opaque with technical and abstruse terms splashed about by L with the confidence of someone who is addicted to solving the Sunday double-crostic in record time using a fountain pen. One is left longing for the clarity and simplicity of expression of his earlier telecasts and the wish that L had trusted more that unique musical insight and expertise which one relied upon never to disenfranchise his listeners. The present reality was, however, that in his enthusiasm within the rarefied intellectual atmosphere of Harvard University L persisted in pursuing musical analogies with linguistics even in areas where his musical logic and theory were sound enough to stand on their own and make his point without analogy. But one must understand that L was searching for a new way to discuss on a higher level brand new concepts and more complex musical ideas with non-professional music lovers. He believed it would be best accomplished by creating analogies between musical functions and comparable language functions related to a linguistic theory to which he sought a parallel within music.

.

Indeed, a bonus of these lectures is that it permits us a fascinating insight into the mind of one of the world's leading musicians. Certainly many of the absorbing propositions and speculations are worthy of the extra input required of anyone acquiring the filmed recordings. I include even those wrong hypotheses which were examined and pursued down several cul-de-sacs in L's search to find genuine parallels between language structure and its innate acquisition and music structure and the intuitive capacity to listen to and simultaneously mentally organise a piece of music. It was L's expressed hope that all his hypothesising and speculation might strike a nugget or two. As we now know, after the passage of thirty-five years, he, in fact, struck the mother-load. But more about that later.

The prelude to the analysis of Beethoven's Sixth Symphony in L's third Lecture on Musical Semantics is a half hour dissertation on *metaphor*. This extended discussion brings L to a reference back to his Young People's Concert of January 18,1958. The YPC program was titled *What Does Music Mean?* and the general thrust of L's text at the time was obviously influenced by statements made by Igor Stravinsky both in his autobiography,

WEST SIDE MAESTRO

Chronicles of my Life (1936) and his Harvard Norton Lectures of 1939/40.[179] L expressed rather dogmatically the same sentiments as Stravinsky, that music is never about *things*, it is only about notes, specifically, in Western music, the notes of the chromatic scale as planned and organised by the composer. Programs superimposed upon specific works, i.e.: *The Sorcerer's Apprentice, The Blue Danube, The William Tell Overture,* etc., were meaningless outside of the possible inspiration they provided for the composer. Musical meaning was only to be found in melody, harmony, instrumental colour and, most important, the way it was developed by the composer.

By the time of the Norton Lectures L had modified his views as had Stravinsky when he expounded his Poetics of Music in his own series of Norton Lectures thirty years earlier. For L, music was now seen to express both *intrinsic* and *extrinsic* meanings expressed by means of *metaphorical transformation* understood on three levels:

1. The *intrinsic* musical metaphor of a purely musical order relates meaning to the musical relationships existing within the notes themselves.

2. The *extrinsic* musical metaphor relates to non-musical meanings associated with the material world and human emotions, such as to be found in Beethoven's *Pastoral* Symphony which contains comments from the composer connecting what he has written to the awakening of cheerful feelings, peasants, birds, a brook and a storm.

3. The third level of *metaphor* creates an analogy between the *intrinsic* and the *extrinsic*, as embodied in the statement, '*musical* transformations are like *verbal* ones.' L now transforms this analogue back into a metaphor by

---

[179] Igor Stravinsky: 'For I consider music is, by its very nature, essentially powerless to express anything at all, whether a feeling, an attitude of mind, a psychological mood, a phenomenon of nature, etc...*Expression* has never been an inherent property of music...To be put into practice, its indispensable and single requirement is construction. Construction once completed, this order has been attained, and there is nothing more to be said.' *Chronicles of my Life*, Simon & Schuster, 1936

deleting the word *like* and now the analogue/ metaphor has become 'musical transformations *are* verbal ones.'

L, as 'devil's advocate',[180] questions his own choice of Beethoven's *Pastoral* for a lecture in which concern had been only with the notes themselves and their internal musical relationships. His justification is the need to clarify and distinguish between the *intrinsic* and *extrinsic* metaphors of music, between the *musical* and the *verbal*.

The entire second half of the lecture is taken up with the Beethoven Symphony. L's first proposition concerns whether it is possible to listen to this work divorced from its extrinsic program especially with all those undeniable extra-musical references imitating the cuckoo and the nightingale, thunder claps, lightning, brooks trickling and all the other references that Disney exploited to a surrealistic degree in his animated feature, *Fantasia*. L challenges his listeners to suspend their programmatic preconceptions and listen afresh as if for the first time. His analysis of the symphony which follows displays a brilliance and clarity that can only be compared to his first *Omnibus* lecture which, as it happens, also concerned a symphony of Beethoven. He continues, as in the first two lectures, to incorporate linguistic terminology within his musical analysis, in this instance to demonstrate that a genuine analogy exists between structural procedures in language and structural procedures in music. The use of language could not be more precise or clear. Great care has been taken not to lose or confuse his novice listeners for an instant. Observing him unfold the creation of the entire first movement, (and, as he proposes, by extension, the entire symphony) from the musical material contained within its opening four bars and, specifically, only the first two notes of the bass line is a display of communicative virtuosity to take ones breath away. There is no rushing this analysis, no tendency towards the sweeping technical-term-dropping prevalent in the previous two lectures. "The Beethovenian style is to develop, to vary, to *transform*", represents the kind of change in language style that has taken place. Three verbs are used to bring us to an unequivocally clear concept of the idea of *transformation* in music. Now

---

[180] The role of *Devil's Advocate* is to prove one of L's most effective techniques in these Lectures.

when L uses Beethoven's symphony to demonstrate the techniques of inversion, fragmentation, deletion, embedding, repetition and inversion, it is so carefully prepared and explained from every angle that we never lose the thread of his thought or the analogous connection he is making which links these techniques to similar manipulations performed by transformations in spoken language. As with the Mozart symphony, there is an analysis of a part of the underlying structure, in this instance a stunning explanation of the simultaneous different structural implications to be discovered in the very long symmetric and asymmetric phrase lengths constructed from a single measure of music profusely repeated by Beethoven. L underlines, in regard to the simultaneous contradictions in one such passage of overt repetition no less than ninety-two bars long, that these contradictions were to be comprehended "as one immense *metaphorical design*", not of peasants and nature but of an *intrinsic* design of purely musical meaning.

To observe L dissect and explain the transformational derivation of every element of the first four bars of the symphony in language his Young People's Concert audience would have understood, which took twenty minutes, constituted in itself a worthwhile reason to attend this lecture. His WGBH audience sat riveted, drinking in his every word, enjoying both the man and the musician, who, at the appropriately judged moment, sensed the need to inject laughter, humanising both himself and his topic.

While the previous two lectures expressed his revolutionary theories of musical innateness within a complex, sometimes ponderous text, this lecture demonstrated them in a direct, sure-footed manner that most certainly must have won over many of the sceptics who were already quite vocal in their criticism.

One would have hoped that the extraordinary textual clarity of the third Lecture was a turning point. This, unfortunately, proves not to be the case in Part I of the three part fourth Lecture, The Delights and Dangers of Ambiguity. One could project that any discussion of *ambiguity* would be fraught with that same quality. The one area in which the fourth Lecture did prove a turning point of the series was with the shift of emphasis on music rather than linguistics. It is a paradox that to L the first three Lectures represented his true passion. They dealt with his theory that wed his belief in a genetic musical competence to Chomsky's established theories of language acquisition. L believed his theories could make a genuine and lasting contribution. At the time, however, the ideas were very new, challenging and unresearched. By L's own admission the questions he was dealing with in linguistics required a much greater depth of understanding than he possessed. He was perceived by his new and concerned friend, Prof. Irving Singer, as "a *genius* experimenting outside his field". Prof. Singer's further concern was that the sum total of L's Norton Lectures would be viewed as tentative. Irving Singer was among the pro-Bernstein supporters who were urging him to use his last three lectures to move the emphasis of his text to more musical matters, the field in which he was a world leader and enjoyed undisputed expertise. It was also Prof. Singer who finally arranged for L to meet Chomsky at an informal dinner for a circle of L's friends and associates at Singer's home following this fourth Lecture.

As already indicated, the fourth Lecture was structured in three sections. Each section dealt with an analysis of a key nineteenth-century orchestral work that pushed the frontiers of musical ambiguity ever forward to the point where the relentlessly growing use of chromaticism no longer seemed able to be contained within former classical diatonic[181] structures. The three orchestral examples chosen to exemplify this were *Romeo Alone* and *The Ball at the Capulets* from Berlioz' Dramatic Symphony, *Romeo and Juliet*, the *Prelude and Love Death* from Wagner's opera, *Tristan and Isolde* and Debussy's *Prelude to An Afternoon of a Faun*.

The published book text in general represents a modest but carefully edited version of the televised programs. This proves even more so in this fourth Lecture. That is all to the good as the small modifications bring greater clarity to the text, remove moments of verbosity and eliminate certain superfluous ad-libs of questionable taste and pretension.

---

[181] Diatonic - L uses this term to denote the tonic/dominant structured relationship of tonal music. The dictionary definition (Musical or Oxford University) is 'using only notes belonging to one key'

WEST SIDE MAESTRO

The opening of the Lecture script attempts to define *ambiguity* in the face of four possible accepted interpretations. L chooses as his definition, "capable of being understood in *two* possible senses" since all previous examples of *ambiguity* encountered in his Lectures have involved *duality*. His opening musical examples demonstrated at the piano are telling. The Adagietto from Mahler's Fifth Symphony, made famous to the general public by the Visconti film, *Death In Venice,* is the perfect *grabber*, to use a *show-biz* term. The generally popular nature of the piece allows L more room to expand technically upon the special nature of its ambiguities. These turn out to be brilliant in their simplicity or, at least, as L explains them. We learn that the instant emotional appeal of the opening theme, based upon only two chords, arises from a vagueness which starts with its introductory harp notes and continues in a variety of other musical shapes, forms and techniques. To stay with linguistics, the variety of ambiguities impart a *syntactic* vagueness to the music. Now for those present at the lectures to whom a music staff and sharps and flats were little more than interesting designs to decorate fabrics, there was nothing for it but to mentally tread water and simply bask in L's personality, enthusiasm and gifts as a performer until they hit a patch of text which dealt with non-technical language they could follow. The reader mustn't assume from this that audience confusion was the order of the day. Following L's line of thought during the technical explanations was analogous to watching foreign language courses on educational television and getting the gist of what was being said even when you did not speak the language.

The time frame of this Lecture encompassed the so-called Romantic Revolution of the nineteenth-century. Although, in music, we tend to associate this new school of thought with composers like Berlioz, Schumann, Chopin and Liszt, in truth Beethoven was its first musical priest and prophet. These Romantic revolutionaries viewed themselves endowed with the divine right to oppose the existing order and make their own rules, create new forms and envision novel, untried concepts in the pursuit of greater expressivity. This movement that swept artistic thought worldwide was not confined to music but encompassed the literary and visual arts as well.

In music, the ambiguities of rhythmic asymmetry, unlikely and surprising modulations and ever increasing chromaticism were key tools in fashioning this new, sought after expressivity. In discussing their use by Schumann and Chopin L splashes about a large chunk of technical references. His swashbuckling musical performance, however, reiterates and helps clarify many of the textual points unclear to the non-musician. It served, as before, to bridge the gap between full understanding and a sufficient enough general grasp of the matters at hand to maintain audience interest and commitment.

We move on to Berlioz who seized the revolutionary banner from Beethoven and extended and magnified the new semantic ambiguities of which the Classical master's Pastoral and Ninth Symphony were portents. The implied programmatic content of the *Pastoral* Symphony was transformed by Berlioz into a symphony, originally titled *Episode in the Life of an Artist, a Fantastic Symphony*, whose programmatic content was not merely implied but wedded and inherent to the understanding of the work itself. In his 'dramatic symphony', *Romeo and Juliet*, Berlioz used soloists and chorus as Beethoven had in his innovative Ninth Symphony. However, where Beethoven used a sung text only in his final movement, Berlioz' vision encompassed the entire Shakespearean tragedy, telling the story using solo, choral and purely instrumental means. Indeed, if we examine Berlioz' total musical output, virtually all of his compositions have literary associations inextricably linked to them.

L chose as his example for analysis one of the purely instrumental interludes which occurs early on in the Berlioz symphony. It depicts Romeo alone, lovesick and restless. We hear sounds from the Capulet ball in the distance. Romeo attends the ball and dances with his beloved, Juliet, in a scene of boisterous gaiety. If only L's explanation was that simple. Key signatures and musical terms are splashed about in a cascading melange. L's straightforward pictorial imagery describing chromatic descents as "dying falls, lovesick sighs" couldn't be more clear especially when demonstrated at the piano in the extrovert Bernstein style but "...*reaching that cadential close in F...it is interrupted by the dance music in D flat, which is not only interrupting but coinciding with the cadence...That final note F of the cadence, which is the tonic note, is suddenly not the tonic, but the third degree of a whole other scale, D flat"* seems a signal to the non-musician to look about for the nearest exit. Although passages like the technical one quoted do appear in chunky bits they never hang about long and vivid pictorial descriptions with just the hint of musical overtones were heralded in to save the day, such as this passage which follows on from the one above, "*The dance tune is created straight out of those chromatic descents we heard in Romeo's reverie. What a transformation: from love sick sighs to highly rhythmic dance music! It's only a short flash...but it's enough to stir up new ambiguities in Romeo, shifty chromatic tremors.*" This is a wonderful mix of imagery and musical terms used as colourful adjectives. What follows is the retelling of this entire segment of the story with L playing a parallel musical blow by blow description at the piano while describing in simplest terms the subtleties of Berlioz' score. As L plays a long, dramatic tremolo he becomes Romeo improvising an impassioned soliloquy as to whether to go to the ball or not. The bass notes of the piano percussively intoning the rhythm of the dance interrupt him. Romeo, depicted by an oboe solo, sings a love song which is punctuated throughout by the dance rhythm played by the percussion. This, we are told, is an example of music's unique ability to depict two happenings simultaneously that can be both perceived and understood by the listener. The Capulet ball reaches its climax as Romeo dances with Juliet and we hear both the ball music and Romeo's love song played concurrently at full orchestral intensity. L labels this happening *contrapuntal syntax,* an analogy which performs both a musical and linguistic function - *counterpoint* which denotes two or more themes performed at the same time and syntax which refers to the resulting new structure created from the combined components of the ball music and Romeo's theme. A complete filmed performance of the excerpt follows.

The text to part two of this Lecture was relatively short but extremely important on several levels. Most important of all, it served as the pivoting point of all the music and text that was to follow. It involved an analysis and performance of the Prelude and Love Death from Wagner's *Tristan and Isolde,* the opera underlined by L as the crisis-work of the nineteenth century, the visionary work that proved to be the turning point after which music was to enter revolutionary realms from which it would never return.

This part of L's Lecture begins with a comparative examination of the similarities between the themes of Berlioz' *Romeo and Juliet* and Wagner's *Tristan.* It proves in turn fascinating, irreverent and amusing. L's lays emphasis on the Wagner/Berlioz friendship.

The historical facts not related to his audience are enlightening and interesting. Wagner, at the age of twenty-seven, became quite friendly with Berlioz during his stay in Paris. At this time he and Berlioz compared compositions and Wagner heard one of the two premiere performances of Berlioz' *Romeo.*[182] Twenty years later he heard a second performance of *Romeo.* In both instances he declared that the music affected him deeply although he had become, after his initial burst of youthful enthusiasm, quite critical of Berlioz.

Wagner had studied the score with Berlioz, attended the initial long rehearsals for the premiere and heard both public performances prior to his composing *Tristan.* L points to a remarkable similarity between themes from *Romeo* and the important motives from *Tristan.* To his audience's amusement L boisterously disclaims any attempt to brand Wagner a "plagiarist". The point he is making, again combining music and linguistics, is that Wagner was "a *transformational* magician". Berlioz, the composer, a living equivalent of a Chomskian *surface structure,* had been transformed into a *deep structure,* specific intellectual components, of another living *surface structure,* namely Wagner. It was a fascinating, new way to view the mental process whereby a creative mind absorbing the ideas of another then transforms, develops and personalises these ideas within his/her own individual and distinct personality. *Romeo* to *Tristan* represented just such an extension from artist to artist. It was a happening, L points out, which

---

[182] November 24, 1840

could be traced throughout music history, each time accompanied by a growth in expressivity and dimension and an increase in ambiguity.

L does go a bit over the top to suggest that *Tristan* is a giant subconscious metaphor of Berlioz' *Romeo and Juliet*. His perceptive musical eye and investigative curiosity was to rebound on him. Michael Steinberg in his previously quoted highly critical NY Times article took L to task for his conjectures in regard to subconscious *borrowing* by Wagner, and, in L's final lecture, by Stravinsky as well. Steinberg dismissively labelled L "a tune detective", thereby invoking the ghost of Sigmund Spaeth whose 'tune detecting' was climaxed in a famous plagiarism trial during which his evidence swayed a jury to view the popular tune, *Avalon,* to be plagiarised from *È lucevan le stelle* from Puccini's opera *Tosca*. Even a superficial investigation by Steinberg would have revealed supporting evidence for L's theories regarding both composers.[183] The voluminous writings on Wagner, which include the composer's auto-biography and various articles, all reveal his long acquaintance with Berlioz and his music and his particular enthusiasm for the *Romeo and Juliet* symphony.

The analysis of the *Tristan* prelude is relatively brief. It concentrates on the increased use of chromaticism by the composer and his avoidance of resolution of harmonies to create a sense of increased *ambiguity*. There is a short semi-technical explanation of *diminished* chords, "the most ambiguous of tonal formations", and Wagner's implied if not overt use of this unstable chord throughout the *Tristan* prelude. L speaks of the Prelude's "timelessness" created through the composer's tempo indication, *slow and languishing*, which is amplified by seeming indeterminate silences and the listener's inability to ascertain a rhythmic pattern during the extended opening. In the closing portion of this segment, there is a flurry of technical jargon that would have been valuable for its Harvard audience in 'instant replay' format. "What gives Tristan its true semantic quality...is the sum of

---

[183] Similarities between their music had already been noted in songs both composers wrote which were inspired by Goethe's *Faust,* Berlioz in 1829 and Wagner in 1832.(Ernest Newman: *Wagner, Man and Artist*, pub. Alfred A Knopf Inc.,1924). Stravinsky's use of quotes from Verdi's *Aida* as musical material for his Oratorio *Oedipus Rex* was confirmed in Robert Craft and Vera Stravinsky's *Stravinsky, In Pictures and Documents,* Simon & Schuster, pub1978

(its) phonological and syntactical transformations, producing (its) highly poetic metaphorical language." Given a second and third look, which is the advantage of owning a permanent record in either book or video format, the quoted statement not only makes perfect sense but also is an accurate summation of the Wagner Prelude *in linguistic terms*. It is, of course, playing armchair general to ponder after the fact whether, having already made and demonstrated his point so tellingly regarding *Tristan* being *the* crisis-work which threatened the framework of tonal containment, the addition of this statement only served to cloud and confuse. Having stated that, could anyone have convinced L to take a *blue pencil* to his script? I doubt it. There are too many evidences to the contrary.

There is a final linguistic cum musical demonstration analysing the principal theme of Isolde's Love Death, the last musical moments of this four hour opera. L sets as his task to show how this theme already exists in nucleus form in the opening phrase of the Prelude. This analysis proves fragmentary, rushed, complex and unclear. As presented, it serves only to 'over-egg the pudding'. It does, however, beautifully set up the line from T.S. Eliot, "In the end is my beginning", which here expresses an analogy to the final Love Death theme developed from the earliest material in the opera. A filmed performance of the *Tristan* excerpts follow.

The final segment of this absorbing if complex lecture takes up the story in 1893. Tristan has burst the dam that contained chromaticism. New and daring post-Wagnerian experiments push the frontiers of music ever forward bringing with them a whole range of new challenges and new ambiguities with which the listener must deal. What was left of the structure that contained the last vestiges of a formal tonal system was to manage to survive into the first twenty years of the new century. L poses the rhetorical question, "How ambiguous can you get before the clarity of musical meaning is lost altogether?" A crisis resulting from uncontained chromaticism taken to its limits could no longer be avoided. It was to split musical thought for the next hundred years. The third part of this lecture sets out to examine through a single work what brought this crisis about. The work is Debussy's

WEST SIDE MAESTRO

Prelude to the Afternoon of a Faun inspired by a poem of the same name by the Symbolist poet, Stéphane Mallarmé.

It was not only music, however, that was in crisis at the turn of the century but all the arts. The beginnings of revolution in the figurative arts had already been underway since 1860 with Manet's shocking *Déjeuner sur l'herbe*. Monet was to usher in Impressionism in 1872 with his *Impression, Sunrise* and Cezanne was to foreshadow the Cubism of Picasso and Braque in his series of late landscapes and final Mt. Saint Victoire paintings. In England, Turner and Whistler were transforming imagery with their subjective view of what they saw and how they translated it onto canvas. World Literature and Poetry had more than their share of early revolutionary figures and *ism's* as well, Zola, Tolstoy, Poe, Whitman, Maupassant, Verlaine, Mallarmé, Gide, Impressionism, Expressionism, Symbolism, and so on.

L draws an important parallel between the rise to dominance of *phonology,* the sheer enjoyment of sound for its own sake, in both the literary and musical Arts. Vagueness in syntax was not only tolerated but pursued in favour of ambiguous dream images and symbolic allusion. Sensual sound and sensual imagery and coloration had taken over. Mallarmé, to whom the euphonic weaving together of words and images was equal to if not more important than their actual meaning, courted an obtuseness that at times defied translation. His philosophy is summed up in the stated purpose, "To evoke in a deliberate shadow the unmentioned object by allusive words."

The Debussy *Afternoon of a Faun* was originally intended as a three part work, a *Prelude*, an *Interlude* and a *Paraphrase Finale* with Mallarmé's poem performed as a monologue by an actor. Although the work was announced in this form only the *Prelude* was ever performed as a concert work. Debussy contradicted himself in letters to colleagues regarding the work's relationship with the poem. At first he stated that "the work conveys the general impression of the poem...(it) illustrates the scene marvellously described in the text." Later he was to speak of it as "a very free illustration...a succession of scenes through which the Faun's desires and dreams move in the afternoon heat." This latter more vague description varies from that associated with typical programme music. Debussy was later to deny that his music was intended as a synthesis of Mallarmé's poem, merely that it was evocative of the poem.

As for L's analysis of the Debussy *Prelude*, it is a mixture, predominantly of technical musical explanation and, to a much lesser degree, poetic description in the music appreciation sense. I have placed great emphasis previously on the necessity of some form of musical background and study to enable the listener or reader to follow L's explication in an informed fashion. Obviously, the better one's grounding in music theory the greater one's understanding of the nuts and bolts that produce Debussy's particular brand of musical poetry and individual orchestral sound palette. With this Lecture, I have come to second thoughts on the matter. Obviously, technical know-how places a listener in a more advantageous position. Nevertheless, the manner in which L reinforces all of his explanations with generously provided and oft repeated piano demonstrations which illustrate and illuminate his text sonically creates a musical lexicon for the non-musician which actually makes it possible for someone without any grounding in music to follow the technical line of thought via what he is hearing, that is, by association with ingested patterns of sound which are identified as the phonological equivalent of technical musical terms with which the listener is unfamiliar.

The understanding of the fourth Lecture in all its parts, analysis included, is especially important as it represents the bridge to the final two programs dealing with music at the crossroads of tonality and atonality. This Lecture, which began by introducing a whole range of new musical ideas, ambiguities and ever-increasing chromaticism in search of ever-greater expressivity, has now reached a point where music has taken a leap into the void. The traditional scales have been discarded, replaced by an arbitrary one invented by Debussy made up only of whole tone intervals.[184]

---

[184] An example of Debussy's whole tone scale would be: C/D/E/F-sharp/G-sharp/A-sharp

WEST SIDE MAESTRO

This new scale, comprised of six tones within the octave instead of the seven of the diatonic scale and the twelve of the chromatic scale, engendered a whole series of new contradictions and ambiguities. As the scale did not include the presence of chromatic semi-tones, (particularly the seventh or *leading* tone of the diatonic scale), the interval of the perfect fifth or the perfect fourth, diatonic stability, based upon a tonic-dominant[185] relationship, ceased to exist. Diatonic major or minor chords could not be constructed from the notes of the whole tone scale. They were replaced by chords which moved about freely and incorporated dissonant, foreign tones without reference to the classical rules of preparation and resolution. This new scale engendered a unique form of *ambiguity* which thwarted, indeed negated the possibility of the traditional *tonic-dominant* relationship upon which the previous two hundred fifty years of music had been based.

L demonstrates the rise in importance in the music of Debussy of the interval of the *augmented fourth*, an interval resulting from the internal structure of the whole tone scale. Baroque, Classical and Romantic composers had avoided this interval. Indeed, its use was forbidden in early church music and given the name, *the devil in music* by the church fathers. Its most famous use in diatonic music was for expressive purposes only in the chorale, *Es ist Genuch,* by Bach which, as we will discover in the fifth Lecture, was later transcribed in its entirety by Alban Berg into the final movement of his *Violin Concerto.* The use of this unusual, exotic and disturbing interval both melodically and to create the tonal ambiguity which pervades *Afternoon of a Faun* throughout helps to concentrate our attention on sensuous sound as an end in itself and on Debussy's unusual use of the orchestra which captures our attention and takes on an individual identity equivalent to "a play within a play". Although, in the truest sense, *The Faun* is modern music, it came to be relatively quickly accepted because of the delicacy, colour and transparency with which Debussy handled his materials. L takes us along an exacting path explaining and demonstrating the complex

---

[185] *Tonic* - the first degree of the major and minor scale. *Dominant* - the fifth degree above the *Tonic* of the major and minor scale *Subdominant* - the fifth degree below the *Tonic* of the major and minor scale *Leading Tone* - the seventh degree of a scale, a semi-tone below the *Tonic* which tends to gravitate, (lead), upwards to the *Tonic.*

WEST SIDE MAESTRO

technical inner workings and logic of this pivotal revolutionary ten minute work but at the same time he constantly refers back in straightforward language, analogy and musical examples to details in other lectures which will help clarify and reinforce the technical points he is making. In the end, he reveals how a contemporary composer even as he turns the order of things upside down can still contain the modernity of his ideas within a communicative framework by making reference at key moments to landmarks which his listeners recognise either consciously or subconsciously and which reflect the creative personality maintaining links with his roots even as he explores new terrain's.

I have chosen not to discuss L's comparative analysis of the Mallarmé poem which inspired Debussy as it was my stated purpose to contain within the first section of my analyses only the music under discussion. It is worthwhile underlining, however, that L's analogy's throughout the six Lectures between the phonology, structure and semantics of poetry and that of music is never less than enlightening. One cannot help but be swept along by L's parallel passion for this musical universe of words.

The fifth and sixth lectures prove less problematic for the non-musician studying the Lectures in filmed format. The text for both falls into the more conventional music appreciation category. L's final two Lectures can be seen to parallel the format of a book by Theodor Adorno titled *The Philosophy of Modern Music*. The Adorno book is constructed as a double essay on Arnold Schönberg and Igor Stravinsky. Adorno, a former pupil of Alban Berg, synthesises the two major streams of musical thought in the twentieth-century, tonal vs. non-tonal music, as personified by these two musical leviathans. As opposing leaders, they represented the galvanising force behind each school of thought, Stravinsky exploring every avenue of possibility in extending and re-freshening musical ambiguity within a tonal framework and Schönberg transforming the entire tonal system into a new metaphorical speech of his own invention which abjured tonality.

L's fifth Lecture is devoted principally to Schönberg and a history and layman's analysis of his *method of twelve-tone,* or *dodecaphonic,*

340

composition. Unlike Adorno in his book, described by L in his introduction as "fascinating, nasty and turgid", L takes a more even handed, one might say ecumenical approach to his examination of these two great composers and the thorny and highly divisive issue that separated them and their followers.

With only a brief introduction, the Lecture begins with a filmed performance of *Feria* (Holiday) from Ravel's *Rhapsodie Espagnole*.

The Ravel work with its undisturbed optimism written in the year of 1908 was a symbol of half of the dichotomy facing European society in this year. On the one hand, there was the general euphoria symbolised in the Ravel work which the prodigious achievements of the nineteenth-century continued to engender. The middle class were prosperous, new inventions, including the automobile, had served to make life more comfortable and held out the promise of new markets and new money. Factories continually belched out their smoke and the railroad's glittering steam engines pulled coaches filled to overflowing with joy-seekers and commercial travellers. What could go wrong?

The other half of the dichotomy pointed to crisis which was already manifesting itself in middle Europe. Germany had begun to arm under the Kaiser. In Italy, Filippo Marinetti, a poet, launched *Futurism* with his *Manifesto*. This radical literary movement that espoused the triumph of science over nature quickly picked up momentum among Italy's painters. Its cryptic war cry with fascist overtones was "Burn the museums! Drain the canals of Venice! Kill the moonlight!" In Austria, in the year 1908, it was music that was at the crossroads. A little known composer named Arnold Schönberg, commanding the interest and support of no lesser personage than Gustav Mahler, had introduced his Second String Quartet, opus 10. Having stretched Wagnerian chromatic harmonies in his early compositions to the very borders of tonality, he had decided to reject traditional forms of harmonic composition totally for a radical solution. Using the unusual inclusion in the final movement of his quartet of a soprano voice, he issued a prophetic warning of the music to come with the words of Stefan George's poem, "I feel the air of other planets." (This short excerpt from the quartet movement is played and sung by L). Schönberg's music of the future was to forsake tonality altogether. In 1911 he completed a treatise on music theory, *Harmonielehre*, dedicated to the memory of Mahler. Though a traditional book on the principles of harmony, it also offered illuminating possibilities of radical new directions in music. It took, however, Schönberg's genius another fourteen years to fully evolve his theories from their early designation of *atonality*, a term he rejected, to his final *System*, "a method of composition with twelve tones related only to one another" or a *dodecaphonic* (dodeca -'12', *phone* - 'sound') *method*.

All of the Schönberg non-tonal works that follow, beginning with a little Waltz from Schönberg's first non-tonal work, *Three Piano Pieces, opus 11*, are demonstrated by L at the piano. Only one other filmed orchestral work is used during the remaining hour-long first part of this Lecture. The year remains1908 but we shift to a small New England town in America and to an unknown Sunday composer named Charles Ives. Ives, very much aware of Mahler, whom he admired, but unaware of Schönberg, has composed a short, highly dissonant work both structurally and sonically far ahead of its time which he titles, *The Unanswered Question*. This is the work which inspired L's Norton Lectures. It was L's projection that Ives instinctively sensed that great changes were in the air and that this short ten-minute work was his response to the musical convulsions taking place.

In his first Lecture L projected that through this piece Ives was really posing the question "Whither music in our time?" The reality was otherwise. Ives, in fact, prefaced this short work with an elaborate metaphysical text involving the priests of the Celts in ancient Britain and "The Perennial Question of Existence" which L reads in part:

"The strings play pianissimo throughout with no change in tempo. They are to represent "The Silences of the Druids - Who Know, See and Hear Nothing." The trumpet intones "The Perennial Question of Existence", and states it in the same tone of voice each time. But the hunt for the "Invisible Answer" undertaken by the flutes and other human beings, becomes gradually more active, faster and louder...[These] "Fighting Answerers, as time goes on...seem to realize a futility and begin to mock "The Question" - the strife is over for a moment. After they disappear, "The Question" is asked for the last time, and "The Silences" are heard beyond in "Undisturbed Solitude"[186].

Ives' preface as it stood held little value for L in his quest. It was discarded as an inconvenient mismatch to the keystone of his inquiry. However, where L at first strongly implied the "Whither music?" question to be Ives' true hidden agenda in composing this work, in the text of his Fifth Lecture he shifts his ground, more by emphasis than by the words employed, and makes it clear that the "Whither Music?" ascription is merely his own projection. As I have already pointed out, L's pursuit, "Whither music?" was no less valid or relevant emanating from his own questioning rather than that of Ives. The consequences merely posed the same legitimate question in a contemporary setting rather than, as L wished, to link it to the revolutionary happenings in Vienna during the first decade of the century through a seeming implicit challenge from an American contemporary, himself an *avant-garde* composer. The reality was even more extraordinary. Ives, viewed in retrospect, despite the most unconventional, incomplete musical training, proved to be a kind of musical Nostradamus, a primitive individualist phenomenon, a pioneer who, in anonymous obscurity, staked his claim to virtually every revolutionary *avant-garde* musical development prior to their advancement by the historic European figures to whom they are generally credited, such as Schönberg, Berg, Webern, Stravinsky and Stockhausen. His music is highly auto-biographical, inspired by everyday happenings from going to church to going to a baseball game. It represents a conglomerate of the sights and sounds of his lifetime fused together with a generous helping of the transcendental philosophy of Ralph Waldo Emerson. Virtually all of his compositions were inspired by or tried to emulate actual happenings from his life, in most cases several remembered happenings sounding cacophonously at the same time in several different keys. *The Unanswered Question* was for Ives merely another of his experiments, specifically in the contrast of consonance and dissonance.

---

[186] Charles Ives' preface note for *The Unanswered Question.*

WEST SIDE MAESTRO

There are no implied questions or sought for answers other than the philosophical ones posed by the preface.

Using a voice-over technique, L analyses his filmed performance with the BSO. If, in the end, after clearly describing the work in its component parts, L's question, "Whither music", is not the one the composer intended, one must agree that it certainly lends itself to the work's musical format. Ives' juxtaposes a *non-tonal* trumpet phrase, (interpreted by L as the "Whither?"question), answered by amorphous *polytonal* babbling in the woodwinds, (*non-tonality*), against a string background of an imperturbably maintained G-major triad, (*tonality*), which, at the conclusion, is left to fade into nothingness leaving behind only its *tonal* ghost hovering around us. Had this Ives opus been performed in its time, one could accurately project that more than one person would have been moved to pose L's fundamental question, "Whither music?".

"Is the final sustained G major chord the answer?", L asks. "Is tonality eternal?" The Ives work represented a summation of the problem for L. The alternatives he presents are rather heavily weighted in one direction, "tonality and syntactic clarity on the one hand - non-tonality and syntactic confusion on the other." L draws back from the brink to which this outlined choice takes him. His pragmatic evaluation is that all composers, whether tonal or non-tonal, search for richer forms of musical speech and increased expressive power. Ergo, Schönberg and Stravinsky, despite the musical chasm that appeared to separate them, were, in fact, pursuing the same goal in different ways.

From this point on we exclusively follow Schönberg's path and that of his disciple, Alban Berg. We sample various of Schönberg's innovations. An excerpt from *Pierrot Lunaire*, a setting of twenty-one poems of Albert Giraud, helps L illustrate *Sprechstimme*, a technique half way between singing and speaking which the soloist must employ in presenting the poetic text. Another excerpt from the same cycle indicates that Schönberg still resorted to fragmentary instances of tonality in the midst of his commitment to his non-tonal system. Thus the composer began working towards perfecting a system that would avoid tonal references of any kind. L allows us to sample other short piano compositions from this development phase. He continues to point out tonal references as well as allusions to other works such as *Tristan*. Finally, L demonstrates Schönberg's fully evolved new System wherein *"all twelve tones are presented in a pre-established order, or series, with no single tone repeated until all other eleven have been sounded."*

The pre-established order, designated a *tone row*, was used as melody or combined into chords. No matter the form taken by the row or the nature of the transformations it undergoes, no note is allowed to be repeated before the other eleven have been employed. We hear as an example of the new system an excerpt from Schönbergs *Opus 23, a Waltz for piano*. However, even this work created from a system of strict controls reveals harmonic implications under L's perceptive microscopic investigation.

After a very brief foray seeking linguistic analogies to Schönberg's *tone-row* and all the material derived from it, the text again centres on the music itself.

Tone-rows and the way they are used can be viewed as analogous to the functions performed by the tonal scale. The twelve tone system with its own idiosyncratic scale offering the possibility of what appears to be endless variations and permutations did seem to present a viable alternative to tonal composition. With the new system and its new language, however, came what L refers to in analogy as "a crisis in syntax". His argument went as follows: since Schönberg's *system* specifically avoids tonal relationships, innate principles of musical perception play no part in the mental organisation of what the listener hears when encountering twelve-tone music. The *system* produces music analogous to a foreign language whose rules must first be learned intellectually. As a result enormous importance is placed upon the logical structure of the music to help bridge the gap of the newness of the musical text. L demonstrates in piece after piece that the strict classical symmetry employed by Schönberg often carries with it subconscious tonal implications resulting from the melodic shape created by the intervals used in its structure. This even appears to be the case in the most highly developed of Schönberg's serial works like the *String Quartet, Opus 30* and the *Variations for Orchestra, Opus 31.* L suggests that *atonality* in a true sense can only be achieved by means of a reconstructed scale comprising a greater number of equidistant intervals, (perhaps thirteen, thirty or even three hundred), than the same twelve equidistant tones used by Bach, Beethoven, Wagner *and* Schönberg.

We are next offered an historic glimpse of the use of melodic sequences resembling *tone rows* found in the music of Bach, Mozart, Beethoven and Franz Liszt. These sequences, shown to be early examples of attempts to transcend tonality in order to evoke a sense of mystery, represent only momentary denials of their harmonic roots. Schönberg, in contrast, worked to construct an entire system totally based upon rootlessness. L's contention was that music can never be rootless as long as it is based upon an octave of twelve equal tones derived from the harmonic overtone series. Given that basis, harmonic relationships survive, either in overt or implied form.

L next points to a compromise solution to this problem as adopted by Schönberg's most famous disciple, Alban Berg. Berg, while employing *dodecaphonic* procedures, deliberately flirted with tonality, balancing the two elements in a fashion that never projected compromise to his commitment to Schönberg. His teacher had in a sense allowed for such modifications by stating that the "rules" of his *system* were no more than guidelines. L uses Berg's last completed composition, his *Violin Concerto*, to demonstrate how the composer managed this fine balancing act between the seeming incompatible schools of strict *twelve-tone* writing and *tonality*.[187]

L's analyses parts of the concerto beginning with the *tone row* upon which the concerto's musical material is based. The tonal implications of the *row* appear virtually self-apparent. Built upon major and minor chords, it concludes with four whole tones that make up the interval of the *augmented*

---

[187] Two other Berg musical excerpts from the opera *Wozzeck* are reprinted in the book of the Lectures but neither was performed during the Lecture itself or is quoted on the accompanying excerpt LP discs.

fourth which had played such an important role in Debussy's *Afternoon of a Faun*. This *row*, L underlines, "has very strong roots in music's traditional past." Berg reinforces these roots by using the same formal music structures to be found in the compositions of Bach, Beethoven, Schumann and the Viennese masters of his youth. The combination of these traditional elements along with the composer's natural, lyric and dramatic gifts brought Berg's music a popularity that far outstripped that of his teacher or his other noted colleague and co-founder of the *Second Viennese School*, Anton Webern.

The concluding section of the first movement of the Berg Concerto, a kind of *Ländler*, a rustic peasant dance and the fore-runner of the Waltz, is L's first chosen excerpt from the concerto. A recording of this *Ländler* excerpt is played for the audience. L first suggests that his listeners compare it with Schönberg's *Opus 23 Waltz for piano* but then strikes out that suggestion in favour of simply listening to it, enjoying its "*mellifluous, tender Wienerisch*ness", (typically Viennese quality). A two-and-a-half minute excerpt follows which must have had those who had never heard the Berg work before wondering at L's choice of adjectives. L even compares the excerpt afterwards to a slice of a popular Viennese chocolate gateau with whipped cream. Let us just say that the chosen excerpt is not among classical music's *top hundred* hummable tunes or even *top thousand*. It is a part of a marvellous and complex work that requires a good deal of hearing and, if one is a musician, studying before one can begin to enjoy its many fascinations.[188] L's over the top enthusiasm is to convince his audience as much as to express his own genuine feelings for the work. Nobody could quarrel with the choice of either composer or work. It makes the point regarding the reconciliation of tonality within strict twelve-tone composition as no other work of this genre. In the second excerpt, taken from the closing pages of the final *Adagio* of the concerto, Berg quotes in its entirety Bach's four part setting of Johann Rudolf Ahle's chorale, *Es ist genug*, (It is enough), upon which he builds a set of variations. The opening soprano line of the chorale is unique among Bach's four hundred and fifty chorale settings. It consists of a rising melody of four whole tones, the augmented

---

[188] L makes this very point just a bit later in his text.

fourth, and the infamous *devil in music* forbidden in church music and in all composed music for three hundred years until its redemption in the whole tone scale of Debussy. These same rising four whole tones form the tail end of Berg's *tone-row* stated at the start of the concerto by the solo violin. L provides a straightforward, non-technical description of the recorded excerpt to be played, Berg's inspired tonal use of the Bach chorale, and the astonishing tonal close of the movement in B flat Major. Following the playing of the recording, L closes the first half of his Lecture posing the question as to whether Berg's hybrid solution solves the *Ultimate Ambiguity* created by Schönberg *twelve-tone system*. Together, he and his listeners have examined the origins of the great tonal split. The methods and an assessment of the leader of the new, radical non-tonal movement, Arnold Schönberg, have been presented in a relatively dispassionate fashion. Accommodation and conclusions have been reached but they point to a compromise solution by a pupil who seems to have outstripped his teacher in achieving public acceptance and relative popularity through the adaptation and modification of his teacher's original ideas. Where is further light to be shed? For L, it is a look backwards to the musical will and testament of Gustav Mahler, his *Ninth Symphony*.

Following the interval, Mahler and his *Ninth Symphony* are discussed within an historical context. I have covered the text of this part of L's Lecture quite exhaustively in the previous section of this chapter. L's analysis of the music of the *Ninth Symphony* occupies only the final five minutes of the Lecture. Again it is a straightforward music appreciation presentation offering no technical challenges to the listener. L describes each movement as a different kind of farewell. The first movement is a farewell to love, the second movement a farewell to nature, the third movement a farewell to urban, cosmopolitan life and the fourth movement a farewell to life itself. It is simple and very moving creating a just atmosphere for the final movement, captured on film during a live concert in Vienna, which follows.

L's final Lecture begins with a problem in aesthetics, "What constitutes *sincerity* in music?" Excerpts from two Verdi operas, *Aida* and *Traviata*, are followed by a *Kinks*[189] tune, a cadenza from a Mozart piano concerto and an excerpt from the third Act of Wagner's opera *Parsifal*. Despite all outward appearances, (an Italian writing Egyptian music, a rock song that shouts you deaf with its declaration of love, a passage from Mozart to display virtuosity and a work depicting 'piety' written by a composer who was the portrait of selfishness, prejudice and impropriety), L maintains that each of these works are "sincere *in their own way.*" *Sincerity* provides a bridge to a discussion of Stravinsky and his music. The link is Theodor Adorno's contentious critique, *The Philosophy of Modern Music*. The noted German critic, philosopher and musician reduces the revolutionary turn of the century split in modern music to a personalised one between Schönberg and Stravinsky. Schönberg is depicted as a hero and Stravinsky as a deceiver, a charlatan, little more than a conjurer with a bag of tricks.

.

We learn that Adorno defines the question of *sincerity* as the direct and subjective expression of feeling, a continuation of the Wagnerian tradition, ergo, the Schönbergian path.[190] He contrasts this to what he views as the cold intellectuality of Stravinsky, slick and stylised, rejecting the personal on every level. Adorno's argument, says L, can be reduced to the relationship between *art* and *artificiality*. L, in an explosion of alliteration, builds a carefully constructed reply to Adorno's polemic beginning with the question, "How artificial can art be, and still be art?" The answer, which he points out is subject to historical modification from one stylistic period to the next and from culture to culture, is that *artifice* has always been a part of the essence of art. Through its application "emotions, from the simple to the most complex, are made aesthetically presentable and intelligible." In a riposte to Adorno, L touches briefly upon his own theory of musical innateness based upon tonal principles. He points out that the twelve-tone row, the essence of Schönberg's *Method*, is a concept that *conflicts with innateness* and,

---

[189] The Kinks - a noted contemporary rock band

[190] *Schoenberg* and his followers *Berg* and *Webern*, despite their radical innovations, were viewed and viewed themselves as continuations of a Viennese tradition of the recent past from *Beethoven, Brahms, Wagner, Bruckner* and *Mahler*. Even as they strove to evolve a new musical language to replace what they viewed as an exhausted *tonality* that had virtually drowned in a sea of harmonic ambiguity, they framed the structure of their music within the traditional strict compositional forms of the past.

therefore, could be construed as the most artificial of musical devices. It would then follow, that the system from which it is derived is itself also *one huge artificiality*. L disclaims such an argument as both pointless and as untrue as Adorno's case against Stravinsky.

Objectivity receives a fair share of prominence in L's text. L's employment of the word as applied to Stravinsky and his music refers to the composer's approach to his craft and the effect he sought his music to project to the listener. *Objectivity* was intended to place the composer and his music at a respectful distance from the final product. The treatment of the subject matter would exhibit all the pertinent details of a complete picture but without being coloured by the feelings or opinions of the writer.

At the turn of the century such an approach was to be exemplified in the music of the Parisian composer, Eric Satie. Satie can be viewed as the first of the revolutionaries to turn his back on the excesses of German Romanticism and to adopt a slightly cool, disengaged approach to his compositions. This approach was to culminate in its full flowering in the music of Igor Stravinsky. It was Stravinsky who elevated what began as a local anti-Romantic reactionary happening to an aesthetic that changed and dominated the face of tonal music for the next forty years.

Music historians divide Stravinsky's musical career into three periods. The first is seen as a *Russian* period. It encompasses his early orchestral works, the *Symphony in E flat Major*, the *Scherzo Fantastique* and *Fireworks*, (all written while still strongly under the influence of his teacher, Nicolai Rimsky-Korsakov), his three famous ballets, *The Firebird*, *Petrouchka* and *The Rite of Spring*, the stage works, *The Wedding, Renard and The Soldier's Tale* concluding with the one act opera *Mavra* written in 1921.

The second and most influential period of Stravinsky's composing career, lasting thirty years, upon which L principally concentrates, bears the label *neo-classic*. It is characterised by an obsession with the distant historical past and was a counter reaction to the weighty romantic emotionalism that burgeoned with Wagner and nurtured those who followed in his footsteps.

WEST SIDE MAESTRO

The ideas and practice of *neo-classicism,* as we have noted in the person of Satie, pre-dates Stravinsky. However, there were others throughout Europe who, by the turn of the century, also stated a need to look backward in order to recapture the spirit of Bach, Mozart and Beethoven.[191] Nevertheless, it was the young Russian Stravinsky to whom the new guard of French music and literature were drawn and who would be *neo-classicism's* greatest, most famous exponent and leader of the movement for the first half of the twentieth-century.

Although music commentators date *neo-classicism* from Stravinsky's composing of his *Pulcinella* ballet for Diaghilev's company, L rightly observes that even in the major works which brought him to fame and pre-date Pulcinella, works of the so-called Russian period, the composer seemed no longer to be expressing himself but had become an observer "contemplating a world to which he was affectively attached." His music had taken on the aspect of an unromanticised "aesthetic document" and thus objectified. It is the composer as reporter, expressing his observations in his own language. The composer "once removed - *objective.*"

L demonstrates the various *artifices* which Stravinsky used to re-freshen tonality and keep the progress of tonal music moving ever forward. Linguistic terminology of earlier lectures again surfaces. L speaks of *phonological* strides in the use of dissonance; of the elements of premeditation and organisation now marshalled to shock one's audience; how the basic *triad,* the very "bread and butter of tonal music", became an ally to discord by the addition of tones which created dissonance without destroying tonal implications. L introduces a new concept called *polytonality* - using two or more tonalities simultaneously. This proved an influential and fashionable Stravinskian *freshener.* Stravinsky had successfully employed *polytonality* in his two ballets, Petrouchka and The Rite of Spring. These masterworks had, in diverse ways, taken Paris by storm

---

[191] One can equally point to Brahms' piano *Variations and fugue on a theme by Handel* as well as his popular orchestra and four-hand setting of *Variations on a theme by Haydn* as examples of taking inspiration from the past. L lists among the Romantics who were reflecting on the past Richard Strauss, Max Reger, Ottorino Respighi and Ferruccio Busoni.

and changed the face of tonal music forever. *Polytonality* became especially popular with Paris' avant-garde musical firebrands, *Les Six*.[192] L explains its use by Stravinsky in his ballets *Petrouchka* and *The Rite of Spring*[193]. He demonstrates at the piano how "the combination of two different chords automatically creates a third chord, a new *phonological* entity." The rapid-fire *polytonal* modulations used in *The Soldier's Tale* illustrate a further extension of the composer's controlled but never confusing use of *ambiguity*. The same work is used to demonstrate yet another tonal freshener, *rhythmic displacement*, a disruption in the continuity of rhythmic patterns. Using an effective metaphor, L describes this addition to the repertoire of *fresheners* as a *rhythmic dissonance*. The use of rhythmic asymmetry became in Stravinsky's hands a new and powerful weapon in the expanding arsenal of tonality.

With the return to linguistic analogy using technical concepts like *transformational procedures, deep-structure deletions, surface structures* and the like, (which harked back to the first Lecture and L's analysis of the Mozart *g minor* symphony using linguistic terms metaphorically to describe Mozart's creative techniques), the book of the Lectures combined with the videos becomes invaluable. Together they permit the interested viewer "a second bite of the cherry", a reference back and the opportunity to take that necessary extra time to gain a deeper understanding of what L was trying to say and accomplish. It also points up the seriousness with which this project was undertaken. Even in those areas where L strayed rather far from the path and lost his way, the importance of this total document, warts and all, in creating a fuller, in depth portrait of the scope and complexity of his mind

---

[192] *Les Six* consisted of young French composers destined to move into the twentieth-century what was then viewed in avant-garde circles to be an anachronistic, fossilised French school of musical thought . The names of their members form a 'Who's-Who' of French contemporary composers, *Georges Auric, Francis Poulenc, Darius Milhaud, Louis Durey, Germaine Tailleferre* and the Swiss-born *Arthur Honnegger*. Originally attracted to *Eric Satie* following Diaghilev's staging of the ballet which scandalised Paris, *Parade*, (which also featured the literary talents of *Jean Cocteau* and decor by *Pablo Picasso*), *Les Six* were to switch allegiance to *Stravinsky* with whom they established, especially *Poulenc*, long friendships and by whom each came to be strongly influenced.

[193] *Petrouchka* is an example of *bi*-tonality, the use of *two tonalities* simultaneously. *The Rite of Spring* is an example of *poly-tonality*, the use of *more than two tonalities* at the same time.

and culture cannot be underestimated. Contrary to Jonathan Miller's petulant and unfathomable description earlier quoted that he viewed these Lectures as being "shallow", one is left to wonder how the majority of those who attended the Lectures were able to follow their complexity with so many multi-discipline, challenging and thought provoking ideas coming at them in such rapid succession.

What exemplifies the individuality of Stravinsky's music? To explain this, L contrasts the difference between the long and mostly symmetrical phrase structures in a Mozart Symphony with Stravinsky's abrupt *asymmetrical* **motivic** *structure*. These *asymmetrical* **motives** are comprised of brief melodic fragments, two, three and four note formations, which are interposed against each other in irregular patterns[194]. Crafted and shaped by Stravinsky with the precision of a diamond cutter, they continually provide the unexpected for the listener.

A somewhat complex ten-minute examination of *polyrhythms*, the *syntactic* equivalent of *polytonality*, follows. In brief, just as one can employ two or more tonalities at the same time to create a new and fresh tonal result so one is capable of juxtaposing two or more rhythms simultaneously to create ever more complex *rhythmic dissonances*. L relates this new polyrhythmic concept to a single page of score from *The Rite of Spring*. **Curtain up!** What follows is razzle-dazzle Bernstein at his most charismatic. First analysing each of the patterns that combines to make up the multiplex of rhythmic polyphony, L then attempts simultaneously to stamp, sing and beat out with his hands on the music rest of the piano the total rhythmic complexity that Stravinsky's genius has created. The heat generated by this incredible display would best be described by evoking a Koussevitzky quote which the maestro used to raise the heat quotient in his rehearsals, "Wild! Wild!!!...but *organised* !!!!!"

Following this show-stopping demonstration, having dealt with two of the linguistic disciplines, *phonology* in terms of harmonic dissonance and

---

[194] L describes these juxtapositions in linguistic terms as '*conjoined, embedded, permuted, expanded*, ...like jagged pieces of glass in some gigantic kaleidoscope.'

syntax as it metaphorically relates to polyrhythmic structures L now moves on to *semantics* as it relates to Stravinsky's use of folk material in both *The Rite of Spring* and *The Wedding (Les Noces)*. L views the deeply rooted expressions of our beginnings in *folk music* and *folklore* as examples of *the Poetry of Earth*. He suggests that their atavistic origin, so deeply embedded in Stravinsky's cultural development, helped shape that *objectivity* which enabled him to place himself at a "respectful distance" from the works he created. He puts forward the challenging thought that the early works of Stravinsky are comparable to "anthropological metaphors". The challenge increases when we contrast the sophistication applied by this twentieth-century composer to music that depicts rituals dating back to pre-history. In a quote that should be read twice, it represented **"a synthesis of earthy vernacular *embedded* in stylistic sophistication."**

A short but highly entertaining interlude follows. Reflecting a euphoric society that had put the terrible rigours of global conflict behind them in the post World War I years, L demonstrates how other composers, inspired by Stravinsky's insatiable acquisition of whatever vernacular suited his creative purpose, began to freely incorporate the vernacular of fun and relaxation in their music as well. Alternatively playing or accompanying his gravel baritone, we are treated to a variety of examples of the transplanting of vernacular in music. It begins with the music of two Frenchmen, Darius Milhaud using the vernacular of Rio de Janeiro in his *Saudade do Brasil* for piano and Francis Poulenc using the vernacular of Montmatre in a delightful Edith Piaf-style *chanson* from his opera *Les Mamelles de Tirésias*. After crooning his way through the Poulenc waltz, L provides us with a taste of American vernacular, Brooklyn-born Aaron Copland's ballet of the Wild West, *Billy The Kid*. As an encore, he offers an example of Kurt Weill's cabaret style, *Mack The Knife* from the *Three Penny Opera*, sung in his best *deutch*. Needless to say, L reminds us that Stravinsky was there first using his dry, musical wit in creating take-offs from lightweight material which transformed them into fresh, humorous and unpredictable music of great sophistication.

WEST SIDE MAESTRO

Humour, in the guise of wittiness, elegance or mockery, is a key Stravinskian component. L reminds us of the basis of all humour, *incongruity*. For example, when our favourite cartoon character slips on a banana skin it produces gales of laughter. In real life we know it can produce a broken limb or fractured skull. Incongruity! The concept of *incongruity* lays the foundation for the greater part of L's thesis which will occupy the second half of this Lecture.

Linguists, L informs us, view that which is *incongruous* to be "the result of ill matched components". L quotes a Chomskian example of incongruity, *Colourless green ideas sleep furiously*. Chomsky constructed this sentence as an example that deliberately thwarted our expectations, (i.e.: something colourless can't be green, ideas can't be green or sleep, and the act of sleeping is a passive experience*)*. Under certain circumstances, L insists, this sentence can be shown to be totally acceptable, for instance, as poetry. For this to be accomplished, what is required is a creative and innovative effort of the imagination. L demonstrates this in a flashy turn of linguistic virtuosity. First he creates a prose twenty-seven-word *deep structure*[195] which lends a sense of credibility to this five word multiple contradiction. Then by using the tools of the linguist, *deletion, condensing* and *embedding*, he reconstructs its original surface form which, with our new understanding of its original deep structure, we can now contemplate as "a line of poetry born of *metaphorical transformation*."

This short linguistic interlude, which at first appearance seems to be another of the obsessive word games in which L revelled in private life, serves two purposes. It re-introduces poetic analysis, first explored in the second and third Lectures, which will occupy virtually a quarter of this final Lecture. As for "colourless green ideas", its incongruous nature, which L has demonstrated can be explained on a non-realistic, aesthetic level, provides a key to that very kind of ambiguity and irony upon which Stravinsky's music thrived.

---

[195] L's prose *deep structure* is: 'Last night I slept badly; my usual *colourless* dreams were invaded by sort of dirty-*green ideas*, which caused me to *sleep* fitfully and toss *furiously*.'

WEST SIDE MAESTRO

It was the composer's Octet of 1923 that set the seal on *neoclassicism*[196]. Stravinsky issued a rather solemn manifesto describing the nature of the work and his relation to it as its composer: "My Octet is a musical *object*. The *object* has a form and that form is influenced by the *musical matter* with which it is composed. The differences of *matter* determine the differences of form. One does not do the same with marble that one does with stone (my italics)." Considering that the Octet is the jolliest of works, this over serious statement makes one wonder whether it had more to do with the attitude the composer wished to engender towards the new direction to which he was now committed than to a comment upon the single work itself.

The ability to thwart the expectation of the listener was to be the trademark of Stravinsky's neo-classic output. It was a technique already highly developed in his earlier works especially in relation to his use of rhythmic and motivic asymmetry. His Pied Piper ability to lead the listener's ear wherever he dictated was now expanded to include his subtle and sudden manipulations of harmony and phrase structure. His repertoire of *freshener* devices seeming to pursue a path in one direction would unexpectedly alter their implied logic without warning and yet continue to project a conviction comparable to that which one feels when listening to a symphony by Beethoven. It remained one of the great attractions as well as challenges of his music. Stravinsky was crafting musical incongruity, the wedding of ill-matched components, to a perfection that would climax four years later with a stage work which was half opera/ half oratorio based upon the classic Greek tragedy of *Oedipus Rex* by Sophocles.

The year is 1923. The Octet and the Piano Concerto, both composed in that year, become the launching pad for Stravinsky's neo-classicism. L draws our attention to the other side of the 'Great Divide'. 1923 was also the year Schönberg revitalised *atonality* by launching his *Twelve-tone System*. That, however, forms only a part of the international Arts picture. Within the Arts in general there was a turning away from the excesses of the previous century. Although L does not mention the neo-classic movement in the

---

[196] *Stravinsky* was later to refer to *neo-classicism* as "a much abused expression meaning absolutely nothing."

figurative arts, Picasso had forsaken *cubism* for monumental figures reminiscent of classical sculptures, Mattisse had begun to look to the 17th and 18th century for his inspiration, The Blue Rider movement in Germany was pushing *Expressionism* to its limits and Kandinsky was soon to produce the first of his abstract paintings which could be viewed as the painterly counterpart to Schönbergs new *Twelve-tone System*.

Just as the situation in the visual and musical arts was boiling over so a similar overheating was taking place within the aesthetics of literature and poetry. In literature, specifically poetry, there had also been an international reaction to the excesses of the Romantics, epitomised in the poet laureates of Eastern and Western Europe as well as America. In this instance, not musical but **verbal** *fresheners* became the order of the day for the young revolutionaries. They brought about what L describes as a "modernistic orgy in poetry".

A poetic intermezzo, designated by L as "a sidelong glance at poetry" now takes center stage. L views an examination of the revolution within poetry to be the most effective way to understand the neo-classic movement as a whole. The entire nature of poetry changed through the use of *fresheners* in a variety of forms just as tonal music had. A key example was the poetry of e e cummings. Placed on the printed page in helter-skelter fashion despite its grammatical sense, it had become poetry for the eye as well as the ear. This was a brand new use of *incongruity* in the literary arts, **visual** *incongruity*, the *mismatching of matter and manner*.

Just as Stravinsky was to be the man of the hour who would lead 'the big save' within the musical Arts so a counterpart would emerge to lead the "big save" in the poetic Arts. That man was T.S. Eliot. What follows is a combination of a superb analogy describing the parallel crisis and its resolution in the musical and poetic Arts. It provides an unspoken declaration of L's life long love affair with poetry and a brilliant example of the interdisciplinary workings of the human mind in seeking out, finding, analysing and reaching its conclusions. This *intermezzo* did not provide the genre of music people came to hear but there is little doubt that they did hear another kind of music enhanced by the performance of a passionate advocate.

A quote from T.S. Eliot precedes and follows the interval, "One has only learned to get the better of words/ For the thing one no longer has to say." Substituting the word *notes* for *words* could be taken, L suggests, to be an autobiographical statement by Stravinsky. Thus begins the final theoretical/analysis portions of these lectures before the final summing up. Over two hours in length it deals with yet another of L's theories which seeks parallels between language and music. It is a journey which again examines possible linguistic parallels between Poetry and Music.

Poetry was first introduced by L in the second Lecture. Its parallel to music was that it brought the basic communicative function of language to a higher level, an *aesthetic* level. Music *only* functions on an *aesthetic* level. There is no equivalent in music to a prose sentence, which is the everyday surface structure of language. The comparable surface structure of music is already at the level of a work of art. Language must, therefore, reach higher than its mundane prose surface structure in order to achieve an aesthetic equivalent to music. This higher language equivalent is found in poetry. L created linguistic diagrams to explain this metaphorical leap from the everyday prose surface structure to what he designated as the *super*-surface structure on which language becomes an aesthetic art form. In his third Lecture on Semantics, he demonstrated the importance of other parallel analogies between language and music. In this instance, he became more specific, dealing with musical equivalents of a variety of smaller operations in language found especially in poetry such as antithesis, alliteration, repetition, anaphora, chiasmus and rhopalism[197], all of which contribute to the aesthetic design of language. In each instance clear, convincing musical examples were provided which illustrated clear parallels to the above listed rhetorical devices. This may have been a form of "game playing", as L frankly

---

[197] *antithesis* - the opposition or contrast between two things   *alliteration* - closely connected words that begin with the same letter or sound   *anaphora* - repetition of a word or phrase at the beginning of successive clauses   *chiasmus* - inversion in the second phrase of a sentence of the order of elements followed in the first phrase, ('What's Hecuba to him, or he to Hecuba?') *rhopalism* - each word has one syllable more than the one immediately preceding

admitted, but it was also both fascinating and enlightening. It opened yet another doorway to the parallels between language and music for the theorists to ponder.

Oedipus Rex, an opera/oratorio, was the first of the large scale musical examples used in these Lectures to employ a text. Having worked to find a correlation between language and music on a *super*-surface level which, for language, required a metaphorical leap upwards from the surface structure of ordinary prose to the *super*-surface structure of poetry, L proposes yet another metaphorical leap upwards. The corollary now sought is in an area of abstraction both for music and language. It is the point where the very concept of musical and linguistic thought reside and intersect. L presents this degree of philosophical speculation as necessary because, unlike his previous purely instrumental examples, *Oedipus Rex* deals with the setting of a text. For L such a union can only be understood on a *supra*-level where Creativity itself resides and concepts, indeed all Art converges and can, through examples, be shown to combine in perfect consummation.

Logically, the expressive success of the union of words and music should depend upon the congruity, the well-matched compatibility, of their musical and linguistic semantics. Examples of such compatibility comprise the entire history of opera and popular song. What happens, L counters, when *ill*-matched components coincide on that *supra*-surface level? "What happens", he states, "is Igor Stravinsky." All the incongruities, modernity, asymmetries, mismatching represent "an encyclopaedia of (Stravinskian) misalliances." They form the essence of his *neo-classicism*. They provide the mask which enables him to describe emotion from the point of view of an observer standing at a distance. Stravinsky's *Symphony of Psalms* demonstrates this amply. The composer totally violates our expectations of the setting of a religious text but still succeeds powerfully in communicating the drama of *Psalm 101* through the use of his ill-matched components, which tread the line between comedy and tragedy.

The list of ill-matched components in Stravinsky's *Oedipus* is long. Eclectic incongruities begin with the creation of a French libretto by Jean Cocteau from the original Greek text by Sophocles which was then re-translated into Latin making the story virtually unintelligible to its audience; borrowings of various styles and accompaniments for the arias from Gluck to Beethoven are to be identified throughout; Queen Jocasta's aria is described by L as sounding like "a hoochy-coochy dance", while Oedipus' aria is said to resembles a Cossack dance; the Messenger's song bears the musical characteristics of a Greek Bouzouki and the Chorus revealing the tragic downfall of the hero and the suicide of Jocasta uncomfortably resembles a football fight song. In his own contribution to irony and absurdity, having explained all this L now tells us that he is *not* going to tell us what he has just spent the last twenty minutes telling us. What he means by this contradiction is that his analysis is going to dig deeper than the surface incongruities he has just described.

Other anomalies gnawed at him, the seemingly endless use by Stravinsky of appoggiaturas[198] in the arias and the diminished seventh chord, that most unstable of all chords, in his harmonies. These were the typical and popular devices to depict pathos and suspense in Romantic opera. At that point, the "penny dropped" and L identified the source of the four note opening *Oedipus* motif as originating from another famous vocal work also depicting 'pity and power', no less than Verdi's *Aida*. In one of his wonderfully uninhibited musical demonstrations, L, singing and accompanying himself at the piano, performs both the parts of *Amneris* and *Aida* in an extended excerpt from the opening scene of Act Two in which *Amneris* tricks *Aida* into revealing her feelings for *Rhadames* whom they both love. Simultaneously playing, explaining and singing in keys totally out of range for his hopelessly terrible voice he gives the most marvellous and informative demonstration of the original four note source of Stravinsky's opening *Oedipus* chorus. The point being stressed is that *using the same motivic notes* both Verdi and Stravinsky in highly contrasted settings were depicting the same theme of "pity and power". Verdi's was one of a slave in an intimate plea for mercy from her mistress while Stravinsky's was an awesome public plea for pity to a king. The former set his motive in rich, romantic harmonies. Verdi's

---

[198] appoggiatura - (from the Italian, *appoggiare* - to lean) - a dissonant note 'leaning' on to a harmony note, and taking part of its time value.

theatrical setting equally matched the romantic demands of the libretto. The various elements meshed to form a set of well-matched musical/language and visual components. The Stravinsky opus, in contrast, placed within a frozen oratorio tableau used stark, ill matched musical, language and visual components to create a harsh, monumental setting of the pity/power theme . In seeking an explanation for this anomaly, L's belief was that within Stravinsky's subconscious the *Aida* metaphor of "pity and power" took root and interacted with Stravinsky's own metaphorical concept of this theme to simultaneously create a third, new, single metaphor. Moving from its abstract, subconscious form, it manifested itself in the surface form we know today in the composer's opera/oratorio. L extends his thesis even further, however, to declare that these matchings and mismatchings created in the *supra* area of the subconscious cannot exist or come to be unless they are obedient to and rooted in our *innate* response governed by the inborn universals of tonality and language. This, for L, is an expression of the eternal nature of the *Poetry of the Earth,* the metaphor expanded to include genetically innate capacity, both musical and linguistic, within the brain. A filmed performance of Oedipus Rex follows.

WEST SIDE MAESTRO

The Dream Team

As far back as 1947, L's name was mooted in connection to an association with the Boston Symphony Orchestra that went beyond the occasional guest appearance provided by his mentor, Serge Koussevitzsky. His close affiliation with the BSO's long serving maestro began when he first became the great Russian maestro's student at Tanglewood in 1940. His senior's immediate musical and emotional response to L's immense talent and youth had blossomed over the years. He became a surrogate son to the aging and childless Koussevitzky. As a result doors flew open to him in Boston that would have, under normal circumstances, been barred to any American conductor no matter how talented. The orchestra responded to and admired his natural gifts from the first and played wonderfully for him, resulting in rave reviews from the most hard-bitten of N.Y. critics. With Koussevitzky at the end of his tenure, three conductors were in contention to replace him as Music Director of the BSO, Fritz Reiner, L's conducting teacher at the Curtis Institute, Dmitri Mitropoulos and L himself. With Koussevitzky's backing and in light of the enormous success he was enjoying both nationally and internationally, for one brief moment it looked as if he might have been in contention. However, with Koussevitzky's retirement in the Spring of 1948, the surprise announcement was that his replacement would be Charles Münch, who had made a sensational U.S. debut in 1946 following the end of World War II. Münch, the former concertmaster of the Leipzig Gewandhaus Orchestra, was a man of immense culture and, thanks to a brilliant marriage, great wealth. He also possessed astonishing good looks which brought him the appellation in France of 'Le Beau Charles'. A slim history of the Boston Symphony titled 'Evening At Symphony'[199] states that Münch's appointment was suggested by Koussevitzky. This seems highly unlikely, as it was known that the elderly Russian was working behind the scenes to influence his powerful Boston friends to choose L. Moreover, I remember being shocked when during an interview on a national radio network, I heard Kousevitzky state in tones and terms that were unmistakable that he would take no responsibility for Münch's appointment!

---

[199] Evening at Symphony by Janet Baker-Carr, Houghton Mifflin Co., Boston pub.1977

WEST SIDE MAESTRO

L continued to guest conduct the orchestra over the years and, indeed, his final concert shortly before his death was with the BSO. Despite Münch's enormously successful residence, followed by two relatively short tenancies by noted conductors of the Austro/German tradition, William Steinberg and Erich Leinsdorf, followed by the long tenure of Seiji Ozawa, the prize of the Boston Symphony as his own instrument was to elude L. Even though the path of his career was to annually take him, with a heavy concentration of time in the UK and Europe, to all parts of the world, one could not help but continue to wonder what a long term partnership of L and the BSO might have produced.

That is the background to the major recording project for his Norton Lectures which again brought L and the BSO together for a concentrated period of time. The complete list of filmed music segments includes the following[200]:

with The Boston Symphony Orchestra - recorded WGBH, Boston, Mass. 1973

W.A. Mozart	Symphony No.40 in g minor, K.550
L. van Beethoven	Symphony No.6 in F Major (Pastoral)
H. Berlioz	Romeo & Juliet : Romeo alone; Festival of the Capulets
	* Love scene in the Garden of the Capulets
	* Queen Mab Scherzo
R. Wagner	*Tristan & Isolde*: Prelude & Love Death
C. Debussy	*Prelude to The Afternoon of a Faun*
M. Ravel	*Spanish Rhapsody*: Prelude*/ Malaguena*/Habenera*
	Festival
C. Ives	*The Unanswered Question*
I. Stravinsky	*Oedipus Rex*, with narator, soloists & the Harvard Glee Club
G. Mahler	*Symphony No.9* : Fourth Movement

with The Vienna Philharmonic Orchestra -Berlin, 1971

---

[200] Using as a definitive reference the listing of films and videotapes from Jack Gottlieb's Complete Catalogue of Bernstein Works, it would appear that an additional forty-five minutes of music was recorded for the Lectures that was never used. Works above listed with a [*]

WEST SIDE MAESTRO

From the outset one is struck by playing of the Boston orchestra. It is of the highest quality, not only in terms of technique but of ensemble, tone and imagination. The orchestra's response to L's smallest gesture is immediate and one can observe the performances being sensitively shaped rather than coming across as routine run-throughs necessitated by time factors and recording costs. The repertoire is broad and certain performances are more successful than others due to a wide variety of factors. Whatever time restrictions existed no work comes off as under-prepared. Though negative comments regarding the sound and pictures were added to the list of Michael Steinberg's critical quibbles, the sound is perfectly acceptable and light years more refined than that encountered on the various Toscanini videos, also made in a recording studio, which sold in large numbers to a receptive music public. The camera work is neither better nor worse than that employed for most orchestral telecasts at the time, visually capturing whatever instrument or instrumental section is featured. Considering the large changes to occur in his music making and podium manner these videos of L's early appearance with the BSO, an orchestra to which he was closely allied historically, are as valid a document of important interest as are the Lectures themselves. A very good case could be made for issuing two commercial DVD's, one of the Beethoven *'Pastoral' Symphony*, the complete Berlioz *Romeo & Juliet* excerpts and the Wagner *Tristan 'Prelude and Liebestod'* and a second video containing Debussy's *L'après-midi d'un Faun*, Ravel's *Rhapsodie Espagnole*, Ives' *Unanswered Question* and Stravinsky's *Oedipus Rex*.

Only the Mozart Symphony No.40 in G minor is a disappointment. It isn't just that it is *big-band* Mozart in these days of original instrument performances. My attitude towards much of this *historic* movement take-over of the *three B's* mirror's that of Pierre Boulez in indifference. It is certainly true that the musician members of this elite brigade have developed a virtuosic expertise in dealing with archaic original instruments or their modern reproduction equivalents. Historic performance practices continue to maintain a curiosity value for audiences and, principally, a record buying public for whom the PR men of the Gramophone industry designed and aimed this elitist *sting*. The truth, should it be revealed, is that

WEST SIDE MAESTRO

if one really desired to hear 17th, 18th and 19th-century music as composers supposedly heard it in their time, one would prepare concerts hopelessly under-rehearsed and badly out of tune. That certainly is not the case in regard to L's Mozart performance with the BSO. It is quite apparent that a strong and special rapport exists between conductor and orchestra. The performance is quite straightforward, cleanly played and phrased but, unfortunately, lacking in tension or excitement. Despite the presence of a large body of strings, it is not heaviness and thickness of tone that is the problem but sluggishness. L's tempos from one movement to the next lack that logic of natural progression that lends a sense of inevitable wholeness to a performance. The Minuet movement begins so underpowered and under tempo that the orchestra does what orchestras always do in such a situation, they slowly nudge the tempo forward to that which feels more comfortable for them. A brilliant last movement infuses some life and drama into the situation but there is no recovering from the lost momentum.

In truth, I think everyone was a bit overawed by the event itself. Being the first of the filmed performances, it was someone's bright idea to have everyone dress in formal eveningwear. This was not a concert. This was supposed to be a laboratory in which the works of music chosen were there specifically to illustrate textual points not to be viewed as an abstract entertainment. The result was a self-conscious sense of occasion. Lacking an audience, none of the frisson of a live music event along with the danger and unpredictability always part of such happenings was present. As a consequence, the music making suffered and the discomfort of having to perform under hot television lighting in this artificial atmosphere must certainly have exacerbated the problem.

Everything changes with the Beethoven symphony and it begins with L's dress fashion. While the orchestra still sport *black tie*, L is casually attired in a turtleneck pullover and a sports jacket. Such a reference in a book about music and musicians may appear the *non sequitur* of the century and of little if any consequence to anyone except L's haberdasher but, in fact, this less formal approach on L's part does have a psychological effect in creating a more informal ambience. From the first this is apparent. The music making is much more relaxed, even 'laid-back' in quality. The starchy formalism in which the Mozart symphony was framed has been discarded and from here on the presence of the cameras becomes secondary.

The Boston Symphony is now at full strength. The variety of music to be recorded serves to point up this great orchestra's virtuosity and versatility. It adjusts its tone quality and weight of sound in each instance to the demands of the work at hand. Their response to L's most subtle gestures, (and 'subtle' is the precise term to describe his conducting of the Beethoven *Pastoral*), is one of total commitment. There is a respect for the man and the musician that inspires them not only to play at their best but to apply their musical imaginations fully to the task at hand. The end results make up a collection of marvellously coloured performances each infused with a spectrum of stylistic nuance and tonal variety. Whether one agrees or disagrees with all of the music making becomes a matter of taste but in regard to the technical performances of both orchestra and conductor, they are of a world class and a consummate example of the fusion of a conductor with an orchestra.

Specifically, in regard to the *Pastoral*, there is a wonderful lightness of touch throughout the first movement. L's gestures shape the music rather than traditionally beat time. He conducts much of the movement in one-beat-to-the-bar rather than the traditional two beats. This creates long melodic patterns and a lovely singing quality of strings and woodwinds riding above the highly rhythmic under-structure of the movement.

The second movement begins slightly under tempo which, although providing a degree of extra clarity, lends a somewhat pedestrian, practice-exercise quality to Beethoven's accompaniment figures. One must understand that the music was recorded in long takes. There was none of the meticulous bar by bar editing which creates the artificial perfection on which today's international recording industry thrives. These films are virtually live, one-take performances. In this instance, you witness and can feel the orchestra straining at the bit to move forward. Indeed, L himself quickly senses the problem and gently urges the tempo notch by notch into one that projects a sense of natural flow. For future observers of this film, I will reveal the trade secret of how this is accomplished without the music lurching forward or the ensemble suffering. L's beat takes on a circular motion rather than the traditional four-to-the-bar called for. This circular pattern was a great favourite of Toscanini and is virtually guaranteed to keep an orchestra from letting the tempo of a texturally complex slow movement, such as Beethoven's *"By The Brook"*, go slack. The image of this wheel-like gesture actually projects the psychological inference of forward motion. It certainly proves effective in this instance.

The Scherzo movement is not rushed, as is often the case, but bounces along in jolly fashion with the lightest staccato string playing and wonderfully long woodwind melodies which create an almost folksong atmosphere. The shift from the one-beat-per-bar scherzo to the Trio, a two-beat-per-bar rustic dance, moves everything up a gear. This movement then proceeds virtually without pause to a short prelude, a calm before the storm, which builds to a Beethovenian tempest of dramatic proportion. This leads, without pause, into a *Hymn of Thanksgiving* which concludes the symphony.

The Boston woodwinds and horns have a field day with this joyful work. The playing throughout is truly superb whether in ensemble or the many lovely solos which proliferate throughout the symphony. As for L's conducting, it couldn't be more straightforward. With the added plus of his musicianship and personality, his most severe critic would be hard put to find fault with his deportment or musical taste in even a single measure of music.

The filmed musical examples used in the next Lecture simply serve to reinforce one's reaction to the first class music making which had marked the Beethoven Symphony in the third Lecture.

Throughout their 100 year history, the Boston Symphony has maintained the highest playing standards. No American orchestra can boast a more distinguished lineage of world class conductors, Henschel, Gericke, Nikisch, Paur, Muck, Monteux, Koussevitzky, Münch, Leinsdorf and, up to the year of the Lectures, William Steinberg, who had just resigned for health reasons. Of this superb list, the succession of Monteux, Koussevitzky and Münch covering a consecutive period of forty-three years had given the orchestra a decidedly *French* accent. Indeed, during Koussevitzsky's tenure a steady stream of outstanding French instrumentalists had made their way to Boston. Just as Stokowski faced a Philadelphia Orchestra for the first time whose rehearsals were carried on in German, so the official language at Boston Symphony rehearsals in the early years of the Koussevitzky reign was French. Under these three great conductors, the orchestra reigned supreme in the area of French music and particularly the 20th-century French moderns. By 1973, the orchestra was mostly made up of American musicians but the traditions of the past had been handed down. A large percentage of the orchestra recording with L had been the same personnel who had worked under Münch. Astonishingly, there were even a few grey heads that I recognised as members of the orchestra under Koussevitzky. The three works to be recorded, instrumental movements from Berlioz's *Romeo and Juliet*, Wagner's *Prelude and Love Death* from *Tristan and Isolde* and Debussy's *Prelude to an Afternoon of a Faun*, were the meat and potatoes of their repertoire. They had recorded Berlioz's *Romeo* under Münch and had performed it under Monteux and L as guest conductors. The Wagner *Prelude* was a favourite of both Koussevitzky and Münch and the Boston tradition of Debussy's miniature tone-poem dated back to 1903 when it received its American premiere by the orchestra. It was a great Münch favourite and found its way into the programs season after season.

Though L had recorded thirty-five minutes of music from the Berlioz work, only twelve minutes from the symphony was used for the Lectures, *Romeo alone, Sadness* and *The Festival of the Capulets*. Again one becomes immediately aware of the orchestra's luminescent tone quality under L even judged by the limited sound resource offered by a television receiver. I own a number of CD transfers of the orchestra under Koussevitzky's direction and their performances under L echo the past. Dynamics are carefully controlled and graded. The orchestra's flexibility is to be marvelled at as L modifies the tempo to reflect the drama depicted in the music. To be noted is Ralph Gomberg's superb oboe solo depicting Romeo alone in the garden. For any watching the tape who might marvel at Mr. Gomberg being able to perform his lengthy solo without apparently having to take a breath, the distinguished instrumentalist does in fact generously supply himself with all the necessary oxygen required for the task. He is, in fact, breathing through his nose as he plays. Were you sitting next to him, the sound an oboist has to make to accomplish this feat could prove distracting but from the audience all you are aware of is the end product, a seamless musical phrase.

The *airborne* Bernstein is beginning to manifest itself although the jumps only occur sparingly and with no attempt to break Mitropoulos' altitude record. There is another moment relating to conducting mannerisms worth mentioning. It occurs at the end of the section titled *Sadness*. The music, building to a climax, comes to a long held chord, which is followed by a short pause and then an outburst of the full orchestra as the masked Romeo attends the Capulet ball. At Tanglewood back in 1951, L had given our conducting class a long lecture on how this difficult musical and technical moment was to be handled. The length of the pause as explained by L verged on the metaphysical and the upbeat to again restart the orchestra required the clearest and most convincing movement of the baton. When it came to that moment at the student orchestra concert a few days later the whole conducting class moved forward in their seats to watch L bring off this difficult conductorial *coup de theatre*. The long chord seemed held interminably, then came the cut-off and the breath pause of dramatic length. We watched L's arm for the upbeat to follow but instead L stamped his foot so loudly on the podium that some of us jumped out of our seats. Needless to say, after such a sonic upbeat the orchestra had no trouble in restarting. I retell that story not so much for its amusement quotient as to report that almost twenty-five years later, at that same place in the music, L was still stamping his foot on the podium. This time, moreover, he also added a loud grunt. Nevertheless, despite a few spare idiosyncrasies, the music is presented in a very relaxed fashion. As previously observed there is an ebb and flow of tempo modifications that mark the best live performances in which a degree of improvisation plays a role.

The execution of the Tristan *Prelude and Love Death* is again a telling example of an interplay between conductor and orchestra born out of mutual involvement and maximum concentration. The orchestra's razor sharp response to each conducting gesture is testimony to this. It is a wonderfully passionate performance ever surging forward, building to a variety of climaxes followed by interludes of reflection.

L's own response to it following the screening of the film at the Lecture was the curious and self-conscious comment that his must have been the slowest performance ever. For a listener to become aware of the slowness of a tempo, its very *slowness* must prove a distraction to one's concentrated listening. This is certainly not the case in this instance. The ever-forward movement and the beautiful shaping of the thematic motives whether played by solo instruments or an entire string section sweep one along. In the wrong hands, Wagner can become very fragmented but here it is all of a piece. The journey to the climax of the Love Death is almost too much for the listener so great is the build up of tension. Perhaps L extends the upbeat to the climax that fraction too long, (one is beginning to note that tendency as an idiosyncratic part of his music making), but nothing can spoil a performance generated at this level of rapport and commitment.

More than the other two works screened at this Lecture, the performance of Debussy's *Faun* projects that of an improvisation caught on film with L merely prompting and the BSO responding to the sensual and tonal needs of this most perfect and poetic of Debussy's creations. I have written about the orchestra's long affiliation and identification with this work. Its authority of presentation and tradition emanated from a seventy-year history of performances under conductors, some of whom enjoyed close associations with the composer. L was the last of the descendants of this great Boston Symphony tradition and this recorded performance bears all its trademarks. Throughout, it is stamped with that special sound that was the mark of the orchestra in its greatest days of triumph.

The inclusion of a portion of a concert with the Vienna Philharmonic filmed in 1971 to close the fifth Lecture was certainly a practical production decision saving both time and a good deal of money. Although I will discuss the complete performance of Mahler's *Ninth Symphony* in Volume 2, the final movement, chosen to mark the Lecture's examination of the farewell to the symphony and tonality and the advent of the revolution to come under Mahler's protégé, Arnold Schönberg, is not a performance representative of L or the Vienna Philharmonic at their best. By this time in his career, L's relation to the symphony had perhaps become almost too intimate. This final movement is truly, as L described it, the composer's personal, autobiographic document. It is also technically a highly contrapuntal work created in the form of a musical jigsaw requiring constant clarification of the principal musical line as it shifts, musically speaking, mid-sentence, mid-phrase, sometimes mid-word from orchestra section to section and solo instrument to solo instrument. Balance and clarity are everything in achieving textual sense from this highly complex work. No less important in achieving these aims are the choice of tempos and the adherence to the exactly noted dynamics and the large number of expressive instructions. L had performed and recorded the symphony with the NY Philharmonic in 1966 and had scheduled it on their tours. He was at the height of his powers at the time and the NY orchestra had truly become *his* instrument. The CBS/Sony recording is testimony to this. The *Ninth*, along with the other symphonies of the Mahler cycle that he recorded for the first time, form one of the most important documents of the Bernstein career. The entire NY performance reveals the portrait of an orchestra at one with its conductor, devoted to fulfilling his every musical wish and applying all their musicality to not only following his baton but to listening carefully to each other so that even in the most congested passages one never loses the intellectual thread or the sense of forward movement until the final peroration which L described as a musical realisation of the very act of dying.

With all the Viennese good will which Humphrey Burton describes as an irresistible magnet which eventually brought L to center much of his European musical activity around that city, the Vienna Philharmonic performance of 1972 isn't a patch on the New York one of six years before. It is very laboured and L's impassioned conducting continually urging more and more tone produces a sound palette of little variety in the more sonorous parts of the movement. His tempos have broadened and he tends to pull and push the music around more than in his earlier performance. The climax of the movement, marked by its composer 'even broader than the beginning', (which at *Molto Adagio* is already approaching one of the slowest tempos one can adopt), is so drawn out that the secondary countersubject in the horns takes on an unbalanced prominence, wiping out the principal string subject which itself has become almost unintelligible in a slowness which its subject matter cannot sustain. This movement also abounds in sudden contrasts requiring the softest playing. In the earlier NY performance these truly surprise the listener while in the later VPO performance they are telegraphed in advance destroying the intended effect. In these quiet passages Mahler contrasts a counterpoint of themes, one at the top of the instrumental range and the other at the bottom. If there is a true balance one can comfortably take in both themes at once. In the Vienna performance, however, the lower strings are just that bit too loud and the meaning of the upper line and, therefore, the passage is lost. Indeed, throughout the performance the lower instruments prove a problem. The bass playing is muddy in the extreme and the rhythmic musical figures which proliferate in their part are unsteadily executed. The entire string ensemble suffers as a result. There seems little question that the players are following L but there appears to be a general lack of security or, that other essential to good ensemble, listening to each other. The internal balance of the strings, as a result, suffers badly. Things fare little better in the woodwinds with the oboe, cor anglais and bass clarinet producing less than their best sound in their low registers or displaying the most consistent dynamic control. The quiet passages featuring the woodwinds project little musical sense as ones ear is pulled 'hither and yon' searching for the design of their interlocking musical puzzle.

"Shouldn't that be the conductor's job?", you might ask. The answer is "yes". But to imagine that L hadn't done this would be absurd. If anything, his rehearsals were so demanding that his constant stopping and starting to make comment about every bar of music could be downright maddening. And now we have come full circle. In my first paragraph discussing this performance I opined that, "L's relation to the symphony had perhaps become almost too intimate." By this I meant that he was incapable of leaving a single measure alone. He wanted to make sure every element was in place no matter how nerve-wracking to the orchestra and the possible havoc it might wreak. It is one thing to take a piece of music minutely apart. It is another to put it all back together again. A conductor of L's command, knowledge and authority creates a presence not to be denied. The orchestra that surrenders all, which may be the case with the Vienna Philharmonic on this occasion, never fully recovers by the time of the performance. All its in-built techniques upon which they create a foolproof playing ensemble, all the internal covert signals and nods of the heads, go straight out the window. Their total concentration is centered upon the conductor. Think of such collective vulnerability in a work with which they are not intimately familiar. They must now adapt a playing style totally foreign to their tradition, indeed to their way of thinking. Any unclear conductorial gesture or musical pitfall, in which the Mahler symphony abounds, is a potential accident waiting to happen. Add to all these problems L's obsessed identification with Mahler. Now he was conducting, so to speak, Mahler's orchestra, the orchestra that rejected him. He was going to right matters once and for all. (That is not merely author's conjecture. That was the way L's mind was capable of working. He was forever drawing parallels between himself and Mahler.) Is it any wonder that L went over the top and that his intense search for the ultimate Mahler performance led him over the years to an almost less than coherent totality? Indeed, L's two later recordings of the Mahler Ninth with the Berlin Philharmonic and the Concertgebouw Orchestra of Amsterdam, both for Deutsche Grammophon, continue along in this direction. They differ one to the other as well as with his earlier Vienna video film, each becoming more and more extended in regard to the final Adagio movement. By the time he made his final recording with the Amsterdam ensemble his performance had moved light years away from his NY performance. One can only muse upon what he might have achieved with the Boston Symphony had not economic and time factors ruled out the possibility of film recording the Adagio with them. At this point in their relationship the orchestra and conductor had obviously bonded in a rare and unique fashion and one could project that they would have produced something very special together.

The largest musical undertaking affiliated with the Lectures was the preparation and recording of *Oedipus Rex*, the opera *cum* oratorio of Igor

WEST SIDE MAESTRO

Stravinsky. This was not a new work to be added to L's vast repertoire with his established virtuoso high speed capacity for learning even the most difficult works in a breathtakingly brief period of time. I had heard him first perform this work at the very beginning of his career with the NY City Symphony. At the time of the Lectures it was a work that he had known and performed over a period of thirty years. Humphrey Burton describes in his biography the first rehearsal with his choral forces, the Harvard Glee Club. The scene is a repeat of one I had witnessed innumerable times in the past, that of a typical L take-over. Any choral conductor who prepared a choir for L had good reason to be nervous. L loved conducting choirs and could produce the most stunning results from them. The problem was always the same, however. Whatever the resident choral conductor had prepared was invariably "completely wrong" and there was nothing for it but to start from the beginning and re-learn the piece under L's personal supervision. God help any host or subsequent reception that might have been planning on his presence later that evening. Once L became involved, it was a guarantee that the next two hours at very least would be spent dissecting and trisecting the music bar by bar. Dishevelled but triumphant he would usually leave the rehearsal with the chorus exhausted but inspired and his evening clothes soaked through with perspiration. For the Harvard rehearsal he was, fortunately, more casually dressed in an outfit reported to have included a red Apache neckerchief and cowboy boots. Nevertheless, the opening minutes were for me pure *deja vu*. The rehearsed tempo for the opening was declared by L to be much too fast; their conductor had probably been listening to Stravinsky's 1961 recording; Stravinsky was a *terrible conductor*; his tempos were completely wrong; and, unless the quote from a Glee Club member [201] at the time is inexact, which I doubt, the opening section should be taken at "half the speed or even less" than that at which they were rehearsing.

A very authoritative and very impressive analysis especially when stated by one of the world's leading conductor's with a charisma count that deserves mention in the Guinness Book of Records. The only problem is that the reality indicates otherwise. It is certainly true that L's performance in Part I

---

[201] The Glee Club member is David Thomas, husband to Jamie Bernstein.

of Stravinsky miniature opera is slower than that of the composer but not to that enormous degree or, sadly, to the enhancement of the inherent drama of the work. The score indicates a metronome mark of 46 pulses per minute. L's tempo is virtually spot on. Stravinsky's tempo is 50 pulses per minute, not that much faster but enough to lend a greater sense of urgency and tension to the dramatic moment. It also gives more impact to the deliberate displaced rhythmic accents which was one of the key Stravinsky *fresheners* that L had spoken about at length in his Lecture. Another contradiction not in L's favour is that though his was the insightful discovery of the Stravinsky/Verdi connection, it is in the Stravinsky performance that the solo vocal parts are phrased and nuanced with the same care one would employ for a Verdi aria. With the exception of L's Oedipus, the other male singers in his performance declaim or simply shout their way through their arias. For the reader not familiar with this esoteric masterwork, one should know that the vocal parts are cruelly constructed. The male vocal parts explore the full range of the tenor and bass voices and in some instances a bit beyond. The highly chromatic vocal lines leap in hugely wide intervals from the top of the singers range to the very bottom requiring both the highest level of musicianship and vocal control on the part of the soloists. The two principal solo bass in L's performance seem so intent upon hitting the right notes, regrettably without total success, that phrasing and dynamics seem the last thing on their minds. *Oedipus* makes the best stab at it of the three but his music lies extremely high and just stays up there. His performance, although phrased intelligently, doesn't reveal much variety of nuance and when the composer takes him to the bottom of his range, not written too low to cause most tenors severe problems, the notes simply aren't there. The Glee Club acquit themselves extremely well note-wise but the slightly slower tempos prove their undoing. They are not actors but undergraduates. The various introspective/retrospective roles of the Greek chorus constantly reacting or relating to the plot action, requires real theatrical know-how. To sustain that extra dimension of drama at L's slower pacing was simply not within their experience or technique and it was not something that could be learned in a handful of rehearsals. All the metaphorical Verdian elements of drama, so abundantly present in the Stravinsky recording, are generally missing in Part I of L's performance. Far from being a 'terrible' conductor, Stravinsky knew exactly how he wanted his music to be performed. I have attended many of his orchestra rehearsals in New York and his sense of rhythm, ear for instrumental mixtures and his exacting instructions to the musicians relating to articulation and phrasing produced that special slightly dry sound unique to all his performances. If his gestures were lacking in theatrical suavity they were precise and indicated exactly what he was after.

When we come to Part II of L's performance, everything changes. Tatiana Troyanos' performance of the part of *Jocasta, Oedipus'* wife/mother, is an absolute triumph and from here on the performance takes wing. Indeed, from the *Gloria* chorus which closes Part I and opens Part II, L's performance builds to a tremendous climax and then fades into a thrilling hushed nothingness at the end. This second part of the drama is instrumentally and rhythmically far more challenging than anything encountered in the opening half hour. Perhaps that pinpoints the difficulty in performing Part I. Its stark directness places the full responsibility on the performers. There is no surface brilliance to protect performances that fall short of the mark, which, where *Oedipus Rex* is concerned, includes several of the commercially available interpretations on recording. With L's performance, there can be little doubt that Troyanos' performance must have inspired her colleagues. Everything moves into high gear and one is swept along even though the Latin text remains an impediment of predictable indecipherability for the listener. Yet the short spoken narrations interposed throughout the work, in a superb new free English translation marvellously performed by Michael Wager, prove all that an audience needs when a performance becomes as vital as had this one in Part II.

Regarding L's conducting, although appearing visually tired, with the exception of two or three small flights into space at climactic moments, it is pure Reiner, simple, direct and straight out of the textbook. L's total knowledge and command of both the musical and Latin texts is immediately obvious. There is no playing to the camera. One almost gets the feeling of a fly-on-the-wall documentary so involved are all the performers in what they are doing. With the exception of the new intrusion of a sedate version of the

WEST SIDE MAESTRO

Mitropoulos jump, the video of L's conducting technique could be used as a teaching tool in music conservatories. Knowledge, command, clarity, control, and personality - everything is there to be seen and learned from.

WEST SIDE MAESTRO

Postlude

Today, thirty-nine years after the event, we can look back and weigh up the results, if any, of this enormous effort. Was the entire undertaking merely *une folie des grandeurs*[202], which was the implication of much of the criticism at the time, or did L make a contribution to the ideas under discussion which is still valid today or, at very least, holds some historical importance? If that is <u>our</u> *Unanswered Question* one would have to reply 'No!' to the first part and a resounding 'Yes!' to the final two parts. We can piece together sufficient documentation from the time of the Lectures to the present day to show that not only were L's efforts truly worthwhile but that they were the catalyst for some of the key research into many of his hypotheses that has taken place since.

Ray Jackendoff's letter quoted in Prof. Irving Singer's reply to Michael Steinberg's polemic summary in the NY Times indicates the immediate results of the Lectures. I quote:

"As a direct result of the Norton Lectures, I have become involved in dozens of serious discussions about musical analysis, musical perception, and aesthetics. Several of my acquaintances are considering setting up seminars and workshops to study the relation of language and music. Thus I feel obliged to point out that the Norton Lectures were in fact an important intellectual event for me and many colleagues, even if not for Mr. Steinberg."

In Joan Peyser's 1987 biography, not exactly the chosen favourite *Book at Bedtime*[203] for the Bernstein family, the author quotes from an article in a 1978 issue of the Musical Quarterly written by Alan Keiler, a musician/linguist, predicating that linguistic theory might prove a crucial link in the study of musical language and that Bernstein would have to be credited as the initial leader in this field.

---

[202] A larger than life way of saying *megalomania.*
[203] *A Book at Bedtime* - a favourite BBC Radio 4 late night reading

Was this not the very hope expressed by L in his second lecture when he said,
"...if I am lucky, I may strike a nugget or two. And if I am really lucky, I may suggest some hints that will stimulate further thought among those of you who are scientifically well-grounded."

With the conclusion of the Lectures, Irving Singer and David Epstein, both members of the faculty of MIT, began serious discussions to set up a new program in aesthetics at their university. L was asked if he would assist them. As a result L went to see Jerome Weisner, the President of MIT, with whom he had become acquainted during the Kennedy administration for which Dr.Weisner had served as Science advisor. L's proposals were positively received and the seminars were subsequently set up. The scope of aesthetic studies in the new project was to include a continuation of the theme of L's Norton Lectures. These were the 'hoped-for' seminars projected in Prof. Jackendoff's letter. Extraordinarily, L's efforts that resulted in these important happenings have not been documented in his many personal biographies that crowd the market place.[204]

Although L was helpful in getting these faculty seminars going his schedule had again closed in upon him and he was not able to commit himself to an amount of time which would have permitted him input into their various undertakings. Nevertheless, an important partnership was to form from within the seminar circle that would take as their stimulus his Lectures and would develop a number of his ideas, as he envisaged, using carefully researched scientific method.

An important group of interested and informed educators and performers in the Boston area were brought together to discuss a wide range of aesthetic disciplines. Two of the members of this group who met for the first time were Ray Jackendoff, an Assistant Professor of Linguistics at Brandeis

---

[204] The seminars are noted in the Preface to the text book, A Generative Theory of Tonal Music by Lehrdahl & Jackendoff but no specific mention is made of the influential role L played in their creation.

WEST SIDE MAESTRO

University who possessed exceptional musical skills and Fred Lehrdahl, a composer with exceptional linguistic skills on the faculty of Harvard.

This was to grow into a formidable partnership[205]. Ten years after the Norton Lectures, having published a series of preliminary articles, they produced one of the most important books in music theory published in the previous half century, A Generative Theory of Tonal Music.[206] As with the Norton Lectures this text approaches music perception from the viewpoint of cognitive science. Analogous to Chomskian theory, contained is a search for a *grammar of music* with the aid of *generative linguistics*. Interestingly enough, their first edition met with criticism from those seeking a traditional and parallel approach to generative grammar which Jackendoff and Lehrdahl found to be incompatible when applied to their examination of music structure. However, by the time of their reprint in 1996 not only had the authors found precedence for the innovations which they had adapted in this area of research but new concepts in cognitive science now paralleled and trailed ideas which were already an intrinsic part of their theories.

Lest one be led to underestimate the original importance of L's Norton Lectures in regard to this later and admittedly far more advanced and developed research, let us again make reference to the words of Ray Jackendoff, first from 1973 and then in a letter to the author in 1996. I again quote Prof. Jackendoff from Irving Singer's 1974 NY Times rebuttal:

---

[205] Since the days of the seminars Ray Jackendoff has continued his association as a full Professor of Linguistics and Cognitive Science at Brandeis University and Fred Lehrdahl is Fritz Reiner Professor of Musical Composition at Columbia University. Both have been prolific writers and the author can especially recommend a collection of articles by Ray Jackendoff, *Languages of the Mind*, MIT Press, dealing with the mind and its cognitive processes to include a formal theory that relates language to a variety of cognitive areas such as mental representation, word learning, subconscious mental powers, the processing of music, the relationship of the mind to the world and the physical functioning of the brain.
[206] A Generative Theory of Tonal Music, Lehrdahl & Jackendoff, MIT Press, 1983.

WEST SIDE MAESTRO

"The value of the Bernstein lectures lay in his attempt to juxtapose linguistic theory and musical analysis, putting a new range of possible interpretations on well-known musical techniques. I agree that Bernstein's particular reinterpretations were often naive, (even by his own admission)...But anyone would have groped with this topic: it is an area where so little is known that even to pose interesting questions is a significant advance. I admire Bernstein for getting as far as he did: I learned a great deal from thinking about the musical and linguistic intuitions behind his proposals."

And in 1996:

"Fred Lehrdahl and I set to work on our research on musical cognition, which eventuated in our book. We felt it was doing what Lenny wanted to do...certainly our inspiration was his Norton Lectures."

It certainly was what L wanted when he projected the hope that others who were truly scientifically well grounded, which he freely admitted he was not, would be stimulated to bring ideas still in their infancy to maturity. One must remember that the entire approach to education at Harvard when L was an undergraduate was far different than that which is employed today. The great emphasis was aimed at meeting the needs of graduate rather than undergraduate students. The hopes of the University were directed at producing from their graduates eminent scholars and leaders in their fields of expertise. As a result it was understandable that L's background in philosophical subjects such as linguistics was somewhat lacking and initially without a solid foundation of the subject. However, as has been verified by Prof. Donald Freeman, L had given a great deal of time and effort, ("homework" was the word Prof. Freeman used), to enable himself to pose his various linguistic parallels with authority. Prof. Morris Hallé also commented to the author that he felt L's use of linguistics was good and acceptable although, at the time, he felt he had little new to say in regard to the science. The authority on L's aims linguistically must be Donald Freeman with whom he worked closely and who discussed and helped edit all linguistic references in the Lectures. Prof. Freeman wrote to me as follows:

WEST SIDE MAESTRO

"The 'innovative and significant' ideas that Lenny had were for the most part his ability to posit interesting analogies between the way Chomskian theory explained language and what he saw as the essential properties of musical exposition...the importance of the lectures was in their potential and suggestiveness, not in their concrete demonstration measured against the standard of scholarly work by a qualified expert in language. Quite a lot of scholarly research has come out of Lenny's Lectures, and I know for a fact that was his primary goal. I think another facet of his career was that he was a seed-planter, a generator of ideas and fashions. Your word 'catalyst' fits perfectly."

In terms of further research in regard to musical innateness and its correlation to innate cognitive ability in language acquisition, 1997 seems to have been a banner year. Throughout the last decade of the century a branch of study of foreign languages has explored an affiliation between language learning and music by creating interactive programs that have juxtaposed music played unobtrusively in the background to spoken foreign language texts. The purpose was to simultaneously stimulate different parts of the brain that deal with language and music processing. The results to date appear to be quite dramatic in terms of accelerating the learning process. Similarly, the London Times reported that research had shown that teaching children music encourages quicker and clearer reasoning. In succinct, down-home American terms, Dr.Gordon Shaw of the University of California stated, "Music improves the hardware in the brain for thinking." To back up this statement was a six month research project showing a 34% improvement in the speed and accuracy in performance of children between three and four years of age who were involved in a music program over children not involved with music who showed no improvement at all. A later program using older pupils registered an improvement in their maths results when their studies were affiliated with a music program. This led to research in the commercial sector where similar results of improved performance were produced within an everyday professional working environment through a judicious use of music[207]. Best of all but receiving the smallest

---

[207] The program to which the author makes reference is scientifically based and should not be mistaken for merely providing a *muzak* wallpaper music environment.

coverage, was an article printed in the back pages of the London Times. Dr. Peter Marler, again at the University of California, stated that birds at the time of their hatching already have their song "hard-wired" into the structure of their brain. Only three of twenty-seven orders of birds studied seemed to learn by imitation and in one of these species, the sparrow, the learning period required was very short and occurred within the first two weeks of life indicating that they appeared to have some sort of built-in head start.

Dr. Marler drew a distinction between "*lexicoding*, which provides the criteria for defining a true sentence and *phonocoding*, which concerns the ability to create new sound patterns by recombination...Lexicoding appears to be uniquely human. Phonocoding is widespread in certain groups, especially songbirds and whales...It is most evident in those animal groups, some of whose vocalisations are learned." Dr. Marler goes on to point out that, "The ability to engage freely in phonological rearrangement of sound elements in order to create new sequences may be regarded as a precurssor, not only of language, but also of the ability to create music. Given that animal songs that are learned, and depend on phonocoding for signal diversity are, like human music, primarily non-symbolic and affective in nature, their study may be a source of insights into the animal origins of human music."[208]

Dr. Marler summed up the above in a letter to the author. He wrote,

"Briefly I make the point that one elementary requirement for music is creativity, for which is the ability to take a complex sound pattern (melody?), break it up into phrases, and then recombine the phrases in many different ways. Such an ability is rare or absent in non-human primates, but commonplace in birds with learned songs, as illustrated by the winter wren. Some birds have huge song repertoires, usually created this way. What drives this creative process is another question, and a primordal esthetic

---

[208] These quotes are from *Animal Origins of Music* by Peter Marler, a condensed version of *Origins of music and speech: insights from animals* which appears in *The Origins of Music,* edited Nils Wallin, MIT Press, 1999.

sense might make a contribution. But my main point is that what I call "phonological syntax" is arguably a prerequisite for music..."[209]

In these matters the author acknowledges that he is a wader in very deep waters. As Dr. Marler freely admits his correlation between music and birdsong is reductionistic. Nevertheless, we are dealing here with years of research by leading authorities in the field. It is not far fetched to take the next step and view the results of such research as powerfully pointing to L's theory of human musical innateness, the caveat being that where music is concerned Creation does not seem to discriminate in its gifts between Man and the Animal Kingdom.

Finally, there is one other pertinent news item which would have deeply affected L in diverse ways. On August 3, 1997, the NY Times devoted a page and a half of their broadsheet publication to a three thousand word editorial on music by K. Robert Schwarz titled *In Contemporary Music, A House Still Divided*. The article well salted with captioned photographs of well and lesser known composers of various ranks within Music's hierarchy regurgitates the same division of "to be or not to be *tonal*" complete with the anger, resentments and recriminations of old. The single consequential change was that the *dodecaphonic* or *serial techniques* of Schönberg and their further elaboration in the 1960's in the United States by Milton Babbitt and in Europe by Pierre Boulez, which had attained dominance in the post-World-War II years, had fallen out of fashion by the late 1970's. What L observed as the "emerging of a synthesis, the merging of the two previously hostile camps...a fusion of extraordinary force" in 1973 had instead become a full fledged rout of the twelve-tone school by the end of the decade. In contrast to L's projection of "one style feeding the other" a full-blown backlash had taken place.

The interviews in Mr. Schwarz's article read like pages out of the script of Kurosawa's film, *Rashoman*. The tonal composers tell a tale of being ridiculed and their music scorned, of a take-over of grant-giving bodies,

---

[209] Correspondence, Dr. Peter Marler, Director, Center for Animal Behavior, Univ. of California to Robert Mandell, 20 October 1998

new-music ensembles and competitions and, most serious of all, of the domination of American academic circles by the *serialists*. The *serial* composers who, with their inspirational leader, Schönberg, suffered forty years of living on the fringe tell a whole different story. The domination of academic circles is rejected by Milton Babbitt as propaganda. "We never dominated anything", he is quoted as saying pointing to an absence of key figures on the faculties of America's prestigious *Ivy League* schools among which he names Columbia University. This view is supported by Charles Wuorinen who speaks of his time as a young composer at Columbia. He describes it as follows, "...the reigning orthodoxy was, on one hand, a kind of Coplandesque Americana and, on the other hand, the symphonism of Howard Hanson and Roy Harris...I have never seen anybody make someone write any particular kind of music...forcing innocent students to do terrible, nameless things...the whole story is a big fake." Powerful words! Yet, John Corigliano[210], a noted, much feted and award-winning composer who attended Columbia University at the same time as Wuorinen, paints a different picture. He remembers *Serialism* at Columbia as "the established official academic manner." One wasn't prohibited from writing in a preferred tonal style but, as Mr. Corigliano understates it, "the general mode of thought was certainly not in my direction." The implication was that student composers were given to view *Serialism* as their only viable option. Certainly, the quote in Mr. Schwarz's article from Wuorinen's manual on composition reinforces such a position, "While the *tonal* system, in an *atrophied* or *vestigial* form, is still used today in popular or commercial music, and even in the works of *backward-looking*[211], serious composers, it is no longer employed by serious composers in the mainstream. It has been replaced or succeeded by the twelve-tone system."[212] A very senior tonal composer, Ned Rorem, was quoted as saying, "We were treated as if we didn't exist."

---

[210] John Corigliano Jr, son of the long serving concert master of the NY Philharmonic during the majority of L's 'golden years' with the orchestra. John Jr., in the early days of his career, with Jack Gottlieb took over my combined duties as L's assistant for the televised Young People's Concerts of the NY Philharmonic.

[211] Author's italics

[212] Charles Wuorenin, *Simple Composition*, pub. 1979, Longman Music Series, N.Y.

WEST SIDE MAESTRO

I have written of Stravinsky's and Copland's conversion to twelve-tone composition, the latter out of personal desperation rather than musical conviction, and the initial profound effect it had on their followers. The crux of the rise and, if not fall, rather injuring stumble of *Serialism* eventually hinged on its rejection by concert-going audiences. It did prove to be an "ambiguity too huge to be grasped" as projected by L in his Lecture on Schönberg. Reactions to the negative response of audiences produced injudicious responses from the serialists. Milton Babbitt, a long-standing acquaintance of the author and the gentlest, most soft spoken and reasonable persons one would care to know, wrote an article in 1958 that was misinterpreted from the first, not least by an editor who gave it the title, "Who Cares if You Listen?". Babbitt lay the onus on the audience to meet the challenge of serial music by acquiring the "appropriate abilities" which would bring understanding. Until that day, he felt it would better serve the creator of music of a complexity comparable to higher mathematics, to restrict performances of their compositions to private events using electronic media to reproduce the musical text thus eliminating "the public and social aspects of musical composition." Needless to say, the contemporary composers who have found an audience have a much repeated, pragmatic reply to the stated aims of a Milton Babbitt. Mr. Schwarz again quotes John Corigliano, " If you want to approach music on a level of scientific research, then you can only expect another scientist to understand it...don't be bitter that the public is not sitting and listening to it."

And so the pendulum has swung yet again. During Schönberg's lifetime, *twelve-tone* music was the shadowy threat and tonal music led by Stravinsky straddled it like a Colossus. Then in the '50's, with Stravinsky's conversion, *twelve-tone* music moved to a position of dominance and *tonal* music moved into the shadows. After twenty-five years, everything shifted yet again but this time, as Milton Babbitt rightly points out, the large majority of today's concert-going audience no longer are as aware or open to the 'new' as audiences of the past. History documents, if one only cares to go back as far as Beethoven, that all innovative composers suffered rejection and were ready to be packed off to the madhouse by their audiences. However, audiences of the past were passionate about the music of their time in a manner that simply doesn't exist today. In time they came, if not to love, to at least accept and be stimulated by the 'new'. In that lies the major difference with audiences of today. Today's passionate listeners are mostly record collectors not concertgoers. Music which was a regular part of our children's school curriculum has become an anathema to the educators and politicians of political correctness. Their priorities lie elsewhere.

Was Schönberg wrong when he projected that "if audiences...listened with open ears and inquiring minds in search of originality and whether the composer has something new and worthwhile to say, within a few decades they would recognise the *tonality* of this music called *atonal*. It would only then be a matter of the gradual recognition between the 'tonality of yesterday and the tonality of today." And further, that "That which is *tonal* is perhaps nothing else than what is understood *today* and *atonal* is what will be understood in the future." Or was the contrary challenge to Schönberg's view tomorrow's reality, "Can an arbitrary new way of organising music be so assimilated (by audiences) or, like chess or quantum mechanics, is its mastery somewhere at the extreme limits of human ability, or even beyond them[213]?"

None of this sad turn of events even hints at the fact that in the year 1997, when the NY Times published K. Robert Schwartz's article reporting the strong division among American contemporary composers, the music of Schönberg, Berg and Webern had risen to its pinnacle of popularity. Today, multiple superb recordings can be acquired of their entire *oeuvre*. Moreover, these recordings sell sufficiently well to justify and indeed encourage international and smaller independent record companies to not only maintain the titles in their catalogues but to record new versions of their various orchestral, chamber and vocal works. This music, rejected yesterday, has indeed become the music of today, certainly throughout Europe and with the young in America. *Moses and Aaron*, which Schönberg never heard performed in his lifetime, exists in no less than three fine recordings and has been mounted in opera houses throughout Europe and Great Britain. Berg's *Wozzeck* and *Lulu* are cheered to the rafters by audiences held spellbound by

---

[213] Ray Jackendoff, Review Article, Language: Volume 53, Number 4 (1977)

these gripping and moving musical works for the opera stage. The minimalist works of Webern now fascinate rather than bewilder audiences. Nothing in this latest positive assessment, however, even begins to point towards the possibility of L's belief in 1973 that there would be "musical progress in friendly competition" or - as Stockhausen would have it - "in communal effort." This positive view of the future, this *Poetry of the Earth*, which L foresaw, remains and looks to remain unspoken.[214]

---

[214] L has since found a new protagonist among the Fourth Estate in the person of the NY Times critic, Anthony Tommasini. Tommasini, a graduate of the music school of Yale University, in the *Critic's Notebook* of the Times on July 28, 1998 confirmed K. Robert Schwartz's article of the previous year relating to the degree of pedagogical control commanded by the *serialists* over university life when he was a Yale undergraduate. His Times article, relating to a week long "Bernstein Celebration at Lincoln Center", concerned itself with a re-assessment of the *Norton Lectures* which were being re-telecast at the time in co-ordination with the Center festivities which included a re-examination of "Bernstein as Teacher". Tommasini, an advocate for twelve-tone music, approached L's theory of human innate *tonal* recognition in a most ecumenical manner, admitting the possibility of its existence and posing the possibility that, perhaps, because twelve-tone music violates this innate sense it, in fact, "titillates, discombobulates, engages the ear." It is for this reason Tommasini finds "the best twelve-tone fun because they disrupt, in a sense, the ear's inclination for tonal bearings." He went on to acknowledge that "Bernstein rightly observed that all tonal music and synthesized experiments would inevitably be 'embedded in a tonal universe', that is, conceived against a contextual background of Tonality." He concludes with a recognition that "it took (L) courage to state his case and call for a cessation of hostilities."

WEST SIDE MAESTRO

5. BERNSTEIN CONDUCTS BERNSTEIN

If the Bernstein Legend has suffered at all it has been in regard to his talents as a composer. There are two arguments that dominate. The first is concentrated on the general critical consensus that L never fulfilled the earlier potential that his talent promised and the second upon whether his music will survive even fifty years hence. In examining the first of these two points rather than bemoan how little music was written during a fifty year career dominated by a series of non-stop performing engagements, a vast number of commercial recordings and an entirely separate career as an educator both on television and *in situ* at music festivals and universities in every part of the globe, the critic should take astonished note of how much music *was* written, the greatest portion of which is on a grand scale for orchestra and includes three symphonies, a Mass, a full scale opera composed in two sections and then integrated after a time span of thirty years and five musicals for Broadway, one of which broke the mould of the established Broadway formula and influenced the shape of musical theatre to follow, two of which have reached 'classic' film status and can be viewed at almost any time anywhere in the world, and a third which, after a chequered series of rewrites, has found acceptance in the operetta repertoire of the world's opera houses, in the repertoire of London's prestigious National Theatre Company and performed successfully in concert both without staging and semi-staged. In addition, there are three ballets, two of which have never been out of the repertoire of America's principal ballet companies, a further huge amount of ballet music written for his Broadway musicals, distinguished incidental music for two straight play Broadway productions[215], a single foray as a film score composer in Hollywood which produced an Academy Award nomination if not the grand prize of an Oscar, a major violin concerto, a song cycle and a choral setting of three Psalms that have become standard repertoire for choral forces both young and veteran throughout the world and a miscellany of works written on commission for various orchestras, noted instrumentalists or prestigious events. To this list one must add solo instrumental works, songs and other miscellaneous

---

[215] J.M. Barrie's *Peter Pan* (1950) and Jean Anouilh's *The Lark* (1955)

compositions mostly the product of early career years. This is no small accomplishment for even a full time composer. L may not be considered within avant-garde circles as having advanced musical thought one jot but unlike much of what the avant-garde has placed before the public his music, employing both tonal and, sometimes, non-tonal contemporary vocabulary and techniques, is notably communicative. As for the size of his lifetime's compositional output, it is vast compared to Pierre Boulez, one of the world's icons among composers, about whom no one utters a word regarding his scant lifetime's output which to date consists of little more than a handful of works which he continues to work and rework without producing anything substantially new or of a communicative quality to rival his earliest compositions influenced by his teacher, the noted French composer, Olivier Messiaen.

As to critical conjecture of what will or won't be played fifty years from now, that is a pointless game of speculation regarding which history has time and again proved critics opinions to be, to put it generously, wanting. What is a fact is that, thanks to L's position as one of the handful of superstar international performers who could dictate what he wished to record, virtually the entire Bernstein *oeuvre* has been personally set down in recordings and films by two of the world's major recording companies in performances that few other conductors could match...Via repackaging, re-engineering and anniversaries which come and go, these remain in the catalogue and continue to find a public. In addition, his *Serenade*, three symphonies, *Songfest* and *Prelude, Fugue and Riffs* along with the more popular and immediately accessible *West Side Story, On The Town, Wonderful Town, On The Waterfront, Candide* and *Fancy Free* all enjoy multiple recordings either in complete or excerpt form by a variety of conductors, artists and orchestras. What now also has taken place since the early days when L was forced to be a virtual one-man-band promoter and performer of his more formal and in some cases, somewhat thornier compositions, is that his music, especially his first two symphonies, his violin concerto, *Serenade,* the ballet, *Fancy Free,* the mega-demanding *Mass,* the overture to *Candide* the concert suites from *West Side Story* and

WEST SIDE MAESTRO

On The Waterfront and *3 Dance Episodes from On The Town* are now firm staples of the concert repertoire.

I have chosen to begin with an examination of the recordings of the Chichester Psalms and the three symphonies. These works generally enjoy superb performances. I prefer L's second recorded version of the Psalmes for Deutsche Grammophon (1977) with the Israel Philharmonic, available in video (Polytel Music), DVD (Kultur Video Int.) and CD format, (DG). L's earlier NY Philharmonic performances of all these works, (SONY), were recorded in 1961, '63 and '65 respectively. The 1965 recording of the Second Symphony, 'The Age of Anxiety' with the NY Philharmonic featuring Philippe Entremont in the important solo piano role replaced L's superb premiere 1950's CBS LP recording with the Philharmonic with Lucas Foss as soloist, a task Lucas was again to undertake in the 1977 DG recording. The 1950 LP recording also represented the Symphony's original version, which was revised in 1955 to include a piano cadenza in the final *Epilogue*. The Third Symphony, subtitled *Kaddish*[216], receives two contrasting performances. The original 1963 version, as explained by the composer at a press conference in Berlin, featured a woman narrator representing *das Ewig-Weibliche*, (the *Eternal Feminine*), "that part of man that intuits God."[217] The revised 1977 version uses a male narrator in an edited and somewhat rewritten spoken text along with some pruning and re-scoring of the music.

The *Psalms*, while using a full contemporary musical vocabulary of dissonance and disjunct rhythms, is very much a traditional work, completely tonal and enjoying the communicative melodic gifts of its composer. In contrast, all three symphonies are atypical in their form, the *First* has only three movements, the third movement employing a mezzo-

---

[216] The *Kaddish* is the traditional Hebrew prayer for the dead. Its meaning is 'sanctification'. It is spoken at the graveside of the deceased and at annual memorials at which a *Jahrzeit* (yearly) candle is burned and, at synagogue services, in remembrance of the departed.

[217] The redisignation of the earlier version of the Speaker's role in *Kaddish* to the abstract idea of the *Eternal Feminine* represented backtracking on the composer's part. In the first version the Speaker is specifically identified as the *Lily of Sharon*. The composer was later to be reminded that the *Kaddish* prayer is never spoken by a woman.

soprano soloist; the *Second* is in two parts housing six movements containing fourteen variations and featuring a piano solo whose prominence is more akin to a concerto than merely that of an *obbligato* or *concertante* part of slight additional prominence[218] as suggested by the composer; and the *Third Symphony*, in seven parts contained within three movements, has been described, not incorrectly in my view, as a hybrid oratorio/monodrama. All three are highly programmatic although the first two symphonies can be listened to as pure music while, in the *Third Symphony*, the spoken and musical texts are inexorably bound to each other.

The earlier NY Philharmonic recordings of the symphonies and *Chichester Psalms* are superb. L had been Music Director for a full three years when the first of his three symphonies was recorded. The orchestra had been transformed, restored to its full glory among the premiere world ensembles. Between the additional recording sessions and television programs, which came in the wake of L's appointment, its members were now among the highest paid contract musicians in the United States. Orchestral musicians show their appreciation fully to those conductors who improve their lot in life. Under everyday professional circumstances they would have given their all for L. In recordings of his own compositions, they would have pushed themselves and, as these recordings are testament to, did push themselves even further to show their appreciation. The results are here to be heard and marvelled at. The ensemble, colour, rhythmic precision and drive are everything one could hope for. Jennie Tourel's performance of the Lamentation movement from the *Jeremiah* Symphony contains all the artistry one would expect from so distinguished a soloist Her voice no longer displays the luxuriant beauty of her earlier recording with L of the Ravel Schéhérazade song cycle but her passion and clear expression of the Hebrew text is deeply moving.

---

[218] *Obbligato* (Italian) obligatory; essential instrumental part performing an important soloistic function; *concertante* (Italian) concertizing; an instrumental part designed for virtuoso display

WEST SIDE MAESTRO

Having reported so glowingly on the early recorded performances what is left to say about the later 1977 recordings and filming for video/DVD - a remarkable amount as it happens.

One has to go back to the beginning, the year 1947, to fully comprehend the highly charged nature of these performances. It was the year L first travelled to what was then Palestine to conduct the Palestine Symphony at the conclusion of their tenth anniversary season. Included in his program was his First Symphony, *Jeremiah*. This was the first of many times over the years that he was to conduct *Jeremiah* and other of his compositions with this Orchestra. The public reception at the time was overwhelming bringing him out again and again, receiving him in a manner described in the news reports as verging on hysteria. At the conclusion of his debut two week engagement, not only had he been invited back to conduct for a two month period the following year but was asked to accept a long term artistic directorship with the orchestra for a minimum of three months a year. Only the following year after the career disappointment of being passed over in Boston despite all of Koussevitzky's behind the scenes endeavours and campaigning on his behalf, did he decided to accept the Palestine offer. Much was to occur before his next visit. In 1948, Palestine, a British protectorate, became the State of Israel. The Palestine Symphony was renamed the Israel Philharmonic. His engagements with the orchestra served to reaffirm the huge success of his previous year's debut. Before his second engagement had concluded the Orchestra extended their offer to L to become Music Director, spending six months a year in Israel. L rejected this proposal. Indeed, he requested that his relationship with the orchestra be officially re-designated to that of 'music advisor' rather than the more committed position of 'artistic director'. Nevertheless, L's empathy with the country, its people and their problems had now indelibly and passionately embedded themselves in his social conscience and his pride in being a Jew. This mutual identification between the musician and the Jewish nation was to grow over the years. Whatever world celebrity L was to enjoy in his career, nothing could compare with his celebrity in Israel. It shattered God's commandments to "not make unto thee any graven images or any likeness of anything that is in heaven above or that is in the earth beneath...(and) not bow down thyself to them..." Those commandments seemed to carry a disclaimer clause in Israel where *our Lenny* was concerned. Reciprocally, the State and the Orchestra were never far from the thoughts of Bernstein, the musician and liberal activist. It was L who was key to the orchestra, following many years of recording for English Decca, being offered a recording contract with Deutsche Grammophon.

In light of this brief biography, consider the scenario surrounding the Israeli orchestra's first tour to Austria, a centre of European anti-Semitic expression, and Germany, the epicentre of the oppression and persecution of World Jewry from the political emergence of Adolf Hitler and his Blackshirts in the 1920's.

Consider the emotional luggage of Second World War memories they brought with them, the extermination of 5,000,000 European Jews in the horrors that were the concentration camps of Dachau, Treblenka and the rest, more than just a memory to the millions of Jews driven from their homes and countries, fleeing for their lives, their plight rejected by many European states and nowhere to go until they finally found refuge in the Middle-East in the newly formed Jewish State of Israel.

Were the events of the Second World War nowadays not merely a distant seventy-five year old memory, replaced in our experience by other atrocities more contemporary, the high feeling in Israel against anything Austro/German, (extending to a ban on the music of Wagner and Richard Strauss whose music was favoured by Hitler as representing the ideals of Germany's Nazi past), would need no further explanation.

One can only imagine the personal grievances held by members of the orchestra who themselves or whose families may have suffered terrible treatment or extermination at the hands of the Nazis. It is not difficult to comprehend the subtext of unprecedented drama that underscored the Israeli orchestra's 1977 European tour under L's direction.

WEST SIDE MAESTRO

The Israel Philharmonic willingness to accept this tour must have awakened both public and political indignation and antagonism throughout their country. The tour was scheduled following a three-week Bernstein festival in Tel Aviv. Only the high stature in which L was held and the unreserved admiration, affection and respect he evoked throughout Israel enabled him to pull off this coup. Some of the cooler heads also judged that there were positive political and propaganda benefits to be accrued.

One needs only examine the ingredients that went into this recipe for high drama. Imagine, if you will, the orchestra of the State of Israel, conducted by the world's leading Jewish conductor/composer, (now the idol of Europe and especially of that most anti-Semitic of cities, Vienna), performing a retrospective of his own music principally inspired by Jewish history and Old Testament Aramaic and Hebrew texts at the Carinthian Festival in Villach, Austria followed by repeat concerts in Germany at the Berlin Philharmonie and the Rheingold-Halle in Mainz, all to be preserved on film.[219] Indeed, at the Carinthian Festival, L went as far as to include a pre-concert talk explaining to his Austrian audience the meaning of his *Kaddish* Symphony.

The first tour program opened with the *Chichester Psalms*, text in Hebrew, sung by the Vienna Boys Choir and the Vienna Youth Choir. Although affinities have been noted between the *Psalms* and the *Kaddish* Symphony even to the degree of inferring that the Psalms could be viewed as an extended *Coda* to the Symphony, one is struck in listening to the first of the three Psalms, *Make A Joyful Noise*, by rhythmic and melodic echoes of the Lamentation and Profanation movements of L's *Jeremiah*. The difference lies in character. This initial setting, after a powerful introduction, becomes transparent and light, expressing joyous optimism in contrast to the Profanation movement of *Jeremiah*, which uses similar rhythmic patterns and formulas, but is dissonant and sardonic. The second Psalm, The Lord is my Shepherd, features the unbroken voice of a boy soprano. It begins

---

[219] This was not the only tour undertaken by L and the Israel Philharmonic featuring his *Kaddish* Symphony. There was a second tour which again visited Vienna as well as Budapest, Athens, Hiroshima, Israel, New York and Washington.

lyrically and reposeful accompanied only by harp, an allusion, no doubt, to the David of the Psalms. It is interrupted abruptly by a choral setting of verses from Psalm 2, Why Do the Heathen Rage. The setting is highly rhythmic and agitated, punctuated by percussion. The 23rd Psalm music is heard again but in a high counterpoint above the agitation. It returns us to a state of repose as we again hear the innocent sound of the solo youthful voice. The chorus peacefully reiterate his words but in the far distance we hear the contrapuntal mutterings of discontent as the movement comes to an abrupt end. The final Psalm 31, Lord, My Heart Is Not Haughty, is unashamedly tonal and lyrical throughout. Its directness and beauty has drawn criticism for being Hollywood saccharine. Such criticism brings one to wonder why any composer should have to justify possessing a talent of direct communicative expression to jaded musical ears and jaundiced attitudes? The *Chichester Psalms* is not only a deeply moving work but an affirmation of L's composing gifts, continually dismissed from one quarter or another by his critics, and his unswerving commitment as a composer to tonality. It was never a lack of talent but a lack of working discipline in a career from which he wanted and expected all, celebrity, adulation and an endless variety of constant stimulation, which created an insurmountable barrier to his fulfilling his own belief in his gifts and destiny as a composer. L often identified himself with Mahler but unlike Mahler, the composer, he was unable to shut himself off from the pleasures of the material world for concentrated periods of time during which no one and nothing but his compositional goals mattered.

The Sony/DG CD's and the Polytel/Kultur Video and DVD respectively contain beautiful performances of the *Psalms*, the slight edge going to DG for the expressive and lovely sounding contribution of the young soloist drawn from the Vienna Boys Choir.

Jeremiah and *The Age of Anxiety* follow on the video and DVD. To observe that the Israel Philharmonic, while a very fine orchestra, were not section for section the equals of the NY Philharmonic would be to beg the question. They are a first class orchestra with a marvellously rich sounding string section needing neither apology nor special consideration. On this occasion, their extra identification with both the music and the circumstances in which they were performing give them the edge. It produced that indefinable communicative magic one longs for when attending any concert. *Jeremiah*, with Christa Ludwig in glorious, blooming, young voice delivers a most moving rendition of the *Lamentation* and the whole is presented in a white-hot performance with a freshness and vitality comparable to a world premiere.

As for *The Age of Anxiety*, one would expect that the jazz passages, which dominate Part Two of the symphony, to give the New Yorkers a slight stylistic edge but the Israelis have the full measure of this very American music and toss it off as if it were everyday standard repertoire. In the solo piano role Lucas Foss recreates the triumph of his 1950 recording with L and the NY Philharmonic. He is a formidable pianist and among the half dozen performers I have heard undertake this work he has no peer. In the end one is again faced with the decision of choosing the best among equals. The decision, in light of the soloist and the Israeli's breathtaking commitment, goes again to them.

Comparing the two performances of the *Kaddish* Symphony carried for me an additional emotional dimension. I could not claim to be a close friend of Felicia Bernstein but I knew her from my days at Tanglewood, spoke to her often when L and I worked at their apartment rather than his studio at the Osborne and did the sound balances for her Carnegie Hall performances of Honneger's *Joan of Arc at the Stake* with L conducting the NY Philharmonic.

The *Kaddish* Symphony was the result of a combined commission by the Koussevitzky Foundation and the Boston Symphony to celebrate the orchestra's seventy-fifth birthday. It was scheduled for premiere during the Boston's 1955-56 season. It was to prove an eight-year struggle in the realisation. L did not settle down seriously to work at the project till 1961. Even then, it seems to have been a spasmodic, on-again, off-again affair over the next two years best described by a phrase much used by creative talent in the music business, 'I've *almost* begun!' It seems to have been the cause of much sympathy, pain and *angst* within the Bernstein household. Humphrey Burton reports that Felicia was so overjoyed on the day L came running from his studio at their home in Connecticut shouting, "I've finished it, I've finished it." that she leaped into the swimming pool fully clothed.

Felicia Montealegre Bernstein's performance, recorded with L and the NY Philharmonic in 1964, is highly intense and, understandably, one of total identification with the work, its creation and its creator. Although the premiere of the Symphony took place in Tel Aviv with the noted Israeli actress, Hannah Rovina, performing the Speaker's role in Hebrew, Felicia was the Speaker for the American premiere performances in January 1964 in Boston with Charles Munch conducting the Boston Symphony and later that April for the New York premiere with L and the Philharmonic, following which the performance was preserved on disc.

The work, which I have referred to earlier as a hybrid creation, owes a debt in regard to its form to the oratorios of the French composer Arthur Honneger, *King David, Joan of Arc at the Stake* and *The Dance of Death*[220]. It is a difficult and complex work to mount requiring a highly skilled adult and children's choir, a soprano soloist, an actor/narrator and a large percussion section within a large orchestra. The spoken text, written by L, is one of struggle on several levels, highly melodramatic and, to those of a conservative religious outlook, controversial to the point of blasphemous. It makes one reflect on the fate of author Salmon Rushdie who now lives everyday of his life under the cloud of a *Fatwa* that has caused the more fanatic of the Moslem *Fundamentalists* to seek his life for writings

---

[220] Arthur Honneger, (1895-1955), a member of the French avant-garde, *Les Six*. His major compositions reflected his religious outlook. His oratorios, highly melodramatic and leaning heavily on religious symbolism, employed, as well as the expected solo singers and choirs, actors as either narator or characters within the dramatic text. Vocal and spoken parts were all integrated within the music text unlike Stravinsky's opera/oratorio, *Oedipus Rex* and ballet, *Persephone*, in which spoken naration only occurs between musical passages.

seemingly far less controversial and offensive about the prophet, Mohammed[221]. Within the history of the Jews, however, the *Kaddish Symphony*'s text in which Man disputes with God can find precedent in the historic biblical figures of the Old Testament beginning with Moses. In light of a parallel line of thought expressed in all of the major biographies and from my own observations during my tenure as L's assistant, the thrust of the text could also be construed as a confrontation with all authority, extending from parental to managerial to governmental. Even musically it could be interpreted to represent a struggle between tonal and non-tonal forces which had been one of the on-running battles L had fought his entire career as a committed tonal composer.

The orchestral writing is extremely confident and uses a wide range of compositional techniques including *twelve tone* and *aleatory* although there is never a question that, in essence, the composition overall is conceived tonally. It is a highly original work. That is not the same as saying that it is a totally successful work. Nevertheless, its failures lie more within the format the composer chose to employ and the spoken text he supplied than with the musical ideas he conceived and the originality and skill with which he developed his materials.

The Symphony is in three parts, performed without pause, in which the composer frames the *Kaddish* prayer within three highly contrasted settings for a variety of combinations employing both choruses and the soprano soloist. These settings reflect in mood the emotions of the Speaker as he/she tries to establish ground for a new beginning, a new relationship with the Creator in light of a past history of catastrophes, which have come to raise a challenge to Faith itself. The Speaker's words spill over with emotion. They are filled with anger, accusation, recrimination and regret but finally acceptance and accommodation. The form of address to God used by the Speaker and the self-importance assumed by His creation form the most contentious portions of the poem. Yet, when L sent the text to Israel to have

---

[221] *Fatwa(h),* from the arabic verb *fata,* to instruct by legal decision. Although we associate violence to the term *fatwa* resulting from the Salmon Rusdie affair, its meaning is simply that of a legal decision or ruling given by an Islamic religious leader.

it approved prior to the Israel Philharmonic's premiere performance, an authority on Hebrew literature and philosophy declared it in keeping with

historic Jewish writings and poetry.[222] The work makes a thrilling and challenging adjunct to the orchestral repertoire presented to a cosmopolitan audience. It would, one could readily project, find a hostile reception in those areas of the U.S. which have become religiously polarised and have been designated as centres of the 'Christian Right'.

The distinguishing nature of the two available Bernstein recorded performances is notable, principally in regard to the role of the Speaker and the individual and highly contrasted approach of the two actors involved. Felicia Montealegre Bernstein is all emotion, Michael Wager is highly contained. Wager had previously collaborated with L as Narrator for the teletaped performance of Stravinsky's *Oedipus Rex* used for L's Harvard Norton Lectures. This second collaboration began with the 1977 Tel Aviv Bernstein retrospective followed by the tour to Austria and Germany and in the following years subsequent tours throughout Europe, Israel and Japan. Plans to film a *Kaddish* performance during a second visit to Vienna were aborted when the director was unable to schedule sufficient camera rehearsal time. The CD was recorded at sessions in Mainz, Germany during the initial European tour but again technical problems, upon which I will later expand, prevented the recording of the Speaker's role which had to be later over-dubbed. A video made by Israeli television during a second tour of Israel has never been commercially released although excerpts from it can be seen in two documentaries, *A Gift of Music* and *Reflections*. Another most moving televised concert performance with L conducting the European Community Youth Orchestra, Barbara Hendricks as soloist and Michael Wager narrating was made by Japanese television in 1985 for the city of

---

[222] Many years after the completion of *Kaddish,* L's close friend, the actor, Michael Wager, who performed the role of the Speaker on world tours with the composer, spoke to L of a Yiddish song he had learned from his father at a very young age which he identified as the *Dudeleh.* The song uses the familiar Yiddish form of address *Di,* (derived from the ur-German *Du*) in a *Din Toirah mit Gott,* (An argument or case put to God according to Jewish law). In this song the singer always uses the familiar *Du* to address and argue with God. Discoursing with God in such familiar terms was a central tradition among Eastern European Jews.

WEST SIDE MAESTRO

Hiroshima's forty-year memorial of the dropping of the world's first atomic bomb on that city. With a mixed superb, young European/Japanese choir and the most passionate and committed of performances by all involved, it is regrettable that this unique performance has not been made generally available. A further technically flawed performance filmed in Budapest exists in a privately owned copy.

In comparing the two Speaker's performances one must take several factors into consideration. Felicia was performing the original highly histrionic text, which was considerably longer than the revised version. Her character was specifically identified as the Lily of Sharon. Many passages from this original text, which sat uncomfortably within the narration, were cut or revised by L. The Speaker's role as performed by Michael Wager in the revised version, was no longer identified in relation to gender. He assumes the more anonymous role of Everyman. Styles of acting had changed considerably in the fifteen years that separated the two performances. None of the biographies list a coach for Felicia to help her prepare so we must assume L coached her exclusively. Considering that the words were of his design, she must have been placed under a severe handicap when it came to disagreements about acting values and general approach. Moreover, Felicia's experience working in this medium was limited to her collaboration with L on Honneger's *Jeanne D'Arc*. The two roles are totally different in nature and pose different acting problems. Honneger's *Jeanne* is a character in a play. Though she is the only non-singing role, she continually interacts with the other vocally portrayed characters. Her reactions, unlike *Kaddish's* original Lily of Sharon, are not confined to external reactions to her own internal conflicts. They are reactions to a myriad of contrasting characters and circumstances. The portrayal of the character of *Jeanne* is not solely self-generated, which is the acting problem confronting the Speaker in *Kaddish*. It is the result of and is shaped by the interrelation and reactions to what the other characters are saying. The end result of Felicia's highly intense performance in *Kaddish* is that one soon becomes aware of her acting technique, that is, of an actor acting, which distracts from her projection of a character in whom we believe and identify and for whom we suspend disbelief in the artificial situation of the concert setting in which the drama takes place.

In contrast, Michael Wager's performance is underplayed from first to last. Such an approach helps ameliorate the unrelenting high drama of the text. With Wager's performance one's attention is concentrated upon the depicted suffering of the character rather than the performer's style and technique. On the few occasions when Wager as Speaker allows himself an emotional outburst, he quickly pulls back. This does not project as mere underplaying; it is the containment of high emotion. By skilfully using small vocal inflections the end result becomes even more powerful. One believes the anger of the character. However, the volatile nature of the text and the rising dynamic level of the orchestra writing at times forces matching contrasting dynamic levels even upon a highly controlled performance. This inevitably results in moments of high melodrama. All in all, however, Michael Wager's proves the more convincing performer. One must not lose sight of Felicia's uphill task, however. She had to find an original conception for a work which taxed her musicianship along with her gifts as an actor while at the same time meet the exacting and ever critical demands of her composer/conductor husband. She was working with a flawed text, which L was later to considerably revise. Michael Wager did enjoy the acting advantage of being able to assess the dramatic pitfalls of the work in advance and he did have a corrected, more compact text with which to work. Indeed, the actor was among several of L's friends and colleagues who attempted to assist in revising the text to Kaddish.[223] Chief among Wager's contributions were in reminding L that the Kaddish prayer of mourning is only spoken by the sons within the family never by the women and also in helping L re-examine and restructure the over impassioned narrative passages. Among other advantages that the actor himself enjoyed, referred to earlier, was the record producer's decision to later over-dub the Speaker's narration in a New York studio. This came about as a result of the concentration of L's time in Mainz being devoted to helping Montserat Caballé perfect the difficult

---

[223] Despite genuine efforts by several hands to help him with rewrites of the text, which included Irving Singer, Richard Wilbur, Frederick Seidel and Harold Brodkey, in the end L chose not to relinquish or share authorship.

solo role which she was singing for the first time. As a consequence, Wager had the opportunity of perfecting his own performance of the work in concert with L throughout Europe and Israel. By the time of the scheduled New York over-dubbing sessions, he had the full measure of the work and all its technical problems. Even with L in the control booth, he was able to perform without the stress normally encountered in having to do battle with concert hall acoustics along with the fierce range of orchestral dynamics that plague any spoken narration used indigenously within a concert work.[224]

Notwithstanding the diverse approach of the two Speakers, two other elements still weigh heavily in favour of the earlier New York recording, the performance of the orchestra throughout and Jennie Tourel's most moving solo in the second movement, *Kaddish II*. The demonic playing of the orchestra in the twelve tone and other *avant- garde* passages depicting anger and rebellion begs one to find or invent adjectives of praise not overworked in countless analyses and reviews. Perhaps it can best be characterised as simply the kind of great playing all orchestras strive for and pray to achieve. The Israel Philharmonic simply cannot match their New York colleagues in power, technique and rhythmic ferocity. Moreover, the NY Philharmonic makes such sense of even the most complex and opaque passages of the symphony and their palette of tonal colours mirror the rainbow oft spoken about in the text. Though the Israel orchestra does not project to the same degree the bite or demonic aspects of the work, all the notes are there and their ensemble is flawless. Where they do score heavily is in the lyrical sections. They capture the quiet drama beautifully and display a marvellous range of dynamics. Atmospheric playing combines with a seamless outpouring of the work's long melodic lines.

As for Miss Tourel, emotion and understanding floods every word she sings and the dark maternal sound of her mezzo-soprano, an alteration from L's original concept of a soprano voice, adds poignancy. One understands why L commented regarding Jennie's performance at both rehearsals and concerts at the premiere in Israel that, "Whenever she stood to sing that stage was the Holy of Holies." Montserrat Caballé, in beautiful voice, delivers the notes for

---

[224] Aaron Copland's *A Lincoln Portrait* is a case in point

the revised edition but little more. Her sheer beauty of sound cannot offset Tourel's added understanding of contemporary music, which produces textual clarity, and phrasing both natural and unforced.

There is little to choose between the choral forces employed on these two occasions. The singing is first class by all involved with a slight edge of boisterous enthusiasm in the more brilliant passages going to the Americans and a notably beautiful sound throughout from the Austrians, especially and predictably by the Vienna Boys Choir.

I have saved comments regarding all aspects of L's involvement for last. His conducting on this occasion can best be appreciated in the video recordings. His stage presence, as always, exudes enormous power reaching both forward to the performers he is guiding and simultaneously filling the hall behind him. With this great array of performers standing before him, conducting music of intense drama and luxuriant lyricism, were one to go along with the characterisation by his critics, one might expect and predict an unbridled, larger than life, physical performance to match the occasion. What we get, however, is the most controlled, precise conducting any orchestra or ensemble could hope for without exaggeration of any kind. His is a guiding force that never imposes itself between the music and the audience. It characterised L's physical presence whenever he conducted contemporary music. His attention was always turned to building a bridge of understanding between composer and audience, at least when he enjoyed or respected the composer involved and had himself specifically chosen the contemporary work to be performed.

Bernstein, the composer, comes off extremely well in these programs. One is struck by the freshness of his earliest symphony, *Jeremiah*. *The Age of Anxiety* poses separate problems for the listener. Surface-wise it is a totally accessible contemporary work which, over repeated hearings, puts you in mind of the Swiss movement of a clock, more interesting in its parts than in its main function. The revised version which, in face of its designation by the composer as a symphony, still projects more as a piano concerto, is a good addition to the repertoire and deserves to be undertaken by pianists with a sympathy and flair for jazz. It represents a challenging and interesting alternative to the endless repetition of the standard piano repertoire of concerti. The *Kaddish* Symphony is a controversial work. Despite its display of originality and enormous compositional skill, it has attracted the same phantom accusations from the past that invariably arise when any discussion of L's music is generated. In the case of *Kaddish*, it is of eclecticism to the point of stealing. One can dismiss the first part of the argument with the truism that all music is eclectic. As to 'stealing', L does tend to borrow or repeat ideas that he has previously used. All composers do, especially those under pressure of a deadline. In L's case, one can readily point to his passion for the disjunct rhythm of seven beats to the bar that dominate his scherzos in *Jeremiah, Kaddish* and the *Chichester Psalms*. If, in relation to his Third Symphony, 'stealing' refers to the obvious Copland quote from the ballet, *Appalachian Spring*, has anyone ever considered that if *Kaddish* truly represents a challenge and final accommodation with all parental authority from 'Big Daddy' to 'Big Brother' what better music to represent the accommodation aspect than with loved music by one of the most loved parental figures in L's life, Aaron Copland. *Kaddish* is worth the time, effort and cost for an orchestra with the budget and a sympathetic conductor possessing an understanding and genuine 'feel for the stage'. In its revised form, presented with a well thought out and modulated acting performance by the Speaker, integrating rather than competing with the orchestra, its textual defects can be minimised and an example of some of L's best symphonic writing will come to enjoy, hopefully, additional deserved outings. Perhaps its form, comparable to the works of Arthur Honneger listed earlier, now very much out of fashion, has deterred and undermined this work finding an audience. If so, one has only to listen to the recordings to assess the potential success it is capable of achieving. Regarding the *Chichester Psalms*, it has already established a firm place for itself in the choral repertoire. Some would attribute this to its conservative tonal writing. However, it is not *that* conservative, its first two movements containing a variety of rhythmic and harmonic contemporary elements. The last movement serves to resolve all forms of dissonance from the preceding two movements.

WEST SIDE MAESTRO

Deciding on preference of performance is extremely difficult. The video of the Chichester Psalms and the First and Second Symphonies is of an historic happening and unique in every way. In regard to the *Kaddish* Symphony, I would want both the Israel and NY Philharmonic CD performances in order to appreciate the full potential of the work. Hopefully, one day the video film of the Hiroshima concert performance of *Kaddish* will be made available.

The Ballets

It was natural as a man of the theatre that L proved so successful in composing for the Dance. At the conclusion of a Gala Dance Evening at the old Metropolitan Opera House during which four American composers helped Ballet Theatre celebrate by each conducting their own scores commissioned especially for that Company[225], Aaron Copland turned to L and declared *Fancy Free* to be the best integration of dance and music he could imagine. That remark was made in my presence almost sixty years ago and *Fancy Free* continues to remain one of the most popular ballets in this same Company's repertoire. This boisterous dance romp brought L together for the first time with the choreographer, Jerome Robbins. Robbins, with whom he would continue to collaborate throughout his career, was to be a seminal influence in the composing of L's most successful stage works. Robbins presence contributed an element of containment, structure, discipline and authority, qualities often lacking in other of L's collaborations. It always produced the best from him even when the best proved less than successful, as was the case with their second collaboration for the ballet, *Facsimile*. Robbins was also to adapt for George Balanchine's NY City Ballet, L's Second Symphony, *The Age of Anxiety*, along with its complex program based upon W.S. Auden's monumental poem. With Robbins, this brilliant partnership was to extend their joint talents to Broadway with two classic shows, *On The Town* and *West Side Story*. While Dance played an unusually prominent but subsidiary role in *On The Town*, in *West Side Story* dance evolved into an equal partnership with the spoken and sung drama. This pivotal theatre work is credited with changing the face of the Broadway

---

[225] Morton Gould conducted *Fall River Legend*; Aaron Copland conducted *Billy The Kid;* Virgil Thomson conducted *Filling Station* and Leonard Bernstein conducted *Fancy Free.*

WEST SIDE MAESTRO

musical and elevating the choreographer/director to a dominant position within the Broadway hierarchy and the dancer/singer/actor, talents in that order, to the casting director's first choice for most musicals AWSS, (after West Side Story). The final Bernstein/ Robbins partnership was on the ballet, *Dybbuk*. Although high hopes were held for this production, (it was chosen for a 'black tie' premiere to open the 1974 season of the NY City ballet at $250 for a pair of tickets, a huge sum of money at the time), it proved a disappointing failure. Robbins without consultation was to re-choreograph the work twice, first in 1975 and then again in 1980. In its reincarnations the Dybbuk theme was to be abandoned in favour of an abstract approach, which the choreographer titled simply, *Suite of Dances*. These also seem not to have found a permanent place in the Company's repertoire.

Other Bernstein compositions adapted for the dance also enjoyed mixed success. *Prelude, Fugue and Riffs* had a short life as a dance sequence in L's second Broadway musical, *Wonderful Town*. It was dropped, however, during the out-of-town tryouts as not being in keeping with the light hearted spirit of the show. It was to resurface in two reincarnated dance forms, the first time in 1966 in choreography especially created for the NY City Ballet and then in 1978 in Amhearst, Massachusetts in another choreographed form for the Hartford Ballet under the jaw breaking title, *Partrasolifutricatramerifu*.

The *Serenade* for Violin, String Orchestra, Harp and Percussion, which I will expand upon separately, was translated to the stage for Ballet Theatre by Herbert Ross five years after its instrumental premiere. Titled *Serenade for Seven*, its ballet premiere took place at the Spoletto Festival and was generally well received. In addition to the Serenade other Bernstein instrumental works that entered briefly into the repertoire of the world of dance include the *Jeremiah* Symphony in 1948 at the Choreographer's Workshop in New York City and the *On the Waterfront* Suite in 1964 by a New York based Jazz-Ballet Company at the Brooklyn Academy of Music.

L's music for the dance, whether listened to in a theatre accompanying stage action, in the concert hall played by a virtuoso symphony orchestra or at

WEST SIDE MAESTRO

home on entertainment centres ranging from costly, lease-breaking matched components to a modestly priced 'boom box' provides, for most part, a highly enjoyable, highly communicative experience. Although an underlying thematic element of loneliness and sadness has been traced throughout his output as a composer and certainly is clearly reflected in his early symphonic and Broadway successes, with the exception of his dramatic First Symphony, *Jeremiah*, music by Bernstein is more likely to provoke a sense of excitement, nostalgia and fun than sadness. Much of the music, while seeming to be unchallenging, is stretching the capacity of its audience to listen to other symphonic music of a more complex nature. In that sense, the music of Leonard Bernstein has for many helped formed a bridge to a much broader palette of listening experience. Neither the Symphonic Dances to *West Side Story* nor the much more sophisticated symphony-cum-ballet, *The Age of Anxiety*, represent too great a stretch in challenging listening even for the novice or less committed listener to symphonic music. The Suite drawn from West Side Story utilises the equivalent form that has been a favourite mainstay of 'pops' concerts since their initiation, the ballet suite. It contains whole sections or excerpts from all of the show's dance music with the exception of the huapango, *America*. It is all brilliantly stitched together out of show sequence but making wonderful sense to the listener as a through-composed piece of music. Its popularity in concert has never diminished since its NY Philharmonic premiere in 1961. The *Age of Anxiety*, a far more complex work, brims over with good tunes, enjoys a vividly colourful orchestration with loads of exciting percussion writing, includes a bit of jazz within its diversely rhythmic content and adds to all this the extra element of a virtuoso soloist, a pianist, to provide an additional fireworks display.

In comparison with the above, L's two other compositions specifically composed for the dance, *Facsimile* and *Dybbuk*, created almost thirty years apart, are far more challenging works even for the experienced listener. The score to *Facsimile*, (1946), written only two years after his first three important successes as a composer, *Jeremiah*, *Fancy Free* and *On The Town*, (1942-44), seems light years away in style from what had preceded it, but is, in fact, very much related to the writing associated with L's short piano pieces of 1943, *Seven Anniversaries*. Indeed, the presence of an important virtuoso solo piano part in *Facsimile* also anticipates by three years a similar use of piano in L's Second Symphony, *The Age of Anxiety*. *Facsimile*, divorced from the brutal, misogynist stage libretto of its failed ballet and after years of neglect by all but its composer, is now, deservedly, being explored to a greater degree by symphonic organisations and record companies.

Dybbuk, perhaps L's most individual and complex orchestral composition, is, in its uncut full ballet form, a hard 'slog'[226] for the most avid Bernstein fan. The composer has created two concert suites from the complete ballet. The first of the two suites, which includes the vocal element from the original score, is the more problematic for the listener. The second suite, shorter and purely instrumental, contains a better balance of elements. It contains four movements of interesting content and contrast well worth investigation.

The techniques employed in *Dybbuk*'s composition, we learn from its composer, are based upon the Jewish mystical system of numerology[227], the caballa. Assigning a numerical value to each of the twenty-two letters of the Hebrew alphabet the composer then translates numerically both the letters of the names of the ballet's principal characters and the letters of the words defining their spiritual qualities, (understanding, grace, strength, etc.). He then devises his musical vocabulary by correlating the numerical substitutions to the twelve notes of the chromatic scale. If that appears somewhat complicated and confusing, I can only comment that my head is still spinning from the program note explanations which became even more dense and convoluted as the panoply of L's metaphysical formulas were expounded in all their aspects.

Music by formula of simple or complex nature is nothing new. A musical formula, however, can only produce a limited result and a limited solution.

---

[226] slog - hard, steady, dogged work, *Oxford Concise Dictionary*
[227] numerology - divination by or study of the occult meaning of numbers, *Oxford*Concise Dictionary

The quality of that result still depends upon the application of personal originality and inspiration. That's what seems to me to be lacking in this work. It isn't just that *Dybbuk* is highly challenging to the listener. In the end, it proves to be less than a rewarding listening experience. Its uninteresting musical materials grind on like a machine without a final cycle to its program that, ultimately, runs out of steam.

L's mental brilliance at word games was legend. Perhaps the lesson to be learned here is that games with words are best left as a pastime for the parlour not as the basis for extended musical compositions. It must be added, despite my criticism, that *Dybbuk* is a work of immense professionalism. It also represents a tonal composer's search for a wider music vocabulary. Was L like his mentor, Aaron Copland, who turned in the end in desperation to twelve tone composition, also searching at this time for *new chords*?

The composer recorded *Facsimile* no less than three times. The first recording for RCA appeared on shellac 78rpm discs in the late 1940's, was later transferred to LP and, more recently to CD. It is an early example of Bernstein, the new, young meteor flashing across the American music scene. It possesses all the energy and youthful exuberance one might expect from its composer/conductor. His *pick-up*[228] RCA Symphony play extremely well. Unfortunately, the recording is harsh and shrill sounding even in its most recent refurbished CD version, and is anaemic on the low end of the sound spectrum as well. Again, the more recent recordings are for CBS/Sony and DG and again the comparison is between performances by the NY Philharmonic and the Israel Philharmonic. *Facsimile*, a Choreographic Essay, forms part of a three CD Bernstein Portrait devoted to his music for the stage. I will refer to it from time to time throughout this chapter. The album contains classic performances by the NY Philharmonic against which all competition fades. Specifically related to the ballet scores, the album encompasses in addition to the *Facsimile* ballet, the complete score to *Fancy Free*, the three dances from *On The Town* and the Symphonic Dances from

---

[228] *pick-up* – a top-flight, freelance orchestra later given a fictitious but impressive sounding title, ie: RCA Symphony.

WEST SIDE MAESTRO

West Side Story for which they gave the premiere and recorded one of CBS's all-time best selling records. If you do not wish to invest in the three disc set, however, there is the re-coupled composer's single DG disc containing the above four ballet titles, three of which are played by the Israel Philharmonic and the fourth, the *West Side Story Dances*, played by the Los Angeles Philharmonic. The disc is very well performed throughout and the West Coast version of the *West Side Story Suite* is almost a match for the New Yorkers. The Israeli's are very good in *Facsimile* and *Fancy Free* if not quite catching the full humour of the latter ballet and the bite and swing required for the popular dance rhythms employed in the score. The *very* idiomatic New York style required for the *On The Town* dances also eludes them. The *West Side Story Dance* suite with the NY Philharmonic was videotaped during their 1976 Bicentennial tour to Europe. It will be discussed in the chapter devoted to video films in Volume 2, later to be published. It is sufficient to state at this juncture that their performance was brilliantly authentic as one might expect and was overwhelmingly received by their German audience.

No commercial video exists of either the Jerome Robbins *Dybbuk* ballet or of any concert performance of the score. Recently re-mastered CD recordings are currently available of the complete ballet score on CBS/Sony and of two suites drawn from the ballet on DG. The composer conducts for both recordings. The earlier complete Sony recording features the NY City Ballet Orchestra and two vocal soloists. The two ballet suites, recorded only four years later for DG, feature the NY Philharmonic. The *Suites*, formerly available separately, have recently been coupled together by DG on a new CD release along with one of the composer's last compositions, the *Concerto for Orchestra*. The DG disc illustrates the composer at his most complex. Both the Sony and DG recordings are equally authoritative performances. However, the NY Philharmonic's drive and breathtaking virtuosity, marvellously captured by a superb and atmospheric DG recording, takes the prize.

WEST SIDE MAESTRO

Overture & Beginners
The works for the Stage

Even L's most vociferous detractors readily admit that, at very least, his contribution to the musical stage will withstand the test of time. This narrow view takes on an even more attenuated aspect when one considers that such pronouncements are, in fact, mostly limited to one of L's several individual contributions to the Broadway stage, *West Side Story*. At the time of its production, *On The Town* was considered equally revolutionary. It is a product of youthful effervescence, Bernstein/ Robbins/ Comden/ Green/ (Oliver)Smith, tempered by the wisdom of age, George Abbott. It is a toast to New York City, not with *Brut* champagne but with a Nathan's *hot dog*[229] and a frosty bottle of *coke*. As I have written earlier, it is the Bernstein show with which I most closely identify as it launched my own career as a conductor and was my introduction to L and the beginning of our ten-year professional relationship. As this first revival took place at a university, The College of the City of New York, it has not seemed to rank of sufficient importance with archivists to have merited mention in the many detailed biographies of the show. Nevertheless, as with the original Broadway production, it was responsible for launching a number of distinguished careers in all areas of the Performing Arts among whom were the noted producer/ director/ choreographer, Herbert Ross, one of America's finest classical actors, Donald Madden and the Broadway producer, Marvin Krauss.

Rarely has a composer enjoyed the kind of close rapport with his working colleagues as existed for the creation of *On The Town*. L and Adolph Green had become friends in 1937 when they both were hired to work at Camp Onota, a summer camp for youngsters in Massachusetts. They were later to share an apartment in the Greenwich Village area of lower New York City. Adolph Green was part of a satirical nightclub act called the *Revuers*. Another member of the act was Betty Comden. L was a *regular* at the Village

---

[229] *Nathan's* frankfurters, originally founded at Coney Island, one of the scene settings in *On The Town*, has long been one of America's most popular fast food restaurants and can be found in most food malls throughout the United States.

WEST SIDE MAESTRO

Vanguard where his friends performed nightly. Often after their final show he would sit at the piano and, with his friends, would sing and wile away the hours till dawn. In the year 1944, L and Jerome Robbins scored a brilliant success with the ballet, *Fancy Free* for Ballet Theatre, set designs by Oliver Smith. Smith recognised that there were greater possibilities to the *Fancy Free* story of three sailors on leave in New York City for a night of high-jinx. The next link in the chain was provided by L who brought in his friends, Betty Comden and Adolph Green, to write the book and lyrics for the new musical, now christened *On The Town*. With it, the association of *Comden & Green* was launched as one of Broadway's newest and wittiest writing partnerships. Oliver Smith's production partner was Paul Feigay, later to become a member of the Robert Saudek Organization and the person who suggested to Mary Ahearn, Saudek's feature editor that she meet with L regarding the *Omnibus* television program they were planning devoted to Beethoven. From this short, Voltaire-like interlocking of lives, events and careers, one can immediately assess the significance of this single show in launching some of most important talents in the theatre, dance and concert worlds of the last half century.

What was it that was so individual, indeed, revolutionary about *On The Town?* After all, running on Broadway that same season was that most revolutionary of new musicals, *Oklahoma,* the product of a new partnership, Richard Rodgers and Oscar Hammerstein. For starters, *On The Town* exploded with a new level of energy, pace, and freshness, those ingredients without which no Broadway musical can succeed. While the tale of three sailors on twenty-four hours leave in New York City, each with his own personal agenda to fulfil, (echoes of the ballet *Fancy Free*), appears to be the plot of the show, I have always viewed the central star of the show to be New York City itself, whose portrait, people and kaleidoscope of attractions would again concern the composer in two further brilliant and individual musicals as well as the score for a major film. To support this theory I point to two subtle but important threads of plot. The character of Miss Subways, Ivy, with whom Gabey, one of our three sailors, falls in love at the first sight of her subway poster photograph, is merely part of a continuous procession of Miss Subways, newly chosen each month. The second plot thread is the arrival of three new sailors on twenty-four hours leave at the very end of the show just as our three erstwhile heroes are leaving to join their ship. Chip, Ossie and Gabey have only been part of a passing parade of lives and happenings that make up the colossal daily jigsaw that is New York City. Add to this the various New York icons that provide the scene settings, the Brooklyn Navy Yard, the subways, the taxi cab with its over-friendly driver, Carnegie Hall, the Museum of Natural History, Times Square and Coney Island. Lenny Bernstein may have been born and brought up in a provincial town in Massachusetts and educated at Harvard, one of America's most distinguished Universities located in Boston, heart of one of America's most elite and sophisticated city of the Arts, but once he was infected by the excitement and volatility of New York, he lost his heart to that city. It became the center of his personal life, friendships, career and creativity, a love affair that, in a unique act of faithfulness, he maintained for virtually two thirds of his life. The score and look of *On The Town* was something Broadway aficionados had neither seen and, certainly, never heard before, not from the cultured Jerome Kern, the sophisticated Cole Porter, the tune master Irving Berlin, the illuminator of drama, Richard Rodgers or even the unique, all-round genius of George Gershwin. It was *On The Town's* veteran director of musicals, George Abbott, ever referring to the brilliant and original ballet music which abounds throughout the show as "that Prokofiev stuff", who was among the first outside the show's creative clique of cohorts to express appreciation in a unique way of L's distinctive musical input. L was concerned that his long, symphonic ballet contributions, calling for a larger than normal pit orchestra and certainly extra costly rehearsals, might become another victim of the "snipping away" of that "ever practical man of the theatre"[230], Mr Abbott. In the end, L reports that George Abbott did not cut a single bar of his symphonic contributions.

It may have been the show's dance music that precipitated the "that Prokofiev stuff" remark. It should be noted that the music for most dance sequences on Broadway is most often pieced together by specialists working to the instructions of the choreographer during dance rehearsals. The names

---

[230] Two direct Bernstein quotes reported in Joan Peyser's coverage of *On The Town,* in her biography of *Leonard Bernstein* .

of Trude Rittman, Peter Howard, Larry Rosenthal are among those that have loomed large in this specialist field. The dance sequences are rarely ever constructed by the composers and almost never composed as anything but endless sequences and variations of the show's main tunes strung together. Certainly they are seldom viewed as works that are suitable to be delivered straight to the concert hall. L's ballet music for *On the Town* was from the first a brilliant and classically skilled top-drawer creation that soon found a permanent place in the light music programs of orchestras throughout the world as well as on disc. Indeed, none of the music in the show is written in traditional Broadway style and form. The tunes or fragments of them have become well known, 'NEW YORK, NEW YORK, a hell-uv-a town' or 'A town's a LONELY TOWN' for example. I have deliberately quoted only the lyrics of these two songs not examples of the tunes themselves. I'm sure many feel they know these tunes well. Just try to sing them, however, and discover how difficult it is to get a handle on them. And if you think *they* are problematic just attempt the chromaticism of *Come Up To My Place* or the huge vocal range of *Lucky To Be Me* or the verses of any of the songs - <u>not</u> easy, I promise you. Yet all of them, appealing in one way or another help to establish the characters and mood and give this show its unique musical profile. Not everything in the show is original in concept, however. The opening is particularly reminiscent of another show. A lonely, solo baritone shipyard worker is starting his early morning shift. With virtually no accompaniment he sings, "I feel that I'm not out of bed yet". Theatrically it is the parallel moment of the opening of Oklahoma when we hear the voice of Curly off-stage, again unaccompanied, again singing in a three-beat-to-the-bar rhythm, "There's a bright, golden haze on the meadow". Once the shipyard whistle blows, (a brilliant dissonance orchestrated for screeching woodwinds), *On The Town* begins to speak with its own musical voice, a voice that rings clear till the fall of the second act curtain.

There have been over the years a number of attempted revivals of *On The Town*, none of which have enjoyed a sustained success. I did attend one of the earliest revivals in the late 1950's, a tatty, scaled down version presented in the small confines of Carnegie Hall Playhouse. I have no personal knowledge of the other productions, which included a London production in

WEST SIDE MAESTRO

1963, a much valued but failed 1973 Broadway revival and a successful outdoor production in Central Park in 1997. *On The Town* requires a big production budget to include the cost of a full sized orchestra to properly display the rich panoply of the Bernstein score, something one rarely encounters in show musicals these days, especially in regard to revivals. It requires a superb, versatile choreographer who understands and rejoices in its period style, is not ashamed of emotion, can depict love without resorting to nudity or blatant crudity, has a broad sense of humour and knows New York inside out. It needs a director who knows how to enjoy the brilliance of good material and who would assiduously avoid an endless search to find an anti-war political agenda to give the show *a contemporary relevance*. As for the stage design, one would have few worries regarding its brilliance. Nowadays, one usually departs an evening's theatre watching most modern musicals *whistling the scenery*. It may be, in any case, that in light of its most successful movie version, made at the height of MGM's *All Talking, All Singing, All Dancing* era, which still figures as a regular family holiday feature of most television networks, that no revival can compete. This is not because it can't be cast better, although your talent search would probably have to extend to the ends of the earth, or lack an effective mounting in the hands of a superb production staff with a generous budget. It is because you could never hope to present a vision of the wonders of New York, the unspoken star of the show, better than it has been captured in glorious Technicolor by its film director, Stanley Donen.

There are two recorded performances of virtually the complete score to consider. The most recent recording was taken from a 1992 concert performance at London's Barbican Centre with Michael Tilson-Thomas conducting the London Symphony Orchestra, an all-star international cast of mostly opera singers and special guest stars Tyne Daly, TV's *Lacy* from *Cagney & Lacey,* performing the Nancy Walker role of *Hildy*, and Cleo Lane singing, in her inimitable fashion, a night club torch song, *Ain't Got No Tears Left*, which was cut from the score prior to the Broadway premiere. The other recording is a studio performance dating from 1960 with the composer conducting a *pick-up* orchestra. The soloists include four members of the original Broadway cast, Betty Comden and Adolph Green, the show's book writers and lyricists, Nancy Walker as *Hildy*, the predator taxi driver, and Chris Alexander as Chip, the Frank Sinatra role in the film. The role of *Gabey* is taken by John Reardon, famous for his performance as *Billy Bigelow* in Rodgers & Hammerstein's *Carousel,* and, in the minor role of *Judge Pitkin W. Bridgework*, George Gaynes, now a film superstar for his role as the addle-brained Captain Lazar in the slapstick *Police Academy* series. On the surface, it appears a *no-contest* with the newer recording of mostly opera superstars walking away with the vocal honours but just the opposite is true. Comden & Green's performance of *the* duet, *Carried Away*, a song with the shortest chorus ever written, is hilarious. It is a nightclub review-style number that might have been straight out of their Greenwich Village act. Frederica von Stade and Kurt Ollman simply can't compete for all their superior vocal equipment. The same holds true for the DG *Gabey* wonderfully sung by Thomas Hampson. However, John Reardon is no slouch in the vocal department and his Broadway know-how and natural acting delivery of the song lyrics creates a real sense of musical comedy in comparison to Hampson's somewhat artificial operetta style. Tyne Daly is the only star performer on the DG album who gives the original *Hildy*, Nancy Walker, more than a run for her money. Daly is the genuine *show-biz* article and she steals the show from her less than authentic colleagues. Finally we come to the conductors and the orchestras. I was surprised how lacking in energy and drive the Tilson Thomas performance projected. The rhythms are sharp and the ensemble is well nigh perfect but there is no bite to the orchestra's playing, all the edges are smoothed out and the big ballet climaxes are all over-cooked, indeed vulgar. L's NY freelancers are fewer in number but their performance of every note of the score is to the manor born and their slightly lean sound is the real Broadway article. My unhesitating vote goes for the older Sony recording, part of an unbeatable box set titled Leonard Bernstein, a Portrait, to which I have referred earlier and which also includes the *West Side Story* Dances, the *On The Waterfront* Suite, the ballets, *Fancy Free* and *Facsimile* and the early one act opera, *Trouble in Tahiti*, later to be incorporated into the three act opera, *A Quiet Place*.

WEST SIDE MAESTRO

Eight years were to pass before L again involved himself in a full scale musical.[231] The sequence of unusual circumstances that brought it about would have provided the prototype script for a typical 1950's movie about a classically schooled musical genius, whose secret love is popular music, drafted in at the eleventh hour by friends to save the day by composing a brilliant score for a musical comedy whose composer had walked out leaving both cast and investors threatened with the loss of jobs and their life savings. That's a much gilded representation of what actually happened but it does follow the general sequence of events which brought L back to Broadway and created for him an even greater personal triumph than had his debut musical, *On The Town*. *Wonderful Town* particularly interested me at the time of its production because, having conducted *On The Town* and spent two summers at Tanglewood studying with L in his scholarship conducting class, I was hoping that he might consider me for the position of conductor with the show. This, of course, proved no more than a young and very ambitious conductor's fantasy since the show's producers correctly sought out the services of one of the most experienced and respected Broadway conductors, Lehman Engel.

To get the full, accurate picture of the sequence of events leading up to the production of *Wonderful Town* one must make reference to at least four of the current Bernstein biographies. It all began with a series of autobiographical stories written in the late 1930's for The New Yorker magazine by Ruth McKinny. These were adapted into a highly successful theatre comedy titled, *My Sister Eileen*, by Joseph Fields and Jerome Chodorov, which enjoyed a successful Broadway run during the 1940 season. In 1942, *Eileen* was successfully transferred to the silver screen starring Rosalind Russell and Janet Blair as the two sisters from Ohio on the hunt in lower New York City for fame, fortune and a fiancé. After a series of aborted tries by various noted Broadway producers, writers and directors to transform the Fields/Chodorov comedy into a musical, the producer Robert Fryer in collaboration with George Abbott bought the rights and signed Rosalind Russell to recreate her successful film role of ten years previous.

---

[231] L did write songs and incidental music for a 1950 production of *Peter Pan* starring Jean Arthur and Boris Karloff.

WEST SIDE MAESTRO

Mr Abbott worked on a book with the original short story author, Ruth McKinny. It was then decided by Fryer to bring in Fields and Chodorov to adapt their original stage play and to obtain the services of either Irving Berlin or Frank Loesser to write the score. This dream ticket did not quite work out as planned and Leroy Anderson, the noted arranger for the Boston *Pops* and composer of *The Syncopated Clock, Blue Tango* and *Fiddle-Faddle*, among the Boston *Pops*' best selling records at the time, was asked to write the score. The necessary chemistry between composer and writers did not, unfortunately, crystallise and five weeks before the show was set to go into rehearsal Anderson bowed out and with him his lyricist. Abbott telephoned Comden and Green. The story is told in more than one version at this point. Whether Comden and Green insisted that they would only come on board if L was asked to write the music or it was Abbott who suggested the three of them work together is not really important in light of the result. The team of Abbott/Comden/Green and Bernstein were again up and running. In five weeks the score and lyrics were delivered. The setting of the book, which had been updated to the 1950's, was restored to its original 1930's time frame. L delivered a new valentine to New York City, again capturing its explosive energy but this time viewed within the madcap, bohemian eccentricities of Greenwich Village. From every point of view, *Wonderful Town* proved to be a superior musical to L's initial young effort eight years before. The pressure of a deadline resulted in a creative heat that produced the very best from the Comden/Green/Bernstein partnership. L's music matched the wit of his partners' brilliant lyrics note by word in a manner that reflected back to and equalled the very best of Rodgers and Hart but with the addition of L's more daring musical vocabulary. There are tributes to be found everywhere in the score, some subtle, some blatant but all integrated and assimilated in a manner that never distracts or seems to be, as was often later the charge, "borrowing". The Eddy Duchin vamp[232], which everyone in America could play on the piano whether or not one ever had a lesson, introduces *Christopher Street,* the musical curtain raiser of the show. Its appearance right at the start of the show for those of us of a certain generation was like being welcomed into your best friend's home. A quote from *Buckaroo Holiday* from Aaron Copland's ballet, *Rodeo,* is both part of

---

[232] Eddy Duchin, pianist and noted band leader of the 1940's & '50's.

the melody and accompaniment of *What A Waste*. Much has been made of L's use of musical fragments to generate development within his symphonic compositions but he was already using something of this same technique as a unifying device in his early theatre work. *Wonderful Town* is filled with examples. Material from both the verse and chorus of *What A Waste* is used to generate the songs *Pass The Football*, *A Quiet Girl* and the hit vocal of the show that sends the audience out into the streets singing, *It's Love*. Incidentally, a much-transformed Eddie Duchin vamp also benefits the chorus of *Pass the Football* and then again, in its transformed guise, becomes the opening phrase of *Wrong Note Rag*.

The integration of book and music in *Wonderful Town* is just that, *wonderful*! The songs move comfortably in and out of dialogue and even internally mix dialogue within the vocals. The show, often viewed as the next step on from Frank Loesser's *Guys and Dolls*, in many ways was ahead of its time and its unanimous reception showed that it did much more than merely please, it struck a chord on several levels simultaneously with audience and critics alike. The show swept the boards of all the major theatre awards. The eminent New York music critic of the NY Times, Olin Downes, assessed *Wonderful Town* as a harbinger of the evolution of American opera. Certainly, the vocal writing pointed towards the future of musical theatre. The vocal line to the verse of *What A Waste* could be straight out of a late Stephen Sondheim musical, including *Sweeny Todd*.

Wonderful Town has remained a perennial favourite on America's summer theatre circuit. In 1958, CBS mounted a two-hour adaptation for television starring Rosalind Russell recreating her role as Ruth and Jackie McKeever playing *Eileen*.[233] Sidney Chaplin, son of *Charlie*, later to be Barbra Streisand's leading man in the Broadway production of *Funny Girl*, played *Robert Baker* and Cris Alexander, (the original *Chip* in *On The Town* and also a member of the original cast of *Wonderful Town*), was on board as well. The show enjoyed a brilliant revival and successful run in London's West End in 1986 starring Maureen Lipman, a favourite comedienne of

---

[233] A kinescope of this black and white production can be viewed at the Museum of Radio & Television in New York City.

WEST SIDE MAESTRO

British television and theatre. An excellent CD original cast recording is available using an imaginative reduced orchestration without strings created especially for this production. Unlike many a British staging of American musicals, this one retains the flavour of the original show and has all the drive and vitality one could hope for and all the clarity that the Bernstein score and Comden and Green lyrics demand[234].

I want to proceed out of sequence with *West Side Story*, saving a discussion of the much revised *Candide* for afterwards. *West Side Story* concludes the trilogy of *New York* shows. Of all the Bernstein shows, this is the best documented, the most well known, the most often revived for major international productions and tours and the most generally publicly accessible. The original NY cast recording is readily available on CD as well as other more recent CD recordings based upon numerous revivals. Virtually every important popular vocalist has recorded the four standards to come out of the show, *Tonight, Maria, Somewhere* and *One Hand, One Heart*. Two best selling videos whose sound tracks are also available on CD are the award winning 1961 Hollywood film of the show and a more recent 1985 documentary of the original studio recording of virtually the entire score under the composer's direction. The 1985 documentary has the distinction of being one of the all-time best selling videos. It also has the distinction of being a record of one of the most ill tempered displays by a powerful personality using his authoritative muscle to bully others for his own errors in judgement. The affair has been generally well documented in two of the most recent Bernstein biographies but there are additional facts and observations that are relevant to further discussion. It is fair comment to summarise the affair as one that began with high purpose, a composer wishing to leave his personal statement on his single, most famous composition, and ended as a tale of greed which, without doubt, was more financially successful than anyone envisioned. Considering how badly L, the principal player, has critically been seen to come off, one might wonder how the video achieved such success. The obvious truth is that the general public

---

[234] To usher in the millennium, EMI has released the complete score to *Wonderful Town* brilliantly conducted by Simon Rattle and featuring Audra Mc Donald, Kim Chriswell and Thomas Hampson.

did not view it in the same manner as the professional community. What they observed was everybody's favourite TV classical music superstar displaying the kind of legendary temperament which film studios had for years exploited to the full in their many *factionalised* biographies of artistic genius stretching from Mozart to Van Gogh. They obviously not only didn't care that the casting of the two vocal principals was patently absurd and totally contradicted the intended concept of the original show characters they represented but that, by surrounding them with a relatively authentic cast and a hand picked theatre orchestra, even their superb voices ended up being something of a handicap and an anomaly. Everyone ended up laughing all the way to the bank so what importance can it hold for the listener/viewer of today? Perhaps only in clarifying the reality of the dangers of being a top rank artist who accepts a role for which they are not suited and are encouraged and permitted to do so by organisations and individuals who are highly paid to be looking out after their best interests, not always compatible with the amount of money involved. In this situation, I am particularly thinking of José Carreras with whom I discussed the video during the coffee break of a concert we were performing together at London's Barbican Centre with the London Symphony Orchestra. José had been made to appear both unprepared and musically incompetent during the recording of *Something's Comin'* and then again during the early takes of *Maria*. Why did he sanction the inclusion of that bit of film? To my astonishment, he told me he had been advised to do so by his management. In again reviewing the video, it is shocking to watch the campaign of aggressive intimidation waged by L during the sessions directed mostly towards two people, Carreras and the record producer, John McClure. Written all over L's face as José began to record *Something's Comin'*, his natural Spanish accent projecting far more than at the private piano rehearsals at which L was present, was his clear realisation turned to displeasure that the wrong choice of singer had been made, a choice he had sanctioned. John McClure trying to help José with his American pronunciation only caused L to explode in anger. One can readily see on the videotape the oncoming explosion building in L's tense and none too pleased expression as he repeatedly stops for corrections during the recording of his tenor soloist's first scheduled song.

WEST SIDE MAESTRO

L's quarrel with McClure served to only further upset José, shaking his confidence. He began to make mistake after mistake each of which L coldly and cavalierly corrected. An orchestral break was called to relieve the tension but L's response to this was to hunch his shoulders and bury his head in his hands, which could not have helped raise the general level of confidence in the studio. Listening to the playbacks, which we are permitted to observe, serves to increase the disquiet and when retakes begin things are seen to get worse. L treats his distinguished soloist like a stupid child and, precipitated by such behaviour, José's mistakes multiply. Finally, when the air is spilling over with stress, anger and just about every other negative emotion you can assemble, John McClure's intervention stating he has enough material to splice together a performance along with L's agreement abruptly ends the session. José, totally excluded from the artistic decision, in a confused state, leaves the studio in a fury. Not a nice situation!

José was certainly aware of what he was getting himself into. In a short interview to camera he summarises the problem, he is the only Spaniard in the cast who is required to play an American. He is equally concerned that in the lyrics of some of his numbers "there are a lot of words to say". I am loathe to be critical of a colleague but as the credits roll at the end of the program among the production staff list is a language coach. One is left to ponder about the approach this technician used which produced, at best, meagre results with José, who needed the most help, and which equally failed to demonstrate to Kiri Te Kanawa how to avoid a broad English 'A' vowel in favour of the required American pronunciation for a simple word like 'half'.

To come to a balanced view of the total result of this enormous and expensive effort, I gave an afternoon to listening and analysing the finished sound recording released on cassette by DG. My views are based upon my knowledge of the original Broadway production, my attendance at Max Goberman's orchestra rehearsals with the original Broadway pit orchestra and my personal involvement with an extended tour for which I served as music director and assistant producer. I view it as pointless to list my criticisms track by track as the three foolscap pages I filled with comments become highly repetitive and, in the end, come down to the basic artistic and theatrical weaknesses which would be apparent to most musical theatre aficionados and certainly any West Side Story fan brought up on the stage production or its film version.

Of the five major classically trained soloists, Kurt Ollmann comes reasonably close to tailoring his voice to a musical theatre style but there are moments in *The Jet Song* when his cultured baritone voice destroys any illusion of a New York teen-age gang chieftain. Kiri Te Kanawa is in wonderful voice but her *operettisch* rolled *R's* make a caricature out of her attempted Puerto Rican accent and the mature, full throated, dark tone she uses does not project any aspect of the teenage character she is supposed to be portraying. Tatiana Troyanos makes a healthy stab at the character of Anita. She is the best actor among the principals but again a mature sound plus her inability to avoid shifting gears vocally in her middle register from what is termed in popular parlance as a *chest voice* to her legitimate, glorious mezzo soprano voice gives the impression that Saint-Saens *Delilah* on a date with *Samson* has got off at the wrong station on the IRT subway[235]. I have already dwelt at some length on the problems that José Carreras faced which he was seen in the video to acknowledge. It should be added that his Spanish accent, seeming even more prominent on the sound recording of his struggling rendition of *Somthing's Comin'*, is modified for his lovely performances of *Maria* and *One Hand, One Heart*. It was someone's wrong call not to permit him to speak *Maria*'s name at the beginning of that song. The actor used, I presume Alexander Bernstein, is so authentically American in his pronunciation of this single word that it is a jolt when José begins to sing despite the obvious enormous effort he is making to overcome his accent. I think, however, Marilyn Horne proved my biggest disappointment. Before achieving her well deserved, brilliant operatic career, Ms. Horne paid the bills by being a session singer with Ray Coniff as well as for television and radio jingles. If any of the soloists knew how to properly deliver what was required, my money would have been on her. Unfortunately, she also succumbs to the big voice syndrome and her performance of *Somewhere* is

---

[235] New York's Independant Rapid Transport whose route covers the lower and upper west side of Manhattan and the Bronx.

sadly overblown beyond any semblance of what the disembodied voice representing young, unrequited love desperately seeking a time and haven of safety requires. Sadly, matters don't improve much with the ensemble numbers when analysed on both an acting and style level. The acting values displayed do not in any way communicate an understanding of the anger and tension of the gang characters. The best 'acting' on the recording is, in fact, provided by Alexander Bernstein and Jamie Bernstein Thomas performing the speaking roles of Tony and Maria. The spoken dialogue provided by the Bernstein progeny allow the listener to experience the full drama of the scene rather than only the big 'tunes' abstracted from the show. It also provides an opportunity to hear long passages of underscore, which serves as connecting tissue between dialogue and songs.

Regarding the *Sharks* and *Jets* ensembles the one number that gets an unequivocal thumb's-up is *America* sung by Tatiana Troyanos and the *Shark* girls. However, the usually electric *Jets'* ensemble, *Cool*, misfires. I would not have thought it possible to render this number in a bland fashion but that is the only word that adequately describes the performance. All the notes are performed by everyone involved but that is the totality of it. Kurt Ollmann's delivery of the *Jet Song* would sound more stylistically correct in *The Pajama Game,* and the first entrance of the Jet gang gave me the feeling that I had been transported to a performance of *The Most Happy Fella* listening to a new verse of *Standin' On The Corner*. Things do improve considerably once the ensemble gets into the *Jet Song* proper. Their best track is *Officer Krupke* but the *Tonight Quintet* sounds like something out of Verdi's *The Force of Destiny*. The freelance American orchestra provides the best contribution to the project. The musicians deliver virtually all the dance and ballet music from the show in brilliant style. They are well recorded with an interesting if old-fashioned audio mix which, in the re-mix, rebalances levels to enable the flute in its weak low register to have greater prominence than the surrounding ensemble. L's tempos are, if a notch under the original Broadway tempos, fairly standard. There is one exception, *I Feel Pretty*, and that seems well off the mark. He defends his choice of speed for this particular number on the video declaring that its was rushed in the original, having been determined because it opened the Second Act and served to

WEST SIDE MAESTRO

settle the audience down. Theatrically, L seems to have forgot the scene setting, a young girl breathless with excitement in anticipation of meeting her forbidden first love. In fact, he composed her vocal phrases throughout to begin after the beat to create this sense of breathless excitement. The words after the phrases, 'I feel pretty. O, *so* pretty.' begin to spill over each other, words like, 'running and dancing for joy'. These are not the words or feelings of contained emotion. They are the breathless, excited utterings of a young girl in love for the first time. There are the chattering Latin brass and woodwind figures throughout the accompaniment, which also contradict the choice of L's slow tempo. But who was there to challenge him on the important but always personal choice of tempo, especially in light of his general black mood clearly on display during the film recording. In the time we worked together, it often fell to me to be the one to bring sensitive matters of this nature to his attention. In the present situation, I'm not sure I would have risked it. In a biography by Paul Meyers, it is implied that L was less than prepared going into the *West Side* sessions. Meyers lists as his credits producer for Columbia Records, (later to become CBS and then Sony); then, for the same Company, as Artists and Repertoire vice-president for Europe. In this role he certainly had some contact with L but never worked with him in a production capacity. To imply that he was not prepared to conduct his own composition or any composition shows little knowledge of the musician. I have never known L to be unprepared in ten years of working in close contact with him. Moreover, his musical gifts were so totally developed that at a Philharmonic rehearsal for a Young People's Concert at which his conducting score for a complex Gabrielli piece, (added to the programme at the eleventh hour), had been mislaid, he not only rehearsed the work without score, which he barely had time to glance at, but corrected all the wrong notes in the brand new set of parts being used. Though my analysis of the DG video and recording of *West Side Story* deals with what I view as flaws in the artistic approach and the final production content, the one undeniable element that is clearly to be observed and realised throughout is L's total command of all matters musical even if he was not always in command of himself.

WEST SIDE MAESTRO

Throughout the video, there is a goodly portion of self-congratulation and self-justification. Who would deny the extraordinary accomplishment of this show or the great credit due to L for his major contribution in the creation of dance drama as a viable new form of the Broadway musical? The core purpose of creating this video/recording was not to reaffirm that West Side was still relevant, even *funky*, as L's proudly boasted. It was to create, as with the later *Candide* video, a permanent record of his theatre compositions conducted by himself, one of the world's leading maestros. The recorded and filmed performances featuring star-name casts were intended to surpass all previous versions and all that might follow. On this level both the recording and video fail. The best recording remains the original Broadway version on Sony which enjoys good sound and a superb cast. It is not merely 'dancers who sing a bit', as implied by L on the video, but wonderful, strong personality Broadway voices who ideally and believably project their characters as real people in a real conflict. The conducting of Max Goberman, who also served as conductor for *On The Town*, is first class in every way as is his orchestra. Goberman, a member along with L in Fritz Reiner's conducting class at the Curtis Institute, was later to become music director of Ballet Theatre. I attended all his orchestra rehearsals for *West Side* and they were as demanding and meticulous as any of L's own. As regards the orchestra for the video, the Meyers' Bernstein biography[236] speaks of the free-lance band gathered for the occasion in terms of legendary status providing "a musical backing that no pit orchestra in the world could match". I suggest that the writer of the above statement listen to the original show recording. Indeed, every NY pit orchestra is made up of a team of all-stars. Pit work is or was the best and steadiest paying job for the top New York free-lance musicians. It not only provided a regular income but also left the instrumentalist free to teach or accept recording sessions, such as the Bernstein video recording, during the day. Musicians such as the flutist, Jule Baker, the oboist, Ronny Roseman, and the cellist, James McCracken, all of whom participated in the Bernstein video, are only three from that band of classy free-lancers, most of whom I had the pleasure to know personally and work with often during my own free-lance years in New York. All that grey hair of experience one sees generously sprinkled among the Bernstein

---

[236] *Leonard Bernstein* by Paul Meyers, Phaidon Press

orchestra was not acquired sitting at home practising, waiting to be called for this single video. These familiar faces on the free-lance scene regularly distributed their top-drawer talents among the many non-permanent concert ensembles and large theatre pit bands that proliferated in New York's many concert halls and theatres until the remorseless invasion of electronic synthesisers which, where Broadway was concerned, became the joy and toy of accountants posing as producers.

Leaving editorials and paeans of praise to my New York colleagues aside, let us take a moment to examine the three New York musicals and try to find a link, if any, to their success in light of the chequered history of *Candide*, which preceded *West Side Story*, and the much later outright failure of *1600 Pennsylvania Avenue*. The obvious immediate link is the production staff. *On The Town* and *Wonderful Town* shared writers, Comden and Green, and director, George Abbott. One could even add to *Wonderful Town* the name of Jerome Robbins who was brought in late in the day without credit[237] to restage Rosalind Russell's numbers after she was dropped by a dance partner in one of Donald Saddler's several athletic stagings that went very wrong during the Boston tryout. *West Side Story* shared both director/choreographer, Jerome Robbins, and set designer, Oliver Smith, with *On The Town* as well as music director, Max Goberman. It did no harm to the creative atmosphere that this list of legendary skilled talent also encompassed long and trusted friendships. However, the one single ingredient which I am convinced augured for the ultimate success of these three productions was the presence of a director of contractually unquestioned and respected authority with a clear vision from the first day of rehearsal of the entire work and a total grasp of the workings of musical theatre and all its production departments from the construction of the book to the construction of the scenery. I have already made the point earlier that a talent of the enormity of a Leonard Bernstein without a degree of control and direction threatens to become a loose canon. Hyperbole? Consider if you will the following creative *Candide recipe*:

---

[237] It was Robbins himself who specifically requested that his work remain uncredited so as not to diminish the contribution of his colleague, Donald Saddler.

WEST SIDE MAESTRO

Take   Voltaire's picaresque novella *Candide*

Then   mix a theatre-wise Leonard Bernstein together with a Lillian Hellman, an equally strong personality of matching culture but admittedly lacking knowledge of musical theatre

Sprinkle this volatile mixture with an assortment of their peers to create song lyrics of a level to measure up to the musical and writing brilliance of the authors[238]

Add   the imperative of a political agenda

Hire   a *Chef* lacking knowledge or experience of musical theatre, short of the ruthless disposition needed to combine and control all of the above volatile ingredients.

Result: an open Pandora's box that sets loose an assortment of evils which eventually consumes both creators and creation.

That is precisely what happened with *Candide*. The analysis proposed has nothing to do with being wise after the fact. The history of *Candide, the Musical*, could be made into a small volume the length of Voltaire's novella. All aspects of it have been reported at length in the various biographies and essays with a surprising variety of additional information from version to version, the best and most perceptive of which is by Humphrey Burton who is the only one among the various writers to pinpoint the problem and wherein the solution lay:

"Tyrone Guthrie, *Candide*'s director, had no experience at all with the Broadway musical...(he) lacked the experience to do his own show-doctoring and nobody was in command of the creative talent in the way that George Abbott had been for Bernstein's two previous musicals."

It was not merely, as Joan Peyser suggests, that there were too many large talents and egos involved. More power to them! It was that, without the guiding hand of an overall absolute authority, each went their merry way

---

[238] Among *Candide*'s parade of distinguished lyricists were a noted *Who's Who* of writers, John LaTouche, Dorothy Parker, Richard Wilbur, (the principal lyricist), Bernstein and Lillian Hellman for the original production, later to be joined in the revivals by Stephan Sondheim.

developing their own agenda in conflict with their colleagues and the overall co-ordinated needs of the show.

Let's begin by examining the fragmented opposing views of the principal parties.

Lillian Hellman wanted *Candide* to take the same form as her adaptation of Jean Anouilh's *The Lark*, a play with incidental music. The underlying motive that drove her was the desire to extract a degree of revenge on the House on Un-American Activities by publicly satirising its workings and that of their leader Senator Joe McCarthy, who had blackened her name and destroyed the career and sent to prison her lover, the novelist Dashiell Hammett.

L convinced a reluctant Hellman to alter the show's form to a full scale musical. Although he was in sympathy with the writer's motives to expose the HOUA he wanted to approach the planned satire as a comic operetta even though he knew by its very nature that the form would water down the serious message Hellman was trying to get across to her public.

A passing parade of distinguished lyric writers came to a standstill when Richard Wilbur joined the show. To begin with, he did not seem to hold a high opinion of Voltaire's novella, viewing it 'a one joke novel that goes on for thirty chapters.' Communication between this lyricist and his colleagues seems to have been an on-again, off-again affair. L's rather sarcastic description of Wilbur's method of working was "...he shuts himself off in a phone booth and talks to God." Wilbur on the other hand was somewhat underwhelmed by Bernstein's claim to a writing talent. He characterised L as "thinking rather highly of himself." He was later to make a self-analytic *mea culpa* confessing to have been "too literary and stubborn."

Had Tyrone Guthrie started with a clear idea of how to create a *Candide* which was the next step in the evolution of the Broadway musical and been of a nature to tame these talented tigers, the end result might have been very different and very successful. Unfortunately, just the opposite proved to be the case. The following is his own description of his contribution or, more accurately, his disservice to *Candide*:

'It was an artistic and fantastic disaster from which I learned almost nothing about everything...My direction skipped along with the effortless grace of a freight train heavy-laden on a steep gradient... But it was fun to be closely associated with a group so brilliantly and variously talented.'

But it was fun! The investors lost $340,000 *but it was fun*!

If the producers had read the published transcript of Tyrone Guthrie's talk delivered before the Royal Society of Arts in 1952 titled, 'An Audience of One',[239] only four years prior to *Candide*'s premiere, they would not have been surprised at the detour his usually reliable direction took when faced with his first Broadway musical. They also might have hesitated before making their initial approach to him to debut with their production in such a specialist field. The approach to directing as advocated in this twenty-five minute address seems to be that of committee. There are a goodly scattering of controversial statements along the way which must have set up a hum in the crowd, such as Guthrie's certainty that the author of "an important work of art...will not have the faintest idea of what he has really written...Shakespeare only had the vaguest idea of what he was writing when he wrote Hamlet...the more important the work of art, the less the author will know what he has written." He based this broad statement, which probably set the Author's Guild alight, on a comment of an English playwright friend with whom he had worked and who probably felt he had better ways of spending his time than to do Guthrie's homework for him in matters he viewed as self-evident. Guthrie stressed the need for principal actors to work step by step with the financial manager, the set designer, the costume designer and the other actors in "a productive exchange of ideas." That seems to be doubly important in the director/actor relationship within which, should a difference of opinion arise, the director must tiptoe around the actor to keep everyone's feelings in tact. One is left to wonder where the traditional Broadway director fits in to this scenario or how the noted British

---

[239] *An Audience of One,* reprinted in Directors On Directing, edited by Cole & Chinoy, published 1953, Bobbs-Merrill, USA

director would have viewed George Abbott's more muscular approach with the *On The Town* authors, Comden and Green. The director told them to cut the prologue flashback to the show. When they protested that it was 'the whole backbone of the show', Mr. Abbott's reply was simple and direct, "OK. I'll tell you what. You can have me or the prologue." Contrast Abbott's no nonsense approach with Guthrie's declaration that the dominance of a director's role in theatre is a fiction. In face of the practical need for a musical to be thought out and meticulously pre-planned prior to each rehearsal especially in regard to the staging of musical numbers involving chorus and dancers as well as principals, Guthrie's expressed convictions were that 'the best ideas are not arrived at by formal, carefully worked out planning but by permitting the creative idea to come straight from the subconscious during rehearsals' or as he so picturesquely expresses it, "...to relax and just trust the Holy Ghost will arrive and the idea will appear...(the director's) function at its best is one of psychic evocation and it is performed almost entirely unconsciously." The title of Guthrie's lecture is understood by his stated view that "the one creative function of the director is to be at the rehearsals, a highly receptive, highly concentrated sounding-board for the performance, *an audience of one*. He is not the drill sergeant, not the schoolmaster...He is simply receiving the thing, transmuting it and giving it back." Such a view and approach may have been ideal working with classic plays starring an Olivier, a Gielgud or an Edith Evans but it bears no relation to the needs of a Broadway musical.

Much in fighting among *Candide's* creative team was reported during the out-of-town try-outs when it became apparent that the show was not working. When trials of strength occur the dominant personalities, whether right or wrong, usually end up bullying the passive, co-operative members. This will occur with any production that lacks a strong director whose pronouncements regarding any department in any matter are the final say. With a powerful, unquestioned authority at the head, all anger and individual frustration are directed towards him, creating a bond among the other departments and the cast. Everyone ends up finding ways of accommodating their colleagues rather than arguing with them. The big moment at the end of each day is the sit-down in the local delicatessen where each production member shares that day's tale of woe with his colleagues over a corned beef sandwich railing against some terrible *artistic injustice* that has been perpetrated by their director which has eliminated 'the best idea they ever had' and without which 'the show is doomed to failure.'

While the above might be judged as jocular speculation, the history of *Candide* proves it to be otherwise. In 1973 the production was refashioned. The Hellman book was revised by Hugh Wheeler, the symphonic orchestration was cut down to a meagre 13 players, uniquely stationed in small groups around the theatre, the music was cut and shuffled about but, most important of all, these changes were conceived by Hal Prince the new director for the revival who had a clear idea from the first of how he wanted this satire to play. Prince was a veteran of stage musicals from the ground up. His executive career with the musical stage had begun and developed in the role of one of Broadway's most respected stage managers. For those unfamiliar with the role of stage manager for American productions, once the director completes his contract and the show opens, it is placed in the hands of the stage manager. He, aided by the dance captain to keep the choreography tidy, is in total charge nightly of every aspect of the production which includes liaison with management, all the staging, lighting, cast performance and discipline, preparing understudies and all full rehearsals which are called when important cast replacements occur. He has become the surrogate, unquestioned director. Prince quickly moved up the ladder into producing and directing his own productions. He continues today in both roles as a force in world musical theatre. Back in 1973 under his direction, whether one agrees or not with the changed conception and approach, he took the raw materials of what had been a commercial failure in musical theatre and turned it into a success that ran profitably both off and on Broadway for more than a year. If nothing else this underlines the potential for success that the original *Candide* might have enjoyed in the hands of a skilled, experienced musical comedy director.

From the first, the one positive element of *Candide* to shine through was the quality of L's score. The general consensus had been that it was the star of the show. There is no denying the retrospective criticism that its brilliant, bubbling character was at odds with Hellman's intended serious message but his instincts were tuned-in to the needs of a Broadway musical where hers were directed elsewhere. In such a contest she was bound to come off the loser in the communicative popularity stakes.

One should not cut short discussion of the L's score without noting that along with the many words of critical praise the music was also the target for scorn. It was accused of being a pretentious *eclectic ragbag*. It had no 'hit tune' to fill the radio airwaves each day. In fact, 'it had no melodies one could recall when leaving the theatre.' The last accusation is the most foolish of the lot. *Candide* is brimming over with melody, as much if not more than his previous hit shows. It may not have been hit parade material but all of it has an emotional sweep and ranges in character from sad to witty to downright funny. It is eminently whistleable upon first hearing with the exception of, *Quiet,* a song constructed upon a *twelve-tone* melody that opens the second act. As for the 'eclectic ragbag' accusation, eclectic it may be but ragbag never. The score is a passing parade of styles, Gilbert and Sullivan, Gounod, Offenbach, Stravinsky and others. However, it doesn't ridicule its forbears, it is an homage to them. Each example represents top-drawer Bernstein, not merely some hack musical conjuring trick or conservatory student assignment to 'write a waltz *a la* Richard Strauss.'

Was the problem with the original concept for *Candide* contained within the truth of the Hollywood cliché, "Messages should be delivered by Western Union!" Although much of the satire that drew analogy with the workings of the HOUA was edited out of the Inquisition scene in Boston when both producers and director lost their nerve, the book was assessed at its premiere to be heavy handed and lacking the light, satiric touch of the Voltaire original. By the time *Candide* reached Broadway, only a psychic could extract from it Lillian Hellman's original political message. The ponderous quality of the libretto and the variety of 'chops and changes' it had endured during rehearsals and the out of town try-out had reduced it to what Richard Wilbur characterised as 'connective tissue' which seemed only to produce confusion for its audience.

WEST SIDE MAESTRO

Transcribing Voltaire's novella, aptly described by the adjective *picaresque*, originally referring to a style of fiction dealing with adventures of a rogue chiefly of Spanish origin, but in this instance referring specifically to Voltaire's ninety-five page tale in which virtually "every page takes us to a different country and every paragraph contains a new adventure"[240], posed an almost insoluble problem for the authors. Voltaire's *Candide* suffers thirty blows of fate, Hellmann's *Candide* only nine on his journey towards an enlightenment that, counter to the philosophy of providentialism[241] which held eighteenth century Europe in its thrall, all is *not* for the best in this *not* so best of all possible worlds. Even reducing the magnitude of *Candide*'s painful Odyssey still involved its authors in a sea of words that threatened to drown the show. The brilliant diversity of the score and the shining wit and seamlessness of the lyrics, despite the many hands involved, kept this from happening - just! However, one does feel a sense of mental exhaustion by the middle of the second act as the *déjà vu* of yet another of Candide's bludgeoning adventures, complete with the questioning hero's inevitable acceptance, moves towards its predictable disastrous end.

Candide enjoyed any number of revivals following its initial commercial failure on Broadway. There was a limited American tour, a failed London opening, college productions and concert performances. The 1973 *Chelsea* one-act version directed by Hal Prince provided the show with its first claim to financial success. This *Chelsea* version was then expanded in 1982 into a two-act opera version with much music restored and additional numbers included which had been cut from the original Broadway production. Again under Hal Prince's direction, this was mounted by the NY City Opera and proved a success.

---

[240] The quotation is taken from the concert naration for *Candide* written by John Wells and Leonard Bernstein.

[241] Providentialism, all that happens is ordained by divine providence, was a philosophy espoused by Wilhelm Leibnitz and Alexander Pope to which Voltaire was a convert until the Lisbon earthquake of 1775 with its senseless, massive loss of life. The French writer's reaction was to mock the philosophy of providentialism in his satirical novella, *Candide*, or *Optimism*.

WEST SIDE MAESTRO

Andrew Porter[242] in his program notes which accompany the cassette tapes, CD's and video created from a performance of *Candide* recorded at a concert at London's *Barbican Centre* under the composer's direction[243] in the last year of his life makes the following acute observations:

"There is a big difference in practical circumstances between Broadway shows and opera house presentations...A new opera...that achieved 73 performances in its first season would be counted a remarkable success; the original *Candide,* with only 73 performances on Broadway, was counted a failure. Commercial consideration has a stronger impact on the form the work finally takes."

Porter, however, expresses strong criticism regarding Hal Prince's restructuring, of the libretto and music in his 1973 'Chelsea' version. The critic actually uses the stronger term *distortion* and extends his criticism to include what he believes to be Prince's misreading of the true spirit behind the original Voltaire classic. To back his views he quotes John Mauceri, the conductor of both the original 'Chelsea' version, the subsequent extended Broadway run and its later enormously successful 1982 expanded opera house version for the New York City Opera again under Prince's direction. In a classic example of biting the hand that feeds you, John Mauceri's quote deprecates Prince's newly conceived production which took a commercial failure and turned it into a commercial success and which, along the way, just happened to establish Mauceri's own career from that of conductor of a college orchestra to a conductor with an international career within two years following the original 'Chelsea' *Candide.* To Mauceri's credit, he subsequently proved of great service to L both in regard to Candide and *A Quiet Place.* Mauceri, during his relatively short tenure at Scottish Opera, mounted a swiftly paced, excellent production of *Candide* in which he restored the original order of scenes and music and assisted the satirical writer, journalist and performer, John Wells, in readapting Hugh Wheeler's

---

[242] Andrew Porter, highly respected music critic of American magazine publication, *The New Yorker.*

[243] It was the case that most of the principal singers, the conductor and members of the London Symphony Orchestra were so ill from flu at the concert that subsequent studio recording sessions had to be scheduled to bring the vocal tracks to a standard acceptable to the artists.

libretto accordingly. John Wells later went on to work with L on a linking narration to accompany a concert version of the operetta based upon the Scottish Opera production. L conducting the LSO and, this time, a wonderfully chosen list of international singers, performed this concert version at London's Barbican Centre in his final year to great critical acclaim. It was filmed for video and simultaneously recorded for CD by Deutsche Grammophon.

Where does the truth regarding the true nature of this much-battered musical version of Voltaire's *Candide* lie? Did Hal Prince do a disservice to it? Has Mauceri's restored and expanded version of the original rescued it from being remembered, to quote its re-re-re-adapter, as "one long joke" - its heart torn out, its tears derided, and the faith of its original author betrayed. One doubts it. It would be valuable to quote at this point Harry Kraut, Executive Vice-president and business brain behind L's company, Amberson, in his letter to Hal Prince dated June 19, 1980 regarding the planned 1982 expanded NY City Opera revival. The tone of the letter is extremely warm. In it Kraut makes suggestions regarding some possible dialogue cuts and the restoration of certain musical numbers from the original version, which he knew to be viewed of particular importance to L. The letter ends as follows, "...may I say again what a witty and entertaining version you and Hugh Wheeler have created. Even if my cuttings and pastings come to naught, (he was referring to his suggestions), once again you've provided me with some evenings of pleasure." Those are not the words of a man who believed his most important client was being done a disservice.

I believe the truth is to be found in my quote from Andrew Porter. *Candide* lives not a double but a triple life. In the Harold Prince/Hugh Wheeler version it contains, or contained, the necessary ingredients delivered in a fashion to make it a hit Broadway show. In the Scottish Opera version it contains all the elements to make it a welcome staple in opera houses throughout the world. Finally, in its concert version with narration, it not only maintains the thrust of the original Voltaire, it accomplishes this with fewer words and greater clarity than the staged opera version. In addition, it rightfully includes an overdue tribute to the original author, Lillian Hellman, by describing in vivid terms the political conditions existing in the United States, which originally inspired her idea for a Voltaire *Candide*, with music. Lastly, it presents the Bernstein score in its full symphonic splendour.

The reader may have noted that in my reference to the Harold Prince version I wrote that 'it contains or *contained...*'. Why my equivocation, having been an advocate for what Prince accomplished from the start? My doubts were raised when yet another revival of *Candide* was mounted by Prince - and it failed! It made me wonder whether it was just possible that *Candide*'s time as a Broadway musical had come to a close and that, from here on, the future of this brilliant but plagued creation, which had struggled long to find its identity and audience, lay either in the world's opera houses or as a full evening's concert entertainment? My doubts regarding Candide's staying power as a viable vehicle for the commercial theatre were to be assuaged in the spring of 1999.

STOP PRESS!
Candide-Addenda

On April 17, 1999, the Royal National Theatre of London opened a newly conceived, edited, rewritten and staged production of *Candide*. In reading advanced notice of the new production in London's Sunday Times ten days prior to its premiere, I became first intrigued by two large photographs, one a portrait of Stephan Sondheim seated at a piano and the other of L in rehearsal clothes deep in thought during a recording session. These photos accompanied a feature article on the Arts page that had the contrived headline "A chance to be perfectly *Candide*" and an even more eye-catching sub-headline, "Stephan Sondheim tells...why he is helping to re-stage *Candide*." As becomes clear rather late in this thousand word article, Sondheim was not to be involved in any part of the new re-staging but had co-operatively consented to revamp the lyrics to one of the songs for which he had forty-five years before served as lyricist. While the theatre critic eventually got around to discussing the new National production in the final three hundred words of his article, the bulk of the article turned out to be for the most part just another potted history of *Candide*'s chequered production past. I can only admit to acquaintance with four of the ten different productions, (to include staged concert versions), which have seen the light of day since *Candide*'s Broadway premiere in 1955, the original production, the Hal Prince *Chelsea* version of 1973, John Mauceri's Scottish Opera version of 1989 and L's final concert version of 1990, which, originally available on videotape is currently available on CD and DVD. The Times critic's brief description of the new presentation was far too general to evoke any immediate interest or enthusiasm. As a result, when I entered the National Theatre for the final matinee and evening performances of *Candide*'s first scheduled repertory run, I still felt heavily prejudiced towards the Scottish Opera production. I viewed it to have solved a sufficient number of the problems L had struggled to correct since its failed Broadway premiere in 1956 and to have provided an entertaining evening of operetta suitable for any of the world's opera houses.

Candide seemed to me a sick child who had undergone a series of operations in an attempt to effect a cure for its many ills. The Hal Prince *Chelsea* version was, if one merely considers the sheer number of performances chalked up, 700 in all, an enormous success in that direction, but it was not the *Candide* envisioned by Bernsein or Lillian Hellman. It was at best a Readers Digest clone of the original show which made use of only a skeleton of the original, lengthy score, none of Hellmann's book or original conception and little of the cutting satire of Voltaire's picaresque novella. Without diminishing its impressive success, it was more about Harold Prince's commercial instincts and sure skill as a producer and director than about Voltaire, Bernstein or Hellmann. With the Scottish Opera production one felt that *Candide* had found a form that could provide opera house if not theatre audiences with blockbuster entertainment. If Voltaire's bite still proved a bit toothless, the general sweep, grandeur and light-hearted theatricality of an evening built around a brilliant Bernstein score guaranteed *Candide* a star place in opera houses the world over. Why was it necessary, then, to make this formerly sick but now reasonably well child endure yet another bout of surgery? That was the question, even challenge, which posed itself internally as I entered the Olivier Auditorium at the

WEST SIDE MAESTRO

National Theatre. The answer was delivered positively and resoundingly over the next three hours and fifteen minutes. I left the National Theatre convinced that *Candide* had at last found a form, which confirmed it as one of the classics of the musical theatre. Let me emphasise the word *theatre* and not opera house, for *Candide* was conceived as a theatre piece. In the National Theatre production book and music coalesced in a manner to produce a theatrical justification that had eluded this stage work for forty-five years. It had vindicated after all this time the never-ending faith of its composer. Yet, it is the Bernstein music, till now the *saving* grace, indeed, saviour of the show, which has been, in a sense, most affected by director John Caird's new book and staging. The music, for the first time, functions in a balanced partnership with the stage drama. It is no longer required to rush in and save the day for an ever-sagging libretto. As with all the great musicals, *Candide*'s score in this version is served by a book that can hold its head high in its company. It does justice to both the score and the classic source from which its text was inspired.

As for the production that I viewed at the National Theatre, John Caird's direction succeeded in imbuing *Candide*'s odd assortment of principal characters, despite the chain of bizarre improbabilities that befall them, with sufficient reality to invite my interest and sympathy. The Bernstein score, no longer required to carry the principal burden of the evening, was able to function in a more tightly integrated fashion within the totality of the production. The entrance of music became a logical extension of the drama, which permitted the characters to reflect and expand at length on the twists and turns in their lives and the happenings around them. It helped drive the plot forward rather than merely interrupt the proceedings for *a jolly good musical romp*. This dramatic and fully motivated integration of book and music for the first time altered the position of the Bernstein score from that of *star turn* and virtual sole reason for mounting a production of *Candide* to that of a key element within an ensemble partnership.

John Caird's staging, (with the assistance of Trevor Nunn, Artistic Director of the National Theatre), was a supreme example of *less is more*. Like the National Theatre's epic production of *Nicolas Nickelby*, the settings were imaginative minimalist creations not huge grandiose structures. The three-quarters round stage was overhung at an acute angle by a huge ring which was echoed in a second ring which served as a path along the circumference of the proscenium. The sight of this vast, suspended, circular symbol as I entered the auditorium put me immediately in mind of scenic designs created for Wagner's *Ring* operas at Bayreuth and Salzburg in the 1960's. It left me wondering whether the designer was deliberately making an analogy between the *Ring* dramas and *Candide*. One witnesses in both epics the self-deception, brutal struggles for power and control, cruelty and greed leading to personal corruption, all of which culminate in the death of innocence, the destruction of false gods and new beginnings. On a less emblematic and philosophical level, there were John Napier's ultra stark stage settings, which were generated from a folderol in the form of a large wooden chest from which were taken six smaller chests each contained within the other. These were employed one, two or several at a time, placed strategically about the stage or piled one upon another and covered with sheets, saddle blankets, or whatever was needed to create the illusion required. They served as a bed, tombstones in a cemetery, an altar, horses, a gondola, a sailboat, a jewellery box - even the mobile half torso of a rebellious slave mutilated by his masters. Jets sunk in the stage emitted clouds of smoke that were coloured by the stage lighting to intensify the scenes of drama and violence. Finally, a marvellous collection of period and character costumes, which included actors dressed as rather colourful monkeys and mountain sheep, plus an array of suitable props helped complete the illusions required.

While the Caird version satirically pursues the same improbable adventures which the original *Candide* librettists extracted from Voltaire's novella, the burlesque and slapstick elements applied with a broad brush in previous major theatre and opera productions are done away with. Thus the characters in this production enact the storyline and perform the songs in a human and real fashion to amplify their internal thoughts and emotions. They may start their lives as little more than puppets chanting a litany of positive determinism taught to them by Voltaire's alter-ego, Dr. Pangloss, but they soon begin to display the individual human qualities which enable them to survive their odysseys of pain, misfortune and disillusionment on their pilgrimage towards mutual reconciliation having finally come to acknowledge that all is *not* "for the best in the best of all possible worlds".

Caird's organisation of the first act restores the scene order of the original Broadway production with the Paris sequence preceding that of the Spanish Inquisition. This version provides a heartier than usual helping of Voltairian satire and irony in the dialogue. More serious and menacing overtones, the Inquisition *auto-da-fé*[244] scene for example, replace the light-hearted, frothy gestures used for the all-purpose *go-for-laughs* approach of earlier productions. The second act is completely restructured with tracts of re-written dialogue and new song lyrics to provide a sharper cutting edge. The most important character transformation is that of the Voltaire/Pangloss figure. He remains constant throughout not assuming a variety of wigs and accents of other subsidiary characters, (i.e. the half-caste, Cacambo and the pessimist, Martin), such as was the preference in the Scottish Opera production. This allows each of these Voltaire characters, when performed by individual actors, to take on a more human persona, Cacambo, as Candide's ever faithful and trusted servant, and Martin, despite his relentless pessimism, as Candide's companion and friend, loyal through thick and thin.

Directors Caird and Nunn and choreographer Peter Darling grouped and distributed their large cast pictorially over the Olivier's enormous stage area in a manner often reminiscent of paintings by William Hogarth, Pietro Longhi and Giambattista Tiepolo. The use of tableaux, employed all too rarely these days in musical theatre, was judiciously and effectively used. Ballet per se was not employed but rather choreographed stage movement, (from military drill sequences to cannibal rituals), and dances in a variety of national styles, (*Paso doblé*, peasant dances, waltzes, mazurkas) which were intrinsic to and complemented the specific stage action. One of the most effective was that of a clamouring mob dancing *La carmagnole*, a round dance performed at the execution of aristocrats during the French Revolution, in the *auto-da-fé* scene which was staged as a *Grande*

---

[244] *auto-da-fé* - the public declaration of sentences passed by the courts of the Spanish Inquisition leading to public execution that included the burning of heretics at the stake.

Guignol[245] of dead bodies, shrieking peasants and chanting prelates bathed in crimson light celebrating the hanging of Dr. Pangloss.

The new theatre orchestration created for the National's *Candide* utilised an orchestra of fourteen players. Bruce Coughlin, who orchestrated L's *Arias and Barcaroles* for Michael Tilson Thomas's recording with the London Symphony, was responsible for this superb reduction. Wonderfully and intelligently conceived, only the paucity of strings in the overture, *Candide's* most familiar musical component, evoked critical complaint. Much credit for the success of the performances I attended was due to the music direction of Mark W. Dorrell. He galvanised the superb, young National Theatre Orchestra and his cast, which he had prepared impeccably to a very high musical standard. I was especially impressed with the pace, energy, crispness of performance and the clarity of diction that he was able to inspire.

Actors of immense skill with remarkable singing voices made up the National Theatre cast which enabled both the dramatic and comedy values of Caird's newly fashioned book to be fully realised alongside the brilliant Bernstein score. I do not begrudge these skilled actors full credit for their individual contributions. Their names and the characters they played can be found listed in the footnotes. But I would like to underline that equal credit must go even to those with the smallest roles in this remarkable production, so tightly knit was this ensemble of players.[246]

John Caird's National Theatre production deserves to be recognised as the new standard theatre text for *Candide*. Through it *Candide* has finally found a balance that has transformed it from a failed musical that has depended

---

[245] *Grande Guignol* - a *guignol* is a *Punch and Judy* show with all its violence and sometimes murder. The *Grande Guignol*, maintaining the aspects of violence, is expanded to a dramatic entertainment consisting of a succession of short, sensational, macabre pieces.

[246] The National Theatre cast was headed by a superb Simon Russell Beale as *Voltaire/Dr. Pangloss*, an engaging Daniel Evans as *Candide*, a funny and touching Alex Kelly as *Cunégonde*, Simon Day's pompous, but happily not burlesqued *Maximilian*, Elizabeth Renihan's charming soubrette *Paquette*, Denis Quilley's dyspeptic but sympathetic *Martin* and Beverly Klein's tour de force acting and singing performance of *The Old Woman*.

upon the brilliance of its score as its sole life support system to a well-proportioned play with music which I believe will now take its deserved place as a classic of musical theatre to stand alongside Brecht/Weill's *Three-Penny Opera*.

The Caird adaptation does not vitiate the John Mauceri/ John Wells version, which leans more towards the style of *Gilbert and Sullivan* operetta. These two viable approaches meet the needs of both the theatre and the opera house. It is my hope that the National Theatre production will find a place one day on Broadway, which may see it equal or surpass in success Harold Prince's *Chelsea* version. I also believe it will find an enthusiastic reception throughout Europe and the Far East translated into the language of each country. It is its deserved due.

There is little else to say except that this musical *cum* operetta *cum* opera *buffa* is extremely well served on disc and video. The original cast album on a single CBS/Sony CD deserves its cult status. For casting and performance it has never been surpassed. It is not complete, however. For this, one turns to the composer's version, (the Scottish Opera stage version has never been released having been caught up in a legal wrangle). In general, L takes a slightly broader view of his score. His recordings on CD and DVD are more sonically glamorous than the original cast album. They enjoy the brilliant playing and wonderful orchestral colour of the LSO and is miraculously performed by a cast, orchestra and conductor decimated by flu right up to the performance itself. With additional recording sessions and over-dubbing over a period of months, DG has produced a marvellously entertaining *Candide* DVD along with a pair of CD's accompanied by an excellent libretto, which should bring pleasure to all Bernstein fans for years to come.[247]

---

[247] The CBS/Sony original cast album featured Robert Rounsville and an astonishing Barbara Cook as Cunegonde with Max Adrian as Pangloss and Irra Petina as the old woman. Sam Krachmalnick is the superb conductor.The composer led the Unitel Video and DG CD. Jerry Hadley and June Anderson feature as the lovers, Christa Ludwig as the Old Woman and Adolph Green as a very 'show-biz' Pangloss. An extra bonus is the presence of Nicolai Gedda performing the various supporting tenor role characters.

WEST SIDE MAESTRO

1600 Pennsylvania Avenue
The black portrait of a White House

When I devised the title for this segment of *B on B*, the subconscious multiplicity of its meanings did not register until I began to consult my notes. As with *Candide*, the genesis of *1600 Pennsylvania Avenue* was a political happening. In this instance it was the 1972 landslide victory enjoyed by the then President, Richard M. Nixon. Alan Lerner depressed by this political event devised the idea of a musical that celebrated not the presidency but the building that was its symbol. The agenda was to be purely political, dwelling on the history of the building's first one hundred years of service during which happenings within it threatened to destroy its meaning as a symbol to the American people of what America stood for. The significant year for its launch was to be 1976, marking the bi-centenary celebrations of the Declaration of Independence.

The 1970's had represented a volatile political period for L. Black rights had been prominent in his thoughts at this time. In 1969, the NY Philharmonic had been brought up on charges of discrimination in their employment practices by two noted black musicians, one of whom, the bass player, Arthur Davis, had been a fellow student of mine at the Juilliard School. The case was heard before the NY State Commission on Human Rights. Davis and Earl Madison, a cellist complained that in an open audition, such as those held by the Philharmonic in which the judging panel could see all those who were auditioning, black players automatically became victims of discrimination of orchestras that were predominantly white. The players offered to perform hidden behind a screen in competition with any of the established members of the Philharmonic's cello and bass sections. This blind testing, they believed, would prove their superiority as performers, worthy to be offered a position with the orchestra. Both men lost their claim but neither the orchestra nor L came out of the affair unscathed. L had given key testimony in support of the orchestra's established method of auditioning. When the commission's final decision was published in the Law Journal, the headline read, "Philharmonic ordered to end racial bias." Indeed, the commission's finding was that there was a "pattern of bias found in the orchestra's hiring of substitutes." Further criticism was to follow from the National Urban League. A virulent attack ended with the words, "Behind the red and gold facade of our major cultural institutions is the rotten stench of racism." L, whose politics were always a bit left of center, was shaken by these events. Felicia, his wife, herself a great supporter of civil rights' causes, became involved at this time in the case of twenty-one members of the Black Panthers who had been held pending trial for nine months. The charges against all were serious and very high levels of bail had been set which none of the accused could pay. The suffering of the Panthers' wives and children resulting from their detention moved Felicia who organised a reception to help raise their bail money. This story and its ending with the Bernsteins being branded *radical chic*[248] is all too familiar to require any further re-telling. What is important is that these two happenings and the unpleasant aftermath which each produced set the stage for Lerner's invitation to L to join him in writing a musical for America's upcoming centennial celebrations about the history of America's best known residence which would include the behind-stairs story of its black servants.

In its final form the musical was constructed as a play within a play. Actors in rehearsal are seen preparing a stage piece based upon the history of the White House. A shift in time span would then bring to life the historic happening about which the rehearsing actors had been arguing. This shifting back and forth remained consistent throughout the show. Much has been made of using such an unlikely form for a musical. Mark Blitzstein's *The Cradle Will Rock*, a work directed and conducted by L in his college days and again as part of his NY City Symphony series, has often been pointed to as *1600*'s antecedent. One only need point out, however, that Cole Porter's *Kiss Me Kate* takes the form of a play within a play. One cannot argue with that musical's success and lasting power. Unlike *Kiss Me Kate*, *1600* took itself much more seriously and the libretto's endless dwelling upon racial injustice was criticised as oppressive. The description of audiences in retreat at the interval never to return put one in mind of the grand Exodus from Egypt. These days, hidden agendas are seen to be lurking everywhere. No doubt, even *Kiss Me Kate* would also be attacked by a barrage of women's groups

---

[248] First coined for a *New Yorker* article and later used as the title of a book by Tom Wolfe

for being a misogynist nightmare. *1600* endured an out of town breaking-in period during which every important director and producer known to its authors told them to close it down and walk away. Notwithstanding, the production, for contractual reasons with its backers, *Coco-Cola*, opened in New York. Historically disastrous reviews, from which the music alone survived, greeted its Broadway arrival. *1600* closed seven performances later.

Until 1997, there was only the chequered history of this star crossed musical to consult. The artistic disaster that opened and closed after seven performances on Broadway was so personally devastating that the composer refused to permit a cast recording to be made. However, in 1997, *1600 Pennsylvania Avenue* made a fresh appearance in a new guise at one of London's major concert halls. Under the guiding hand of Sid Ramin, the original orchestrator for the show, a stab was made at creating a concert cantata out of a goodly portion of the historical music from the show. This new musical entity traced the history of the White House, its presidential residents and their wives, (the first ladies), from George Washington to Theodore Roosevelt, (with the exception of Andrew Jackson and Abraham Lincoln). Using a huge symphony orchestra, solo and choral forces and short spoken narratives between numbers for text continuity, short scenes, which originally formed the substance of the complex play within a play flashbacks, were performed in sequence without any attempt to create musical links to tie the whole together as a single continuous work. The London performance did not make a large number of converts to the work. However, it is my contention having attended both dress rehearsal and the concert, following the text with a libretto, and afterwards having studied in close detail a recording made from the BBC broadcast of the concert transmitted the week following, that with a bit of pruning and reshuffling in part two an important addition could be made to the Bernstein catalogue.

Regarding the London performance, as presented, the concert adaptation didn't stand a chance. It was virtually impossible to follow the considerable and complex lyrics without a libretto in hand. The conductor for the event, whose curriculum vitae included a fair bit of opera conducting, simply did not seem to have a clue as to what was required. His tempos were reasonably sound but his sense both of theatrical timing and balancing of soloists with orchestra was, for the most part, virtually non-existent. The London Symphony played stylishly throughout but was permitted to overwhelm solo voices and chorus. The broadcast tape only served to underline the problems the listener experienced at the live performance. A knowledgeable musical theatre conductor would have from the first insisted upon the orchestra adhering to accompanying dynamics rather than the full range of concert dynamics employed. He would also have circled, that is, *taceted* any number of music figurations in the winds, brass and especially the percussion, which again and again covered the vocal lines. A maxim when accompanying singers is, 'If you can't hear the words clearly, you are playing too loudly!'

Performance problems extended, unfortunately, beyond the orchestra. Notewise the chorus was superb but they might as well at times have been singing in a foreign language. What projected when they sang with orchestra was for the most part gorgeous sounding mulch with hardly a clear consonant to be identified, especially at the end of their words. In understanding the art of singing, it is important to stress that only vowels produce the sounds. It is the consonants, however, that shape the words.

Among the soloists, Dietrich Henschel performed all the presidents and Nancy Gustafson represented the various first ladies. Henschel's German accent brought to mind the casting of Carreras as Tony for the *West Side* recording. Nevertheless, he performed his various roles with distinction and, despite having to belt out his part at times in order simply to be heard over the overpowering accompaniments, he made a genuine effort to find individual characterisations for each of the presidents. Ms. Gustafson, rushing back and forth from the Royal Opera to LSO rehearsals, did not have time to learn her various *1600* roles from memory. She is, however, the most reliable of performers and projected her characters stylishly although not always with the best word clarity. Among the supporting roles, the British singer, Neil Jenkins, was outstanding for his crystal-clear projection of the text. Thomas Young and Jaqueline Miura, two of the three featured black singers, performed movingly and equally displayed excellent diction.

WEST SIDE MAESTRO

Several months after the London premiere of the *1600 Cantata*, speaking with an executive at Amberson, it quickly became clear that plans based upon the London performance had been put on hold. Certainly, as presented at the concert, there was still work to be done to bring the *Cantata* to a form that would best represent it in recorded form. There had been discussion about possibly removing the spoken narration, which, in the performance, was very professionally and clearly presented by the composer's son, Alexander. I suggested to the Amberson executive that the work might even attract interest as a staged oratorio but that possibility had already been considered and rejected by the Bernstein family.

It would be a shame for the score and parts of this new addition to the Bernstein catalogue to again end up on a shelf gathering dust for another twenty years. It is a viable work and it, at very least, deserved to be represented on disc. Deutsche Grammophon did just that in Millenium Year, releasing a nicely packaged CD complete with a libretto containing the history of the project and the full text of the Cantata. Except for one supporting artist, the tenor, Neil Jenkins, all the principal singers from the concert were replaced. Thomas Hampson took the various roles of the several American Presidents depicted and June Anderson was the First Lady wife to each of them. Barbara Hendricks, Kenneth Tarver and Keel Watson sang the roles of the White House servants. Kent Nagano again conducted the London Symphony.

Even in the flawed London concert performance, *1600*'s potential was there to be recognised by anyone who knew and was sympathetic to L's theatre music. The newly constructed *White House Cantata* has a deserved life ahead of it certainly beyond that which the composer conceived possible when he closed its Broadway production without even permitting a scheduled recording to take place of his score. The fate of the Cantata will depend on the theatrical quality and textual clarity of its future performances. It deserves to and, one hopes, it will be given its moment to shine.

WEST SIDE MAESTRO

MASS
A Theatre Piece for singers, players and Dancers

Humphrey Burton refers to *Mass* as a "musical" in terms of its resources. Viewed in that limited frame it might be considered to come under the 'musical' category but from no other aspect does it comfortably fit the genre. It seems more a parallel to an elaborately staged oratorio or morality play. Its Victorian sized assemblage of performers exceeds the demands of the most lavish of Broadway musicals. Burton based much of his analogy upon the 'panic stations' atmosphere which marked *Mass*'s genesis, often encountered in the mounting of Broadway musicals with their last minute changes and daily rewrites leading up to opening night. This was certainly the scenario for the creation of *Mass*. Despite his huge commitment to the Kennedy Center staring him in the face, L accepted a calendar of European concert engagements, tours, recordings and film documentaries which, as in the past, found him composing to meet his deadline under the most stressed and pressured conditions. For him, that was merely par for the course. What is astonishing, in light of the dimension and seriousness of purpose of the work, is that not only did he end up with a good result but that he created perhaps his most original work for the stage.

The reports of shock and offence that *Mass* caused in certain very high and powerful circles is well documented in several of the existing biographies. It is not every work that sets out to challenge the authority of American government from the President down as well as question the contemporary relevance of the Catholic Church and the Supreme Being Himself. With the passing of years, the initial controversy surrounding the work has died down and we can examine *Mass* and its message in a clearer, more dispassionate light. Not withstanding that within today's seemingly limitless concept of 'free speech', certain aspects of the text's challenge to held traditional viewpoints might still offend, it would be difficult for the most partisan anti-Bernstein, anti-*Mass* theatre-goer to deny its impact as a powerful and original fusion work of the theatre, capable of producing an overwhelming theatrical experience. 'Fusion', it seems to me, most clearly and accurately describes this highly original creation, which combines elements of ritual, pageant, theatre, concert and opera in tandem with a variety of music styles from the Baroque to a Woodstock 'happening'.

While the general view of this original hybrid, encouraged by the composer's own statements, is that of another Bernstein composition dealing with 'a crisis of faith', it projects a far wider agenda. *Mass* concerns itself with the loss of innocence and essence, both of the individual and that of the Church. It also represents a challenge to the concept of 'separation of Church and State'. Doubtless, behind it all is a search for an affirmation of faith, a reconciliation between a God/Father/Creator of all things human and environmental, whom we look to as the embodiment of perfection, and his creations whose imperfections manifested daily cause the ever growing questioning, self-doubt and alienation that separates us from our Creator. It is just as logical to perceive it as another example of L's rebellion against authority in all its forms to include the Ultimate Authority. He already had challenged God from the view of Orthodox Judaism in his *Kaddish* Symphony using ancient Hebrew and Aramaic texts. Now he again turned to address God in Christian terms using the traditional Church service and language. As with his Third Symphony, historic prayer was only to provide the catalyst for a very volatile situation of confrontation, rejection and reconciliation. In that sense, Mass represents another step along the path towards the parallel universal affirmation and accommodation that the composer was seeking with a personal God in *Kaddish* and even as far back as *Candide*. Mere speculation on another individual's intention often proves neither helpful nor illuminating but, in the case of *Mass*, not to accept the provocative intellectual/moral/emotional challenges set up by its form and its sacred and composed texts is not to participate fully in a powerful, thought provoking experience in theatre. Once the pebble has dropped into the pool, one must feel free to pursue the ever-widening circle of events set into motion by the initial happening.

WEST SIDE MAESTRO

Mass inaugurated the opening of the JFK Center of the Performing Arts in Washington, DC in 1971 and the Center chose to remount this massive work for its tenth anniversary celebrations as well. Fortunately, we have a telecast record of this revival from Public Service Broadcasting, (PBS). The revival was a no-expense- spared, magnificent affair wonderfully cast, rehearsed and brilliantly staged by Tom O'Horgan with choreography by Wesley Fata and music direction by John Mauceri[249]. For this anniversary production, the composer provided a short introductory explanation of the work. His purpose, he said, was 'to communicate as directly and as universally as (he) could a reaffirmation of faith.' He went on to explain this musical hybrid as 'a theatre piece *in the form of a Mass*', (my italics). Its symbolism was as follows:

'The Celebrant represents the struggle of Man in his search for faith in God. The dancers represent the ritual of the Church. The on-stage choir sings the liturgical text of the Catholic Service while the band of street people question in their own secular way these traditional beliefs. Finally, a boys' choir represents an innocence which carries their faith on to a hopeful conclusion of the work.'

While one is treading upon thin ice to disagree with an author regarding the symbolic meaning of his own creation, *Mass* has certainly sustained a wide degree of interpretation from the several writers who have chosen to tackle its *inner* meaning. The depiction of the Celebrant as 'Man in search of faith', for instance, doesn't jibe with the character we encounter in *Mass*. The individual introduced to us is one who fully enjoys a simple, straightforward relationship with his faith and judging by the words he sings drawn from the Psalms of the Old Testament, an ecumenical God. He renews this faith each day through the performance of the Mass. It is only when he takes on the responsibility of Celebrant, the human instrument of the Mass, and is forced to face the unrelenting challenges to belief in contemporary society, that he suffers a personal crisis of faith to which he must seek accommodation and

---

[249] Mauceri was also artistic director and conductor for the 1974 Yale University production of *Mass* which had been filmed at its European premiere in Vienna by L's production company, Amberson.

reaffirmation. Among the several flawed, off-the-beaten-track constructions attributed to *Mass* found in the now large catalogue of Bernstein biographies is the one by Joan Peyser. Ms. Peyser views the role of Celebrant as analogous to L himself and his years with the NY Philharmonic during which she alludes to his having become the servant, conformist representative of the 'Establishment', what L once characterised in a moment of self-mockery as being 'a trained monkey'. Peyser goes as far as to trace within *Mass* autobiographical overtones of virtually L's whole professional life, from the early influence of Mitropoulos, to his *Broadway* period, to his 'assumption of the robes of authority' with the NY Philharmonic, to his composer *persona* and "*inclusion of the **Kaddish** in a mass...*" With imperfect logic she concludes, "There can be no explanation for a *Kadd**ish*** in a mass unless *Mass* is in fact the story of Bernstein's own life." Unfortunately, for Ms. Peyser's hypothesis, there is no *Kadd**ish*** in *Mass*. What is quoted from the Hebrew service is not the Kad*dish* but the Ka*dosh*. Both are prayers but serve two different and distinct hierarchical functions in the Hebrew liturgy. The Kad*dish* is the more important of the two. It is the prayer of glorification and sanctification of God to help the mourner come to terms with bereavement and find peace within himself. It is the closing prayer of the synagogue service. Spoken only by the male members of the congregation who have lost a parent, it is intoned initially during the first seven days of mourning, then twice a day for the next month and then continued once a day for the remainder of the first year of bereavement. Thereafter, it is spoken once a year, the *Jahrzeit,* as a commemoration, of the day of passing. The *Kadosh* is the equivalent to the *Sanctus* of the Mass, 'Holy, holy, holy, Lord, God of Hosts.' It serves only as a subsidiary part to *The Prayer of 18 Blessings* but is not a prayer in itself as is the case with the *Kaddish*.

It may be that L was, in a sense, hedging his bets by including the Hebrew service *Kadosh* within his setting of the Sanctus of the Catholic Mass. Who is to know? Certainly ten years after *Mass*'s premiere, he felt it necessary to provide an explanation of the symbolism attached to the work's various characters and factions. By including the *Kadosh* taken from the ancient synagogue prayer service, the challenge to faith can be viewed to take on an ecumenical aspect covering the whole of the Judaic-Christian ethic, lending a universality to the writers' protest against the failure of all religions to afford leadership in providing answers to the challenges of our contemporary world.

I have taken time to scrutinise Joan Peyser's provocative interpretation because it is endemic of much speculation of a similar nature that has detracted from a proper appreciation of this and other original Bernstein compositions. There has been some redressing of the balance marked by a degree of backtracking, (the more erudite and preferred critical term is *rethinking*), in recent times. In assessing not only *Mass* but all the Bernstein compositions written from 1971 onwards, we are no longer deafened by the endless mantra regarding this most versatile and gifted musician of "his never having fulfilled his potential" or that of its variant, chanted on Tuesdays, Thursdays and Saturdays, that he will *only* be remembered as the composer of *West Side Story*. In reviewing the contemporary critical commentaries written following various Bernstein premieres, one is taken aback by the degree of nastiness that marks the language used. The *bandwagon* effect of negative senior critics can be viewed in the writings of their acolytes at the time and continue to be perpetuated in contemporary articles and biographies. These perpetuated echoes of the past reveal the lack of new, in-depth research. Of even greater concern are writings which lack a depth of knowledge for proper musical analysis and, in regard to the stage works, a well rounded understanding of this many faceted medium.

Since *Mass*'s debut, Stephan Schwartz's participation in the writing of the libretto has been strongly and consistently criticised. Schwartz was L's enthusiastic choice of writing partner after he attended a performance of *Godspell* at the behest of his sister, Shirley, who was Schwartz's literary agent. A good starting point for examination would be the melange of harsh adjectives meted out to the libretto, "*superficial, pretentious, cheap, vulgar, sloppy, banal, inane, cliché ridden, embarrassing...*" The writer of the last four adjectives also chose to describe the violent and aggressive setting of the *Agnus Dei* of *Mass* as one of 'great charm', casting doubt as to whether he had ever listened to the work. Perhaps the most damaging bit of gossip at the time was Stephan Sondheim's pronouncement that the lyrics ought be translated into Latin so one wouldn't have to listen to the words. With such a witty, tantalising quote in circulation by so important a theatre personality as Sondheim, it didn't take long for other negative opinions to gain currency.

Critics of the librettist's writing style might have taken a moment to discern the qualities that had attracted so eminent a musician as Leonard Bernstein to him. It certainly wasn't only the few superficial external similarities between Schwartz and Stephan Sondheim often mentioned in biographies, (both shared the same initials as well as Christian name, both were composer/writers, both, at the time, were young... No doubt some super-sleuth could find a dozen more). If any of the librettist's critics had seen *Godspell* or at least listened to the show recording, they would have known exactly what to expect. Schwartz's text for *Mass*, using simple sentence and attractive, if obvious, rhyming patterns easily and clearly communicated to the listener, are a mirror of the structure of his lyrics for his hit show. Did or could anyone expect him to be transformed into TS Eliot as a result of working with Leonard Bernstein? The attraction of his writing talent was its simplicity. *Mass* has certainly suffered its share of criticism from the professional community and from the pulpit but no one can deny that its message, whether you agree with it or not, comes over loud and extremely clear. It is the dichotomy of contrasting simple and intricate elements; Schwartz's clear language used in tandem with L's complex music and varied asymmetrical rhythms, which creates *Mass*'s theatrical brilliance and communicative power. Moreover, it is accomplished by that most direct and simple of writing devices, an essential for text clarity whether in the construction of lyrics for 'pop' tunes or the setting of a Da Ponte libretto by a Mozart, *repetition*. Not only does one find a consistent methodical repetition of simple key phrases and ideas within *Mass*'s English texts but the Latin texts of the Catholic Mass are treated exactly in the same manner. One might fantasise that a Richard Wilbur or Stephan Sondheim would have produced a more subtly complex dramatic structure along with far more intricate rhyming patterns and gracefully turned phrases but, in light of Schwartz's undeniable communicative result, it is fair to ask whether such would have served the composer any better or duplicated the achieved clarity and punch of his intended message?

WEST SIDE MAESTRO

The Roman Mass has been referred to as a form of theatre - ritual theatre. As such, its presence within the *Theatre Piece* created by Leonard Bernstein and Stephan Schwartz serves to intensify the totality of this hybrid drama, which lends itself to several layers of meaning. Such a use of the central act of worship for the world's Catholics does impart weight to the question posed by the then archbishop of the city of Cincinnati, Paul F. Leopold, as to whether any artist has the right to use the key elements of the Catholic faith as a vehicle to present his theme? Unfortunately, the archbishop issued his strong statement that branded Mass "a blatant sacrilege" and "offensive to our Catholic sense and belief" without having seen the work he was condemning. His words only served to guarantee sold-out performances of *Mass* when it was later mounted in Cincinnati. This was, after all, the post-Vietnam United States not *fundamentalist* Iran of the deposed Shah.

Let us examine the theatrical bones of the work. Mass begins in a rather startling cinematic fashion. For the premiere staging, the work began in darkness but for its 10th anniversary revival at the Kennedy Center the stage area was lit revealing a progression of levels with stairs leading upward from the center of each elevation to a central altar with tape machines pre-set on different levels. Dancers in dark robes, Acolytes representing, according to L, 'the ritual of the Church', switch on each tape console. And, indeed, the ritual of the Church does begin as we hear the Antiphon of the Roman Mass, *Kyrie eleison! Christe eleison!* 'Lord, have mercy! Christ, have mercy!', sung responsively by five pre-recorded voices in solo or duet combination, each response emanating from one of four loudspeakers located in the four corners of the auditorium. This quadraphonic effect which had been developed for the home sound components market, had been one of the enhancing effects developed by the Cinerama process for the ear crushing sound tracks of block-buster movies. These individual antiphonal replies, each composed in a different rhythm and accompanied by varied combinations of percussion instruments, join together and reach a wild pitch of confused excitement which is suddenly silenced by a single guitar chord sounded by a young man simply dressed in shirt and jeans who has entered. In keeping with his attire, he sings 'A Simple Song' in praise of God accompanied by a solo flautist who has appeared from behind the highest level. Three members of the Boys' Choir enter. One takes the singer's guitar, the other two vest him with a simple robe. From this moment he becomes the Celebrant. The Roman Mass continues to unfold but with the addition of tropes, a medieval practice in western church music, usually sung by the choir, which was, at first, merely ornamental embellishment to the Mass. It later developed into a poetic moral discourse with its own musical setting. The trope as used in this *theatre piece* is a very different animal from its medieval origin. Here it is used to question the pertinence of the various orders of the Mass in contemporary life and to challenge the very relevance of organised religion.

As the Celebrant conducts the Mass, he finds himself confronted by individuals and groups of street people in conflict with the dogma of renewed faith which he is bringing. To the many challenging questions his only reply is one that demands unquestioning faith, "Let us pray!" spoken each time with greater insistence and increasing desperation. The Celebrant's initial projected simplicity of loving innocence changes with his each subsequent appearance. He continues to be vested with ever more elaborate clerical garments which, like layers of veneer, symbolise his separation from the child-like essence and 'simple' message of faith which marked his 'Simple Song', itself an analogy to Christianity's modest beginnings and the humble men who first carried its message. Soon he finds himself in conflict with the street people around him whose confrontations now interrupt the Mass interposing their protests regarding specific issues of faith and commitment encountered within its Latin text. With the invocation of the *Credo*, "I believe in one God", the protests become more confrontational and mocking, forming a dominant counterpoint to the Mass itself. Sacred objects are brought on by choirboys to be blessed in preparation for Communion as the *De Profundus*, "Out of the depths I call Thee", is intoned. Having blessed the objects, the Celebrant leaves. With the exit of the Celebrant the *De Profundus* is turned into a wild secular dance around the sacred objects, an Old Testament 'golden calf' analogy. The Celebrant returns, interrupting the orgiastic scene. In the silence that follows the area clears and the Celebrant is left alone. He goes to the piano and picks out a melody with one finger to which he sings *The Lord's Prayer* which leads without pause into a trope in which the Celebrant expresses his continuing faith but also reveals the many daily doubts that he has to face and overcome. The trope ends with the *Lauda, Laudé* from his *Simple Song*. But when he repeats these words of praise, what was first sung in a bright, positive F major key now takes on the shadowed implication of the minor.

With the ringing of the *Sanctus Bell* preparations for Communion begin. *Sanctus, Sanctus, Sanctus,* "Holy, *Holy, Holy*", sing the Boys' Choir. The Celebrant adds his voice in joyful expression but when his turn comes to sing the *Sanctus* the words are not Latin but the Hebrew, *Kadosh, Kadosh, Kadosh.* A large adult choir, upstage in pews, that has participated in the Mass from the beginning, respond with the full *Kadosh* prayer from the Hebrew Prayer Service. Then in a further ecumenical gesture, the Sanctus is sung in English followed by a repeat of the Hebrew prayer. The crowd that has gathered for the Communion Service breaks apart to reveal the altar. As the Celebrant grasps the *Monstrance*, he is interrupted by the *Agnus Dei*, "Lamb of God', sung by the Street Singers. Its mood is not tender and reverential but aggressive, punctuated by foot stamps. The Celebrant tries to continue the consecration but his way to the altar is barred. He appeals to the ensemble but his cries become weaker. The crowd does not plead but shouts a demand, *Dona nobis pacem!* 'Give us peace!' He tries to protect himself with the words of the Mass but the Street People use the words of his faith to assault him. 'Let us pray!' he weakly whispers and the crowd kneels. The *Agnus Dei* begins again, this time quietly and mysteriously. The Celebrant holding the Chalice and Monstrance moves towards the altar. As the Celebrant climbs the staircase to the altar with ever-greater effort, the crowd, which have become more and more disorganised, again shouts the *Agnus Dei.* The violent cry, *Dona nobis pacem,* is again taken up and becomes an hypnotically repeated mantra over which the street chorus sings a counterpoint of threats of violence if they do not witness a manifestation of God righting the wrongs of the world. The *Dona nobis,* now at a fever pitch, is interrupted by three cries of '*Pacem!*' from the Celebrant. On the third cry, to the shock of the onlookers, he hurls the Chalice and Monstrance, smashing them. There is a stunned silence. As the Celebrant descends the staircase, all fall to the ground and are frozen by the happening. The violent protest of the mob and his failure to communicate the message of the Mass and make them accept the symbols of Communion that represent Christ's sacrifice seem to have unhinged the Celebrant's mind. Dramatically, although the performance of the Mass has been shattered, the act of transubstantiation from the Communion of the Mass takes place[250]. The spilled wine from the smashed Chalice, representing the blood of Christ in the performance of the Mass, has indeed turned to blood. "How easily things get broken.", aberrantly reflects the Celebrant as he continues to smash the fragments of the Holy Vessels, referring not only to things material but his own faith.[251] 'What are you staring at?' he challengingly asks. "Haven't you ever seen an *accident* before?" What proceeds is an eighteen-minute soliloquy of the wanderings of an unhinged mind. It is an extraordinary *tour de force* during which the Celebrant taunts his taunters, admits his loss of faith and re-lives fragmentary events from the various challenges he has faced from the time we first heard him sing *Lauda*. As his mind wanders, memories of the Mass and his failure to accomplish the transubstantiation of the wafers and the wine into the body and blood of Christ thus manifesting the presence of God to the chanting mob continue to haunt him. Then, to the accompaniment of wild, calliope-like circus music, he desecrates the alter and rends his vestments. During all this the shocked mob is silent. In the face of his powerful challenge, with the Mass shattered and its representative rejecting his commitment to it and to them, they have no answer. It had been easy for them to protest when the opposition was passive in its response. The Celebrant's words become more halting and spasmodic. He slowly descends to the orchestra pit pausing only to again comment, 'How easily things get broken.' Silence.

---

[250] Transubstantiation occurs during the Eucharist of the Catholic Mass. The Celebrant prepares the bread and wine and tells the story of what Jesus did and said at The Last Supper. In doing so, according to Catholic doctrine, a conversion of the whole substance of the bread into the body and of the wine into the blood of Christ takes place. While the appearance of bread and wine remain the presence of the real Christ, God made man, is revealed within the bread and wine.

[251] From this moment the Celebrant is no longer a priest. One could create an analogy to this dramatic schismatic happening in *Mass* with the vocal and physical anti-war protests coming from within the Catholic Church itself.

WEST SIDE MAESTRO

The flautist who first greeted and accompanied the Celebrant in his *Lauda* reappears and plays an extended solo. As she concludes a young choirboy with whom she has entered begins an elaborate and melismatic version of the *Simple Song* and *Lauda*[252]. It is the essence and innocence of the child, perhaps a reference to the Biblical exhortation "to become as little children[253]", that restores the original message of the *Simple Song*. He goes to stir one of the stricken, silenced mob of protesters who joins him in the *Lauda*. The choirboy embraces the protesters one at a time. They too join in the *Lauda* until the entire stage rings with a song of praise. The anger has been dissipated. Everything comes together including the stage setting, which split apart during the schism. All take hands as various choir boys walk into the auditorium and, as a *Sign of Peace*, an integral part of the Catholic Mass, touch hands with members of the audience urging them "to pass the message on."

The Celebrant enters again dressed as the Simple Man. He unites with the choirboy in singing the *Lauda* and they, in turn, are joined by the flautist. All on stage band together in a block chord hymn-like song to the Almighty Father seeking His blessing. As they sing a final *Amen*, both the Celebrant and choir boy speak, "The *Mass* is ended; go in peace."[254] The stage slowly goes dark.

The late Roger Stevens, legendary Broadway producer, long time associate and friend of L and the leading figure in the creation of the Kennedy Center for the Performing Arts, declared the opening night of *Mass* to be the most exciting evening he had ever spent in theatre. He described the audience reaction as follows:

---

[252] melisma: from the Greek = song; in plainsong a group of notes sung to a single syllable

[253] The New Testament: Matthew 18: 3

[254] In the 1971 premiere production the closing statement, 'The Mass is ended. Go in peace!' was heard on a pre-recorded tape. Only a Celebrant can close the Mass. The Simple Man is no longer a Celebrant. While it is dramatically valid for his character to speak this final benediction as he was directed to do in the 1981 revival production, it is wrong in relation to the performance of the Catholic Mass since he is no longer a priest. The director's decision to have him do so is as theologically incorrect as L's use of a female speaker for his *Kaddish* Symphony since the *Kaddish* prayer is only to be spoken by a man.

WEST SIDE MAESTRO

"When it was finished, there was silence for three minutes. Then everyone stood and applauded for half an hour."

Compare this reportage with some of the negative critiques that followed:

"...pseudo serious ...cheap and vulgar...an ill considered effort to be *trendy*...a combination of superficiality and pretentiousness and the greatest melange of styles since the ladies magazine recipe for steak fried in peanut butter and marshmallow sauce."
Harold Schonberg, chief critic, NY Times

"Some of this music is...merely derivative and attitudinising drivel. The trouble is not so much that it is eclectic, as that it is banal, inappropriate and rather vulgar...it is set to ideas by Bernstein and lyrics by Bernstein and Stephan Schwartz that are simplistic, pretentious, pedestrian and not a little distasteful."
John Simon, critic, New York Magazine

"Subliterate rubbish!"   Eric Bentley, critic, NY Times

"What cripples *Mass* at last, however, is...its inability to persuade the sympathetic listener that the banalities have been given meaning...We are unmoved."
Donal Henahan, critic, NY Times

"...Radical *Sheik* of American middle-brow culture has done it again...the nadir of the evening for me personally comes in the Sanctus when the Celebrant suddenly segues from Latin into Hebrew...I was offended at hearing a Hebrew prayer ripped off and stuck into this high-fashion equivalent of the Great Easter Show at the Radio City Music Hall for the benefit of Mr. Bernstein's smarmy ecumenism."
Julius Novick, critic, The Village Voice

WEST SIDE MAESTRO

The reviews were not all a tidal wave of negativity. Note the following:

"The greatest music Leonard Bernstein has ever written...The entire *Mass* is a shattering experience that signally honours its creator, the Center and the memory of the man for whom the Center is named...*Mass* moves in an unbroken line from beginning to end. But Bernstein scatters through it a brilliant array of musical forms and styles."
Paul Hume, critic, The Washington Post

"A magnificent work, masterly contrived, marvellously performed."
Herbert Kupferberg, critic

"It shook, exalted and moved me as have few statements in recent years."
John Ardoin, critic

And a revised opinion by Donal Henahan of the NY Times following the remounting of *Mass* for a limited engagement *at* the Metropolitan Opera under Sol Hurok's management in July 1972:

"Mass is one of those rare theatrical works that sum up their time and place, like it or not, and that is never a simple or useless thing to do...The score is a minor miracle of skilful mixing, mortising together folksy ballads, blues, rock, Broadway-style song and dance numbers, Lutheran chorales, plainchant and bits of 12-tone music."

What do all these contradictory opinions prove? Perhaps, most importantly, that a critic is merely another member of the public with personal likes and dislikes along with a range of personal prejudices. Taking that one step further, where the fraternity of critics are concerned, the most apt cliché which marks the wide divergence of opinion, which occurs more often than most readers of one periodical realise, is, "One man's meat is another man's poison." There is, however, a caveat. When one's opinion is given currency and circulation in print, responsibility becomes part and parcel of your contract with your readers. What sticks out like the proverbial 'sore thumb' in the quoted reviews is the lack of balance in the reporting for which a cleverly turned or witty phrase is no substitute. It would be useful to recall Roger Stevens' description of the public response at the premiere and underline that his reputation for honesty and reliability were rare if not unique in the world of theatre. The critics couldn't have been on a deadline in covering so important a premiere that embraced the first official opening to the public of the Kennedy Center itself. *Mass*, even with an extended interval which would have been the norm for so festive an evening, would have concluded in little more than two and a half hours leaving little excuse for the critics to rush away in the middle of the second half. If, in fact, the work was greeted with a lengthy silence before the public showed its reaction, and not only has Roger Stevens' integrity in describing the event never been questioned but there are other eyewitness reports to confirm it, this in itself was news. If Stevens' Rolex wasn't functioning that night and the audience only applauded for twenty minutes rather than his estimated half hour, that still would have represented an extraordinary response to so controversial a theatre work created for such a unique occasion in memory of an American icon whose life and dramatic death paralleled the great tragedies of theatre. Whatever the reality of the situation, the question remains, why did not so unusual and positive an audience response deserve mention in critiques of such an important national cultural event, especially if its writer had chosen to assume a minority position? The answer has to lie somewhere in the realm of that most overused political phrase in the final decade leading to the millennium, 'the pursuit of a hidden agenda' and/or a concern with self-promotion. Donal Henahan's second review is worthy of attention, not because it was a reversal of his first review which was generally negative, but because he showed the rare courage to admit publicly that his first assessment, whatever its tone, had been wrong and that it was important to correct it with the same degree of detail as that of his initial statement.

Criticism of *Mass* seems to incorporate a sum total of every criticism levelled at every other work L ever composed. *Eclecticism* is the most frequent charge and perhaps most easily answered. The compendium of all that has gone before forms the roots of the contemporary Arts, whether it be painting, sculpture, architecture or music and all concomitant sub-sections.

WEST SIDE MAESTRO

It is how the artist uses the heritage, which has shaped his artistic being that matters, and whether, in the end, it is the personality of the new creative mind that shines through. The fact that critics can play 'name that composer' when they listen to a Bernstein composition indicates a certain erudition on their part which may be the result of solid professional training or merely their catholic tastes in record collecting, but it doesn't direct itself to the central question: Does the work merely stylistically sound like composer X, Y or Z or, within its context, does it sound like Bernstein? Listening to *Mass,* even if one is accomplished at the 'spot the composer' game, it is difficult to understand how one would come to any other conclusion except that it is a work by Bernstein and, for the most part, pretty much 'top drawer' Bernstein at that. The problem facing the listener/viewer with any new theatrical creation is his or her willingness to suspend disbelief in order to fully participate in an experience that may, at times, challenge or offend. Theatre cannot function without this commitment. If the viewer/listener becomes bored, offended or insulted, he or she has a variety of remedies that include sleep, walking out or staying to shout, hiss and boo those who have offended him. Only one Bernstein biography mentions such outrage at the premiere of *Mass.* The recount is of *one* person shouting out, 'Sacrilege' and there should be more substantiation for the reader than the second-hand reportage offered without detail by a single author.

Another criticism centres upon the composer's use of recycled material from other projects. One would not like to be at a séance recalling the spirits of Rossini, Berlioz or many other of the great composers who kept detailed sketchbooks. This question would bring blushes to even their ectoplasmic, ghostly pallor. Such critical disclosure would be a valid if the recycled material had not been transformed to fit the character and shape of the new work. That is the startling and, perhaps, unique aspect of *Mass.* Referring back to Donal Henahan's second review he comments that anyone caught up in its stage drama would only marvel at "a minor miracle of skilful mixing, mortising together" of so many different and diverse styles.

There was much harsh contemporary and later post-criticism of the music composed in what were the current 'pop', 'rock' and jazz styles of the period.

WEST SIDE MAESTRO

One must start from the reality that L was not composing an album of twelve rock song titles aimed at Billboard's 'top ten' best-sellers[255] nor was he sufficiently immersed and experienced in the style had he wanted to do so. He was attempting to wed styles of contemporary *pop* music to characters in his drama whom he felt matched that musical profile. He certainly achieved some success though, in musical terms, not to the degree as with other styles with which he was far more experienced in practice. Moreover, the weakness within some of these numbers centres as much on the text as the music. The Trope, 'Easy', sung following the *Confiteor*, 'I Confess to Almighty God', of the Mass, is gratuitously offensive. It typifies the deliberate outspoken tendency L displayed throughout his career and which those close to him attempted to modify in his interest. He remained a law unto himself but was always quick to blame others following any 'fallout'. Another of his rock genre tropes whose music and lyrics fail to convince is "I believe in God but does God believe in me?" which closes the *Credo*. The lyric, of Bernstein origin, with its obscure metaphysical references, 'I believe in F sharp, I believe in G, in A flat, in C', notes and intervals which held special personal meaning only for the composer, is confusing, weak and gratuitously confrontational. It's musical setting ranks very low on a scale of one to ten revealing little of the heat of inspiration so evident throughout the work.

Mass contains several dramas running parallel. There is the inherent drama of L's new, contemporary setting of the Ordinary of the Mass[256] and his use of historical elements such as the *trope* last associated with The Order of Mass in medieval times. There is the metamorphosis of the final *Dona nobis pacem*, 'Give us peace'. The composer converts this introspective moment within the Catholic Mass to a setting of intense, violent drama that is *Mass, A Theatre Piece*. *Dona nobis pacem* is transformed into his personal anti-war rallying cry. This was, after all, the time of the Pentagon Papers in the

---

[255] Bilboard, one of the music industry's most authoritative periodicals.

[256] The Ordinary of the Mass consists of five main sections: Kyrie, Gloria, Credo, Sanctus with Hosanna and Benedictus, and Agnus Dei with Dona nobis pacem. These sections of the Mass, which are invariable throughout the year, have provided the texts traditionally set to music by composers over the centuries such as Bach, Mozart, Schubert and Beethoven. Latin, as in the past, remains the prefered language of composers when setting the Mass although the Second Vatican Council ruled that the Mass be performed in the vernacular of each country.

nation's capital and, with their disclosure, the beginning of the end of the presidency of Richard Nixon. In this *Theatre Piece* it is this anti-war outburst that overwhelms the *Celebrant* and brings about the disintegration of the celebration of the Mass at his hands. Speaking through the voices of his diverse cast of *street people* the composer poses a challenge to the relevance of the Mass and, indeed, the Church itself in contemporary life. The final drama is the Celebrant's own expression of personal doubt, a reflection of what was actually taking place from within the Church itself at the time.[257] These principal themes combine throughout to express the work's anti-authoritarian, anti-war sub-plots.

L's musical setting of the Ordinary of the Mass in Latin is highly imaginative. The quality of the interposed *Tropes* proves more problematic and variable. One must straightaway modify so general a statement by noting that those Tropes which are lyrically inspired are beautifully conceived and those in the more popular style of the Gospel-Sermon, 'God said, "Let there be light!"', genuine 'toe-tappers' and 'hand-clappers'. The instrumental writing throughout is powerful and assured and two of the three Meditations from *Mass* have been sufficiently strong to find an independent life for themselves in the concert hall.

If one is examining the work for anomalies in its dramatic structure, one need only start with the impassioned ballad, 'The Word of the Lord' assigned to the Celebrant. The Celebrant throughout *Mass* projects passivity towards the protests that surround him, pursuing a straight line of religious worship and dogma. It is his inability to deal with and face the contemporary challenges of the *street people* that eventually fractures his faith and causes him in turn to fracture the performance of the Mass at its climax. For him to be assigned this outspoken statement with its highly politicised anti-war lyrics obviously aimed at the time towards the government, the military and,

---

[257] An extreme example of this was the case of Father Philip Berrigan with whom L consulted when he was creating *Mass*. Father Berrigan along with his brother and other peace protesters against the Vietnam war were imprisoned at the Danbury Federal Correctional Institute in Connecticutt for the alleged attempted kidnapping of the noted presidential adviser Henry Kissinger. Their challenge to Catholic authority at the time was not that they were leaving the Church but that the Church had left them.

had he not avoided attending the performance upon advice from the F.B.I., President Richard Nixon himself, is totally alien to the Celebrant's character as developed by its authors to that point in the drama. Another weakness involves the rather pat manner in which the authors tie a pink ribbon around the final scene. 'A new beginning' as represented in the image of the choir boy, a new generation, passing on the message of renewed faith to the *street people*, ('And a child shall lead them'), is developed sufficiently both visually and musically to gain audience acceptance following the drama of the explosive interruption of the Mass. However, the re-appearance of the Celebrant in the final two minutes of the work as if nothing had previously taken place is far from satisfactory. It is not only unclear but confusing. His was a fall from grace from a great height, which rendered both his faith and his sanity. To see him casually walk on stage seven minutes later and join the *Lauda* as if he had solved the greatest crisis of his life while offstage with two aspirin is dramatically invalid, saccharine, and a rather forced Hollywood 'all's well that ends well' conclusion. It dissipates the power and the validity of the crisis he has suffered.

This problematical and, in my opinion, less than satisfactory closing is the result of a series of personal choices by the composer which can be better understood by examining the history of the writing of *Mass* especially in the short period leading up to its premiere. We know from documented reports that only four months prior to opening night its composer was suffering from writer's block. He did not acquire the services of Stephan Schwartz, his co-writer, until a month later. This provided him with the new stimulus he needed. However, with barely three months till the premiere, L left for California to attend rehearsals and performances of the Los Angeles Civic Light Opera production of *Candide* thus increasing the pressure on him and everyone else. His return East to begin work in earnest on completing *Mass* found him in euphoric mood but time was now very short. In the run up period to the premiere a typical Broadway 'panic stations' atmosphere, referred to at the beginning of this analysis, now served as a cattle prod on all its participants. L, working in his hotel room, would pass his piano sketches to three of Broadway's finest orchestrators, Hershey Kay, Sid Ramon and Jonathan Tunick, working nearby. They in turn would pass on their completed orchestrations to a team of five copyists holed up at a hotel working day and night to complete manuscript copies of all the individual parts to deliver to the director, music director, choreographer and cast of two hundred. Wayne Dirkson, organist and choirmaster at Washington Cathedral, who performed one of the two organ parts in *Mass*'s orchestra is quoted as reporting that the ending of Mass was not written until a few days before opening night. The theatrical problem for the composer and his co-librettist, quite obviously, was how to follow and satisfactorily resolve in the final nine minutes of *Mass* the Celebrant's fifteen-minute 'mad scene' which precedes it. Humphrey Burton in an interview with the author revealed that since 1953, after working with Maria Callas at La Scala, Milan, on Cherubini's *Médée*, (Medea), L had had a burning passion to compose a 'mad scene'. The difference between the *Celebrant's* 'mad scene' and the classical 'mad scenes' of a *Médée, Lucia di Lammemoor* or a *Salomé* is what comes afterward. Those operas along with others of that genre all end the same way, with a violent tragedy that exceeds the drama of the moment of madness. In contrast, *Mass* ends in positive resolution with the person gone mad completely restored to his senses. You can't theatrically explain that away in two minutes. My own thoughts on the matter are that the Celebrant might have been brought on earlier and shown to be reluctant and afraid to join in with the others. Then, at the urging of the child and some of those who, like himself, have also suffered a crisis of faith, he makes the effort to enter into the song of praise. That approach doesn't attempt to fully resolve the major crisis so recently experienced but it does point a somewhat more valid way forward then the original contradictory solution.

After having set down my thoughts on *Mass*, I was presented with the opportunity of viewing a video filmed in Vienna in 1974 of the Yale University production I discovered to my great interest that this production sought new solutions in two of the problem areas which had caused me concern. In the Yale production, the Epistle, *The Word of the Lord*, is performed by the Celebrant in a less accusative, more pastoral fashion, as if it is being quoted from the text of the open Bible from which he is reading. This is very much in keeping with *The Liturgy of the Word* from the Catholic Mass, which includes readings from the Old, and New Testaments from which the priest bases his sermon of the day. It is somewhat of a fudge but it does to a degree solve the problem of maintaining the Celebrant's non-confrontational character. The Yale production ending also represents a revision of the original stage directions. To my not unpleasant surprise, it proved to be much along lines paralleling my own thinking. In the Yale production the *Celebrant*, now defrocked, never leaves the stage at the conclusion of his outburst that fractures the performance of the Mass, but sits huddled among the *Street People*, his head buried in his arms. After all around him have recovered from the shock of the previous scene and joined together with the young boy who has brought a fresh and innocent message of praise, they leave the central stage area. Only the boy and the former *Celebrant* remain. The boy brings him out of his trance and succeeds in inducing him to join in the *Lauda* albeit, as I have suggested, reluctantly. As they stand together, representing the voice of the past and the voice of the future, we hear the choir all around them sing the final hymn quietly asking God to bestow His blessings. The boy moves off leaving the man alone. Though liturgically incorrect, he, no longer the Celebrant, announces that the Mass is ended.

Does this newly conceived ending work? Having independently arrived at a somewhat similar solution for what I felt was a glaring dramatic weakness in its original ending, my feeling is that the Yale conclusion is undeniably valid and superior to the authors' original concept. The best resolution, without doubt, would require more time to establish itself. Michael Tilson Thomas kept telling L that he felt the ending needed more music. For Tilson Thomas it was "about two minutes of extremely fast, angry music at the moment where the Celebrant has his breakdown." L's suggestion to his persistent young colleague's urgings was that perhaps *he* should write it. Perhaps, one day he will, resolving more satisfactorily at the same time the problematic ending as well. Whether such an approach is judged more valid than the present less than satisfactory solution will be for the esteemed conductor, the Bernstein family and another director to decide for a production not yet in rehearsal.

WEST SIDE MAESTRO

No commercial videotape exists of the opening night at Kennedy Center, which was directed by Gordon Davidson and featured the Alvin Ailey Dance Theatre. We have authoritative written accounts by Schuyler Chapin and Roger Stevens leading up to and including a brilliantly received preview night but no available visual documentation of the staging. The preview represented a slightly cut version of Mass by its artistic directors undertaken with the composer's permission. Although reported to have successfully tightened the work dramatically, producing a thirty-minute standing ovation at the end, the composer insisted upon restoring all the cut music the following night. A superb sound recording produced immediately following the premiere performances is available on Sony Classical with L conducting the full original cast. It has been excellently re-engineered and made available in a three CD package accompanied by the full text and the addition of the composer's ballet score to *Dybbuk*. The two subsequently recorded videos are both conducted by John Mauceri. The first, the Yale University production, was produced by Amberson in 1974 for the European premiere of *Mass* at the Konzerthaus in Vienna with soloists, singers, dancers and orchestra from the American university assisted by the Vienna Singakademie and the Vienna Boys Choir. The Bernstein/Schwartz text is sung in English and the performance is introduced by the composer. A massive undertaking, it is a tribute to the Arts Department of Yale University and the enormous dedication of Mauceri who was both conductor and artistic director for the show. The stage direction by James Shaffer is skilled and sound and, as underlined by the composer in his spoken preface, represents a new concept and visual approach to *Mass*. The choreography for the Yale production, like the Mass itself, is a mixture of styles, with elements of the Broadway rock musical, quite a bit of Martha Graham and Contemporary Dance ensemble influence and even a bit of *Seven Brides For Seven Brothers* thrown in. All this is insured a solid video presentation under the experienced hand of director, Brian Large. If the Yale production values didn't benefit from a 'theatre angel's' blank check, the audience was not short changed in regard to the full impact of the work, its outstanding musical preparation and the seemingly limitless energy of its young cast.[258] I

---

[258] It is an interesting sidelight to this production is that its telecast by the BBC produced a protest registering 'disgust and distress' by two thousand of Great Britain's Catholic priests.

have earlier described the inexpressibly fine quality of the second video produced live for the tenth anniversary celebrations at Kennedy Center in 1981. It is stunning and deservedly should be assessed alongside the composer's sound recording. Both can be considered equally definitive performances of the work, the video providing not only the full power but also the visual splendour of the work. It is imaginatively directed and choreographed and represents, lacking a live presentation, the ideal medium with which to project the total communicative experience that this unique work offers. One must single out from the 1981 production Joseph Kolinski for his performance of the Celebrant. His eighteen-minute long crisis of faith 'mad' scene is a *tour de force*. It is photographed in the cruellest of close-ups, a test of any actor's ability to convincingly sustain so long a scene of such dramatic intensity, and provides an overwhelming and memorable moment of television drama.

Humphrey Burton points out that *Mass* is 'practical, popular and suitable for entire communities to undertake.' The only word in Burton's assessment with which I would take issue is that of "practical". The organising and mounting of a production of *Mass* is a huge undertaking and challenge. Nevertheless, since the time I first wrote this overview there were already encouraging signs that professional organisations, colleges and communities were eagerly accepting this challenge. Between 1997 -99, virtually thirty years after its premiere, *Mass* was produced in Germany, Canada and, in the U.S.A., in Colorado, Oregon and in multiple productions in California. Since then, *Mass* has continued to chalk up an extraordinary number of performances, not only on the college campuses of America but in its concert halls, as well as those of the UK and Europe. This continued interest in a work of such complexity both in its preparation and physical demands provides convincing affirmation of its continued relevance as an important and deserving communicative work of Art that will carry on finding and expanding its audience.

A Quiet Place/Trouble in Tahiti

WEST SIDE MAESTRO

'A Quiet Place' proves a disturbing dichotomy; a composite of two stage works composed thirty years apart employing totally diverse musical styles and language. Character development and stagecraft for each opera also sit at opposite ends of the theatrical spectrum. The librettos to both operas contain autobiographical aspects and several of the subsidiary characters are equally drawn from life.

Although composer and librettist, Stephen Wadsworth, began work on this project in 1980 as an independent 'work in progress', the impetus of a negotiated triple commission by the Houston Grand Opera, Italy's famed La Scala and the Kennedy Center in Washington D.C. for the 1983/84 seasons provided the necessary pressure of a target completion date without which the predictable pattern of procrastination and delay typical of its composer might have resulted in yet another project in waiting rather than a project in progress. As the librettist was later to diary, even with the commission date hanging like a sword over their heads, it was no easy task to discipline this most gifted but reluctant of composers to any kind of regular work schedule until the deadline pressure became inexorable.

Initially, the structure of the new work involved L's 1952 chamber opera *Trouble in Tahiti* serving as the first half of a double bill. Following an intermission, *A Quiet Place*[259], an opera in four scenes, picked up the dramatic thread of *Tahiti* presenting a contemporary portrait of its principal characters thirty years on. Other characters were added to the drama, some new and some only referred to but never seen in the earlier opera.

After the premiere, the work underwent several metamorphoses and was still viewed by L as "a work in progress" when his untimely death ended speculation regarding further changes to its form and content. In its final mould, the work was restructured into a three act opera with a prologue, some plot changes and cuts were instituted in *A Quiet Place*, its orchestration was lightened to help textual clarity and, most important of all, *T in T* was divided into two entities and incorporated into the body of the new opera as flashbacks serving as the second and fourth scenes of a newly

---

[259] For future reference, *Trouble in Tahiti* and *A Quiet Place* will be referred to as T in T and AQP

devised Act Two. It is this version that is examined in detail with reference at times to the earlier material that was discarded.

The addition of a Prologue and the incorporation of *T in T* quite late into the opera creates certain problems relating to text clarity for the audience. Although the minutiae of the lives of the plot's two principal and pivotal characters, Sam and Dinah, are eventually detailed in the flashback scenes of Act Two, it is important, indeed a key to our understanding of the violent and emotional Prologue and the following Scene One into which we are thrust when the curtain goes up, that we possess some knowledge of their life together before *AQP* begins. This is easily solved by inserting a written Preface in the program incorporating the following:

"Despite all the idyllic external promise that life in Suburbia, USA, complete with white-picket-fenced luxury house with all modern conveniences appears to offer, Sam and Dinah's marriage had become a sham. Communication had broken down and the pattern of their daily domestic existence was relegated to and dominated by quarrels at the breakfast table. In their struggle to achieve personal peace at any price, each created an individual life that excluded the other. Dinah retreated into the world of psychiatry to try to help her find some peace of mind and perhaps a place of accommodation in which her marriage could again function. Sam, who viewed himself as one of life's natural 'winners', whether in business or in his passion for sports competition, made 'success' his mistress. He created a life away from his home and the drudgery of responsibility it symbolised for him as a husband and father. Meanwhile, their children, Junior and Dede, the latter born ten years after the conclusion of *T in T*, suffered a pattern of parental neglect which left both emotionally scarred."

My above suggested Program Preface was written before viewing the video film of the 1986 production mounted by the Vienna State Opera which followed the opera's international premieres by its various commissioning Arts bodies, the Houston Grand Opera (1983), The Kennedy Center and the La Scala Opera House, Milan (both in 1984). The librettist, Stephen Wadsworth, directed all but the Houston premiere and in viewing the video it is obvious that he himself sought a solution to the problem of lost clarity created by a newly added Prologue and the radical decision to combine *T in T* and *AQP* into a single entity following the Houston premiere. Wadsworth's final solution was quite brilliant although it did create other problems, which I will later detail. Initially, the new Prologue was performed in a darkened theatre before the proscenium curtains. We hear but do not see a re-enactment of a fatal car accident in which one of the principal *T in T* characters, Dinah, is killed. In addition to the comments out of the darkness of bystanding witnesses to the accident, we hear the voices of an unseen chorus. Not only are the words they sing important clues as to what lies ahead, 'My Heart shall be the Garden' and 'Give All for Love, for Love is strong as death', but also their musical setting provides dramatic motives employed throughout the opera. For his Vienna production, the librettist/director staged the Prologue still in darkness, but looking onto an open proscenium rather than, as originally conceived, upon closed house curtains. There was now the addition of a projection screen on which, immediately following the sound of the fatal automobile crash, we view silent home movies of our leading characters, Sam and Dinah with their children Junior and Dede. We are outside their *little white house in Suburbia, USA,* at a much earlier time in their marriage. At the same time, to either side of the projection screen we begin to see the flashing lights of police cars and an ambulance. As we hear the voices of unseen bystanders and the choir, we view films of 'young' Sam trying to engender his love for sport to a very young, clumsy Junior who is seen to be hopeless at it. Junior's affection is directed towards his younger sister, an important plot seed to be planted early. Equally important is Dede's obvious need to be her Daddy's girl. She proudly shows off to the camera his silver sport's trophy. The need for a father's love and approval as well as the symbolic sporting object will later prove to be of key significance. An unsteady hand held camera, obviously being managed by Junior, photographs Sam and Dinah dancing. The only things we do not witness are the early signs of growing dysfunction within the family, which is the basic plot of *T in T*. If the audience is to fully comprehend the climactic events they are to witness when the first scene of *AQP* finally begins, they should possess some knowledge of the total alienation that exists between Sam and his children these many years later.

WEST SIDE MAESTRO

It helps us to comprehend better the reasons behind Dinah's violent death or possible suicide as depicted in the Prologue and the emotional wreckage we witness in the scenes to follow.

This new staging concept added by Wadsworth, an inspired director's solution, did have its downside. The simultaneous juxtaposition of both the car accident staged in darkness to either side of the projection screen and the viewed *T in T* film flashback is difficult for an audience to take in at one go. One tends to either concentrate only on the accident, taking in only bits of meaning from the film, or one concentrates on the film trying to extract its full significance, thus missing out the important details of the accident. Perhaps, if the home movie, relatively short in length, were to be shown in silence and then at a final frozen image it was interrupted by the short orchestral and choral prelude to the opera followed by the accident sequence, one would then achieve 'the best of all possible worlds.'

The Prologue moves without pause into the first scene. Our initial introduction to the cast of characters does not enlist our sympathy even though the action takes place at a funeral home and incorporates a final memorial tribute to the deceased, Dinah. Anger and resentment rather than condolence and regret pervade the atmosphere. Emotions are spewed out in diverse forms indiscriminately by the various characters depending upon their personal agenda.

Sam sits in morose silence for the greater part of the Act. When he finally gives vent to his rage, we discover him to be even more resentful, selfish, self-righteous and self-absorbed than in the past. The other guests attending the funeral don't improve the social atmosphere. Mr. Doc, the family physician, attends with his wife, Mrs. Doc. He proves to be a beleaguered husband, constantly apologising and compensating for his wife, a rude, vulgar aggressive virago. In the premiere version of the opera, Mrs. Doc was also presented as being sexually fixated on Dinah. Bill, Dinah's brother, who has taken charge of the funeral arrangements, reveals himself to be neurotically possessive towards his dead younger sister and obviously loathes Sam. Susie, Dinah's best friend, tries to boost everyone's general level of spirits as she deals with her own confusion trying to understand and come to terms with the violence of Dinah's death. Dinah's analyst of forty years spends all his time avoiding questions regarding his former patient's possible motives for committing suicide and the funeral director, attempting to glean enough information about the deceased and her mourning family, discovers that his 'clichés' for all occasions' don't seem to fit the highly neurotic situation into which he is thrust and for which he has been hired to provide a semblance of dignity and order. The chorus play a dual role, both introspective and retrospective, much as the chorus in Bach's St Matthew Passion. They are stationed unseen in the orchestra pit. Their vocal comments range from pertinent active participation in the stage dialogue to reflective comment pointing the way forward to resolution.[260]

Last to enter are Dede, her Canadian husband, Francois, and finally, Junior, who bursts in while the memorial service is taking place. There has been much gossip about the three of them spread about by Mrs. Doc prior to their entrance. Junior, now forty years old, is homosexual and deeply psychotic. He has been living in Canada, looked after by Dede and Francois who, in this highly convoluted exposition, turns out to have been Junior's lover before marrying Dede. The chorus pithily sums up the situation with the choice vernacular phrase, 'What a fucked-up family!'

Despite the overall cosmetic appearance of a plot and characters that would only engage an audience of a morbid disposition who thrived on misery and neurosis, *A Quiet Place* proves to be a riveting, moving experience for the listener who suspends judgement until he/she obtains a deeper understanding of the characters and permits them to interact within and come to terms with the new circumstances in which they have been thrust.

In what we must now accept as the final statement of the composer, all subsidiary characters disappear once the funeral service is over. Andrew Porter, critic of the New Yorker magazine, in the second of two positive

---

[260] The vocal score indicates that non-singing super-numeraries are to be used on stage to fill out the number of mourners. This group appear to be making the participating comment actually being supplied by the unseen chorus.

reviews of the opera, felt that this created an imbalance in restricting the remainder of the opera to the family quartet after the heavily populated interaction of characters in the first scene. Porter also regretted the incorporation of *T in T* into the body of the opera believing it to weaken the structure. He went even further, viewing the new opera as strong enough to stand on its own without its thirty-year-old antecedent.

While I admired both of Porter's reviews, superb examples of well-researched, well thought out, highly original essays, I disagree strongly with his revised conclusions. *T in T* and *AQP* both represent an ongoing family tragedy classically resulting from the inherent character defects of its principals. The new *AQP* characters of Bill and Susie were only names of unidentified, unseen characters in *T in T*. They first achieve specific substance in *AQP* and serve their purpose fully in the plot exposition of the first scene. The plot twist of Mrs. Doc's sexual fantasies regarding Dinah, said to be autobiographically based upon the composer's marriage, only served to 'over-egg the pudding'. By the end of the Act 1 funeral scene, Sam and Dinah's dysfunctional marriage has already revealed to us a legacy of family neurosis and psychosis. To bring this domestic tragedy to a dramatically satisfying conclusion, the librettist's full concentration in his re-write had to be directed towards clarifying and developing the principal family relationships without distracting, confusing and, perhaps, further alienating the audience from the already complex plot and its initially unattractive main characters. The two sub-plots involving Dinah's brother and Susie, Dinah's best friend, on the one hand and Mrs. Doc on the other only served to add additional sexual confusion to an already erotically drenched story line. For the sake of clarity alone, they had to go. As for the incorporation of *T in T* into the body of the opera, it was both a brilliant theatrical and musical stroke. It was the suggestion of the conductor, John Mauceri, who premiered the revised version of *AQP* at La Scala. L and his librettist were fortunate to have so stage-wise a colleague. Not immersed in the daily *sturm und drang* of their collaborative, creative process, Mauceri was able to take a fresh look at the entirety and come up with a simple, (always the best), and most effective theatrical solution for welding such two disparate works together and have them integrate logically. While *T in T* is only forty-five minutes in length it is packed with detail regarding every aspect of Sam and Dinah's life together. Among its sub-plots, the parental indifference towards Junior strikes the strongest chord followed by Dinah's dependence upon an analyst. All other unseen but named characters serve only as anonymous foils to help reveal other aspects of Sam and Dinah's personality complexities.

For audiences new to the work in its original form, the debut of *AQP* in Houston presented the following theatrical and musical problems:

T in T with its vast amount of character and plot detail preceded a long intermission. *AQP* then opened with a funeral scene exploding with catharsis, accusation, recrimination, innuendo, guilt, denial and three additional sub-plots mostly regurgitating from characters we have never met before and all of who sing in a musical style light years removed from that of *T in T*.

It is not surprising that the work opened to generally hostile reviews. On the surface it seemed to demand from its audience a collective Mensa brain and the gift of total recall. It took an Andrew Porter to see past the work's teething problems and to assess the originality of its creators' accomplishment in terms of its theatrical form and musical treatment of vernacular language sung in an inchoate fashion by characters interacting under emotional stress. He went as far as to liken its plot to Richard Wagner's *Ring* trilogy whose pervading father figure, the mythological Teutonic god, Wotan, through his personal behaviour, errors in judgement in both his family and business dealings. Above all, his neglect and withholding of love from his children, who possessed the devotion to save him from himself, eventually crushes his family and brings about the destruction of everything for which he believed he stood.

The insertion of *T in T* as two flashback sequences in Act Two creates a new validity for the earlier work on several levels. The consistent tonal and musical theatre oriented melodic style offers relief contrast to the much more complex and contemporary musical setting of words encountered in

AQP up to that point. At the same time, as flashbacks to a period thirty years previous, its more conservative musical language reflecting that period comes off as a theatrical stroke, as logical as if planned as an integral part of the AQP's musical structure. There are additional echoes of 'other times' that occur in *AQP*. The librettist speaks of the thread of *remembered intimacies* with which the principal characters of the drama must deal and come to terms. Contemporary situations serve to trigger off past memories. Following the funeral service, Sam, the guests now gone and alone with his guilt, faces the three young people, Dede, Francois and Junior, who are living symbols of his failure. He rails against all three as well as his dead wife. He was born to win and they have all made him a loser. His words form a rambling accusation filled with contradictions. Throughout his asides to himself, which are admissions of his own culpability and guilt, we hear quoted musical fragments from *T in T*. This huge outpouring of self-pity brings no reaction from either his children or Francois. They are frozen in time, his outburst precipitating for each a memory, a difficult youthful moment when, seeking understanding, they reached out in personal need not to their mother but to their father. The child's need of a father's love, approval and forgiveness is the underlying thread of *AQP*. Later, in Act Three, another flashback occurs, again at a moment of stress, when a children's game of tag between Junior and Dede is interrupted by the arrival of Francois. Dede rushes to embrace Francois. Junior senses a new kind of intimacy that has developed between them. Again time stops and we relive the moment in Canada at Dede's birthday party when Junior first introduced her to Francois, his then lover. Then, as now, Junior, seeing them together, experiences a sense of jealousy towards both Dede and Francois, each of whom he views as his personal possession.

To express its panoply of emotions musically, *AQP* uses a variety of tonal, polytonal and non-tonal techniques, which are closely wedded to its text. The non-tonal techniques dominate in moments of stress and conflict while emotions expressing need, care, concern, or resolution is expressed tonally. The music for Junior, whose unseen character was established and essential to the plot of *T in T*, is invariably tonal in keeping with the musical character of the earlier opera. This is exemplified in both his two Act I arias, *I'm sorry*

WEST SIDE MAESTRO

I'm late, and his outpouring of paternal resentment, *Hey, Big Daddy,* performed in Broadway-style. Again in Act Two, during his psychotic episode when he taunts Francois with his confession of incest with his sister when they were children, and in Act Three, when brother and sister recreate the childhood game of tag that they invented in their dead mother's garden, the music is rooted in tonality. Indeed, the Act Three aria is created from and accompanied by a fragment of the third movement of Mendelssohn's Violin concerto. In contrast, the music for the Dede character, born ten years after the events of *T in T,* is, generally, twelve tone in style, in keeping with the writing for most of the new first act characters of *AQP.* As she and her father, influenced by the memory of her mother, begin to rebuild their relationship, her music becomes more and more tonal. It is Francois, however, Dede's husband, who will prove to be the force for reconciliation. It is through his presence that Sam and his children begin their journey towards accommodation and acceptance. Even in the midst of complex twelve-tone ensemble passages in Act I, the sung contributions of Francois remain completely tonal. The subtlest use of ambiguous tonal techniques occurs in the final fifteen minutes of the opera at a moment of euphoria when 'all seems right with the world, God is love and all are going to live happily-ever-after.' At this moment of seeming positive resolution, the musical language suddenly becomes non-tonal. This rejection of tonality when one might expect the richest of diatonic settings is as brilliant as it is subtle. It is a subtext that reveals the fragility of the bond that the principal characters have forged and anticipates the collision of personalities about to take place. When the first disagreement arises regarding something as simple as the assigning of bedrooms, a huge row ensues which climaxes in Junior suffering another psychotic episode, snatching his dead mother's diary from which his father has just been reading and throwing it into the air with such force that its pages are scattered everywhere. It is this sobering act that shocks all to silence. Still in the middle of his episode Junior, now regressed to his childhood, once again reaches out desperately for his father by re-enacting that moment when, having been caught in a compromising situation with his younger sister, he came to fantasise that his father had shot him in punishment. Sam, in his confusion, does not fully understand what is taking place or the meaning of his son's hand stiffly formed into the shape of a gun but he hears Junior's cry for help and takes the boy in his arms to comfort him. Dede and Francois approach Sam. She reaches out tentatively and takes her father's hand as the unseen chorus intones an *Amen*. This *Amen* is very much rooted in the key of C but with other interposed dissonant tones which could conceivably form another chord. More likely, they are intended as overtone partials of the C chord itself to include that famous *F sharp* which became the composer's public, passionate declaration in *Mass*, "I believe in *F sharp*". In terms of the drama, this second interpretation of an unstable final chord implies that what has taken place within this dysfunctional family is far from resolution. It is not an ending but only a beginning.

The video and CD recordings of the opera both emanate from live performances given at the Vienna State Opera in 1986. The sound recording with an excellent libretto containing biographies of the artists, the story of the creation of the opera by the librettist, Stephen Wadsworth, a synopsis of the various scenes, the full text in four languages and photographs of the Vienna production has been produced by Deutsche Grammophon. The video, produced by ORF, Austrian Radio and Television, not commercially available, would provide an important adjunct to the schedules of Public Service and Arts Television Networks.

The telecast and compact disc recording represent the same definitive performance in two different media. The casting is quite good throughout. Sung in American English, the diction is impressively clear. So clear, in fact, that one can listen without the aid of the libretto except during the several complex ensembles that occur in each act. One is loathe to single out any individual from such a uniformly fine group of singers but deserving special mention is Beverly Morgan as *Dede* for her exceptional diction and musical accuracy in a singing role of enormous range and difficulty and Chester Ludgin as *'Old' Sam* for the rich acting values he brings to an extremely taxing dramatic and musical role. Ludgin, a veteran of American musical theatre, uses his vast wealth of stage experience to give 'Old' Sam genuine dimension. Among the cameo roles, Clarity James as *Mrs. Doc* creates a character who is as nasty a bit of work as one would never hope to meet socially. Hers is a standout performance of an interesting sub-principal role. Wendy White's Dinah in the *T in T* flashbacks combines both a wonderful mezzo-soprano with beautiful sound and security at both the top and bottom ends of her vocal range with a strong theatrical sense. Little, subtle inflections applied to her words provide both clarity and that extra bit of meaning to the text. The *T in T* Jazz Trio, that serves as a kind of Greek Chorus, unfortunately suffer at times from poor internal balance. Their three generally excellent, well matched voices capture the style beautifully in the quiet sections but when they are required to sing out, the girl vocalist asserts herself far too strongly and all semblance of trio balance ceases to exist. This could have resulted from a rush of performer's adrenaline or it may simply be bad microphone placement. This recording is, after all, the composite result of several *live* performances. More than likely, however, it is the consequence of too much encouragement during coaching rehearsals.

Although *Trouble in Tahiti* has now been integrated into *A Quiet Place*, as far as recording, video and live performance are concerned, it continues to enjoy a highly popular separate life. As a separate entity, the public has long had the opportunity to become familiar with it for over forty-five years as a mini-opera, available on record, television or, as most often presented, as part of an operatic double bill. I first came to know it as a student at Tanglewood. It was mounted by the Berkshire Music Center opera department in a newly revised version during the summer of 1952 following its premiere, the previous June, at Brandeis University. I attended many of the rehearsals that summer in L's company as one of his students. Sarah Caldwell directed and Seymour Lipkin conducted. A young mezzo, an unknown newcomer, Beverly Wolff, sang *Dinah*. To describe her performance as sensational is to understate everyone's view at the time. In Broadway tradition, she 'stopped the show' at each performance with her rendition of Dinah's parody of the movies, *Trouble in Tahiti*, ("What a terrible, awful movie"). Less than three months following that summer's Berkshire Festival, Beverly, with David Atkinson as Sam, repeated her Tanglewood success in the NBC Opera Company's television production of *T in T*. During my research, I was able to relive this marvellous early telecast at New York's unique Museum of Television and Radio which possesses a kinescope of this 1952 production among its more than two hundred Leonard Bernstein listings of televised and film recordings available for viewing to anyone who walks through its doors. *T in T* was then recorded for LP by MGM Records with the same cast under the direction of Arthur Winograd. In 1973, L conducted a version for London Weekend Television. Produced by Humphrey Burton, its highly original approach combined animation that surrounded and interacted with the live performers. Well cast and superbly executed, it is now commercially available on video[261]. The soundtrack of this performance is also on release by Sony Classical as part of a three CD musical portrait of L's Theatre Works. This London production features the best sung and acted 'Young Sam', Julian Patrick, and an all-round good performance by Nancy Williams as Dinah. Miss Williams, however, doesn't quite match the secure vocal quality and sheer beauty of Wendy White's Dinah in the *T in T* portions of *AQP*. Miss White possesses a naturally produced voice, which she uses skilfully and expressively, without any noticeable sign of the very fast vibrato which marks Nancy Williams' vocal performance throughout the video. In addition, her complete change of pace in Dinah's show-stopping send-up of the movies, *Trouble in Tahiti*, reveals a genuine flair for musical comedy. All this is topped off by a charming and youthful appearance, which combine to project the right *thirty-something* age for the character.

Sony's re-mix for the CD version of London Television's video soundtrack is very close up and the brilliant orchestra writing becomes fierce at times in competition with the singers. This problem doesn't exist in the video version of the same performance. In contrast, the newer DG recording of AQP displays a more natural balance between voice and orchestra in the *T in T* portions.

The staging for *T in T* in the video of *A Quiet Place* is conceived in natural, realistic terms. Props, a desk for Sam's office, a leather reclining couch for Dinah's visit to her psychiatrist, etc., and projected backdrops serve for the various changes of scene. One other important dramatic element is added,

---

[261] This version of *TinT* is at present commercially available only in the U.S.A. from KULTUR International Films.

that of the presence of 'Old' Sam. As the flashbacks are his memories he is seen observing and reacting but never speaking within the whole framework of the revised *T in T* scenes within the newer opera. It is an interesting theatrical touch. The original Austrian telecast of *AQP* enjoyed two distinct pluses. It was introduced with effulgent Viennese panache, in German, of course, by a popular Austrian presenter who provided listeners with a very full background of the opera and all the additional plot information regarding its characters dating back to *T in T*, making the drama totally comprehensible from the rising of the first curtain. There was also a half hour intermission feature on L and his musical love affair with Vienna and all things Viennese which included one of their popular comedian/impersonators doing an hilarious send-up comparing Bernstein with Karajan. It is iconoclastically backstabbing, done as only the Viennese know how.

The choice comes down to the interest and developed tastes of the listener/viewer. If one is not a fan of grand opera the clear choice is the video of *T in T*. I cannot envision that any devotee of L's music would want to be without the Sony / Bernstein Theatre Album with its high-powered performances of *T in T* accompanied by classic NY Philharmonic performances of his most famous show, film and ballet music[262].

For the committed opera lover, I view *A Quiet Place* as a must. I don't begin to pretend that one will instantly go around the house whistling dodecaphonic tunes from Act I, but it is a riveting work for the theatre and, in agreement with Andrew Porter's assessment, one of the tiny handfuls of truly important American operas. Unfortunately, there has been far too much written about Bernstein, the man of unlimited indiscretion, and this has served to drown everything that he has composed in a surrounding ocean of psycho-babble. None of his original compositions since the *Kaddish*

---

[262] A 'must' for all Bernstein fans and anyone else who enjoys first rate theatre music, this album includes all the ballet and vocal music from *On The Town* with a cast that includes its authors, Betty Comden and Adolph Green plus other members of the original Broadway cast, the Symphonic Dances from *West Side Story* and the Symphonic Suite from the film *On The Waterfront* definitively performed by the NY Philharmonic, two ballet suites, *Fancy Free* and *Facsimile* and the opera, *Trouble in Tahiti*.

WEST SIDE MAESTRO

Symphony has escaped analysis for its autobiographical meanings and I have to plead 'guilty' along with the rest, certainly in terms of examining his relationship with authority figures on every conceivable level. If I beg 'special privilege', I can at least claim to have witnessed ten years of it at first hand and viewed its influence on his personal behaviour as it affected his musical persona. In the final analysis one must or, at least, should, listen to the music composed from the Philharmonic years onward without external preconceptions and associations, especially in regard to the two major compositions surrounding which the greatest storms of controversy have arisen, *Mass* and *Quiet Place*. Listening on a one to one basis to this music, products of his mature and ripening old age, without preconceptions or attempts to search out external meanings beyond those peripheries set up by the texts themselves, will reveal whether we, as individuals, can relate to and empathise not only to the told tale but the manner in which it is told. The secret, as with most things in life, is not to leap to judgement but to allow oneself time to acquire familiarity before forming an opinion. In both instances where these two works are involved, it is a pity that two brilliant videos are not available, the 1981 Kennedy Center 10th anniversary production for *Mass* and the ORF/Vienna Opera production of *A Quiet Place*. Seeing them performed as works for the theatre, the medium for which they were created makes the best and most powerful case for both. Lacking these, there are John McClure's astonishing Sony album production of *Mass* and Hans Weber's equally well-produced live recording of *A Quiet Place*.

Without gaining familiarity and public acceptance via some innovative opera management or a colourful entrepreneur with the perception of the legendary Sol Hurok, these two works, especially *A Quiet Place*, may be forced to languish for the next twenty years. Perhaps then, when all the Bernstein biographies have been long remaindered and forgotten and all that remains is the music to stand or fall on its own merits, these works will find the public recognition that this musician believes they deserve.[263]

---

[263] Indeed, in less than twenty years since I first began work on this two volume compendium of memories, research, analysis and, as I hope my readers agree, informed opinion, A Quiet Place has resurfaced in New York as part of the New York City Opera Company's 2010 season. It has

WEST SIDE MAESTRO

received a generally good critical reception and it is hoped that it will remain in that company's repertoire.

Other Works for Solo Instruments & Orchestra

Serenade
after Plato's 'Symposium'

The composition of *Serenade* served L in a multiplicity of ways. It fulfilled a much-delayed commission for the Koussevitzky Foundation dating back to 1951 [264]. It also served to fulfil a commitment to his friend, the noted violinist, Isaac Stern, who had approached him to write a solo work for violin and orchestra. The five movement concerto was begun in the autumn of 1953 and was completed in the white heat of inspiration during the summer months of 1954. It is scored for solo violin, strings, harp and a large variety of percussion. An elaborate program is printed in the score revolving about an imagined *Symposium* at the home of the Greek poet Agathon during which, after a goodly quantity of wine has been consumed, a heated discourse between Socrates and other Greek philosophers takes place upon the various aspects of love. L's biographer, Humphrey Burton, writes that there is no known record of when L conceived the idea to base the concerto on Plato's *Symposium* but projects that it was shortly before the completion of the work. Knowledge of the program makes an interesting sidelight but bears no importance in lending greater pleasure to the listener of this inspired addition to the concerto repertoire.

Isaac Stern performed both the world premiere in Italy at the Venice Festival in the autumn of 1954 with the composer conducting the Israel Philharmonic and the American premiere in New York in April of the following year with L conducting the Symphony of the Air, (the former NBC Symphony Orchestra), the latter performance subsequently recorded by CBS Records. As mentioned earlier, *Serenade* also served as the score for Herbert Ross's ballet *Serenade for Seven* introduced at the Spoletto Festival in Italy in 1959.

---

[264] *Serenade* is dedicated to the memory of his mentor, Serge Koussevitzky and his first wife, Natalie

WEST SIDE MAESTRO

No Bernstein work is any one thing and as with all his compositions *Serenade* is a mix of many influences and many styles but, as is also invariably the case, it all comes out sounding like Bernstein. From the implication of its title derived from the Italian word *sereno (calm)* to its claimed inspiration from Greek antiquity, this work is neo-classic with a vengeance. It is explosively exuberant in the best Bernstein tradition on the one hand and movingly lyric in an unusually unsentimental fashion on the other. The writing for the solo violin is superbly idiomatic and the sound palate achieved with relatively modest orchestral means equals Bartok's imaginative masterpiece written for a similar combination of instruments.[265] Indeed both composers choose to open their works with a slow fugue. It is the voice of the solo violin that introduces *Serenade*.

Within its solo statement is embodied the thematic material which will generate the entire concerto. The composer further refines the method of composition he employed in the *Age of Anxiety*, that of using elements from a previous movement or variation to generate material for what follows, analogous to the continuous generation of one idea from another. In this instance, a three second fragment that opens Serenade originates the entire movement. This single idea gives birth to a chain of ideas all born from each other and this process extends itself to the end of the piece. As the composer explains in a Preface to his orchestra score, "The *relatedness* of the movements does not depend on common thematic material, but rather on a system whereby each movement evolves out of elements in the preceding one." The fourth movement of *Serenade* has been singled out for special praise. It is by any standard a truly beautiful creation with its opening serene mood whose combined bowed and plucked murmuring string accompaniment evokes the pastoral spirit of a Vivaldi concerto. Much has been written regarding this movement as the crowning achievement of the concerto but that is to underrate the quality of writing and originality throughout. Critical attention, although not of the same positive tone as that applied to the lyric *Adagio*[266], has been drawn to the use of jazz syncopations and chordal writing in the final movement. I refer to printed comment by

---

[265] Bartok: *Music for Strings, Percussion and Celeste*
[266] *Adagio*: from the Italian, meaning 'slowly'.

WEST SIDE MAESTRO

Howard Taubman of the NY Times, "Mr. Bernstein writes jazz with a flair, but does it really belong in the context of this piece? ... Just as this work...has begun to persuade that it is going to be all music, it fritters away the opportunity. Then fine passages appear and are again dissipated in easy excitement. Too bad!" One must judge such criticism in light of the actual overt use of traditional jazz sounds all of which are logically arrived at and treated convincingly in its relation to and interplay with the solo part. Within the final movement, it consists of only thirty-six measures of music within a three hundred-seventy measure concerto. The composer may have lead with his chin when he volunteered in advance, "If there is a hint of jazz in the celebration, I hope it will not be taken as anachronistic Greek party-music, but rather the natural expression of a contemporary American composer imbued with the spirit of that tireless dinner party."

As with every Bernstein premiere, there were detractors of considerable high musical profile, in this instance yet again Virgil Thompson and, as already reported, the soon to become powerful Bernstein supporter, Howard Taubman of the NY Times. Certainly if you poll the number of internationally established violinists along with the present group of 'fiddle' prodigies, all of whom have made *Serenade* a part of their repertoire or are represented by recordings of this concerto, Virgil Thompson's characterisation of the work as "a negligible contribution to music" holds no currency whatever. In time, *Serenade* has come to be hailed by performers and critics alike as one of L's best and most original works.

Regarding videotapes and CD recordings, the work is very well represented. The two original LP performances recorded by the composer for CBS initially revealed a variety of problems, both musical and technical. The earliest with Isaac Stern, for whom *Serenade* was composed, features the Symphony of the Air as the accompanying ensemble. This monaural recording has now been impressively improved through digital technology for the new Sony Bernstein *Century* issue. The SOA string section tends to be a bit ponderous but Stern, in top form, delivers a performance that is quite special. With the disc's coupling of L's 1950 first recording of his *Age of Anxiety* symphony with Lucas Foss as soloist and the NY Philharmonic in great form, these performances are very much in contention with the more modern stereo recordings. The second CBS/Sony Bernstein recording featuring Zino Francescatti as soloist, recorded eleven years later, suffers from an ultra close microphone set-up for both soloist and orchestra. By the time both the NY Philharmonic violins and violas join the soloist the orchestra accompaniment has already begun to dominate. With the next entrance of ponderous and overblown cellos and basses, any chamber quality of the work has flown. Francescatti takes a romantic view of the solo part. As with any of this soloist's recordings, it is technically sure from start to finish, especially the finish, but, except for the lyric Adagio, which he projects exquisitely, he comes across as somewhat uncomfortable with the work. Certainly with all the overpowering scrambling for notes and the forcing of tone from the instruments around him, he must have felt a bit under siege. The fault for the rough and ready, unbalanced orchestral accompaniment was the result of a combination of factors. The sound set-up using very close miking, which the composer must have approved and perhaps even requested, is the major problem. The choice of the over-resonant acoustic of Manhattan Center for a work whose musical implications lean more towards chamber orchestra proportions did not serve the work well either. Finally, it is quite obvious that the composer opted for all the string players to play everything in sections where his initial thoughts were to avoid any more than half of the first and second violin sections to be playing at any given time. In fact, specific addenda score instructions advise the conductor to follow such a procedure. I view these second thoughts a miscalculation and this recording is more than proof of this. There is, happily, a third recording with L at the helm that reveals all the marvels of this exquisite work, recording and performance-wise. The soloist is Gidon Kremer with the Israel Philharmonic Orchestra on the Deutsche Grammaphon label. All the participants are in top form. Their slightly dry, impersonal neo-classic approach to performance, usually associated with the music of Stravinsky beginning with his early *Octet*, suit this work to perfection. *Serenade* is listed in the Unitel Catalogue as part of an all Bernstein concert performed at the Barbican in 1986, which was recorded for video in stereo. Again the soloist is Gidon Kremer and the composer conducts the London Symphony Orchestra. The performance and sound are of high quality although there are small ensemble problems experienced in the first and fourth movements. The tape also contains the Chichester Psalms with a young Aled Jones the boy soprano soloist and the *Age of Anxiety* featuring Krystian Zimmerman in the difficult piano role. L's conducting is quite controlled throughout. This concert was performed in the presence of Her Majesty, the Queen and the Duke of Edinburgh. An amusing sidelight of the concert was L beginning the national anthem, God Save The Queen, before Her Majesty and the Duke were seated forcing them to stand in the aisle waiting for it to be concluded before they could take their seats. Oh, to have been a Royal fly on the wall of the breakfast room of Buckingham Palace the following morning. There must have been a good deal of interesting chat over the toast and kippers that day.

Halil
Nocturne for Solo Flute

Prior to my first listening encounter with *Halil,* I underestimated the full scope of what L had in store for this simply named but unusual, harmonically hybrid composition for solo Flute. The word *Halil* itself is Hebrew for 'flute'. Its subtitle delineates its character and orchestral makeup, Nocturne for Solo Flute with Piccolo, Alto Flute, Percussion, Harp and Strings which, except for the solo woodwind contribution, is very much the same accompaniment for *Serenade*. The principal difference between the handling of the orchestra accompaniment for *Halil* and that of *Serenade* is that the flute presence is much more dominant throughout than the violin in *Serenade*, which, incidentally, is twice the length of this 'nocturne'. *Halil* has enjoyed a very good press so it seems rather begrudging taking a minority view, which in quite obvious ways finds me writing about the work in a manner for which I have criticised others. It strikes me that this sixteen-minute miniature concerto attempts to be all things to all people. Its musico/philosophical antecedence dates back to L's Harvard Norton Lectures and his own 'Unanswered Question', to be or not to be *tonal?*' This work reveals that same "ambiguous tug-of-war between being rooted and *partly* rooted in *tonality*"[267] upon which L expounded so eloquently in his

---

[267] See chapter 7, The Unanswered Question, pgs. 323

quest to find an answer to *The Unanswered Question*. Much has been made of the work beginning with a dodecaphonic tone row. The reality is that no sooner has the row been set out then you have disclaimers in the form of immediate tonal references. L spoke at great length in his sixth Norton Lecture regarding *sincerity* in music. I found myself thinking back to this challenging question, which was posed in relation to compositions by Verdi, the Kinks, Mozart, and Wagner, and wondering whether *Halil* met L's own criteria for '*sincerity*'. Was it written out of a genuine need for self-expression or was it the product of a cold intellectual decision to provide his publishers with a relatively short work that filled a gap in the classical music market and, at the same time, continued to mark him as 'a player' among American composers? I find the program note L supplied as less than helpful in shedding light on this short and, in many ways, effective mini-concerto. One has no call to doubt that L was moved by the story of Yadin Tannenbaum, a nineteen-year-old Israeli flautist, who, as a serving member in the Israeli army, was killed in his tank in the Sinai desert in 1973. L's love and commitment to the country and its ongoing struggles mirrored in the microcosm of its orchestra, the Israel Philharmonic, had held a special and particular place in his life and affections since his first working visit to Israel in 1947. However, *Halil* was written eight years after Tannenbaum's death in the Sinai War not in the white heat of the emotion of the happening.

L describes *Halil* as unlike any work he has ever written, a struggle between tonal and non-tonal forces, which seems to describe the developing musical scenario for everything he composed from 1954 onward. He also widens the sense of struggle to include war and the threat of war. If that were not sufficient he broadens his agenda even further to include the overwhelming desire to live, and the consolations of art, love and the hope for peace, which just about covers all bases. He then generalises upon the nature of the work as "a kind of night music...an ongoing conflict of nocturnal images"; and further from the general to the particular - "wish-dreams, nightmares, repose, sleeplessness, night-terrors and sleep itself", and, to end melodramatically with a poetic analogy to "sleep itself" - "*Death's twin brother*".

WEST SIDE MAESTRO

If we accept the general designation of *night music* to describe *Halil*, and many of the sounds and moods of *Halil* certainly conform to works of Mahler and Bartok to which we have applied this label, and then proceed on to L's long list of specifics, the programme takes on an autobiographical allusion to the composer himself who was a chronic insomniac. Such an interpretation seems to hold greater validity than the Israeli connection. However, as I have underlined previously, lack of knowledge of the elaborate programs attached to his instrumental compositions does not impede the enjoyment of the music itself.

What is it about this music that I find unconvincing, even 'insincere'? I have previously taken an opposing view to the strong criticism levelled at L for *eclecticism*, i.e.: borrowing stylistically from other composers. That which, for the most part ignored by L's critics in trying to gather support for the repetitive, negative *eclecticism* argument they put forward, is the litmus test as to whether the music sounds more like the composer whose style L has adapted or like an original Bernstein work indelibly stamped with his own personality. I have invariably opted for the latter view. Michael Tilson Thomas in conversation with the writer and music critic Edward Seckerson made the following pertinent remarks, "...all of (L's) music is filled with references to his, and to the whole world's, musical past, but he has a unique way of presenting even the most familiar material, and then seeing whether it will hold its own against an all-out attack of compositional techniques...What's interesting about his music is that one senses *him*; the more you are aware of his personality, the better it is." These statements of Michael Tilson Thomas, with which I totally agree, do not, in my opinion, validly describe *Halil*. I have carefully studied and analysed the score and then listened a multiplicity of times to the DG recording with Jean-Pierre Rampal as soloist. I find my attention consistently distracted by its stylistic references to other composers, such as Bartok and Copland. The unusual opening of the work and the lovely slow theme that follows are pure Bernstein. The opening displays the composer's new voice, a row of notes one would more readily associate with an Alban Berg melody than with the typical Bernstein instantly whistle-able tune. But this tone row is far from unpleasant or uncommunicative. It is intriguing in shape and has a natural flow. Out of this strange introduction evolves a lovely slow and gentle tonal theme played by the solo flute accompanied by the harp, a vibraphone and the barest of string accompaniments. This is the Bernstein voice we have come to know which eventually surfaces even in his most complex compositions. The flute becomes silent as the strings and harp take up a rich setting of its lyric theme which subtly and without warning, moves to a new and brighter sounding key. This is violently interrupted by what appears to be new musical material but is, in fact, completely constructed from melodic fragments we have already heard. Its seeming unfamiliarity results from a variety of composer's 'tricks-of-the-trade' handled with all the cleverness at L's command, which is considerable.[268] For this listener, this phrase immediately presents two problems; the first, it projects as a *non sequitur* in style and substance to that which has come before, that is, it does not seem to proceed inevitably from what has preceded despite its musical antecedence. Secondly, and unfortunately, it sounds uncomfortably not merely like a passage reflecting Bartokian influence but one lifted directly from Bartok's Concerto for Orchestra. This association with another work without deliberately intending to be a quote, I view as genuinely distracting. The work, only sixteen minutes in length, is jam packed with all manner of musical complexities, which, for this listener, do not create a logical, and satisfying total musical experience. The composer, in conversation with Peter Gradenwitz, described it as "musically like an *essay*, a *study* on the struggle between tonality and non-tonality, almost like a Ph.D. dissertation." The mechanics of *Halil's* serious agenda seems to me to take precedence over the composer's inspiration. *Halil* certainly requires the listener's full concentration without distraction of any kind. Had the work's eclecticism been confined to a single, short instance, I would deserve to take my place

---

[268] Having aimed this volume at the non-musician music lover, I have purposely avoided the use of technical terms which would only confuse the reader. For those with theoretical knowledge the seemingly new Bartokian theme results from *augmentation,* the enlargement of a musical figure or phrase by lengthening the note values. It is accompanied by its own *diminution,* the opposite of augmentation.That occurs in a single bar of music. In the second bar of music the augmentation and diminution of the first bar are transformed into the continuation of the melody and accompaniment by the device of retrograde, repeating a musical phrase or theme backwards note for note. For readers interested in a more technical discussion of L's music, the only general reference available is Peter Gradenwitz's *Leonard Bernstein.*

among the nitpickers of America who constantly subjected L's music to this same kind of *Name That Tune* criticism. However, Bartok's shadow proves to be ubiquitous right up to the cadenza except for an intervening Allegro con brio, (fast and lively), section during which the spirit of Aaron Copland takes over with passages that might have come from the Copland of the 1920's. The *cadenza* for solo flute and percussion proves to be a watershed. It is brilliant, virtuoso, and fascinatingly inventive. It explores both the orchestral possibilities of the flute in all its registers from its lowest to highest notes and musically it continually juxtaposes tonal and non-tonal writing. The dramatic use of the timpani against the solo woodwind echoes Berlioz's similar juxtaposition in his *Scene in the Fields* from the *Fantastic Symphony*. Despite this possible reference, *Halil* takes on a more individual persona from the cadenza to the end, which is fully half the work. The freshness of the *cadenza* seems to cleanse the ears from the work's previous disjointed references and one does get caught up in the many moods still to come which lead along obscure tonal pathways until the return of the gentle tonal tune of the opening. Although welcome, in light of the work's fragmented nature it rings somewhat less true upon its return. The work ends unequivocally tonally in the key of D flat, alluded to from the start but never genuinely resolved till the very end.

The only recording in the catalogue is the DG compact disc featuring Jean Pierre Rampal with the composer conducting the Israel Philharmonic. No concert film is listed in Unitel's catalogue. As a performance it contains all the brilliance, colour and virtuosity the work demands. Among his late works, it represents an interesting and important experiment that moved L another step closer to evolving a fusion of a panoply of tonal and non-tonal techniques into a single personal and valid form of expression.

Three Meditations from *Mass* for Violoncello & Orchestra

This fine addition to the meagre repertoire for cello and orchestra is very welcome. In a preface note for the orchestral score, the composer expresses his thanks to his associate John Mauceri and his former assistant Jack Gottlieb for their assistance in preparing this work. Jack Gottlieb confirmed to me that the work evolved initially from a short score created by L, that is, some kind of shorthand outline of the new work from which his associates worked. The process most probably took the following form. Copies of the original orchestral scores to the first two Meditations, which in the final cello version are note for note transcriptions of the originals, were marked with pencilled instructions and crossings out to indicate L's transformational modifications. The third Meditation, however, unlike the first two, is a composite creation from three disparate excerpts from *Mass*. This would have required very detailed written instructions to piece it together as effectively as the final results reveal. Everything would then have been put into proper score form by his two assistants with perhaps their list of further editing suggestions and then presented to L for approval and further modification. A second score containing all the changes would then have been produced which, once approved, would have been sent to the publisher.

The *Three Meditations for Cello* were created for his friend and colleague, Mstislav Rostropovich on the occasion of Rostropovich's inaugural concert as music director of the National Symphony Orchestra at the Kennedy Center, Washington, DC, in the autumn of 1977. The program, an all-Bernstein affair, included three premiers, the overture, *Slava*, the *Three Meditations* and, most significant, *Songfest*, L's most notable song cycle based upon selected American poems encompassing themes of love, art and politics.

Mass, A Theatre Piece for Singers, Players & Dancers, lists three *Meditations* within its content structure. The first two Meditations are purely instrumental but the third Meditation is a polyphonic setting for choir of one of the seven Penitential Psalms, *De Profundus*, (Out of the depths I call thee, Lord). This did not lend itself to an instrumental transcription. The transformation of the first two *Meditations* was a matter of redistribution of parts in the creation of a solo cello line followed by subsequent editing of the instrumental texture to create a proper balance. The third Meditation, however, had to be entirely reconceived. This was done in the following manner. The Meditation begins with three pitched drums quietly repeating *ad libitum* a disjunct rhythmic pattern. This will serve as the connective tissue for the entire work and, at the same time, anticipate the music of the middle section of this movement. Over this quietly repeated rhythmic introduction, the solo cello plays a note for note transcription, (an octave lower), of the Epiphany from the Mas,s (scored originally for solo oboe with keyboard and percussion interjections). At the end of this long cello cadenza, the pitched drums, which have given way to other percussion instruments, restart their disjunct rhythm Now comes music from the Second Introit, *In Nomine Patris*, (In the Name of the Father), re-composed in the disjunct pattern of the drums. An instrumental dance within *In Nomine Patris*, also used in part two of the original *De Profundis*, forms the central section of this *Meditation*. This passionate dance music reaches a climax and fades away leaving only the rhythm of the pitched drums sounding. This pulsating drum beat links us to the closing section of this third Meditation. It begins with the solo cello leading the lower strings in the first verse of the final hymn that closes *Mass*. In the second verse of the hymn, the upper strings take over from the cello and at the cadence of each phrase the soloist intones yet another fragment of the Epiphany melody with which he opened this *Meditation*. At the final hushed string cadence, the solo cello completes the Epiphany melody and upon its final sustained note we hear for the last time the disjunctive rhythm of the pitched drums that fades to nothingness.

No video exists but the DG recording featuring Rostropovich with the composer conducting the Israel Philharmonic is everything one could ask for. Moreover the newly mastered coupling on this disc of five Bernstein works to include the *Divertimento* and *Halil* with Rampal as soloist makes this compact disc a must for all Bernstein aficionados.

Jubilee Games - Concerto For Orchestra

The *Concerto for Orchestra*, L's hybrid of hybrids, started life as a two movement work titled *Jubilee Games* written to celebrate the 1986 fiftieth anniversary of the Israel Philharmonic. L had first set pen to paper on this, for him, groundbreaking composition in the summer of '85. Predictably, the scenario of his work pattern for this commission was not to be any different than for others in the past. Its progress was understandably slow in light of yet another log jammed work calendar, which over-committed his services to other causes and events about which he felt equally passionate. There was the Journey for Peace tour during which he travelled to Japan for a commemorative Hiroshima concert, then back to Europe, on to Israel, a second tour to Japan, then Germany, followed by United States. A return to Europe marked important concert, recording and opera commitments, (*A Quiet Place)*, in Vienna followed by a Bernstein festival in London with the London Symphony Orchestra. One could go on with the list, enumerating the awards bestowed during this period, further concert recordings and tours but what it all adds up to composing-wise is yet another last minute rush towards another deadline. As on previous occasions, with his back against the wall, he again called upon the reliable services of always dependable colleagues, in this instance Sid Ramon and Jack Gottlieb, to help with the orchestration.

Jubilee Games was first heard on a two continent tour undertaken in the last months of 1986 by the Israel Philharmonic. The two movement version consisted of *Free-style Events*, the single most complex musical construction ever undertaken by L, and the *Diaspora Dances*, genuine Bernstein which, if lacking an instantly whistle-able tune did not lack energy, verve, a Hassidic touch plus a bit of Hindemith, Stravinsky, *Dybbuk* and *West Side Story*. As L once stated to Michael Tilson Thomas, "If you are going to steal, *steal classy.*" The composer himself describes the musical allusions of the *Diaspora Dances* as encompassing the flavour of the Middle East, the ghettos of Central-Europe plus a healthy helping of New York Jazz.

Jubilee Games continues the thread of L's profound identification with his Jewish heritage and deeply rooted sense of family, which serve as key unifying factors throughout his personal and creative life. This double identification held special relevance in his relationship with the Israel Philharmonic. All the orchestras with which he had long-term relationships were viewed as *his* families. Even the Vienna Philharmonic, whose history is scarred with rabid anti-Semitic behaviour and among whose ranks during

WEST SIDE MAESTRO

Bernstein's long tenure was numbered a former Nazi SS officer, was spoken of as his 'little brothers', his *Brüderlein*. With the Israelis, however, there was a *special* bond, perhaps *the* most 'special bond' of all. Not only were they his 'brothers', they were his *Jewish brothers*, God's chosen people inhabiting the land God had chosen for them, whose Biblical history and traditions he had learned at the feet of his father and from the synagogue elders who had helped him towards his official Jewish confirmation of manhood, his *bar-mitzvah*. L became an *ex-officio* Israeli citizen from the moment he first set foot in the Holy Land in 1947, not only in his own mind but in the minds of all that country's citizenry. Now he was helping their orchestra celebrate their fifty-year jubilee. How better than with a work inspired from an Old Testament parallel to a jubilee celebration of that exact number of years. In the book of *Leviticus*, chapter 25, verses 8-17, God commands Moses to say to the children of Israel to celebrate seven years of Sabbaths seven times, "forty and nine years", then "cause the trumpet of the Jubilee to sound ...on the Day of Atonement, (*Yom Kippur*), throughout all your land." The fiftieth year shall then be declared holy, a Jubilee year, and God directs, "ye shall proclaim Liberty throughout the land and unto the inhabitants thereof."[269]

With that as his starting point, L's fertile imagination went into top gear. Numerology had played a key role in the musical construction of his themes for the ballet *Dybbuk*. He came to *Jubilee Games* well practised in translating the Hebraic letters which made up his cardinal inspirational words, in this instance *sheva* and *hamishim*, (seven and fifty), into equivalent musical expression. Next there was the original meaning of the Hebrew word *Jovel*, from which the word *jubilee* is derived. *Jovel* in Hebrew is a homonym whose original ancient meaning was 'rams horn', the *shofar* of Biblical fame, the trumpet of Joshua, sounded by the Hebrews at the conclusion of all religious celebration as well as in battle. That's quite a stirring mix for a mind such as L's, addicted to playing word and numbers games. To these components he decided for the first time to employ *aleatoric* techniques. This unusual feature, already somewhat passé among contemporary composers who had made it their trademark, brought the

---

[269] This quote from Leviticus is inscribed upon America's famed *Liberty Bell* hanging in Independance Hall in Philadelphia, Pennsylvania.

element of chance into compositional techniques. *Aleatory* quite literally means 'a throw' of the dice' with all the mathematical implications and permutations it connotes. In musical terms it means 'involving random choice by the performer'. L's final solution in handling these materials in light of his decision to use *aleatory* techniques is quite complex and produces a certain degree of the resulting unpredictability expected. I will come back to my choice of phrase 'a certain degree' when I discuss the recording of this work.

Let me try to summarise this most unusual first movement, *Free Style Events*, the only one to use *aleatory* techniques. It is unique in sound among all of L's compositions except, perhaps, the taped quadraphonic opening of Mass with its four separate vocal group entries who eventually sing simultaneously in four different disjunct rhythmic patterns creating an aural sense of organised confusion and improvisation, the very essence and end result sought after in aleatory composition.

L's opening *idée fixe* is the word *sheva*, the Hebrew for the number seven. Amidst an energetic outburst of percussion, strings and horns, *sheva* is shouted or whispered by the players a total of seven times, which symbolically fulfils the Biblical injunction 'to celebrate seven years of Sabbaths seven times.' There is a final shout, *hamishim*, the Hebrew for fifty, the year of *Jubilee*. This entire first section is notated improvisationally without any specific indication of pitch. The composer instructs the players merely to freely choose seven tones rising scale-wise from any diatonic scale[270], preferably avoiding C Major. These free-choice scales are to be performed in a range of the instrument specifically indicated. The shout of *Hamishim* is the signal for the sounding of the *shofar*, the ram's horn here depicted by the brass section. The entrances for each of the brass instruments are roughly staggered. There are four traditional blasts played by the *shofar*, a short but sustained signal, a repetitive signal, a staccato

---

[270] Diatonic from the Greek *dia tonikis, 'at intervals of a tone'*. In the Western tonal system, diatonic music, major or minor, only uses notes that exclusively belong to one key. Therefore, if a strictly diatonic composition is in C Major all the melodies and chords would be derived only from the tones which comprise a C Major scale.

signal, and a signal sustained as long as possible by the player. The order in which the four signals are performed are the choice of each performer as he enters and begins to play. However, the pitches of the signal for each player are specifically prescribed by the composer. There is no attempt to co-ordinate these signals. They are to be played as the title of the movement suggests, in *free-style*. A kind of bridge section follows played very softly, *pianissimo*, by strings and woodwinds. As this fades a brass chorale begins for which the rhythmic structure, phrasing and register are precisely notated. The note pitches, however, are again 'freely chosen' by the performers from seven note scales provided by the composer. On a given cue, a taped version of the opening of the movement complete with shouts of *sheva* and ending with *hamishim* is played as a counterpoint against the live brass chorale. This ends in a final burst of energy as a new, totally improvised section begins with instrumental entrances controlled by a nod or a glance from the conductor. The improvised but exactly structured brass chorale returns, this time in counterpoint to another tape recording, this one of the earlier varied calls of the *shofar*. There is a composed short coda and the movement ends sharply with a much used Bernstein signature motif, perhaps best recognised from its use in *West Side Story* when *Rick* is stabbed by *Bernado* during the Act One *Rumble*. This *motif* appears in other movements of *Jubilee Games*. Studying the score of this most complex movement is fascinating and in this instance very precisely organised even if the end results seem less so.

Two movements were added to *Jubilee Games* but in the reverse order to their position in the score. The *Benediction* movement which now closes the four movement work had two previous reincarnations, first as a piano *Anniversary* dedicated to Aaron Stern, dean of the American Conservatory of Music in Chicago, and next as *Benediction*, a work for Baritone and Orchestra, composed for the rededication of a much refurbished Carnegie Hall in celebration of its reopening in 1986. It was then included and premiered by the Israel Philharmonic in 1988 as the central section of a three movement *Jubilee Games*. Still dissatisfied L added a fourth movement composed in January 1989 titled *Seven Variations of an*

WEST SIDE MAESTRO

Octatonic Theme[271]. The four movement work was re-titled *Concerto for Orchestra* and given its world premiere by the Israel Philharmonic in April 1989. The *Seven Variations* became the new second movement, *Mixed Doubles*. The *Diaspora Dances* were moved to the position of third movement and the *Benediction*, sung in Hebrew, now served as a logical conclusion.

It has been suggested that the newly-renamed *Mixed Doubles* was inspired by *Game of the Couples*, the second movement of Bela Bartok's *Concerto for Orchestra*. Except for the duple implication of their titles and their position within two works of the same title, there is nothing in form or content that would suggest any resemblance. The Bernstein *Mixed Doubles* is very sparely written, virtually chamber music, featuring in the first three variations couplings from dissimilar instrumental families, (flute/horn - trumpet/double bass - clarinet/trombone) and in variations four to seven couplings from the same family, (timpani/tuned percussion - two solo violins - alto flute/bass clarinet - oboe/bassoon). A coda for viola and cello follows and the work concludes with a unison tone played by all the solo instruments featured with the exception of the percussion. L wrote a short program note in which he explained that the *octatonic scale, which he had already employed when composing Dybbuk,* resulted in lending to the work 'a Near-Eastern, possibly Hebraic coloration.'

The *Diaspora Dances*, described earlier, provide an ideal example of the kind of mental gamesmanship that stimulated L's imagination. Each letter of the Hebrew alphabet, which predated the Arabic numerical system, also serves as a number. This assigning of a numerical value to each letter is called *gematria*. The rabbis would seek hidden meaning into words or phrases in the *Torah,* (The Five Books of Moses), or *Prophets* by adding the numerical value of their letters, totalling them, and then breaking them down into other combinations of letters which revealed further and deeper knowledge into the writings contained within this most holy of books to the Jewish nation. L's never-ending obsession with word and number games gave rise to his applying this system of *gematria* to music. For example, as

---

[271] *Octatonic* - eight tones

the dance element establishes itself at the opening of the *Diaspora Dances* we hear whispered the Hebrew word *chai* which means 'alive' and *chayim* which means 'life'. *Chai*, using numerical substitutions, adds up to the number 18. Ergo, L assigns an unusual rhythmic meter to the opening of the movement, 18 beats to each measure of music. The dance tune itself is divided into two parts and each part is made up of nine beats, which again total 18. The number 36 also joins this mystical cabalistic group. It is interpreted as *double hai*, **'twice** alive', and twice *hai*, (18), equals 36. Further explanations provided by the program note regarding the work's *gematria*, cabalistic numerical manipulations, expound upon all manner of the composer's philosophical ferreting out and mathematical exploitations. In the end, the best news is that whatever highways and byways of thought progression it took to produce the *Diaspora Dances*, the end result was very worthwhile which was not my judgement in regard to a similar cabalistic approach to *Dybbuk*. As already pointed out this jolly piece offers a wonderful smorgasbord of elements Middle-Eastern/Middle-European/Broadway and Harlem. The *West Side Story* three note *motif* which ended the first movement is here exploited dramatically and dynamically to the full and L's brilliant jazz finale goes its Hindemith antecedent one better.[272] Terrific stuff!

The final *Benediction* movement was not planned for *Jubilee Games* but for a celebratory evening of the reopening of Carnegie Hall. *Benediction* was not performed as the central movement of the *Games* until 1988, two years after the premiere of the original two-movement version. Its first page of score bears a written inscription by the composer, 'For Carnegie Hall, 15 Dec.'86, Remembering Dmitri M., Harold G., Alma M., Bruno W.'[273] Although a movement of introspection, *Benediction* begins with triumphant brass. The several elements that make up this celebratory brass opening generate all instrumental and vocal material for the movement. What begins as an introduction of stirring brilliance is developed and transformed into long, introspective melodies spun out first by the oboe, then the violins and finally

---

[272] Paul Hindemith, *Metamorphosis on Themes of Carl Maria von Weber* : see *Turendot Scherzo.*
[273] 'Dimitri Mitrpoulos, Harold Gomberg, NY Philharmonic Principal Oboe, Alma Mahler, Bruno Walter and all the others'

WEST SIDE MAESTRO

by the baritone soloist who sings the Hebrew *Benediction* which brings the four movement *Concerto for Orchestra* to a close.

The DG recording of the *Concerto for Orchestra* with the composer conducting the Israel Philharmonic benefits from as confident a presentation in regard to the *aleatoric* elements of the first movement as one could hope for. I commented cryptically earlier that L succeeded admirably in producing *a certain degree* of the resulting unpredictability expected. Let me elaborate on this equivocation. It is accepted that L's position as one of a handful of superstar international conductors in the second half of this century allowed him to regularly program his own music virtually without restriction. He also was contractually guaranteed his own choice of repertoire by two of the world's largest recording companies. Unlike his beloved Mahler, who rarely promoted his own music with his own orchestra, the Vienna Philharmonic, L exploited to the full his position as a composer/conductor with the orchestras with whom he was most closely associated, The New York, Israel and Vienna Philharmonics and the London Symphony Orchestra, as well as those orchestras who invited him to guest conduct. His own music was programmed not only for individual concerts but also for tours, televised events, recordings and commercial video films. He is, in fact, probably the best and most completely commercially documented of American composers of the 20th century with the possible exception of Aaron Copland. Consider that for the 1986 fifty year Jubilee of the Israel Philharmonic, he was able to extensively tour the two movement *Jubilee Games* with them over two continents. In 1988, he performed the three movement *Jubilee Games* with them at least twenty times in their own subscription series of concerts in Israel and then in 1989 he again performed a similar series of repeat subscription concerts that included the four movement version now renamed *Concerto for Orchestra*. The commercial recording consists of recordings made in both 1988 and 1989. It would be naive to think that with all this exposure to and experience with the work the Israel orchestra continued to perform the *aleatoric* sections as if for the first time. Not only did they more than any other orchestra know how to make the *Free-Style Events* movement work but I would even suggest that in regard to the brass chorale for which the note pitches are 'freely chosen' from seven note scales provided by the composer, that the brass section had pre-arranged among themselves which notes sounded best together while still projecting a dissonant improvisation. I don't believe or suggest for a moment that the composer colluded in such a solution. This is merely my own projection having listened carefully to the recorded result and based upon my experience of working with orchestras over the past fifty years. As a former brass player in student days as well as a conductor, I possess a certain functional knowledge of how musicians think and the practical recourses they are moved to when faced with such problems as presented by *aleatoric* composition. I have witnessed to what lengths a brass section will go in order to sound their best. Even opting for such an approach there was still room for sufficient communal spontaneity to produce what Humphrey Burton perspicaciously describes as "the sheer ugliness produced by a group improvisation selected from an infinite variety of pitches."[274] Nevertheless, this was an interesting experiment for L to undertake and very much in keeping with his philosophy of the *new eclecticism* "where mismatched components can unite - tonal, non-tonal, electronic, serial, aleatory - in a magnificent eclectic union."

The other three movements offer no special challenge to the Israelis. Their identification with this work created especially for them with its Middle-Eastern rhythms and melodies, so much an expression of their culture, gave them a unique insight and inspired them in a manner which no other orchestra could hope to match.

There are two discs produced by DG. The first couples the Bernstein *Concerto* with Ned Rorem's *Violin Concerto* and David Del Tredici's *Tattoo*. A later release is all-Bernstein, which couples the most challenging of L's instrumental works, the *Concerto for Orchestra* with the *Dybbuk Suites Nos. 1 & 2*. The performances are, as might be expected, definitive. As the

---

[274] It is also to be noted in relation to future performances of *Free-style Events* that in the sections requiring taped recordings of the opening and of the adlib *shofar* calls, played on cue simultaneously with the live performance, two pre-recorded tapes taken from the L's commercial recording are supplied by the publisher. To create a truly aleatoric result the tapes should be made during the live performance itself and instantly played back at the required times. The expense and danger involved in such a venture make it much more practical to use the pre-recorded tapes.

complete ballet score to *Dybbuk* is available on the Sony label with L conducting, one might wish to choose the earlier release of the Concerto with its coupling of Rorem and Del Tredici as it offers the listener the opportunity of becoming acquainted with two interesting and accessible contemporary American composers who deserve to find a wider public.

A Little Light Music

The number of L's compositions which fall into the category of *Light* Music or *Pops* provide a rather significant repertoire for summer concerts or special event evenings celebrating theatre, ballet and cinema. To do it full justice, much of his music that falls into this genre has never been limited merely to 'Pop' concert programs but has enjoyed full repertoire status during regular subscription seasons everywhere. Indisputably, the two most famous concert standards are the Overture to *Candide* and the Symphonic Dances from *West Side Story*. Two other works based upon *West Side Story* have been adapted by two arrangers, Jack Mason and Maurice Peress. The Mason arrangement, the most accessible to orchestras of all levels of technical ability, is a *pot-pourri* of the best known songs along with snatches of the dance music and the Peress work is a symphonic reworking of the overture to the show[275]. Among the other popular extracts are the superb 'Three Dance Episodes' from *On The Town* and the 'Three Dance Variations' from *Fancy Free*. To this list must be added the Symphonic Suite drawn from the film *On The Waterfront*. With the exception of the Mason and Peress arrangements, all of the above are available in superb recorded performances by the composer both on the Sony and DG labels. There are videotaped performances dating from a 1976 Centenary tour with the NY Philharmonic of the *Candide* Overture and the *West Side* Symphonic Dances. They are part of a mixed bag program of American music tele-videoed in Germany which includes Gershwin, a Sousa March and, most important, Copland's *Symphony No. 3*. A revised version of this program substituting Roy Harris's *Symphony No. 3* as the major symphonic work and excluding the *West Side Story* Dances was televised at the Albert Hall in

---

[275] L chose not to include the show overture in his famous recording of *West Side Story*.

London. The videotape of the concert in Germany is the more distinguished of the two but the London concert does include just about the best performance ever of Copland's *Lincoln Portrait* with the American bass, William Warfield, delivering a moving and inspiring narration. The London concert displays a rather sluggish, sometimes slap-dash and careless Bernstein, especially in his performance of the Gershwin *Rhapsody in Blue*. Nevertheless, an ever-attentive NY Philharmonic respond with style even at tempos that are lethargic in comparison to his notable recorded versions of this work. These videos form part of the Unitel/Bernstein catalogue available to Public Service and Arts Television Channels. They can also be viewed at the Museum of Radio and Television in New York City.

The recorded versions of L's lighter compositions do not lack for top class recordings by various top flight orchestras led by Bernstein specialists like Tilson Thomas, Slatkin, Litton and Ozawa and, most recently, Marin Alsop, who is a Bernstein protégé. Leading the field, unsurprisingly, are those by the composer. I have already indicated preference for the older, original CBS/Sony NY Philharmonic performances which are available in 3 CD box sets but that is not to diminish the newer individual DG discs that have been recompiled with other, non-Bernstein popular classics at least three times. Perhaps the most comprehensive and generous all Bernstein CD combines the *West Side Story* and *On The Waterfront* Suites with the Three Dances from *On The Town*, the Three Dance Variations from *Fancy Free* plus the *Candide* Overture and, as an important bonus, the *Prelude, Fugue and Riffs* which I will discuss with other of his later *crossover*[276] works for orchestra. The Los Angeles Philharmonic in the Candide and West Side tracks and the Israel Philharmonic for the rest of the disc share the orchestra honours on this disc.

The *Divertimento* commissioned by the Boston Symphony Orchestra for their Centenary was premiered in the autumn of 1980 by the BSO under its then music director, Seiji Ozawa. It was the most extended and singular of

---

[276] *Crossover* is an adjective created by the recording industry to delineate vocal or instrumental music that is suitable for either light music or full symphonic concerts or in reference to concert performers who combine both serious and light music on their programs.

four compositions that could be designated as *light* or *occasional* music composed between 1977 and 1980. The other three works are *Slava! A Political Overture* (1977), *CBS Music* (1978) and *A Musical Toast* (1980). The Divertimento is high class *classical light music*, a wonderful addition to the sparkling repertoire produced by the American musical influences in L's formative years and list of friends. It joins the ranks of American 'Pop' classics such the ballet suite, *The Incredible Flautist,* by one of L's teachers, Walter Piston, or *Ives' Variations on America* and *Chester* by his good friend, the former president of the Juilliard School of Music when this writer was pursuing his post-graduate studies, William Schuman, or the four dances from the ballet *Rodeo* by L's dearest friend and mentor, Aaron Copland.

As I studied the score and listened to L's recording of *Divertimento*, it revealed itself to be much more than just a highly sophisticated and entertaining fifteen minute piece written to order for another of the many *special* occasions which seemed to have been the starting point of several of L's compositions for the concert hall. The work is a musical riddle, a kind of *Enigma Variations* inhabited by hidden references throughout to specific works of music that held special meaning and evoked special memories and relationships for the composer. Some of these are easily discernible, others are transformed by a brilliant mind that thrived upon game playing and puzzling. There are those 'clevernesses' revealed by the composer himself, such as the creation of all his thematic material from only two notes, B and C, (which signify 'Boston Centenary'). There is the repeated use of the interval of a half tone, which is the interval between the two tones B and C[277]. There is the recurrence of a horn signal theme that closely resembles

---

[277] The half or semi-tone is the smallest interval between two notes in western music, one of twelve semi-tones that make up the *chromatic* scale which encompasses within an octave all the notes available to composers working in a traditional western styles. Other cultures, such as those of India and Asia, and much of today's avant-garde electronic music deal in scales which encompass *microtones*, intervals smaller than a semi-tone, fractional notes, most simplistically expressed, all the frequencies that exist in the cracks between the notes on the piano. In Western music, these *microtones* can be readily identified in the performance of jazz especially in the flattened notes in *blues* songs where the player will inflect a note expressively by attacking it just under the pitch and then bend it upward to that which we associate with being *in tune*. Perhaps the most famous example of *microtones* is the opening clarinet solo in Gershwin's *Rhapsody in Blue*.

the famous horn solo from Richard Strauss' *Till Eulenspiegel*, a renowned legendary prankster. The key to *Divertimento*'s riddles, in my view, lies in the sixth movement titled *Sphinxes*. We rarely, if ever, make plural references to this noun, the mythological Sphinx. It was the Sphinx who accosted and was defeated by *Oedipus* who, by solving its riddle, freed the people of Thebes. This title alludes not to mythological beasts but to riddles. In reference to this particular movement L made the following comments: "I take the basic motive of the *Divertimento*, (the notes B and C), which everything is based on, and from this I make...two tone rows, and the first row ends in a *dominant* cadence, and the second one ends in a *tonic*. That's the joke. You make these tone rows out of the basic motive and in the end you have to make *dominant* and *tonic*. The question - I find it very funny!"[278]

In a true sense, this was L answering *The Unanswered Question* that he felt Ives' composition implied and that he had posed in his fifth Harvard Norton Lecture. When, at the conclusion of his final lecture, he remarked rather obscurely that he was no longer sure of the question but that the answer was 'Yes', I believe he was referring to his rhetorical question regarding the sustained, undisturbed major chord that, after the non-tonal voices and dissonance's were silenced, continued to sound to the conclusion of the Ives' work. "Is tonality eternal, immortal?" L's comments regarding *Sphinxes* simply reiterate his personal commitment to the inevitability of tonality. He was again saying "Yes" to the *Unanswered Question*.

Some of *Divertimento*'s musical riddles are not difficult to solve. The allusions to Beethoven, Johann and Richard Strauss, Berlioz, Satie, and the composer himself are quite evident. A program note, which accompanies the orchestral score, indicates that personal notes to musicians are also contained within the musical fabric. Perhaps one day one of L's close colleagues or some other musician puzzler will reveal or unravel all of the

---

[278] *Tone-row*: A row of twelve different notes upon which both melody and chords of a *dodecaphonic,* (twelve-tone) composition are based. (See Chapter: The Norton Lectures, page 46) *Dominant*: The fifth note of the major and minor scales above the *tonic* note. In classical harmony the progression from a *dominant* chord to a *tonic* chord is the principal cadential formula.

works secrets. I don't believe it will tell us anything new but it will be a reminder of the loss of a most clever and brilliant musical mind[279].

The work is in eight short movements six of which describe their form, a waltz that isn't a waltz, a mazurka, a samba, a turkey trot, a blues and a march. The titles of the other two movements allude to historical or literary reference. *Sennets and Tuckets* are trumpet flourishes to be found in the stage directions of Elizabethan plays and *Sphinxes* alludes to the winged monster of Greek mythology which, as a proper name, exists only in the singular. The final march movement, *The BSO Forever*, recycles music from *1600 Pennsylvania Avenue*. The score indicates that the piccolos and brass section should stand the second time the main march theme appears. This bit of added theatrical fun is a performance tradition associated with Sousa's *Stars and Stripes Forever* march when it is performed at the Boston *Pops*. That is where the resemblance to Sousa ends for the rest of this disjunct march is pure Bernstein in the highest of spirits. This is preceded by a short prelude, a *fughetta*[280] for three flutes titled *In Memoriam*. We are not told whose memory this commemorates but due to the work's association with the BSO the first name that comes to mind is that of L's mentor, Serge Koussevitzky.

A Musical Toast was written in memory of Andre Kostelanetz, one of America's two most famous and recorded conductors of light music, the other being Arthur Fiedler. Kostelanetz, who had personally commissioned works from a number of important composers such as William Walton, William Schuman and Aaron Copland, enjoyed a long affiliation with the NY Philharmonic as conductor of a sold-out subscription series of Saturday

---

[279] As always, Humphrey Burton's biography comes to the rescue. Burton writes that the *Samba* and the *Turkey Trot* are an allusion to the Boston *Pops*' typical bill of fare, and that the latter of the two represents another rescue job from the Bernstein bottomless trunk of discards, specifically from an abandoned film score to *Tucker*. The "waltz that isn't a waltz" goes Tchaikovsky's *Pathétiqe* five-beats-to-the-bar-waltz two beats better. L's opus is in *seven*-beats-to-the-bar and in family circles was sung to lyrics spiced with the vernacular composed by his daughter, Jamie Bernstein Thomas.

[280] *fughetta*: a small fugue. A short melodic theme once introduced is taken up successively by other voices which, according to strict rules, interweave with each other.

evening popular concerts. I think *Kosty*, as he was affectionately known, would have, in one respect, been confused by this slightly-over-two-minute funfest. It seems that a 'popular' American party game which fills in the name of famous people to the rhythm of George Gershwin's song *Fascinatin' Rhythm* was the inspiration for this brief *Toast*. The little bit that has been written about this concert *lollypop*[281] gives the impression that the rhythm Gershwin devised for his song was borrowed by L. Obviously none of the writers were familiar with the Gershwin tune because nothing could be further from the truth. This work is mostly in L's favoured seven-beats-to-the-bar rhythm and one would not be hard pushed to find some resemblance with the oddball seven-beats-to the-bar *Waltz* from *Divertimento*. The actual *Toast* to the dedicatee comes at the very end when the orchestra shouts out the name of '**An**-dre **Ko**-ste-**la**-netz'. The work proves to be very versatile as one can easily substitute '**Mi**-chael **Til**-son **Thom**-as' or '**Sla**-va **Ro**-stro-**po**-vich' among others. Chalk this one up as a delightful *hors-d'oeuvre*.

Slava! A Political Overture is a slightly longer affair lasting four minutes. *Slava* is the affectionate form of address used by close colleagues and friends of the great cellist/conductor, Mstislav Rostropovich. L wrote this short overture to mark the occasion of Rostropovich's appointment as Music Director of the National Symphony Orchestra in Washington DC in 1977. In October of that year a Gala Concert was mounted at the Kennedy Center for the Performing Arts at which both Rostropovich and L conducted an all Bernstein program. Included were three world premieres, *Slava!*, *Three Meditations from Mass* for Cello and Orchestra and *Songfest*. *Slava*! is a proper romp filled with shouts, a pre-recorded tape containing multiple political speeches in counterpoint to each other complete with crowd reactions, a dog bark and three very good tunes, two borrowed from 1600 Pennsylvania Avenue, *The Grand Ol' Party* and *Lud's Wedding,* and the third a typical Bernstein metamorphoses of a fragment from the Coronation Scene from Moussorgsky's opera *Boris Godounov*. All these add up to an affectionate musical portrait of the many aspects of the complex character

---

[281] *Lollypop* was Sir Thomas Beecham's designation for popular light concert works which he performed as encores to the delight of his audiences.

and multiple involvements of Rostropovich, one of the world's truly great musicians, as well as dog lover and political dissident. The overture is a short but quite formal affair. It is carefully constructed which lends it good shape but does not rob it of its fun. L has provided another excellent addition to the *Pops* repertoire.

Two recordings exist of the *Divertimento* as well as a Unitel filmed performance, part of a concert with the Vienna Philharmonic which includes Haydn's *Sinfonia Concertante* and Robert Schumann's *Spring* Symphony. The video is very enjoyable although the performance of the *Spring* Symphony with the NY Philharmonic in Japan (Kultur video) is preferred. The *Divertimento* shows L at his most relaxed sometimes dropping his hands to his sides and conducting with merely a nod, a smile or a twinkle in his eye. The compact disc recordings are performed by different orchestras. The most readily available is the DG recording, an outstanding all-Bernstein disc that happily includes both *A Musical Toast* and *Slava!* as well as Rostropovich performing the Three Meditations from *Mass* for Cello and Rampal playing *Halil*. This disc, featuring the Israel Philharmonic, is an absolute must for Bernstein aficionados and for those who would like to become familiar with his lesser-known compositions.

Finale: Songfest and Arias and Barcaroles

Initially, I pondered whether these two important song cycles were linked to or inspired by L's strong commitment to the music of Gustav Mahler as well as his personal identification with the composer himself. In conversation with Humphrey Burton, we discussed this possibility and the suggestion arose that *Songfest*'s place in the Bernstein catalogue might be viewed as his *Lied von der Erde*. When, following *A Quiet Place,* L's efforts to initiate another opera proved fruitless, his creative drive was drawn to and manifested itself in another song cycle which proved to be his very last composition, *Arias and Barcaroles*. While it would be difficult to conceive that Mahler's shadow, cast so large over his career, did not insinuate its presence in his creative thinking for *Songfest*, other obvious relevance's point towards a larger picture. Unlike Mahler's *Das Lied*, which is a farewell to life, *Songfest* is a celebration, of poetry, things American, the human condition and song itself as the most powerful messenger of communication. In retrospect, the art of song writing provides an inspirational force from the very beginning of L's efforts at composition and is a principal connecting link throughout the composing side of his career. One need only consider the large number of his compositions that incorporate a vocal element. What remains is but a tiny percentage of purely instrumental compositions.

L's early works for the stage dominate the general public's view of his diverse talents. They far from represent a full picture of his outstanding gifts as a composer especially when writing for the human voice. His consummate skill in this realm culminated in four complex, late works, the failed Broadway musical, *1600 Pennsylvania Avenue, Songfest*, the opera, *A Quiet Place*, and his final work, *Arias and Barcaroles*. These challenging works form a quartet of substance and style and are the summation of a personal, fully evolved eclectic but tonal musical philosophy to which L remained loyal and totally committed for his entire career. Aspects of this final mature style had been gestating within his thinking since his earliest days as a composer. During his time at Harvard delivering his Norton Lectures, he came to think out and crystallise for himself not only the route he believed the music of the future would take but his own journey along this route. It is perfectly described in his final paragraphs of his Norton valediction:

'We are in a position where one style can feed the other, where one technique enriches the other, thus enriching all of music. We have reached that supra-level of abstract musical semantics...where those apparently mismatched components can unite - tonal, non-tonal, electronic, serial, aleatory - all united in a magnificent new eclecticism. But the eclectic union can take place only if all the elements are combined with and embedded in the tonal universal - that is, conceived against a contextual background of tonality.'

That paragraph summarises a Bernstein compositional style that had already been conspicuously exploited in *Mass* in 1971, whose unbridled eclectic roots could be traced back to *Candide*, and his *Kaddish* Symphony and which would come into full flower with the two song cycles and *AQP*. The 1973 *Norton Lectures*, televised and later made available as commercial videos and in elaborate book form, allowed L the unique privilege of presenting his ideas internationally regarding what he viewed as the only way forward for contemporary composers if they wanted to communicate with and hold the attention of present and future audiences as well as each other. No other composer or classical musician previously had ever been provided with so notable or international a platform with which to present his ideas. While other living musicians with strongly differing views possessed the knowledge, commitment and distinctness to put forward before an audience their contrasting, challenging ideas, none combined L's enormous charisma, intellect, broad tastes in all areas of the Arts, experience in media communication, natural gifts as both a script writer and teacher, an enormous international public profile and, which cannot be excluded, his own commercial empire ready to serve and promote his doctrines. It is not hyperbole to state that his position was unparalleled among the world's music community in being able to use so unique an opportunity to his own full advantage in advancing his ecumenical and, speaking realistically, self-serving musical theories. From the 1970's onward the variety of compositional styles and techniques that he employed no longer merely combined fragments of a wide variety of methods to include tone rows, chromaticism, pan- and polytonality and neo-classicism among others. He freely exploited them all unselfconsciously. Earlier compositions such as *The Age of Anxiety*, *Serenade* and the *Kaddish* Symphony already had shown him in command of techniques associated with the *avant-garde*. They were used in many instances as contrasting passages within what was overwhelmingly conceived as a broad tonal canvas. Following the Norton Lectures, however, he exemplified the composer of *the new eclecticism*, which he envisaged as the way forward for the future of contemporary music. His personal commitment was now to fully incorporate in his compositions all the techniques available to him, expressively and skilfully while never losing his identification as a composer rooted in *tonality*.

WEST SIDE MAESTRO

Among composer/conductors, L's career can only find an historical parallel with that of Gustav Mahler.[282] . The core difference between the manner in which the two men balanced both careers, as I have earlier pointed out, was that of discipline. Mahler would apportion his summers at a secluded retreat to devote himself exclusively to composition. L often spoke about following such a regime. He made great public declarations towards this end, taking much publicised sabbaticals in order to meet composing commitments. But rarely could he be pinned down to following through if some interesting conducting or teaching project appeared on the horizon. The musical revolutionaries of the twentieth century were only taking their first steps when Mahler died. The changes they wrought were to be far reaching, beyond anything Mahler had envisaged. His music had already proved to be a catalyst for one of the most radical of revolutionary schools of musical thought, that of Arnold Schönberg's New Viennese School. L's role as an influential conductor and composer within a century of change that had witnessed the music world split apart for one hundred years has been to date far less profound. There can be little doubt that among contemporary American composers his commercial success set him apart and was the cause for both jealousy and resentment. What made his position even more fragile was his outspoken commitment to tonality against the background of a constant seesaw power struggle between tonal and non-tonal composers. At the time of the Norton Lectures, the non-tonal composers were occupying the seat of power internationally. L, I believe wisely, attempted to assume in his Norton Lectures a more Mosaic profile, that of a codifier more than an innovator. In seeking unification of the many compositional schools of thought that had not only developed over the century but which waged a

---

[282] One might also wish to include the names of Pierre Boulez, Esa-Pekka Salonen, the late Giuseppe Sinopoli and Peter Maxwell Davies to this list. However, Salonen, although a skilled avant-garde contemporary composers, devotes the greatest part of his time to conducting, as did Sinopoli, and neither are well known to or identified by the public as composers. Boulez and Davies, on the other hand, gained fame as composers only later falling into and establishing careers for themselves as conductors Both these noted musicians continue to guest conduct to support their principal interest and commitment to composing, teaching or, in Boulez's case, proselytising for his most contemporary avant-garde composers colleagues.

perpetual uncompromising war with one another, he himself had to lead by example to demonstrate that a viable possibility existed for all these styles to converge into 'a new eclecticism' with a lexicon that would encompass and satisfy the needs of all. *Songfest* is just such an example of this new eclecticism. Its framework contains a diversity of styles and forms of poetic and musical expression which is the very essence of the melting pot that is America. The poetry spans three hundred years, as does the politics of the poems, politics of culture, love, marriage and creativity. The music encompasses a multiplicity of tonal, polytonal polyrhythmic and serial techniques in a meaningful, assured and skilful manner. It is one of L's most accomplished works. Unfortunately, it cannot be said to have readily found a wide audience, as have his other 'popular' compositions. That is the burden of a hugely gifted and famous composer who wishes to be recognised for his more profoundly conceived compositions but whose public image was accrued not in the concert hall but on Broadway, television and in film. When the casual concert-goer encounters the Bernstein name on the program he expects to hear, if not the standard popular items like *West Side Story*, *On The Town*, *On The Waterfront* or the Overture to *Candide*, something that is immediately accessible. A cycle of Art Songs, one of which is composed using a strict twelve-tone approach, doesn't exactly fill the bill. Thus, in 1982, the composer had to suffer the indignity of having the audience at an open air concert in Concord, California "leave in droves during Songfest" with "some of those who stayed...heard to boo."[283] To add insult to injury, the critics as well have proved very slow to accept this very accomplished work. As always, a panoramic view of their writings reveals huge contradictions, not only within the fraternity but within individual reviews. Staying with the positive aspect of this inspired work before discussing the critical response, I will deal with the songs and texts both individually and collectively.

Observing L's fascination with numbers, one cannot but wonder whether the number six or at very least multiples of three, a mystic Masonic number, held some special significance in relation to *Songfest*. The cycle is performed by six singers, three male and three female. Each is assigned a solo and are

---

[283] Humphrey Burton, *Leonard Bernstein*, pg. 467

combined in duets and trios as well and there are three sextets which open and close the work and provide the centrepiece. The texts for the songs represent a 300 year journey of ideas based upon the American experience as seen through the eyes of thirteen poets. The song cycle itself consists of only twelve songs but for the highly charged, racially inspired song about black America, the composer conceived the design of two contrasting poems dealing with the same idea from opposite ends of the political spectrum. Thus the Langston Hughes and June Jordan poems share one song but are conceived in two styles both tonally and in substance. They are pitted one against the other, first in turn and then simultaneously in a struggle for supremacy of idea, in true Charles Ives style. The other poems span a period from the first days of colonisation to twentieth century America.

Although the work began its creation as a commission for America's Bi-centennial celebrations in 1976, only four songs were composed by the required date and the commission had to be vacated. The complete cycle was premiered late the following year on October 11, 1977 with the composer conducting the National Symphony Orchestra of Washington. Nevertheless, the composer, in a BBC televised prelude to a live performance of *Songfest* in 1982, continued to refer to the work as having been written in honour of the Bi-centenary celebrations in 1976. Other comments on his song cycle during this telecast help shed light on his creative approach to the work:

"*Songfest* is just what its name suggests, a festival of songs though not all of them are exactly festive. I wrote the work...not so much to celebrate the glory of my nation as that of its artists, specifically its poets. Since this song cycle is a musical setting of American poems ranging over 300 years of American life, it naturally reveals some of our more shadowed sides as well as our more euphoric ones. But it *is* a celebration - performed by six singers who sing in a 'friendly' manner as if they were entertaining after a dinner party. I hope you will find these songs festive in the true sense no matter whether they are joyful, reflective, sad or even bitter. They all combine to celebrate the American experience."

WEST SIDE MAESTRO

This cogent summing up of this forty-two minute work seems applicable except in L's description of the manner of performance as 'friendly' and as if 'entertaining after a dinner party.' Such a description would seem more applicable to *Arias and Barcaroles*, the final work to be discussed. *Songfest* is not a casual work for the drawing room but a song symphony certainly in the mould of and inspired to a degree by Mahler's late masterpiece, *The Song of the Earth*. Its emotions of love, anger, elation, frustration, joy and sadness are set in a big manner for the concert hall with a brilliant, powerful and sometimes overgenerous symphonic accompaniment. The Bernstein personality was always a melange of positive and negative qualities as well as contradictions. Modesty, however, was rarely, if ever, a trait one associated with this most outspoken of individuals. Yet his above quoted allusion of what was from the first intended to be a 'big' work for a big occasion to a diminutive, after- dinner entertainment does not ring true. Moreover, he was further to expand this outpouring of untypical humility in his concluding televised remarks. In enlarging upon the meaning of the opening and closing poems of his cycle, those by Frank O'Hara and Edgar Allen Poe, L presents this self-effacing description of the American artist:

"We American artists do not pretend to greatness. We are not Schillers and Shakespeares. We are what we are. If we lived elsewhere, says Poe, that is, if we were other than we are, if we were angels or supermen or the ideal Americans, then, perhaps, we could *try* for greatness. But as we are, basically immigrants and minorities, we create only what O'Hara called our 'real right thing', grand but small, important because it must be said, yet not pompous, not bidding for immortality. And that is the fundamental ambiguity of *Songfest*...I hope what Poe and O'Hara meant, and all the other poets in-between as well, is what eventually emerges in my music. That we are not gods, only artists. We struggle with our words and notes, we create the best we can and we praise God for giving us the chance to do so."

Modesty may not have been one of L's virtues but insecurity certainly revealed itself in his personality in expressed fears regarding his position in the history of twentieth century music. He constantly voiced concern that his serious music would not be listened to by future generations and that he would not be remembered as anything more than a composer of Broadway musicals. Was he on this occasion echoing such fears, perhaps even apologising for this most sophisticated, contemporary work to a television audience whose experience with his music may have been limited to *On The Town* and *West Side Story*?

While reviews of *Songfest* had been generally mixed, L could take pride in the many good things that had been written about it. Two of the most discerning and respected American critics, Paul Hume in the Washington Post and Andrew Porter in the New Yorker, received it with glowing reviews. To counter this there was his negative California experience of a large number of the audience walking out and the 'booing' at its conclusion. Certainly regarding his reference to the O'Hara poem, L had composed other music that could be described as 'grand but small' but *Songfest* did not fit this profile. It was one of his important works, 'grand' on all fronts. As for "not bidding for immortality", that was not an idea he ever countenanced despite all his outpourings of insecurity. That phrase carries a hollow ring in face of his multi-faceted super-star career celebrated by audiences internationally and documented in all its aspects on film, television, hundreds of recordings and in printed publications. In point of fact, as we celebrate the commemoration of twenty-years since L's passing, the legend of Bernstein, the composer, is still very much with us thanks to the advocacy on recordings and in concert of the next two generations of important international American Conductors many of whom he directly influenced, among them Leonard Slatkin, Michael Tilson Thomas, Andrew Litton, Kent Nagano, Marin Alsop and John Mauceri.

Turning now to the cycle itself, Jack Gottlieb's writes of *Songfest*'s 'unabashed eclecticism', perhaps the understatement of the decade. I do not imply this in any way in a negative fashion. *Songfest* is a no-holds-barred display of L's commitment to "those apparently mismatched components ...-tonal, non-tonal, electronic, serial, aleatory - all united in a magnificent new eclecticism." When examining the work, one can only admire the accomplishment of such an act of musical bravura. The true wonder of the work, however, is the consummate skill with which it is carried out.

WEST SIDE MAESTRO

The *bookends* of the cycle, both Sextets, are hymns of praise, the first to Poetry, the last to inspired creativity. The poems chosen are contrasts, one to another. Frank O'Hara's *To The Poem,* which opens the cycle, is devoid of frills. Barely a dozen lines in length it is an ode to simplicity, demonstrating that that which is small can also be important. And in this 'un-American' lack of pretension, "in a defiant land of its own", it can be "a real right thing". The cycle's concluding poem, Edgar Allen Poe's *Israfel,* in contrast, is a full-blown eight stanza romantic ode characterised by L as "an artist's credo". Where O'Hara's language is simple and direct, Poe's purple patterned poem is a Fourth of July fireworks celebration overflowing with classical illusion as befits its title hero, *Israfel,* the archangel of music in the *Koran.* The musical settings are equally varied. The O'Hara begins as a kind of foursquare celebratory, even military hymn but with an ironic difference. The words are set so that the strong musical accents come on all the wrong word syllables. Thus, "Let us do some-THING grand...someTHING small AND IMporTANT etc." This, rightly to my view, has been compared to the kind of satire readily associated with Charles Ives' 'outdoor celebration' settings. Even the snare drum flourishes in the opening hymn sound as if the drummer had been to the beer keg one too many times. The hymn gives way to a slower hushed six voice contrasting polyphonic fantasy[284]. The obscurity of the setting matches precisely the obscurity of the lines of the poem: "Some fine thing /will resemble a human hand/ and really be merely a thing/Not needing a military band". With the mention of a 'military band', however, the hymn tune returns and with it the displaced accents which marked the opening word setting. The song ends triumphantly with the words, "But be In a defiant land of its own, *a real right thing.*" [285]

Why the irony? Why the mockery? Is it, as has been suggested, merely "a satire on patriotic hymns"?[286] I view the irony as occupying a much broader canvas. O'Hara's words struck a deep chord in L. The poet, having called for the creation of something 'grand', looks to the reverse not only of the general

---

[284] polyphony: music which combines two or more independant melodic lines
[285] author's italics
[286] From program notes by Jack Gottlieb accompanying the vocal score and the composer's CD recording.

concept of what is conceived to be 'grand' but what we Americans expect *grand*ness to encompass - a military band, an elegant premiere, spotlights, applause, mass recognition. O'Hara seeks *importance* not in grandiose concepts but in "Something small" which, in defiance of convention, is in itself ***a real right thing***.

The seeming simplicity of this mostly homophonic[287] opening hymn is in high contrast to the cycle's closing hymn set to the florid words of Edgar Allen Poe. This complex finale calls for virtuosity from first to last not only from the singers but the orchestra as well. The musical setting matches the floridity of the text, note for word. For its musical setting L chose to emulate the style of Benjamin Britten. If it should be discovered to be meant as an homage to his British colleague and friend who had only recently died, it is certainly the best of tributes. It is an enormously accomplished outpouring celebrating the fire of artistic creativity that looks for its inspiration to the heavens and an angel whose heart strings are a lute, whose singing silences the stars and enamours the moon and who despises "the unimpassioned song". In the blinding light of such heavenly fire it also underlines, as L pointed out in his televised analysis of Poe's poem, that the creative personality is not a god only an artist struggling to do the best he or she can.

The tempo marking in the score, 'strong waltz, with passion' has led to a good deal of critical misunderstanding and resulted in a fair amount of misinformed writing. I won't pretend to know what the composer actually intended when he wrote the direction 'waltz' but as a performing musician I can make an educated guess. He wanted the work to go with a kind of swing, that is, a forward movement, a lightness and a lift that we usually associate with the waltz. In reality, only dance partners possessing five legs apiece could ever hope to waltz to this paean to creativity. This song, the final statement in *Songfest*, serves to again reinforce the composer's total commitment to *tonality* ending in a blazing C Major coda.

These two poems that frame *Songfest* encompass large concepts addressed directly to the artist. The remaining poems deal with aspects of love,

---

[287] homophonic: characterised by the movement of all parts to the same melody.

marriage, the socially disenfranchised and one oddball who defies a category.

L chose poems which celebrated four kinds of love, unrequited first love, (Lawrence Ferlinghetti, *The Candystore Beyond The El*), the hidden and, at the time it was written, forbidden love of one man for another, (Walt Whitman, *To What You Said*), the heartbreak of a bereaved love, (Conrad Aikin, *Music I Heard With You*), and the lament for faceless loves come and gone which, in the winter of our years, silences the song of summer that sang in our hearts, (Edna St.Vincent Millay, *What Lips My Lips Have Kissed*).

The Candy Store Beyond The El is a reminiscence of youth. A man recalls a windy, rainy autumn day of his adolescence standing around in his local candystore, that tiny one-room neighbourhood shop which was a monument to juvenile self-indulgence. It could be found on virtually every neighbourhood street corner in New York but here it is located just beyond the *El*, general slang for New York's elevated trains which, when they run underground, are called subways. He recalls the counter, (always made of marble), crowded with all those cavity-creating delights which bring pleasure to the young but are forbidden fruit to their elders, Tootsie Rolls, liquorice sticks and Oh Boy Gum, (with which, for those old enough to remember, you could blow a gum bubble as big as your head). Then he recalls the girl who suddenly rushed in bringing with her the first awakening glimmers of physical love as he noticed her 'rainy' hair and her breasts 'breathless in the little room.' All 'Too soon! Too Soon!'

For this superbly remembered reminiscence, L creates a kind of modern jazz accompaniment built on a strict *tone row*. For those who have shunned *twelve tone* composition in the past declaring it un-tuneful, this song is the perfect antidote. It is handled by L with complete confidence and skill creating a marvellous contrast to the opening sextet and providing a crystal clear setting of the poem along with a thoroughly enjoyable listening experience.

WEST SIDE MAESTRO

The Walt Whitman poem, *To What You Said,* his homosexual confession, was discovered pencilled into the fly-leaf of a book and first published more than seventy-five years after his death. This poem was his 'dark' secret masked by an outpouring of poetry that came to represent everything rugged and virile in nineteenth century America. It is a poem of pain and alienation more than of love, describing a life of hiding and of enforced, self-disciplined correctness.

Among the collected songs of *Songfest, To What You Said* has been singled out by colleagues, critics and the public as the most beautiful. Although the poem lends itself to an emotion once removed from committed love, the song setting provides a deeply emotional representation of Whitman's words. L did not pursue such deep sentiment when setting Anne Bradstreet's poem of married life and love. In that instance his decision was to take one step back. He deliberately assigned it to three women's voices to depersonalise it and avoid sentimentality. With the Whitman poem, however, he threw caution to the winds and gave himself up to the big emotion that it evoked in him. This song is certainly one of the most melodious and beautiful among all of his compositions. It was, however, not original to *Songfest*. It began life as the Prelude to *1600 Pennsylvania Avenue*. Wisely, as with *Slava!* written at this same time, and *Divertimento*, composed three years later, the fruit of his failed partnership with Alan Lerner continued to flower in other forms from the tree of his imagination. In this instance, although L kept the entire introduction and, more important, the main theme of *1600*'s Prelude in tact, he gave this beautiful melody to a solo cello later to be joined by a humming chorus of the remaining quintet of singers while the solo bass reveals Whitman's proud confessional, singing a simple but impassioned descant in counterpoint.[288] One, of course, is left to wonder what L might have come up with if he had started from scratch with only Whitman's words in front of him. Nevertheless, it is true to state that in his present solution, though the shape and character of the re-used melody taken from *1600* was not altered in any way, the addition of the descant for the setting of the poem gave a whole new meaning and validity to the salvaged Prelude.

---

[288] descant: the upper part of a polyphonic composition used as a counterpoint to the main melody

WEST SIDE MAESTRO

The next aspect of love to be examined is that of bereaved love, revealed to us in Conrad Aitkin's classic *Music I Heard with You*. This song is another example of skilled eclectic mixtures. The poignancy of grief is depicted combining diatonic and serial textures. The Coplandesque tonal writing depicts the spiritual aspects of the relationship while the serial sections evoke the imagined ghostly presence that the bereaved relates to material things such as silverware and glassware that were touched by the fingers of the departed. This is an imaginative but challenging setting, complex in its parts but simple, delicate and direct in its presentation.

The last of our four contrasting images of love is a setting of Edna St.Vincent Millay's sonnet, *What Lips My Lips Have Kissed*. This was said to be L's favourite song of the cycle. His highly chromatic setting, a lonely portrait of bitterness over loves passion lost in the winter of life, is anything but lacking in passion. Wonderfully and clearly set for the Alto voice, it is one of those works following which one almost dares not breathe for fear of breaking the spell that both poet and composer have created.

One could have included a fifth poem within this category of love but it seemed to fit best within L's settings of two contrasting poems on marriage, Anne Bradstreet's *To My Dear And Loving Husband*, a wife's passionate declaration of love for her husband, and Gertrude Stein's *Storyette H.M.*, a marriage gone sour with husband and wife going their opposite ways along the path of 'peace at any price' to end their bickering.

The Anne Bradstreet poem dates back to 1650, the early days of colonisation of America. Mrs. Bradstreet, a British born, Massachusetts housewife has the distinction of being America's very first poet. Her poem, *To My Dear And Loving Husband*, is simple and direct, an outpouring of love from a wife to her husband, more remarkable in its sentiment when viewed through present day Society's disenchantment with the estate of marriage.

L chose not to pursue musically such deep sentiment when setting Anne Bradstreet's thoughts of married life and love. Unlike the setting of the

Whitman poem, his decision in this instance was to take one step back. He is quoted as deliberately assigning the song to a trio of women's voices to depersonalise it and avoid the very direct sentimentality, which is the essence of Mrs. Bradstreet's heartfelt tribute to her husband.[289] Even before checking the printed music my first reaction to L's decision to use three women's voices was to check the date of his Vienna recording of Richard Strauss' *Der Rosenkavalier*. A cursory glance at the score, however, prior to determining that almost ten years spanned the gap between his immersion in Strauss' backward sentimental glance at 18th century Vienna and the composition of *Songfest*, revealed straightaway little if any connection between the approach of the two composers in setting text for a trio of women's voices. My knee-jerk reaction to compare the two scores, however, would seem not to have been a-typical. Such a view was anticipated in the Bernstein camp and well answered by Jack Gottlieb in his program notes to the CD. "This is not a *Rosenkavalier* kind of female trio with three independent thoughts," he writes, " but rather a multi-layered abstraction of one individual's feelings." L's setting for the Bradstreet poem is unique within Songfest in that the composer reconstructs the poem to create an ABA song form.[290] The three voices enter one at a time in the A section each singing an overlapping imitation of the same musical phrase to different words before joining together to express a single thought. In the B section the composer assigns each voice a long solo line before again joining the trio together. The return of the A section is an exact repeat except for a short, unusual extended closing. The final cadence measure poses the question, 'When is a dissonance *not* a dissonance?' Although the work clearly ends in D flat Major, the final chord sung by the trio is not one of mellifluous thirds but three neighbouring tones a whole step apart, what we would normally designate as a dissonance. However so skilfully is this final chord approached and the voices spaced within the total texture that the serenity of the poem is not in the slightest disturbed. It is a brilliant final stroke of L's musical brush.

---

[289] see program note 5

[290] ABA or *ternery* song form is most simply described as a composition in three distinct sections, the third of which is a repetition of the first.

WEST SIDE MAESTRO

Immediately following this hymn to marital love is a neo-classic setting of the Gertrude Stein's *Storyette HM*, the initials referring to the painter, Henri Matisse, a close friend of the poem's author who was one of the leading collectors of his works. The poem is of a marriage in a rut with the partners going round in a perpetual circle getting nowhere. Logically, to depict such a scenario, L created a duet with an accompaniment in the form of a perpetual motion. As with the plot, the music goes round and round, mostly in a deliberately expressionless fashion. The chat between the couple never stops. They interrupt each other, talk at the same time or instantly resume when the other has to take a breath from his or her incessant chattering. There are two short outbursts depicting the husband's joy at the thought of leaving and the wife's anger at the thought of being left. The husband wins the battle of wills by perpetually grinding away at his wife barely letting her get a word in until she agrees in a frustrated shout which ends the song.

The final group of poems deals with the disenfranchised, the *no-hope*-ers and those that never fit in, those we label in modern vernacular, the *weird-o*'s. I want to begin with one of *Songfest*'s most powerful statements, both in regard to its ideas and its music, *A Julia De Burgos*, (To Julia De Burgos). Had Manuel de Falla's life not been so tragically cut short, surely he would have come to produce contemporary music of this complexity and power to reflect his culture. The song, sung in Spanish[291], is a monologue in which Julia de Burgos, the poet and liberated woman, addresses her alter ego, De Burgos, the woman who conforms to her husband's and society's demands. Her tone is angry, defiant but her declaration is positive. She rejects the safety of a life of gentility and the acceptance awarded to a woman who is only a painted facade and submissive to the whims of men. Her kingdom is not the confines of the housebound subservient. She is Don Quixote's faithful steed, worn out but now unbridled, independent, a runaway "sniffing out the horizons of God's retribution." This song not only celebrates De Burgos, the politically and socially liberated women years ahead of her time and the emergence of the *women's lib* movement, but also the place of her birth, Puerto Rico. L's setting, which one noted broadsheet dismissed as 'a

---

[291] The English translation of Julia De Burgos' poem, which is printed in the score and the program notes accompanying the CD recording, is by Jamie Bernstein.

WEST SIDE MAESTRO

West Side Story offshoot'[292], is one of the most brilliant and original of the entire cycle. Wildly polyrhythmic from start to finish, it modulates from key to key with the poem's every changing thought. It enjoys an orchestration that matches, even surpasses the greatest of the many well known tributes to Spanish culture which have absorbed not only Spain's native composers but European, South American, Mexican and American composers throughout the 20th century.[293]

Two poems deal with the struggle of the black man in America. It traces his history from his days of slavery to those of acceptance and further to those of ridicule at the hands of other blacks who, politically scornful of the 'whitening' of the black man, forced him to seek , (long after but as a result of public declarations by black activists like the poets, Langston Hughes and June Jordan), his eventual identity as an African/American. I have discussed this unusual duet for mezzo-soprano and baritone, *I, Too, Sing America / Okay "Negroes"* earlier, and the manner in which L combined them within a single song first structuring them sequentially and then simultaneously in counterpoint. I have also described these poems as thematically polarised politically. To personalise this conflict of outlook, try to conceive a debate over the perception of the black American between Martin Luther King and Malcolm X.

In style L has used his themes in a kind of chameleon fashion. The Langston Hughes poem of the black man struggling for recognition and a place at the white man's table, biding his time to grow sufficiently strong so no man will dare refuse him his place, is set tonally but in a highly chromatic style with a challenging vocal line that only one well practised in the more difficult arias from Benjamin Britten operas would confidently take on. There is even a short twelve-tone passage. It is set to the words, "Besides, They'll see how beautiful I am And be ashamed." Its unique twelve-tone setting within the song creates for it a cryptic importance. I could not help but indulge myself

---

[292] Financial Times, April 9, 1994

[293] This refers not only to the superb orchestrations of Spain's de Falla and Enrique Granados but those many classic *homage*s to Spain by Debussy and Ravel, as well as the native South Americans, Villa Lobos, Guarnieri, Fernandez, the Mexicans, Chavez and Revueltas and, not to forget , L's friend and mentor, Aaron Copland.

in wondering whether it was L personally addressing those avant-garde composers who have begrudged him *his* place at the table? I haven't a shred of proof of this but it struck me as a muse worth reflecting upon.

The setting of the June Jordan poem is in total contrast, very simple, very direct. Its first part is crafted as a kind of blues spiritual and its contrasting part as a jazz scherzo. Her words mock the pride and humility with which Langston Hughes begins his poem, "I, too, sing America" and his reference to "the darker brother". In the Jordan poem the word *Negroes* is framed by quotation marks underlining the poet's disdain for the word's implied characterisation. With the re-entry of the Hughes poem a short, lyrical scherzo like duet ensues. Jordan's words outline the reality of what it is to be black while Hughes laughs at the black man's temporary exclusion while he bides his time, growing in strength. The Hughes poem continues. His protagonist again chromatically sings of tomorrow and of his established place at the white man's table, which no one will dare take away from him. The Jordon spiritual tune begins again but in its first chameleon like alteration. The addition of muted brass in its orchestra accompaniment has transformed it into a Dixieland blues. As this fades away we again hear Hughes voice lyrically projecting that twelve tone *double entendre*, (at least to this author), "Besides, they'll see how beautiful I am and be ashamed." In her swinging scherzo style the Jordan words mock those who emulate the white man, deluding themselves that clean fingernails, shined shoes, a crucifix around the neck and good manners will get them something. She shouts, "**who's gonna give *you* something**?!!!" The orchestra now takes the spiritual tune and turns it into a raunchy, low-down, burlesque blues. The antagonists try to out shout each other with their previously stated messages. Again and again the Hughes protagonist sings, "I, *too*, am America" and then reaffirms his future rise from his present subservience, all the while being mocked by his antagonist. The argument gets louder and louder till it climaxes to the crash of a gong. But the woman gets in the last words in street jive. "Come a little closer. Where you from?" As at the very opening, there are three strokes on the timpani - soft, louder, and a smashing blow. Then silence! This double setting of two highly contrasting texts simultaneously underlines the composer's daring and originality among contemporary songsmiths.

ee cummings poem, "if you can't eat you got to", completes the cycle of poems dealing with social awareness. I have characterised it as the voice of the *no-hope'r*. The poem also serves the song cycle structurally. It is the centrepiece of the three sextets that give Songfest its symmetrical balance. Returning to the poem's theme, I would like to make reference to two interpretations that have appeared in print. In the accompanying program notes for the composer's definitive 1978 recording, Jack Gottlieb interprets cummings' poem as the expression of a "Bohemian artist...speaking of his poverty...his life style, and his artistic compulsion". The second reference is taken from Piers Burton–Page's program notes for a 1988 performance of *Songfest* at London's Royal Albert Hall with the composer conducting professional soloists and the student orchestra of the new Tanglewood-oriented summer music school and festival that he helped establish in Schleswig-Holstein, Germany. Burton-Page's program note interprets the cummings' poem as "a disillusioned commentary on the American dream." My own reading of the poem finds me leaning towards the latter interpretation. Without the knowledge of the poem's 1940 copyright date one could have projected cummings' small opus as a product of America's Depression Years of the very early 1930's. It is not stretching an interpretative point to view it as a reflective remembrance of that soul-destroying time. Both published program notes must have been seen and approved by the composer. They were written eleven years apart and may reflect a change or at least a broadening of L's view of both the poem and his setting of it.

The cummings Sextet has been described as an *Intermezzo* although no such designation appears in the vocal score. It begins in a wonderfully lightweight fashion using the kind of group vocal swing popular in the '30's and 40's. Its words speak of escape into sleep from the everyday deprivations of no food and nothing to smoke. Even lacking every day necessities, says the poem, "you got to sing" but, it continues, "we ain't got nothing to sing" and so again only sleep offers a solution. Now both the poem and song assume a more serious tone and take on greater weight. "If you can't sing - you got to die..." This key poetic phrase, hidden within cummings' deliberate avoidance of punctuation and capitals plus his imposition of arbitrary line endings, is allowed more space and time by L to bring its point home. The note values are lengthened up to four times as long per word and the sense of expanded time is created by the serious and sustained expressive style which contrasts to the song's bubbly, bouncing, lightweight opening section. The illusion created is of a much slower tempo when, in fact, the basic underlying pulse of the song never changes from start to finish. This switch of styles, for those whose memory goes back far enough, is the equivalent of turning the radio dial to change programs from the Mills Brothers to Fred Waring's Pennsylvanians, both of whom, without doubt, inspired the vocal writing for this song. For the composer, expanding the time frame was a way of underlining the importance of the poet's message to the creative artist. A wonderfully subtle touch in word setting is achieved at the end of this section. L, through repetition, has placed great emphasis on the word 'die'. The three upbeats and the inevitable downbeat which return us to the bright spirited tempo of the opening are sung by the soprano to the words, "die, die, die, die". On the fourth 'die' the five other members of the sextet come bouncing in. In retrospect, the four times spoken 'die' now becomes transformed in our ear and brain from the verb, *to die,* to a vocalised meaningless syllable long associated with close part harmony singing of which the most famous variants are *du, du, du, du* and Bing Crosby's *bu, bu, bu, bu.*

The last stanza of cummings' poem, "if you can't die you got to dream and we ain't got nothing to dream (come on kid - let's go to sleep)" is set much as the opening with the double meaning 'die' syllable forming a short accompanying vocalise for the top soprano line. With the repeat of the words, 'let's go to sleep' the mood again changes, this time to a quiet, reflective tone. Against sustained chords, the tenor sings 'die, die, die' and on the last repeat of the word all the singers join him singing only the vowel 'aye'. The ensemble sings a sweet wordless melody harmonised in six parts. The tenor repeats, 'die, die, die' as the accompanying melody continues, but this time hummed by the others. One last time, the tenor enters, "let's go to sleep", (actually only 'let's go to *slee-*), the others join him singing '*slee-*' one measure later, creating a gorgeous and complex version of a six part G major chord. The chord is quietly held for five plus full measures at which point, on the conductor's signal, all add the 'p'(puh!) consonant to *slee-* completing both the word 'sleep' and the song. This sextet provides a wonderful change of pace in regard to both vocal sound and the composer's choice of setting while making a profound statement related to the creative personality.

The final song defies a category, for me at any rate. Gregory Corso's *Zizi's Lament* is a hymn to hedonism, an idea one might have expected to flow from the pen of Paul Bowles. It is funny, sad and disturbing all at the same time. The poem requires a fair bit of detective work in regard to "Who?, What?, When?, Where?, and Why?" 'Where(?)' seems the easiest to solve, somewhere in North Africa I would hazard a guess - probably Morocco, a famous hangout for Artists and *weirdo's* looking for some new bizarre, hedonist experience. 'When(?)' might be post World War 2, perhaps the 1950's, but certainly at a time of little or no conflict in the area so as to permit the wide freedom of travel described by the protagonist in the poem. 'What?' remains problematical, for 'what' is the unidentified *laughing sickness*, for which the protagonist *Zizi* longs and searches for as if it were some Holy Grail. 'Why(?)' seems to be the sheer boredom in which our bizarre boaster finds himself after a life of experimentation in exoticism and eroticism that has not succeeded in achieving what he believes to be the ultimate physical experience. 'Who(?)', just by following the trail of clues, seems to suggest an ageing, ex-patriot, burned out, homosexual cross-dresser. L's reaction to this poem, a product of the *Beat Generation*, was that "it is either androgynous or a poem *in drag*[294]." Though unsure which of his two analyses was correct, he professed at any rate to hear a belly dancer's lament and this is pretty much the manner in which he has set the song and coloured the orchestration. It is the only song of the cycle where the tenor voice is given an opportunity to shine. In regard to clarity with which the text is set, whether you fathom what the poem is about or not, it is an admirable creation. The melody is authentically derived from a variety of tetrachordal, (four note), scales associated with music originally derived from Ancient

---

[294] *in drag* : a synonym for cross-dressing

Greece which spread to the Arab countries, Turkey and the former Persia and which, today, is native to Morocco, Algeria and Tunisia. Although it projects as very melodious, even simple, due to the pattern of phrases built upon only four successive tones at a time, it is crafted by L in a highly complex fashion as he moves freely from one tonality to another. This song, poem-wise and setting-wise, is odd man out in the cycle but it is no less accomplished for all that and it fulfils its role as part of the panorama of the culture and range of America's poetic heritage just as the entire cycle is testimony to the culture, range of versatility and vivid imagination of the composer. It may represent L's "unabashed eclecticism" but it is an integrated whole for all that and every bar is stamped with the Bernstein personality. *Songfest* is a work immediately accessible in part to the listener. The entire cycle requires time and repeated hearings to gain a full appreciation of what I have come to view as one of L's finest compositions and among the best, if not *the* best American song cycle composed to date. The work requires meticulous preparation especially in the ensembles in regard to diction and the balancing of principal and secondary voices to insure the clear projection of the words. This is doubly true of the conductor who must have an impeccable sense of rhythm and the courage to halve the written orchestral dynamics when they threaten to overpower the singer. One concert solution in regard to creating a full appreciation of *Songfest's* important poetic texts has been to have the poems read in advance by actors. A 1982 telecast of the composer's performance with the BBC Symphony Orchestra included a reading of all the poems as an intermission feature with L serving as annotator. A 1988 performance at the BBC Proms again under the composer's direction also featured a reading of the poems but in this instance as a preface to the performance of each appropriate song. In this instance, there was merit in the several critical complaints that in doing so it interfered with the listener's ability to sustain the natural flow and broad contrasts that make up *Songfest's* carefully proportioned structure. Whether actors are used or not, it is vitally important to the appreciation of the broad musical, intellectual and emotional scope of the cycle that its internal flow not be interrupted. With the poems printed in the concert program and the houselights lifted to halfs for those who wish to follow them, an appreciation of both the text and L's imaginative settings is achieved.

I have analysed *Songfest* not in composed order but in relation to topical groupings, to give a sense to the reader of the work's dimension and variety. The following diagram will provide a broad if pithy view of the cycle on both musical and textual levels, (Author / Title / Poem Description / Musical Setting):

The Poems

1. *Frank O'Hara*

To The Poem

(short/ simple/direct/ironic)

Sextet

(Opening Hymn: Freshly Cheerful/Tonal)

Three Settings for Solo Voice

2. *Lawrence Ferlinghetti*	3. *Julia de Burgos.*	4. *Walt Whitman*
The Pennycandystore Beyond The El	**A Julia De Burgos**	**To What You Said**
(pictorial/sensual)	(fierce/angry/passionate)	(sexual/direct/lyrical)
Baritone	**Soprano**	**Bass**
(Light & quick/Jazz/12 tone)	(Fast with fire/Tonal/a la DeFalla)	(Serious/slow/ Expressive/tonal)

Three Ensembles

5 L.Hughes/.J.Jordan	6.Anne Bradstreet	7.Gertrude Stein
I, Too,Sing America/OK Negroes	**To My Dear And Loving Husband**	**Storyette H.M.**
(identity/pride/mockery)	(ideal conjugal love)	(humorous/wry/ deadpan)
Duet:	**Trio**	**Duet**:
Mezzo-Soprano/Baritone	**Soprano/Mezzo-Soprano/Alto**	**Soprano/Bass**
(declamation vs blues/	(tranquil/tonal)	(perpetual motion/
(chromatic vs diatonic)		neo-classic)

WEST SIDE MAESTRO

----

8. ee cummings
: **if you can't eat you got to**
(disillusion/despair/surrender)
Sextet
(1930's Swing and Sway)

Three Solos

9. Aiken	10. Corso	11. Millay
Music I Heard With You	**Zizi's Lament**	**What My Lips Have Kissed**
(heartbreak)	(exotic/erotic/obscure)	(intense/ evocative/moving)
Mezzo Soprano	**Tenor**	**Alto**
(Moderate but moving	(Exotic Dance/Middle-Eastern/	(Very Slow/Expressive/
/Coplandesque/	Modal)	Chromatic)
Diatonic & Serial)		

----

12. E.A. Poe:
Israfel
(impassioned/inspired/rejoicing)
Sextet
(Closing Hymn: With Passion/Brilliant/Positive/ Britten-esque/**Unequivocally Tonal!**)

As these short descriptions underline, *Songfest* is a portrait of ideals and diversity. Both qualities are what America is all about or, at least, America *thinks* what it is all about.

Why, with all its direct qualities and brilliance has *A Julia De Burgos* come to be ignored by the criticsw? Out of nine British press reviews only one responded to it by name, one obliquely dismissed it as a *West Side Story* reject and the rest ignored it. Could it be that its very directness, its immediate appeal to the listener automatically labels it as a *not-sufficiently-*

esoteric-enough reject? - *Lenny* doing his *thing*??? Certainly *Julia De Burgos* is surrounded by much more textually and harmonically challenging settings but none is more brilliantly constructed or better captures the spirit of the poem and its writer and, most important of all, of such inevitable musical consequence that not one note, rhythm or harmonic decision can be challenged by the most skilful of analysts. It is not lack of originality that has made Bernstein the composer a critical target but his ability to use and combine all the possibilities at his disposal to create both simple and complex music of such immediate accessibility to audiences as to make both the writer and his creations suspect. He is not a Wagner, Schönberg or Stravinsky, revolutionaries all, supreme architects of everything composed for the past one-hundred-fifty years, but he is one of the many skilled, creative craftsmen who has appeared on the scene in the last half of the 20th century whose intellect and imagination was broad enough to combine the lessons of all three of his revolutionary forbears to create for himself a musical language which communicates to people of all ages and backgrounds. Will his music be part of our future heritage? I don't know but I hope so. Only through contemporary music that communicates will audiences open themselves to the possibilities of more radical musical ideas than those that appealed to Leonard Bernstein. If he was not the most radical of the century's original thinkers or revolutionaries, he was nevertheless among the leaders who helped shape musical tastes for half a century. His music represents a bridge to all contemporary music. It is not the only road but it is one of the roads over which audiences, at this time, are more willing to travel. To close access to so valuable a route under the mistaken belief that only by struggling along the bumpiest and rockiest of highways will one arrive at the proper destination threatens the halt of all movement in that direction. A bridge is not a highway but it is a connection. Without it, the way to a given destination can take much, much longer and even end up discouraging the traveller from wishing to continue on, perhaps resulting in his turning his back on travelling in that direction ever again.

Arias and Barcarolles

Irony plays an important part in both *Songfest* and *Arias and Barcarolles*. It is doubly ironic, therefore, that *Arias*, a work whose act of composition provided L with one of the most joyful creative experiences within his lifetime, was written to commemorate the passing of an old friend, Jack Romann, of the Baldwin Piano Company who had only recently died of AIDS. In 1978, ten years previously, in an interview with Paul Hume, L had fantasised about writing an "American kind of opera" using his *Songfest* cast of singers. "We could all go off somewhere for a month and talk for ten hours a day," he idealised, " and out of that would evolve the scenario for an opera."[295] The act of creating *Arias* provided him with a scenario analogous to this daydream. It is wonderfully documented in the published reminiscences of Michael Tilson Thomas in conversation with the critic Edward Seckerson[296]. Tilson Thomas had agreed to join L in a piano four-hand duet to accompany a new composition, which L was composing within the short space of three weeks for a fund-raising event in memory of Romann. As bits and pieces of the work came together, their rehearsals seemed to become as much an improvisation of possibilities as practise sessions. The following is one of Tilson Thomas's recollections,

"...sometimes I would play something a bit differently, and he'd say, 'Oh, you didn't play what I wrote but it sounded better. Do that again!...And then in a couple of places there were spots where it wasn't quite filled in musically, and I would improvise something, and he would say, 'Oh, what was that? Do something like that again!

We would go on for hours and hours. When Michael Barrett and Bright Sheng[297] came over, Lenny and I would play it, and then they would play it. Lucas Foss would come over and he'd play it through with Lenny. So there

---

[295] Humphrey Burton: *Leonard Bernstein*, pg.444

[296] Michael Tilson Thomas, *Viva Voce, Coversations with Edward Seckerson*, Faber & Faber 1994

[297] Michael Barrett, Bernstein conducting protege and distinguished pianist. With pianist Steven Blier he was responsible for the premiere recording of *Arias and Barcaroles*. Bright Sheng, Chinese-American composer, responsible for creating the first orchestration of Arias and Barcaroles under L's guidance.

was this whole little community of people who were all on the scene, working with Lenny at making this piece happen. It was so exciting to see the piece growing every day, and having fun improvising something in rehearsal. And then overnight he would have transformed and refined it into something special."

This joyful creative time radiates throughout the song cycle. One finds the usual comments, questions and doubts on aspects of love, which were an ever-present Bernstein preoccupation, but there is no inextinguishable anger, dysfunctional neuroses or political, social or religious commentary with which many of his vocal compositions are usually preoccupied. As with *Songfest*, there are musical 'bookends'. A long dissonant instrumental opens the *Prelude*. The singers in unison join in but in contrast to the jagged accompaniment they sing with undisturbed calm, and without expression, "I love you, it's so easy to say it". Again there is a ferocious instrumental interlude and when calm is once more restored our singers neutrally repeat, "I love you". Only the setting of their final, "I love you" reveals the possibility of dissonance between them. The irony of this contrast has been noted in other writings on *Arias*, but this opening song, which introduces a cycle dealing with various aspects and types of love, can also be interpreted as demonstrating that what appears on the surface does not always reflect the true depth of the emotional situation. The closing song to the cycle, *Nachspiel*, (Epilogue), sub-titled *in memorium*, is in complete contrast, a quiet and touching introspective Mahler-esque waltz tune to be played in a simple, sustained fashion, while the singers hum a descant *pianissimo* throughout in counterpoint[298].

In-between these 'bookends' are six songs, a duet, four solos, (soprano and baritone alternating), and a second duet. All of the songs, according to Jack Gottlieb's *Prefatory Note* to the score, are autobiographically derived or related. With the exception of two of the songs, which are credited to L's

---

[298] *Arias* provided a second reincarnation for the *Prelude* and a the third for the *Nachspiel*. The *Prelude* was derived from a song written for his daughter, Jamie's wedding. *Nachspiel*, originally a song titled "First Love (for my Mother, March 1986)" was also published as one of *Thirteen Anniversaries* for piano in memory of his friend Ellen Goetz.

mother, Jennie, and the Yiddish poet, Yankev-Yitskhok Segal, all other texts were written by the composer. Gottlieb points out that *Arias* encompasses those possible elements that form a life cycle from birth, *(Greeting)*, to death, *(Nachspiel)*; although the various events depicted, (childhood, loving/un-loving relationships, marriage and married life), are not dealt with by the composer in chronological order.

The second song, *Love Duet*, poses a lyric with a double meaning. Endless questions pass between a married couple. At first they seem to be examining the inner structure of the song they are singing. In truth they are examining and questioning the structure of their marriage and relationship. A second batch of questions are more directly concerned with themselves, some self-examining, some, slightly cruel, towards the other and better not voiced. When all the endless questioning becomes too repetitious and boring, the couple just stop and there is silence between them. This is one of two quite personal, autobiographical songs. Much as I had promised myself that I would avoid any involvement with L's private life, in this cycle of songs he simply doesn't permit it. The words to this and the fourth song, *The Love of my Life*, are the memories come to life of a man who had never buried his ghosts. They are the confessions of a man who insisted on using the world as a stage for what was best left said behind closed doors. They are, nevertheless, interestingly constructed songs, like *Songfest*, part of an unbridled eclectic whole that somehow manages to create a logical entity from all the different styles and ideas.

The third song, *Little Smary*, words credited to L's mother, is a memory of childhood and a child's reliving of a bedtime story which in turn frightened, saddened and then, as is only proper, gladdened him at the inevitable 'happy ending'. Each of the child's reactions is embellished with stylistically varied segments of musical onomatopoeia to fit the emotion and the physical goings on in the story. This song with its *twee* constructed lyric had most of the critics up in arms for what they viewed as irrelevant foolishness. The satirical send-up of the Disney-style cartooned adventure so exciting to children with its musical soundtrack containing a hundred classical borrowings in every style to match every gesture and emotion of our animated heroes, heroines and most loveable animals to the point of absurdity seems to have totally escaped them.

The fourth song, *The Love of My Life*, is an erotic confessional of a man of ambiguous sexuality incapable of a living love of any kind. Love to him exists only in a fantasy which may come or that which, unawares, may have been and gone. That which is experienced in the present is only a forgettable physical happening to be described in monosyllabic erotic phrases and which always ends in predictable disappointment.

A free-flowing tone row purveying on-going sadness opens the long slow introduction launching an implied but unfulfilled fughetta that reaches a highly dramatic climax before settling into the song proper. The song itself is of a not-too-strict twelve-tone construction. Its lack of tonal center creates an unsettled ambience that mirrors the copious, unsettled thoughts of its protagonist.

The fifth song, *Greeting*, found its way to *Arias* from L's ever trusty trunk of musical memorabilia where it had been placed for safe-keeping more than thirty years previously. Originally inspired by every Jewish father's pride and joy, the birth of his first son, in this instance Alexander Serge (after Koussevitzky) Bernstein, the song was revised for the cycle in 1988. In three pithy couplets it muses upon the individual qualities of renewal to life, which the birth of both male and female child bestow, and then upon the wonder of birth itself. Although the song is written for the mezzo soprano voice, the thoughts expressed seem to be that of the Patriarch to whom birth is the eternal symbol of personal continuity. By wisely assigning the song to the maternal warmth of the mezzo voice the song takes on a broader sense of expression rather than the air of personal, sentimental comment. Its presence in the cycle provides a needed moment of tranquillity. Musically it is atmospherically reminiscent of *Grover's Corner* from Aaron Copland's score to the film, *Our Town*.

Oif Mayn Khas'neh, (At My Wedding), is the second of two texts employed in the cycle not authored by the composer. Based upon a *Yiddish* poem by

WEST SIDE MAESTRO

Yankev-Yitskhok Segal, it tells of a young Jewish fiddler who spends his days and evenings in small villages being fed by local *shikses*[299], playing at all-night gentile drinking parties, learning their customs and incorporating what he has learned in wonderful ways with his native Jewish style of performing. The elder Jewish musicians are in awe of his new kind of music and do not understand how a boy ignorant even in Hebrew is able to accomplish such things. At the wedding of the narrator we hear that he played with such passion that people were torn from their seats and began to dance wildly. Not only did he stir them to uncontrolled excitement but his melodies cut across their heartstrings till they bled and caused them to beg for mercy.

Jack Gottlieb alludes to a possible sub-conscious link with this text to L's father, Samuel Bernstein, who, like the elders of the poem, initially showed little faith in his son's aspirations. Such descriptions leave this writer in a somewhat compromised position in trying to avoid the psycho-babble that, with the exception of the Burton biography, proliferates in regard to writings on L's career and relationships. Michael Barrett, another Bernstein associate, offers a simpler, more picturesque explanation, as L's description to him of the uninhibited singing and dancing of his father's Hassidic friends who first instilled the joy of music making in him as a boy. If one is not to shy away from seeking out other autobiographical allusions, it seems not a great stretch to easily find a career parallel to the Jewish musician who captures the imagination of Western Christian society even in their most exclusive anti-Semitic strongholds such as Vienna, making all dance to his tune and awarding him both riches and their greatest honours. In the end, however, all is speculation.

Oif Mayn Khas'neh is a concert art song of a dimension enabling it to be extrapolated from the cycle for performance on its own. It is the second longest song of the cycle. Its *Yiddish* text lends it a unique word sound setting. It is filled with the drama and humour of a song by Mussorgsky, a composer quoted in its musical text. The other songs of *Arias and Barcaroles* are more personal and intimate even when their texts are

---

[299] *shikse* - (Yiddish) A non-Jewish woman, especially a young one.

WEST SIDE MAESTRO

deliberately obscure. *At My Wedding* is highly pictorial, exotic and extrovert in the manner of Ravel's *Asie* in his orchestra song cycle, *Schéhérazade*. Using a variety of tonal and non-tonal techniques, *At My Wedding's* auto-biographical musical quotes include not only Mussorgsky's *Pictures at an Exhibition* but melismatic sung passages in describing the wedding service characteristic of those one might hear intoned within the synagogue.

The penultimate song, *Mr. and Mrs. Webb Say Goodnight*, depicts an imagined mini-drama in the bedroom of Charles Webb, the Dean of the Indiana University School of Music, during a night of sleeplessness experienced by the entire family. Mrs. Webb, (Kenda), reproves the on-going high-jinx of the Webb teenage sons, Malcolm and Kent, who refuse to settle down to a nights sleep. (In performance the jazzy, *scat* singing of the two boys is performed by either the accompanying pianists in the chamber music version or by two members of the ensemble in the orchestrated version).

Mrs. Webb is having a bad night. She is upset at her husband's last minute change of plan to stay in Indiana rather than to relocate to a more important position in a new city. She sings of the embarrassment she will experience having told friends, social organisations, the milkman and the newsagents that they were moving. Mr. Webb, the soul of warm reassurance, calms his wife by first joining her in evening prayers and then recalling romantic memories from their past. He succeeds admirably in reducing his wife's anxiety and they complete their evening prayers together. Quiet descends on their bedroom and the scene closes but not before we again hear the whispering voices of the Webb boys still larking about, this time communicating ever so quietly in their *jazz scat*-speak. The scene fizzles out.

L had met Charles Webb and his family in 1982 when he was honoured by Indiana University as its first fellow of a new Institute for Advanced Study. It was while at the University that recently completed portions of *A Quiet Place* were first tried out at specially organised opera workshops. Although L and the Webbs did not extensively socialise during his stay, they seem to have hit it off astonishingly well from the first. This certainly would account for L's liberty in creating so personal a fantasy about the Webb's for his song cycle.

WEST SIDE MAESTRO

This song in structure and style seems a subconscious salute to Stephan Sondheim, easily identified with a scene from any of his colleague's *Sweeney Todd*-and-beyond music dramas[300]. It is a self-contained mini-musical with relationships and characters fully delineated, and a plotline that ties together the time, the place and the emotional state of mind of its cast of Webb family members. It is all done within a highly varied and contrasting musical setting without the use of spoken dialogue of any kind. It is funny, fraught, warm and tender in turns with a happy ending that contains a bit of a twist to it. This is Broadway Bernstein at its best and most sophisticated.

The cycle closes with *Nachspiel*, an Epilogue, during which the singers, in accompaniment to a slow, nostalgic waltz, hum a wordless descant. This bittersweet, Mahler-like setting represents the third metamorphoses of this valuable fragment of musical memorabilia. The piano as a symbol threads its way through all three settings. *Nachspiel* began life as the song, *First Love*, created for a family occasion and dedicated to his mother on her eighty-eighth birthday. In his song lyric, L declared his eighty-eight year old mother his 'first love' but the piano with its eighty-eight keys his second love. It was later published as an *Anniversary*, one of twenty-nine *Anniversaries* for piano composed and dedicated over his lifetime, in this instance to the memory of a yet another departed friend, Ellen Goetz. As the conclusion to his song cycle it would again be recreated for piano and voice as a memorial to a friend, in this instance to a friend who represented L's career-long association with the Baldwin Piano Company. *Nachspiel* projects as a work of utter simplicity, but its complexity is sufficient and subtle enough for Jack Gottlieb to identify its genesis as Schubertian. Gottlieb is quoted by Joseph Horowitz, in his program note for Gerhard Schwarz's New York performance of the Bright Sheng orchestration of the song cycle. One can further identify echoes of Schumann and, in my own view, in every turn of phrase and unresolved cadence, echoes of Mahler.

---

[300] L actually identified *Love Duet* with its parody on word games as the *Sondheim* song of the cycle. He used to play these word games with Sondheim into the wee hours. Sondheim was among the few people, much to his chagrin, who could beat him at it.

WEST SIDE MAESTRO

Whatever the source of its inspiration, *Nachspiel's* exquisite simplicity allows the listener a moment of reflection after the variety and complexity of what has preceded it. Let us take a short overall view of the cycle itself. There has been the enigma posed by the first two songs as to what is or isn't love and its expression, which along the way has touched upon expressive dissonance and the minimalism of composer John Adams. There are the personal remembrances of the next two songs, the first a happy one of childhood, the second of the ongoing barrenness of the emotionally unfulfilled. These two have brought us in contact with the varied dodecaphonic approaches of Alban Berg and Arnold Schönberg. The fifth song observes the joys and rewards of parental love expressed in the tonal fashion of Aaron Copland. The sixth song is the odd man out. Its autobiographical allusions are not immediately apparent, as is the case with the preceding songs. Through two of L's close associates, Jack Gottlieb and the conductor/pianist, Michael Barrett we gain two rather different views of the possible source of its inspiration, both relating to L's father and his Jewish upbringing but neither providing an obvious logical reason for its place in the cycle beyond its central character, the Jewish musician who conquers all through his unique talent. Its musical content seems a mixture of everything that has preceded it. *Mr & Mrs Webb Say Goodnight* provides the most positive, affectionate picture of marriage or a heterosexual relationship ever musically depicted by L[301], light years away from his own *Trouble in Tahiti* and *A Quiet Place* or even the characters in his musicals. Perhaps that was its and the Webb's special appeal to the composer. The style is modern Broadway as it has matured through L's influence and beyond him via Stephan Sondheim. The final Epilogue is a farewell and how better to express it than in the language of Mahler, the composer whose many musical expressions of farewell had helped shape cornerstones in L's career. *Arias and Barcaroles* is not of the dimension of *Songfest* but it is a wonderfully crafted work that, with its two predecessors, *Songfest* and *A Quiet Place*, set the stamp on a maturely evolved Bernstein style which

---

[301] The one exception would be L's setting of Anne Bradstreet's *To My Dear and Loving Husband* from *Songfest*. The special appeal of the Webbs, a genuine, uncomplicated, loving family, were that they were real to his experience after a lifetime of having witnessed and been part of failed personal family experiences.

demonstrated everything he believed the contemporary music of the future would encompass.

Aria and Barcaroles has come to us in four forms, the first two consisting of the original 1988 chamber version for the private premiere that called for piano four hands with four singers and the world premiere version introduced in Israel one year later, the published version, calling for two singers only, soprano and baritone. This second version exists in a definitive performance on KOCH records recorded under the composer's supervision. The singers are Judy Kaye and William Sharp with Michael Barrett and Steven Blier performing the piano four hands accompaniment. If one recalls L's description of the manner in which *Songfest* should be performed, "by singers who sing in a 'friendly' manner as if they were entertaining after a dinner party, one is struck by how much more appropriate such an instruction would apply to this vocal chamber work.

There can be no question that the cycle works perfectly in this intimate setting. *Arias and Barcaroles* projects a personal quality by the very nature of its texts with the one exception of the song with the big ring about it, Yankev-Yitskhok Segal's *Oyf Mayn Khas'neh*, (*At My Wedding*). The absolute word clarity that the chamber version produces is quite obviously a big plus in its favour. Nevertheless, being an intimate work does not necessarily imply that *Arias* is conceived as a small, incidental work. It has real dimension and colour and this was later realised in two orchestrations. The first, by Bright Sheng, was created under the composer's watchful eye. It is relatively simple and chamber-like, using only strings and percussion. It is wonderfully recorded and performed by Jane Bunnell & Dale Duesing with the strings and percussion of the Seattle Symphony conducted by Gerard Schwarz on the Delos label.[302] The second setting, by Bruce Coughlin, is a grandiose, symphonic orchestration created three years after the composer's death and premiered in London in 1993 under the direction of Michael Tilson Thomas with the London Symphony and the same soloists with whom

---

[302] Schwarz conducted the premiere of Sheng's orchestration at Long Island University in September 1989 with Susan Graham and Kurt Ollmann as his soloists.

he later recorded it for DG that same year, Frederica von Stade & Thomas Hampson.

The orchestration by Bright Sheng works wonderfully well from first to last but especially so in the first four movements where not only does the Coughlin orchestration tend to overwhelm the singers but the songs themselves. The violence of a big orchestra opening the *Prelude* is enormous, more befitting some three act tragic opera. The woodwind/string combinations of the second song, *"Love Duet"* allow for a good balance between voice and orchestra but the repetitious use of bright instrumental colours tends to draw our attention away from the words being sung. Bright Sheng's gentle string backing and his use of pizzicato for variety are quite sufficient and perfect. The third song, a child's fairy tale for bedtime, with its musical overtones of Alban Berg for the scary parts of the story, begins wonderfully but as it progresses becomes so overwritten by Coughlin as to put one in mind of the use of a sledge-hammer to crack a walnut. I appreciated the Coughlin orchestration more in the fourth song, *The Love of my Life*. The long instrumental opening is effectively and atmospherically set. Problems begin, however, with the entry of the voice and the brilliant instrumental touches that again tend to upstage the soloist, especially in the erotic word association section of the lyric. There is no question that Coughlin is a brilliant orchestrator. I am surprised, however, that between the live performance and the subsequent recording a blue pencil was not more judiciously used on the more thickly scored portions of the orchestration out of consideration for the needs of the singers. From the fifth song onward, I have not a further single complaint. Coughlin's orchestration is gentle and tender for *Greeting*, wildly but appropriately colourful for the *Wedding* scene, funny, jazzy and sentimental in turns in a *show-biz* way for *Mr. and Mrs.Webb* and their family's nocturnal high jinx and very moving in a simple fashion for the closing *Nachspiel*. Perhaps the ideal solution would be to combine the first four movements of Bright Sheng's arrangement with last four movements of Coughlin's. Copyright law and egos being what they are, I would not hold my breath waiting for that to happen.

WEST SIDE MAESTRO

The recording of the piano four-hand version of *Arias* (Koch) offers in addition an attractive selection of Bernstein showtunes and can be highly recommended. The Tilson Thomas recording of the Coughlin orchestration (DG) is an all-Bernstein disc which includes an interesting debut recording of an instrumental suite drawn from the opera *A Quiet Place* and an explosive performance of the Symphonic Dances from *West Side Story*. The Delos disc, (Schwarz and the Seattle Symphony), is my first choice if you want the best overall orchestrated version, (Bright Sheng), of *Arias and Barcaroles*. The rest of the repertoire chosen for the disc is a bit of a mixed bag. Listen to each one before you make up your mind! I am happy to own all three versions.

How does one sum up the accomplishments and place in musical history of a Leonard Bernstein? What is left to us is an incomplete portrait even though so much was known about the subject. These days the word *genius* is tossed about so indiscriminately that its depth of meaning and application has been devalued to little more than *PR hype*. The term *Renaissance man* has been used to describe L's multiplicity of talents, interests and accomplishments and, perhaps, since individuals who possess such vast gifts and enquiring minds are so rare, viewing them in an historical perspective better serves to define their uniqueness. His huge, regenerative resources of energy permitted him to pour himself wholeheartedly into a wealth of creative activities, while maintaining the continuum of an international career in conducting in which, whether one always agreed or not with the final results he achieved, he deservedly rose to world pre-eminence. However, even that single musical thread that occupied the greatest part of his professional life left many unanswered questions for those who followed his many-faceted career with undiminishing interest.

Whatever were his own feelings and expressed desires, *conductor* is properly the first listing to follow his name in the music dictionaries, encyclopaedias and various compendium *Who's-who* publications. Among his several *creative* gifts[303], *Composer* would have been his own choice to follow and based upon the sustained international fame of one theatre work alone, *West Side Story*, one would find it hard to resist that option. Such reasoning, however, would have been a metaphorical blade in L's heart. He aspired to a different kind of recognition as a composer. However, the life of a classical composer takes time, self-imposed isolation and loneliness and a good deal of instant frustration and emotional pain not to mention the *post partum* pain at the hands of critics. The material rewards for a composer that will provide not only the good things but the very finest luxuries are usually slow in arriving as well. For a compulsively gregarious, impatient individual whose other immense talents could bring about fame and fortune much more quickly, the choice was less difficult than the many Bernstein disclaimers given in interviews over his lifetime would lead us to believe. He had the talent but as a composer *er hat kein sitzfleisch*. That descriptive German expression which has been incorporated in *Yiddish* describes someone who is "unable to sit down for long", the deeper implication being "to lack perseverance." If Lenny persevered towards any goal it was to seduce the goddess of success, and as quickly as possible. This he accomplished at the remarkably young age of 25 years. When interviewers would imply that things came to him easily he would protest that he worked very hard for what he had accomplished. No one can testify to that better than myself having worked with him in close association over a ten-year period. Nevertheless, a graph created to measure the direction his career took from the moment he was appointed assistant conductor of the NY Philharmonic[304] would show a line moving in an ever upward direction without troughs of any kind right to the end of his life - disappointments, certainly, troughs never. Career-wise, he lived a charmed life.

---

[303] One must not lose sight of the differentiation between L's creative activities as a composer and writer on subjects musical and the career of a conductor which involves re-creating the creative works of others.

[304] One could chart L's rise to fame from the moment he met Serge Koussevitzky.

WEST SIDE MAESTRO

If recognition as a serious composer was withheld from him over the course of his career, it was by other composers and critics, not the public. But it was the approval of his peers that he sought. Staying with hypothetical graphs, his symphonic output for orchestra and the stage from 1942-57 was his single longest and most fertile period of composing activity. As was to be his life's pattern, it was followed by a period during which creative output was reduced to a trickle or ceased altogether. The years that followed were marked by sporadic bursts that produced a major work of consequence only upon occasion. The early creative career, however, is impressive by any standard. These years were dominated by his four most famous major musicals plus the incidental music and songs he supplied for a fifth Broadway production, a revival of *Peter Pan*. There was also a first foray into opera, the forty-five minute, one Act miniature, *Trouble in Tahiti,* two symphonies, *Jeremiah* and *The Age of Anxiety*, the ballets *Fancy Free, Facsimile,* and *Prelude, Fugue and Riffs*[305], the violin concerto *Serenade,* the film score to *On The Waterfront* and a host of smaller chamber works mostly for voice and piano or solo piano.

Following this initial fifteen-year productive period, no new composition of consequence was to appear for the next five years, 1958-63. These years represent the first half of his tenure as Music Director of the NY Philharmonic. 1963 was to mark an end to the creative drought with the premiere of his Third Symphony, *Kaddish*. This new symphony augurs the fresh direction L's creative output was to take. The question arises as to whether Copland's 1962 conversion to twelve-tone techniques was the major influence that brought this about. The fact is that the *Kaddish* Symphony marks the first of the Bernstein compositions to extensively fuse twelve-tone techniques with his established commitment to tonality. In ten years time, he would make the strongest possible argument for such a fusion in his series of lectures at Harvard University. Yet, it is one thing to lecture on such matters and another to be creatively demonstrating its rightness and potency. The historic fact is that between 1958 and 1970 L produced only two works of consequence, the *Kaddish* Symphony in '63, which represents a

---

[305] Originally written as ballet music music for the musical, *Wonderful Town.*

daring shift in style, and the *Chichester Psalms* in '65, which could not be more traditionally tonal[306].

Having departed the halls of Lincoln Center in 1969, leaving behind his time consuming responsibilities as Music Director of the NY Philharmonic, his creative juices again began to flow. It didn't happen instantly but considering what was on the horizon there must have been a good deal of internal creative gestation going on for in 1971 *Mass* shook the Kennedy Center in Washington to its foundations. No work written by L had previously created such controversy and so polarised his audience or critics. In every sense the work is autobiographical of the man and the musician, eclectic, brash, iconoclastic, daring, pretentious, shocking, political, trendy and unbelievably talented. It was a work that stated in no uncertain terms, "I'm still here!" 1972-73 was devoted to another totally different creative project - thinking out, developing, putting into some kind of form and finally delivering his six Charles Eliot Norton Lectures at Harvard University. Subsequent to the Harvard Lectures, he was again seriously immersed in composing producing the following year an hour-long ballet, perhaps his most complex contemporary score to date, for Jerome Robbins' ballet *Dybbuk*. His next major theatre partnership with Alan Lerner resulted in the first unmitigated disaster of his career, the 1976 production of *1600 Pennsylvania Avenue*. Nevertheless, one must recognise the huge amount of music he produced for the show, much of it, as we now know from the ninety minute *White House Cantata* which has been posthumously constructed from his score, of a high and often outstanding quality. The following year L produced what I believe may come to be viewed as his masterpiece of this period, the song cycle, *Songfest*. *Songfest* represents a sophisticated synthesis of his vision of the contemporary music of the future, an eclectic

---

[306] I do not view the Symphonic Dances from *West Side Story* from 1961 or other future reworkings of past triumphs or failures as examples of fresh creativity but more akin to the metaphoric treading of water until rescue in the form of a commission deadline or the undeniable internal need to compose shook or panicked L out of his creative hybernation.The Symphonic Dances are exactly what the title suggests, long stretches of ballet and dance music lifted whole and note for note from the *West Side* score, resequenced to provide continuity, (that was L's contribution), and then re-scored for symphony orchestra by Sid Ramon and Irwin Kostal, the show's original orchestrators.

fusion of tonal and non-tonal techniques. This stunning work is for L the final demonstration in the musical evolution he envisaged and advocated. It had developed within him over fifteen years from conceptual pupa to caterpillar to butterfly.

The next two years were barren but creative activity resumed from 1980-82. Two lightweight commissions, *Divertimento* and *A Musical Toast*, appeared in 1980 and the extended soliloquy for flute and small Orchestra, the Nocturne, *Halil* in 1981. While *Halil* is instantly communicative, musically it is a look backwards, lyrically reminiscent of *On The Waterfront* plus a good deal of Copland and Bartok. In the background during this period was, however, another major work bubbling to the surface, the opera *A Quiet Place*, the dramatic sequel to the 1952 one-act opera, *Trouble in Tahiti*. *A Quiet Place* is Wagnerian in all its trappings with its composer involved as co-writer of the text, with the wide application of musical motives for characters and events, with its symphonic development of all its musical material which includes its prequel, *Trouble in Tahiti,* now integrated into the fabric of the new opera, and with an assured application of the composer's new musical language which represented an intermarriage of tonal and non tonal music.

Only two large scale works of substance emerged over the next eight years, Jubilee Games, in 1986 which, through a process of accretion over the next four years was to expand to the 1989 *Concerto for Orchestra*, and the brilliant and witty song cycle, *Arias and Barcaroles* which, in my opinion, was only fully realised in its deserved large scale dimension in the composer approved orchestration by Bright Sheng.

In the face of this brief summary of creative accomplishment that fills two and a half pages of Jack Gottlieb's *Leonard Bernstein*: A Complete Catalogue of his Works, L, nevertheless, after 1957 was, at best, a part time composer Before that time, it could have been a toss up which of two careers he could or would pursue, a full time composer who was a first class conductor, or a first class conductor who was a part-time composer[307].. History now views Mahler first as a composer not primarily as a conductor despite his pursuing the latter career on a full time basis during his lifetime. Mahler reserved every summer for his composing and at each summer's end his continued growth in his creative craft was revealed in new and ever more remarkable works. For L, forever announcing sabbaticals or taking time off to reacquaint himself with his muse became more and more a matter of the road to hell being paved with good intentions. I have limited my brief to only dealing with his stage works and works for orchestra, twenty-eight in all. The totality of his output, however, consists of five Broadway musicals plus songs, choruses and incidental music for two straight plays, two operas, three symphonies, three ballets, a Mass, two major song cycles and two miniature ones, a violin concerto, a film score, a varied miscellany to include the *Chichester Psalms, Concerto for Orchestra, Three Meditations* for cello, *Halil, Divertimento, Slava, A Musical Toast, Prelude, Fugue and Riffs*, plus twenty-nine *Anniversaries,* sixteen chamber music works for piano or small ensembles, about thirty songs to include compositions for chorus, (many for projects that never came to fruition in their original form), and about thirteen other works, some merely a reworking or rehashing of compositions written from the earlier part of his career. It should be noted that his facile ability to recycle even small fragments of discarded efforts was remarkable and helped extricate him from many ticklish situations when deadlines stared him in the face. The single factor that stands out, as one studies the chronological list, is the ever-diminishing creative output during the course of his career. Still the list is impressive and one cannot help but admire what he accomplished as a composer during an over-committed lifetime. One also must not forget the song of a different creative *siren* calling to him from another rock in the ocean of his creativity, *Television. This* major

---

[307] Jack Gottlieb's: Leonard Bernstein, A Complete Catalogue Of His Works. This short volume is much more than its title implies. It is not only a comprehensive detailed listing of every composition L ever wrote but those that have been withdrawn in their original form and which now exist in other published forms recycled into compositions dating from 1975 till his death in 1990. One can also find lists of L's own writings to include articles, books and television scripts, a comprehensive list of books on Bernstein to include dissertations and six pages of honors and awards bestowed upon him over the years. It is an indispensable catalogue for anyone doing research on Bernstein.

professional distraction, which instantly launched him into a far wider public orbit than that of the concert hall or even Broadway, tipped the scales in another creative direction.

It all began in 1954 and continued annually for the next thirty-five years. His appearances which instantly placed his several musical gifts on display, writer, presenter, conductor, pianist, teacher, a virtual music guru to the family, transformed him into a national star with international stardom not far behind. As a classical musician he already enjoyed an unusual fame as a result of his work on Broadway. Leonard Bernstein, the composer of *On The Town*, brilliantly transferred to the Silver Screen with a superstar cast, was certainly a name if not yet a face recognised by millions, if only in the major capital cities of America. Television bestowed upon him a more personal immediacy with an immense public in small town America. In headcount he reached an audience during a single telecast greater than that which he could encompass in a lifetime of giving concerts. His Hollywood good looks and cultivated accent, combined with his gifts as a communicator and charismatic conductor who made learning about music compelling television watching even for a complete novice, made culture fashionable in homes where the average viewer tended to turn on football and baseball programs in their spare time rather than long *hair* musical essays on Beethoven, opera or how to conduct a symphony orchestra. It catapulted him into a most extraordinary position. Not only did he become America's favourite and most famous musician, but an international super-star of Elvis Presley proportion.

Considering the impact television had upon his professional life, the consistency of his commitment to the medium and the amount of time and mental energy he devoted to developing his image as one of its unique educational communicators, it would not be unwarranted to view this area of his *creative* professional life as the one with greatest continuity. On balance, it commands that position much more than the part time career to which his composing was relegated in the pecking order of his priorities. After all, while his stature as a composer continues to be the subject of critical debate, his position as one of the important figures within the history of the development of television is unquestioned.

It is pointless to even muse upon the future compositions he might have produced. His undisciplined work habits as a composer throughout his career set in stone a pattern which would have been virtually impossible to alter even if one believed his repetitiously regular and passionately professed good intentions to do just that. What is astonishing in the midst of the constant internal intellectual tug of war among the many interests that vied for his attention is the manner in which he continued effortlessly to shift his focus at will within so many areas of the musical Arts. These several disciplines were not merely the collected interests of an enquiring and brilliant mind. The pursuit and conquest of each possessed him with a Faustian passion. That is why his failures were as magnificent in their own way as his successes. One can only be grateful that he continued to produce right to the end works that, when even of variable quality and importance, still represented the best of his inventive mind and creative gifts. In retrospect they allow us to construct a cubistic musical profile of a composer/performer whose divergent talents illuminated the lives of all with whom he came in contact.

For those genuinely interested in the musician, and I assume that if you have travelled with me this far on this extended musical journey that your fascination lies as much with the musician as with the controversial private individual sometimes luridly described in his several biographies, that you, both listener and professional, are interested in taking the time to develop a more considered, in depth examination of not only the quality and originality of the totality of what Bernstein the musician, composer and teacher accomplished but a more objective evaluation of his creative gifts and his contribution to American music and the Arts in general.

To form such an evaluation, one really must start afresh. If a new, valid and balanced view is to be constructed, both L's creative and re-creative output must be separated from the reams of titillating gossip which scarred our perception of the artist throughout his career and for which he himself, through his open and indiscriminate life style and compulsion for public confession must shoulder the largest portion of blame. One must be wary of taking a predetermined partisan view that villainizes and then summarily dismisses critics such as Harold Schonberg and Virgil Thomson. Their powerful positions as chief critics of New York's two most influential broadsheets conditioned and set patterns for much of the way L's compositions and music making were long evaluated, not only in America in his lifetime but even to a degree in Europe which, in general, readily and enthusiastically embraced both the man and his multi-faceted musical gifts. One wonders whether to be astonished or amused to read record reviews written eight years after his death churning out the same equivocal, cliché terminology of the old American reviews. Opinions continue to echo like some sort of gospel from a new generation of critics who, not having appeared as yet to have formed a researched, thoughtful view of their own, continue to lean upon the convenient, past views of others without examining whether a genuine basis exists within their own experience to make similar pronouncements.

In many ways L's talent defied criticism because of the quirky nature of the man, which spilled over into both the creative and re-creative pursuits of the artist. The volatility of his mind and his seeming non-ending curiosity in all matters intellectual caused him to constantly shift from one of his several talents or thought-provoking projects to another, not always leading to the most consistent or positive results. This intellectual over-commitment manifested itself early on in his career as a composer resulting in a noted lack of dependability in delivering his compositions at the promised time. Documentation over L's entire career support my own ten year experience of non-stop highly pressurised, panic conditions out of which were produced an astonishing long list of accomplishments in every field to which he applied his talents. It is not surprising with so much on his plate all the time that dependability became less and less the strong suit or even a concern of this musician of potential consummate artistry. Every aspect of his wide ranging career as conductor, composer for Broadway and the concert hall, solo performer, writer/teacher and television personality evoked in him high passions. If that was not enough to fill his jam-packed schedule, he remained politically active throughout his lifetime, supporting a wide variety of social causes, many politically dangerous in terms of his career, resulting in his being viewed with suspicion by the F.B.I., or subjecting him at times to public and press ridicule.[308] His passion for politics went beyond the shores of America. The politics of Israel remained a constant concern to him and he devoted himself to numerous fund raising causes on behalf of the Jewish state and its national orchestra with whom he enjoyed a close association to the very end of his life. Becoming a member of the *establishment* with his appointment to the NY Philharmonic did not, as one might expect, concentrate his mind towards a more practical, organised schedule of undertakings but made him even more profligate in his commitments and public pronouncements. In his remaining seventeen years following the Norton Lectures this lack of dependability became exacerbated. As one of the handful of superstar conductors, he became a law unto himself, alone determining the projects to be undertaken, the consistency or lack thereof of his work patterns as they related to performing and composing commitments and, in regard to the latter, completion dates. Most important, he had reached a stage of independence in which he became answerable to no one. The chronicle of Bernstein the composer from the early days of his career regarding his several commissions is one of delay following delay while he wilfully permitted himself to be distracted and his work patterns broken at crucial moments of his involvement in a creative project[309]. Even when the importance of the occasion was the American Bi-centennial, pressing completion dates for *Songfest* were ignored and barely a third of the work was completed on schedule. As a result the commission had to be vacated. Happily, on this occasion L did not resort to his pattern of panic last minute completions accomplished by dragging existing compositions out of

---

[308] His surveillance by the FBI resulted in his passport being temporarily confiscated. His activity in social politics resulted in his being branded *radical chic* in print by Tom Wolfe after he threw a much heralded glamourous party at his home for a cause supported by his wife, Felicia, the raising of money for the families of the jailed leaders of the Black Pather movement,

[309] A flagrant example occurred at the start of rehearsals for *Mass*. With the cast of two hundred in rehearsal and with the score still incomplete L left for Los Angeles to attend rehearsals and the opening of the Civic Light Opera's production of *Candide*. His West Coast stay was for more than two weeks after which he had conducting engagements to fulfill at Tanglewood. *Mass* was completed in the usual last minute panic.

his trunk and quickly reworking them, sometimes, it should be added, to marvellous effect. One would like to believe that, in this instance, he realised the outstanding quality of his initial efforts and was unwilling to rush through a cobbled together 'work in progress' for later revision just to deliver the commission on time and save face.   The additional year that L took to complete the song cycle, however, produced one of his finest compositions. I am not a composer, but during the activities of a sixty-year concert and recording career I have often been called upon to arrange and/or orchestrate[310] music in all styles. The general rule of which I became quickly aware regarding any learned musical skill is that 'if you don't use it, you lose it'. It is no different with composing. L's fragmented on again/off again approach to the composing side of his career, certainly from the 1970's onwards must have made each new beginning that much more difficult. We have the published detailed descriptions confirming this from Stephen Wadsworth's *Librettist's Notes* for *A Quiet Place*:

"Our next prolonged period of working together was in Bloomington, Indiana, as guests of Indiana University, who workshopped what there was of the opera *as we wrote it*. (my italics). Before actually setting pen to paper, however, Lenny went to bed for nine days, terrified. We hadn't written very much up to then and both knew if we didn't produce now we probably never would. Eventually, and suddenly, he awakened and composed most of what is now Act I with me close by, nodding approval or disapproval at his urging."

L was very fortunate indeed that those who worked with him and for him never ceased their belief in him or deserted him in his times of need,

---

[310] Arranging and orchestration are two separate crafts. The arranger provides the concept which will not only transform a composition from one medium to another, (ie: adapting a song to an instrumental composition), but he might choose to create a new musical profile that may entirely alter our view of the original composition. An example would be the author's arrangement of the Beatles tune, *When I'm 64,* as a literal instrumental paraphrase of Johann and Josef Strauss' *Pizzicato Polka.* It was created in the middle of a busy touring concert schedule and I did not have time to complete the orchestration and write out the string and percussion parts for the orchestra. In this instance, I simply instructed a skilled colleague to execute the orchestration according to my musical design and he, as orchestrator, added his mechanical skills to my creative skills.

whether professional or personal, no matter how difficult he made their lives.

It is highly unlikely that we will encounter L's like again, certainly not in the millennium century which enters with the profession of conducting itself in crisis, starved of a level of talent that brought the craft to its pinnacle in the 20th century. In the last half-century, only Karajan attracted the same mass audiences which greeted L whenever and wherever he appeared. But where Karajan was shy and a very private person, remaining aloof from people outside the concert hall, L was regarded as a public treasure, a man who relished the cheering of the crowd and the adoration the young. Among 20th century musicians, only the composer Giuseppe Verdi was held in equal esteem by the public at large. Consider the touching moment retold in the documentary *Leonard Bernstein, Reaching For The Note* when L's funeral cortege passed a New York construction sight and the workers stopped to wave and call out, "Goodbye, Lenny!" Only the passing of Verdi had evoked such a similar outpouring of emotion from the general public for a musician. The vastness of L's talent, his intensity, versatility, total commitment, his seeming endless energies to pursue multiple major projects simultaneously with an undiminished passion and, not to be underestimated, his glamorous, movie star public image never ceased to dazzle an ever worshipping public. To some, without doubt, there was a vulgarity about such celebrity. The pedestal on which the public placed him made him a clear target for his critics and they proved to be a small army. In the end, however, not critics but future audiences will properly assess and determine L's place in the pantheon of musicians. One can predict even now with a certain confidence a longevity for his early theatre works, the three New York musicals and *Candide,* as well as his first two symphonies, his violin concerto *Serenade,* the Suites from *On The Waterfront* and *West Side Story,* the ballet *Fancy Free* and the *Chichester Psalms.* The number of international performances of all L's major orchestral and vocal works with the exception of *A Quiet Place* has continued unabated since his death. Perhaps the success of the recent New York City Opera production for *A Quiet Place* will accomplish for it what John Caird's Royal National Theatre production has done for

Candide. When this happens, opera lovers are in for an intensely stimulating and moving evening of music drama.

Thanks to an impressive number of Bernstein disciples who are now key players on the world's concert stages, Michael Tilson Thomas, Seiji Ozawa, Leonard Slatkin, Eiji Oue, Yutaka Sado, Marin Alsop, John Mauceri along with a large number of conductors who served as his assistants at the NY Philharmonic, plus a younger generation now making their mark world-wide who came under his influence at Tanglewood, UCLA, Salzau, Germany and Japan, the number of annual performances of a wide variety of music from the Bernstein catalogue seems on the increase. Even L's early short jazz effort, *Prelude, Fugue and Riffs,* and his musical, *Wonderful Town,* have attracted the attention of no less an important conducting personality than Sir Simon Rattle[311]. Bernstein recordings, twice sonically refurbished and repackaged by Sony, are finding a large new audience. DG has begun to repackage their Bernstein catalogue at mid-price to boost their sales but as of this writing their *Bernstein on Bernstein* issue, a repackaged box set of Mahler symphonies and orchestra songs plus a large slice of core symphonic repertoire from Beethoven to Milhaud have reached the market place with hardly a flourish much less a fanfare. DG did take some care in heralding the initial premiere release of L's posthumously constructed *1600 (White House) Cantata.* Unfortunately, the work had a very mixed reception at its lack-lustre London concert premiere and this may have cast a shadow over the lukewarm manner in which the recording was received. This work contains much top drawer Bernstein theatre music. Its present somewhat rambling form needs tightening and the orchestration, rearranged for large symphony orchestra, made the delivery of the text almost incoherent at times. A *blue pencil* wielded generously by its knowledgeable orchestrator, Sid Ramon, would go far to solving that problem. A musical *show doctor*[312] could deal with the rest, modestly editing and reshaping the various sections depicting life in the White House under various American presidents. As the

---

[311] Maestro Rattle has been knighted by Her Royal Majesty, Queen Elizabeth.
[312] *Show doctors* are skilled technicians in the theatre, usually directors, who, when shows are in trouble, are noted for their ability to quickly pinpoint the weaknesses and suggest the remedies.

WEST SIDE MAESTRO

Cantata is a posthumous creation, it is within the jurisdiction and power of the Bernstein family to accomplish this.

Whatever the weaknesses of the original Lerner/Bernstein musical as a whole, L's score to *1600 Pennsylvania Avenue,* taken on its own merits, reveals a self-contained validity. Within the newly constructed *White House Cantata,* it has been transformed into a crossover work of musical theatre for the concert hall. Once given a refreshed form through which it can communicate and convince future audiences of its rightful place within the Bernstein catalogue, it can stand alongside the body of his established works which have continued to bring pleasure and stimulation to a world audience, an audience which Lenny envisioned and hoped would take pleasure from and find an evergreen credibility in his music long after his life had come to its final cadence.

WEST SIDE MAESTRO

6. PORTRAIT OF A TEACHER

A Final Testament

The Student Festivals
SALZAU 1987: '...so that we go forward...'

In the final three years of his life L, suffering from ever-worsening emphysema but not yet diagnosed with the cancer that was to manifest itself, rather than conserve his energies to a limited schedule of major concert and recording commitments, pushed his physical and mental capacities to the limit. Among his important new achievements was to help establish two legacies for the future in the form of summer music festivals for youth in Germany and Japan created along the lines of the Berkshire Music Centre at Tanglewood. Videos produced at the Schleswig-Holstein Summer Festival at Salzau and at The Pacific Music Festival in Sapporo, Japan document these accomplishments.

Humphrey Burton graphically describes L's deteriorating physical condition in these final years. The former svelte, athletic figure is now badly overweight, the imbibing of scotch whisky has gone far beyond the social stage, the lifetime addiction to cigarettes has turned his velvet toned voice to a rasp which is interrupted by constant coughing fits. The picture Burton paints, however, pales alongside the image revealed on film. L looks much older than his sixty-eight years; his face and dark circled heavy eyelids reveal the wear and tear of chronic insomnia. His sunken cheeks and heavily lined face tend to exaggerate the now larger nose and longer ears, one of the characteristics of old age. He still displays vigour at rehearsals but he noticeably runs out of 'puff' much more quickly. Nevertheless, not until his final year during the founding season of the Pacific Music Festival is he observed trying to use his energies sparingly. Not only did L not conserve himself during these three final years but he seemed to increase his pattern of activities and pressures. In terms of priorities and commercial interests, his doctors could easily have made a strong case for striking off his calendar these predictably, physically demanding Youth Festivals. Yet L pushed himself right to the edge where his commitments to these youngsters were involved. These videos are extraordinarily moving, the image of a father figure educating the young. They are both a testament *of* a teacher and *to* a teacher.

There are seven videos encompassing the years 1987-89 at the Schleswig-Holstein Festival. Five of these deal with the student orchestra in rehearsal and performance under L's tutelage, one is of L's International Conducting Competition which is combined with the Master Class held at the Festival that followed and one is purely a Documentary about the Festival itself and its origins. There is only one video of the Pacific Music Festival filmed the summer before L's death.

The first of the documentaries, The Birth of an Orchestra, subtitled, "...so that we go forward...", introduces Justus Frantz, a young pianist whom L first met in the Spring of 1973 when he was a guest in the Canary Islands at the home of the concert pianist and conductor, Christoph Eschenbach. Years later, Frantz, after visiting the Berkshire Music Centre at Tanglewood, was determined to establish just such an international summer training school and festival for young musicians in Germany. He prevailed upon L, with whom a warm friendship and professional relationship had grown over the years, to help him. In 1985, L made a special trip to Germany to speak personally with Helmut Kohl regarding the project and committing himself to becoming its musical patron.

The school and festival were centred in the magnificent Schloss Salzau, a palatial residence and surrounding grounds, set in the idyllic countryside of Schleswig Holstein. We meet Justus Frantz, the students, teachers and conductors attending the premiere Festival in the summer of 1987 preparing the groundwork for L's arrival. The young musicians, one hundred-twenty in number, were gleaned from among eight hundred potential finalists from the thousands of applicants who applied from every part of the Americas, Europe, Great Britain and the Middle and Far East. The scope of the musical program they were about to undertake at Salzau was conceived in extremely broad terms, centering not only upon mastering the wide range of technical and ensemble problems of the Stravinsky masterwork L was to rehearse and conduct in concert, *Le Sacre du Printemps*, but a wide variety of other music for strings, winds, brass and percussion ensemble as well as chamber music and jazz.

Various teachers, all noted symphony orchestra section leaders, and students speak to camera of their expectations in coming to the Festival, of life at the Schloss, of problems faced by young musicians wanting to enter the profession and of the exacting standards that will be required of them in professional life. The students, from all parts of the globe, not only speak excitedly of the unique coming opportunity offered by the Festival to work with L but of their resplendent if isolated ambience in the rural countryside of North Germany in which they have come for a summer to live, work and make music and new friends. All agree that the isolation concentrates their minds to the task at hand but a few, reflecting upon the structured Festival life of mostly 'all work and no play...' miss the many distractions and attractions of normal urban living.

At the beginning and at carefully placed intervals L speaks to camera of the enormous enthusiasm of his friend Justus Frantz, which convinced him to help make what was only an idea of a summer Festival into a reality created along the lines of the Berkshire Music Center at Tanglewood.

Although L appears only spasmodically in this hour-long documentary his presence dominates throughout. The film opens with this retrospective quote: "What impressed me most in Salzau was to see how strongly people loved other people, who loved music." In truth, L was the magnet that drew these young musicians from all parts of the world to this tiny village in North Germany, which one is hard pressed to find either listed in an Atlas or located on a map.

For Justus Frantz, the Festival represented an opportunity to raise the musical standards of young orchestral musicians studying throughout Germany, which compared poorly to the standards of accomplishment of the students at the Royal College of Music, witnessed during an extended professional period concertising in London. After securing L's support for his project and the necessary funding, he acquired Schloss Salzau and had it converted from a private residence into a combined living and working area "where one hundred and twenty students could live and work in harmony, make music and celebrate."

The administration planned a concert to launch the Festival not long after the arrival and housing of their orchestra. Their aim was to garner the support of the diplomats from the many nations whose young nationals were represented among the participating chosen musical elite. On a rotunda before the entrance to the Schloss, the flags of all the nations represented were raised.

Following the concert, under the direction of one of the Festival's faculty, there was a reception for the distinguished audience and students. One has reason to smile wryly at the honoured guests proceeding to supper in the grand dining room through the Schloss's palatial entrance while the students proceed to their post-concert repast 'below stairs' through the back entrance to the castle. As is commented upon in the accompanying narration, not much has changed since Mozart's time.

The majority of the rest of the film shows the various sections of the orchestra, the strings, the woodwinds, the brass and the percussion, preparing the Stravinsky ballet separately under specialist instrumental tutors in advance of L's arrival. These rehearsals are highlighted by a wide variety of faculty and student comment upon the positive and negative aspects, (mostly overwhelmingly positive), of life and work at Salzau. We see the students taken on arranged tours to the surrounding environs of natural scenic beauty characteristic of the holiday area of Schleswig Holstein to help *change the vibes* from their intensive daily work schedule. They also organise for themselves evening outdoor picnics with dancing in the grounds of the Schloss. We are never in doubt, that except for their musical gifts, these are normal boys and girls who know how to have a good time and to whom life is more than endless hours of practice towards perfection.

WEST SIDE MAESTRO

As the orchestra arrives closer to the mastery of the technical challenges set by Stravinsky, the students spend time watching videos of L in rehearsal with the Vienna Philharmonic to judge how he works and to anticipate what he will expect. Two days prior to his arrival, they are taken as a group to observe L live in concert. This serves to electrify the atmosphere at Salzau. As one of the instrumental tutors comments, "This orchestra is already very well prepared. I can predict it is going to be a strong orchestra and that L can begin at a very high level."

L has the final word. " I am trying to do in Europe what Europe has done for me." By this he was referring to his own heritage assimilated from a European tradition transmitted to him by the influential European musical figures in his life, his teachers Koussevitzky and Reiner and his senior colleagues who had encouraged him as a young musician, Dmitri Mitropoulos and Bruno Walter.

L reminds us that not too long ago Germany was the vitriolic enemy of the world's free and democratic nations but that today it is the young people of Europe, especially Germany and Austria who, in the face of their recent brutal histories, have become the great protagonists for World Peace.

The last images we see are of L arriving at Schloss Salzau to the blare of welcoming brass. The stage is set for a week of music making that will change the lives of these young people, many of whom have come half way round the world to Salzau.

SALZAU 1987, Part II: 'With him up front...'

The second part of this 1997 video trilogy, "...with him up front...", takes up the story with L in charge. From this point on, all the remaining videos in this series will be dominated by his presence in a musical capacity as well as teacher, father figure, father confessor and standard-bearer for the most exacting ideals in Art.

WEST SIDE MAESTRO

As the film begins we see L and the orchestra in concert. We hear the final moments of Stravinsky's ballet, *Le Sacre du Printemps,* (The Rite of Spring). The images represent the end of a musical and personal journey that this young orchestra has made with this haggard, worn, ill but ever charismatic maestro.

Rehearsals had begun a week earlier and from the first they were a learning experience for the players. L's approach to his task echoed his own experiences as a student at Harvard University and the structured manner in which he chose to present his Norton Lectures at that University thirty-five years later, that of applying interdisciplinary techniques to engender a broader understanding. Much later in the video he speaks of having used this approach successfully with his young orchestra and of both the positive and negative reactions one would receive to such an approach in the 'real' and hard world of commercial music making. "Out there", L states, "it is invariably *business as usual*". There are classic conducting stories that serve to underline the black reality of the analogy that L has used. Among the most famous are tales of two of music's greatest maestros, Otto Klemperor and Willem Mengelberg. Klemperor was stopped short in a lengthy explanation by the Principal Oboe of the NY Philharmonic, Bruno Labate. "Mr. *Klemps*", interrupted Labate, "you *talk-a* too much." As for Mengelberg, it was again a member of the same NY orchestra, a violinist, who, after the Dutch conductor's lengthy, romantic explanation filled with poetic similes of how a particular passage should be performed, turned to his partner and said succinctly, "Play it *softer!*"

But this is not *out there*, this is a scenario far removed from strict timetables, union rules and jaundiced attitudes. There is nothing to disturb or distract from the sense of purpose that has brought these young people together with this unique musical figure.

The first rehearsal begins in a purposeful if pedantic fashion. L does not plunge into the music at hand to judge the orchestra's technical ability, he asks them merely to play a rising and descending two octave C Major scale. As he conducts his beat becomes deliberately wayward, slowing down and speeding up capriciously, indicating certain notes be extended or sudden accents and dynamics to be applied. This has a two-fold purpose, to judge the flexibility of the players and to give them fair warning to keep their eyes glued upon him for any modification in tempo or nuance that he may wish to improvise, even in performance.

The atmosphere between players and conductor remains relaxed throughout the days of preparation. There are many lengthy explanations and repetitions of individual musical passages to achieve the precise balance, colour and ensemble required yet the viewer never perceives restlessness or boredom on the part of the players. This is summed up succinctly by a percussionist in one of the many inserted players' reactions to their maestro liberally sprinkled through the film, "It's fun to play even when you don't have so much to do."

L reaches each of these young people on various levels, whether emotional, intellectual or through sheer fascination. In the end their musical response is summed up by another of the players, "It is rare at our age to perform with such a conductor. Normally, you play for a time beater, not one who really makes music. This is something more sublime. One has to learn that, too."

It is not only musical preparation problems that occupy L's time. Many of the young musicians come to him with career and personal problems and he gives his time, attention and concern to each of them. It is extraordinary to watch this man who bristled against authority figures his whole life, something which had its roots in his own troubled relationship with his father, himself now the prototype father figure to the vast number of young people whose lives he was to directly touch in the final three years of his life. We hear him protest against such an image accepting only that working with the new generation of musicians rejuvenates and energises him. Despite all his protests, the paternal relationship is clear for all to see. However, now, even while seemingly still physically fit, another shadow associated with the elderly parental figure is already very much in his thoughts, if only in jest. It is that of death. After handing back an autographed sheet of music to one of the players he jokes, "You'll be a rich man after I die...which may be tomorrow."

This documentary creates the full flavour, if, albeit, in a very unique situation, of what takes place at an orchestra rehearsal. We observe how a conductor works with various sections of the orchestra on a specific passage, taking it apart and rehearsing small groups to achieve specific effects and then putting all the various pieces together again like a puzzle. In L's case he uses all variety of imagery to create a visual as well as a musical understanding of *Le Sacre*. In one instance he describes a particular bassoon passage as a Duke Ellington *lick*.[313] He imitates the actions of the dinosaurs in Walt Disney's animated interpretation of *Le Sacre* in his film *Fantasia* that provokes huge laughter. Even his lack of inhibition describing the sexual nature of the Stravinsky ballet is a cause for fascination and admiration among the older players. What is indisputably obvious is that the orchestra adores him and would walk over hot coals at his request.

The rehearsal sequence ends with L rehearsing the most challenging final moments of the ballet, the *Danse Sacrale*. The scene dissolves to the night of the concert. We are backstage and our musicians are in formal eveningwear. As we view the scene the sound track is of the closing moments of the Stravinsky. Only for the final chord do we see them again seated on the stage with L on the podium just as in the opening credits of the film. He brings his baton down for the final chord; the audience explodes into applause and cheers. There is much shaking of hands, a dispensing of the famous Bernstein bear hug, a fatherly approving kiss on the cheek for the young concertmaster of the orchestra and the scene is frozen while we continue to hear the echo of the cheers of the crowd.

The only quibble one might have regarding what for the viewer will be a fascinating new view of music making is that one never achieves a complete

---

[313] Should *Duke Ellington* need any introduction to my readers, he was one of the great black, American jazz band leaders from the end of World War I up until his death in the early 1970's. A composer as well an instrumentalist, he was among the most important and influential figures on the jazz scene. A *lick* refers to a solo instrumental jazz passage in most instances improvised.

sense of the music performed. Only about a third of the Stravinsky work, at most, is heard within this hour long documentary, mostly in fragmentary bits. Progressively, the director, Horant H. Hohlfeld solves this problem, and brilliantly, one should add, over the next two years. His filming of L's work with the students at subsequent Salzau Festivals was to reveal in depth the level of accomplishment achieved.

SALZAU 1987, Part III:'Beating time is very basic but...'

The final film from the Trilogy produced during the first year of the Festival is titled, "Beating time is very basic but..." and sub-titled International Conductor's Competition and Master Course. While I view this film as an interesting, dramatic and extraordinarily honest documentary, it is not for the reasons the Festival directors intended. It exposes a serious lapse in judgement on the part of whoever was in charge of auditioning and choosing the conductor candidates. The end result as viewed here, far from being a Master Course, proved to be, even putting the best face on what took place, little more than a course for beginners.

As with the orchestra, the conductor semi-finalists were chosen from among the many applications received and, one must assume, some kind of audition process. These semi-finalists, having arrived in Salzau, were then re-auditioned to pick a select four who would be coached by L both privately and in rehearsal with the student orchestra. As a prize, each student finalist would perform the work they had been preparing and rehearsing in an evening concert.

To choose the four finalists, each of the eleven semi-finalists were allowed to conduct a work of their choice and given fifteen minutes to rehearse with the orchestra. To the average person fifteen minutes would not seem to be sufficient to demonstrate the best of one's talents. Indeed, one of the semi-finalists was later to make that exact comment. The truth is that five minutes is sufficient, not to determine the full depth of talent but to judge baton technique, communicative qualities, confidence, the level of preparation, musicianship and a host of other subtleties which are immediately apparent to anyone with a trained eye.

Before I begin my analysis in detail it is only right to point out virtually twenty years have passed since this film was made. Much could and may have happened within that time in regard to the development of the conducting skills and musical advancement of all the personalities involved. The inborn gift of a communicative personality, however, which is not a specific musical trait but a *sine qua non* for every orchestra conductor, is not something one can teach or be learned from a textbook. The perception of genuine communicative gifts, or the lack thereof, weighed heavily, therefore, in forming my stated opinion of the Salzau candidates. All the standards I applied in the evaluation of the skills of each candidate were those expected of a professional conductor by a professional orchestra. and based upon their audition segment with the student orchestra at the rehearsals recorded in this film. All comments or criticisms formulated must, therefore, be viewed in this context.

The young talent brought together consisted of four Americans, one of whom was female, a Frenchman, an Englishman, a Brazilian, a Swede and three Germans. Giving all eleven the benefit of the doubt regarding their musical competence, I would categorise the degree of their conducting expertise as follows:

1. The very first conductor to mount the podium, not identified by name or country, by process of elimination must have been the Swedish representative. He conducted Schumann's *Fourth Symphony*. He projected insecurity and his baton technique proved quite basic. From his first unclear downbeat one knew he wasn't to be among the finalists

2. Two of the Americans displayed a reasonably schooled baton technique and sufficient confidence in front of the orchestra. One conducted Dvorak, the other a Beethoven overture. Of these two, only one already displayed what is most often referred to as a flair for the craft. The other had the look and manner of the Conservatory student. Another of the Americans,

whose musical credentials seemed impressive, talked far too much and displayed a highly tense, overwrought personality combined with a rather primitive, ungainly stick technique. The lady conductor was assertive and competent with a basic textbook technique but little more.

3. The Brazilian produced the most beautiful sound from the orchestra of all the conductors. His chosen work was Brahms' *First Symphony*. Unfortunately, he fell at the first technical hurdle in the ninth bar of music.

4. The Frenchman oozed confidence from the moment he walked up to the podium and shook hands with the concertmaster. His chosen work was among the most difficult, the *Danse Generale* from Ravel's *Daphnis and Chloe Suite No 2*, a brilliantly fast work mostly in an irregular *five-beat-to-the-bar* rhythm[314]. Though the orchestra's sight-reading left a bit to be desired, the young Frenchman was unflappable, with a crystal clear baton technique, oodles of temperament and a genuine ability to communicate. He reminded me in style of a French version of Lorin Maazel.

5. The first German candidate conducted Beethoven's *Egmont Overture*. His genuine conducting gifts were immediately apparent. In a very professional manner, he gave clear, spoken directions to the orchestra while he conducted. This is a valuable and much used professional technique when rehearsal time is in short supply. Like the French candidate who preceded him, he stood out from the crowd.

6. The single British entry displayed an unfortunate manner. He possessed all the necessary confidence but it projected as arrogance. He also patronisingly peppered his comments to the orchestra with a light sprinkling of German words, not enough to impress anyone that he was fluent in the language but enough to be off-putting. His organisation of his time left something to be desired, at one point indicating that he wished to restart at one place, then changing his mind, shuffling pages causing confusion which

---

[314] Other famous examples of *five-beat-to-the-bar* compositions are the Second Movement to Tchaikowsky's Sixth Symphony and Dave Brubeck's *Take Five.*

then necessitated him having to repeat no less than ten times the rehearsal number of the new place at which he had decided to begin.

7. There was no comparison between the two remaining German semi-finalists. The first to conduct was brimming with self-confidence as he raised his baton to begin Mendelssohn's Fourth Symphony. His technique was clear if somewhat inexpressive and his rhythm was slightly unsteady at the start. He acquitted himself reasonably well in the end and spoke quite confidently of his performance after he finished. The last to conduct hailed from the former Bundesrepublik. He conducted Tschaikowsky's *Sixth Symphony*. To me this last young conductor was the least commanding of the eleven who conducted. He showed little authority or technical control. This created insecurity in the orchestra which then began dragging the tempo, getting progressively slower and slower. From an audition point of view, his was the poorest showing.

As the rehearsal is breaking up and the musicians are packing up their instruments, we hear the voice of Justus Frantz, the Artistic Director of the Festival. He tells us of the difficult and controversial debate that took place among the jury panel following the auditions. After three hours of enjoying the work of these new and *'excellent'* young conductors, the judges were all especially aware of their responsibility in having to choose at most only three or possibly four finalists.

In light of such a statement of high purpose, the announcement of the names of the finalists sent a shock wave not only through the assembled group of conductors but the orchestra as well. Those who weren't struck dumb by the judges' choices were very vocal in displaying their confusion and displeasure. The four chosen were the German who conducted Beethoven, (I agree), plus three whom I never would have rated, the highly-strung, nervous American, the English representative and the final competitor from the Bundesrepublik Deutschland. The biggest PR *faux pas,* however, was, having given the orchestra a vote regarding the finalists, totally ignoring their opinion.

WEST SIDE MAESTRO

Having myself been a member of L's private conducting class for three seasons at Tanglewood, I was not prepared for the manner in which he imposed himself in his students' rehearsals at Salzau. At Tanglewood we worked in a private studio. L would play the piano, reading brilliantly straight from the orchestra score rather than a piano transcription and make his comments and corrections in private. He would sometimes play deliberate wrong notes to check if we were listening properly or he would pose questions about the orchestration expecting in reply the right answers without our checking the score. When we rehearsed with the orchestra, L would sit in their midst, usually with the woodwinds, surrounded by other conductors and make quiet comments to the onlookers regarding any imperfections in the baton technique, musical approach or the comments of the conductor on the podium. Afterwards, he would discuss the rehearsal with us in private or analyse the problems openly with the large group of conducting auditors using his small scholarship class as guinea pigs to demonstrate the various points. Two important features to stress are that he never interfered in our rehearsals and he continually worked to develop uniqueness in each of his students rather than to merely create clones of himself.

Salzau proved to be just the opposite. L stood by the podium, hovering over each conductor's shoulder. He often interrupted and interposed himself. He seemed little interested in the ideas or individuality of the young conductors themselves. As I commented earlier, baton technique can be anything that works, the most obvious examples of this being the frenetic and obscure gestures of a Furtwängler or a Dmitri Mitropoulos. L chose not to consider this historically established reality on this occasion. He would demonstrate in front of the orchestra *his* method of executing a particular passage, many times mounting the podium to conduct the passage himself while the student stood impotently by. Each of the student conductors reacted in different degree to this daily happening over which they had no control. The overwrought American simply fell apart. Close-ups show him in despair pulling his hair. It struck me that the lesser of the two German conductors simply didn't involve himself in what L was doing or saying to the orchestra. He simply withdrew to the sidelines waiting for L to finish so that he could carry on much in the way he had prior to the interruption. In one instance, during the rehearsal of the first movement and *Scherzo* from Sibelius' *Fifth Symphony*, a Bernstein speciality, L seemed to have completely lost his perspective regarding his position and responsibilities as a teacher as well as the position and feelings of one of his students. In this case in point, it was not merely a handful of measures of music he chose to illustrate but, beginning with the final climax of the first movement, conducting totally from memory, he took the orchestra through the entire *Scherzo*, some seven minutes of music. The young German conductor, the most gifted of the finalists, stood next to L as he conducted not a straightforward demonstration of specific conducting techniques for a few key passages but a full blown personality performance of the Sibelius symphony. His charisma swept over the orchestra as he called out the wrong notes they were playing, threw cues to every section of the orchestra in rapid succession, and took control with an authority none of his students could ever hope to emulate. And to top it all, as I have already pointed out, it was all done from memory. I can't think of a professional conductor who would have wanted or dared to follow that act. The orchestra's applause at the end brings a protest from L. They have misunderstood, he tells them. His only reasons for conducting were to demonstrate "certain techniques" to his young colleague. Unfortunately, when you view this seven minutes of film out of context, one cannot be faulted for concluding that it is a document of L simply having a wonderful time conducting a work with which he had long been associated.

Unlike the other Salzau documentaries there are no post Master Course reactions of the participants recorded on film. In retrospect, the inclusion of the conducting Master Class this first year proved to be neither a good nor practical idea. L was already an ill man with limited energies. The training of the Salzau student orchestra in very difficult repertoire sapped him both mentally and physically. I would project that he was very disappointed, in general, with the entire organisation of the conducting course and most certainly with the level of expertise of the conducting candidates. I am convinced that he would have dealt with them differently had the class been made up of young conductors on the verge of being launched into major careers. Why then choose the lesser candidates among those in attendance?

WEST SIDE MAESTRO

During my own ten-year experience working with him, over and over again I observed the positive pleasure he took from playing 'God'. Perhaps he thought he could produce a biblical miracle and, under his guidance and inspiration, truly "the *last* would be *first*." Though the Master Class added little distinction to the Festival, it could not diminish the inspirational miracles L wrought with the orchestra. A video record of human drama!

SALZAU 1988

For his return to the Salzau Festival the following year, L chose a young symphony to challenge his young orchestra, Dmitri Shostakovich's *Symphony No.1*, written when the composer was barely nineteen years old, as his graduation piece when a student at the Petrograd Conservatory. The interdisciplinary approach L had adopted in working with the student orchestra in the Festival's debut year is now even more in evidence. What is also in evidence is that the positive experience of his first summer in Salzau has made him more relaxed. Any qualms or fears he may have had prior to his very first rehearsal the previous summer were immediately dispelled by the quality of the orchestra's preparation prior to his arrival. He expects no less now and he is not disappointed.

L begins his rehearsal by explaining the nature of Shostakovich's First Symphony. He describes its quirky character, traditional to the point of Tschaikovskian, but always coming up with an unexpected twist. He regards the first two movements, youthfully anti-authoritarian, as the weakest of the symphony. The third movement, however, is where he views Shostakovich as finding his own voice. While overtones of Mahler, a composer the Russian strongly admired, are to be found, L suggests that equally this movement may have started life as an anti-Wagnerian protest, a mockery of the high levels of emotion identified with the German composer's equally revolutionary music. It is in this movement in which we experience a new lyrical level in the symphony. Paradoxically it contains all the Wagnerian passion it set out to mock.

WEST SIDE MAESTRO

As we have already witnessed in the documentary of the previous year, L's rehearsals are stop-and-start affairs. He is meticulous in correcting every aspect of performance, whether rhythmic, dynamic, (degrees of loudness or softness), ensemble, (togetherness), tone colour or pitch accuracy. However, his positive experience of the previous year has led him to be immediately more demanding of this year's Festival orchestra, many of whom had worked with him the previous summer. At the very start of the rehearsal he places the very gifted young lady principal clarinettist under tremendous pressure by having her repeat an exposed solo passage again and again. Many a professional would have cracked under the circumstances but this young lady afterwards just commented that while it was a difficult moment it pointed up that she must practice more.

Nothing escapes L's attention. Once he has projected his message that he will not let the slightest deviation from what he is seeking get past him, the orchestra plays ever more attentively and carefully to meet his wishes and to satisfy him musically. As the camera pans to the various sections of the Festival orchestra it is quite obvious that the young players spend as much time keeping their conductor in their focus as the music sitting before them on their stands.

The rehearsal is intercut with short interviews with the players. The common thread running through their comments is their total identification with the high level of standard L is demanding. They are inspired by his presence, learning to listen more carefully to what is going on around them and achieving a better overall grasp of the music. These interviews and the orchestra's sensitivity in rehearsal are testament to and a perfect example of a conductor fusing with an orchestra and the two functioning as a single mind.

By the second day, L's manner of rehearsing at this second Festival parallels his methods with a professional orchestra. He permits the orchestra to play longer excerpts before stopping to make corrections and, when the dynamic of the music permits, he speaks over the orchestra to individual players making corrections while continuing to conduct. As the orchestra becomes more and more sensitive to his spoken requests and, even more important, to his silent gestures, his demands become more exacting. The tempo modifications inherent in the Shostakovich work require constant vigilance on the part of the players. On this second day, L is taking improvisatory musical freedoms, which would require the total attention of even the most experienced orchestra. He remains always awake to the musical and technical challenges of the music by helping individuals analyse specific solos or by rehearsing with, for example, the entire violin section, practising difficult passages slowly in order to perfect them. In the final movement, he sets the trumpets a task in the Coda[315] so fierce that it would tax any of the world's great orchestra brass sections. L insists on conducting certain measures in one beat to the bar within which the trumpets must maintain a steady quick pulsation of notes. The problem arises when L alters the tempo within these one beat bars, not too clearly, one should add, leaving the trumpets to swim their way through to the next big full orchestra ensemble, happily only a few bars later. That these young, relatively inexperienced players manage as well as they do is astonishing. How did they manage it? The only explanation is that it was L's presence that inspired them to this super-effort. I had witnessed Koussevitzky do the very same thing with the Juilliard Orchestra in my student days. He had come to the conservatory to conduct Beethoven's *Ninth Symphony*. In the demonic scherzo, the Russian maestro began to beat more quickly and the orchestra rushed to follow him. Koussevitzky stopped and commanded, "Don't hurry!" He repeated the passage and again began to accelerate and again the orchestra followed. Again he stopped and ordered, **"Don't hurry!"** The orchestra somewhat confused and terrified began again. The third time K began to quicken the orchestra held rock steady to the point where this imperious force moved a full measure of music ahead of them at which point he adjusted and both conductor and orchestra proceeded exactly together to the end of the movement. The tension following the final chord was so thick you could cut it with a knife but it was one of the most thrilling musical moments one could ever hope to witness. As with L on this occasion it was accomplished by the compelling force of a huge musical personality. It is awesome to

---

[315] Coda from the Italian meaning *tail*. It refers to an addition occurring as the last part of a piece of music or melody at the conclusion of any standard musical form.

behold. In retrospect one could ask, 'Why did L do it?' He could have made the trumpets' task that much easier if he had simply maintained a *two-beats-to-the-bar* orientation. Perhaps the purpose behind this gesture was to teach these young musicians yet another discipline that would be required of and test them in the 'real world'. It certainly seemed Koussevitzky inspired in origin which, as I have demonstrated, required at times and remarkably achieved what appeared to be a level of clairvoyance between orchestra and conductor.

Unlike the first 1987 Salzau rehearsal documentary, this second Salzau film consists of two parts, the second of which is a complete concert performance of the Shostakovich symphony rehearsed in Part I. It provides for a much more fulfilling viewing experience. What is immediately apparent in this second part is that the orchestra has gelled as a unit and absorbed fully the long days of rehearsal tuition. Their performance is assured to a high professional level. The Scherzo movement featuring the young lady clarinettist unremittingly pressured in rehearsal by L is virtuoso, taken at a tempo that would have struck fear into the hearts of the Vienna Philharmonic. Yet these youngsters take it all in their stride.

L's conducting is very economical but extremely clear, still making no concessions to his young orchestra. It is quite obvious that the orchestra has done a good deal of growing up in the short time they have been with him. They perform at the point of his baton with tempo variations never catching them out or revealing a fault in their ensemble. Even the impossible task set the trumpets manages to come off. As an experienced conductor, I cannot begin to explain to you how that particular bit of sleight-of-hand was accomplished except to instinctively project that it was through the sheer will power, stature and inspiration of their conductor. One cannot pretend that the performance was totally without blemish. There is an overheated moment in the final measure of the work that causes an untidy final chord which produces just the glimmer of reaction on their maestro's countenance. Yet one is left with little doubt that many of the world's concert subscribers would gladly have paid a premium price to have been treated to a performance at this level of candle power

WEST SIDE MAESTRO

SALZAU
1989

For the 1989 Festival at Salzau, L chose orchestral movements from Hector Berlioz's Choral Symphony, *Romeo and Juliet,* with which to challenge the fresh batch of young musicians who had won their places at this new but already prestigious European Tanglewood. Again the use of an interdisciplinary teaching approach is implicit to L's method of working with young orchestras. On this occasion, to point up the close relationship between Shakespeare's tragic love story and Berlioz's musical metamorphosis, L reads to the orchestra throughout his rehearsals parallel passages from the Elizabethan play which the French composer has, with graphic exactitude, mirrored in his symphonic canvas through a dynamic, expressive and melodically created lexicon of musical onomatopoeia.

Much of what L has to say historically regarding the Berlioz work is a recapitulation of his long commentary on this same work from his Norton Lectures of 1973. The rehearsal begins with an eight minute spoken exposition taking in the "star crossed" lovers, Berlioz's Shakespearean-based masterwork and Wagner as sub-conscious plagiarist of Berlioz for his opera *Tristan and Isolde.*

L is exacting with his new group of charges. His corrections begin before the violins have played even their first notes of *Romeo alone in the garden of the Capulets.* "Vibrate the string before you play", he insists. (This is to insure that the very first note is alive, *vibrant,* from the instant the audience hears it). The first violins are not permitted to proceed very far, however. L has them rehearsing again and again to perfect barely a dozen notes. Indeed, he is to stop fourteen times within the next five minutes perfecting the sound, phrasing and ultra quiet dynamics of the first four opening measures of music.[316] Then, suddenly, we are no longer in rehearsal but in the concert hall with the orchestra executing the finished performance of the same passage they have been viewed meticulously rehearsing plus a subsequent three additional minutes of music. Their playing is exquisite under L's gentle direction, detailed in its execution and filled with colour. Then, without breaking the continuity of the music, we again find ourselves back in the rehearsal hall.

This technique of intercutting between rehearsal and concert, which is adhered to throughout, was the major new change in the documentary technique to which I referred earlier. The film's director, Horant Hohlfeld, employs it effortlessly to powerful effect. It demonstrates to the viewer in greater dimension, far beyond that of the film of the previous year's Festival, the ongoing process from rehearsal to finished performance. It is a wonderfully theatrical innovation and increases the pleasure for multiple viewings of the video.

The rehearsal segments tend to be dominated by L's musical explanations. He not only elucidates the music in terms of its history, but he speaks of the composer's musical methods and philosophy of composition and of the technical problems the work presents for the performer. The entire thrust of explanation is to impart a deeper understanding of the music. The concert segments serve to lend musical continuity to the film, allowing us to hear a

---

[316] There is a conducting psychology behind meticulous, detailed rehearsing. It is to create awareness and attention. Different conductors accomplish this in different ways. *Fritz Reiner* would sit on a high stool before the orchestra, his head slightly bowed, only occasionally turning his head from one side to the other to glance towards a section or solo player through the narrow slits of his eyes. He was the challenging image of someone intently listening for every detail in every part of the orchestra. This projected so overpoweringly to the musicians that, instead of casually playing their own part without concern to what was going on around them, an attitude quite common among orchestra players, the orchestra became an amalgamated set of giant eyes and ears watchful of every dynamic nuance, listening, integrating, balancing, accompanying and emphasising only those parts intended by the composer as indicated by the commanding figure on the podium. One has only to listen to Reiner's recordings with the Chicago Symphony to marvel at the clarity and transparency of playing along with the rainbow of orchestral colour he was able to evoke when conducting even the most complex of scores.

sufficient amount of the totality of each of the two Berlioz movements rehearsed to impart a genuine sense of the each work.

Most professional orchestras would have become restless in a rehearsal dominated by so much explanation but the young orchestra, absorb it all with riveted interest. It should be added that once the historical discussion of the work is out of the way, the practical wisdom L dispenses regarding performance and playing techniques is pure platinum. It represents pedagogy at its highest level. My own thoughts while viewing this memorable video wandered back to my days at Tanglewood and to a young Bernstein, barely out of his twenties, performing similar miracles with the Berkshire Center student orchestra.

Part I of this video is devoted to a rehearsal and performance of the movement, *Romeo alone and the Festival of the Capulets*. Part 2 involves the preparation and performance of the *Balcony Love Scene*, another purely instrumental movement from the Berlioz symphony. The same format of intercutting rehearsal with finished performance is retained by the director throughout and L's interdisciplinary approach is preserved as well. Each of Berlioz's close musical parallels with the Shakespeare text and play action continues to fascinate the young orchestra just as they continue to be amused by L's banter and sideline comments. At one point, conducting the introduction to the *Love Scene* in a rhapsodically free manner, he expresses his dissatisfaction with their inability to follow his beat. He performs a cruel caricature of those conductors who are little more than strict time beaters. He explains that he feels it only necessary to conduct that particular introductory passage in a manner which coincides with the movement of the music on the page; sometimes beating only one beat to the bar, sometimes two, sometimes six beats to the bar. This is a lesson of great importance. There is no simplification or compromise in the execution of his conducting technique in deference to his young and relatively inexperienced orchestra. This is the real world of concert performance and an orchestra must be able to correctly interpret even the most obscure of conducting gestures. Lessons such as these are what made the Salzau Festival such a valuable happening for the young orchestra. Working with L provided a forecast of what awaited and what would be expected of them in the tough and highly competitive professional world in which they would later compete. By the time they had completed their short summer tenure at the Festival, they had had a genuine taste of the best that music had to offer. Their final segment in the concert hall served to underline that they had learned their lessons well. This summer would provide each of them with a memory they would carry with them throughout their lives and careers. A stunning film!

VALEDICO:

The Pacific Music Festival
(1990)

Although now dangerously ill, L made a last odyssey to Japan just four months before his death to help launch yet another music festival for youth. Originally scheduled to take place in Beijing, China, the now re-named Pacific Music Festival was transferred to Sapporo on Hokkaido, the northern-most island of Japan, following the suppression of the student protest in Tiananmen Square in 1989. Originally conceived along the lines of Tanglewood by L and Michael Tilson Thomas, the Festival brought together a wealth of talent that included the London Symphony Orchestra, a hand picked student orchestra from nineteen countries, and noted young soloists and aspiring young conductors. L's role as succinctly summed up by Humphrey Burton "was to be the guiding spirit, the Koussevitzky figure, of the entire festival." Once again emulating his mentor, L was to communicate to a gathered microcosm of the world's youth, leaving with them his legacy of knowledge, intelligence, dedication and, above all, passionate love of music.

A concerned and watchful personal entourage of L's most trusted associates were in attendance to help alleviate the obvious strain this commitment placed upon his weakened state. Nevertheless, he persisted when working with these young people in taxing all his powers without thought for himself. Observing him on the video, one is witness to an indomitable spirit clinging tenaciously to keep the flame of life not only burning but burning brightly.

His speech of welcome to the students, however, is also an *Abschied*, a farewell. References to mortality are scattered throughout the text. He speaks of his "*very advanced **old** age*" of 71, the need to "*now* make the choice how best to serve music"., to spend "whatever *days* the good Lord grants me", and again, "...most of the *remaining time the Lord grants me*",

WEST SIDE MAESTRO

and *"...in the years that remain...*this commitment which I make *for the rest of my life..."* [317]

Although there are daily reminders of his physical fragility, one would be hard pressed to believe when watching him vigorously throw himself into his rehearsals with the student orchestra that at the eleventh hour he would not again arise, reborn like a phoenix from the flames. To communicate with these young players, this desperately ill man held nothing back, giving every drop of whatever energy he possessed, and it still was astonishingly considerable, to the task at hand.

Standing on the sidelines before the orchestra L observes one of the student conductors, Eije Oue, preparing for him the Scherzo from Schumann's *Second Symphony.* If Oue, who has since built a considerable international reputation as a conductor, represented the young apprentice conductors who attended the Pacific Festival, one must comment that the standards set for Japan produced candidates far beyond the virtual beginner conductors who were filmed in the first year of the Salzau Festival. As for L, while he is openly appreciative of Oue's professional efforts on his behalf, the instant he takes the podium one is put in mind of the moment on any bright morning in Rome when Bernini's Trevi Fountain bursts into life after its dormant overnight vigil. He immediately begins to teach and conduct the young players with an intensity and enthusiasm that must have taken everyone, including his concerned staff, by surprise. One cannot underestimate the psychological challenge that the more than competent Oue set him. Conductors are a breed apart. It is one thing for a Principal Conductor to be preceded by a répétiteur, an adequate coach, who rehearses in a

---

[317] In light of the legendary mystique surrounding conductor's longevity, (Toscanini, 89, Stokowski, 95, Adrian Boult, 94, Monteux, 89, **Klemperer, 88!!!**, Karl Böhm, 87, Bruno Walter, 86, etc.) 71 years labels L as a mere 'boy'.I have put Otto Klemperer's name in bold print as he is perhaps the most extraordinary example of the indomitable spirit of conductors. His longevity of 88 years is especially astonishing in light of a medical history which included a brain tumour which left him partially paralysed, being clinically diagnosed as manic/depressive causing him to suffer severe bouts of emotional stress sending him to the heights of euphoria or the depths of despair, breaking his legs descending from an airline forcing him to conduct for many years sitting down and setting fire to himself in a hotel room having fallen asleep with a cigarette still burning between his lips.

straightforward manner without frills. It is another to be preceded by a young firebrand who represents the talent of the future that will eventually replace you. Subconsciously, this must have galvanised L as it would any ageing maestro visited by Dickens' *Ghost of Christmas to come*.[318]

From his first downbeat, L begins to correct a quantity of detail, indeed, such a plethora of detail in regard to playing and various specific music passages that even his new, young, alert orchestra is hard pressed to keep up with him. In order to help them not lose the thread of his corrections, he works at each passage section by section, first the winds, then the strings and, only then, the entire orchestra. As we have witnessed at Salzau, he stops for everything without thought of limiting or conserving his energies. He is in high gear and loving it, not only the *now* of conducting and teaching but the universal ideal of imparting one's knowledge to those who will come after.

We receive an instant poll reaction from a sampling of young musicians at the interval. "He was really great...He really knew things...He was on top of everything..." volunteered an excited Japanese violinist, and from the Principal Cellist, "It was so interesting to see how one hundred people who've never come across each other before can suddenly come together and understand everything that is being said...to produce a musical whole. It was like the whole orchestra had become one." This young and most sensitive musician had stumbled upon the *one mind* concept that I wrote of earlier as the ideal fusion towards which both conductor and orchestra strive.

The interval is over and the rehearsal proceeds. L continues to drive himself, straining his energies to their maximum capacities. It soon becomes obvious that Music itself is the key source of that drive. His communion with it and his commitment to it is what energises him. At one point he stops and scolds the orchestra for its slow response and making him work so hard. It produces precisely the effect sought after. From his next downbeat, the orchestra floats on his baton. No longer is there need to merely beat a metric pattern. Now he is free to guide and shape the musical flow in a totally

---

[318] This reference is to the third Ghost in Dickens' novel *A Christmas Carol* who conjures up a vision of the future.

relaxed fashion. It is marvellous to observe. L sums up this wondrous inter-reaction as follows, "I can't imagine life without people. People are as essential in my life as music is essential in my life."

By the second day, no doubt to everyone's amazement, L appeared rejuvenated. Although he had a raft of people and pills with him to look after his medical needs, I'm convinced the playing of the orchestra and the response of Youth proved to be the best medicine of all.

Even during his explanations to the orchestra he makes no attempt to conserve his energies, sometimes shouting in his worn, grating voice or singing a passage in demonstration in what he once caricatured as his naturally *atonal* style.

The orchestra by now is astonishingly quick. The difficult transition accelerating from the slow sustained introduction of Schumann's *Second Symphony* to the nervously rhythmic Allegro proper is so perfectly managed by the second try that L decides to devise a bit of fun which is still soundly based in pedagogy. He repeats this opening transition several times, each time choosing a different improvisational approach including one that is totally impractical. The orchestra follows him closely each time without question. This rehearsal routine will insure maximum attention and flexibility in the final concert. In the midst of the obvious pleasure L is taking from his new orchestra family, a crisis moment occurs as his voice gives out causing him to express concern. This is followed by a loss of concentration after stopping to make a correction and suddenly realising that he has forgotten his reason for stopping. He confesses this to be a by-product of his old age and he rails against it complete with an uninhibited expletive which causes much amusement among his younger colleagues. An intermission is called. During it L seems relaxed, posing for photographs with the players and receiving a caricature drawing sketched of him during rehearsal, which gives him much pleasure.

Back on the podium at the end of the interval, however, L is obviously physically exhausted, breathing laboriously. "I'll tell you what...", he says,

WEST SIDE MAESTRO

"Let's play the *Adagio*! Let's skip the *Scherzo*...The *Scherzo* is the hardest..." he says, trying to summon up a bit more energy. "But... I think you've worked so hard already on the first movement..." (he is, in truth, speaking of himself), "...that it may be time for a little...very personal...intimate...music making..."

The dots represent pauses as L struggles for breath. However, he regains his composure and turns to the solo oboe. "Get your *Schumann-est* reed ready...oboe...make sure your entrance is...inaudible...You sneak in...until it's burning...this *piano*...", (referring to the dynamic at which the solo should be performed. He tries to sing to demonstrate, but cannot) "...but always the pulse..."(he just manages a semi-singing demonstration of the accompanying syncopated rhythm for the strings), "...panting, but very slowly...This is the ultimate test in left hand *forte*...right hand...*piano*." (He imitates the left hand manner in which a violinist vibrates the strings of his instrument. Then, he turns to his right to address the Double Basses). "...This is also true of the bass line...*wonderful* bass line..." He tries to sing but it is a toneless groan. Restarting the movement, he quietly sings one measure of the accompanying string figure. He gives the downbeat but there is confusion and he must stop. "It's in four, dear," he says gently to the young lady who is concertmistress. Once more he sings one bar of string accompaniment and begins again to conduct. Perspiration is pouring down his brow. This time the strings make a superb start but L is disturbed by certain phrasing deficiencies and stops to explain. For the next five minutes pearls of musical wisdom are dropping in every direction. He conducts the first violins alone, shaping and moulding their solo theme. This imparting of wisdom is the essence of what the Festival and L himself represent. Earlier I commented that despite the huge fees he could command for Young People's Concerts, lectures such as the ones he gave at Harvard or the many youth Festivals he helped found or, like Tanglewood, continually supported, where the act of teaching was involved, it was a life's compulsion to which L would have gladly devoted himself without fee of any kind. Here, on this small Japanese island, his physical super efforts are testament that he will be a teacher to the last.

WEST SIDE MAESTRO

He has somehow by now recaptured his second wind and is again in full flow, stopping to correct and explain everything with a thousand similes at his disposal. He begins the slow movement again and this time, with the orchestra supersensitive to his every gesture, he makes progress well into the movement. He stops finally at a cadence looking very pleased.

"This is going to be the most beautiful *Adagio* you've ever heard. *But it isn't yet*! It's *going* to be."("Yet!", another caveat from L! Here is the teacher still striving for that extra *something* from his pupils, pressing them not only to the limits of their abilities but beyond, if possible). However, L is not so unappreciative of their efforts to begrudge them a final word of encouragement. "Bravo!" he adds, "Really beautiful!"

The orchestra bursts into applause.

There is one last rehearsal sequence. L, looking extremely fragile and exhausted, conducts through the *Adagio* undeterred by his failing strength. He is taking genuine joy from this young orchestra performing the work he, like them, had first experienced as an aspiring young musician. It was the memory of Dmitri Mitropoulos' performance with the Boston Symphony that proved a constant inspiration to him as a young conductor not much older than the players sitting before him. Now, through this same music, he would leave with these young musicians a similar indelible memory to carry with them as an inspiration. The rehearsal melts into the live concert as L completes the movement, lowers his baton and stands a silent figure. The scene fades to black as a simple, thin bordered commemoration appears:

> **LEONARD BERNSTEIN**
> **Born 25 Aug. 1918 - died 14 Oct. 1990**

In interviews with musicians both great and less great, most interviewers sooner or later come to that frequently posed and virtually unanswerable conundrum, "Who is your favourite composer?" or that even more narrowly

WEST SIDE MAESTRO

posed riddle of the Sphinx, "What is your favourite piece of music?" Yet, having listened to and viewed the enormous output of L's performances on CD, film as well as in video format, which includes a large sampling of his television Specials, I find myself posing that same genre of question to myself. Do I have a favourite performance, film or video? Can one settle on a single *favourite* in the face of so great and diverse an accomplishment? I would have been among the first to deflect such an inquiry with the reply, "Next question, please!", that is until I viewed *Sharing*. This final view of so unique a musician transcends the idea of individual personality. It is a portrait of man's indomitable spirit when facing his own finality. It also reveals new depths of meaning in the words, *legacy* and *commitment,* the *legacy* being the unstinting transmission of a dying Master's lifetime knowledge, intelligence and passionate love of his calling to those who will follow after him, the *commitment* his viewed example of unceasing efforts in seeking the highest standards and pursuing even those goals beyond one's energies and reach.

Sharing delivers a subtext of meaning which echoes far beyond its relatively short fifty-five minute length. It is the summing up of L's life and his achievements, even more-so than the documentaries *A Life in Music* or the even more admirable *Leonard Bernstein, Reaching For The Note,* the former a pocket biography and the later a memorial and retrospective of L's career complete with a goodly sprinkling of most of his major compositions for the concert hall and the stage. *Sharing* goes beyond places, dates and musical milestones. It paints a picture of continuity, an uninterrupted line of teaching and teachers, of the transmission of knowledge to the young who themselves will be the teaching conduits of the future. Were I asked to make the impossible choice of a single video of L to be deposited in a time capsule, I would choose *Sharing* as the most fitting musical memorial. It represents the musical bookends of his life, from his youthful foray into teaching, coaching his siblings within his family circle, to his final documented statement, still as a teacher serving the young. His life can, perhaps, best be summed up in the lines that serve as bookends in one of L's favourite poems, *The Four Quartets,* composed by one of his favourite poets, TS Eliot:

WEST SIDE MAESTRO

©Friedrun Reinhold

'Lenny'

"In my beginning is my end...

In my end is my beginning."

WEST SIDE MAESTRO

ACKNOWLEDGEMENTS

It is difficult to come to terms with the reality that a personal odyssey, which I began sixteen years ago, is now at an end. When I began I did not know where it would lead me or what conclusions I would draw. I was simply intent upon writing about a unique musician, perhaps the most famous and diverse American musical talent the world has ever known or would ever know, not merely as a reporter taking bits and pieces from a mountains of news clippings or a professional biographer from hours of interviews with family members, professional associates and friends but as my teacher, then, a close working colleague and, if not a lifetime friend, a friend and mentor for ten of the most important career years in both his and my life. Although there was a time when one could not walk into a retail record outlet without noting huge window displays and a variety of dramatic posters all trumpeting his photogenic good looks and dramatic conducting personality, one is hard pressed nowadays to find among the huge plethora of current biographies and 'I knew Lenny' books, writings which dwell specifically upon the unique musician rather than 'Peck's *unbelievably* bad boy'.

Lenny courted controversy his entire life. He danced with danger both in his personal life and in his music making, constantly confronting, challenging and defying all authority from parental to medical to management to his most tenacious and severest professional critics. The cost in the end was exorbitant physical disintegration followed by a relatively premature death.

While we were robbed of the immediate presence of so great a talent, we are fortunate to have virtually a complete biographical documentation in photographs, films and sound recordings of his entire professional career from his impromptu historic debut with the NY Philharmonic to his final concert with the Boston Symphony barely two months before his passing. Once one begins to take stock of the diversity contained within this most complete living biography, the enormity of L's lifetime's output and accomplishments can only be described as staggering. It is one, which, most probably, will remain unduplicated in the near future, if ever again. His career of forty-five years of undiminished public acclaim encompassed every area of both live and mechanically transmitted musical performance. He authored best selling books on music, he published poetry and was also a music publisher. He was a theorist and original thinker, a university lecturer, a teacher to the young and old and, in his autumn days, a patron, philanthropist and founder of several international music festivals for young musicians.

Although he often protested that all that interested him was the musical side of life, the picture painted by his biographers is that Lenny developed into a very astute and sharp businessman over the years. Herbert von Karajan's business empire, similarly built around a unique musical personality, was the only other commercial force created for a classical musician of a magnitude to match L's organisation, Amberson, which controlled his varied financial interests. Now twenty-two years after his death, Amberson continues to function as a high powered, high profile organisation which publishes quarterly its own Leonard Bernstein news bulletin, *Prelude, fugue and riffs,* has a permanent Internet site, **www.leonardbernstein.com,** which is encyclopaedic in its coverage of his professional career and accomplishments, and encompasses a group of philanthropic, educational and commercial ventures with which the name of Leonard Bernstein continues to resound internationally.

I suffered from the delusion when I began this musical memoir that I could complete a fairly accurate musical portrait of Leonard Bernstein in three hundred pages but I underestimated the complexity of the man and his accomplishments. This, then, is the first of two volumes with which I will try to capture a comprehensive portrait of this truly unique musican. I also underestimated the help and encouragement that would be offered to me by a range of people in the arts and sciences, one of whom, Mary Ahearn, a long time colleague, former feature editor for the production organisation, Robert Saudek Associates, producers of the Bernstein *Omnibus* and *Ford and Lincoln presents* programs, and the dearest of friends, deserves special thanks for her reading and correction of many of the chapters, for constantly reminding me of the importance to double check and source all opinions and documents quoted and, most of all, to avoid getting caught up in the *psycho-babble* which has become a trend in the writing of biographies.

Among others of importance to my researches, I want to thank Humphrey Burton who took time from his busy schedule to allow me a half dozen extended recorded interviews and who was always at the end of a telephone line when additional factual information was needed. Among those who helped and advised on my extended chapter on the Charles Eliot Norton Lectures at Harvard University special mention should go to Ray Jackendoff, Professor of Linguistics at Brandeis University and Irving Singer, Professor of Philosophy at MIT. Both of these friendly and learned gentlemen were generous in supplying important documentary material and information relating to the Lectures and also opening doors for me to others in the field of Linguistics who could help me with my pursuits.

The viewing of the huge number of Bernstein videos/film performances beyond the relatively few still commercially available was made possible through the hospitality of the Museum of Television and Radio in New York City, the Unitel International Music Films in Munich, Germany (with special thanks to Horant Hohlfeld and his assistant Renata Münzel), to Ronald Davis of Kultur Performing Arts Videos, New Jersey, USA, to Sony's Classical Division in London, Deutsche Grammophon in Hamburg, Germany, and, again, to Humphrey Burton.

There also accrued for me along the way the benefits of valued friendships. Initial mention must go to Raymond Monk of the Elgar Trust who was the first to read my early efforts and to urge me to persevere; to Dr Richard Haigh of the University of Leicester who was ever on hand to advise upon and solve my computer problems; to Pam Richardson for her unstinting encouragement that helped me to fulfil my commitment.

There are yet four others to whom special mention must now be made. At the head of a queue of supporters stood the most tolerant and forbearing of wives, my dearest, late wife, Ruth, to whom I dedicate this book. In the fiftieth year of my non-stop, sixty-five year career, neither of us conceiving what the future held, she allowed our plans to leisurely travel the world together to be placed on hold while I took on the last musical task of completing this one final octave. Ever lending key support and encouragement were other family members; my son David who conceived the title of the book and the book cover and served as legal council; my son, Jonathan for his management skills and proofing of the volume and, finally, my nephew James Cohen, himself an author, who took on the preparation and launching of this first volume of West Side Maestro on the Internet.

ROBERT MANDELL
Leicester, England
March 2012

ROBERT MANDELL

Humphrey Burton, author of "Leonard Bernstein" and director of over 170 Bernstein documentaries and filmed concerts, writes of West Side Maestro:

"Robert Mandell's detailed analyses and level headed assessments of Bernstein's recorded legacy and of his equally extraordinary work as a teacher, (from The Young People's Concerts to the Norton Lectures), break new ground in Bernstein studies and will serve as the standard work for future generations: we owe him a huge debt of gratitude."

CPSIA information can be obtained
at www.ICGtesting.com
Printed in the USA
FSHW021950300819
61617FS